D1626047

THE TIMES MINI
ATLAS OF THE WORLD

TIMES BOOKS
LONDON

Times Books, 77-85 Fulham Palace Road,
London W6 8JB

The Times is a registered trademark of
Times Newspapers Ltd

First published 1991
Published as The Times Atlas
of the World Mini Edition 1994
Second Edition 1999
Third Edition 2006

Fourth Edition 2009

Copyright © Times Books Group Ltd 2009

Maps © Collins Bartholomew Ltd 2009

The contents of this edition of The Times Atlas
of the World Mini Edition are believed correct at
the time of printing. Nevertheless the publisher
can accept no responsibility for errors or omissions,
changes in the detail given or for any expense or
loss thereby caused.

Printed and bound in Hong Kong

British Library Cataloguing in Publication Data
A catalogue record for this book is available from the British Library

ISBN 978-0-00-727638-7

All mapping in this atlas is generated from Collins Bartholomew™
digital databases. Collins Bartholomew™, the UK's leading
independent geographical information supplier, can provide a
digital, custom, and premium mapping service to a variety of markets.
For further information:
Tel: +44 (0) 141 306 3752
e-mail: collinsbartholomew@harpercollins.co.uk

or visit our website at: www.collinsbartholomew.com

www.timesatlas.com
The world's most authoritative and
prestigious maps and atlases

Pages	Title	Scale

GEOGRAPHICAL INFORMATION

Pages	Title	Scale
6–19	**COUNTRIES** OF THE **WORLD**	
20–21	**OCEANIA PHYSICAL** Features	
22–23	**ASIA PHYSICAL** Features	
24–25	**EUROPE PHYSICAL** Features	
26–27	**AFRICA PHYSICAL** Features	
28–29	**NORTH AMERICA** Physical Features	
30–31	**SOUTH AMERICA** Physical Features	
32–33	**OCEANS** AND **POLES** Physical Features	
34–35	**CLIMATE**	
36–37	**LAND COVER**	
38–39	**POPULATION**	
40–41	**URBANIZATION**	
42–43	**SYMBOLS** AND **ABBREVIATIONS**	

WORLD

Pages	Title	Scale
44–45	**WORLD** Physical Features	1:170 000 000
46–47	**WORLD** Countries	1:170 000 000

OCEANIA — 1:70 000 000

Pages	Title	Scale
48–49	OCEANIA	1:70 000 000
50–51	**AUSTRALIA**	1:25 000 000
52–53	**AUSTRALIA** Southeast	1:10 000 000
54	**NEW ZEALAND**	1:10 000 000

ANTARCTICA

Pages	Title	Scale
55	ANTARCTICA	1:60 000 000

ASIA

Pages	Title	Scale
56–57	ASIA	1:70 000 000
58–59	**SOUTHEAST ASIA**	1:30 000 000
60–61	**MALAYSIA** AND **INDONESIA** West	1:15 000 000
62–63	**CONTINENTAL SOUTHEAST ASIA**	1:15 000 000
64	**PHILIPPINES**	1:15 000 000

CONTENTS

Pages	Title	Scale
65	**NORTH KOREA** AND **SOUTH KOREA**	1:9 000 000
66–67	**JAPAN**	1:10 000 000
68–69	**CHINA** AND **MONGOLIA**	1:30 000 000
70–71	**CHINA** Central	1:15 000 000
72–73	**SOUTH ASIA**	1:20 000 000
74–75	**PAKISTAN, INDIA** AND **BANGLADESH**	1:15 000 000
76–77	**CENTRAL ASIA**	1:20 000 000
78–79	**ARABIAN PENINSULA**	1:15 000 000
80–81	**EAST MEDITERRANEAN**	1:15 000 000
82–83	**RUSSIAN FEDERATION**	1:42 000 000
84–85	EUROPE	1:40 000 000
86–87	**EUROPEAN RUSSIAN FEDERATION**	1:20 000 000
88–89	**NORTHEAST EUROPE**	1:8 000 000
90–91	**UKRAINE** AND **MOLDOVA**	1:8 000 000
92–93	**SCANDINAVIA** AND **ICELAND**	1:10 000 000
94–95	**BRITISH ISLES**	1:8 000 000
96	**SCOTLAND**	1:4 000 000
97	**IRELAND**	1:4 000 000
98–99	**ENGLAND** AND **WALES**	1:4 000 000
100–101	**NORTHWEST EUROPE**	1:4 000 000
102–103	**CENTRAL EUROPE**	1:8 000 000
104–105	**FRANCE** AND **SWITZERLAND**	1:8 000 000
106–107	**SPAIN** AND **PORTUGAL**	1:8 000 000
108–109	**ITALY** AND **THE BALKANS**	1:8 000 000
110–111	**GREECE, ROMANIA** AND **BULGARIA**	1:8 000 000
112–113	AFRICA	1:60 000 000
114–115	**NORTHWEST AFRICA**	1:26 000 000

CONTENTS

Pages	Title	Scale
116–117	**NORTHEAST AFRICA**	1:26 000 000
118–119	**CENTRAL AFRICA**	1:20 000 000
120–121	**SOUTHERN AFRICA**	1:20 000 000
122–123	**REPUBLIC OF SOUTH AFRICA**	1:10 000 000
124–125	NORTH AMERICA	1:70 000 000
126–127	**CANADA**	1:30 000 000
128–129	**CANADA** West	1:15 000 000
130–131	**CANADA** East	1:15 000 000
132–133	**UNITED STATES OF AMERICA**	1:25 000 000
134–135	**USA** West	1:11 000 000
136–137	**USA** North Central	1:11 000 000
138–139	**USA** South Central	1:11 000 000
140–141	**USA** Northeast	1:11 000 000
142–143	**USA** Southeast	1:11 000 000
144–145	**MEXICO**	1:15 000 000
146–147	**CARIBBEAN**	1:20 000 000
148–149	SOUTH AMERICA	1:70 000 000
150–151	**SOUTH AMERICA** North	1:25 000 000
152–153	**SOUTH AMERICA** South	1:25 000 000
154–155	**BRAZIL** Southeast	1:10 000 000
	OCEANS	
156–157	**PACIFIC OCEAN**	1:120 000 000
158	**ATLANTIC OCEAN**	1:120 000 000
159	**INDIAN OCEAN**	1:120 000 000
160	**ARCTIC OCEAN**	1:60 000 000
161–256	INDEX	

AFGHANISTAN
Islamic State of Afghanistan
Capital Kābul

Area sq km	652 225	**Currency**	Afghani
Area sq miles	251 825	**Languages**	Dari, Pushtu,
Population	27 145 000		Uzbek, Turkmen

ALBANIA
Republic of Albania
Capital Tirana (Tiranë)

Area sq km	28 748	**Currency**	Lek
Area sq miles	11 100	**Languages**	Albanian, Greek
Population	3 190 000		

ALGERIA
People's Democratic Republic of Algeria
Capital Algiers (Alger)

Area sq km	2 381 741	**Currency**	Algerian dinar
Area sq miles	919 595	**Languages**	Arabic, French,
Population	33 858 000		Berber

ANDORRA
Principality of Andorra
Capital Andorra la Vella

Area sq km	465	**Currency**	Euro
Area sq miles	180	**Languages**	Spanish,
Population	75 000		Catalan, French

ANGOLA
Republic of Angola
Capital Luanda

Area sq km	1 246 700	**Currency**	Kwanza
Area sq miles	481 354	**Languages**	Portuguese,
Population	17 024 000		Bantu, local lang.

ANTIGUA AND BARBUDA
Capital St John's

Area sq km	442	**Currency**	East Caribbean
Area sq miles	171		dollar
Population	85 000	**Languages**	English, creole

ARGENTINA
Argentine Republic
Capital Buenos Aires

Area sq km	2 766 889	**Currency**	Argentinian peso
Area sq miles	1 068 302	**Languages**	Spanish, Italian,
Population	39 531 000		Amerindian lang.

ARMENIA
Republic of Armenia
Capital Yerevan (Erevan)

Area sq km	29 800	**Currency**	Dram
Area sq miles	11 506	**Languages**	Armenian, Azeri
Population	3 002 000		

AUSTRALIA
Commonwealth of Australia
Capital Canberra

Area sq km	7 692 024	**Currency**	Australian do
Area sq miles	2 969 907	**Languages**	English, Italia
Population	20 743 000		Greek

AUSTRIA
Republic of Austria
Capital Vienna (Wien)

Area sq km	83 855	**Currency**	Euro
Area sq miles	32 377	**Languages**	German,
Population	8 361 000		Croatian, Tu

AZERBAIJAN
Republic of Azerbaijan
Capital Baku (Bakı)

Area sq km	86 600	**Currency**	Azerbaijani n
Area sq miles	33 436	**Languages**	Azeri, Armen
Population	8 467 000		Russian, Lez

THE BAHAMAS
Commonwealth of The Bahamas
Capital Nassau

Area sq km	13 939	**Currency**	Bahamian do
Area sq miles	5 382	**Languages**	English, creo
Population	331 000		

BAHRAIN
Kingdom of Bahrain
Capital Manama (Al Manāmah)

Area sq km	691	**Currency**	Bahraini dina
Area sq miles	267	**Languages**	Arabic, Englis
Population	753 000		

BANGLADESH
People's Republic of Bangladesh
Capital Dhaka (Dacca)

Area sq km	143 998	**Currency**	Taka
Area sq miles	55 598	**Languages**	Bengali, Engl
Population	158 665 000		

BARBADOS
Capital Bridgetown

Area sq km	430	**Currency**	Barbados do
Area sq miles	166	**Languages**	English, creo
Population	294 000		

BELARUS
Republic of Belarus
Capital Minsk

Area sq km	207 600	**Currency**	Belarus rouble
Area sq miles	80 155	**Languages**	Belorussian,
Population	9 689 000		Russian

BELGIUM
Kingdom of Belgium
Capital Brussels (Bruxelles)

Area sq km	30 520	**Currency**	Euro
Area sq miles	11 784	**Languages**	Dutch (Flemish),
Population	10 457 000		French (Walloon),
			German

BELIZE
Capital Belmopan

Area sq km	22 965	**Currency**	Belize dollar
Area sq miles	8 867	**Languages**	English, Spanish,
Population	288 000		Mayan, creole

BENIN
Republic of Benin
Capital Porto-Novo

Area sq km	112 620	**Currency**	CFA franc*
Area sq miles	43 483	**Languages**	French, Fon,
Population	9 033 000		Yoruba, Adja,
			local lang.

BHUTAN
Kingdom of Bhutan
Capital Thimphu

Area sq km	46 620	**Currency**	Ngultrum,
Area sq miles	18 000		Indian rupee
Population	658 000	**Languages**	Dzongkha,
			Nepali, Assamese

BOLIVIA
Republic of Bolivia
Capital La Paz/Sucre

Area sq km	1 098 581	**Currency**	Boliviano
Area sq miles	424 164	**Languages**	Spanish, Quechua,
Population	9 525 000		Aymara

BOSNIA-HERZEGOVINA
Republic of Bosnia and Herzegovina
Capital Sarajevo

Area sq km	51 130	**Currency**	Marka
Area sq miles	19 741	**Languages**	Bosnian, Serbian,
Population	3 935 000		Croatian

BOTSWANA
Republic of Botswana
Capital Gaborone

Area sq km	581 370	**Currency**	Pula
Area sq miles	224 468	**Languages**	English, Setswana,
Population	1 882 000		Shona, local lang.

BRAZIL
Federative Republic of Brazil
Capital Brasília

Area sq km	8 514 879	**Currency**	Real
Area sq miles	3 287 613	**Languages**	Portuguese
Population	191 791 000		

BRUNEI
State of Brunei Darussalam
Capital Bandar Seri Begawan

Area sq km	5 765	**Currency**	Brunei dollar
Area sq miles	2 226	**Languages**	Malay, English,
Population	390 000		Chinese

BULGARIA
Republic of Bulgaria
Capital Sofia (Sofiya)

Area sq km	110 994	**Currency**	Lev
Area sq miles	42 855	**Languages**	Bulgarian,
Population	7 639 000		Turkish, Romany,
			Macedonian

BURKINA
Democratic Republic of Burkina Faso
Capital Ouagadougou

Area sq km	274 200	**Currency**	CFA franc*
Area sq miles	105 869	**Languages**	French, Moore
Population	14 784 000		(Mossi), Fulani,
			local lang.

BURUNDI
Republic of Burundi
Capital Bujumbura

Area sq km	27 835	**Currency**	Burundian franc
Area sq miles	10 747	**Languages**	Kirundi (Hutu,
Population	8 508 000		Tutsi), French

CAMBODIA
Kingdom of Cambodia
Capital Phnom Penh

Area sq km	181 035	**Currency**	Riel
Area sq miles	69 884	**Languages**	Khmer,
Population	14 444 000		Vietnamese

CAMEROON
Republic of Cameroon
Capital Yaoundé

Area sq km	475 442	**Currency**	CFA franc*
Area sq miles	183 569	**Languages**	French, English,
Population	18 549 000		Fang, Bamileke,
			local lang.

CANADA
Capital Ottawa

Area sq km	9 984 670	**Currency**	Canadian dollar
Area sq miles	3 855 103	**Languages**	English, French
Population	32 876 000		

CAPE VERDE
Republic of Cape Verde
Capital Praia

Area sq km	4 033	**Currency**	Cape Verde
Area sq miles	1 557		escudo
Population	530 000	**Languages**	Portuguese, creole

CENTRAL AFRICAN REPUBLIC
Capital Bangui

Area sq km	622 436	**Currency**	CFA franc*
Area sq miles	240 324	**Languages**	French, Sango,
Population	4 343 000		Banda, Baya,
			local lang.

CHAD
Republic of Chad
Capital Ndjamena

Area sq km	1 284 000	**Currency**	CFA franc*
Area sq miles	495 755	**Languages**	Arabic, French,
Population	10 781 000		Sara, local lang.

CHILE
Republic of Chile
Capital Santiago

Area sq km	756 945	**Currency**	Chilean peso
Area sq miles	292 258	**Languages**	Spanish,
Population	16 635 000		Amerindian lang.

CHINA
People's Republic of China
Capital Beijing (Peking)

Area sq km	9 584 492	**Currency**	Yuan, HK dollar,
Area sq miles	3 700 593		Macao pataca
Population	1 313 437 000	**Languages**	Mandarin, Hsiang,
			Cantonese, Wu,
			regional lang.

COLOMBIA
Republic of Colombia
Capital Bogotá

Area sq km	1 141 748	**Currency**	Colombian peso
Area sq miles	440 831	**Languages**	Spanish,
Population	46 156 000		Amerindian lang

COMOROS
Union of the Comoros
Capital Moroni

Area sq km	1 862	**Currency**	Comoros franc
Area sq miles	719	**Languages**	Comorian,
Population	839 000		French, Arabic

CONGO
Republic of the Congo
Capital Brazzaville

Area sq km	342 000	**Currency**	CFA franc*
Area sq miles	132 047	**Languages**	French, Kongo,
Population	3 768 000		Monokutuba,
			local lang.

CONGO, DEMOCRATIC REPUBLIC OF THE
Capital Kinshasa

Area sq km	2 345 410	**Currency**	Congolese franc
Area sq miles	905 568	**Languages**	French, Lingala,
Population	62 636 000		Swahili, Kongo,
			local lang.

COSTA RICA
Republic of Costa Rica
Capital San José

Area sq km	51 100	**Currency**	Costa Rican col
Area sq miles	19 730	**Languages**	Spanish
Population	4 468 000		

CÔTE D'IVOIRE
Republic of Côte d'Ivoire
Capital Yamoussoukro

Area sq km	322 463	**Currency**	CFA franc*
Area sq miles	124 504	**Languages**	French, creole,
Population	19 262 000		Akan, local lan

CROATIA
Republic of Croatia
Capital Zagreb

Area sq km	56 538	**Currency**	Kuna
Area sq miles	21 829	**Languages**	Croatian, Serb
Population	4 555 000		

CUBA
Republic of Cuba
Capital Havana (La Habana)

Area sq km	110 860	**Currency**	Cuban peso
Area sq miles	42 803	**Languages**	Spanish
Population	11 268 000		

EAST TIMOR
Democratic Republic of Timor-Leste
Capital Dili

Area sq km	14 874	**Currency**	US dollar
Area sq miles	5 743	**Languages**	Portuguese, Tetun, English
Population	1 155 000		

CYPRUS
Republic of Cyprus
Capital Nicosia (Lefkosia)

Area sq km	9 251	**Currency**	Euro
Area sq miles	3 572	**Languages**	Greek, Turkish, English
Population	855 000		

ECUADOR
Republic of Ecuador
Capital Quito

Area sq km	272 045	**Currency**	US dollar
Area sq miles	105 037	**Languages**	Spanish, Quechua, and other Amerindian lang.
Population	13 341 000		

CZECH REPUBLIC
Capital Prague (Praha)

Area sq km	78 864	**Currency**	Czech koruna
Area sq miles	30 450	**Languages**	Czech, Moravian, Slovak
Population	10 186 000		

EGYPT
Arab Republic of Egypt
Capital Cairo (Al Qāhirah)

Area sq km	1 000 250	**Currency**	Egyptian pound
Area sq miles	386 199	**Languages**	Arabic
Population	75 498 000		

DENMARK
Kingdom of Denmark
Capital Copenhagen (København)

Area sq km	43 075	**Currency**	Danish krone
Area sq miles	16 631	**Languages**	Danish
Population	5 442 000		

EL SALVADOR
Republic of El Salvador
Capital San Salvador

Area sq km	21 041	**Currency**	El Salvador colón, US dollar
Area sq miles	8 124		
Population	6 857 000	**Languages**	Spanish

DJIBOUTI
Republic of Djibouti
Capital Djibouti

Area sq km	23 200	**Currency**	Djibouti franc
Area sq miles	8 958	**Languages**	Somali, Afar, French, Arabic
Population	833 000		

EQUATORIAL GUINEA
Republic of Equatorial Guinea
Capital Malabo

Area sq km	28 051	**Currency**	CFA franc*
Area sq miles	10 831	**Languages**	Spanish, French, Fang
Population	507 000		

DOMINICA
Commonwealth of Dominica
Capital Roseau

Area sq km	750	**Currency**	East Caribbean dollar
Area sq miles	290		
Population	67 000	**Languages**	English, creole

ERITREA
State of Eritrea
Capital Asmara

Area sq km	117 400	**Currency**	Nakfa
Area sq miles	45 328	**Languages**	Tigrinya, Tigre
Population	4 851 000		

DOMINICAN REPUBLIC
Capital Santo Domingo

Area sq km	48 442	**Currency**	Dominican peso
Area sq miles	18 704	**Languages**	Spanish, creole
Population	9 760 000		

ESTONIA
Republic of Estonia
Capital Tallinn

Area sq km	45 200	**Currency**	Kroon
Area sq miles	17 452	**Languages**	Estonian, Russian
Population	1 335 000		

ETHIOPIA
Federal Democratic Republic of Ethiopia
Capital Addis Ababa (Ādīs Ābeba)

Area sq km	1 133 880	**Currency**	Birr
Area sq miles	437 794	**Languages**	Oromo, Amharic,
Population	83 099 000		Tigrinya,
			local lang.

GEORGIA
Republic of Georgia
Capital T'bilisi

Area sq km	69 700	**Currency**	Lari
Area sq miles	26 911	**Languages**	Georgian, Russian,
Population	4 395 000		Armenian, Azeri,
			Ossetian, Abkhaz

FIJI
Sovereign Democratic Republic of Fiji
Capital Suva

Area sq km	18 330	**Currency**	Fiji dollar
Area sq miles	7 077	**Languages**	English, Fijian,
Population	839 000		Hindi

GERMANY
Federal Republic of Germany
Capital Berlin

Area sq km	357 022	**Currency**	Euro
Area sq miles	137 849	**Languages**	German, Turkish
Population	82 599 000		

FINLAND
Republic of Finland
Capital Helsinki (Helsingfors)

Area sq km	338 145	**Currency**	Euro
Area sq miles	130 559	**Languages**	Finnish, Swedish
Population	5 277 000		

GHANA
Republic of Ghana
Capital Accra

Area sq km	238 537	**Currency**	Cedi
Area sq miles	92 100	**Languages**	English, Hausa,
Population	23 478 000		Akan, local lang.

FRANCE
French Republic
Capital Paris

Area sq km	543 965	**Currency**	Euro
Area sq miles	210 026	**Languages**	French, Arabic
Population	61 647 000		

GREECE
Hellenic Republic
Capital Athens (Athina)

Area sq km	131 957	**Currency**	Euro
Area sq miles	50 949	**Languages**	Greek
Population	11 147 000		

GABON
Gabonese Republic
Capital Libreville

Area sq km	267 667	**Currency**	CFA franc*
Area sq miles	103 347	**Languages**	French, Fang,
Population	1 331 000		local lang.

GRENADA
Capital St George's

Area sq km	378	**Currency**	East Caribbean
Area sq miles	146		dollar
Population	106 000	**Languages**	English, creole

THE GAMBIA
Republic of The Gambia
Capital Banjul

Area sq km	11 295	**Currency**	Dalasi
Area sq miles	4 361	**Languages**	English, Malinke,
Population	1 709 000		Fulani, Wolof

GUATEMALA
Republic of Guatemala
Capital Guatemala City

Area sq km	108 890	**Currency**	Quetzal, US dollar
Area sq miles	42 043	**Languages**	Spanish,
Population	13 354 000		Mayan lang.

Gaza
semi-autonomous region
Capital Gaza

Area sq km	363	**Currency**	Israeli shekel
Area sq miles	140	**Languages**	Arabic
Population	1 586 008		

GUINEA
Republic of Guinea
Capital Conakry

Area sq km	245 857	**Currency**	Guinea franc
Area sq miles	94 926	**Languages**	French, Fulani,
Population	9 370 000		Malinke,
			local lang.

GUINEA-BISSAU
Republic of Guinea-Bissau
Capital Bissau

Area sq km	36 125	**Currency**	CFA franc*
Area sq miles	13 948	**Languages**	Portuguese,
Population	1 695 000		crioulo, local lang.

GUYANA
Co-operative Republic of Guyana
Capital Georgetown

Area sq km	214 969	**Currency**	Guyana dollar
Area sq miles	83 000	**Languages**	English, creole,
Population	738 000		Amerindian lang.

HAITI
Republic of Haiti
Capital Port-au-Prince

Area sq km	27 750	**Currency**	Gourde
Area sq miles	10 714	**Languages**	French, creole
Population	9 598 000		

HONDURAS
Republic of Honduras
Capital Tegucigalpa

Area sq km	112 088	**Currency**	Lempira
Area sq miles	43 277	**Languages**	Spanish,
Population	7 106 000		Amerindian lang.

HUNGARY
Republic of Hungary
Capital Budapest

Area sq km	93 030	**Currency**	Forint
Area sq miles	35 919	**Languages**	Hungarian
Population	10 030 000		

ICELAND
Republic of Iceland
Capital Reykjavík

Area sq km	102 820	**Currency**	Icelandic króna
Area sq miles	39 699	**Languages**	Icelandic
Population	301 000		

INDIA
Republic of India
Capital New Delhi

Area sq km	3 064 898	**Currency**	Indian rupee
Area sq miles	1 183 364	**Languages**	Hindi, English,
Population	1 169 016 000		many regional lang.

INDONESIA
Republic of Indonesia
Capital Jakarta

Area sq km	1 919 445	**Currency**	Rupiah
Area sq miles	741 102	**Languages**	Indonesian,
Population	231 627 000		local lang.

IRAN
Islamic Republic of Iran
Capital Tehrān

Area sq km	1 648 000	**Currency**	Iranian rial
Area sq miles	636 296	**Languages**	Farsi, Azeri,
Population	71 208 000		Kurdish, regional lang.

IRAQ
Republic of Iraq
Capital Baghdād

Area sq km	438 317	**Currency**	Iraqi dinar
Area sq miles	169 235	**Languages**	Arabic, Kurdish,
Population	28 993 000		Turkmen

IRELAND
Republic of Ireland
Capital Dublin (Baile Átha Cliath)

Area sq km	70 282	**Currency**	Euro
Area sq miles	27 136	**Languages**	English, Irish
Population	4 301 000		

ISRAEL
State of Israel
Capital Jerusalem* (Yerushalayim) (El Quds)

Area sq km	20 770	**Currency**	Shekel
Area sq miles	8 019	**Languages**	Hebrew, Arabic
Population	6 928 000		

* De facto capital. Disputed.

ITALY
Italian Republic
Capital Rome (Roma)

Area sq km	301 245	**Currency**	Euro
Area sq miles	116 311	**Languages**	Italian
Population	58 877 000		

JAMAICA
Capital Kingston

Area sq km	10 991	**Currency**	Jamaican dollar
Area sq miles	4 244	**Languages**	English, creole
Population	2 714 000		

Jammu and Kashmir
Disputed territory (India/Pakistan/China)
Capital Srinagar

Area sq km	222 236
Area sq miles	85 806
Population	13 000 000

JAPAN
Capital Tōkyō

Area sq km	377 727	**Currency**	Yen
Area sq miles	145 841	**Languages**	Japanese
Population	127 967 000		

JORDAN
Hashemite Kingdom of Jordan
Capital 'Ammān

Area sq km	89 206	**Currency**	Jordanian dinar
Area sq miles	34 443	**Languages**	Arabic
Population	5 924 000		

KAZAKHSTAN
Republic of Kazakhstan
Capital Astana (Akmola)

Area sq km	2 717 300	**Currency**	Tenge
Area sq miles	1 049 155	**Languages**	Kazakh, Russian,
Population	15 422 000		Ukrainian, German,
			Uzbek, Tatar

KENYA
Republic of Kenya
Capital Nairobi

Area sq km	582 646	**Currency**	Kenyan shilling
Area sq miles	224 961	**Languages**	Swahili, English,
Population	37 538 000		local lang.

KIRIBATI
Republic of Kiribati
Capital Bairiki

Area sq km	717	**Currency**	Australian dollar
Area sq miles	277	**Languages**	Gilbertese,
Population	95 000		English

KOSOVO
Republic of Kosovo
Capital Prishtinë (Priština)

Area sq km	10 908	**Currency**	Euro
Area sq miles	4 212	**Languages**	Albanian, Serbian
Population	2 070 000		

KUWAIT
State of Kuwait
Capital Kuwait (Al Kuwayt)

Area sq km	17 818	**Currency**	Kuwaiti dinar
Area sq miles	6 880	**Languages**	Arabic
Population	2 851 000		

KYRGYZSTAN
Kyrgyz Republic
Capital Bishkek (Frunze)

Area sq km	198 500	**Currency**	Kyrgyz som
Area sq miles	76 641	**Languages**	Kyrgyz, Russia
Population	5 317 000		Uzbek

LAOS
Lao People's Democratic Republic
Capital Vientiane (Viangchan)

Area sq km	236 800	**Currency**	Kip
Area sq miles	91 429	**Languages**	Lao, local lang
Population	5 859 000		

LATVIA
Republic of Latvia
Capital Rīga

Area sq km	63 700	**Currency**	Lats
Area sq miles	24 595	**Languages**	Latvian, Russi
Population	2 277 000		

LEBANON
Republic of Lebanon
Capital Beirut (Beyrouth)

Area sq km	10 452	**Currency**	Lebanese pou
Area sq miles	4 036	**Languages**	Arabic, Armen
Population	4 099 000		French

LESOTHO
Kingdom of Lesotho
Capital Maseru

Area sq km	30 355	**Currency**	Loti,
Area sq miles	11 720		S. African rand
Population	2 008 000	**Languages**	Sesotho, Englis
			Zulu

LIBERIA
Republic of Liberia
Capital Monrovia

Area sq km	111 369	**Currency**	Liberian dollar
Area sq miles	43 000	**Languages**	English, creole
Population	3 750 000		local lang.

LIBYA
Great Socialist People's Libyan Arab
Jamahiriya
Capital Tripoli (Ṭarābulus)

Area sq km	1 759 540	**Currency**	Libyan dinar
Area sq miles	679 362	**Languages**	Arabic, Berber
Population	6 160 000		

LIECHTENSTEIN
Principality of Liechtenstein
Capital Vaduz

Area sq km	160	**Currency**	Swiss franc
Area sq miles	62	**Languages**	German
Population	35 000		

LITHUANIA
Republic of Lithuania
Capital Vilnius

Area sq km	65 200	**Currency**	Litas
Area sq miles	25 174	**Languages**	Lithuanian,
Population	3 390 000		Russian, Polish

LUXEMBOURG
Grand Duchy of Luxembourg
Capital Luxembourg

Area sq km	2 586	**Currency**	Euro
Area sq miles	998	**Languages**	Letzeburgish,
Population	467 000		German, French

MACEDONIA (F.Y.R.O.M.)
Republic of Macedonia
Capital Skopje

Area sq km	25 713	**Currency**	Macedonian denar
Area sq miles	9 928	**Languages**	Macedonian,
Population	2 038 000		Albanian, Turkish

MADAGASCAR
Republic of Madagascar
Capital Antananarivo

Area sq km	587 041	**Currency**	Malagasy franc
Area sq miles	226 658		Malagasy Ariary
Population	19 683 000	**Languages**	Malagasy, French

MALAWI
Republic of Malawi
Capital Lilongwe

Area sq km	118 484	**Currency**	Malawian kwacha
Area sq miles	45 747	**Languages**	Chichewa,
Population	13 925 000		English, local lang.

MALAYSIA
Federation of Malaysia
Capital Kuala Lumpur/Putrajaya

Area sq km	332 965	**Currency**	Ringgit
Area sq miles	128 559	**Languages**	Malay, English,
Population	26 572 000		Chinese, Tamil,
			local lang.

MALDIVES
Republic of the Maldives
Capital Male

Area sq km	298	**Currency**	Rufiyaa
Area sq miles	115	**Languages**	Divehi
Population	306 000		(Maldivian)

MALI
Republic of Mali
Capital Bamako

Area sq km	1 240 140	**Currency**	CFA franc*
Area sq miles	478 821	**Languages**	French, Bambara,
Population	12 337 000		local lang.

MALTA
Republic of Malta
Capital Valletta

Area sq km	316	**Currency**	Euro
Area sq miles	122	**Languages**	Maltese, English
Population	407 000		

MARSHALL ISLANDS
Republic of the Marshall Islands
Capital Delap-Uliga-Djarrit

Area sq km	181	**Currency**	US dollar
Area sq miles	70	**Languages**	English,
Population	59 000		Marshallese

MAURITANIA
Islamic Arab and African Rep. of Mauritania
Capital Nouakchott

Area sq km	1 030 700	**Currency**	Ouguiya
Area sq miles	397 955	**Languages**	Arabic, French,
Population	3 124 000		local lang.

MAURITIUS
Republic of Mauritius
Capital Port Louis

Area sq km	2 040	**Currency**	Mauritius rupee
Area sq miles	788	**Languages**	English, creole,
Population	1 262 000		Hindi, Bhojpuri,
			French

MEXICO
United Mexican States
Capital Mexico City

Area sq km	1 972 545	**Currency**	Mexican peso
Area sq miles	761 604	**Languages**	Spanish,
Population	106 535 000		Amerindian lang.

13

MICRONESIA, FEDERATED STATES OF
Capital Palikir

Area sq km	701	**Currency**	US dollar
Area sq miles	271	**Languages**	English,
Population	111 000		Chuukese,
			Pohnpeian,
			local lang.

MOLDOVA
Republic of Moldova
Capital Chişinău (Kishinev)

Area sq km	33 700	**Currency**	Moldovan leu
Area sq miles	13 012	**Languages**	Romanian,
Population	3 794 000		Ukrainian,
			Gagauz, Russian

MONACO
Principality of Monaco
Capital Monaco-Ville

Area sq km	2	**Currency**	Euro
Area sq miles	1	**Languages**	French,
Population	33 000		Monégasque,
			Italian

MONGOLIA
Capital Ulan Bator (Ulaanbaatar)

Area sq km	1 565 000	**Currency**	Tugrik (tögrög)
Area sq miles	604 250	**Languages**	Khalka
Population	2 629 000		(Mongolian),
			Kazakh,
			local lang.

MONTENEGRO
Republic of Montenegro
Capital Podgorica

Area sq km	13 812	**Currency**	Euro
Area sq miles	5 333	**Languages**	Serbian
Population	598 000		(Montenegrin),
			Albanian

MOROCCO
Kingdom of Morocco
Capital Rabat

Area sq km	446 550	**Currency**	Moroccan dirham
Area sq miles	172 414	**Languages**	Arabic, Berber,
Population	31 224 000		French

MOZAMBIQUE
Republic of Mozambique
Capital Maputo

Area sq km	799 380	**Currency**	Metical
Area sq miles	308 642	**Languages**	Portuguese,
Population	21 397 000		Makua, Tsonga,
			local lang.

MYANMAR (Burma)
Union of Myanmar
Capital Nay Pyi Taw/Rangoon (Yangôn)

Area sq km	676 577	**Currency**	Kyat
Area sq miles	261 228	**Languages**	Burmese, Sha
Population	48 798 000		Karen, local la

NAMIBIA
Republic of Namibia
Capital Windhoek

Area sq km	824 292	**Currency**	Namibian doll
Area sq miles	318 261	**Languages**	English, Afrika
Population	2 074 000		German, Ovan
			local lang.

NAURU
Republic of Nauru
Capital Yaren

Area sq km	21	**Currency**	Australian dola
Area sq miles	8	**Languages**	Nauruan, Engl
Population	10 000		

NEPAL
Capital Kathmandu

Area sq km	147 181	**Currency**	Nepalese rupee
Area sq miles	56 827	**Languages**	Nepali, Maithi
Population	28 196 000		Bhojpuri, Engl
			local lang.

NETHERLANDS
Kingdom of the Netherlands
Capital Amsterdam/The Hague ('s-Gravenh

Area sq km	41 526	**Currency**	Euro
Area sq miles	16 033	**Languages**	Dutch, Frisian
Population	16 419 000		

NEW ZEALAND
Capital Wellington

Area sq km	270 534	**Currency**	New Zealand
Area sq miles	104 454		dollar
Population	4 179 000	**Languages**	English, Maori

NICARAGUA
Republic of Nicaragua
Capital Managua

Area sq km	130 000	**Currency**	Córdoba
Area sq miles	50 193	**Languages**	Spanish,
Population	5 603 000		Amerindian lar

NIGER
Republic of Niger
Capital Niamey

Area sq km	1 267 000	**Currency**	CFA franc*
Area sq miles	489 191	**Languages**	French, Hausa,
Population	14 226 000		Fulani, local lang.

NIGERIA
Federal Republic of Nigeria
Capital Abuja

Area sq km	923 768	**Currency**	Naira
Area sq miles	356 669	**Languages**	English, Hausa,
Population	148 093 000		Yoruba, Ibo,
			Fulani, local lang.

NORTH KOREA
Democratic People's Republic of Korea
Capital P'yŏngyang

Area sq km	120 538	**Currency**	North Korean won
Area sq miles	46 540	**Languages**	Korean
Population	23 790 000		

NORWAY
Kingdom of Norway
Capital Oslo

Area sq km	323 878	**Currency**	Norwegian krone
Area sq miles	125 050	**Languages**	Norwegian
Population	4 698 000		

OMAN
Sultanate of Oman
Capital Muscat (Masqaṭ)

Area sq km	309 500	**Currency**	Omani riyal
Area sq miles	119 499	**Languages**	Arabic, Baluchi,
Population	2 595 000		Indian lang.

PAKISTAN
Islamic Republic of Pakistan
Capital Islamabad

Area sq km	803 940	**Currency**	Pakistani rupee
Area sq miles	310 403	**Languages**	Urdu, Punjabi,
Population	163 902 000		Sindhi, Pushtu
			English

PALAU
Republic of Palau
Capital Melekeok

Area sq km	497	**Currency**	US dollar
Area sq miles	192	**Languages**	Palauan, English
Population	20 000		

PANAMA
Republic of Panama
Capital Panama City

Area sq km	77 082	**Currency**	Balboa
Area sq miles	29 762	**Languages**	Spanish, English,
Population	3 343 000		Amerindian lang.

PAPUA NEW GUINEA
Independent State of Papua New Guinea
Capital Port Moresby

Area sq km	462 840	**Currency**	Kina
Area sq miles	178 704	**Languages**	English,
Population	6 331 000		Tok Pisin (creole),
			local lang.

PARAGUAY
Republic of Paraguay
Capital Asunción

Area sq km	406 752	**Currency**	Guaraní
Area sq miles	157 048	**Languages**	Spanish, Guaraní
Population	6 127 000		

PERU
Republic of Peru
Capital Lima

Area sq km	1 285 216	**Currency**	Sol
Area sq miles	496 225	**Languages**	Spanish, Quechua,
Population	27 903 000		Aymara

PHILIPPINES
Republic of the Philippines
Capital Manila

Area sq km	300 000	**Currency**	Philippine peso
Area sq miles	115 831	**Languages**	English, Filipino,
Population	87 960 000		Tagalog, Cebuano,
			local lang.

POLAND
Polish Republic
Capital Warsaw (Warszawa)

Area sq km	312 683	**Currency**	Złoty
Area sq miles	120 728	**Languages**	Polish, German
Population	38 082 000		

PORTUGAL
Portuguese Republic
Capital Lisbon (Lisboa)

Area sq km	88 940	**Currency**	Euro
Area sq miles	34 340	**Languages**	Portuguese
Population	10 623 000		

QATAR
State of Qatar
Capital Doha (Ad Dawḥah)

Area sq km	11 437	**Currency**	Qatari riyal
Area sq miles	4 416	**Languages**	Arabic
Population	841 000		

ROMANIA
Capital Bucharest (Bucureşti)

Area sq km	237 500	**Currency**	Romanian leu
Area sq miles	91 699	**Languages**	Romanian,
Population	21 438 000		Hungarian

RUSSIAN FEDERATION
Capital Moscow (Moskva)

Area sq km	17 075 400	**Currency**	Russian rouble
Area sq miles	6 592 849	**Languages**	Russian, Tatar,
Population	142 499 000		Ukrainian,
			local lang.

RWANDA
Republic of Rwanda
Capital Kigali

Area sq km	26 338	**Currency**	Rwandan franc
Area sq miles	10 169	**Languages**	Kinyarwanda,
Population	9 725 000		French, English

ST KITTS AND NEVIS
Federation of St Kitts and Nevis
Capital Basseterre

Area sq km	261	**Currency**	East Caribbean
Area sq miles	101		dollar
Population	50 000	**Languages**	English, creole

ST LUCIA
Capital Castries

Area sq km	616	**Currency**	East Caribbean
Area sq miles	238		dollar
Population	165 000	**Languages**	English, creole

ST VINCENT AND THE GRENADINES
Capital Kingstown

Area sq km	389	**Currency**	East Caribbean
Area sq miles	150		dollar
Population	120 000	**Languages**	English, creole

SAMOA
Independent State of Samoa
Capital Apia

Area sq km	2 831	**Currency**	Tala
Area sq miles	1 093	**Languages**	Samoan, English
Population	187 000		

SAN MARINO
Republic of San Marino
Capital San Marino

Area sq km	61	**Currency**	Euro
Area sq miles	24	**Languages**	Italian
Population	31 000		

SÃO TOMÉ AND PRÍNCIPE
Democratic Rep. of São Tomé and Prín
Capital São Tomé

Area sq km	964	**Currency**	Dobra
Area sq miles	372	**Languages**	Portuguese, cr
Population	158 000		

SAUDI ARABIA
Kingdom of Saudi Arabia
Capital Riyadh (Ar Riyāḍ)

Area sq km	2 200 000	**Currency**	Saudi Arabian
Area sq miles	849 425		riyal
Population	24 735 000	**Languages**	Arabic

SENEGAL
Republic of Senegal
Capital Dakar

Area sq km	196 720	**Currency**	CFA franc*
Area sq miles	75 954	**Languages**	French, Wolof
Population	12 379 000		Fulani, local la

SERBIA
Republic of Serbia
Capital Belgrade (Beograd)

Area sq km	77 453	**Currency**	Serbian dinar,
Area sq miles	29 904	**Languages**	Serbian,
Population	7 788 000		Hungarian

SEYCHELLES
Republic of Seychelles
Capital Victoria

Area sq km	455	**Currency**	Seychelles rup
Area sq miles	176	**Languages**	English, Frenc
Population	87 000		creole

SIERRA LEONE
Republic of Sierra Leone
Capital Freetown

Area sq km	71 740	**Currency**	Leone
Area sq miles	27 699	**Languages**	English, creole
Population	5 866 000		Mende, Temne
			local lang.

SINGAPORE
Republic of Singapore
Capital Singapore

Area sq km	639	**Currency**	Singapore dollar
Area sq miles	247	**Languages**	Chinese, English,
Population	4 436 000		Malay, Tamil

SLOVAKIA
Slovak Republic
Capital Bratislava

Area sq km	49 035	**Currency**	Euro
Area sq miles	18 933	**Languages**	Slovak,
Population	5 390 000		Hungarian, Czech

SLOVENIA
Republic of Slovenia
Capital Ljubljana

Area sq km	20 251	**Currency**	Euro
Area sq miles	7 819	**Languages**	Slovene, Croatian,
Population	2 002 000		Serbian

SOLOMON ISLANDS
Capital Honiara

Area sq km	28 370	**Currency**	Solomon Islands
Area sq miles	10 954		dollar
Population	496 000	**Languages**	English, creole,
			local lang.

SOMALIA
Somali Republic
Capital Mogadishu (Muqdisho)

Area sq km	637 657	**Currency**	Somali shilling
Area sq miles	246 201	**Languages**	Somali, Arabic
Population	8 699 000		

SOUTH AFRICA, REPUBLIC OF
Capital Pretoria (Tshwane)/Cape Town

Area sq km	1 219 090	**Currency**	Rand
Area sq miles	470 693	**Languages**	Afrikaans,
Population	48 577 000		English, nine
			official local lang.

SOUTH KOREA
Republic of Korea
Capital Seoul (Sŏul)

Area sq km	99 274	**Currency**	South Korean
Area sq miles	38 330		won
Population	48 224 000	**Languages**	Korean

SPAIN
Kingdom of Spain
Capital Madrid

Area sq km	504 782	**Currency**	Euro
Area sq miles	194 897	**Languages**	Spanish, Castilian,
Population	44 279 000		Catalan, Galician,
			Basque

SRI LANKA
Democratic Socialist Republic of Sri Lanka
Capital Sri Jayewardenepura Kotte

Area sq km	65 610	**Currency**	Sri Lankan rupee
Area sq miles	25 332	**Languages**	Sinhalese,
Population	19 299 000		Tamil, English

SUDAN
Republic of the Sudan
Capital Khartoum

Area sq km	2 505 813	**Currency**	Sudanese pound
Area sq miles	967 500		(Sudani)
Population	38 560 000	**Languages**	Arabic, Dinka,
			Nubian, Beja,
			Nuer, local lang.

SURINAME
Republic of Suriname
Capital Paramaribo

Area sq km	163 820	**Currency**	Suriname guilder
Area sq miles	63 251	**Languages**	Dutch,
Population	458 000		Surinamese,
			English, Hindi

SWAZILAND
Kingdom of Swaziland
Capital Mbabane

Area sq km	17 364	**Currency**	Emalangeni,
Area sq miles	6 704		South African
Population	1 141 000		rand
		Languages	Swazi, English

SWEDEN
Kingdom of Sweden
Capital Stockholm

Area sq km	449 964	**Currency**	Swedish krona
Area sq miles	173 732	**Languages**	Swedish
Population	9 119 000		

SWITZERLAND
Swiss Confederation
Capital Bern (Berne)

Area sq km	41 293	**Currency**	Swiss franc
Area sq miles	15 943	**Languages**	German, French,
Population	7 484 000		Italian, Romansch

SYRIA
Syrian Arab Republic
Capital Damascus (Dimashq)

Area sq km	185 180	**Currency**	Syrian pound
Area sq miles	71 498	**Languages**	Arabic, Kurdish,
Population	19 929 000		Armenian

TAIWAN
Republic of China
Capital T'aipei

Area sq km	36 179	**Currency**	Taiwan dollar
Area sq miles	13 969	**Languages**	Mandarin, Min,
Population	22 880 000		Hakka, local lang.

The People's Republic of China claims Taiwan as its 23rd province.

TAJIKISTAN
Republic of Tajikistan
Capital Dushanbe

Area sq km	143 100	**Currency**	Somoni
Area sq miles	55 251	**Languages**	Tajik, Uzbek,
Population	6 736 000		Russian

TANZANIA
United Republic of Tanzania
Capital Dodoma

Area sq km	945 087	**Currency**	Tanzanian shilling
Area sq miles	364 900	**Languages**	Swahili, English,
Population	40 454 000		Nyamwezi,
			local lang.

THAILAND
Kingdom of Thailand
Capital Bangkok (Krung Thep)

Area sq km	513 115	**Currency**	Baht
Area sq miles	198 115	**Languages**	Thai, Lao,
Population	63 884 000		Chinese, Malay,
			Mon-Khmer lang.

TOGO
Republic of Togo
Capital Lomé

Area sq km	56 785	**Currency**	CFA franc*
Area sq miles	21 925	**Languages**	French, Ewe,
Population	6 585 000		Kabre, local lang.

TONGA
Kingdom of Tonga
Capital Nuku'alofa

Area sq km	748	**Currency**	Pa'anga
Area sq miles	289	**Languages**	Tongan, English
Population	100 000		

TRINIDAD AND TOBAGO
Republic of Trinidad and Tobago
Capital Port of Spain

Area sq km	5 130	**Currency**	Trinidad and
Area sq miles	1 981		Tobago dollar
Population	1 333 000	**Languages**	English, creole
			Hindi

TUNISIA
Tunisian Republic
Capital Tunis

Area sq km	164 150	**Currency**	Tunisian dinar
Area sq miles	63 379	**Languages**	Arabic, French
Population	10 327 000		

TURKEY
Republic of Turkey
Capital Ankara

Area sq km	779 452	**Currency**	Lira
Area sq miles	300 948	**Languages**	Turkish, Kurdis
Population	74 877 000		

TURKMENISTAN
Republic of Turkmenistan
Capital Aşgabat (Ashkhabad)

Area sq km	488 100	**Currency**	Turkmen mana
Area sq miles	188 456	**Languages**	Turkmen, Uzbe
Population	4 965 000		Russian

TUVALU
Capital Vaiaku

Area sq km	25	**Currency**	Australian dolla
Area sq miles	10	**Languages**	Tuvaluan, Engl
Population	11 000		

UGANDA
Republic of Uganda
Capital Kampala

Area sq km	241 038	**Currency**	Ugandan shillii
Area sq miles	93 065	**Languages**	English, Swahil
Population	30 884 000		Luganda,
			local lang.

UKRAINE
Capital Kiev (Kyiv)

Area sq km	603 700	**Currency**	Hryvnia
Area sq miles	233 090	**Languages**	Ukrainian,
Population	46 205 000		Russian

UNITED ARAB EMIRATES
Federation of Emirates
Capital Abu Dhabi (Abū Ẓabī)

Area sq km	77 700	**Currency** UAE dirham
Area sq miles	30 000	**Languages** Arabic, English
Population	4 380 000	

UNITED KINGDOM
United Kingdom of Great Britain and
Northern Ireland
Capital London

Area sq km	243 609	**Currency** Pound sterling
Area sq miles	94 058	**Languages** English, Welsh,
Population	60 769 000	Gaelic

UNITED STATES OF AMERICA
Capital Washington D.C.

Area sq km	9 826 635	**Currency** US dollar
Area sq miles	3 794 085	**Languages** English, Spanish
Population	305 826 000	

URUGUAY
Oriental Republic of Uruguay
Capital Montevideo

Area sq km	176 215	**Currency** Uruguayan peso
Area sq miles	68 037	**Languages** Spanish
Population	3 340 000	

UZBEKISTAN
Republic of Uzbekistan
Capital Toshkent

Area sq km	447 400	**Currency** Uzbek som
Area sq miles	172 742	**Languages** Uzbek, Russian,
Population	27 372 000	Tajik, Kazakh

VANUATU
Republic of Vanuatu
Capital Port Vila

Area sq km	12 190	**Currency** Vatu
Area sq miles	4 707	**Languages** English,
Population	226 000	Bislama (creole), French

VATICAN CITY
Vatican City State or Holy See
Capital Vatican City

Area sq km	0.5	**Currency** Euro
Area sq miles	0.2	**Languages** Italian
Population	557	

VENEZUELA
Republic of Venezuela
Capital Caracas

Area sq km	912 050	**Currency** Bolívar fuerte
Area sq miles	352 144	**Languages** Spanish,
Population	27 657 000	Amerindian lang.

VIETNAM
Socialist Republic of Vietnam
Capital Ha Nôi

Area sq km	329 565	**Currency** Dong
Area sq miles	127 246	**Languages** Vietnamese, Thai,
Population	87 375 000	Khmer, Chinese, local lang.

West Bank
Disputed territory

Area sq km	5 860	**Currency** Jordanian dinar,
Area sq miles	2 263	Isreali shekel
Population	2 676 284	**Languages** Arabic, Hebrew

Western Sahara
Disputed territory (Morocco)
Capital Laâyoune

Area sq km	266 000	**Currency** Moroccan dirham
Area sq miles	102 703	**Languages** Arabic
Population	480 000	

YEMEN
Republic of Yemen
Capital Şan'ā'

Area sq km	527 968	**Currency** Yemeni riyal
Area sq miles	203 850	**Languages** Arabic
Population	22 389 000	

ZAMBIA
Republic of Zambia
Capital Lusaka

Area sq km	752 614	**Currency** Zambian kwacha
Area sq miles	290 586	**Languages** English, Bemba,
Population	11 922 000	Nyanja, Tonga, local lang.

ZIMBABWE
Republic of Zimbabwe
Capital Harare

Area sq km	390 759	**Currency** Zimbabwean dollar
Area sq miles	150 873	**Languages** English, Shona,
Population	13 349 000	Ndebele

Total Land Area 8 844 516 sq km / 3 414 868 sq miles
(includes New Guinea and Pacific Island nations)

HIGHEST MOUNTAIN
Puncak Jaya
5 030 m / 16 502 feet

Line of cross section

Joseph
Bonaparte Gulf

Arnhem Land

Gulf of
Carpentaria

Cape York
Peninsula

Great Dividing
Range

Tasman Sea

North Cape

North Island

Cook Strait

Oceania perspective view and cross section

HIGHEST MOUNTAINS	metres	feet	Map page
Puncak Jaya, Indonesia	5 030	16 502	59 D3
Puncak Trikora, Indonesia	4 730	15 518	59 D3
Puncak Mandala, Indonesia	4 700	15 420	59 D3
Puncak Yamin, Indonesia	4 595	15 075	—
Mt Wilhelm, Papua New Guinea	4 509	14 793	59 D3
Mt Kubor, Papua New Guinea	4 359	14 301	—

— LARGEST ISLAND
New Guinea
808 510 sq km /
312 167 sq miles

LARGEST ISLANDS	sq km	sq miles	Map page
New Guinea	808 510	312 167	59 D3
South Island, New Zealand	151 215	58 384	54 B2
North Island, New Zealand	115 777	44 701	54 B1
Tasmania	67 800	26 178	51 D4

LONGEST RIVERS	km	miles	Map page
Murray-Darling	3 750	2 330	52 B2
Darling	2 739	1 702	52 B2
Murray	2 589	1 609	52 B3
Murrumbidgee	1 690	1 050	52 B2
Lachlan	1 480	920	53 C2
Macquarie	950	590	53 C2

LARGEST LAKES	sq km	sq miles	Map page
Lake Eyre	0–8 900	0–3 436	52 A1
Lake Torrens	0–5 780	0–2 232	52 A1

LARGEST LAKE AND LOWEST POINT
Lake Eyre
0 – 8 900 sq km / 0 – 3 436 sq miles
16 m / 53 feet below sea level

LONGEST RIVER AND
LARGEST DRAINAGE BASIN
Murray-Darling
3 750 km / 2 330 miles
1 058 000 sq km / 408 000 sq miles

Total Land Area 45 036 492 sq km / 17 388 686 sq miles

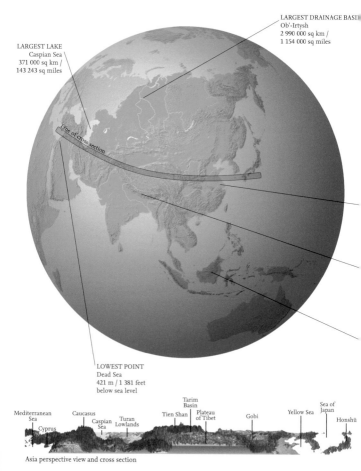

LARGEST DRAINAGE BASIN
Ob'-Irtysh
2 990 000 sq km /
1 154 000 sq miles

LARGEST LAKE
Caspian Sea
371 000 sq km /
143 243 sq miles

Line of cross section

LOWEST POINT
Dead Sea
421 m / 1 381 feet
below sea level

Mediterranean Sea · Cyprus · Caucasus · Caspian Sea · Turan Lowlands · Tien Shan · Tarim Basin · Plateau of Tibet · Gobi · Yellow Sea · Sea of Japan · Honshū

Asia perspective view and cross section

HIGHEST MOUNTAINS	metres	feet	Map page
Mt Everest (Sagarmatha/Qomolangma Feng), China/Nepal	8 848	29 028	75 C2
K2 (Qogir Feng), China/Pakistan	8 611	28 251	74 B1
Kangchenjunga, India/Nepal	8 586	28 169	75 C2
Lhotse, China/Nepal	8 516	27 939	—
Makalu, China/Nepal	8 463	27 765	—
Cho Oyu, China/Nepal	8 201	26 906	—

LARGEST ISLANDS	sq km	sq miles	Map page
Borneo	745 561	287 861	61 C1
Sumatra (Sumatera)	473 606	182 859	60 A1
Honshū	227 414	87 805	67 B3
Celebes (Sulawesi)	189 216	73 056	58 C3
Java (Jawa)	132 188	51 038	61 B2
Luzon	104 690	40 421	64 B1

LONGEST RIVER
Yangtze (Chang Jiang)
6 380 km /
3 965 miles

LONGEST RIVERS	km	miles	Map page
Yangtze (Chang Jiang)	6 380	3 965	70 C2
Ob'-Irtysh	5 568	3 460	86 F2
Yenisey-Angara-Selenga	5 550	3 449	83 H3
Yellow (Huang He)	5 464	3 395	70 B2
Irtysh	4 440	2 759	86 F2
Mekong	4 425	2 750	63 B2

HIGHEST MOUNTAIN
Mt Everest
8 848 m / 29 028 feet

LARGEST LAKES	sq km	sq miles	Map page
Caspian Sea	371 000	143 243	81 C1
Lake Baikal (Ozero Baykal)	30 500	11 776	69 D1
Lake Balkhash (Ozero Balkhash)	17 400	6 718	77 D2
Aral Sea (Aral'skoye More)	17 158	6 625	76 B2
Ysyk-Köl	6 200	2 394	77 D2

LARGEST ISLAND
Borneo
745 561 sq km /
287 861 sq miles

Total Land Area 9 908 599 sq km / 3 825 710 sq miles

LARGEST ISLAND
Great Britain
218 476 sq km /
84 354 sq miles

Line of cross section

HIGHEST MOUNTAIN
El'brus
5 642 m / 18 510 feet

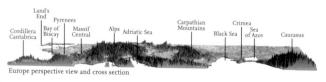

Cordillera
Cantabrica
Land's
End
Bay of
Biscay
Pyrenees
Massif
Central
Alps
Adriatic Sea
Carpathian
Mountains
Black Sea
Crimea
Sea
of Azov
Caucasus

Europe perspective view and cross section

HIGHEST MOUNTAINS	metres	feet	Map pages
El'brus, Russian Federation	5 642	18 510	87 D4
Gora Dykh-Tau, Russian Federation	5 204	17 073	—
Shkhara, Georgia/Russian Federation	5 201	17 063	—
Kazbek, Georgia/Russian Federation	5 047	16 558	76 A2
Mont Blanc, France/Italy	4 808	15 774	105 D2
Dufourspitze, Italy/Switzerland	4 634	15 203	—

LARGEST ISLANDS	sq km	sq miles	Map pages
Great Britain	218 476	84 354	95 C3
Iceland	102 820	39 699	92 A3
Novaya Zemlya	90 650	35 000	86 E1
Ireland	83 045	32 064	97 C2
Spitsbergen	37 814	14 600	82 C1
Sicily (Sicilia)	25 426	9 817	108 B3

LONGEST RIVER AND
LARGEST DRAINAGE BASIN
Volga
3 688 km / 2 292 miles
1 380 000 sq km / 533 000 sq miles

LONGEST RIVERS	km	miles	Map pages
Volga	3 688	2 292	89 F2
Danube	2 850	1 771	110 A1
Dnieper	2 285	1 420	91 C2
Kama	2 028	1 260	86 E3
Don	1 931	1 200	89 E3
Pechora	1 802	1 120	86 E2

LARGEST LAKE AND LOWEST POINT
Caspian Sea
371 000 sq km / 143 243 sq miles
28m / 92 feet below sea level

LARGEST LAKES	sq km	sq miles	Map pages
Caspian Sea	371 000	143 243	81 C1
Lake Ladoga (Ladozhskoye Ozero)	18 390	7 100	86 C2
Lake Onega (Onezhskoye Ozero)	9 600	3 707	86 C2
Vänern	5 585	2 156	93 F4
Rybinskoye Vodokhranilishche	5 180	2 000	89 E2

Total Land Area 30 343 578 sq km / 11 715 721 sq miles

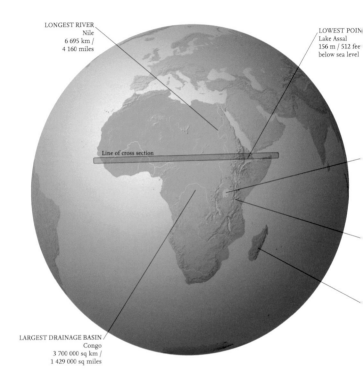

LONGEST RIVER
Nile
6 695 km /
4 160 miles

LOWEST POINT
Lake Assal
156 m / 512 feet
below sea level

Line of cross section

LARGEST DRAINAGE BASIN
Congo
3 700 000 sq km /
1 429 000 sq miles

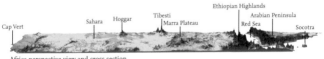

Cap Vert   Sahara   Hoggar   Tibesti   Ethiopian Highlands   Arabian Peninsula
                              Marra Plateau   Red Sea   Socotra

Africa perspective view and cross section

HIGHEST MOUNTAINS	metres	feet	Map page
Kilimanjaro, Tanzania	5 892	19 330	119 D3
Mt Kenya (Kirinyaga), Kenya	5 199	17 057	119 D3
Margherita Peak, Democratic Republic of the Congo/Uganda	5 110	16 765	119 C2
Meru, Tanzania	4 565	14 977	119 D3
Ras Dejen, Ethiopia	4 533	14 872	117 B3
Mt Karisimbi, Rwanda	4 510	14 796	—

LARGEST ISLANDS	sq km	sq miles	Map page
Madagascar	587 040	226 656	121 D3

LARGEST LAKE
Lake Victoria
68 870 sq km /
26 591 sq miles

LONGEST RIVERS	km	miles	Map page
Nile	6 695	4 160	116 B1
Congo	4 667	2 900	118 B3
Niger	4 184	2 600	115 C4
Zambezi	2 736	1 700	120 C2
Webi Shabeelle	2 490	1 547	117 C4
Ubangi	2 250	1 398	118 B3

LARGEST LAKES	sq km	sq miles	Map page
Lake Victoria	68 870	26 591	52 B2
Lake Tanganyika	32 600	12 587	119 C3
Lake Nyasa (Lake Malawi)	29 500	11 390	121 C1
Lake Volta	8 482	3 275	114 C4
Lake Turkana	6 500	2 510	119 D2
Lake Albert	5 600	2 162	119 D2

HIGHEST MOUNTAIN
Kilimanjaro
5 892 m / 19 330 feet

LARGEST ISLAND
Madagascar
587 040 sq km /
226 656 sq miles

Total Land Area 24 680 331 sq km / 9 529 076 sq miles
(including Hawaiian Islands)

HIGHEST MOUNTAIN
Mt McKinley
6 194 m / 20 321 feet

LARGEST ISLAND
Greenland
2 175 600 sq km /
839 999 sq miles

Line of cross section

LOWEST POINT
Death Valley
86 m / 282 feet
below sea level

Coast Ranges

Rocky Mountains

Great Plains

Lake Michigan

Lake Huron

Lake Erie

Chesapeake
Bay

Appalachian
Mountains

Long
Island

Cape
Cod

Nova
Scotia

North America perspective view and cross section

HIGHEST MOUNTAINS	metres	feet	Map page
Mt McKinley, USA	6 194	20 321	124 F2
Mt Logan, Canada	5 959	19 550	126 B2
Pico de Orizaba, Mexico	5 610	18 405	145 C3
Mt St Elias, USA	5 489	18 008	126 B2
Volcán Popocatépetl, Mexico	5 452	17 887	145 C3
Mt Foraker, USA	5 303	17 398	—

LARGEST LAKE
Lake Superior
82 100 sq km /
31 699 sq miles

LARGEST ISLANDS	sq km	sq miles	Map page
Greenland	2 175 600	839 999	127 I2
Baffin Island	507 451	195 927	127 G2
Victoria Island	217 291	83 896	126 D2
Ellesmere Island	196 236	75 767	127 F1
Cuba	110 860	42 803	146 B2
Newfoundland	108 860	42 031	131 E2
Hispaniola	76 192	29 418	147 C2

LONGEST RIVERS	km	miles	Map page
Mississippi-Missouri	5 969	3 709	133 D3
Mackenzie-Peace-Finlay	4 241	2 635	126 C2
Missouri	4 086	2 539	137 E3
Mississippi	3 765	2 340	142 C3
Yukon	3 185	1 979	126 A2
Rio Grande (Río Bravo del Norte)	3 057	1 900	144 B1

LONGEST RIVER AND
LARGEST DRAINAGE BASIN
Mississippi-Missouri
5 969 km / 3 709 miles
3 250 000 sq km / 1 255 000 sq
miles

LARGEST LAKES	sq km	sq miles	Map page
Lake Superior	82 100	31 699	140 B1
Lake Huron	59 600	23 012	140 C2
Lake Michigan	57 800	22 317	140 B2
Great Bear Lake	31 328	12 096	126 C2
Great Slave Lake	28 568	11 030	128 C1
Lake Erie	25 700	9 923	140 C2
Lake Winnipeg	24 387	9 416	129 E2
Lake Ontario	18 960	7 320	141 D2

Total Land Area 17 815 420 sq km / 6 878 534 sq miles

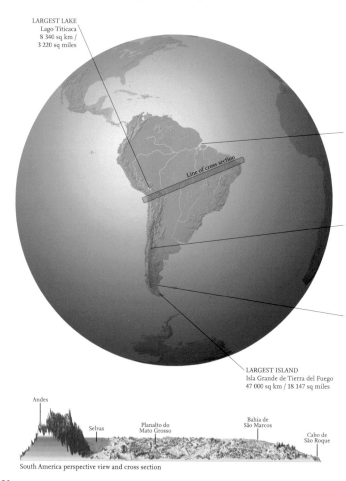

LARGEST LAKE
Lago Titicaca
8 340 sq km /
3 220 sq miles

Line of cross section

LARGEST ISLAND
Isla Grande de Tierra del Fuego
47 000 sq km / 18 147 sq miles

Andes

Selvas

Planalto do
Mato Grosso

Bahía de
São Marcos

Cabo de
São Roque

South America perspective view and cross section

HIGHEST MOUNTAINS	metres	feet	Map page
Cerro Aconcagua, Argentina	6 959	22 831	153 B4
Nevado Ojos del Salado, Argentina/Chile	6 908	22 664	152 B3
Cerro Bonete, Argentina	6 872	22 546	—
Cerro Pissis, Argentina	6 858	22 500	—
Cerro Tupungato, Argentina/Chile	6 800	22 309	—
Cerro Mercedario, Argentina	6 770	22 211	—

LARGEST ISLANDS	sq km	sq miles	Map page
Isla Grande de Tierra del Fuego	47 000	18 147	153 B6
Isla de Chiloé	8 394	3 241	153 A5
East Falkland	6 760	2 610	153 C6
West Falkland	5 413	2 090	153 B6

LONGEST RIVER AND
LARGEST DRAINAGE BASIN
Amazon
8 516 km / 4 049 miles
7 050 000 sq km / 2 722 000 sq miles

LONGEST RIVERS	km	miles	Map page
Amazon (Amazonas)	6 516	4 049	150 C1
Río de la Plata-Paraná	4 500	2 796	153 C4
Purus	3 218	2 000	150 B2
Madeira	3 200	1 988	150 C2
São Francisco	2 900	1 802	151 E3
Tocantins	2 750	1 709	151 D2

HIGHEST MOUNTAIN
Cerro Aconcagua
6 959 m / 22 831 feet

LARGEST LAKES	sq km	sq miles	Map page
Lake Titicaca	8 340	3 220	152 B2

LOWEST POINT
Laguna del Carbón
105 m / 345 feet below sea level

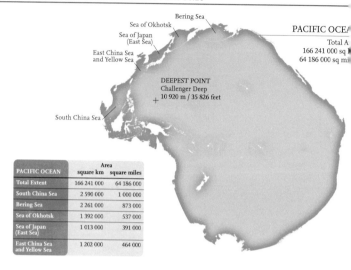

Bering Sea

Sea of Okhotsk

Sea of Japan
(East Sea)

East China Sea
and Yellow Sea

South China Sea

DEEPEST POINT
Challenger Deep
10 920 m / 35 826 feet

PACIFIC OCEA

Total A
166 241 000 sq
64 186 000 sq m

PACIFIC OCEAN	Area	
	square km	square miles
Total Extent	166 241 000	64 186 000
South China Sea	2 590 000	1 000 000
Bering Sea	2 261 000	873 000
Sea of Okhotsk	1 392 000	537 000
Sea of Japan (East Sea)	1 013 000	391 000
East China Sea and Yellow Sea	1 202 000	464 000

ANTARCTICA

Total Land Area 12 093 000 sq km /
4 669 107 sq miles (excluding ice shelves)

HIGHEST MOUNTAIN
Vinson Massif
4 897 m / 16 066 feet

HIGHEST MOUNTAINS	Height	
	metres	feet
Vinson Massif	4 897	16 066
Mt Tyree	4 852	15 918
Mt Kirkpatrick	4 528	14 855
Mt Markham	4 351	14 275
Mt Jackson	4 190	13 747
Mt Sidley	4 181	13 717

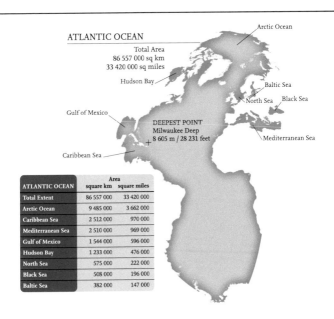

ATLANTIC OCEAN

Total Area
86 557 000 sq km
33 420 000 sq miles

Arctic Ocean

Hudson Bay

Baltic Sea

North Sea   Black Sea

Gulf of Mexico

DEEPEST POINT
Milwaukee Deep
8 605 m / 28 231 feet

Mediterranean Sea

Caribbean Sea

ATLANTIC OCEAN	Area	
	square km	square miles
Total Extent	86 557 000	33 420 000
Arctic Ocean	9 485 000	3 662 000
Caribbean Sea	2 512 000	970 000
Mediterranean Sea	2 510 000	969 000
Gulf of Mexico	1 544 000	596 000
Hudson Bay	1 233 000	476 000
North Sea	575 000	222 000
Black Sea	508 000	196 000
Baltic Sea	382 000	147 000

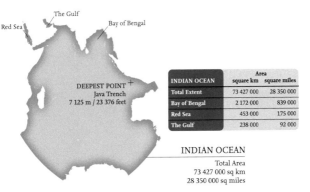

The Gulf

Red Sea   Bay of Bengal

DEEPEST POINT
Java Trench
7 125 m / 23 376 feet

INDIAN OCEAN	Area	
	square km	square miles
Total Extent	73 427 000	28 350 000
Bay of Bengal	2 172 000	839 000
Red Sea	453 000	175 000
The Gulf	238 000	92 000

INDIAN OCEAN

Total Area
73 427 000 sq km
28 350 000 sq miles

MAJOR CLIMATIC REGIONS AND SUB-TYPES

Köppen classification system
Winkel Tripel Projection
scale 1:200 000 000

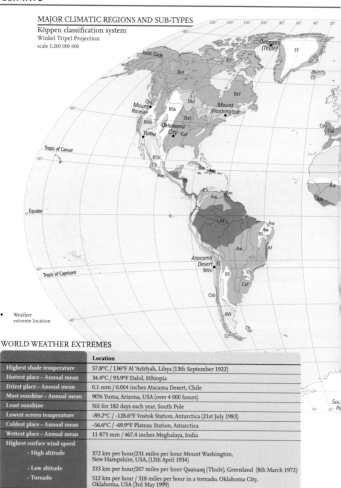

- Weather
  extreme location

WORLD WEATHER EXTREMES

	Location
Highest shade temperature	57.8°C / 136°F Al 'Azīzīyah, Libya (13th September 1922)
Hottest place – Annual mean	34.4°C / 93.9°F Dalol, Ethiopia
Driest place – Annual mean	0.1 mm / 0.004 inches Atacama Desert, Chile
Most sunshine – Annual mean	90% Yuma, Arizona, USA (over 4 000 hours)
Least sunshine	Nil for 182 days each year, South Pole
Lowest screen temperature	-89.2°C / -128.6°F Vostok Station, Antarctica (21st July 1983)
Coldest place – Annual mean	-56.6°C / -69.9°F Plateau Station, Antarctica
Wettest place – Annual mean	11 873 mm / 467.4 inches Meghalaya, India
Highest surface wind speed	
- High altitude	372 km per hour/231 miles per hour Mount Washington, New Hampshire, USA, (12th April 1934)
- Low altitude	333 km per hour/207 miles per hour Qaanaaq (Thule), Greenland (8th March 1972)
- Tornado	512 km per hour / 318 miles per hour in a tornado, Oklahoma City, Oklahoma, USA (3rd May 1999)
Greatest snowfall	31 102 mm / 1 224.5 inches Mount Rainier, Washington, USA (19th February 1971 – 18th February 1972)

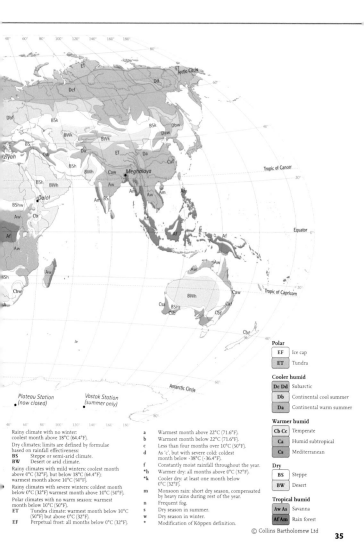

Plateau Station (now closed)

Vostok Station (summer only)

Antarctic Circle

Rainy climate with no winter:
coolest month above 18°C (64.4°F).
Dry climates; limits are defined by formulae
based on rainfall effectiveness:
BS Steppe or semi-arid climate.
BW Desert or arid climate.

Rainy climates with mild winters: coolest month
above 0°C (32°F), but below 18°C (64.4°F);
warmest month above 10°C (50°F).
Rainy climates with severe winters: coldest month
below 0°C (32°F) warmest month above 10°C (50°F).
Polar climates with no warm season: warmest
month below 10°C (50°F).
ET Tundra climate: warmest month below 10°C
  (50°F) but above 0°C (32°F).
EF Perpetual frost: all months below 0°C (32°F).

a	Warmest month above 22°C (71.6°F).
b	Warmest month below 22°C (71.6°F).
c	Less than four months over 10°C (50°F).
d	As 'c', but with severe cold: coldest month below -38°C (-36.4°F).
f	Constantly moist rainfall throughout the year.
***h**	Warmer dry: all months above 0°C (32°F).
***k**	Cooler dry: at least one month below 0°C (32°F).
m	Monsoon rain: short dry season, compensated by heavy rains during rest of the year.
n	Frequent fog.
s	Dry season in summer.
w	Dry season in winter.
*****	Modification of Köppen definition.

Polar

EF	Ice cap
ET	Tundra

Cooler humid

Dc Dd	Subarctic
Db	Continental cool summer
Da	Continental warm summer

Warmer humid

Cb Cc	Temperate
Ca	Humid subtropical
Cs	Mediterranean

Dry

BS	Steppe
BW	Desert

Tropical humid

Aw As	Savanna
Af Am	Rain forest

© Collins Bartholomew Ltd

WORLD LAND COVER

Winkel Tripel Projection
scale: 1:190 000 000

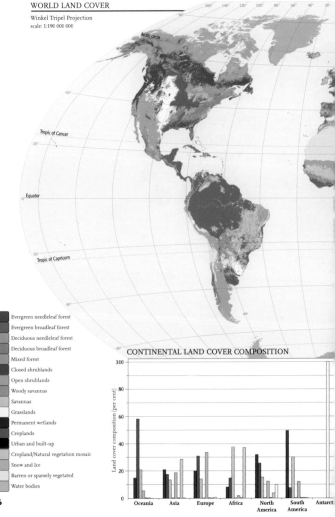

160° 140° 120° 100° 80° 60° 40° 20°

Arctic circle

Tropic of Cancer

Equator

Tropic of Capricorn

Evergreen needleleaf forest
Evergreen broadleaf forest
Deciduous needleleaf forest
Deciduous broadleaf forest
Mixed forest
Closed shrublands
Open shrublands
Woody savannas
Savannas
Grasslands
Permanent wetlands
Croplands
Urban and built-up
Cropland/Natural vegetation mosaic
Snow and Ice
Barren or sparsely vegetated
Water bodies

CONTINENTAL LAND COVER COMPOSITION

Land cover composition (per cent)

100

80

60

40

20

0

Oceania   Asia   Europe   Africa   North   South   Antarct
                                     America America

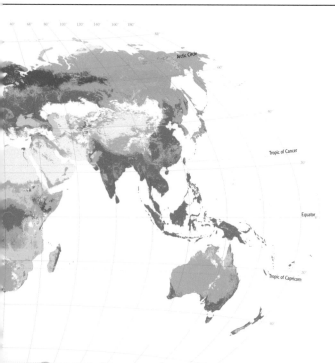

Arctic Circle

Tropic of Cancer

Equator

Tropic of Capricorn

Antarctic Circle

LAND COVER GRAPHS - CLASSIFICATION

Class description	Map classes
Forest/Woodland	Evergreen needleleaf forest
	Evergreen broadleaf forest
	Deciduous needleleaf forest
	Deciduous broadleaf forest
	Mixed forest
Shrubland	Closed shrublands
	Open shrublands
Grass/Savanna	Woody savannas
	Savannas
	Grasslands
Wetland	Permanent wetlands
Crops/Mosaic	Croplands
	Cropland/Natural vegetation mosaic
Urban	Urban and built-up
Snow/Ice	Snow and Ice
Barren	Barren or sparsely vegetated

GLOBAL LAND COVER COMPOSITION

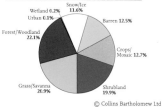

Snow/Ice 11.6%
Wetland 0.2%
Urban 0.1%
Forest/Woodland 22.1%
Barren 12.5%
Crops/Mosaic 12.7%
Shrubland 19.9%
Grass/Savanna 20.9%

© Collins Bartholomew Ltd

WORLD POPULATION DISTRIBUTION

Population Density
Winkel Tripel Projection
scale 1:190 000 000

KEY POPULATION STATISTICS FOR MAJOR REGIONS

	Population 2007 (millions)	Growth (per cent)	Infant mortality rate	Total fertility rate	Life expectancy (years)
World	6 671	1.2	49	2.6	67
More developed regions[1]	1 223	0.3	7	1.6	77
Less developed regions[2]	5 448	1.4	54	2.8	65
Africa	965	2.3	87	4.7	53
Asia	4 030	1.1	43	2.3	69
Europe[3]	731	0.0	8	1.5	75
Latin America and the Caribbean[4]	572	1.2	22	2.4	73
North America	339	1.0	6	2	79
Oceania	34	1.2	26	2.3	75

Except for population (2007) the data are annual averages projected for the period 2005–2010.

1. Europe, North America, Australia, New Zealand and Japan.

2. Africa, Asia (excluding Japan), Latin America and the Caribbean and Oceania (excluding Australia and New Zealand).

3. Includes Russian Federation.

4. South America, Central America (including Mexico) and all Caribbean Islands.

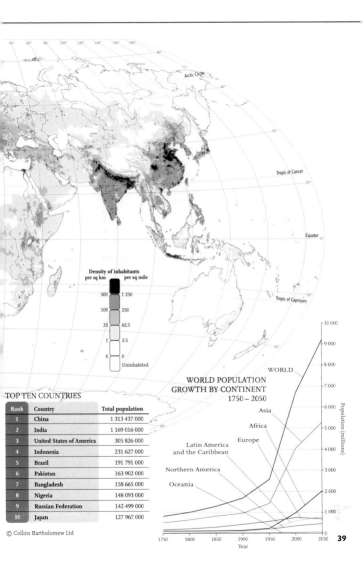

Density of inhabitants
per sq km | per sq mile
500 | 1 250
100 | 250
25 | 62.5
1 | 2.5
0 | 0
| Uninhabited

TOP TEN COUNTRIES

Rank	Country	Total population
1	China	1 313 437 000
2	India	1 169 016 000
3	United States of America	305 826 000
4	Indonesia	231 627 000
5	Brazil	191 791 000
6	Pakistan	163 902 000
7	Bangladesh	158 665 000
8	Nigeria	148 093 000
9	Russian Federation	142 499 000
10	Japan	127 967 000

© Collins Bartholomew Ltd

WORLD POPULATION GROWTH BY CONTINENT
1750 – 2050

WORLD

Asia

Africa

Europe

Latin America and the Caribbean

Northern America

Oceania

Population (millions)

Year

THE WORLD'S MAJOR CITIES

Urban agglomerations with over
1 million inhabitants.
Winkel Tripel Projection
scale 1:190 000 000

LEVEL OF URBANIZATION BY MAJOR REGION 1970–2030

Urban population as a percentage of total population

	1970	2010	2030
World	35.9	50.8	59.9
More developed regions[1]	64.6	75.2	80.8
Less developed regions[2]	25.2	45.5	56.1
Africa	23.4	40.5	50.7
Asia	22.7	42.5	54.1
Europe[3]	62.6	72.9	78.3
Latin America and the Caribbean[4]	57.2	79.1	84.3
Northern America	73.8	82.1	86.7
Oceania	70.8	71.2	73.8

1. Europe, North America, Australia,
New Zealand and Japan.
2. Africa, Asia (excluding Japan), Latin
America and the Caribbean, and
Oceania (excluding Australia and
New Zealand).
3. Includes Russian Federation.
4. South America, Central America
(including Mexico) and all Caribbean
Islands.

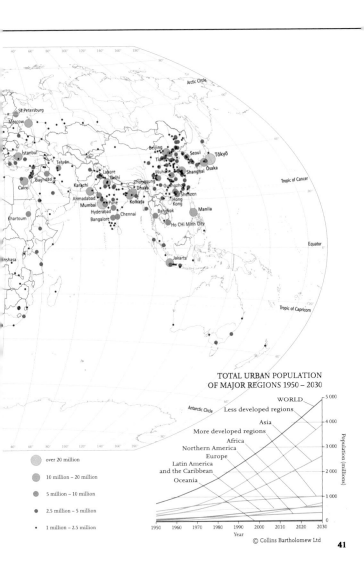

St Petersburg
Moscow
Istanbul
Tehrān
Baghdād
Cairo
Khartoum
Kinshasa

Lahore
Karachi
Ahmadabad
Mumbai
Pune
Hyderabad
Bangalore
Delhi
Kolkata
Chennai
Dhaka

Beijing
Tianjin
Wuhan
Shanghai
Chongqing
Guangzhou
Hong Kong
Shenzhen

Seoul
Ōsaka
Tōkyō

Bangkok
Ho Chi Minh City
Manila
Jakarta

Arctic Circle
Tropic of Cancer
Equator
Tropic of Capricorn
Antarctic Circle

over 20 million
10 million – 20 million
5 million – 10 million
2.5 million – 5 million
1 million – 2.5 million

TOTAL URBAN POPULATION
OF MAJOR REGIONS 1950 – 2030

WORLD
Less developed regions
Asia
More developed regions
Africa
Northern America
Europe
Latin America
and the Caribbean
Oceania

Population (millions)
5 000
4 000
3 000
2 000
1 000

1950   1960   1970   1980   1990   2000   2010   2020   2030
Year

© Collins Bartholomew Ltd

SYMBOLS

Map symbols used on the map pages are explained here. The depiction of relief follows the tradition of layer-colouring, with colours depicting altitude bands. Ocean pages have a different contour interval. Settlements are classified in terms of both population and administrative significance. The abbreviations listed are those used in place names on the map pages and within the index.

LAND AND WATER FEATURES

Lake		River	
Impermanent lake		Impermanent rive	
Salt lake or lagoon		Ice cap / Glacier	
Impermanent salt lake		123 Pass height in metres	
Dry salt lake or salt pan		.·. Site of special inter	
		⌒⌒⌒ Wall	

RELIEF

Contour intervals used in layer-colouring for land height and sea depth

	METRES FEET		Ocean pages METRES FEET
			0 0
	5000 16404		200 656
	3000 9843		2000 6562
	2000 6562		3000 9843
	1000 3281		4000 13124
	500 1640		5000 16404
	200 656		6000 19686
	0 0		7000 22967
	LAND B.S.L.		9000 29529
	200 656		
	4000 13124	123	Ocean deep In metres.
	6000 19686		

BOUNDARIES

▬▬▬ International boundary

·▬·▬· Disputed international boundary or alignment unconfirmed

Undefined international boundary in the sea. All land within this boundary is part of state or territory named.

▬▬ Administrative boundary Shown for selected countries only.

●●●● Ceasefire line or other boundary described on the map

TRANSPORT

═══ Motorway

▬▬ Main road

--- Track

▬▬ Main railway

⊥⊥⊥⊥ Canal

✈ Main airport

1234 Summit
△ Height in metres

1234 Volcano
▲ Height in metres

CITIES AND TOWNS

Built-up area
SCALE 1:4 000 000 only

Population	National Capital	Administrative Capital Shown for selected countries only	Other City or Town
over 10 million	BEIJING ▣	São Paulo ◉	New York ◉
5 to 10 million	PARIS ▣	St Petersburg ◉	Chicago ◉
1 to 5 million	KUWAIT □	Sydney ○	Seattle ○
500 000 to 1 million	BANGUI □	Winnipeg ○	Jeddah ○
100 000 to 500 000	WELLINGTON □	Edinburgh ○	Apucarana ○
50 000 to 100 000	PORT OF SPAIN □	Bismarck ○	Invercargill ○
under 50 000	MALABO ▫	Charlottetown ○	Ceres ○

STYLES OF LETTERING

Cities and towns are explained separately

			Physical features	
Country	**FRANCE**		Island	*Gran Canaria*
Overseas Territory/Dependency	**Guadeloupe**		Lake	*Lake Erie*
Disputed Territory	AKSAI CHIN		Mountain	*Mt Blanc*
Administrative name Shown for selected countries only.	**SCOTLAND**		River	*Thames*
Area name	PATAGONIA		Region	*LAPPLAND*

CONTINENTAL MAPS

BOUNDARIES

———— International boundary

- - - - - - Disputed international boundary

•••••••• Ceasefire line

CITIES AND TOWNS

National capital

Kuwait □

Other city or town

Seattle ○

ABBREVIATIONS

Arch.	Archipelago				Mts	Mountains Monts	French	hills, mountains
B.	Bay		bay		N.	North, Northern		
	Bahía, Baía	Portuguese	bay		O.	Ostrov	Russian	island
	Bahía	Spanish	bay		Pt	Point		
	Baie	French	bay		Pta	Punta	Italian, Spanish	cape, point
C.	Cape				R.	River		river
	Cabo	Portuguese, Spanish	cape, headland			Rio	Portuguese	river
	Cap	French	cape, headland			Río	Spanish	river
Co	Cerro	Spanish	hill, peak, summit			Rivière	French	river
E.	East, Eastern				Ra.	Range		
Est.	Estrecho	Spanish	strait		S.	South, Southern		saltpan, saltpans
Gt	Great					Salar, Salina, Salinas	Spanish	
I.	Island, Isle				Sa	Serra	Portuguese	mountain range
	Ilha	Portuguese	island			Sierra	Spanish	mountain range
	Islas	Spanish	island		Sd	Sound		
Is	Islands, Isles				S.E.	Southeast, Southeastern		
	Islas	Spanish	islands		St	Saint		
Khr.	Khrebet	Russian	mountain range			Sankt	German	saint
L.	Lake					Sint	Dutch	
	Loch	(Scotland)	lake		Sta	Santa	Italian, Portuguese, Spanish	saint
	Lough	(Ireland)	lake					
	Lac	French	lake		Ste	Sainte	French	saint
	Lago	Portuguese, Spanish	lake		Str.	Strait		
M.	Mys	Russian	cape, point		W.	West, Western		watercourse
Mt	Mount					Wadi, Wādī	Arabic	
	Mont	French	hill, mountain					
Mt.	Mountain							

NORTH AMERICA

Mt McKinley
6194
Mt Logan
5959
Aleutian Islands
Gulf of Alaska
Rocky Mountains
Great Lakes
Hawaiian Islands
St Maria Occidental
Rio Grande
Gulf of Mexico
Mississippi
Appalachian Mts
St Lawrence
Hudson Bay
Labrador
Newfoundland
Baffin Island
Greenland
Iceland
British Isles
Azores
Canary Islands
Atlas Mountains
Sahara
AFRICA

PACIFIC
OCEAN

Galapagos Islands
Hispaniola
Caribbean Sea
Orinoco
Cuba
Cape Verde
Gulf of Guinea
Niger

ATLANTIC
OCEAN

SOUTH AMERICA
Amazon
Brazilian Highlands
Andes
Paraná
Cerro Aconcagua
6959
Patagonia
Pampas
Tierra del Fuego
Falkland Islands
Cape Horn
South Georgia
South Sandwich Islands
Ascension
St Helena
Tristan da Cunha

Tuamotu Islands
Tubuai Islands
Pitcairn Is
Easter Island
Polynesia
Line Islands

Antarctic Peninsula
Amundsen Sea
Vinson Massif
4897
Weddell Sea
ANTA

Winkel Tripel Projection

1 : 170 000 000

MILES 0   1000   2000   300

0   1000   2000   3000   4000   5000 KILOMETRES

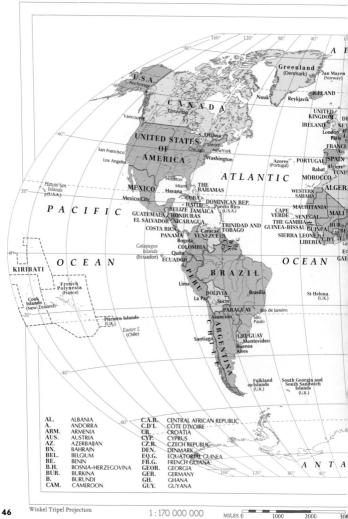

AL.	ALBANIA	C.A.R.	CENTRAL AFRICAN REPUBLIC
A.	ANDORRA	C.D'I.	CÔTE D'IVOIRE
ARM.	ARMENIA	CR.	CROATIA
AUS.	AUSTRIA	CYP.	CYPRUS
AZ.	AZERBAIJAN	CZ.R.	CZECH REPUBLIC
BN.	BAHRAIN	DEN.	DENMARK
BEL.	BELGIUM	EQ.G.	EQUATORIAL GUINEA
BE.	BENIN	FR.G.	FRENCH GUIANA
B.H.	BOSNIA–HERZEGOVINA	GEOR.	GEORGIA
BUR.	BURKINA	GER.	GERMANY
B.	BURUNDI	GH.	GHANA
CAM.	CAMEROON	GUY.	GUYANA

Winkel Tripel Projection

1 : 170 000 000

MILES 0   1000   2000   300

Svalbard
(Norway)

Arctic Circle

ARCTIC OCEAN

NORWAY
FINLAND
ESTONIA
LATVIA
LITH.
BELARUS
POLAND Kiev
CZ. UKRAINE
SVK. MOL.
HUN. ROMANIA
ALB. BULGARIA GEOR.
GREECE TURKEY
CYP. SYRIA
LEB. ISR. IRAQ
JOR. IRAN
EGYPT KUWAIT
SAUDI ARABIA
LIBYA
Cairo
Tripoli
Khartoum
CHAD SUDAN
C.A.R.
DEM. REP. CONGO
UGANDA KENYA
TANZANIA
COMOROS
MOZAMBIQUE
MADAGASCAR
MAURITIUS
Réunion (France)
ZAMBIA
ZIM- BABWE
NAMIBIA BOTS- WANA
Windhoek
Pretoria SWAZILAND
LESOTHO
REP. OF SOUTH AFRICA

Moscow
Yekaterinburg
Novosibirsk

RUSSIAN FEDERATION

Magadan

Astana
KAZAKHSTAN
Ulaanbaatar
MONGOLIA

UZBEK. KYR.
TURKM. TAJIK.
AFGHAN.
Tehrān
PAKISTAN
Islamabad
New Delhi
NEPAL BHUTAN
INDIA BANGLA- DESH
MYANMAR
Nay Pyi Taw
Rangoon
THAILAND
Bangkok CAM- BODIA
SRI LANKA
MALDIVES

Mumbai
Chennai

SEYCHELLES

Nairobi
Dodoma
Mogadishu
SOMALIA
ETHIOPIA
Addis Ababa
ERITREA
DJIBOUTI
YEMEN

Beijing
Tianjin
CHINA
Xi'an
Chengdu Wuhan
Chongqing
Shanghai
T'aipei
TAIWAN
Hong Kong
Hà Nôi
VIETNAM
Manila
PHILIPPINES

N.KOREA
Seoul
S.KOREA
JAPAN
Tōkyō
Osaka

BRUNEI
MALAYSIA
SINGAPORE
INDONESIA
Jakarta
EAST TIMOR

PACIFIC OCEAN

Tropic of Cancer

Northern Mariana Islands (U.S.A.)

MARSHALL ISLANDS

FEDERATED STATES OF MICRONESIA
PALAU

Equator

NAURU
KIRIBATI

PAPUA NEW GUINEA
Port Moresby

SOLOMON ISLANDS

VANUATU

New Caledonia (France)

FIJI
TONGA
SAMOA
American Samoa
TUVALU

Tropic of Capricorn

INDIAN OCEAN

French Southern and Antarctic Lands
Îles Kerguélen

AUSTRALIA
Perth
Sydney
Canberra

Wellington
NEW ZEALAND

ANTARCTICA

Antarctic Circle

HUN.	HUNGARY	Q.	QATAR
ISR.	ISRAEL	R.	RWANDA
JOR.	JORDAN	S.	SERBIA
K.	KUWAIT	SLA.	SLOVAKIA
KYR.	KYRGYZSTAN	SL.	SLOVENIA
LEB.	LEBANON	SUR.	SURINAME
LITH.	LITHUANIA	SW.	SWITZERLAND
LUX.	LUXEMBOURG	TAJIK.	TAJIKISTAN
M.	MACEDONIA	T.	TOGO
MO.	MOLDOVA	TURKM.	TURKMENISTAN
NETH.	NETHERLANDS	U.A.E.	UNITED ARAB EMIRATES
NI.	NIGERIA	UZBEK.	UZBEKISTAN

0   1000   2000   3000   4000   5000 KILOMETRES

© Collins Bartholomew Ltd

1 : 72 000 000

MILES 0   500   100

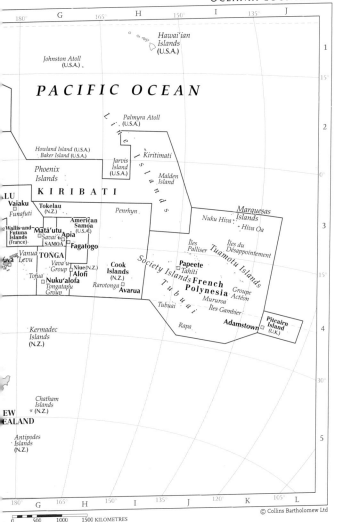

PACIFIC OCEAN

Hawai'ian Islands (U.S.A.)

Johnston Atoll (U.S.A.)

Palmyra Atoll (U.S.A.)

Howland Island (U.S.A.)
Baker Island (U.S.A.)

Phoenix Islands

Jarvis Island (U.S.A.)

Kiritimati

Malden Island

KIRIBATI

LU
Vaiaku
Funafuti

Tokelau (N.Z.)

Penrhyn

Marquesas Islands
Nuku Hiva · Hiva Oa

Wallis-and-Futuna Islands (France)

American Samoa
Matā'utu
Savai'i
SAMOA
Apia (U.S.A.)
Fagatogo

Îles du Désappointement

Vanua Levu

TONGA

Vava'u Group

Niue (N.Z.)
Alofi

Cook Islands (N.Z.)

Îles Palliser

Tuamotu Islands

uva

Tofua

Nuku'alofa
Tongatapu Group

Rarotonga
Avarua

Society Islands
Papeete
Tahiti
French Polynesia

Groupe Actéon

Tubuai

Tubuai

Mururoa
Îles Gambier

Pitcairn Island (U.K.)

Rapa

Adamstown

Kermadec Islands (N.Z.)

Chatham Islands (N.Z.)

EW
EALAND

Antipodes Islands (N.Z.)

0   500   1000   1500 KILOMETRES

© Collins Bartholomew Ltd

49

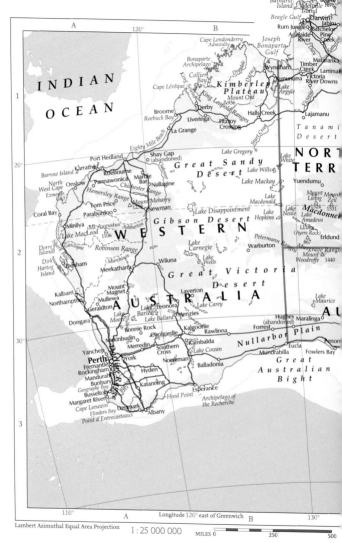

INDIAN

OCEAN

Bathurst
Island
Beagle Gulf · Darwin · Jabiru
Rum Jungle · Batchelor
Adelaide · Pine
River · Creek
Joseph
Cape Londonderry · Bonaparte · Timber · Mataranka
Admiralty Gulf · Creek · Larrimah
Gulf · Wyndham · Victoria
Bonaparte · Kununurra · River Downs
Archipelago · Kimberley · Lake
Collier · Plateau · Argyle · Lajamanu
Bay · Mount Ord
Cape Lévêque · King Leopold Ranges · 1936 · Halls Creek
Broome · Derby · Fitzroy · Tanami
Roebuck Bay · Liveringa · Crossing · Desert
La Grange

Eighty Mile Beach · NOR
Lake Gregory · TERR
Port Hedland · Shay Gap · Lake
Karratha · (abandoned) · White
Barrow Island · Roebourne · Marble · Great Sandy · Lake Wills · Yuendumu
North · Pannawonica · Bar · Desert · Lake Mackay
West Cape · Onslow · Chichester · Nullagine · Mount Mount
Exmouth · Hamersley Range · Range · Liebig · Zeil
Gulf · Tom Price · Mount Meharry · Lake Disappointment · 1524 1531
Coral Bay · Paraburdoo · 1249 · Newman · Gibson Desert · Lake · Macdonne
Macdonald · Lake · Amadeus
Minilya · Mt Augustus · Ashburton · Neale · Uluru
Lake MacLeod · 1106 · WESTERN · Lake · (Ayers Rock) · Erldund
Dorre · Robinson Range · Hopkins · 867
Island · Gascoyne · Lake · Petermann Ranges
Dirk · Denham · Murchison · Carnegie · Warburton · Musgrave Range
Hartog · Meekatharra · Lake · Mount
Island · Wiluna · Wells · Woodroffe 1440

AUSTRALIA · Great Victoria
Mount · Desert · AU
Kalbarri · Magnet · Lake
Northampton · Mullewa · Leonora · Laverton · Lake Carey · Lake
Geraldton · Lake · Barlee · Menzies · Maurice
Dongara · Moore · Hughes · Maralinga
Bonnie Rock · Kalgoorlie · (abandoned)
Mukinbudin · Coolgardie · Rawlinna · Forrest · Nullarbor Plain · Eucla · Penon
Yanchep · Merredin · Kambalda · Mundrabilla · Fowlers Bay
Perth · Southern · Lake Cowan · Great
Fremantle · York · Cross · Norseman · Australian
Rockingham · Hyden · Balladonia · Bight
Mandurah
Bunbury · Katanning
Geographe Bay · Esperance
Busselton
Margaret River · Hood Point · Archipelago of
Cape Leeuwin · Denmark · the Recherche
Flinders Bay · Albany
Point d'Entrecasteaux

1 : 25 000 000

MILES 0 · 250 · 500

Wessel Is *Cape Wessel*
ngham Bay
Nhulunbuy
Cape Arnhem
Arnhem Bay
Cape York
Bamaga
C. Grenville
Cape York
Arnhem
Land
Isle Woodah
Alyangula
Groote
Eylandt
Gulf of
Carpentaria
Cape
York
Albatross Bay Weipa
Coen
C. Direction
Princess
arche Charlotte Bay
Peninsula
Cape
Melville

Sir Edward
Pellew Group
Borroloola

Daly
Waters
Lake
Woods

Mornington
Island
Wellesley
Islands
Laura
Cape
Flattery
Cooktown

CORAL
SEA

Barkly Tableland
Burketown
Gilbert
Mossman
Mount Bartle Frere
Cairns
Innisfail

GREAT

D

150°

E

Tennant
Creek
Camooweal
Forsayth
Tully Hinchinbrook
Island

HERN
TORY
Mount
Isa
Kajabbi
Cloncurry
Gregory
Range
Townsville
Ayr
Bowen
Whitsunday I.
Proserpine
BARRIER

1

Barrow
Creek
Dajarra
Richmond
Charters
Towers
Mt Dalrymple
1277
Mackay
Sarina
REEF

20°

Alice
Springs
Ranges
Boulia
Winton
QUEENSLAND
Longreach
Clermont
Emerald
Percy Islands
Arthur Point
Curtis I. Tropic of Capricorn
Rockhampton
Yeppoon
DIVIDING

Simpson
Desert
Cluny
Barcaldine
Moura
Gladstone
Biloela
Monto

Birdsville
Yaraka
Blackall
Windorah
Buckland
Tableland
Maryborough
Bundaberg
Hervey Bay
Sandy Cape
Fraser Island

Bilpa Morea
Claypan
Charleville
Mitchell
Roma
Kingaroy
Gympie
Tewantin
Nambour

Oodnadatta
Lake Eyre
(North)
Coober Pedy
Lake Eyre (South)
Birdsville
Track
Sturt
Stony
Desert
Quilpie
St George
Balonne
Dalby
Toowoomba
Caboolture
Brisbane
Beenleigh
Gold Coast

SOUTH
TRALIA
Lake
Blanche
Tibooburra
Hungerford
Cunnamulla
Dirranbandi
Goondiwindi
Moonie
Warwick
Casino
Ballina

arcoola
Lake
Gairdner
Woomera
Lake
Torrens
Lake
Frome
Innamincka
Bourke
Brewarrina
Mungindi
Moree
Inverell
Narrabri
Grafton
Macksville

eduna
Streaky
Bay
Whyalla
Port Augusta
Broken Hill
Wilcannia
Cobar
Warren
Armidale
Tamworth
Port Macquarie

Kyancutta
Eyre
Peninsula
Port Pirie
Jamestown
Burra
Ivanhoe
NEW SOUTH WALES
Dubbo
Muswellbrook
Taree

Cape Carnot
Gawler
Adelaide
Murray
Bridge
Mildura
Swan
Hill
Griffith
Wagga Wagga
Parkes
Orange
Bathurst
Newcastle
Sydney
Botany Bay
Wollongong

Kangaroo
Island
Cape Jaffa
Lake
Terrell Hills
Bendigo
Shepparton
Albury
Yass
Goulburn
CANBERRA
A.C.T.
Nowra
Batemans Bay

Mount Gambier
Hamilton
VICTORIA
Ararat
Ballarat
Melbourne
Mt Kosciuszko
Bega
Cape Howe

TASMAN
SEA

Portland
Cape Otway
Geelong
Colac
Moe Sale
Bairnsdale
Warrnambool
Wilson's Promontory

Bass Strait
Flinders Island
Furneaux Group
Cape Barren I.

Currie
King Island
Hunter Islands
Burnie
Devonport
Eddystone Pt
Launceston
Scottsdale

Queenstown
Mount Ossa
TASMANIA
Lake Gordon
Hobart
Bicheon

40°

C

140°

150°

E

© Collins Bartholomew Ltd

51

0   250   500 KILOMETRES

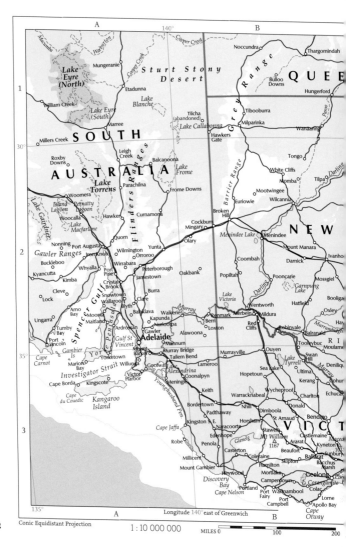

Conic Equidistant Projection

1 : 10 000 000

Longitude 140° east of Greenwich

MILES 0   100   200

45'   C   150°   D

Moonie
Oakey Gatton Laidley
Toowoomba Pittsworth Ipswich Brisbane
Cunnamulla Bollon St George Nindigully Inglewood Millmerran Boonah Beenleigh Gold
Murra Murra Goondiwindi Warwick Murwillumbah Coast
Dirranbandi Talwood Boggabilla Stanthorpe Kyogle Casino Byron Bay
Barringun Wellmoringle Goodooga Lightning Hebel Mungindi Garah Texas Tenterfield Coraki Ballina
Ridge Boomi Yetman Ashford Deepwater Evans Head
Eulo Enngonia Dilllabenron Moree Warialda Glen Innes Maclean Iluka
Fords Bridge Rowena Bellata Bingara Yamba
Bourke Brewarrina Gongolgon Walgett Bundarra Grafton
Collarenebri Gravesend Inverell Woolgoolga
Byrock Carinda Pilliga Narrabri Barraba Guyra Dorrigo Coffs Harbour
Coolabah Baradine Manilla Armidale Sawtell
Louth Coonamble Mullaley Gunnedah Uralla Walcha Macksville Nambucca Heads
Nyngan Warren Gilgandra Coonabarabran Tamworth Werris Creek South West Rocks
Cobar Hermidale Coolabah Gulargambone Premer Quirindi Kempsey
Nevertire Eumungerie Merrygoen Murrurundi Wingham Port Macquarie
Gilgunnia Mount Hope Nyngan Narromine Dubbo Wellington Scone Gloucester Taree Lake Cathie
Bobadah Tomingley Mudgee Denman Muswellbrook Stroud Bulahdelah
Condobolin Yeoval Molong Kandos Dungog Tea Gardens
Roto Buabalong Forbes Parkes Orange Glen Davis Cessnock Raymond Terrace Nelson Bay
Lake Cargelligo Ungarie Marsden Blayney Portland Lithgow Kurri Kurri Newcastle
Hillston West Canowindra Bathurst Richmond Morisset Swansea
Wyalong Cowra Oberon Katoomba Gosford
Griffith Ardlethan Grenfell Young Crookwell Windsor
Leeton Temora Wallendbeen Yass Camden Sydney
Narrandera Cootamundra Burrinjuck Goulburn Picton Botany Bay
Coleambally Junee Reservoir Bungendore Mittagong Wollongong
Darlington Point Coolamon Wagga Wagga Tarcutta Gundagai CANBERRA Bowral Kiama
Forest Hill The Rock Tumut AUSTRALIAN Queanbeyan Nowra Greenwell Point
Tocumwal Culcairn Tumbarumba CAPITAL Beecroft Peninsula
Cobram Howlong TERRITORY JERVIS BAY
Nathalia Corowa Holbrook Cooma Batemans Bay TERRITORY
Numurkah Rutherglen Mount Adaminaby Moruya
Shepparton Wangaratta Kosciuszko Jindabyne Narooma
Myrtleford 2228 Dalgety Bermagui
Benalla Bright Mount Beauty Mount Bega TASMAN
Mansfield Bogong Nimmitabel Tathra
Alexandra Omeo Bombala Merimbula
Healesville Delegate Eden SEA
Melbourne Dargo Buchan Cann River
Woods Pt Ensay Cape Howe
Droubin Orbost Mallacoota Inlet
Warragul Moe Yallourn Bairnsdale Lakes Entrance Mallacoota
Traralgon Sale Lake Wellington
Morwell
Worthaggi Yarram Corner Inlet
Wilson's Promontory

0   100   200   300 KILOMETRES

© Collins Bartholomew Ltd

53

C   150°   D   155°

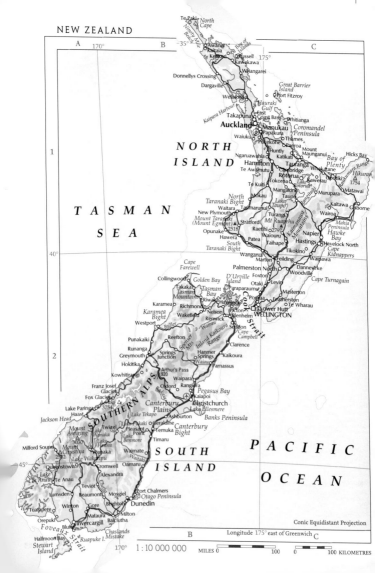

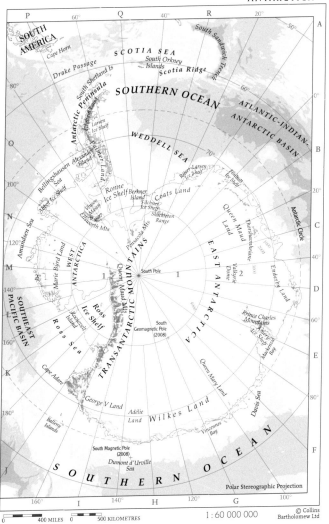

SOUTH AMERICA

Cape Horn

SCOTIA SEA

South Orkney Islands

Scotia Ridge

South Sandwich Trench

Drake Passage

South Shetland Is

SOUTHERN OCEAN

ATLANTIC-INDIAN-ANTARCTIC BASIN

Antarctic Peninsula

Palmer Land

Larsen Ice Shelf

WEDDELL SEA

Antarctic Circle

Bellingshausen Sea

Alexander Island

Ronne Ice Shelf

Wilkins Ice Shelf

Berkner Island

Riiser Larsen Ice Shelf

Brunt Ice Shelf

Coats Land

Queen Maud Land

Thorshavnheane

Amundsen Sea

Marie Byrd Land

WEST ANTARCTICA

Ellsworth Mts

Vinson Massif

Filchner Ice Shelf

Shackleton Range

Pensacola Mts

Valkyrie Dome

Enderby Land

SOUTHEAST PACIFIC BASIN

Ross Ice Shelf

Roosevelt Island

South Pole

South Geomagnetic Pole (2008)

EAST ANTARCTICA

Prince Charles Mountains

Amery Ice Shelf

Mackenzie Bay

Ross Sea

TRANSANTARCTIC MOUNTAINS

Cape Adare

Queen Mary Land

Davis Sea

George V Land

Adélie Land

Wilkes Land

Vincennes Bay

Balleny Islands

South Magnetic Pole (2008)

Dumont d'Urville Sea

SOUTHERN OCEAN

Polar Stereographic Projection

0   400 MILES   0   500 KILOMETRES

1 : 60 000 000

© Collins Bartholomew Ltd

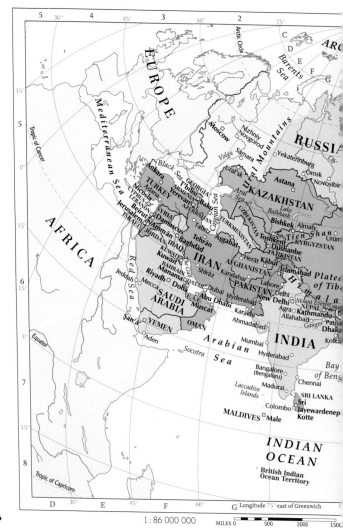

1 : 86 000 000

MILES 0   500   1000   1500

IC OCEAN

oril'sk

Bering
Sea

Magadan

N FEDERATION

Sea
of
Okhotsk

Petropavlovsk-
Kamchatsky

Irkutsk
Lake
Baikal

Ulan Bator   Harbin   Sapporo

Vladivostok   Hakodate

MONGOLIA

Shenyang   NORTH   Sea of
KOREA   Japan   JAPAN
(East Sea)

Beijing   Dalian   P'yŏngyang   Tōkyō
Tianjin   Seoul   SOUTH   Ōsaka
KOREA   Fukuoka   Hiroshima

Lanzhou   Xi'an   Yellow
Sea

HINA   Nanjing   Shanghai   East
China
Sea

Chengdu   Yangtzu   Wuhan

Chongqing   Hangzhou

PACIFIC

OCEAN

Kunming   T'aipei
Liuzhou   Guangzhou   TAIWAN
Nanning   Kaoshiung

ADESH   Ha Nôi   Hong Kong   Luzon Strait
ANMAR   Hai Phong
RMA)
Nay Pyi Taw   Quezon City

ngoon   Vientiane   South   Manila   PHILIPPINES
LAOS   China
THAILAND   Sea
Bangkok

damand   Phnom   Ho Chi Minh City   Davao   Melekeok
nds   Penh   PALAU
ia)
icobar   Kota
lands   Kinabalu   Celebes
dia)   Kuala   Bandar Seri   Sea
Lumpur   Begawan   Jayapura

edan   MALAYSIA   BRUNEI
Putrajaya   SINGAPORE   Kuching   New
Singapore   Borneo   Guinea

Pontianak   INDONESIA   OCEANIA

Sumatra   Palembang   Banjarmasin   Laut Banda

Jakarta   Laut Jawa   Makassar
Bandung   Surabaya   Dili   EAST TIMOR
Semarang
Java   Timor
Sea

MONGOLIA   Yellow River

Lena

0   1000   2000 KILOMETRES

Albers Equal Area Conic Projection

1 : 30 000 000

Longitude 105° east of Greenwich

MILES 0   200   400   600

PHILIPPINE

SEA

PACIFIC

OCEAN

Northern

Mariana

Islands

(U.S.A.)

Pagan

CAPITOL HILL   Saipan

Tinian

Rota   HAGÅTÑA

Guam

(U.S.A.)

PHILIPPINES

olillo

lands

aet *Catanduanes*

Sorsogon

Catarman

Samar

Catbalogan

Tacloban

acolod

Cebu

hilaran

Surigao

Butuan

Cagayan de Oro

roquieta

gadian *Mindanao*

Davao

Cotabato   Mati

oro

General Santos

ulf

Ulithi   Fais

Yap

FEDERATED STATES

Ngulu   Sorol

OF MICRONESIA

Eauripik   *Caroline*

Islands

PALAU

MELEKEOK

bes

Kepulauan

Talaud

Morotai

Kepulauan

a   *Sangir*

Manado   Tobelo

indhasa

Tondano   Ternate   Halmahera

Gorontalo   Sao-sio

an   *Laut Maluku*

wuk   (Molucca Sea)   Waigeo

Bacan   Obi   Salawati   Sorong

Peleng   Misoöl

Bangga   Dofa   *Laut Seram*

Taliabu Mangole

ggai   Sula   Namlea   Piru

ndari   *S*   Ambon   Saparua

Anui   *Kepulauan*

Wowoni   *Banda*

ua   Watubela

Buton   *Kepulauan*

bau   *Tukangbesi*

Equator   0°

Pelieluhu Is

Hermit Is

Biak

Manokwari

Numfoor   Selat Yapen   Tanjung d'Urville

Nabire   Sarmi   Jayapura   Vanimo   Aitape

Taritatu

Enarotali   *Pegunungan Van Rees*   Wewak

Sepik   Manam I.

PAPUA

Madang

Long

Island

Umbo

4000   *NEW GUINEA*

Mendi   Mount   Goroka   Lae

Hagen   Kerema   Morobe

Balimo   Mt   Wau

Victoria

Daru   Gulf   Bereina

Morehead   of   PORT

Papua   MORESBY

Arafura Sea

C. York

Bamaga

AUSTRALIA   Weipa

Gulf

of

Carpentaria

Coen

Melville

Island

DILI   EAST

Kupang   Timor

Rote

ea

Laut Banda

(Banda Sea)

Kepulauan Barat

Alor   Pulau Roma   *Kepulauan Tanimbar*

Wetar   Wuliaru

Pulau

Wokam

Dobo

Benjina

Larat

Sia   Saumlakki

Selaru

Pulau

Dolok

Digul

Merauke

© Collins Bartholomew Ltd

0   500   1000 KILOMETRES

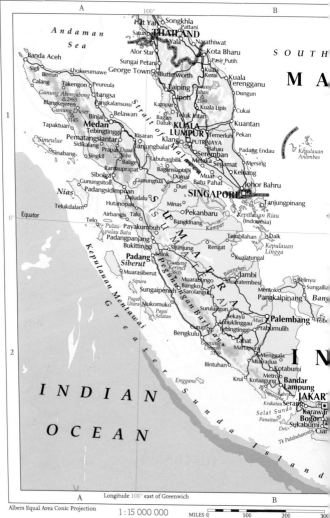

A map showing the northern part of Sumatra and the Malay Peninsula.

Andaman Sea

THAILAND
Hat Yai · Songkhla
Pattani
Satun · Yala · Narathiwat
Kangar · Alor Star
Sungai Petani · Kuala Kerai · Kota Bharu
Banda Aceh · Pasir Putih
Sigli · Bireun
Calang · Lhokseumawe · George Town · Butterworth · Kuala Terengganu
Takengon · Peureula · Taiping · Gunung Tahan 2189 · Dungun
Gunung Abongabong △2985 · Langsa · Ipoh
Blangkejeren · Pangkalansusu · Kampar · Kuala Lipis · Cukai
Gunung Leuser △3145 · Belawan · Binjai · Bagan Datuk · Kuantan
Tapaktuan · Medan · Teluk Intan
Tebingtinggi · KUALA LUMPUR · Temerluh · Pekan
Simeulue · Pematangsiantar · Kisaran · Klang · PUTRAJAYA
Sidikalang · Prapat Danau · Tanjungbalai · Seremban · Padang Endau
Sinabang · Singkil · Baligé · Toba · Labuhanbilik · Melaka · Mersing
Ranauprapat · Bagansiapiapi · Segamat · Keluang
Sibolga · Gunungtua · Dumai · Muar · Batu Pahat
Nias · Gunungsitoli · Duri · Johor Bahru
Padangsidimpuan · Daludalu · SINGAPORE · Tanjungpinang
Telukdalam · Hutanopan · Minas · Kepulauan Riau (Indonesia)
Equator · Airbangis · Talu · Pekanbaru
Telo · Payakumbuh · Bangkinang · Kampar · Tembilahan · Daik
Pulau-pulau Batu · Padangpanjang · Bangkinang · Rengat · Kepulauan Lingga
Bukittinggi · Sijunjung · Kualatungal
Padang · Solok · Gunung Kerinci △3805
Siberut · Muarasiberut · Batanghari · Jambi · Muaratembesi
Sipura · Muarabungo · Bangko · Sarolangun
Sungaipenuh · Surulangun · Sekayu · Belinyu
Pagai Utara · Mukomuko · Lubuklinggau · Musi · Palembang
Pagai Selatan · Curup · Tebingtinggi · Prabumulih
Bengkulu · Gunung Dempo △3159 · Lahat · Martapura
Menggala · Muaradua · Kotabumi
Bintuhan · Krui · Kotaagung · Bandar Lampung
Enggano · Metro · Serang
Krakatau · Karawa
Selat Sunda · JAKARTA · Bogor · Sukabumi · Cian
Panaitan · Deli · Tk Palabuhanratu

INDIAN OCEAN

SUMATRA

SOUTH
MA

Kepulauan Anambas

IN

Strait of Malacca

Kepulauan Mentawai

Greater Sunda Islands

Pegunungan Barisan

60 · Albers Equal Area Conic Projection · 1 : 15 000 000 · MILES 0 · 100 · 200 · 300

Longitude 100° east of Greenwich

110°

Banggi

SULU SEA

Kudat

Kota Belud
Gunung
Kinabalu
Kota 4095
Kinabalu
Ranau
Sandakan

CHINA SEA

Beaufort

Labuan
SABAH

Lamag
Lahad
Datu

LAYSIA

BANDAR SERI
BEGAWAN
Kuamut

Pensiangan

BRUNEI

Kuala Belait
Lutong
Miri
Seria

Tawau

Semporna

Tuaran

Natuna Besar

Panarik

Lumbis

CELEBES

Kepulauan
Natuna

Bintulu

Long
Akah

Kubuang

Tarakan

SEA

1

Igan Mukah

Sibu
Belaga

Sarikei
Rajang Kapit

Tanjungredeb

Tanjungselor

Sepinang

Liku
Sematan
Kuching
Saratok
Debak

Datadian

2988

Sambaliung

Sambas
Kota
Samarahan
Pemangkat Serian Sri Aman
Lubok
Antu
Putusibau

KALIMANTAN

Sangkulirang

ngkawang

Semitau

Bontang

Bengkayang

Sanggau
Sintang
BORNEO

pulauan
mbelan
Mempawah

Ngabang
Kapuas

Longiram

Pontianak

Nangahpinoh

Muaralaung

Samarinda

Tenggarong

0

Balaiberkuak

Muarateweh

Balikpapan

Selat Makassar

(Macassar Strait)

Pulau-pulau
Karimata

Telukbatang

Nangatayap
Rantaupanjang

Tanahgrogot

Babana

Ketapang

Schwaner
Palangkaraya

Amuntai

Mamuju

elat Ka

Kendawangan

Sukaraja

Sampit
Barito
Kandangan

Bukit
3074
Gandadiwata

anjungpandan

Pangkalanbuun

Kotabaru

Polewali

Manggar
*Tanjung
Sambar*

Kualapembuang
Martapura

Majene

Banjarmasin
Pagatan

elitung

*Tanjung
Puting*
*Tanjung
Selatan*

Laut

DONESIA

2

LAUT JAWA
(JAVA SEA)

*Kepulauan
Laut Kecil*

Pulau-pulau
Karimunjawa

Sabalana

Kemujan

Bawean

*Tanjung
Indramayu*

*Kepulauan
Kangean*

*Tanjung
Bugel*

Madura

Kepulauan
Tengah

akarta
ebon
TegalPekalongan
Pati
Tuban
Bangkalan
Sumenep

Sumbawa

andung
3428
Semarang
Surabaya
Jombang
Kudus

Raas

Garut

Temanggung
Surakarta
Pasuruan
Situbondo

Laut Bali
(Bali Sea)

Alas

Dompu
Raba

mis
Kebumen
Madiun
G. Raung
3142
Banyuwangi

Sumbawabesar

Cilacap

Yogyakarta
Malang

Mataram

Praya
Taliwang

JAVA
(JAWA)

Lumajang Jember
Barung
Gilimanuk

Bali

Singaraja

Lombok

Denpasar

110°

C

© Collins Bartholomew Ltd

0   250   500 KILOMETRES

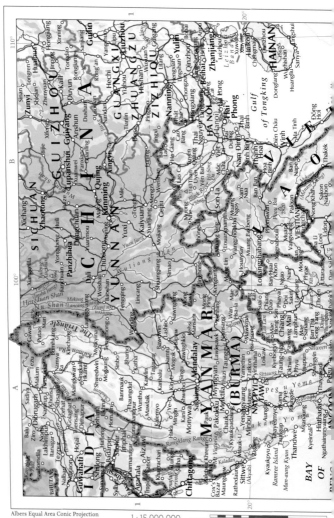

Albers Equal Area Conic Projection

1 : 15 000 000

MILES 0   100   200   300

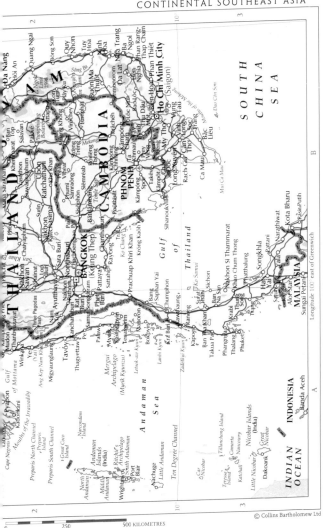

© Collins Bartholomew Ltd

Albers Equal Area Conic Projection

1 : 15 000 000   MILES 0   100

0   250 KILOMETRES

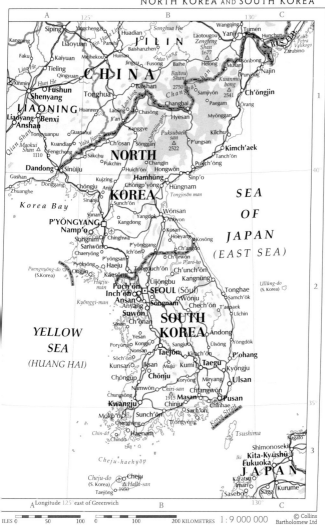

SEA
OF

JAPAN
(EAST SEA)

HOKKAIDŌ

La Pérouse Strait

Albers Equal Area Conic Projection

1 : 10 000 000

MILES 0   100

Places and labels:

Ostrov Kunashir
Ostrov Kunashir
Yuzhno-Kuril'sk
Shiretoko-misaki
Nemuro
Mys Anīva
Mys Kril'on
Ostrov Monzeron
Rebun-tō
Rishiri-tō
Sōya-misaki
Wakkanai
Monbetsu
Abashiri
Kitami
Nayoro
Teshio-gawa
Kushiro
Kussharo-ko
Shibetsu
Meakan-dake 1503
Asahi-dake 2290
Asahikawa
Obihiro
Hidaka-sammyaku
Erimo-misaki
Samani
Takikawa
Ishikari-gawa
Asahikawa
Bibai
Yūbari
Iwamizawa
Otaru
Sapporo
Ishikari-wan
Tomakomai
Shakotan-misaki
Iwanai
Suttsu
Yakumo
Muroran
Uchiura-wan
(Volcano Bay)
Okushiri-tō
Ō-shima
Mori
Hakodate
Matsumae
Shiriya-zaki
Tsugaru-kaikyō
Mutsu
Goshogawara
Aomori
Noshiro
Oga-hantō
Noshiro
Hachinohe
Towada
Ōdate
Hanawa
Akita
Kitakami-gawa
Hiraizumi
Honjō
Kitakami
Ichinoseki
Sakata
Tsuruoka

Sikhote-Alin'
Amgu
Amur
Terneye
Dal'negorsk
Rudnaya Pristan'
Kavalerovo
Chuguyevka
Arsen'yev
Spassk-Dal'niy
Ussuriysk
Mikhaylovka
Yaroslavskiy
Pol'tavka
Artëm
Bol'shoy Kamen'
Vladivostok
Nakhodka
Nakhodka
Vrangel'
Zaliv Petra Velikogo
Zarubino

RUSSIAN

FEDERATION

CHINA

Mudan Jiang
Mudanjiang
Boli
Linkou
Jixi
Qitaihe
Baoqing
Wanda Shan
Jidong
Dongning
Dalneretchensk
Lesozavodsk
Hulin
Mishan
Lake Khanka
Suifenhe
Muling
Ning'an
Hunchun
Tumen
Wangqing
Hailin
Jilin
Yanji
Tumen

NORTH
KOREA

Najin
Ch'ŏngjin
Onsong
Hoeryŏng
Kyŏnghŭng
Unggi

N

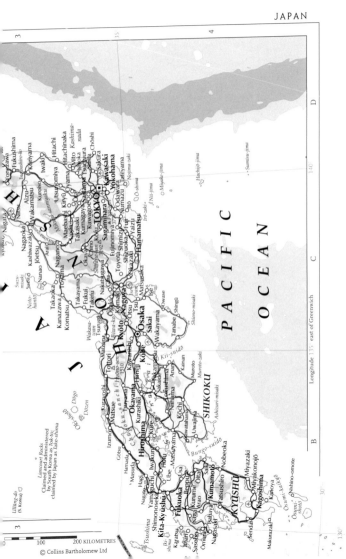

3

35

4

D

Ulleung-do (S. Korea)

Lancourt Rocks
Claimed and administered
by South Korea as Tok-to;
claimed by Japan as Take-shima

O-Ki O-shidō Dōgo
Dōzen

C

Niigata
Nagaoka
Oetsu
Nanao
Suzu-misaki
Noto-hantō
Takaoka
Toyama
Kanazawa
Takazawa
Komatsu
Takayama
Fukui
Takefu
Tsuruga
Wakasa-wan

Kashiwazaki

Fukushima
Koriyama
Iwaki

Aizu
Wakamatsu

Utsunomiya
Kiryū
Maebashi
Kumagaya
Takasaki
Nagano
Kōfu

TOKYO
Kawaguchi
Kawasaki
YOKOHAMA
Odawara
Numazu
Atami

Mito
Hitachinaka
Hitachi

Kashima-nada
Chōshi
Sakura

Kuroiso

Nojima-zaki
Ō-shima
Nii-jima
Miyake-jima
Hachijō-jima

PACIFIC

OCEAN

Longitude 135° east of Greenwich

140

Samisu-jima

30

130

Gifu
Ichinomiya
Nagoya
Okazaki
Toyota
Toyohashi
Hamamatsu
Shizuoka
Fuji
Shimizu
Ōmi
Yaizu
Irō-zaki
Ōno

Ōtsu
Komaki
Kōnan
Yokkaichi
Suzuka
Tsu
Ise
Iwase

Maizuru
Miyazu
Kyōto
Osaka
Sakai
Wakayama

Tottori
Matsue
Izumo
Gōtsu
Kurayoshi
Hamada
Masuda
Hagi
Nagato
Shimonoseki
Kita-Kyūshū
Yamaguchi
Iwakuni
Hōfu
Ube

Kurashiki
Okayama
Himeji
Akashi
Kōbe
Kawanishi

Hiroshima
Kure

Matsuyama
Imabari
Niihama
Saijō

Uwajima
Ōzu

Anan
Tokushima
Komatsushima
Naruto

KŌCHI
Aki

Muroto
Muroto-misaki
Ashizuri-misaki

SHIKOKU

Kii-suidō
Kainan
Tanabe
Shingū
Owase

Shio-no-misaki

B

Tsushima
Iki
Karatsu
Imari
Sasebo
Ōmura
Nagasaki
Isahaya

Fukuoka
Iizuka
Ōmuta
Kurume
Saga

Kumamoto
Ōita
Beppu
Usuki
Saiki

Nobeoka
Miyazaki
Miyakonojō

Kagoshima
Kanoya

KYŪSHŪ

Sendai
Akune

Makurazaki
Ōsumi-shotō
Ōsumi-hantō

Nishino-omote

Bungo-suidō

A

0   100   200 KILOMETRES

© Collins Bartholomew Ltd

67

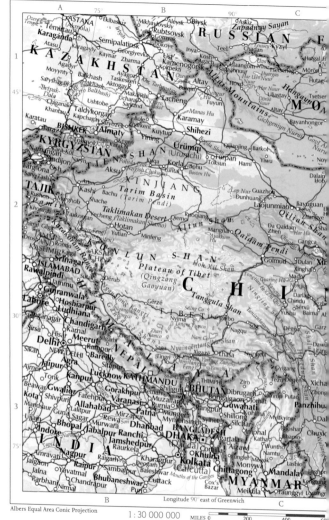

Albers Equal Area Conic Projection

1 : 30 000 000

MILES 0   200   400   600

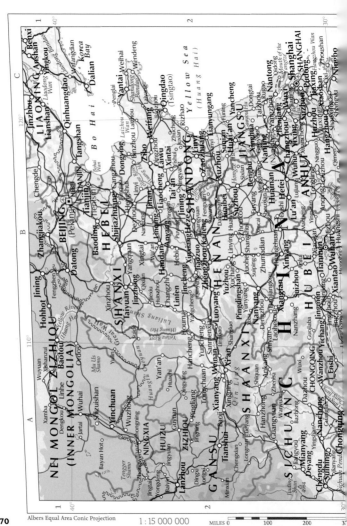

1 : 15 000 000

MILES 0   100   200

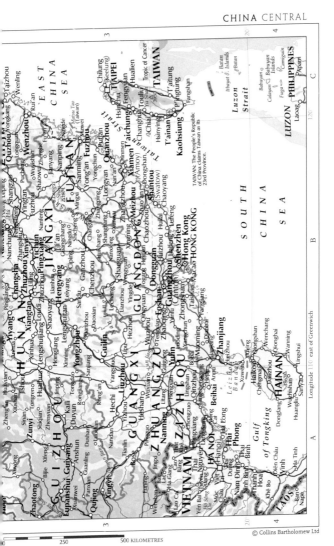

TAIWAN: The People's Republic
of China claims Taiwan as its
23rd Province.

250   500 KILOMETRES

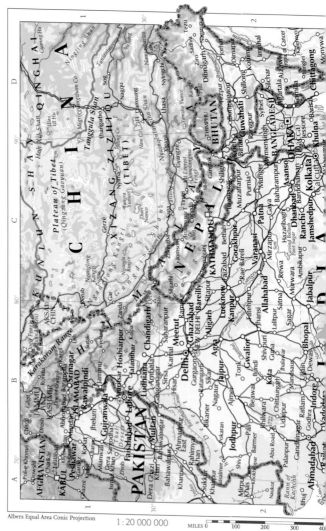

Albers Equal Area Conic Projection

1 : 20 000 000

MILES 0   100   200   300   400

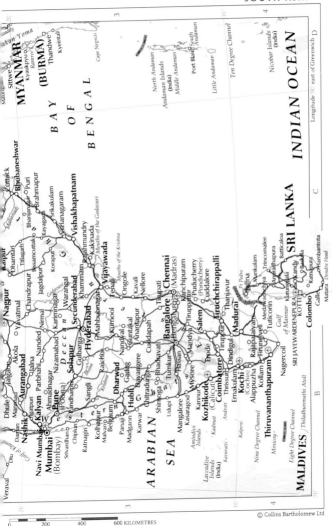

MYANMAR
(BURMA)

Sittwe
Thandwe
Kyaikkami
Kyaukpyu
Ramree
Cape Negrais

BAY

OF

BENGAL

North Andaman
Andaman Islands
(India)
Middle Andaman
South Andaman
Little Andaman
Port Blair

Ten Degree Channel

Nicobar Islands
(India)

INDIAN OCEAN

Cuttack
Bhubaneshwar
Puri
Dhamtari
Brahmapur
Bhanjanagar

Nagpur
Kanker

Chandrapur
Jagdalpur
Rayagada
Srikakulam
Vizianagaram
Vishakhapatnam

Bhadrachalam
Koraput
Kakinada
Rajahmundry
Mouths of the Godavari

Godavari

Khammam
Vijayawada
Mouths of the Krishna

Warangal
Secunderabad
Hyderabad
Mahbubnagar
Kurnool
Ongole
Nellore
Kavali

Nalgonda
Nandyal
Anantapur
Kadapa
Tirupati

Bangalore
(Bengaluru)
Chennai
(Madras)
Kanchipuram
Puducherry
(Pondicherry)
Cuddalore

ARABIAN

SEA

Nagpur
Akola
Yavatmal
Nirmal
Nanded
Karimnagar
Nizamabad
Parbhani
Deccan

Gulbarga
Raichur
Bhima
Gadag
Navalgere
Chitradurga

Shimoga
Bhadravati
Tumkur
Mysore
Hassan
Erode
Tiruppur

Salem
Namakkal
Dindigul
Madurai

Coimbatore
Tiruchirappalli
Thanjavur

Thrissur
(Cochin)
Kochi
Alappuzha
Kollam
Nagercoil
Thiruvananthapuram

Tuticorin
Tirunelveli
Rajapalaiyam
Virudhunagar

Gulf
of Mannar
Pt Pedro
Jaffna

Mannar
Trincomalee
Anuradhapura
Batticaloa

SRI LANKA

Kandy
Ratnapura
Negombo
Colombo
SRI JAYEWARDENEPURA
KOTTE
Galle
Matara   Dondra Head
Hambantota

Amindivi
Islands
Laccadive
Islands
(India)
Andrott
Kadmat
Kavaratti
Kalpeni
Minicoy

Nine Degree Channel

Eight Degree Channel

MALDIVES
Thiladhunmathi Atoll

Kolkata
Nashik
Navi Mumbai
Kalyan
Mumbai
(Bombay)
Pune
Solapur
Aurangabad
Ahmadnagar
Nashik
Dhule
Jalgaon
Malegaon
Kolhapur
Sangli
Belgaum
Panaji
Madgaon
Karwar
Mangalore
Kasaragod
Kannur
(Calicut)
Kozhikode
Udupi
Hubli
Dharwad

Veraval
Diu

ARABIAN
SEA

© Collins Bartholomew Ltd

0   200   400   600 KILOMETRES

Albers Equal Area Conic Projection

1 : 15 000 000

MILES 0   100   200   300

Longitude 70° east of Greenwich

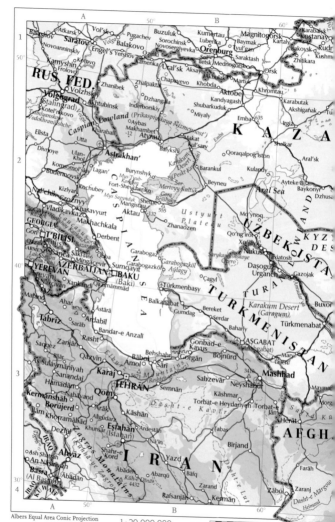

Albers Equal Area Conic Projection

1 : 20 000 000

MILES 0   100   200

Petropavlovsk
kishkeneko
Saumalkol' Kokshetau
Ozero
Siletitenjz
Ruzayevka Makiosk
Yesil' Akkol'
Atbasar Yereymentau
Zhaltyr
Derzhavinsk
Arkalyk Ozero
Kypshak
Amangel'dy
Kazakhskiy
Melkosopochnik

RUS. FED.
Kulunda Aléysk
Pavlodar
Ekibastuz Mikhaylovskiy Rubtsovsk
Semipalatinsk
koryak
Glubokoye Inyal
ASTANA (Akmola)
Temirtau
Karaganda Karagayly Ust'-Kamenogorsk
1559 Kaynar Zharma Georgiyevka
Atasu Ayagoz Kokpekti
Agadyr' Taskesken Khrebet Tarbagatay
Balkhash Aktogay Makanchi Tacheng
Moyynty Ucharal Karamay
Saryshagan Sarkand
Chiganak Ushtobe

K H S T A N
Betpak-Dala
Zhezkazgan
Zhezkazgan Gora Ayet
464

Kyzylorda
Khr. Karatau
Kentau Syrdar'ya
Turkestan Karatau
Shymkent
TOSHKENT Tarazo
(Tashkent) Chirchiq
Angren Namangan
Andijon Osh
Guliston Jizzax Khujand Qullai Lenin
Qurghonteppa

Taldykorgan
Khr. Dzhungarskiy Alatau
Saryozek Bole Yining Shihezi
Zharkent
Kapchagay Kapchagayskoye
Almaty Kegen
Esik
Khr. Küngey Alatau
Balykchy Issyk-Köl
Karakol
BISHKEK TIEN SHAN
KYRGYZSTAN Naryn Poberla Peak
Toktogul Aksu Kuga
Jalal-Abad Pass Kuytun
Sary-Tash XINJIANG UYGUR ZIZHIQU
Artux Tarim Basin (Tarim Pendi)
Kashi (SINKIANG)
Taklimakan Desert

TAJIKISTAN Shache
Pamir Yecheng CHINA
DUSHANBE Rushon Murghob Hotan
Khorugh Yutian Minfeng
Fayzabad Taxkorgan
Mazar
KUNLUN SHAN

Mazar-e Khanabad
Sharif
Baghlan Gilgit Aksai
Chitral JAMMU Chin XIZANG ZIZHIQU
Drosh AND (TIBET)
Charikar Astor KASHMIR Plateau of
KABUL Jalalabad Baramulla Srinagar Tibet
Peshawar Mardan Kargil
Abbottabad HIMALAYA
Rawalpindi ISLAMABAD Jammu
PAKISTAN Srinagar
Mianwali Sutak
Sargodha Gujranwala
Lahore Amritsar
Faisalabad Jalandhar Hoshiarpur
Ludhiana Chandigarh
Abohar Ambala NEPAL
INDIA

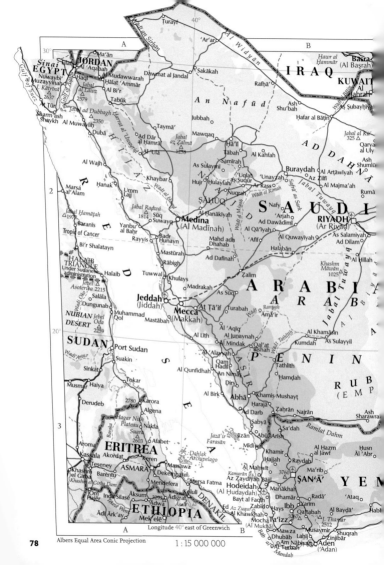

Albers Equal Area Conic Projection

Longitude 40° east of Greenwich

1 : 15 000 000

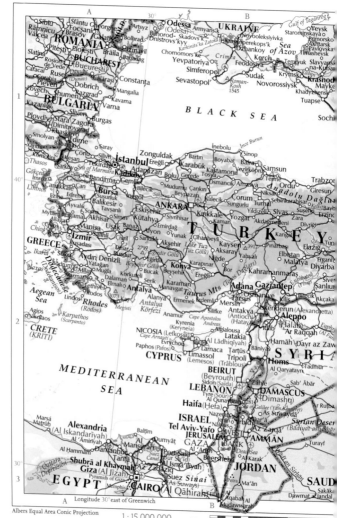

Albers Equal Area Conic Projection

1 : 15 000 000

MILES 0   100   200   300

© Collins Bartholomew Ltd

0   250   500 KILOMETRES

Conic Equidistant Projection

1 : 42 000 000

MILES 0   250   500   750

Longitude 75° east of Greenwich

1 : 39 000 000

MILES 0   250   500   750

60°   A   50°   B   40°   C   30°   D   20°   E   10°   F   0°   G

Arctic Circle

2

60°

Jan Mayen
(Norway)

Reykjavík   ICELAND

3

Norwegian
Sea

Tórshavn   Faroe
Islands
(Denmark)

Bergen

Oslo

ATLANTIC

OCEAN

50°

Glasgow   Edinburgh

Aalborg

North
Sea

DENMARK

Copenhagen

IRELAND

Belfast

Manchester

UNITED
KINGDOM

Hamburg

AL.	ALBANIA
B.H.	BOSNIA-HERZEGOVINA
CR.	CROATIA
CZ.R.	CZECH REPUBLIC
HUN.	HUNGARY
K.	KOSOVO
LIE.	LIECHTENSTEIN
LUX.	LUXEMBOURG
M.	MACEDONIA
MO.	MONTENEGRO
NETH.	NETHERLANDS
SER.	SERBIA
SW.	SWITZERLAND

Dublin

Birmingham

The Hague

Amsterdam

Cardiff

NETH.

London   Brussels

Essen

GERMANY

English Channel

BELGIUM

Frankfurt
am Main

Channel Islands
(U.K.)

Paris   Luxembourg

Dan

Nantes

Strasbourg

Zürich

Mün

40°

Orléans

Bern

SW.

Vaduz

Bay of
Biscay

FRANCE

Geneva

Milano

Ljublj

Lyon

Turin

Azores
(Portugal)

Bordeaux

Marseille

MONACO

Ponta
Delgada

Oporto

Andorra
la Vella

ANDORRA

Corsica

Vatican City

SP.
MAI

Lisbon

Madrid

Tagus

PORTUGAL

Valencia

Barcelona

Palma
de Mallorca

Roma

Sardinia

Na

SPAIN

Seville

Cartagena

Balearic
Islands

Tyrrhe

Madeira
(Portugal)

Cádiz   Gibraltar
(U.K.)

Mediterr

Palermo

Se

30°

Valle
MA

6

AFRICA

D   20°   E   Longitude 10° west of Greenwich   F   0°   G   10°

0   500   1000 KILOMETRES

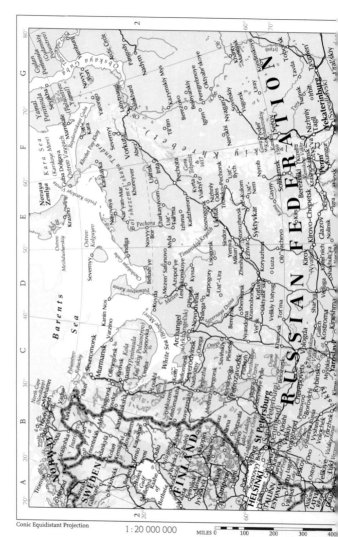

Conic Equidistant Projection

1 : 20 000 000

MILES 0   100   200   300   400

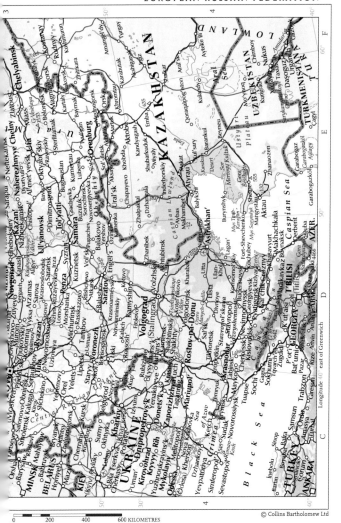

0   200   400   600 KILOMETRES

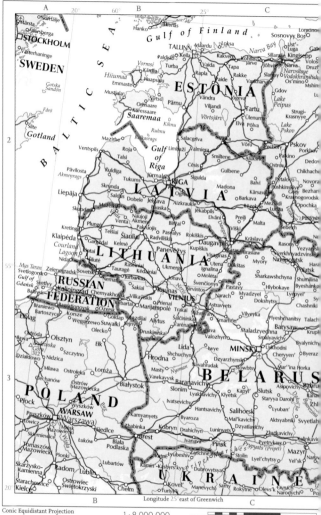

Conic Equidistant Projection

1 : 8 000 000

MILES 0   50   100   15

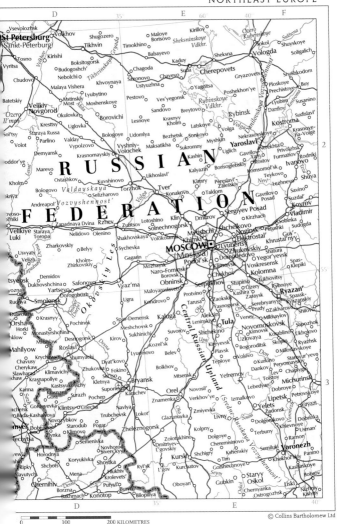

0   100   200 KILOMETRES

© Collins Bartholomew Ltd

Conic Equidistant Projection

Longitude 25° east of Greenwich

1 : 8 000 000

MILES 0   50   100   150

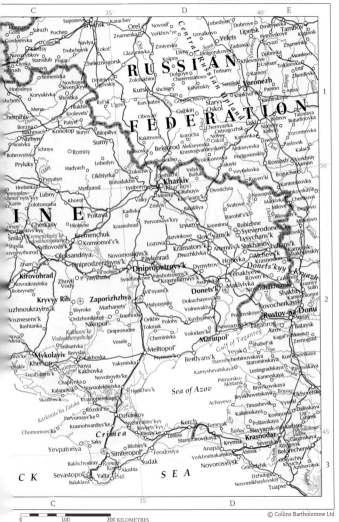

0   100   200 KILOMETRES

© Collins Bartholomew Ltd

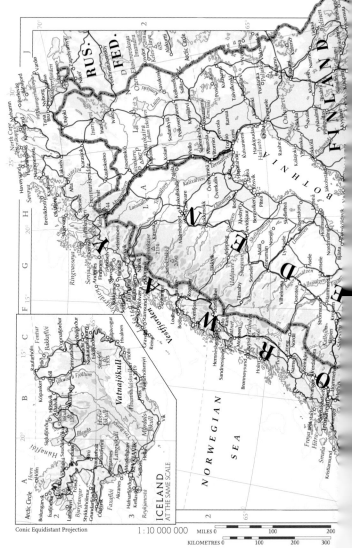

Conic Equidistant Projection 1 : 10 000 000 MILES 0 · 100 · 200

KILOMETRES 0 · 100 · 200 · 300

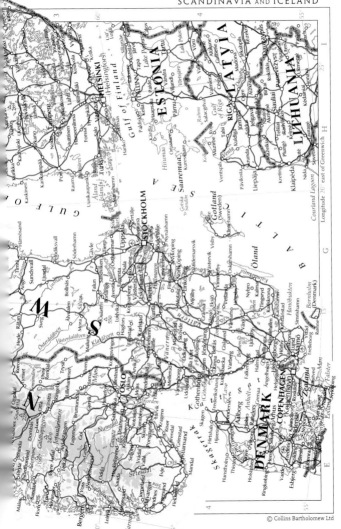

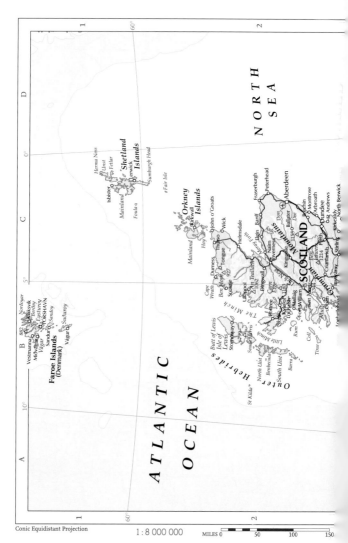

NORTH SEA

ATLANTIC OCEAN

Faroe Islands (Denmark)

Vestmanna
Mykines
Vágur
Sørvágur
Sandur
Sandoy
Norðoyar
Klaksvík
TÓRSHAVN
Eysturoy
Suðuroy
882

Shetland Islands

Herma Ness
Unst
Fetlar
Isbster
Mainland
Lerwick
Sumburgh Head
Foula
Fair Isle

Orkney Islands

Mainland
Kirkwall
Hoy
John o'Groats
Wick

SCOTLAND

Cape Wrath
Durness
Tongue
Scourie
927
Ben Hope
Helmsdale
Ullapool
Dingwall
Nairn
Elgin
Banff
Fraserburgh
Peterhead
Cairn
Loch Ness
Loch Maree
Kingussie
Inverness
Aberdeen
Brechin
Montrose
Arbroath
St Andrews
Dundee
Kirkcaldy
North Berwick
Stirling
Chatelrault
Dee
Ballater
1154
Don
Spey

The Minch

Butt of Lewis
Isle of Lewis
Stornoway
Harris
North Uist
Benbecula
South Uist
Barra
St Kilda
Little Minch
Rum
Coll
Tiree

Outer Hebrides

Conic Equidistant Projection

1 : 8 000 000

MILES 0   50   100   150

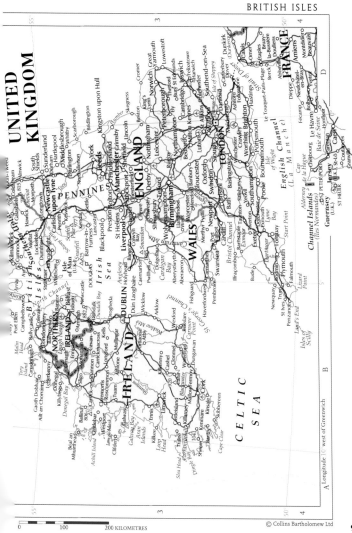

© Collins Bartholomew Ltd

0   100   200 KILOMETRES

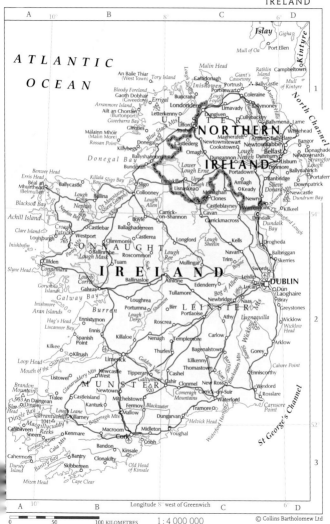

0   50   100 KILOMETRES   1 : 4 000 000

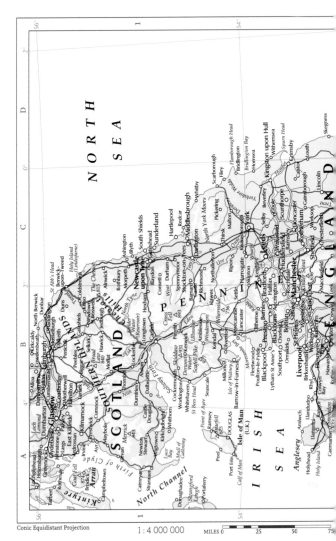

Conic Equidistant Projection

1 : 4 000 000

MILES 0   25   50   75

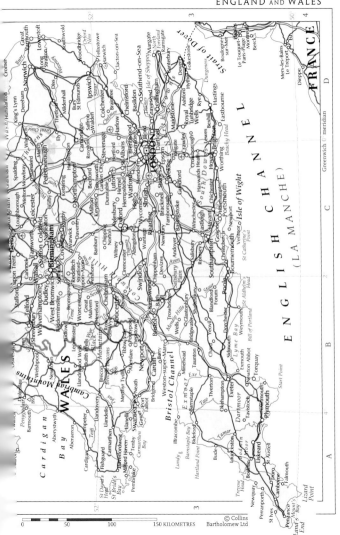

© Collins
Bartholomew Ltd

0   50   100   150 KILOMETRES

Longitude 6° east of Greenwich

Conic Equidistant Projection

1 : 4 000 000

MILES 0   25   50   75

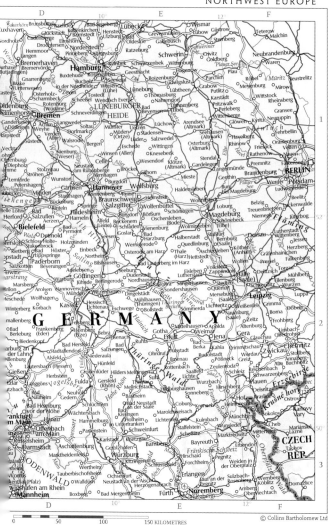

0   50   100   150 KILOMETRES

Conic Equidistant Projection

1 : 8 000 000

MILES 0   50   100   15

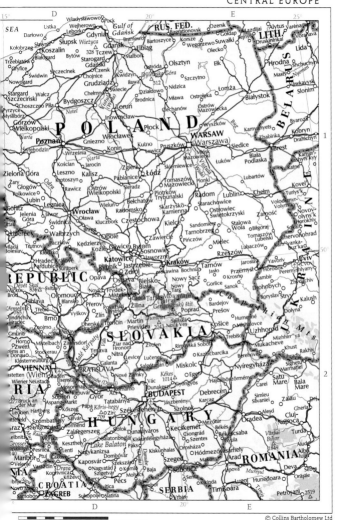

© Collins Bartholomew Ltd

0   100   200 KILOMETRES

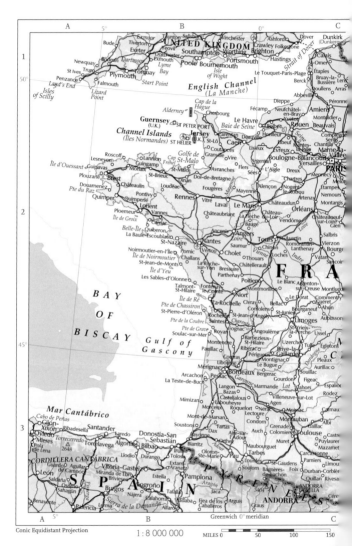

Conic Equidistant Projection

1 : 8 000 000

MILES 0   50   100   150

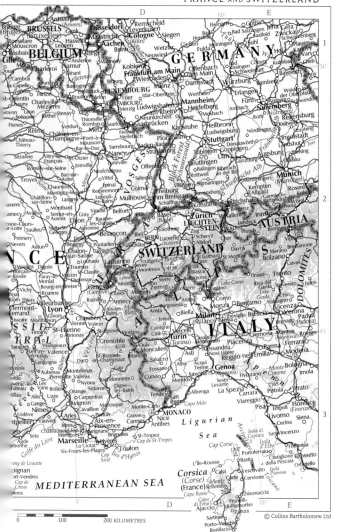

© Collins Bartholomew Ltd

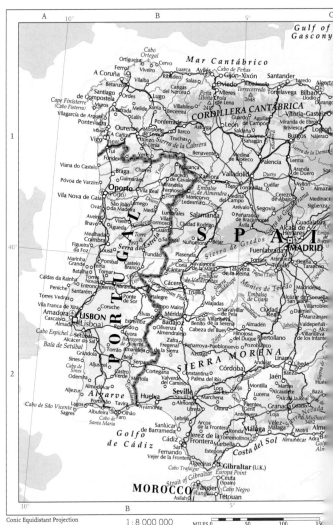

Conic Equidistant Projection   1 : 8 000 000   MILES 0   50   100   150

0   D   5   E

Langon Marmande Cahors Rodez Florac Sévérac-le-Château Ales Uzès Bollène Orange Sisteron
Bazas Villeneuve-sur-Lot Agen Moissac Montauban Gaillac Albi Millau Ganges Nîmes Avignon Carpentras Digne les-Bains
Mimizan Castelialoux Labouheyre Roquefort Nérac Condom Lectoure Montbrun-Muret Castres Lodève Montpellier Vauvert Arles Aix-en-Provence Manosque
Soustons Morcenx Mont-de-Marsan Tartas F R A N C E Toulouse Puylaurens Mazamet Béziers Sète Châteauneuf-les-Martigues Marseille Brignoles
Baydonne Dax Aire-sur-l'Adour Colomiers Carcassonne Narbonne Agde Golfe du Lion La Ciotat Six-Fours-les-Plages Toulon Hyères
Biarritz Oloron-Ste-Marie Pau Tarbes Pamiers Limoux Rivesaltes l'Étang de Leucate Cap Sicié
Irún Donostia-San Sebastián P Y R É N É E S Lourdes Bagnères-de-Luchon St-Gaudens Foix Quillan Port-Vendres
Errenteria Pamplona Aragón Jaca ANDORRA LA VELLA Perpignan Céret Cap de Creus
Estella Tafalla Arguis Graus Tremp Berga Ripoll Banyoles Figueres Cap de Begur
Calahorra Sábada Caballeros Huesca Olot Girona Torroella de Montgrí
Alfaro Tudela Ejea de los Barbastro Monzón Manresa Vic Palamós
Alagón Zaragoza Binéfar Lleida Tàrrega Igualada Sabadell Blanes Costa Brava
Quinto Fraga El Prat de Mataró
Calatayud Cariñena Estarrón Caspe Reus Valls Llobregat Martorell Barcelona
Medinaceli Daroca Calamocha Alcañiz Gandesa Tortosa Vilanova i la Geltrú
Molina de Aragón Monreal del Campo Morella Amposta Golf de Sant Jordi
Tordesillos Perales del Alfambra Peñarroya 2019 Vinaròs Minorca (Menorca)
N Teruel Torreblanca Cap de Formentor Ciutadella Mahón
Sierra de Cuenca Santa Cruz de Moya L'Alcora Castellón de la Plana Majorca (Mallorca) Alcúdia Cap des Freu
Embalse de Alarcón Sarrión Burriana La Vall d'Uixó Calvià Manacor
Motilla del Palancar Minglanilla Utiel Requena Lliria Sagunto Sa Dragonera Palma de Mallorca Felanitx
La Roda Torrent Valencia Cap de ses Salines
Albacete Algemesí Sueca Cullera Golfo de Valencia Illa de Cabrera
Almansa Alcoy Xàtiva Gandia Sant Joan de Labritja BALEARIC ISLANDS (ISLAS BALEARES) (Spain)
Alcaraz Hellín Villena Benidorm Oliva Ibiza (Eivissa)
Segura Elda Cabo de la Nao Sant Antoni de Portmany
Caravaca de la Cruz Cieza Orihuela Alicante Ibiza (Eivissa)
Moral Elche-Elx Costa Blanca San Francisco Javier
Murcia Formentera
Lorca Alhama de Murcia Torrevieja Cabo de Palos
Cartagena
Águilas
Cabo de Gata

M E D I T E R R A N E A N   S E A

ALGIERS (Alger) Aïn Taya Dellys Tizi Ouzou Bejaïa
Koléa Rouïba Thénia Bordj Menaïel
Djebel Tipasa Blida Bouira Bougaa
Ténès Bou Ismaïl Gouraya Médéa Berrouaghia Bordj Bou Arréridj
Sidi Aïn Defla Khemis Miliana Sour el Ghozlane Sidi Aïssa M'Sila
Mostaganem Ain Tédeles Relizane Bordj Bounaama Ksar el Boukhari
Gap Carbon Oran Arzew Oued Tlélat Tissemsilt
Oued Zemmora Mohammadia Greenwich 0° meridian ALGERIA

D   5

© Collins Bartholomew Ltd

0   100   200 KILOMETRES

Conic Equidistant Projection   1 : 8 000 000   MILES 0   50   100   150

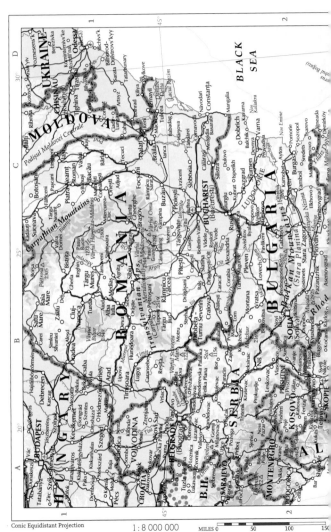

Conic Equidistant Projection

1 : 8 000 000

MILES 0   50   100   150

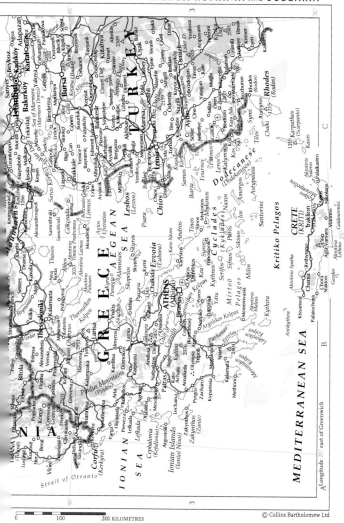

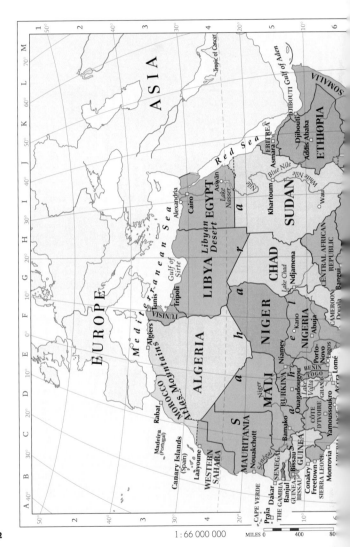

1 : 66 000 000   MILES 0   400   80

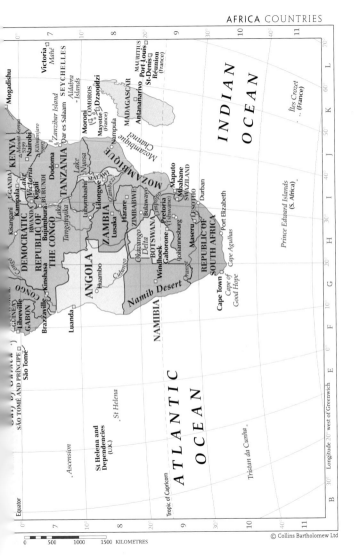

ATLANTIC
OCEAN

A

20°   10°

SPAIN
Strait of Gibraltar   Málaga Almería
Gibraltar   Cartage
Tangier (Tanger)   Ceuta (Spain) Oran Mostaganem
Larache   Kar el Kebir Oujda Tlemcen
Kenitra   Tétouan Sidi Bel
RABAT   Meknes Fès (Fez)
El Jadida   Settat   MOROCCO
Casablanca

Madeira
(Portugal)   Safi   Beni
FUNCHAL   Mellal
Essaouira   Marrakech   Tbel Atlas (High Atlas) ATLAS MOUNTAIN
Taroudannt   167 Haut Atlas (High Atlas) Rachidia
Agadir   Ouarzazate   Figuig (Sa
Tiznit   Anti-Atlas   Abadla
Sidi Ifni   Guelmim   Hamada du Drâa   Beni
Tabelbala   Abbes   Occider
Grand E
SANTA CRUZ DE   Lanzarote   Ksabi   Timimo
TENERIFE   Tarfaya   Tindouf   Adrar Sbaa
La Palma   Gran   Fuerteventura
Tenerife   Canaria
El Hierro   LAS PALMAS   LAÂYOUNE   AL G
Canary Islands   DE GRAN   Es Semara
(Islas Canarias)   CANARIA   El Eglab   Sal
(Spain)   Reggane   Sebkha
Boujdour   Chenachane   Mekerr
Galtat   'Ain   Sebkha Azzel
Zemmour   Ben Tili   Chegga   Matti
Bir   El Hammâmi
Mogrein   ERG CHECH
Ad Dakhla   Zouérat   Taoudenni
Tropic of Cancer   WESTERN   fdérik   A
SAHARA   S   Tanezrouft
Tichla   Choûm
Nouâdhibou   Atâr   OURÂNE
Akjoujt
Nouâmghâr   Araouane   M A L I
NOUAKCHOTT   MAURITANIA   Tidjikja Tichît
Boutilimit   Anéfis   Adra
Magta   HÔDH   des
Rosso   Lahjar   Oualâta   Ifoghas
St-Louis   Aleg   Ayoûn el   IRÎGUI   Kidal
Louga   Dagana   Kaédi   Kiffa   Atroûs   Néma   Gourma-
DAKAR   Linguère   Matam   Sélibaby Bakel   Gao   Rharous Menaka
Mbour   Diourbel   Ould   Nioro   Balléi Nara   Nampala   Niger   Bourem
SENEGAL   Gossas   Goudiry   Kayes   Diéma   S   Douentza Hombori Ansongo
Kaolack   Tambacounda   Kolokani   Ségou   Mopti   Bandiagara
BANJUL   Kédougou   Bafoulabé   Kati   Koutiala   Djibo Dori   Tillabéri
THE GAMBIA   Kolda   Satadougou   BAMAKO   Kangaba   Bougouni San   Tougan Ouahigouya Bogandé NIAMEY
Ziguinchor   Cachéu   Gabú   Mali   Siguiri Dabola Kita   Sikasso Manga   Hada   Gorom-Gorom   Diapaga
GUINEA-   Labé   Koussanar   BURKINA   Fada N'Gourma Koudou
BISSAU   Arquipélago   Dalaba   Kankan   Odienné   Banfora OUAGADOUGOU   Pama
dos Bijagós   Fria   GUINEA   Mandiana   Boundiali   Tehini   Léo Tenkodogo   Kan   BENI
Dubréka   Kissidougou   Korhogo   Bouna Batié   Natitingou   Djoug
CONAKRY   Macenta   Séguéla   Bondoukou   Tamale   Kara
Forécariah   Beyla   CÔTE   Ferkessédougou   Bouaké   GHANA   Parakou
SIERRA   Kono   Man   D'IVOIRE   Bondoukou Sunyani   ACCRA
LEONE   Kenema   Danané   Daloa   Yamoussoukro   Kumasi PORTO
FREETOWN   Robertsport   Zuénoula   Gagnoa   Abengourou   Koforidua   LOMÉ
Zorzor   Gbarnga   Divo   Winneba
MONROVIA   Buchanan   Abidjan   ACCRA Lag
Greenville   Grand-   Sekondi   Cape Coast   Bigh
Harper   Bassam   Axim   Three Points Cape Coast
Cape Palmas   San-Pédro   Tabou   GULF OF GUINEA   Gold Coast
of Beni

GUINEA-BISSAU

LIBERIA

Lambert Azimuthal
Equal Area Projection

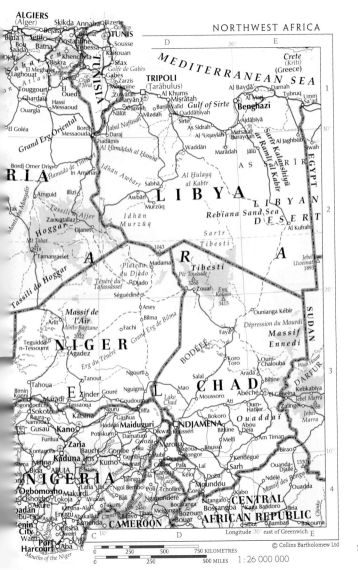

ALGIERS
(Alger)
Skikda Annaba
Blida Sétif Bizerte
Bou Batna Constantine TUNIS
Saâda El Kef Tébessa Sousse
Djelfa Biskra Kairouan
Laghouat Gafsa Sfax
El Meghaïer Zarzis Golfe de Gabès Gabès
Touggourt El Oued Médenine
Ouargla Hassi Nalut Zuwārah TRIPOLI Al Khums Mişrātah
Messaoud Gharyān (Ṭarābulus)
El Goléa Ghadāmis Banī Walīd Gulf of Sirte Benghazi Al Baydā' Darnah Tubruq Umm
Bordj Darāj Al Qaddāḥīyah Ajdābiyā Marsā al Sa'd
Messaouda Al Ḥamādah al Ḥamrā Mizdah As Sidrah Sirte Burayqah Jaghbūb Sīwah
Bordj Omer Driss In Amenas Jabal Nafūsah Waddān Marādah Jālū
R I A Ḥamāda de Tinrhert Idhān Awbārī As Sarīr Kalanshiyū
Amguid Illizi Sabhā Al Ḥulayq Sarīr Rimāl al Kabīr
Zaouatallaz Tassili n'Ajjer L I B Y A Rebiana Sand Sea L I B Y A N
Hoggar Idhān Awbārī Murzūq Al Kufrah D E S E R T
Djanet Murzūq
Mt Tahat A R Sarīr Tibesti A
2918 1043 Tibesti Jebel
Tamanrasset Plateau Madama Pic Toussidé Uweinat
du Djado 3265 1893
Tassili du Hoggar Ténéré du Djado Zouar Emi
Tafasasset Séguédine Koussi
Massif de Aney 3415 Ounianga Kébir
l'Aïr Bilma Dépression du Mourdi
Arlit Monts Bagzane Fachi Faya Massif
Teguidda- 2022 Ennedi
n-Tessoumt N I G E R Grand Erg de Bilma BODÉLÉ Koro Oum-
Agadez Toro Chalouba
Erg du Ténéré Arada D A R F U R
Tahoua L C H A D Biltine Kebkabiya
Birnin Zinder Ngourti Mao Abéché El Geneina Jebel Marra
Konni Tanout Salal Ati Oum- Zalingei 3088
Maradi Tessaoua Goudoumaria Lake Moussoro Hadjer Am Jebel
Dogondoutchi Goudoumaria Chad Bokoro Ouaddaï Marra
Kaura Katsina Nguru Diffa NDJAMENA Bitkine Abou Zalingei
Namoda Gashua Maiduguri Dikwa Kousséri Melfi Déïa
Gusau Haddejia Potiskum Maroua Bousso Am Timan Birao
Funtua Kano Damaturu Gwoza Mubi Bongor Kendégué Ouanda-
Kontagora Zaria Gombe Biu Guider Laï Djallé
KADUNA Bauchi Kumo Pala Sarh Ndélé Ouadda
Minna Jos Mubi Garoua Doba Massif des Bongo
Bida Lafia Ngol Bembo Poli Kélo Moundou Ouadda
NIGERIA Benue Bali Kabo Batangafo Bria
Ogbomosho Lokoja Wukari Ngaoundéré Bocaranga Bossangoa CENTRAL Bakouma
Oshogbo Enugu Abakaliki Tibati Meiganga Bozoum Bambari
Akure Asaba Bamenda Bafoussam Bouar AFRICAN REPUBLIC
Ife Onitsha CAMEROON Sibut Bambari
Benin Oweri Bangui
City Port Aba Mouths of the Niger
Warri Harcourt

Longitude 20° east of Greenwich

0 250 500 750 KILOMETRES
0 250 500 MILES

1 : 26 000 000

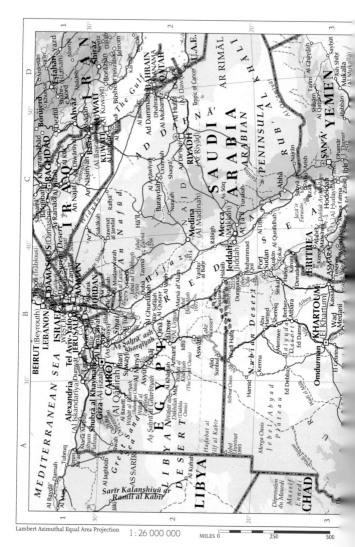

Lambert Azimuthal Equal Area Projection   1 : 26 000 000

MILES 0   250   500

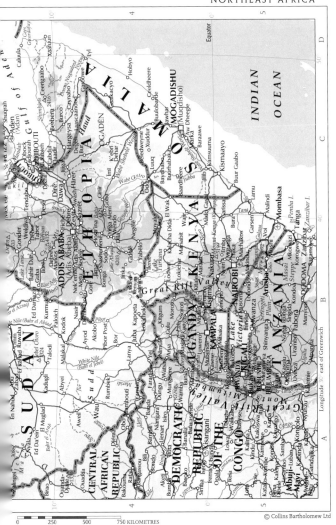

117

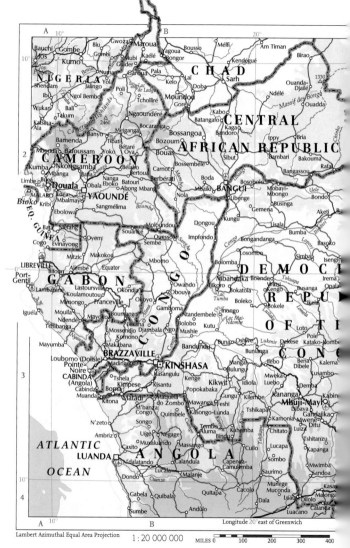

Lambert Azimuthal Equal Area Projection   1 : 20 000 000   MILES 0   100   200   300   400

0   200   400   600 KILOMETRES

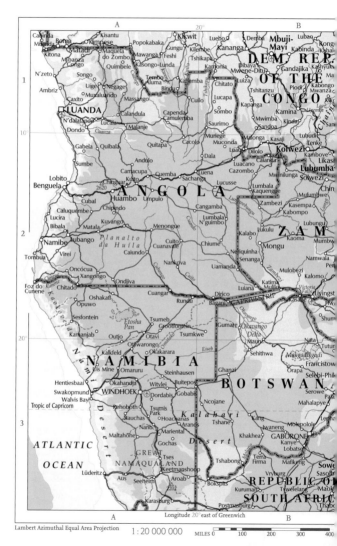

Lambert Azimuthal Equal Area Projection   1 : 20 000 000   MILES 0   100   200   300   400

yunzu oKalemie   Ugalla   Manyoni   oDODOMA   Bagamoyo
oKiambi   Moba   Mpanda   Myonga   Kilosa   Morogoro   oZanzibar   Zanzibar I.
          Lake Tanganyika   Dar es Salaam
          Sumbawanga   Makongolosi   Iringa   Ifakara   Nangulangwa   Mafia I.
2458   Mbeya   Mafinga   Mohoro   INDIAN
wa   Lake Mweru   oMbala   Nakonde   Chimala   Njombe   Luhombero   Kilwa Masoko   OCEAN
Nchelenge   Mnorokoso   Chitipa   Karonga   Liwale   Mitole
oga   Mwenda   Mingoyo   Mtwara
Kasama   Chinsali   Chambeshi   Mbinga   Songea   Tunduru   Masasi   Quionga   Cabo Delgado
Mansa   Lake Bangweulu   Chama   Mzimba   Mzuzu   Lupilichi   Macaloge   Salimo   Mueda   Mocimboa da Praia   COMOROS
ililabombwe   Mpika   Lundazi   Nkhotakota   Lichinga   Márrupa   Montepuez   MORONI   Njazidja
Mufulira   Chitambo   Mfuwe   Kasungu   Salima   Mangochi   Muite   Pemba   Mayotte (France)
itwe   oNdola   Chipata   Katete   Mutuali   Lúrio   Nacala   DZAOUDZI
ansh'va   LILONGWE   Dedza   Alto Molócuè   Ribáuè   Nampula
Kapiri Mposhi   Bene   Zomba   Murrupula   Tanjona Bobaomby
Kabwe   Ruf'nsa   Blantyre   Mt Mulanje   Nsanje   Angoche   Antsiranana
LUSAKA   Zumbo   Songo   Lake Cabora Bassa   Tete   Milange   3002   Mocuba   Pebane   Andoany   Ambilobe
Chirundu   Changara   Nhamalabué   Caia   Marromeu   Quelimane   Nosy Be   Ambanja   Massif du Maromokotro 2876   Sambava
ke Kariba   Karof   Mount Darwin   Bindura   Chinde   Benanamar   Antsohihy   Tsaratanana   Andapa
Kariba   HARARE   Chitungwiza   Nyanga   Rusape   Pingué   Mahajanga   Maroantsetra   Antalaha
Chinhoyi   Norton   Marondera   Mutare   Chimoio   Dondo   Beira   Soalala   Marovoay   Mandritsara   Mahalevona
Kadoma   Kwekwe   Chivhu   Gutu   Chiboma   Buzi   Ambato   Maevatanana   Mananara   Nosy Boraha
MBABWE   Gweru   Masvingo   Chipinge   Machanga   Besalampy   Boeny   Avaratra   Andilamena
ilawayo   Zvishavane   Kandreho   Fenoarivo Atsinanana
anda   Mwenezi   Chiredzi   Jofane   Mabote   Maintirano   Andilanatoby   Ambatondrazaka
Thuli   Mazunga   Massangena   Machaila   Mapinhane   Antsalova   Tsiroanomandidy   Morarnanga
Musina   Limpopo   Sango   Mabote   Massinga   Miandrivazo   Miarinarivo   Toamasina
wang   Thohoyandou   Chigubo   Inhambane   ANTANANARIVO
opane   Phalaborwa   Mapai   Mabalane   Chókwè   Quissico   Morondava   Antsirabe   Mahanoro
a-Bela   2274   Nelspruit   Manhica   Xai-Xai   INDIAN   Mandabe   Ambositra   Ambato Finandrahana   Ambohimahasoa
ETORIA   MBABANE   MAPUTO   OCEAN   Beroroha   Fianarantsoa   Ifanadiana   Mananjary
iwane   eyton   SWAZILAND   Morombe   Ihosy   Ikongo   Manakara
nnesburg   Manzini   Boby 2658   Farafangana
hadi   Vukuzakhe   Lavumisa   Toliara   Betroka   Vangaindrano   INDIAN   Tropic of Capricorn
adeni   Osizweni   Mondlo   Betioky   Bekily   OCEAN
Dundee   Androka   Amboasary   Tôlañaro
          Ejeda   Beloha   Ambovombe

INDIAN OCEAN

MADAGASCAR

MOZAMBIQUE

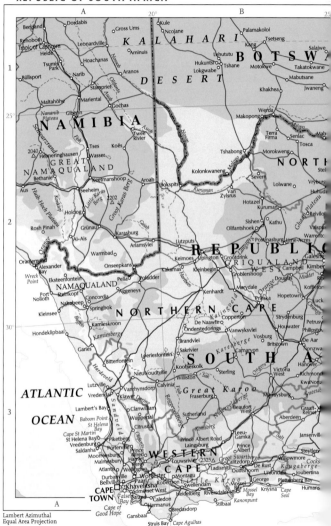

Lambert Azimuthal
Equal Area Projection

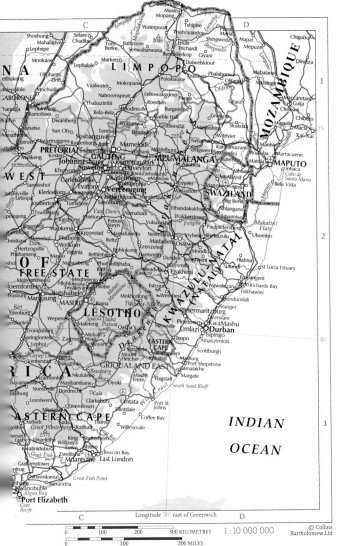

INDIAN

OCEAN

Longitude 30° east of Greenwich

0   100   200   300 KILOMETRES   1 : 10 000 000

0   100   200 MILES

© Collins
Bartholomew Ltd

123

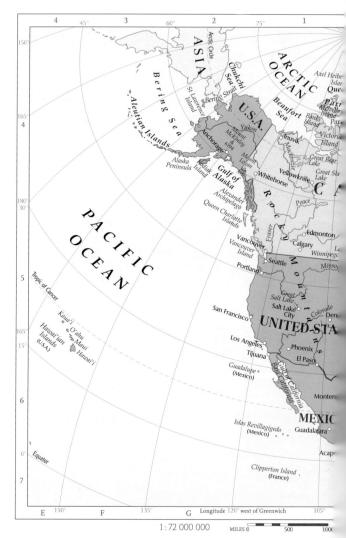

124

1:72 000 000

MILES 0   500   1000

Greenland Sea

Ellesmere Island

Elizabeth Islands

Devon Island

Baffin Bay

Baffin Island

Denmark Strait

Greenland

Davis Strait

Nuuk

Cape Farewell

EUROPE

Foxe Basin

Southampton Island

Hudson Strait

Labrador Sea

Hudson Bay

Belcher Islands

Nelson

James Bay

Île d'Anticosti

Newfoundland

St John's

Gulf of St Lawrence

St-Pierre

St Pierre and Miquelon (France)

Azores

Lake Winnipeg

Lake Nipigon

Québec

Montreal

ATLANTIC

Thunder Bay

Great Lakes

Ottawa

Portland

Halifax

Cape Sable

OCEAN

Minneapolis

Toronto

Boston

Detroit

Cleveland

New York

Mississippi

Pittsburgh

Philadelphia

Chicago

Columbus

Washington

St Louis

Bermuda (U.K.)

S OF AMERICA

Cape Hatteras

Memphis

Kansas

Atlanta

Dallas

Jacksonville

Houston

Orlando

New Orleans

THE BAHAMAS

Nassau

Turks and Caicos Islands (U.K.)

Virgin Islands (U.S.A.)

Virgin Islands (U.K.)

ST KITTS AND NEVIS

ANTIGUA AND BARBUDA

Guadeloupe (France)

DOMINICA

Gulf of Mexico

Miami

Havana

CUBA

Santo Domingo

San Juan

Puerto Rico (U.S.A.)

ico City

Mérida

Cayman Islands (U.K.)

Kingston

HAITI

JAMAICA

Port-au-Prince

DOMINICAN REPUBLIC

ST LUCIA

Martinique (France)

BARBADOS

Veracruz

Yucatán

BELIZE

Pico de Orizaba

Belmopan

Caribbean Sea

GRENADA

ST VINCENT AND THE GRENADINES

GUATEMALA

HONDURAS

Tegucigalpa

Aruba (Neth.)

Netherlands Antilles

TRINIDAD AND TOBAGO

temala City

San Salvador

EL SALVADOR

NICARAGUA

Managua

Lake Nicaragua

Canal de

San José

COSTA RICA

Panama City

PANAMA

SOUTH AMERICA

© Collins Bartholomew Ltd

0   500   1000   1500 KILOMETRES

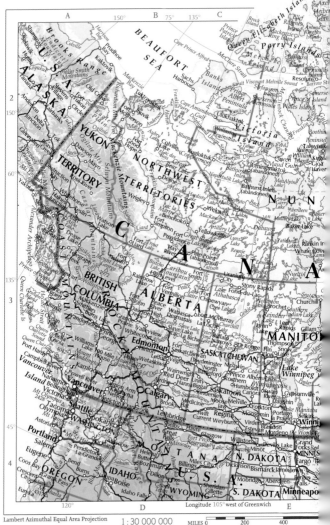

Lambert Azimuthal Equal Area Projection   1 : 30 000 000   MILES 0   200   400

Ellesmere Island
Nares Strait
Kane Basin
Thule
Qaanaaq
Dundas
Grise Fiord

CANADA
J

Kangerlussuaq
Arctic Circle

Kong Christian IX Land
Kong Frederik VIII Land

Nuussuaq
Kangaatsiaq
Ukkusissat
Qeqertarsuaq
Uummannaq
Upernavik

Greenland
(Kalaallit Nunaat)
(Denmark)

Uummannaq
Qaasuitsup
Ilulissat
Qasigiannguit

Kong Christian IX Land

Ammassalik
Kulusuk
Qillak

Kong Frederik VI Kyst

Lancaster Sound Cape
Liverpool
Bylot Island
Arctic Bay
Pond Inlet

Clyde River

Baffin
Bay

Cape
Christian

Davis
Strait

Napassoq
Maniitsoq

Nuuk
(Godthåb)

Kangaatsiaq

Sisimiut

Qeqertarsuatsiaat

Paamiut
Ivittuut
Qassimiut
Nanortalik

Cape Farewell
(Nunap Isua)

Prince
Charles
Island

Barnes
Icecap
Henry Kater
Home Bay

Penny
Icecap

Baffin Island

Qikiqtarjuaq

Broughton
Island
Cape Dyer

NUNAVUT

Fury and Hecla Strait
Igloolik
Hall
Beach

Foxe
Basin

Melville
Peninsula

Foxe
Channel

Resolution
Island

Labrador
Sea

ATLANTIC
OCEAN

45

60

Repulse Bay

Rowley
Island

Amadjuak
Lake

Nettilling
Lake

Iqaluit
Frobisher
Bay

Meta Incognita
Peninsula

Lake Harbour

Coral
Harbour

Southampton
Island

Coats
Island

Mansel
Island

Evans Strait

Ivujivik

Hudson
Strait

Akpatok
Island

NEWFOUNDLAND
AND LABRADOR

D
A

HUDSON
BAY

King George Islands

Fort
Severn
Winisk
(abandoned)
Winisk

Belcher
Islands

Kangiqsualujjuaq
Kangirsuk
Kangiqsujuaq
Puvirnituq

NUNAVIK

Ungava
Bay

Leaf
Bay

Labrador

Nain

Cape
Harrison

Happy Valley-
Goose Bay

St Anthony

Schefferville

Churchill
Falls

Petit

Gander
St John's

Newfoundland

Grand Lake

Corner
Brook

Cape Race

3

45

Fort
George
James
Bay

Ekwan

Attawapiskat

Chisasibi
(Fort George)

La
Grande
Rivière de la Baleine

Grande
Rivière

Eastmain
Rupert

Réservoir
La Grande 2

QUÉBEC

Gagnon

Havre-
St-Pierre

Réservoir
Manicouagan

Anticosti
Island

Gulf of
St Lawrence

Grand Falls-
Windsor

Îles-de-la-
Madeleine

Sable
Island

Trout Lake
Trout

Webequie

ONTARIO
Fort Albany
Moosonee

Waskaganish

Chapleau

Matagami

Chibougamau

Lac
St-Jean

Baie-
Comeau

Tadoussac

Gaspé

Sept-Îles

Matane
Mont-Joli

Campbellton
Bathurst

Edmundston

NEW
BRUNSWICK

PR. EDWARD
ISLAND

Charlottetown

Summerside

Cape Breton
Island

Sydney

St Pierre and
Miquelon
(France)

NOVA SCOTIA

ATLANTIC
OCEAN

45

60

Nakina
Beardmore
Hearst

Nipigon
Lake
Nipigon

Kapuskasing
Hornepayne

Smooth
Rock Falls

Amos

Val-d'Or

Rouyn-
Noranda

La Sarre

La Tuque

Shawinigan

Trois-Rivières

Jonquière
Chicoutimi

Roberval

Sherbrooke

MAINE

Fredericton
Saint John

Moncton

Yarmouth

Digby

Bridgewater

Liverpool

Halifax
Dartmouth

Cape
Sable

Île Royale
Marathon

Thunder Bay

Nipigon

Timmins

Kirkland
Lake

New
Liskeard

Lake
Temiskaming

Mattawa

Pembroke

North
Bay

Rivière-du-Loup

Québec

Lévis

VERMONT
N.H.

Montréal

MICHIGAN
WISCONSIN
Wausau

Green Bay
Oshkosh

Cadillac

Grand
Rapids

Flint

Lansing
Ann Arbor

Detroit

Lake
Superior

Sault
Sainte Marie

Sudbury

Espanola

Lake
Huron

Parry
Sound

Georgian
Bay

Orillia

Peterborough

OTTAWA

Kingston

Belleville

Cornwall

Lake Ontario

Toronto

Hamilton

Buffalo

Utica

Albany

MASS.
Boston

Lowell

Portland

Concord

CONN.

Cape Cod

Nagara Falls

St Catharines

Lake Erie

Cleveland

© Collins Bartholomew Ltd

0   500   1000 KILOMETRES

Lambert Azimuthal Equal Area Projection   1 : 15 000 000   MILES 0   100   200   30

Longitude 120° west of Greenwich

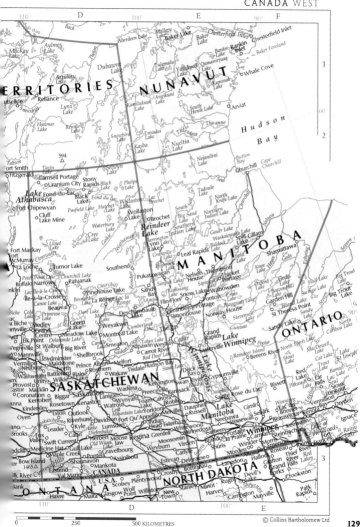

500 KILOMETRES

© Collins Bartholomew Ltd

129

Lambert Azimuthal Equal Area Projection   1 : 15 000 000   MILES 0   100   200   30

Lambert Azimuthal Equal Area Projection   1 : 25 000 000   MILES 0   250   50

GULF

OF

MEXICO

ATLANTIC

OCEAN

THE
BAHAMAS

250   500   750 KILOMETRES

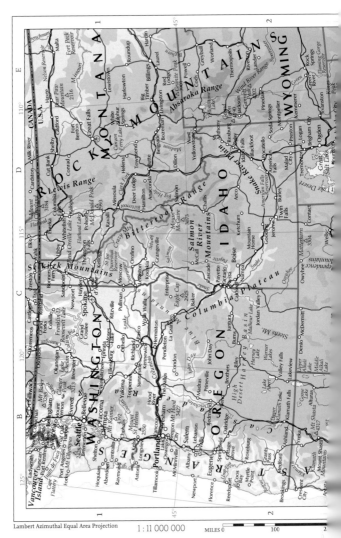

Lambert Azimuthal Equal Area Projection   1 : 11 000 000   MILES 0   100   2

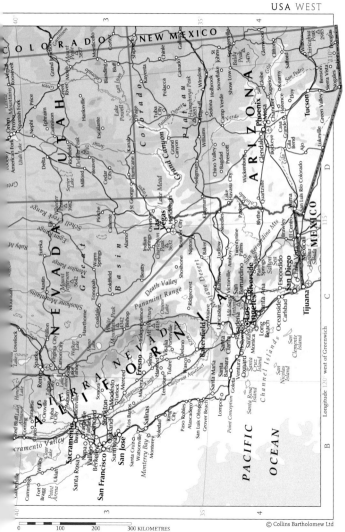

© Collins Bartholomew Ltd

0   100   200   300 KILOMETRES

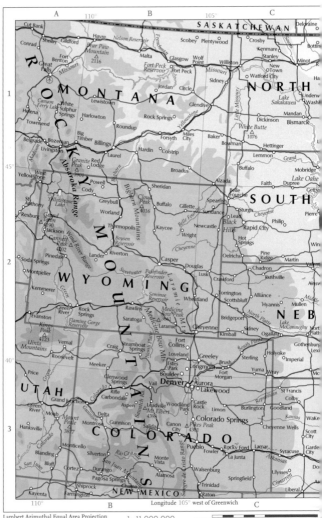

Lambert Azimuthal Equal Area Projection   1 : 11 000 000   MILES 0   100   200

© Collins Bartholomew Ltd

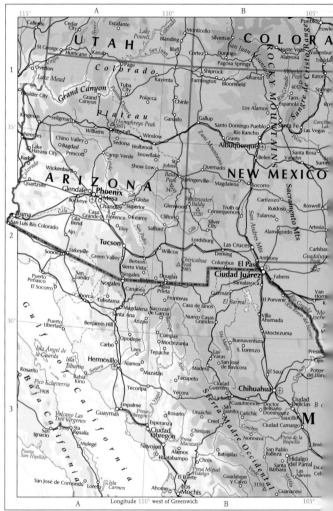

Lambert Azimuthal Equal Area Projection

1 : 11 000 000

MILES 0   100   20...

Longitude 110° west of Greenwich

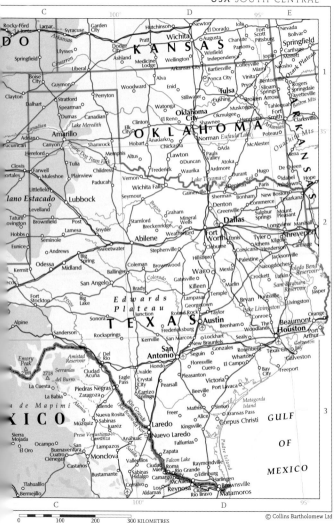

Lambert Azimuthal Equal Area Projection   1 : 11 000 000   MILES 0   100   200

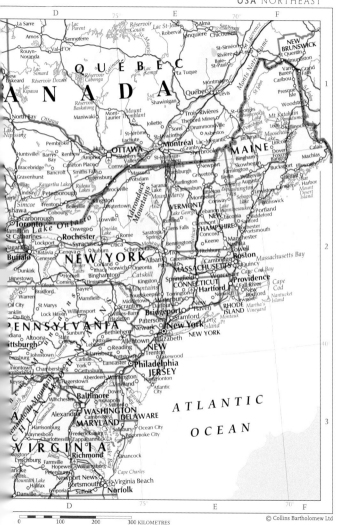

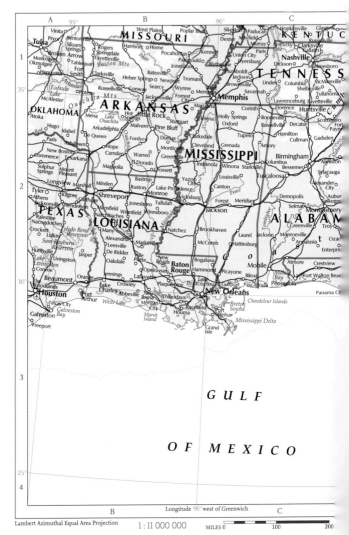

Lambert Azimuthal Equal Area Projection   1 : 11 000 000   MILES 0   100   200

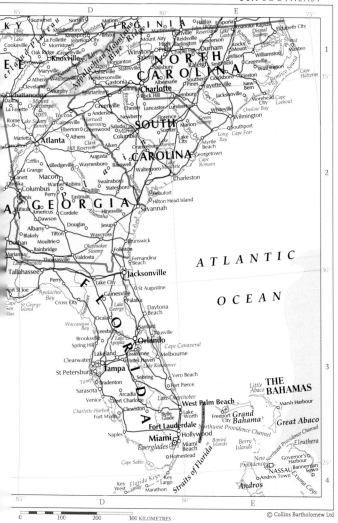

© Collins Bartholomew Ltd

Tijuana
Ensenada
Mexicali
San Colorado
Rio Colorado
El Golfo
de Sta Clara
Ajo
Tucson
ARIZONA
Willcox
Lordsburg
NEW MEXICO
Deming
Las Cruces
Hobbs
Callsbad
Seminole Lamesa
Eunice
Andrews
Midland
Big
Spring
San
Vicente
Presa
del Diablo
Puerto
Peñasco
El Socorro
San
Felipe
Green
Valley
Nogales
Sierra
Vista
Bisbee
Columbus
Ciudad Juárez
El Paso
2985
Fabens
Salaveca
Pecos
Fort
Stockton
Big
Lake
Vicente
Guerrero
3096
C. San
Quintin
Cárdenas
Rosario
San Fernando
Tubutama
Caborca
Nogales
Agua Prieta
Cananea
Fronteras
Nacozari
Arizpe
Casas
Grandes
Janos
Nuevo
Casas
Grandes
El Barreal
Guzmán
El Porvenir
Villa Ahumada
Moctezuma
Buenaventura
San
Lorenzo
Mt Livermore
Alpine
Marfa
Sanderson
UNITED
30°
Magdalena
Benjamín Hill
Cumpas
Tepache
San
José
de Bavicora
Madera
Presidio
Ojinaga
Emory
Peak
Amistad
Reservoir
Serranías
del Burro
La Babia
Gulf
Isla Angel
de la Guarda
Puerto
Libertad
Carbó
Moctezuma
La Junta
Chihuahua
Ciudad
Delicias
Bolsón
de Mapimí
2718
Múzquiz
La Cuesta
Bahía Rosario
Sebastián Vizcaíno
I. Cedros
Guerrero Negro
Punta
Eugenia
Tiburón
Echeverría
Bahía Kino
Hermosillo
Mazatán
Tecoripa
Yécora
San
Juanito
Cuauhtémoc
Doctor B.
Domínguez
Saucillo
Presa de
Camargo
Sierra
Mojada
Ocampo
El Oro
Buenaventura
Gustavos
30°
Vizcaíno
Tortugas
Pta San
Hipólito
Vol. Las
Tres
Vírgenes
1996
Santa Rosalía
Ignacio
Mulegé
Guaymas
Empalme
Esperanza
Rosario
Presa
Macuzari
Uruáchic
Creel
Norboya
Balleza
San Pablo
Hidalgo del Parral
Jiménez
Escalón
Indé
Ceballos
Las Nieves
Bermejillo
Mapimí
Gómez Palacio
Tlahualilo
San Pedro
de las Colonias
Monclova
2
San José de Comondú
Ciudad
Obregón
Navojoa
Alamos
Chinipas
Batopilas
Choix
El Fuerte
Presa M.
Hidalgo
Guadalupe
y Calvo
Santa
Bárbara
3150
Guanaceví
Topia
Indé
Torreón
Matamoros
Viesca
Parras
Concepción
Isla
San
Carmen
Loreto
Villa Insurgentes
Ciudad Constitución
Topolobampo
Los Mochis
Ahome
Guasave
Guamúchil
Mocorito
Pericos
Tepehuanes
Nuevo
Ideal
Santiago
Papasquiaro
Canatlán
Durango
Guadalupe
Victoria
Miguel
Auza
Camacho
Bahía
Magdalena
Puerto
Cortés
La Paz
San Pedro
Pichilingue
Isla
Espíritu Santo
Isla Cerralvo
Piaxtla
Culiacán
Navolato
Costa
Rica
Cosalá
Co Huehueto
El Salto
Villa
Unión
Sombrerete
Río Grande
Villa de
Cos
3150
Picnocho de la Laguna
2163
Todos Santos
Santiago
El Dorado
La Cruz
Villa
Unión
Cañitas de
Felipe Pescador
2
San Lucas
San José del Cabo
Mazatlán
Escuinapa
Rosario
3550
San
Alto
Fresnillo
MEX
Jerez
Salinas
20°
Teacapán
Acaponeta
Tecuala
Nayar
Ruiz
Tuxpan
Santiago Ixcuintla
San Martín
de Bolaños
Colotlán
Mezquitic
Villanueva
Zacatecas
Calvillo
Aguascalient
2985
Islas
Marías
Tepic
Compostela
Las Varas
Teul de
Ortega
Yahualica
Jalpa
Encarnación
Tepatitlán
León
Irapuat
Silao
Puerto Vallarta
Bahía de Banderas
Cabo Corrientes
Ameca
Tequila
Guadalajara
La Piedad
Zamora
Hidalg
Zacapu
20°
Tomatlán
Autlán
Zacoalco
Lago de Chapala
Sahuayo
Ciudad
Guzmán
Uruap
Islas Revillagigedo
(Mexico)
Isla San
Benedicto
Nevado de Colima
4339
Cihuatlán
Manzanillo
Tepalcatepec
Colima
Armería
Tecomán
Aguililla
3859
Apatzing
Isla
Socorro
PACIFIC
Colcomán
Arteaga
Lázaro Cárdenas
Zihuatanej
Peta
3
OCEAN
A
110°
Longitude 110° west of Greenwich
B

Lambert Azimuthal Equal Area Projection
1 : 15 000 000
MILES 0   100   200   300

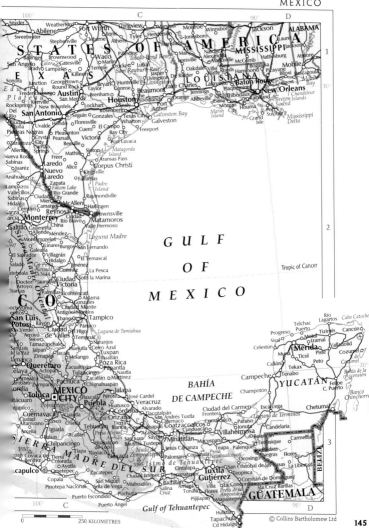

© Collins Bartholomew Ltd

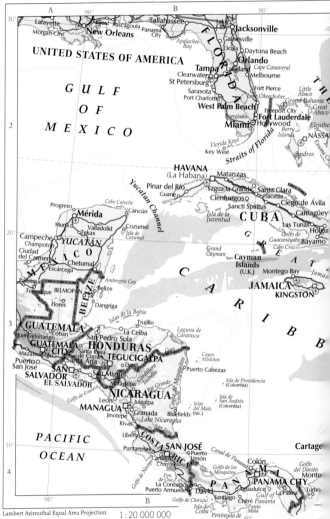

Lambert Azimuthal Equal Area Projection   1 : 20 000 000

C   70°   D   60°   E

30°

A T L A N T I C

O C E A N

2

Tropic of Cancer

BAHAMAS

Cat Island

Long Island

Mayaguana

Acklins
Island

Great
Inagua

Caicos
Islands

**Turks and
Caicos Islands** (U.K.)
GRAND TURK (Cockburn Town)

Baracoa

Guantánamo   Cap-Haïtien

Port-de-
Paix   Santiago

Hispaniola

W E S T   I N D I E S

20°

Gonaïves

Puerto
Plata

Jérémie

Île de
la Gonâve

HAITI   **DOMINICAN
REPUBLIC**

**PORT-AU-
PRINCE**

**SANTO
DOMINGO**

Puerto Rico
(U.S.A.)

SAN JUAN

LEEWARD ISLANDS

Virgin Is
(U.K.)

Anguilla
(U.K.)

Les
Cayes

Jacmel

Barahona

La Romana

Virgin Is
(U.S.A.)

St Maarten
(Neth.)

**ANTIGUA AND
BARBUDA**

Isla Beata   Cabo Beata

Ponce

St Croix
(U.S.A.)

BASSETERRE

Antigua

ST JOHN'S

ST KITTS AND NEVIS

Plymouth
(abandoned)

BRADES

Montserrat
(U.K.)

Guadeloupe (Fr.)

Marie-Galante
(Fr.)

BASSE-TERRE

C   A   R   I   B   B   E   A   N   S   E   A

A N T I L L E S

Lesser
Antilles

DOMINICA
ROSEAU

Martinique
(Fr.)

**FORT-DE-
FRANCE**

ST LUCIA
CASTRIES

**ST VINCENT AND THE
GRENADINES**

BARBADOS
BRIDGETOWN

KINGSTOWN

ST GEORGE'S

GRENADA

**Netherlands
Antilles**
(Neth.)

Aruba
(Neth.)

Curaçao

Ptа
Gallinas

Península
de la Guajira

WILLEMSTAD

Bonaire

Islas Los
Roques

Scarborough
Tobago

PORT OF
SPAIN

**TRINIDAD
AND
TOBAGO**

WINDWARD ISLANDS

Ríohacha

Punto Fijo

Coro

Golfo de Venezuela

San
Felipe   Maiquetía

La Asunción   Isla de
Margarita

Cumaná

G. of Paria

Güiria

Trinidad

10°

Santa
Marta

arranquilla

Valledupar

Cabimas

Machiques

Maracaibo

Lake Maracaibo

Barquisimeto

San Carlos
del Zulia

Valencia

San Carlos

Los Teques

CARACAS

Barcelona

Fernando

Maturín

Orinoco
Delta

Plato

El Banco

Trujillo

Valera

Acarigua

Valle de
la Pascua

Zaraza

Guanipa

4

ncelejo

OLOMBIA

El Tigre   **VENEZUELA**

Mérida

Barinas

Guanare

El Baúl

Calabozo

Libertad

Ciudad Bolívar

Orinoco

El Tigre

Tucupita

Ciudad
Guayana

Longitude 70° west of Greenwich

C   D   60°

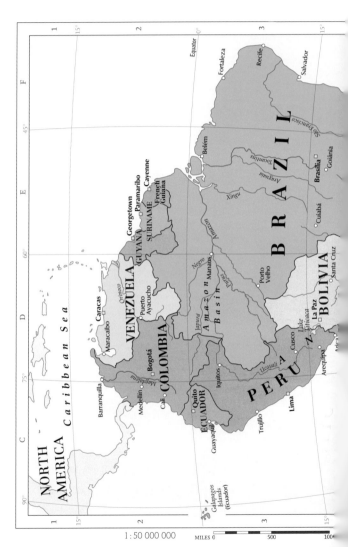

1 : 50 000 000

MILES 0   500   100[...]

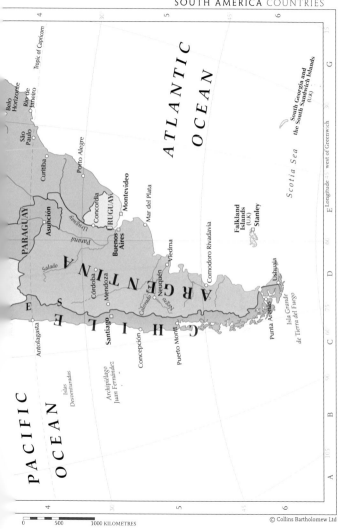

© Collins Bartholomew Ltd

GEORGETOWN
New Amsterdam
inden Nieuw Nickerie
SURINAME
Professor van Blommestein Meer
Pontoetoe

PARAMARIBO
St-Laurent-du-Maroni
Kourou
CAYENNE
French Guiana
Oiapoque

ATLANTIC
OCEAN

Serra Tamucumaque
Lourenço
Calçoene
Ilha de Maracá
Amapá

Equator

Arere
Paru
Porto Santana
Mazagão
Macapá
Chaves
Cabo Maguarinho
Mouths of the Amazon
Baía de Marajó

Oriximiná
Óbidos
Almeirim
Ilha de Marajó
Breves
Portel
Belém
Salinópolis
Bragança
Viseu

rucara
Parintins
Santarém
Monte Alegre
Cametá
Castanhal
Gurupi

Uruçituba
Altamira
Pinheiro
Viana
São Luís
Parnaíba
Camocim

Itaituba
Tucuruí
Represa Tucuruí
Jacundá
Baía de São Marcos
Itapicuru Mirim
Codó
Luzilândia
Tianguá
Sobral
Fortaleza
Caucaia

Maraba
Grajaú
Barra do Corda
Pedreiras
Caxias
Timon
Pres. Dutra
Teresina
Crateús
Taua
Aracati

acareacanga
Araras
São Félix
Tocantinópolis
Balsas
Jerumenha
Floriano
Picos
Iguatu
Sousa
Mossoró
Natal

Manuelzinho
Imperatriz
Araguaína
Conceição do Araguaia
Carolina
Canto do Buriti
Oeiras
Crato
Juazeiro do Norte
Campina Grande
João Pessoa

R A Z I L
Santa Maria das Barreiras
Pedro Afonso
São Raimundo Nonato
Paulistana
Petrolina
Juazeiro
Floresta
Salgueiro
Garanhuns
Caruaru
Olinda
Recife
Jaboatão
dos Guararapes

Serra do Cachimbo
Palmas
Porto Nacional
Dianópolis
Natividade
Barreiras
Ibotirama
Senhor do Bonfim
Paulo Afonso
Monte Santo
Arapiraca
Maceió

Porto Gaúchos Óbidos
Porto Artur
Ilha do Bananal
São Félix
Correntina
Irecê
Jacobina
Serrinha
Feira de Santana
Estância

amantino
Rosário Oeste
Cavalcante
Posse
Santana
Bom Jesus da Lapa
Brumado
Itaberaba
Sto Antônio de Jesus
Salvador

Cuiabá
Barra do Garças
Porangatu
Uruaçu
Niquelândia
Januária
Janaúba
Guanambi
Ubaitaba
Ilhéus
Una

áceres
Rondonópolis
Alto Garças
Iporá
Goiás
BRASÍLIA
Formosa
Arinos
Montes Claros
Espinosa
Vitória da Conquista
Itapetinga
Porto Seguro

Itiquira
Coxim
Jataí
Rio Verde
Itumbiara
Anápolis
Goiânia
Unaí
Paracatu
Jequitaí
Salinas
Almenara
Teófilo Otoni
Alcobaça

Rio Verde de Mato Grosso
Araguari
Patos de Minas

0 250 500 750 KILOMETRES

© Collins Bartholomew Ltd

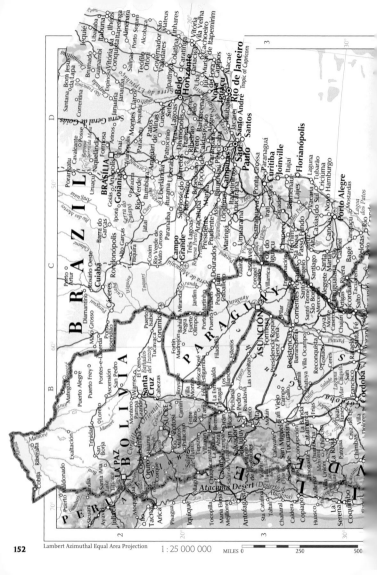

Lambert Azimuthal Equal Area Projection

1 : 25 000 000

MILES 0   250   500

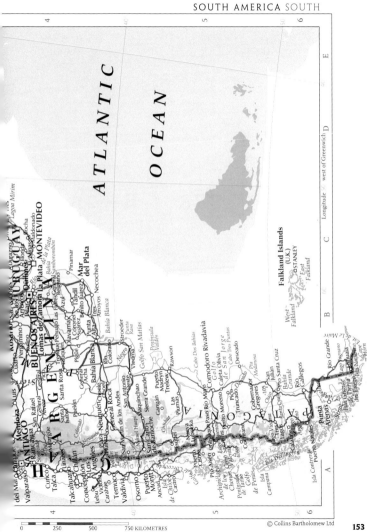

ATLANTIC

OCEAN

Falkland Islands
(U.K.)
STANLEY
West
Falkland
East
Falkland

URUGUAY

MONTEVIDEO

Mar
del Plata

BUENOS AIRES

A R G E N T I N A

SANTIAGO

Valparaíso

Mendoza

Bahía Blanca

Comodoro Rivadavia

P A T A G O N I A

Río
Gallegos

Punta
Arenas

Cape Horn

Concepción

Temuco

Valdivia

Osorno

Puerto
Montt

Isla Chiloé

C H I L E

0   250   500   750 KILOMETRES

© Collins Bartholomew Ltd

153

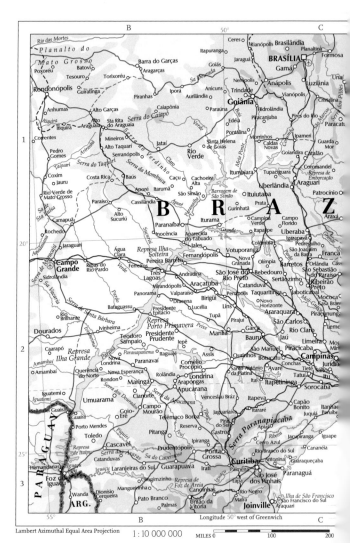

B 50° C

Rio das Mortes
Planalto do
Mato Grosso
Poxoréu
Batovi
Barra do Garças
Ceres ○ Rianópolis Brasilândia
Itapuranga ○ ○ Planaltina
Jaraguá ○ BRASÍLIA □ Formosa
Tesouro Torixoréu Aragarças
Guiratinga
Gamã ○
Rondonópolis
Piranhas ○ Ipora ○ Nerópolis ○ Trindade ○ Anápolis Luziânia Unaí
Anicuns Vianópolis Cristalina
Aurilândia ○ Goiânia ○ Hidrolândia ○ ○ Pires do Rio Paracatu
Anhumas Calapônia ○ ○ Paraúna Piracanjuba ○
Alto Garças
Itaquira Alto Sta Rita Mineiros ○ Edéia ○ Santa Helena ○ Caldas Ipameri Guarda
Itiquira ○ Araguaia do Araguaia Jataí ○ Serra Verdinho ○ de Goiás Pontalina Morrinhos Novas Goiandira Catalão Mor
Correntes Serra do Caiapó Rio Verde Itumbiara ○ Tupaciguara Coromandel Araguari
Pedro Alto Taquari Caçu ○ ○ Cachoeira Uberlândia Represa de
Gomes Serranópolis Alta Prata ○ Ituiutaba Emborcação Patrocínio
Coxim Serra do Taquari Costa Rica ○ Baús Aporé Itarumã São Simão ○ Gurinhatã ○ B R A Z Araxá
Jauru Barragem de
Rio Verde de Paraíso ○ Cassilândia São Simão Iturama ○ Campina Campo
Mato Grosso Alto Camapuã Inocência Aparecida ○ Verde Itapagipe Uberaba
Rochedo Sucurió Paranaíba do Tabuado Jales ○ ○ Colômbia Igarapava
Jaraguari Água ○ Fernandópolis Votuporanga ○ São Joaquim Pedregulho
Campo Clara Represa Ilha Nova ○ Olímpia da Barra Franca
Grande Ribas do Solteira Pereira Barreto Granada ○ Barretos Orlândia Cass
Sidrolândia Rio Pardo Ferreiras Três ○ Bebedouro São Sebastião do Paraíso
Lagoas Andradina ○ São José do Sertãozinho Ribeirão
Mirandópolis ○ Araçatuba Rio Preto Catanduva ○ Taquaritinga Jaboticabal Preto Mococa
Panorama ○ Valparaíso Birigüi ○ Penápolis Novo ○ Araraquara Casa Bran
Bataguassu Dracena ○ Lucélia Tupã ○ Horizonte ○ São Carlos Piracununga
Dourados Represa Presidente Lins Marília Garça ○ Rio Claro Leme
Rio Porto Primavera Epitácio Pirajuí ○ Bauru ○ Jaú Limeira Mog
Brilhante Teodoro Presidente Iepê ○ São Manuel ○ Piracicaba Campinas
Caarapó Represa Sampaio Prudente Paranapanema Itaguaje Assis ○ Ourinhos Botucatu ○ Avaré Conchas Tietê Jund
Ivinheima Londrina Santo Antônio Itapetininga Sorocaba
Amambaí Ilha Grande Querência Nova Esperança Paranavaí Rolândia ○ da Platina Ital Tatuí Itu
do Norte Rondon ○ Cornélio ○ Londrina
Iguatemi Umuarama Maringá Apucarana Procópio Arapongas Venceslau Bráz Itapeva Capão Itanhae
Campo Cianorte Serra da Apucarana Bonito Juquiá Peruib
Salto del Guaíra Goio- Mourão Telêmaco Borba Jaguariaíva Itararé
Guaíra Erê Reserva ○ Pira Apiaí ○ Jacupiranga Iguape
Porto Mendes Pitanga do Sul Castro Ribeira ○ Cerro Azul Cananéia
Toledo Cascavel ○ Ipiranga Serra Paranapiacaba
Hernandarias Catanduvas Prudentópolis Ponta ○ Rio Branco do Sul
Foz do Represa Serra das Araras Sa do Cavernoso Grossa ○ Antonina Guaraqueçaba
Iguaçu de Itaipu Laranjeiras do Sul Guarapuava ○ Palmeira ○ Curitiba
Wanda Iguaçu Mangueirinha Represa de São José Paranaguá
Dionísio Pato Branco Foz de Areia Lapa ○ dos Pinhais
Cerqueira Chapecozinho Canoinhas Rio Negro Ilha de São Francisco
Palmas União da Mafra ○ São Francisco do Sul
ARG. Vitória ○ Joinville Araquari

154 Lambert Azimuthal Equal Area Projection   1 : 10 000 000   MILES 0   100   200

Longitude 50° west of Greenwich

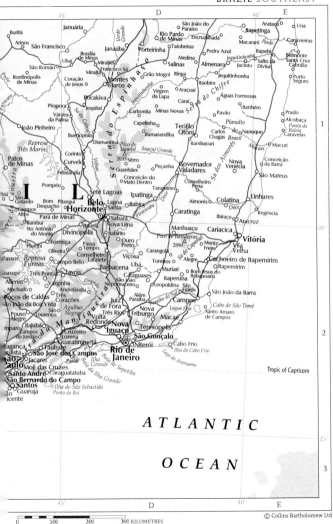

ATLANTIC

OCEAN

Tropic of Capricorn

0   100   200   300 KILOMETRES

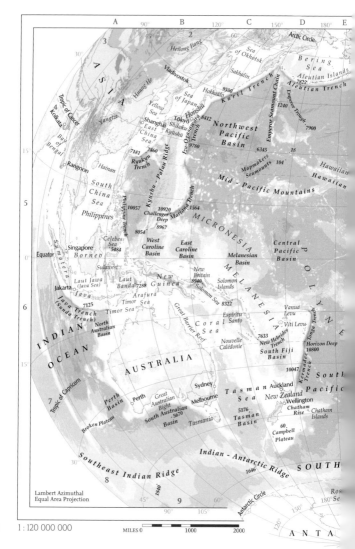

A 90° B 120° C 150° D 180° E

Arctic Circle

Heilong Jiang

Sea of Okhotsk

Bering Sea

Aleutian Islands

ASIA

Vladivostok

Sakhalin

Kuril Trench

Aleutian Trench

Tropic of Cancer

Himar He

Hokkaido

9550

Emperor Seamount Chain

2822

1240

Emperor Trough

Yangtze

Sea of Japan

Honshū

Tokyo

7900

Kolkata

Yellow Sea

Shanghai

Kyūshū

Izu-Ogasawara Trench

8412

Northwest Pacific Basin

Bay of Bengal

East China Sea

9780

6345

18

Rangoon

Hainan

7181 7460

Ryukyu Trench

Kyushu - Palau Ridge

Mapmakers Seamounts

104

Hawaiian

Hawaii

South China Sea

Philippine Trench

10057

10920 1564

Mariana Trench

Mid - Pacific Mountains

Philippines

Challenger Deep

8967

MICRONESIA

8054

Celebes Sea 5484

Singapore

West Caroline Basin

East Caroline Basin

Central Pacific Basin

Equator

Borneo

Sumatera

Sulawesi

Melanesian Basin

POLYNESIA

Laut Jawa (Java Sea)

New Guinea

New Britain

8940

Solomon Islands

Jakarta

Java

Laut Banda 7288

Arafura

8322

Timor Sea

Java Trench (Sunda Trench)

7125

Timor Sea

North Australian Basin

Great Barrier Reef

Coral Sea

Espiritu Santo

7633

Vanua Levu

Viti Levu

MELANESIA

Nouvelle Calédonie

New Hebrides Trench

Tonga Trench

Horizon Deep 10800

INDIAN OCEAN

South Fiji Basin

10047

Kermadec Trench

South Pacific

AUSTRALIA

Tasman Sea

Auckland

New Zealand

Wellington

Chatham Rise

Chatham Islands

Sydney

Melbourne

5176

Tasman Basin

Perth Basin

Perth

Great Australian Bight

South Australian Basin

5670

Tasmania

60

Campbell Plateau

Tropic of Capricorn

Broken Plateau

1646

Indian - Antarctic Ridge

SOUTH

Southeast Indian Ridge

8

1340

9

45° 60°

90° 105°

Antarctic Circle

120°

150°

180°

Ros Se

Lambert Azimuthal Equal Area Projection

156   1 : 120 000 000

MILES 0   1000   2000

ANTA

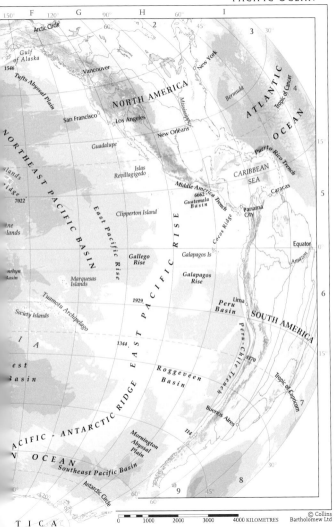

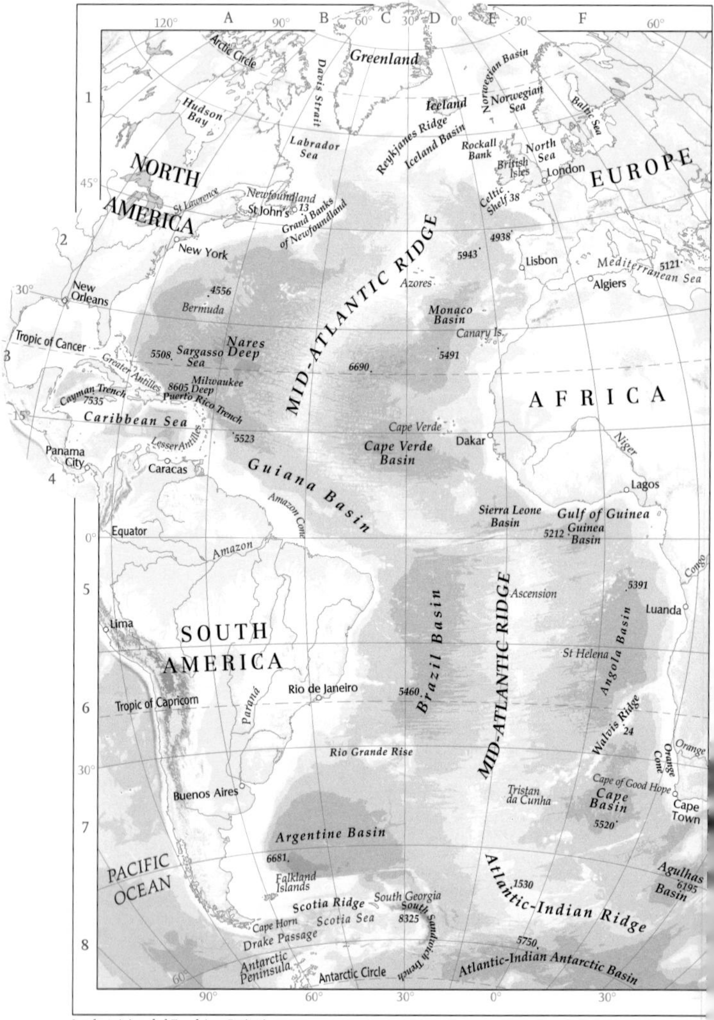

A B C D E F

120° 90° 60° 30° 0° 30° 60°

Arctic Circle
Greenland

1
Hudson Bay
Davis Strait
Iceland
Norwegian Basin
Norwegian Sea
Baltic Sea

NORTH
Labrador Sea
Reykjanes Ridge
Iceland Basin
Rockall Bank
North Sea
British Isles
London
EUROPE

AMERICA
St Lawrence
Newfoundland
St John's
Grand Banks of Newfoundland
13
Celtic Shelf 38

New York
4938
Lisbon
Mediterranean Sea
5121

2
5943
Azores
Monaco Basin
Algiers

Tropic of Cancer
4556
Bermuda
Canary Is.

Nares Deep
Sargasso Sea
5508
6690
5491
AFRICA

Greater Antilles
Cayman Trench
7335
Milwaukee Deep
8605 Deep
Puerto Rico Trench

3
Caribbean Sea
Lesser Antilles
5523
Cape Verde
Dakar

Panama City
Cape Verde Basin

Caracas
Guiana Basin
Sierra Leone Basin
Gulf of Guinea
5212
Guinea Basin
Lagos

Niger

Amazon Cone

4
Equator
Amazon
5391
Luanda
Congo

Lima
SOUTH
Ascension
St Helena Basin
Angola Basin

AMERICA
Brazil Basin
MID-ATLANTIC RIDGE

5
Tropic of Capricorn
Paraná
Rio de Janeiro
5460
Walvis Ridge
24
Orange Cone

Rio Grande Rise
Cape of Good Hope
Cape Basin
Cape Town

6
Buenos Aires
Tristan da Cunha
5520

Argentine Basin
Atlantic-Indian Ridge
Agulhas Basin
6195

PACIFIC OCEAN
6681
1530

7
Falkland Islands
Cape Horn
Scotia Ridge
South Georgia
Drake Passage
Scotia Sea
8325
5750
Atlantic-Indian Antarctic Basin

Antarctic Peninsula
Antarctic Circle
Atlantic-Indian Ridge

8

90° 60° 30° 0° 30°

158 Lambert Azimuthal Equal Area Projection 1 : 120 000 000 MILES 0   1000   200

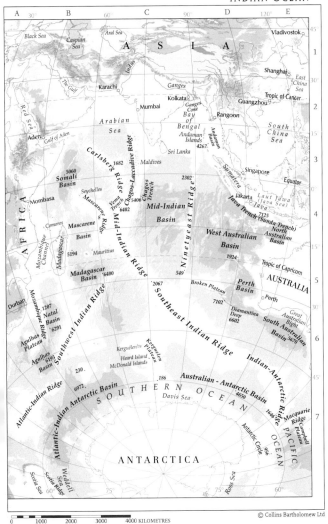

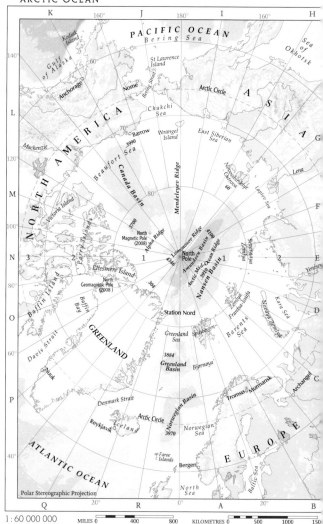

PACIFIC OCEAN

Bering Sea

Kodiak Island

Gulf of Alaska

St Lawrence Island

Nome

Bering Strait

Arctic Circle

Anchorage

A S I A

Sea of Okhotsk

Chukchi Sea

N O R T H A M E R I C A

70°

Barrow

Wrangel Island

East Siberian Sea

Mackenzie

Beaufort Sea

3990

Canada Basin

Mendeleyev Ridge

Novosibirskiye Ostrova

60

Lena

Laptev Sea

G

80°

3700

Victoria Island

Parry Islands

North Magnetic Pole (2008)

Alpha Ridge

3

2

1

Lomonosov Ridge

4346

North Pole

Amundsen Basin

Arctic Mid-Ocean Ridge

Severnaya Zemlya

2100

3910

F

Nansen Basin

1

2

E

Yenisey

Ellesmere Island

North Geomagnetic Pole (2008)

3014

Baffin Island

Buffin Bay

Zemlya Frantsa Iosifa

Novaya Zemlya

Kara Sea

Davis Strait

G R E E N L A N D

Station Nord

Greenland Sea

Spitsbergen

Barents Sea

D

Nuuk

3884

Greenland Basin

Bjørnøya

Tromsø

Murmansk

Archangel

C

Denmark Strait

Norwegian Basin

Arctic Circle

Reykjavík

Iceland

Norwegian Sea

3970

Bergen

E U R O P E

Faroe Islands

Baltic Sea

B

ATLANTIC OCEAN

North Sea

MILES 0   400   800   KILOMETRES 0   500   1000   150

INTRODUCTION TO THE INDEX

The index includes all names shown on the maps in the Atlas of the World. Names are referenced by page number and by a grid reference. The grid reference correlates to the alphanumeric values which appear within each map frame. Each entry also includes the country or geographical area in which the feature is located. Entries relating to names appearing on insets are indicated by a small box symbol: □, followed by a grid reference if the inset has its own alphanumeric values.

Name forms are as they appear on the maps, with additional alternative names or name forms included as cross-references which refer the user to the entry for the map form of the name. Names beginning with Mc or Mac are alphabetized exactly as they appear. The terms Saint, Sainte, etc, are abbreviated to St, Ste, etc, but alphabetized as if in the full form.

Names of physical features beginning with generic, geographical terms are permuted – the descriptive term is placed after the main part of the name. For example, Lake Superior is indexed as Superior, Lake; Mount Everest as Everest, Mount. This policy is applied to all languages.

Entries, other than those for towns and cities, include a descriptor indicating the type of geographical feature. Descriptors are not included where the type of feature is implicit in the name itself.

Administrative divisions are included to differentiate entries of the same name and feature type within the one country. In such cases, duplicate names are alphabetized in order of administrative division. Additional qualifiers are also included for names within selected geographical areas.

INDEX ABBREVIATIONS

admin. div.	administrative division	Fin.	Finland		Guinea
		for.	forest	Pol.	Poland
Afgh.	Afghanistan	g.	gulf	Port.	Portugal
Alg.	Algeria	Ger.	Germany	prov.	province
Arg.	Argentina	Guat.	Guatemala	reg.	region
Austr.	Australia	hd	headland	Rep.	Republic
aut. reg.	autonomous region	Hond.	Honduras	Rus. Fed.	Russian Federation
aut. rep.	autonomous republic	imp. l.	impermanent lake	S.	South
Azer.	Azerbaijan	Indon.	Indonesia	Switz.	Switzerland
Bangl.	Bangladesh	isth.	isthmus	Tajik.	Tajikistan
Bol.	Bolivia	Kazakh.	Kazakhstan	Tanz.	Tanzania
Bos.-Herz.	Bosnia Herzegovina	Kyrg.	Kyrgyzstan	terr.	territory
Bulg.	Bulgaria	lag.	lagoon	Thai.	Thailand
Can.	Canada	Lith.	Lithuania	Trin. and Tob.	Trinidad and Tobago
C.A.R.	Central African Republic	Lux.	Luxembourg	Turkm.	Turkmenistan
		Madag.	Madagascar	U.A.E.	United Arab Emirates
Col.	Colombia	Maur.	Mauritania		
Czech Rep.	Czech Republic	Mex.	Mexico	U.K.	United Kingdom
Dem. Rep.	Democratic	Moz.	Mozambique	Ukr.	Ukraine
Congo	Republic of the	mun.	municipality	Uru.	Uruguay
Congo		N.	North	U.S.A.	United States of America
depr.	depression	Neth.	Netherlands		
des.	desert	Nic.	Nicaragua	Uzbek.	Uzbekistan
Dom. Rep.	Dominican Republic	N.Z.	New Zealand	val.	valley
		Pak.	Pakistan	Venez.	Venezuela
esc.	escarpment	Para.	Paraguay		
est.	estuary	Phil.	Philippines		
Eth.	Ethiopia	plat.	plateau		
		P.N.G.	Papua New		

1

128 B2 **100 Mile House** Can.

A

93 E4 **Aabenraa** Denmark
100 C2 **Aachen** Ger.
93 E4 **Aalborg** Denmark
100 B3 **Aalst** Belgium
100 B2 **Aarschot** Belgium
68 C2 **Aba** China
115 C4 **Aba** Nigeria
81 C2 **Ābādān** Iran
81 D2 **Ābādeh** Iran
81 B1 **Abadla** Alg.
115 C4 **Abakaliki** Nigeria
83 H3 **Abakan** Rus. Fed.
150 A3 **Abancay** Peru
81 D2 **Abarqū** Iran
66 F3 **Abashiri** Japan
117 B4 **Abaya, Lake** Eth.
82 G3 **Ābay Wenz** r. Eth./Sudan see **Blue Nile**
82 G3 **Abaza** Rus. Fed.
108 A2 **Abbasanta** Sardegna Italy
104 C1 **Abbeville** France
142 B3 **Abbeville** U.S.A.
55 O2 **Abbot Ice Shelf** Antarctica
74 B1 **Abbottabad** Pak.
115 E3 **Abéché** Chad
114 B4 **Abengourou** Côte d'Ivoire
114 C4 **Abeokuta** Nigeria
99 A2 **Aberaeron** U.K.
96 C2 **Aberchirder** U.K.
99 B3 **Aberdare** U.K.
99 A2 **Aberdaron** U.K.
122 B3 **Aberdeen** S. Africa
96 C2 **Aberdeen** U.K.
141 D3 **Aberdeen** MD U.S.A.
137 D3 **Aberdeen** SD U.S.A.
134 B1 **Aberdeen** WA U.S.A.
129 E1 **Aberdeen Lake** Can.
119 D2 **Abert, Lake** U.S.A.
134 B2 **Abert, Lake** U.S.A.
99 A2 **Aberystwyth** U.K.
86 F2 **Abez'** Rus. Fed.
78 B3 **Abhā** Saudi Arabia
Abiad, Bahr el r. Sudan/Uganda see **White Nile**
114 B4 **Abidjan** Côte d'Ivoire
137 D3 **Abilene** KS U.S.A.
139 D2 **Abilene** TX U.S.A.
99 C3 **Abingdon** U.K.
91 D3 **Abinsk** Rus. Fed.
130 B2 **Abitibi, Lake** Can.
Åbo Fin. see **Turku**
74 B1 **Abohar** India
114 C4 **Abomey** Benin
60 A1 **Abongabong, Gunung** mt. Indon.
118 B2 **Abong Mbang** Cameroon
64 A2 **Aborlan** Phil.
115 D3 **Abou Déia** Chad
106 B2 **Abrantes** Port.
152 B3 **Abra Pampa** Arg.
136 A2 **Absaroka Range** mts U.S.A.
81 C1 **Abşeron Yarımadası** pen. Azer.
78 B3 **Abū 'Arīsh** Saudi Arabia
79 C2 **Abu Dhabi** U.A.E.
116 B3 **Abu Hamed** Sudan
115 C4 **Abuja** Nigeria
81 C2 **Abū Kamāl** Syria

152 B1 **Abunã** r. Bol./Brazil
150 B2 **Abunã** Brazil
74 B2 **Abu Road** India
116 B2 **Abū Sunbul** Egypt
117 A3 **Abū Ẓabad** Sudan
Abū Ẓabī U.A.E. see **Abu Dhabi**
117 A4 **Abyei** Sudan
145 B2 **Acambaro** Mex.
106 B1 **A Cañiza** Spain
144 B2 **Acaponeta** Mex.
145 C3 **Acapulco** Mex.
151 D2 **Acará** Brazil
150 B1 **Acarigua** Venez.
145 C3 **Acatlán** Mex.
145 C3 **Acayucán** Mex.
114 B4 **Accra** Ghana
98 B2 **Accrington** U.K.
74 B2 **Achalpur** India
97 A2 **Achill Island** Ireland
101 D1 **Achim** Ger.
96 B2 **Achnasheen** U.K.
91 D2 **Achuyevo** Rus. Fed.
111 C3 **Acıpayam** Turkey
109 C3 **Acireale** Sicilia Italy
147 C2 **Acklins Island** Bahamas
153 B4 **Aconcagua, Cerro** mt. Arg.
106 B1 **A Coruña** Spain
108 A2 **Acqui Terme** Italy
103 D2 **Ács** Hungary
145 C2 **Actopán** Mex.
139 D2 **Ada** U.S.A.
79 C2 **Adam** Oman
Adamstown Pitcairn Is
49 J4 **'Adan** Yemen see **Aden**
80 B2 **Adana** Turkey
111 D2 **Adapazarı** Turkey
Adapazari Turkey see **Adapazarı**
108 A1 **Adda** r. Italy
78 B2 **Ad Dafinah** Saudi Arabia
78 B2 **Ad Dahnā'** des. Saudi Arabia
78 B2 **Ad Dahnā'** des. Saudi Arabia
114 A2 **Ad Dakhla** Western Sahara
Ad Dammām Saudi Arabia see **Dammam**
78 A2 **Ad Dār al Ḥamrā'** Saudi Arabia
78 B3 **Ad Darb** Saudi Arabia
78 B2 **Ad Dawādimī** Saudi Arabia
Ad Dawḥah Qatar see **Doha**
78 B2 **Ad Dilam** Saudi Arabia
116 C2 **Ad Dir'īyah** Saudi Arabia
117 B4 **Addis Ababa** Eth.
81 C2 **Ad Dīwānīyah** Iraq
52 A2 **Adelaide** Austr.
50 C1 **Adelaide River** Austr.
101 D2 **Adelebsen** Ger.
55 J2 **Adélie Land** Antarctica
78 B3 **Aden** Yemen
117 C3 **Aden, Gulf of** Somalia/Yemen
100 C2 **Adenau** Ger.
79 C2 **Adh Dhayd** U.A.E.
59 C3 **Adi** i. Indon.
78 A3 **Adī Ark'ay** Eth.
116 B3 **Adigrat** Eth.
75 B3 **Adilabad** India
141 E2 **Adirondack Mountains** U.S.A.
Ādīs Ābeba Eth. see **Addis Ababa**
117 B4 **Ādīs Alem** Eth.
110 C1 **Adjud** Romania
50 B1 **Admiralty Gulf** Austr.
128 A2 **Admiralty Island** U.S.A.
104 B3 **Adour** r. France
106 C2 **Adra** Spain
114 B2 **Adrar** Alg.

140 C2 **Adrian** MI U.S.A.
139 C1 **Adrian** TX U.S.A.
108 B2 **Adriatic Sea** Europe
116 B3 **Adwa** Eth.
83 K2 **Adycha** r. Rus. Fed.
91 D3 **Adygeysk** Rus. Fed.
114 B4 **Adzopé** Côte d'Ivoire
111 B3 **Aegean Sea** Greece/Turkey
101 D1 **Aerzen** Ger.
106 B1 **A Estrada** Spain
116 B3 **Afabet** Eritrea
76 C3 **Afghanistan** country Asia
78 B2 **'Afīf** Saudi Arabia
80 B2 **Afyon** Turkey
115 C3 **Agadez** Niger
114 B1 **Agadir** Morocco
77 C2 **Agadyr'** Kazakh.
74 B2 **Agar** India
75 D2 **Agartala** India
81 C2 **Ağdam** Azer.
105 C3 **Agde** France
104 C3 **Agen** France
122 A2 **Aggeneys** S. Africa
111 C3 **Agia Varvara** Greece
111 B3 **Agios Dimitrios** Greece
111 C3 **Agios Efstratios** i. Greece
111 B3 **Agios Nikolaos** Greece
110 B1 **Agnita** Romania
75 B2 **Agra** India
81 C2 **Ağrı** Turkey
Ağrı Dağı mt. Turkey see **Ararat, Mount**
108 B3 **Agrigento** Sicilia Italy
111 B3 **Agrinio** Greece
109 B2 **Agropoli** Italy
154 B3 **Água Clara** Brazil
146 B4 **Aguadulce** Panama
144 B2 **Aguanaval** r. Mex.
144 B1 **Agua Prieta** Mex.
154 B2 **Águas Formosas** Brazil
106 B1 **Águeda** Port.
106 C1 **Aguilar de Campóo** Spain
107 C2 **Águilas** Spain
144 B3 **Aguililla** Mex.
122 B3 **Agulhas, Cape** S. Africa
155 D2 **Agulhas Negras** mt. Brazil
111 C2 **Ağva** Turkey
81 C2 **Ahar** Iran
100 C1 **Ahaus** Ger.
81 C2 **Ahlat** Turkey
100 C2 **Ahlen** Ger.
74 B2 **Ahmadabad** India
73 B3 **Ahmadnagar** India
74 B2 **Ahmadpur East** Pak.
74 B1 **Ahmadpur Sial** Pak.
144 B2 **Ahome** Mex.
79 C2 **Ahram** Iran
101 E1 **Ahrensburg** Ger.
104 C2 **Ahun** France
81 C2 **Ahvāz** Iran
122 A2 **Ai-Ais** Namibia
80 B2 **Aigialousa** Cyprus
111 B3 **Aigio** Greece
143 D2 **Aiken** U.S.A.
97 B1 **Ailt an Chorráin** Ireland
155 D1 **Aimorés** Brazil
155 D1 **Aimorés, Serra dos** hills Brazil
114 B2 **'Aïn Ben Tili** Maur.
107 D2 **Aïn Defla** Alg.
114 B1 **Aïn Sefra** Alg.
136 C2 **Ainsworth** U.S.A.
Aintab Turkey see **Gaziante**
107 D2 **Aïn Taya** Alg.
107 D2 **Aïn Tédélès** Alg.
115 C3 **Aïr, Massif de l'** mts Niger
60 A1 **Airbangis** Indon.

28 C2 Airdrie Can.
04 B3 Aire-sur-l'Adour France
01 E2 Aisch r. Ger.
28 A1 Aishihik Lake Can.
00 A3 Aisne r. France
59 C3 Aitape P.N.G.
10 B1 Aiud Romania
05 D3 Aix-en-Provence France
05 D2 Aix-les-Bains France
62 A1 Aizawl India
67 C3 Aizkraukle Latvia
18 C3 Aizu-Wakamatsu Japan
05 D3 Ajaccio Corse France
15 E1 Ajdābiyā Libya
74 B2 Ajmer India
38 A2 Ajo U.S.A.
87 E3 Akbulak Rus. Fed.
87 B2 Akçakale Turkey
80 B2 Akdağmadeni Turkey
66 D3 Åkersberga Sweden
18 C2 Aketi Dem. Rep. Congo
87 A4 Akhalk'alak'i Georgia
79 C2 Akhḍar, Jabal mts Oman
1 C3 Akhisar Turkey
87 D4 Akhtubinsk Rus. Fed.
30 B1 Akimiski Island Can.
66 D3 Akita Japan
14 A3 Akjoujt Maur.
77 D1 Akkol' Kazakh.
88 B2 Akmenrags pt Latvia
     Akmola Kazakh. see Astana
17 B4 Akobo Sudan
74 B2 Akola India
78 A3 Akordat Eritrea
27 G2 Akpatok Island Can.
92 A3 Akranes Iceland
24 C2 Akron U.S.A.
75 B1 Aksai Chin terr. Asia
81 A2 Aksaray Turkey
76 B1 Aksay Kazakh.
76 B1 Aksay Rus. Fed.
80 B2 Akşehir Turkey
91 D1 Akshiganak Kazakh.
77 E2 Aksu China
78 A3 Āksum Eth.
76 B1 Aktau Kazakh.
76 B2 Aktobe Kazakh.
77 D2 Aktogay Kazakh.
88 C3 Aktsyabrski Belarus
15 C4 Akure Nigeria
92 B2 Akureyri Iceland
42 C2 Alabama r. U.S.A.
42 C2 Alabama state U.S.A.
81 C1 Alaçatı Turkey
81 C1 Alagir Rus. Fed.
51 E3 Alagoinhas Brazil
07 C1 Alagón Spain
78 B2 Al Aḩmadī Kuwait
77 E2 Alakol', Ozero salt l. Kazakh.
32 J2 Alakurtti Rus. Fed.
78 B3 Al 'Alayyah Saudi Arabia
78 B2 Al 'Amādiyah Iraq
80 A2 Al 'Āmirīyah Egypt
45 C3 Alamo U.S.A.
48 B2 Alamogordo U.S.A.
44 B2 Alamos Sonora Mex.
44 B2 Alamos Sonora Mex.
44 B2 Alamos r. Mex.
24 A3 Alamosa U.S.A.
93 G3 Åland Islands Fin.
70 B2 Alanya Turkey
3 B4 Alappuzha India
8 B2 Al 'Aqabah Jordan
8 B2 Al 'Aqiq Saudi Arabia
7 C2 Alarcón, Embalse de resr Spain
0 B2 Al 'Arīsh Egypt

78 B2 Al Arţāwīyah Saudi Arabia
61 C2 Alas Indon.
111 C3 Alaşehir Turkey
128 A2 Alaska state U.S.A.
124 F3 Alaska, Gulf of U.S.A.
81 C2 Alät Azer.
87 D3 Alatyr' Rus. Fed.
150 A2 Alausí Ecuador
93 H3 Alavus Fin.
52 B2 Alawoona Austr.
108 A2 Alba Italy
107 C2 Albacete Spain
110 B1 Alba Iulia Romania
109 C2 Albania country Europe
50 A3 Albany Austr.
130 B1 Albany r. Can.
143 D2 Albany GA U.S.A.
141 E2 Albany NY U.S.A.
134 B2 Albany OR U.S.A.
     Al Başrah Iraq see Basra
51 D1 Albatross Bay Austr.
116 A2 Al Bawīti Egypt
115 E1 Al Bayḍā' Libya
78 B3 Al Bayḍā' Yemen
143 D1 Albemarle U.S.A.
143 E1 Albemarle Sound sea chan. U.S.A.
108 A2 Albenga Italy
51 C2 Alberga watercourse Austr.
52 A2 Alberta prov. Can.
100 B2 Albert Kanaal canal Belgium
119 D2 Albert, Lake Dem. Rep. Congo/Uganda
137 E2 Albert Lea U.S.A.
104 C3 Albi France
78 A2 Al Bi'r Saudi Arabia
78 B3 Al Birk Saudi Arabia
78 B2 Al Biyāḍh reg. Saudi Arabia
     Alborz, Reshteh-ye mts Iran see Elburz Mountains
106 B2 Albufeira Port.
138 B1 Albuquerque U.S.A.
79 C2 Al Buraymī Oman
53 C3 Albury Austr.
106 B2 Alcácer do Sal Port.
106 C1 Alcalá de Henares Spain
106 C2 Alcalá la Real Spain
108 B3 Alcamo Sicilia Italy
107 C1 Alcañiz Spain
106 B2 Alcántara Spain
106 C2 Alcaraz Spain
106 C2 Alcaraz, Sierra de mts Spain
106 C2 Alcaudete Spain
106 C2 Alcázar de San Juan Spain
91 D2 Alchevs'k Ukr.
155 E1 Alcobaça Brazil
107 C2 Alcoy-Alcoi Spain
107 D2 Alcúdia Spain
145 C2 Aldama Mex.
83 J3 Aldan Rus. Fed.
83 J2 Aldan r. Rus. Fed.
95 C4 Alderney i. Channel Is
114 A3 Aleg Maur.
155 D2 Alegre Brazil
152 C3 Alegrete Brazil
83 K3 Aleksandrovsk-Sakhalinskiy Rus. Fed.
91 D1 Alekseyevka Belgorodskaya Oblast' Rus. Fed.
91 D1 Alekseyevka Belgorodskaya Oblast' Rus. Fed.
89 E3 Aleksin Rus. Fed.
109 D2 Aleksinac Serbia
118 B3 Alèmbé Gabon
151 D2 Além Paraíba Brazil
93 F3 Ålen Norway
104 C2 Alençon France

80 B2 Aleppo Syria
150 A3 Alerta Peru
128 B2 Alert Bay Can.
105 C3 Alès France
110 B1 Aleşd Romania
108 A2 Alessandria Italy
93 E3 Ålesund Norway
124 C3 Aleutian Islands U.S.A.
83 L3 Alevina, Mys c. Rus. Fed.
128 B2 Alexander Archipelago is U.S.A.
122 A2 Alexander Bay S. Africa
142 C2 Alexander City U.S.A.
55 O2 Alexander Island Antarctica
53 C3 Alexandra Austr.
54 A3 Alexandra N.Z.
111 B2 Alexandreia Greece
     Alexandretta Turkey see İskenderun
116 A1 Alexandria Egypt
110 C2 Alexandria Romania
123 C3 Alexandria S. Africa
142 B2 Alexandria LA U.S.A.
137 D1 Alexandria MN U.S.A.
141 D3 Alexandria VA U.S.A.
52 A3 Alexandrina, Lake Austr.
111 C2 Alexandroupoli Greece
131 E1 Alexis r. Can.
128 B2 Alexis Creek Can.
77 E1 Aleysk Rus. Fed.
107 C1 Alfaro Spain
81 C3 Al Fāw Iraq
101 D2 Alfeld (Leine) Ger.
155 C2 Alfenas Brazil
     Al Fujayrah U.A.E. see Fujairah
     Al Furāt r. Iraq/Syria see Euphrates
106 B2 Algeciras Spain
107 C2 Algemesí Spain
78 A3 Algena Eritrea
     Alger Alg. see Algiers
114 C2 Algeria country Africa
79 C3 Al Ghaydah Yemen
108 A2 Alghero Sardegna Italy
116 B2 Al Ghurdaqah Egypt
79 B2 Al Ghwaybiyah Saudi Arabia
115 C1 Algiers Alg.
123 C3 Algoa Bay S. Africa
137 E2 Algona U.S.A.
106 C1 Algorta Spain
81 C2 Al Ḩadīthah Iraq
79 C2 Al Hajar al Gharbī mts Oman
107 C2 Alhama de Murcia Spain
80 A2 Al Ḩammām Egypt
78 B2 Al Ḩanākīyah Saudi Arabia
81 C2 Al Ḩasakah Syria
81 C2 Al Ḩayy Iraq
78 B3 Al Ḩazm al Jawf Yemen
79 C3 Al Ḩibāk des. Saudi Arabia
78 B2 Al Ḩillah Saudi Arabia
79 B2 Al Ḩinnāh Saudi Arabia
     Al Ḩudaydah Yemen see Hodeidah
79 B2 Al Ḩufūf Saudi Arabia
115 D2 Al Ḩulayq al Kabīr hills Libya
79 C2 'Alīābād Iran
111 C3 Aliağa Turkey
111 B2 Aliakmonas r. Greece
107 C2 Alicante Spain
139 D3 Alice U.S.A.
109 C3 Alice, Punta pt Italy
51 C2 Alice Springs Austr.
75 C2 Aligarh India
81 C2 Aligūdarz Iran
69 E1 Alihe China
118 B3 Alima r. Congo

Aliova

111 C3 Aliova r. Turkey
117 C3 Ali Sabieh Djibouti
Al Iskandarīyah Egypt see Alexandria
116 B1 Al Ismā'īlīyah Egypt
123 C3 Aliwal North S. Africa
115 E2 Al Jaghbūb Libya
78 B2 Al Jahrah Kuwait
79 C2 Al Jamalīyah Qatar
115 D1 Al Jawsh Libya
106 B2 Aljezur Port.
Al Jīzah Egypt see Giza
79 B2 Al Jubayl Saudi Arabia
78 B2 Al Junaynah Saudi Arabia
106 B2 Aljustrel Port.
78 B2 Al Kahfah Saudi Arabia
79 C2 Al Kāmil Oman
80 B2 Al Karak Jordan
79 C2 Al Khābūrah Oman
78 B2 Al Khamāsīn Saudi Arabia
116 B2 Al Khārijah Egypt
79 C2 Al Khaṣab Oman
78 B3 Al Khawkhah Yemen
79 C2 Al Khawr Qatar
115 D1 Al Khums Libya
79 B2 Al Khunn Saudi Arabia
79 C2 Al Kir'ānah Qatar
100 B1 Alkmaar Neth.
115 E2 Al Kufrah Libya
81 C2 Al Kūt Iraq
Al Kuwayt Kuwait see Kuwait
Al Lādhiqīyah Syria see Latakia
75 C2 Allahabad India
83 K2 Allakh-Yun' Rus. Fed.
141 D2 Allegheny r. U.S.A.
140 C3 Allegheny Mountains U.S.A.
97 B1 Allen, Lough l. Ireland
145 B2 Allende Coahuila Mex.
145 B2 Allende Nuevo León Mex.
141 D2 Allentown U.S.A.
101 D1 Aller r. Ger.
136 C2 Alliance NE U.S.A.
140 C2 Alliance OH U.S.A.
78 B2 Al Līth Saudi Arabia
96 C2 Alloa U.K.
131 C2 Alma Can.
Alma-Ata Kazakh. see Almaty
106 B2 Almada Port.
106 C2 Almadén Spain
Al Madīnah Saudi Arabia see Medina
116 B1 Al Mafraq Jordan
78 B3 Al Maḥwīt Yemen
78 B2 Al Majma'ah Saudi Arabia
135 B2 Almanor, Lake U.S.A.
107 C2 Almansa Spain
80 B2 Al Manṣūrah Egypt
79 C2 Al Mariyyah U.A.E.
115 E1 Al Marj Libya
77 D2 Almaty Kazakh.
106 C2 Almazán Spain
151 C2 Almeirim Brazil
100 C1 Almelo Neth.
155 D1 Almenara Brazil
106 B1 Almendra, Embalse de resr Spain
106 B2 Almendralejo Spain
106 C2 Almería Spain
106 C2 Almería, Golfo de b. Spain
87 E3 Al'met'yevsk Rus. Fed.
78 B2 Al Mindak Saudi Arabia
116 B2 Al Minyā Egypt
79 B2 Al Mish'āb Saudi Arabia
106 B2 Almodôvar Port.
106 B2 Almonte Spain
75 B2 Almora India
79 B2 Al Mubarrez Saudi Arabia

79 C2 Al Muḍaibī Oman
80 B3 Al Mudawwarah Jordan
Al Mukallā Yemen see Mukalla
Al Mukhā Yemen see Mocha
106 C2 Almuñécar Spain
78 A2 Al Muwaylih Saudi Arabia
111 B3 Almyros Greece
96 B1 Alness U.K.
98 C1 Alnwick U.K.
49 G4 Alofi Niue
111 B3 Alonnisos i. Greece
59 C3 Alor i. Indon.
59 C3 Alor, Kepulauan is Indon.
60 B1 Alor Star Malaysia
Alost Belgium see Aalst
86 C2 Alozero Rus. Fed.
140 C1 Alpena U.S.A.
139 C2 Alpine U.S.A.
105 D2 Alps mts Europe
79 B3 Al Qa'āmīyāt reg. Saudi Arabia
115 D1 Al Qaddāḥīyah Libya
Al Qāhirah Egypt see Cairo
78 B2 Al Qa'īyah Saudi Arabia
81 C2 Al Qāmishlī Syria
80 B2 Al Qaryatayn Syria
79 B3 Al Qaṭn Yemen
106 B2 Alquexa, Barragem de resr Port.
80 B2 Al Qunayṭirah Syria
78 B3 Al Qunfidhah Saudi Arabia
116 B2 Al Quṣayr Egypt
78 B2 Al Quwayyah Saudi Arabia
101 D2 Alsfeld Ger.
92 H2 Alta Norway
92 H2 Altaelva r. Norway
68 B1 Altai Mountains Asia
143 D2 Altamaha r. U.S.A.
151 C2 Altamira Brazil
109 C2 Altamura Italy
68 B1 Altay Mongolia
105 D2 Altdorf Switz.
107 C2 Altea Spain
101 F2 Altenburg Ger.
100 C2 Altenkirchen (Westerwald) Ger.
111 D3 Altınoluk Turkey
111 D3 Altıntaş Turkey
152 B2 Altiplano plain Bol.
154 B1 Alto Araguaia Brazil
107 C1 Alto del Moncayo mt. Spain
154 B1 Alto Garças Brazil
121 C2 Alto Molócuè Moz.
129 E3 Altona Can.
141 D2 Altoona U.S.A.
154 B1 Alto Sucuriú Brazil
154 B1 Alto Taquarí Brazil
102 C2 Altötting Ger.
68 B2 Altun Shan mts China
134 B2 Alturas U.S.A.
139 D2 Altus U.S.A.
88 C2 Alūksne Latvia
78 A2 Al 'Ulā Saudi Arabia
115 D1 Al 'Uqaylah Libya
Al Uqṣur Egypt see Luxor
91 C3 Alushta U.K.
139 D1 Alva U.S.A.
145 C3 Alvarado Mex.
93 F3 Älvdalen Sweden
93 F3 Älvdalen val. Sweden
92 H2 Älvsbyn Sweden
78 A2 Al Wajh Saudi Arabia
74 B2 Alwar India
81 C2 Al Widyān plat. Iraq/Saudi Arabia
Alxa Youqi China see Ehen Hudag

Alxa Zuoqi China see Bayan Hot
51 C1 Alyangula Austr.
136 C1 Alytus Lith.
121 C2 Alzada U.S.A.
100 D3 Alzey Ger.
50 C2 Amadeus, Lake imp. l. Austr.
127 G2 Amadjuak Lake Can.
106 B2 Amadora Port.
78 B2 Amā'ir Saudi Arabia
93 F4 Åmål Sweden
111 B3 Amaliada Greece
59 D3 Amamapare Indon.
154 A2 Amambaí Brazil
154 B2 Amambaí r. Brazil
69 E3 Amami-Ō-shima i. Japan
69 E3 Amami-shotō is Japan
77 C1 Amangel'dy Kazakh.
109 C3 Amantea Italy
123 D3 Amanzimtoti S. Africa
151 C1 Amapá Brazil
106 B2 Amareleja Port.
139 C1 Amarillo U.S.A.
108 B2 Amaro, Monte mt. Italy
80 B1 Amasya Turkey
150 C1 Amazon r. S. America
151 D1 Amazon, Mouths of the Brazil
Amazonas r. S. America see Amazon
74 B1 Ambala India
121 D3 Ambalavao Madag.
121 D2 Ambanja Madag.
150 A2 Ambato Ecuador
121 D3 Ambato Boeny Madag.
121 D3 Ambato Finandrahana Madag.
121 D3 Ambatolampy Madag.
121 D2 Ambatondrazaka Madag.
101 E3 Amberg Ger.
146 B3 Ambergris Cay i. Belize
75 C2 Ambikapur India
121 D2 Ambilobe Madag.
98 B1 Ambleside U.K.
121 D3 Amboasary Madag.
59 C3 Ambon Indon.
59 C3 Ambon i. Indon.
121 D3 Ambositra Madag.
121 D3 Ambovombe Madag.
135 C4 Amboy U.S.A.
120 A1 Ambriz Angola
145 B2 Amealco Mex.
144 B2 Ameca Mex.
100 B1 Ameland i. Neth.
134 D2 American Falls U.S.A.
134 D2 American Falls Reservoir U.S.A.
135 D2 American Fork U.S.A.
49 G3 American Samoa terr. S. Pacific Ocean
143 D2 Americus U.S.A.
100 B1 Amersfoort Neth.
55 F2 Amery Ice Shelf Antarctica
137 E2 Ames U.S.A.
111 B3 Amfissa Greece
83 J2 Amga Rus. Fed.
66 C1 Amgu Rus. Fed.
115 C2 Amguid Alg.
83 K3 Amgun' r. Rus. Fed.
131 D2 Amherst Can.
104 C2 Amiens France
73 B3 Amindivi Islands India
122 A1 Aminuis Namibia
74 A2 Amir Chah Pak.
129 D2 Amisk Lake Can.
139 C3 Amistad Reservoir Mex./U.S.
98 A2 Amlwch U.K.
80 B2 'Ammān Jordan

.27 I2 Ammassalik Greenland
78 B3 Am Nābiyah Yemen
81 D2 Amol Iran
11 C3 Amorgos i. Greece
42 C2 Amory U.S.A.
30 C2 Amos Can.
Amoy China see Xiamen
55 C2 Amparo Brazil
07 D1 Amposta Spain
75 B2 Amravati India
74 B1 Amritsar India
00 B1 Amstelveen Neth.
00 B1 Amsterdam Neth.
03 C2 Amstetten Austria
E3 Am Timan Chad
76 B2 Amudar'ya r. Asia
26 E1 Amund Ringnes Island Can.
26 C2 Amundsen Gulf Can.
55 M2 Amundsen Sea Antarctica
61 C2 Amuntai Indon.
Amur r. China see Heilong Jiang
78 A3 'Amur, Wadi watercourse Sudan
83 I2 Anabar r. Rus. Fed.
83 I2 Anabarskiy Zaliv b. Rus. Fed.
34 C1 Anaconda U.S.A.
39 D1 Anadarko U.S.A.
80 B1 Anadolu Dağları mts Turkey
83 M2 Anadyr' r. Rus. Fed.
C2 'Ánah Iraq
45 B2 Anáhuac Mex.
60 B1 Anambas, Kepulauan is Indon.
37 E2 Anamosa U.S.A.
80 B2 Anamur Turkey
67 B4 Anan Japan
73 B3 Anantapur India
74 B1 Anantnag India
90 B2 Anan'yiv Ukr.
91 D3 Anapa Rus. Fed.
54 C1 Anápolis Brazil
52 B3 Añatuya Arg.
97 B1 An Baile Thiar Ireland
65 B2 Anbyon N. Korea
04 B2 Ancenis France
08 B2 Ancona Italy
53 A5 Ancud Chile
Anda China see Daqing
97 A2 An Daingean Ireland
93 E3 Åndalsnes Norway
42 C2 Andalusia U.S.A.
73 D3 Andaman Islands India
63 A2 Andaman Sea Indian Ocean
21 D2 Andapa Madag.
00 B2 Andelst Neth.
92 G2 Andenes Norway
04 B2 Andenne Belgium
00 B2 Anderlecht Belgium
26 C2 Anderson r. Can.
26 B2 Anderson AK U.S.A.
40 B2 Anderson IN U.S.A.
43 D2 Anderson SC U.S.A.
50 Andes mts S. America
77 D2 Andijon Uzbek.
21 D2 Andilamena Madag.
21 D2 Andilanatoby Madag.
21 D2 Andoany Madag.
Andong China see Dandong
65 B2 Andong S. Korea
07 D1 Andorra country Europe
07 D1 Andorra la Vella Andorra
99 C3 Andover U.K.
54 B2 Andradina Brazil
89 D2 Andreapol' Rus. Fed.
55 D2 Andrelândia Brazil
42 C2 Andrews U.S.A.
09 C2 Andria Italy
21 D3 Androka Madag.

146 C2 Andros i. Bahamas
111 B3 Andros i. Greece
143 E4 Andros Town Bahamas
73 B3 Andrott i. India
90 B1 Andrushivka Ukr.
92 G2 Andselv Norway
106 C2 Andújar Spain
120 A2 Andulo Angola
114 C3 Anéfis Mali
115 D3 Aney Niger
83 H3 Angara r. Rus. Fed.
69 C1 Angarsk Rus. Fed.
93 G3 Ånge Sweden
144 A2 Ángel de la Guarda, Isla i. Mex.
64 B1 Angeles Phil.
150 B1 Angel Falls Venez.
93 F4 Ängelholm Sweden
92 G3 Ångermanälven r. Sweden
104 B2 Angers France
129 E1 Angikuni Lake Can.
98 A2 Anglesey i. U.K.
121 C2 Angoche Moz.
79 C2 Angohrān Iran
120 A2 Angola country Africa
140 C2 Angola U.S.A.
128 A2 Angoon U.S.A.
104 C2 Angoulême France
77 D2 Angren Uzbek.
147 D3 Anguilla terr. West Indies
75 C2 Angul India
93 F4 Anholt i. Denmark
71 B3 Anhua China
70 B2 Anhui prov. China
154 B1 Anhumas Brazil
154 C1 Anicuns Brazil
66 D1 Aniva, Mys c. Rus. Fed.
65 B2 Anjŭ N. Korea
70 A2 Ankang China
80 B2 Ankara Turkey
71 B3 Anlu China
91 E1 Anna Rus. Fed.
115 C1 Annaba Alg.
101 F2 Annaberg-Buchholtz Ger.
78 B2 An Nafūd des. Saudi Arabia
81 C2 An Najaf Iraq
96 C3 Annan U.K.
141 D3 Annapolis U.S.A.
75 C2 Annapurna I mt. Nepal
140 C2 Ann Arbor U.S.A.
150 C1 Anna Regina Guyana
81 C2 An Nāşirīyah Iraq
105 D2 Annecy France
78 B3 An Nimāş Saudi Arabia
62 B1 Anning China
142 C2 Anniston U.S.A.
105 C2 Annonay France
79 B2 An Nu'ayriyah Saudi Arabia
121 D2 Anorontany, Tanjona hd Madag.
71 B3 Anpu China
70 B2 Anqing China
102 C2 Ansbach Ger.
70 C1 Anshan China
71 A3 Anshun China
114 C3 Ansongo Mali
150 A3 Antabamba Peru
80 B2 Antakya Turkey
121 E2 Antalaha Madag.
80 B2 Antalya Turkey
80 B2 Antalya Körfezi g. Turkey
121 D2 Antananarivo Madag.
55 Q3 Antarctic Peninsula Antarctica
96 B2 An Teallach mt. U.K.
106 C2 Antequera Spain
138 B2 Anthony U.S.A.
114 B2 Anti-Atlas mts Morocco

105 D3 Antibes France
131 D2 Anticosti, Île d' i. Can.
131 D2 Antigonish Can.
147 D3 Antigua i. Antigua
147 D3 Antigua and Barbuda country West Indies
145 C2 Antiguo-Morelos Mex.
111 B3 Antikythira i. Greece
Antioch Turkey see Antakya
49 F6 Antipodes Islands N.Z.
152 A3 Antofagasta Chile
154 C3 Antonina Brazil
97 C1 Antrim U.K.
97 C1 Antrim Hills U.K.
121 D2 Antsalova Madag.
121 D2 Antsirabe Madag.
121 D2 Antsirañana Madag.
121 D2 Antsohihy Madag.
100 B2 Antwerp Belgium
An Uaimh Ireland see Navan
74 B2 Anupgarh India
73 C4 Anuradhapura Sri Lanka
Anvers Belgium see Antwerp
51 C3 Anxious Bay Austr.
70 B2 Anyang China
65 B2 Anyang S. Korea
108 B2 Anzio Italy
66 D2 Aomori Japan
54 B2 Aoraki mt. N.Z.
108 A1 Aosta Italy
143 D3 Apalachee Bay U.S.A.
150 B2 Apaporis r. Col.
154 B2 Aparecida do Tabuado Brazil
64 B1 Aparri Phil.
86 C2 Apatity Rus. Fed.
144 B3 Apatzingán Mex.
100 B1 Apeldoorn Neth.
100 C1 Apen Ger.
108 A2 Apennines mts Italy
49 G3 Apia Samoa
154 C2 Apiaí Brazil
64 B2 Apo, Mount vol. Phil.
101 E2 Apolda Ger.
52 B3 Apollo Bay Austr.
143 D3 Apopka, Lake U.S.A.
154 B1 Aporé Brazil
154 B1 Aporé r. Brazil
80 B2 Apostolos Andreas, Cape Cyprus
133 E3 Appalachian Mountains U.S.A.
53 D2 Appin Austr.
140 B2 Appleton U.S.A.
108 B2 Aprilia Italy
91 D3 Apsheronsk Rus. Fed.
154 B2 Apucarana Brazil
154 B2 Apucarana, Serra da hills Brazil
78 A2 Aqaba, Gulf of Asia
154 A1 Aquidauana r. Brazil
75 C2 Ara India
117 A4 Arab, Bahr el watercourse Sudan
Arabian Gulf Asia see The Gulf
78 B2 Arabian Peninsula Asia
56 G5 Arabian Sea Indian Ocean
151 E3 Aracaju Brazil
151 E2 Aracati Brazil
154 B2 Araçatuba Brazil
155 D1 Aracruz Brazil
155 D1 Araçuaí Brazil
110 B1 Arad Romania
115 E3 Arada Chad
156 C6 Arafura Sea Austr./Indon.
154 A1 Araguarças Brazil
107 C1 Aragón r. Spain
151 D2 Araguaia r. Brazil
151 D2 Araguaína Brazil

Araguari

154 C1 Araguari Brazil
67 C3 Arai Japan
115 C2 Arak Alg.
81 C2 Arāk Iran
62 A1 Arakan Yoma mts Myanmar
81 C2 Arak's r. Armenia
76 C2 Aral Sea salt l. Kazakh./Uzbek.
76 C2 Aral'sk Kazakh.
Aral'skoye More salt l.
Kazakh./Uzbek. see Aral Sea
106 C1 Aranda de Duero Spain
109 D2 Aranđelovac Serbia
97 B2 Aran Islands Ireland
106 C1 Aranjuez Spain
122 A1 Aranos Namibia
139 D3 Aransas Pass U.S.A.
67 B4 Arao Japan
114 B3 Araouane Mali
151 E2 Arapiraca Brazil
154 B2 Arapongas Brazil
154 C3 Araquari Brazil
78 B1 'Ar'ar Saudi Arabia
154 C2 Araraquara Brazil
151 C2 Araras Brazil
154 B3 Araras, Serra de mts Brazil
52 B3 Ararat Austr.
81 C2 Ararat, Mount Turkey
155 D2 Araruama, Lago de lag. Brazil
155 E1 Arataca Brazil
Aratürük China see Yiwu
150 A1 Arauca Col.
154 C1 Araxá Brazil
81 C2 Arbīl Iraq
96 C2 Arbroath U.K.
74 A2 Arbu Lut, Dasht-e des. Afgh.
104 B3 Arcachon France
143 D3 Arcadia U.S.A.
134 B2 Arcata U.S.A.
145 B3 Arcelia Mex.
86 D2 Archangel Rus. Fed.
51 D1 Archer r. Austr.
134 D2 Arco U.S.A.
106 B2 Arcos de la Frontera Spain
127 F2 Arctic Bay Can.
160   Arctic Ocean
126 C2 Arctic Red r. Can.
81 C2 Ardabīl Iran
81 C1 Ardahan Turkey
93 E3 Årdalstangen Norway
100 B3 Ardennes plat. Belgium
81 D2 Ardestān Iran
53 C2 Ardlethan Austr.
139 D2 Ardmore U.S.A.
96 A2 Ardnamurchan, Point of U.K.
52 A2 Ardrossan Austr.
96 B3 Ardrossan U.K.
135 B3 Arena, Point U.S.A.
93 E4 Arendal Norway
101 E1 Arendsee (Altmark) Ger.
150 A3 Arequipa Peru
151 E2 Arere Brazil
106 C1 Arévalo Spain
108 B2 Arezzo Italy
104 C2 Argentan France
153 B4 Argentina country S. America
153 A6 Argentino, Lago l. Arg.
104 C2 Argenton-sur-Creuse France
110 C2 Argeș r. Romania
74 A1 Arghandab r. Afgh.
111 B3 Argolikos Kolpos b. Greece
111 B3 Argos Greece
111 B3 Argostoli Greece
107 C1 Arguís Spain
69 E1 Argun' r. China/Rus. Fed.
50 B1 Argyle, Lake Austr.
93 F4 Århus Denmark
122 A2 Ariamsvlei Namibia

152 A2 Arica Chile
96 A2 Arinagour U.K.
155 C1 Arinos Brazil
150 C3 Aripuanã Brazil
150 B2 Aripuanã r. Brazil
150 B2 Ariquemes Brazil
154 B1 Ariranhá r. Brazil
138 A2 Arizona state U.S.A.
144 A1 Arizpe Mex.
78 B2 'Arjah Saudi Arabia
92 G2 Arjeplog Sweden
142 B2 Arkadelphia U.S.A.
77 C1 Arkalyk Kazakh.
142 B2 Arkansas r. U.S.A.
142 B1 Arkansas state U.S.A.
137 D3 Arkansas City U.S.A.
Arkhangel'sk Rus. Fed. see
Archangel
97 C2 Arklow Ireland
102 C1 Arkona, Kap c. Ger.
82 G1 Arkticheskogo Instituta,
Ostrova is Rus. Fed.
105 C3 Arles France
115 C3 Arlit Niger
100 B3 Arlon Belgium
97 C1 Armagh U.K.
116 B2 Armant Egypt
81 C1 Armavir Rus. Fed.
150 A1 Armenia Col.
81 C1 Armenia country Asia
150 A1 Armenia Col.
144 B3 Armería Mex.
53 D2 Armidale Austr.
130 B1 Armstrong Can.
81 C1 Armyans'k Ukr.
80 B2 Arnauti, Cape Cyprus
100 B2 Arnhem Neth.
51 C1 Arnhem, Cape Austr.
51 C1 Arnhem Bay Austr.
51 C1 Arnhem Land reg. Austr.
108 B2 Arno r. Italy
52 A2 Arno Bay Austr.
130 C2 Arnprior Can.
100 D2 Arnsberg Ger.
101 E2 Arnstadt Ger.
122 A2 Aroab Namibia
101 D2 Arolsen Ger.
78 A3 Aroma Sudan
108 A1 Arona Italy
144 B2 Aros r. Mex.
81 C2 Ar Ramādī Iraq
96 B3 Arran i. U.K.
97 B1 Arranmore Island Ireland
80 B2 Ar Raqqah Syria
104 C1 Arras France
78 B2 Ar Rass Saudi Arabia
145 C3 Arriagá Mex.
79 C2 Ar Rimāl reg. Saudi Arabia
Ar Riyāḍ Saudi Arabia see
Riyadh
145 C2 Arroyo Seco Mex.
79 C2 Ar Rustāq Oman
80 C2 Ar Ruṭbah Iraq
81 D3 Arsenaján Iran
66 B2 Arsen'yev Rus. Fed.
111 B3 Arta Greece
144 B3 Arteaga Mex.
66 B2 Artem Rus. Fed.
91 D2 Artemivs'k Ukr.
104 C2 Artenay France
138 C2 Artesia U.S.A.
51 E2 Arthur Point Austr.
54 B2 Arthur's Pass N.Z.
152 C4 Artigas Uru.
129 D1 Artillery Lake Can.
90 B2 Artsyz Ukr.
77 D3 Artux China
81 C1 Artvin Turkey

59 C3 Aru, Kepulauan is Indon.
119 D2 Arua Uganda
147 D3 Aruba terr. West Indies
119 D3 Arusha Tanz.
69 C1 Arvayheer Mongolia
129 E1 Arviat Can.
92 G2 Arvidsjaur Sweden
93 F4 Arvika Sweden
87 D3 Arzamas Rus. Fed.
107 C2 Arzew Alg.
100 C2 Arzfeld Ger.
101 F2 Aš Czech Rep.
115 C4 Asaba Nigeria
74 B1 Asadābād Afgh.
66 D2 Asahi-dake vol. Japan
66 D2 Asahikawa Japan
78 B3 Asālē l. Eth.
75 C2 Asansol India
131 C2 Asbestos Can.
109 C2 Ascea Italy
152 B2 Ascensión Bol.
113 D7 Ascension i. S. Atlantic Ocean
145 D3 Ascensión, Bahía de la b. Mex.
101 D3 Aschaffenburg Ger.
100 C2 Ascheberg Ger.
101 E2 Aschersleben Ger.
108 B2 Ascoli Piceno Italy
92 G3 Åsele Sweden
110 B2 Asenovgrad Bulg.
76 B3 Aşgabat Turkm.
50 A2 Ashburton watercourse Austr.
54 B2 Ashburton N.Z.
142 B2 Ashdown U.S.A.
143 D1 Asheville U.S.A.
53 D1 Ashford Austr.
99 D3 Ashford U.K.
Ashgabat Turkm. see Aşgabat
98 C1 Ashington U.K.
67 B4 Ashizuri-misaki pt Japan
136 D3 Ashland KS U.S.A.
140 C3 Ashland KY U.S.A.
140 C2 Ashland OH U.S.A.
134 B2 Ashland OR U.S.A.
140 A1 Ashland WI U.S.A.
88 C3 Ashmyany Belarus
78 B3 Ash Sharawrah Saudi Arabia
Ash Shāriqah U.A.E. see
Sharjah
81 C2 Ash Sharqāt Iraq
81 C2 Ash Shaṭrah Iraq
79 B3 Ash Shiḥr Yemen
79 C2 Ash Shināş Oman
78 B2 Ash Shu'bah Saudi Arabia
78 B2 Ash Shumlul Saudi Arabia
140 C2 Ashtabula U.S.A.
131 D1 Ashuanipi Lake Can.
106 B2 Asilah Morocco
108 A2 Asinara, Golfo dell' b.
Sardegna Italy
82 G3 Asino Rus. Fed.
88 C3 Asipovichy Belarus
78 B2 'Asīr reg. Saudi Arabia
93 F4 Askim Norway
68 C1 Askiz Rus. Fed.
116 B3 Asmara Eritrea
93 F4 Åsnen l. Sweden
116 B2 Asoteriba, Jebel mt. Sudan
103 D2 Aspang-Markt Austria
136 B3 Aspen U.S.A.
54 A2 Aspiring, Mount N.Z.
117 C3 Assab Eritrea
Aş Şaḥrā' al Gharbīyah des.
Egypt see Western Desert
Aş Şaḥrā' ash Sharqīyah des.
Egypt see Eastern Desert
78 B2 As Salamiyah Saudi Arabia
81 C2 As Samāwah Iraq

79	C2	Aş Şanām reg. Saudi Arabia
115	E2	Aş Sarīr reg. Libya
100	C1	Assen Neth.
115	D1	As Sidrah Libya
129	D3	Assiniboia Can.
128	C2	Assiniboine, Mount Can.
154	B2	Assis Brazil
78	B2	Aş Şubayḩīyah Kuwait
81	C2	As Sulaymānīyah Iraq
78	B2	As Sulaymī Saudi Arabia
78	B2	As Sulayyil Saudi Arabia
78	B2	As Sūq Saudi Arabia
80	B2	As Suwaydā' Syria
79	C2	As Suwayq Oman
		As Suways Egypt see Suez
111	B3	Astakos Greece
77	D1	Astana Kazakh.
81	C2	Āstārā Iran
108	A2	Asti Italy
74	B1	Astor Pak.
106	B1	Astorga Spain
134	B1	Astoria U.S.A.
87	D4	Astrakhan' Rus. Fed.
88	C3	Astravyets Belarus
111	B3	Astypalaia i. Greece
152	C3	Asunción Para.
116	B2	Aswān Egypt
116	B2	Asyūţ Egypt
		Atacama, Desierto de des.
		Chile see Atacama Desert
152	B3	Atacama, Salar de salt flat
		Chile
152	B3	Atacama Desert des. Chile
114	C4	Atakpamé Togo
111	B3	Atalanti Greece
150	A3	Atalaya Peru
77	C3	Atamyrat Turkm.
78	B3	'Ataq Yemen
114	A2	Atâr Maur.
135	B3	Atascadero U.S.A.
77	D2	Atasu Kazakh.
111	C3	Atavyros mt. Greece
116	B3	Atbara Sudan
116	B3	Atbara r. Sudan
77	C1	Atbasar Kazakh.
137	D3	Atchison U.S.A.
108	B2	Aterno r. Italy
108	B2	Atessa Italy
100	A2	Ath Belgium
128	C2	Athabasca Can.
129	C2	Athabasca r. Can.
129	D2	Athabasca, Lake Can.
111	B3	Athens Greece
143	D2	Athens GA U.S.A.
140	C3	Athens OH U.S.A.
143	D1	Athens TN U.S.A.
139	D2	Athens TX U.S.A.
		Athina Greece see Athens
97	C2	Athlone Ireland
111	B2	Athos mt. Greece
97	C3	Athy Ireland
115	D3	Ati Chad
130	A2	Atikokan Can.
87	D3	Atkarsk Rus. Fed.
137	D2	Atlanta U.S.A.
137	D2	Atlantic U.S.A.
141	E3	Atlantic City U.S.A.
158		Atlantic Ocean
122	A3	Atlantis S. Africa
114	B1	Atlas Mountains Africa
114	C1	Atlas Saharien mts Alg.
128	A1	Atlin Can.
128	A2	Atlin Lake Can.
142	C2	Atmore U.S.A.
139	D2	Atoka U.S.A.
75	C2	Atrai r. India

78	B2	Aţ Ţā'if Saudi Arabia
63	B2	Attapu Laos
130	B1	Attawapiskat Can.
130	B1	Attawapiskat r. Can.
130	B1	Attawapiskat Lake Can.
100	C2	Attendorn Ger.
116	B2	Aţ Ţūr Egypt
78	B3	At Turbah Yemen
76	B2	Atyrau Kazakh.
105	C3	Aubenas France
126	C2	Aubry Lake Can.
142	C2	Auburn AL U.S.A.
135	B3	Auburn CA U.S.A.
137	D2	Auburn NE U.S.A.
141	D2	Auburn NY U.S.A.
104	C2	Aubusson France
104	C3	Auch France
54	B1	Auckland N.Z.
48	F6	Auckland Islands is N.Z.
101	F2	Aue Ger.
102	C2	Augsburg Ger.
109	C3	Augusta Sicilia Italy
143	D2	Augusta GA U.S.A.
137	D3	Augusta KS U.S.A.
141	F2	Augusta ME U.S.A.
50	A2	Augustus, Mount Austr.
100	A2	Aulnoye-Aymeries France
62	A2	Aunglan Myanmar
122	B2	Auob watercourse Namibia/
		S. Africa
74	B3	Aurangabad India
100	C1	Aurich Ger.
154	B1	Aurilândia Brazil
104	C3	Aurillac France
136	C3	Aurora CO U.S.A.
140	B2	Aurora IL U.S.A.
137	D2	Aurora NE U.S.A.
122	A2	Aus Namibia
137	E2	Austin MN U.S.A.
135	C3	Austin NV U.S.A.
139	D2	Austin TX U.S.A.
50	B2	Australia country Oceania
159		Australian-Antarctic Basin
		Southern Ocean
53	C2	Australian Capital Territory
		admin. div. Austr.
102	C2	Austria country Europe
144	B3	Autlán Mex.
105	C2	Autun France
105	C2	Auxerre France
105	C2	Auxonne France
105	C2	Avallon France
131	E2	Avalon Peninsula Can.
154	C2	Avaré Brazil
49	H4	Avarua Cook Is
91	D2	Avdiyivka Ukr.
106	B1	Aveiro Port.
109	B2	Avellino Italy
100	A2	Avesnes-sur-Helpe France
93	G3	Avesta Sweden
108	B2	Avezzano Italy
96	C2	Aviemore U.K.
108	A2	Avigliano Italy
105	C3	Avignon France
106	C1	Ávila Spain
106	B1	Avilés Spain
109	C3	Avola Sicilia Italy
99	B3	Avon r. England U.K.
99	C3	Avon r. England U.K.
104	B2	Avranches France
54	B1	Awanui N.Z.
117	C4	Āwash Eth.
117	C3	Āwash r. Eth.
115	D2	Awbārī Libya
115	D2	Awbārī, Idhān des. Libya
117	C4	Aw Dheegle Somalia
96	B2	Awe, Loch l. U.K.

117	A4	Aweil Sudan
126	E1	Axel Heiberg Island Can.
114	B4	Axim Ghana
150	A3	Ayacucho Peru
77	E2	Ayagoz Kazakh.
68	B2	Ayakkuum Hu salt l. China
106	B2	Ayamonte Spain
83	K3	Ayan Rus. Fed.
150	A3	Ayaviri Peru
76	A2	Aybas Kazakh.
91	D2	Aydar r. Ukr.
77	C2	Aydarko'l ko'li i. Uzbek.
111	C3	Aydın Turkey
77	C2	Ayeat, Gora h. Kazakh.
		Ayers Rock h. Austr. see Uluru
99	C3	Aylesbury U.K.
106	C1	Ayllón Spain
129	D1	Aylmer Lake Can.
117	B4	Ayod Sudan
83	M2	Ayon, Ostrov i. Rus. Fed.
114	B3	'Ayoûn el 'Atroûs Maur.
51	D1	Ayr Austr.
96	B3	Ayr U.K.
98	A1	Ayre, Point of Isle of Man
76	C2	Ayteke Bi Kazakh.
110	C2	Aytos Bulg.
145	C3	Ayutla Mex.
63	B2	Ayutthaya Thai.
111	C3	Ayvacık Turkey
111	C3	Ayvalık Turkey
114	C3	Azaouagh, Vallée de
		watercourse Mali/Niger
		Azbine mts Niger see
		Aïr, Massif de l'
81	C1	Azerbaijan country Asia
86	D2	Azopol'ye Rus. Fed.
84	D5	Azores aut. reg. Port.
91	D2	Azov Rus. Fed.
91	D2	Azov, Sea of Rus. Fed./Ukr.
		Azraq, Bahr el r. Eth./Sudan
		see Blue Nile
106	B2	Azuaga Spain
146	B4	Azuero, Península de pen.
		Panama
153	C4	Azul Arg.
80	B2	Az Zaqāzīq Egypt
80	B2	Az Zarqā' Jordan
78	B3	Az Zaydīyah Yemen
114	C2	Azzel Matti, Sebkha salt pan
		Alg.
78	B2	Az Zilfī Saudi Arabia
78	B3	Az Zuqur i. Yemen

B

63	B2	Ba, Sông r. Vietnam
117	C4	Baardheere Somalia
77	C3	Bābā, Kūh-e mts Afgh.
110	C2	Babadag Romania
111	C2	Babaeski Turkey
117	C3	Bāb al Mandab str. Africa/Asia
61	C2	Babana Indon.
59	C3	Babar i. Indon.
119	D3	Babati Tanz.
89	E2	Babayevo Rus. Fed.
128	B2	Babine r. Can.
128	B2	Babine Lake Can.
59	C3	Babo Indon.
81	D2	Bābol Iran
122	A3	Baboon Point S. Africa
88	C3	Babruysk Belarus
64	B1	Babuyan i. Phil.
64	B1	Babuyan Islands is Phil.
151	D2	Bacabal Brazil
59	C3	Bacan i. Indon.

Bacău

110 C1 Bacău Romania
52 B3 Bacchus Marsh Austr.
77 D3 Bachu China
129 E1 Back r. Can.
109 C1 Bačka Palanka Serbia
63 B3 Bắc Liêu Vietnam
64 B1 Bacolod Phil.
130 C1 Bacqueville, Lac l. Can.
106 B2 Badajoz India
62 A1 Badarpur India
101 E2 Bad Berka Ger.
101 D2 Bad Berleburg Ger.
101 E1 Bad Bevensen Ger.
100 C2 Bad Ems Ger.
103 D2 Baden Austria
102 B2 Baden-Baden Ger.
101 E2 Bad Harzburg Ger.
101 D2 Bad Hersfeld Ger.
102 C2 Bad Hofgastein Austria
101 D2 Bad Homburg vor der Höhe Ger.
74 A2 Badin Pak.
Bādiyat ash Shām des. Asia see Syrian Desert
101 E2 Bad Kissingen Ger.
100 C3 Bad Kreuznach Ger.
101 E2 Bad Lauterberg im Harz Ger.
101 D2 Bad Lippspringe Ger.
101 D3 Bad Mergentheim Ger.
101 D2 Bad Nauheim Ger.
100 C2 Bad Neuenahr-Ahrweiler Ger.
101 E2 Bad Neustadt an der Saale Ger.
101 E1 Bad Oldesloe Ger.
101 D2 Bad Pyrmont Ger.
78 A2 Badr Ḩunayn Saudi Arabia
101 D1 Bad Salzuflen Ger.
101 E2 Bad Salzungen Ger.
101 E1 Bad Schwartau Ger.
101 E1 Bad Segeberg Ger.
100 C3 Bad Sobernheim Ger.
73 C4 Badulla Sri Lanka
100 D1 Bad Zwischenahn Ger.
106 D1 Baeza Spain
114 A3 Bafatá Guinea-Bissau
160 O2 Baffin Bay sea Can./Greenland
127 G2 Baffin Island Can.
118 B2 Bafia Cameroon
114 A3 Bafing r. Africa
114 A3 Bafoulabé Mali
118 B2 Bafoussam Cameroon
76 B3 Bāfq Iran
80 B1 Bafra Turkey
79 C2 Bāft Iran
119 C2 Bafwasende Dem. Rep. Congo
119 D3 Bagamoyo Tanz.
60 B1 Bagan Datuk Malaysia
120 B2 Bagani Namibia
60 B1 Bagansiapiapi Indon.
138 A2 Bagdad U.S.A.
152 C4 Bagé Brazil
97 C2 Bagenalstown Ireland
81 C2 Baghdād Iraq
77 C3 Baghlān Afgh.
104 C3 Bagnères-de-Luchon France
88 B3 Bagrationovsk Rus. Fed.
Bagrax China see Bohu
64 B1 Baguio Phil.
115 C3 Bagzane, Monts mts Niger
Bahamas country West Indies see The Bahamas
146 C2 Bahamas, The country West Indies
75 C2 Baharampur India
Bahariya Oasis Egypt see Baḥrīyah, Wāḩāt al
76 B3 Baharly Turkm.

60 B1 Bahau Malaysia
72 B2 Bahawalnagar Pak.
74 B2 Bahawalpur Pak.
153 B4 Bahía Blanca Arg.
144 B3 Bahía Kino Mex.
152 C3 Bahía Negra Para.
144 A2 Bahía Tortugas Mex.
117 B3 Bahir Dar Eth.
75 C2 Bahraich India
79 C2 Bahrain country Asia
116 A2 Baḥrīyah, Wāḩāt al oasis Egypt
79 D2 Bāhū Kālāt Iran
110 B1 Baia Mare Romania
69 E1 Baicheng China
131 D2 Baie-Comeau Can.
Baie-du-Poste Can. see Mistissini
131 C2 Baie-St-Paul Can.
65 B1 Baihe China
69 D1 Baikal, Lake Rus. Fed.
110 B2 Băilești Romania
143 D2 Baima China
48 F2 Bainbridge U.S.A.
Bairiki Kiribati
Bairin Youqi China see Daban
53 C3 Bairnsdale Austr.
65 B1 Baishan Jilin China
65 B1 Baishanzhen Jilin China
65 B1 Baitou Shan mt. China/N. Korea
70 A2 Baiyin China
116 B3 Baiyuda Desert Sudan
103 D2 Baja Hungary
144 A1 Baja California pen. Mex.
78 B3 Bājil Yemen
114 A3 Bakel Senegal
135 C3 Baker CA U.S.A.
136 C1 Baker MT U.S.A.
134 B2 Baker OR U.S.A.
134 B1 Baker, Mount vol. U.S.A.
129 E1 Baker Foreland hd Can.
49 G2 Baker Island N. Pacific Ocean
129 E1 Baker Lake Can.
129 E1 Baker Lake l. Can.
135 C3 Bakersfield U.S.A.
91 C1 Bakhchysaray Ukr.
91 C1 Bakhmach Ukr.
Bākhtarān Iran see Kermānshāh
Baku Azer. see Baku
111 C2 Bakırköy Turkey
92 C2 Bakkaflói n. Iceland
118 C2 Bakouma C.A.R.
81 C1 Baku Azer.
64 A2 Balabac Phil.
64 A2 Balabac i. Phil.
64 A2 Balabac Strait Malaysia/Phil.
61 C2 Balaiberkuak Indon.
52 A2 Balaklava Austr.
91 C3 Balaklava Ukr.
91 D2 Balakliya Ukr.
87 D3 Balakovo Rus. Fed.
145 C3 Balancán Mex.
111 C3 Balan Dağı h. Turkey
64 B1 Balanga Phil.
87 D3 Balashov Rus. Fed.
103 D2 Balaton, Lake Hungary
103 D2 Balatonboglár Hungary
150 C2 Balbina, Represa de resr Brazil
97 C2 Balbriggan Ireland
52 A2 Balcanoona Austr.
110 C2 Balchik Bulg.
54 A3 Balclutha N.Z.
129 E2 Baldock Lake Can.
129 D2 Baldy Mountain h. Can.
138 B2 Baldy Peak U.S.A.

Baleares, Islas is Spain see Balearic Islands
107 D2 Balearic Islands is Spain
155 E1 Baleia, Ponta da pt Brazil
130 C1 Baleine, Grande Rivière de la r. Can.
131 D1 Baleine, Rivière à la r. Can.
75 C2 Baleshwar India
108 A2 Balestrieri, Punta mt. Sardegna Italy
61 C2 Bali i. Indon.
115 D4 Bali Nigeria
60 A1 Balige Indon.
75 C2 Baliguda India
111 C3 Balıkesir Turkey
61 C2 Balikpapan Indon.
59 D3 Balimo P.N.G.
102 B2 Balingen Ger.
Bali Sea Indon. see Laut Bali
76 B3 Balkanabat Turkm.
110 B2 Balkan Mountains Bulg./Serbia
77 D2 Balkhash Kazakh.
77 D2 Balkhash, Lake Kazakh.
Balkhash, Ozero l. Kazakh. see Balkhash, Lake
50 B3 Balladonia Austr.
97 B2 Ballaghaderreen Ireland
92 G2 Ballangen Norway
52 B3 Ballarat Austr.
50 B2 Ballard, Lake imp. l. Austr.
96 C2 Ballater U.K.
114 B3 Ballé Mali
53 D1 Ballina Austr.
97 B1 Ballina Ireland
97 B2 Ballinasloe Ireland
139 D2 Ballinger U.S.A.
97 B2 Ballinrobe Ireland
97 C1 Ballycastle Ireland
97 C1 Ballycastle U.K.
97 C1 Ballyclare U.K.
97 C1 Ballymena U.K.
97 C1 Ballymoney U.K.
97 C1 Ballynahinch U.K.
97 B1 Ballyshannon Ireland
95 B2 Ballyvoy U.K.
51 D2 Balonne r. Austr.
74 B2 Balotra India
75 C2 Balrampur India
52 B2 Balranald Austr.
110 B2 Balș Romania
151 E3 Balsas Brazil
145 C3 Balsas Mex.
90 B2 Balta Ukr.
90 B2 Bălți Moldova
93 G4 Baltic Sea g. Europe
111 C3 Baltım Egypt
123 C1 Baltimore S. Africa
141 D3 Baltimore U.S.A.
88 A3 Baltiysk Rus. Fed.
62 A1 Balu India
88 C2 Balvi Latvia
77 D2 Balykchy Kyrg.
87 E4 Balykshi Kazakh.
79 C2 Bam Iran
51 D1 Bamaga Austr.
130 A1 Bamaji Lake Can.
114 B3 Bamako Mali
118 C2 Bambari C.A.R.
101 E3 Bamberg Ger.
119 C2 Bambili Dem. Rep. Congo
118 C2 Bambouti C.A.R.
155 C2 Bambuí Brazil
118 B2 Bamenda Cameroon
74 A1 Bāmiān Afgh.
119 C2 Banalia Dem. Rep. Congo
151 C3 Bananal, Ilha do i. Brazil

168

74 B2 Banas r. India
111 C3 Banaz Turkey
62 B2 Ban Ban Laos
97 C1 Banbridge U.K.
99 C2 Banbury U.K.
130 C2 Bancroft Can.
119 C2 Banda Dem. Rep. Congo
75 C2 Banda India
75 C3 Banda, Kepulauan is Indon.
59 C3 Banda, Laut sea Indon.
60 A1 Banda Aceh Indon.
79 C2 Bandar-e ʿAbbās Iran
81 C2 Bandar-e Anzalī Iran
81 C2 Bandar-e Chārak Iran
81 C2 Bandar-e Emām Khomeynī Iran
79 C2 Bandar-e Lengeh Iran
79 C2 Bandar-e Maqām Iran
61 C1 Bandar Lampung Indon.
61 C1 Bandar Seri Begawan Brunei
Banda Sea Indon. see Banda, Laut
155 F2 Bandeiras, Pico de mt. Brazil
123 C1 Bandelierkop S. Africa
144 B2 Banderas, Bahía de b. Mex.
114 B3 Bandiagara Mali
111 C3 Bandırma Turkey
97 B3 Bandon Ireland
118 B3 Bandundu Dem. Rep. Congo
60 B2 Bandung Indon.
128 C2 Banff Can.
96 C2 Banff U.K.
114 B3 Banfora Burkina
64 B2 Banga Phil.
73 B3 Bangalore India
118 C2 Bangassou C.A.R.
59 C3 Banggai Indon.
59 C3 Banggai, Kepulauan is Indon.
61 C1 Banggi i. Sabah Malaysia
60 B2 Bangka i. Indon.
61 C2 Bangkalan Indon.
60 B1 Bangkinang Indon.
60 B2 Bangko Indon.
63 B2 Bangkok Thai.
75 C2 Bangladesh country Asia
63 B2 Ba Ngoi Vietnam
97 D1 Bangor Northern Ireland U.K.
98 A2 Bangor Wales U.K.
141 F2 Bangor U.S.A.
63 A2 Bang Saphan Yai Thai.
64 B1 Bangued Phil.
118 B2 Bangui C.A.R.
121 C2 Bangweulu, Lake Zambia
62 B2 Ban Huai Khon Thai.
116 B2 Bani Suwayf Egypt
115 D1 Banī Walīd Libya
80 B2 Bāniyās Syria
109 C2 Banja Luka Bos.-Herz.
60 B2 Banjarmasin Indon.
114 A3 Banjul Gambia
128 A2 Banks Island B.C. Can.
126 C2 Banks Island N.W.T. Can.
48 F3 Banks Islands Vanuatu
129 E1 Banks Lake Can.
54 B2 Banks Peninsula N.Z.
75 C2 Bankura India
62 A1 Banmauk Myanmar
62 B2 Ban Mouang Laos
97 C1 Bann r. U.K.
62 B2 Ban Napè Laos
63 A3 Ban Na San Thai.
143 E4 Bannerman Town Bahamas
74 B1 Bannu Pak.
74 B2 Banswara India
63 A3 Ban Tha Kham Thai.
62 A2 Ban Tha Song Yang Thai.
63 B2 Ban Tôp Laos

97 B3 Bantry Ireland
97 B3 Bantry Bay Ireland
118 B2 Banyo Cameroon
107 D1 Banyoles Spain
61 C2 Banyuwangi Indon.
Bao'an China see Shenzhen
69 D2 Baochang China
70 B2 Baoding China
70 A2 Baoji China
62 B1 Bao Lac Vietnam
63 B2 Bao Lôc Vietnam
66 B1 Baoqing China
62 A1 Baoshan China
70 B1 Baotou China
81 C2 Baʻqūbah Iraq
109 C2 Bar Montenegro
117 C4 Baraawe Somalia
147 C2 Baracoa Cuba
53 C2 Baradine Austr.
147 C3 Barahona Dom. Rep.
116 B3 Baraka watercourse Eritrea/Sudan
61 C1 Baram r. Sarawak Malaysia
74 B1 Baramula India
88 C3 Baranavichy Belarus
78 A2 Baranīs Egypt
90 B1 Baranivka Ukr.
76 B2 Barankul Kazakh.
128 A2 Baranof Island U.S.A.
59 C3 Barat Daya, Kepulauan is Indon.
155 D2 Barbacena Brazil
147 E3 Barbados country West Indies
107 D1 Barbastro Spain
104 B2 Barbezieux-St-Hilaire France
51 D2 Barcaldine Austr.
107 D1 Barcelona Spain
150 B1 Barcelona Venez.
105 D3 Barcelonnette France
150 B2 Barcelos Brazil
Barcoo Creek watercourse Austr. see Cooper Creek
103 D2 Barcs Hungary
75 C2 Barddhaman India
103 E2 Bardejov Slovakia
79 C2 Bardsīr Iran
75 B2 Bareilly India
160 B2 Barents Sea Arctic Ocean
78 A3 Barentu Eritrea
75 C2 Barh India
141 F2 Bar Harbor U.S.A.
109 C2 Bari Italy
81 C1 Barīkot Afgh.
150 A1 Barinas Venez.
75 C2 Baripada India
75 D2 Barisal Bangl.
60 B2 Barisan, Pegunungan mts Indon.
61 C2 Barito r. Indon.
79 C2 Barkā Oman
88 C2 Barkava Latvia
51 C1 Barkly Tableland reg. Austr.
68 C2 Barkol China
110 C1 Bârlad Romania
105 D2 Bar-le-Duc France
50 A2 Barlee, Lake imp. l. Austr.
109 C2 Barletta Italy
53 C2 Barmedman Austr.
74 B2 Barmer India
99 A2 Barmouth U.K.
101 D1 Barmstedt Ger.
98 C1 Barnard Castle U.K.
53 B2 Barnato Austr.
82 G3 Barnaul Rus. Fed.
127 G2 Barnes Icecap Can.
100 B1 Barneveld Neth.
98 C2 Barnsley U.K.

99 A3 Barnstaple U.K.
99 A3 Barnstaple Bay U.K.
143 D2 Barnwell U.S.A.
Baroda India see Vadodara
150 B1 Barquisimeto Venez.
96 A2 Barra i. U.K.
53 D2 Barraba Austr.
151 D2 Barra do Corda Brazil
154 B1 Barra do Garças Brazil
150 C2 Barra do São Manuel Brazil
150 A3 Barranca Lima Peru
150 A2 Barranca Loreto Peru
152 C3 Barranqueras Arg.
150 A1 Barranquilla Col.
151 D3 Barreiras Brazil
154 C2 Barretos Brazil
130 C2 Barrie Can.
128 B2 Barrière Can.
52 B2 Barrier Range hills Austr.
53 D2 Barrington, Mount Austr.
129 D2 Barrington Lake Can.
53 C1 Barringun Austr.
97 C2 Barrow r. Ireland
51 C2 Barrow Creek Austr.
98 B1 Barrow-in-Furness U.K.
50 A2 Barrow Island Austr.
126 E2 Barrow Strait Can.
99 B3 Barry U.K.
130 C2 Barrys Bay Can.
74 B2 Barsalpur India
135 C4 Barstow U.S.A.
105 C2 Bar-sur-Aube France
80 B1 Bartın Turkey
51 D1 Bartle Frere, Mount Austr.
139 D1 Bartlesville U.S.A.
103 E1 Bartoszyce Pol.
69 D1 Baruun-Urt Mongolia
91 D2 Barvinkove Ukr.
53 C2 Barwon r. Austr.
88 C3 Barysaw Belarus
110 C2 Basarabi Romania
105 D2 Basel Switz.
91 C2 Bashtanka Ukr.
64 B2 Basilan i. Phil.
99 C3 Basildon U.K.
99 C3 Basingstoke U.K.
81 C2 Başkale Turkey
130 C2 Baskatong, Réservoir resr Can.
Basle Switz. see Basel
118 C2 Basoko Dem. Rep. Congo
81 C2 Basra Iraq
128 C2 Bassano Can.
114 C4 Bassar Togo
63 A2 Bassein Myanmar
147 D3 Basse-Terre Guadeloupe
147 D3 Basseterre St Kitts and Nevis
114 B3 Bassikounou Maur.
51 D3 Bass Strait Austr.
79 C2 Bastak Iran
101 E2 Bastheim Ger.
75 C2 Basti India
105 D3 Bastia Corse France
100 B2 Bastogne Belgium
142 B2 Bastrop U.S.A.
Basuo China see Dongfang
118 A2 Bata Equat. Guinea
83 J2 Batagay Rus. Fed.
154 B2 Bataguassu Brazil
106 B2 Batalha Port.
71 C3 Batan i. Phil.
118 B2 Batangafo C.A.R.
64 B1 Batangas Phil.
60 B2 Batanghari r. Indon.
71 C3 Batan Islands Phil.
141 D2 Batavia U.S.A.
91 D2 Bataysk Rus. Fed.

130	B2	Batchawana Mountain *h.* Can.
50	C1	Batchelor Austr.
63	B2	Bătdâmbâng Cambodia
53	D3	Batemans Bay Austr.
142	B1	Batesville U.S.A.
89	D2	Batetsky Rus. Fed.
99	B3	Bath U.K.
74	B1	Bathinda India
53	C2	Bathurst Austr.
131	D2	Bathurst Can.
126	D2	Bathurst Inlet Can.
126	D2	Bathurst Inlet (abandoned) Can.
50	C1	Bathurst Island Austr.
126	E1	Bathurst Island Can.
78	B1	Bāţin, Wādī al *watercourse* Asia
81	C2	Batman Turkey
115	C2	Batna Alg.
142	B2	Baton Rouge U.S.A.
144	B2	Batopilas Mex.
118	B2	Batouri Cameroon
154	B1	Batovi Brazil
92	I1	Båtsfjord Norway
73	C4	Batticaloa Sri Lanka
109	B2	Battipaglia Italy
129	D2	Battle *r.* Can.
140	B2	Battle Creek U.S.A.
135	C2	Battle Mountain U.S.A.
74	B1	Battura Glacier Pak.
117	B4	Batu *mt.* Eth.
60	A2	Batu, Pulau-pulau *is* Indon.
81	C1	Bat'umi Georgia
60	B1	Batu Pahat Malaysia
59	C3	Baubau Indon.
115	C3	Bauchi Nigeria
104	B2	Baugé France
105	D2	Baume-les-Dames France
154	C2	Bauru Brazil
154	B1	Baús Brazil
88	B2	Bauska Latvia
102	C1	Bautzen Ger.
144	B2	Bavispe *r.* Mex.
87	E3	Bavly Rus. Fed.
62	A1	Bawdwin Myanmar
61	C2	Bawean *i.* Indon.
114	B3	Bawku Ghana
146	C2	Bayamo Cuba
		Bayan Gol China *see* Dengkou
68	C1	Bayanhongor Mongolia
70	A2	Bayan Hot China
69	D1	Bayan-Uul Mongolia
64	B2	Bayawan Phil.
81	C2	Bayburt Turkey
140	C2	Bay City MI U.S.A.
139	D3	Bay City TX U.S.A.
86	F2	Baydaratskaya Guba Rus. Fed.
117	C4	Baydhabo Somalia
81	C2	Bayjī Iraq
		Baykal, Ozero *l.* Rus. Fed. *see* Baikal, Lake
83	I3	Baykal'skiy Khrebet *mts* Rus. Fed.
76	B1	Baykonyr Kazakh.
87	E3	Baymak Rus. Fed.
64	B1	Bayombong Phil.
104	B3	Bayonne France
111	C3	Bayramiç Turkey
101	E3	Bayreuth Ger.
78	B3	Bayt al Faqīh Yemen
106	C2	Baza Spain
106	C2	Baza, Sierra de *mts* Spain
74	A1	Bāzārak Afgh.
76	A2	Bazardyuzyu, Gora *mt.* Azer./Rus. Fed.
104	B3	Bazas France
74	A2	Bazdar Pak.
70	A2	Bazhong China

79	D2	Bazmān Iran
79	D2	Bazmān, Kūh-e *mt.* Iran
121	D2	Bé, Nosy *i.* Madag.
99	D3	Beachy Head U.K.
123	C3	Beacon Bay S. Africa
50	B1	Beagle Gulf Austr.
121	D2	Bealanana Madag.
97	B1	Béal an Mhuirthead Ireland
130	B2	Beardmore Can.
		Bear Island Arctic Ocean *see* Bjørnøya
134	E1	Bear Paw Mountain U.S.A.
147	C3	Beata, Cabo *c.* Dom. Rep.
147	C3	Beata, Isla *i.* Dom. Rep.
137	D2	Beatrice U.S.A.
135	C3	Beatty U.S.A.
53	D1	Beaudesert Austr.
52	B3	Beaufort Austr.
61	C1	Beaufort *Sabah* Malaysia
143	D2	Beaufort U.S.A.
160	L2	Beaufort Sea Can./U.S.A.
122	B3	Beaufort West S. Africa
96	B2	Beauly *r.* U.K.
100	A2	Beaumont Belgium
54	A3	Beaumont N.Z.
139	E2	Beaumont U.S.A.
105	C2	Beaune France
100	B2	Beauraing Belgium
129	E2	Beauséjour Can.
104	C2	Beauvais France
129	D2	Beauval Can.
129	D2	Beaver *r.* Can.
135	D3	Beaver U.S.A.
126	B2	Beaver Creek Can.
140	B2	Beaver Dam U.S.A.
129	E2	Beaver Hill Lake Can.
140	B1	Beaver Island U.S.A.
128	C2	Beaverlodge Can.
74	B2	Beawar India
154	C2	Bebedouro Brazil
101	D2	Bebra Ger.
106	B1	Becerreá Spain
114	B1	Béchar Alg.
140	C3	Beckley U.S.A.
117	B4	Bedelē Eth.
99	C2	Bedford U.K.
140	B3	Bedford U.S.A.
100	C1	Bedum Neth.
53	D2	Beecroft Peninsula Austr.
101	F1	Beelitz Ger.
53	D1	Beenleigh Austr.
80	B2	Beersheba Israel
139	D3	Beeville U.S.A.
53	C3	Bega Austr.
107	D1	Begur, Cap de *c.* Spain
128	C1	Behchokò Can.
81	D2	Behshahr Iran
69	E1	Bei'an China
71	A3	Beihai China
70	B2	Beijing China
100	C1	Beilen Neth.
96	A2	Beinn Mhòr *h.* U.K.
121	C2	Beira Moz.
80	B2	Beirut Lebanon
123	C1	Beitbridge Zimbabwe
106	B2	Beja Port.
115	C1	Bejaïa Alg.
106	B1	Béjar Spain
74	A2	Beji *r.* Pak.
103	E2	Békés Hungary
103	E2	Békéscsaba Hungary
121	D3	Bekily Madag.
74	A2	Bela Pak.
123	C1	Bela-Bela S. Africa
118	B2	Bélabo Cameroon
109	D2	Bela Crkva Serbia
61	C1	Belaga *Sarawak* Malaysia

88	C3	Belarus *country* Europe
		Belau *country* N. Pacific Ocean *see* Palau
123	D2	Bela Vista Moz.
60	A1	Belawan Indon.
83	M2	Belaya *r.* Rus. Fed.
103	D1	Bełchatów Pol.
130	C1	Belcher Islands Can.
117	C4	Beledweyne Somalia
151	D2	Belém Brazil
138	B2	Belen U.S.A.
89	E3	Belev Rus. Fed.
97	D1	Belfast U.K.
141	F2	Belfast U.S.A.
105	D2	Belfort France
73	B3	Belgaum India
100	B2	Belgium *country* Europe
91	D1	Belgorod Rus. Fed.
109	D2	Belgrade Serbia
134	D1	Belgrade U.S.A.
60	B2	Belinyu Indon.
61	B2	Belitung *i.* Indon.
146	B3	Belize Belize
146	B3	Belize *country* Central America
83	K1	Bel'kovskiy, Ostrov *i.* Rus. Fed.
128	B2	Bella Bella Can.
104	C2	Bellac France
128	B2	Bella Coola Can.
53	C1	Bellata Austr.
136	C2	Belle Fourche U.S.A.
136	C2	Belle Fourche *r.* U.S.A.
143	D3	Belle Glade U.S.A.
104	B2	Belle-Île *i.* France
131	E1	Belle Isle *i.* Can.
131	E1	Belle Isle, Strait of Can.
130	C2	Belleville Can.
140	B3	Belleville *IL* U.S.A.
137	D3	Belleville *KS* U.S.A.
134	B1	Bellevue *ID* U.S.A.
134	B1	Bellingham U.S.A.
55	O2	Bellingshausen Sea Antarctica
105	D2	Bellinzona Switz.
108	B1	Belluno Italy
122	A3	Bellville S. Africa
155	E1	Belmonte Brazil
146	B3	Belmopan Belize
69	E1	Belogorsk Rus. Fed.
121	D3	Beloha Madag.
155	D1	Belo Horizonte Brazil
140	B2	Beloit U.S.A.
86	C2	Belomorsk Rus. Fed.
91	D3	Belorechensk Rus. Fed.
87	E3	Beloretsk Rus. Fed.
		Belorussia *country* Europe *see* Belarus
86	F2	Beloyarskiy Rus. Fed.
86	C2	Beloye, Ozero *l.* Rus. Fed.
		Beloye More *sea* Rus. Fed. *see* White Sea
86	C2	Belozersk Rus. Fed.
77	E2	Belukha, Gora *mt.* Kazakh./Rus. Fed.
86	D2	Belush'ye Rus. Fed.
89	D2	Belyy Rus. Fed.
82	F2	Belyy, Ostrov *i.* Rus. Fed.
101	F1	Belzig Ger.
137	E1	Bemidji U.S.A.
118	C3	Bena Dibele Dem. Rep. Congo
53	C3	Benalla Austr.
106	B1	Benavente Spain
96	A2	Benbecula *i.* U.K.
134	B2	Bend U.S.A.
123	C3	Bendearg *mt.* S. Africa
52	B3	Bendigo Austr.
121	C2	Bene Moz.
102	C2	Benešov Czech Rep.

109 B2 Benevento Italy
159 C2 Bengal, Bay of *sea* Indian Ocean
Bengaluru India *see* Bangalore
70 B2 Bengbu China
115 E1 Benghazi Libya
61 B1 Bengkayang Indon.
60 B2 Bengkulu Indon.
120 A2 Benguela Angola
96 B1 Ben Hope *h.* U.K.
152 B2 Beni *r.* Bol.
119 C2 Beni Dem. Rep. Congo
114 B1 Beni Abbès Alg.
107 C2 Benidorm Spain
114 B1 Beni Mellal Morocco
114 C3 Benin *country* Africa
114 C4 Benin, Bight of *g.* Africa
115 C4 Benin City Nigeria
153 C3 Benito Juárez Arg.
150 B2 Benjamim Constant Brazil
144 A1 Benjamín Hill Mex.
59 C3 Benjina Indon.
96 B2 Ben Lawers *mt.* U.K.
96 B2 Ben Lomond *h.* U.K.
96 A2 Ben Macdui *mt.* U.K.
96 A2 Ben More *h.* U.K.
96 B1 Benmore, Lake N.Z.
96 B1 Ben More Assynt *h.* U.K.
128 C2 Bennett *r.* Can.
83 K1 Bennetta, Ostrov *i.* Rus. Fed.
96 B1 Ben Nevis *mt.* U.K.
141 E2 Bennington U.S.A.
123 C2 Benoni S. Africa
101 D3 Bensheim Ger.
138 A2 Benson U.S.A.
58 C3 Benteng Indon.
140 B2 Benton Harbor U.S.A.
142 B1 Bentonville U.S.A.
115 C4 Benue *r.* Nigeria
97 B1 Benwee Head Ireland
96 A2 Ben Wyvis *mt.* U.K.
70 C1 Benxi China
Beograd Serbia *see* Belgrade
75 C2 Beohari India
67 B4 Beppu Japan
109 C2 Berane Montenegro
109 C2 Berat Albania
59 C3 Berau, Teluk *b.* Indon.
116 B3 Berber Sudan
117 C3 Berbera Somalia
118 B2 Berbérati C.A.R.
104 C1 Berck France
91 D2 Berdyans'k Ukr.
91 D2 Berdychiv Ukr.
90 A2 Berehove Ukr.
59 D3 Bereina P.N.G.
76 B3 Bereket Turkm.
129 E2 Berens River Can.
90 A2 Berezhany Ukr.
90 A2 Berezivka Ukr.
90 B1 Berezne Ukr.
86 D2 Bereznik Rus. Fed.
86 E3 Berezniki Rus. Fed.
86 F2 Berezovo Rus. Fed.
107 D1 Berga Spain
111 C3 Bergama Turkey
108 A1 Bergamo Italy
102 C1 Bergen *Mecklenburg-Vorpommern* Ger.
101 D1 Bergen *Niedersachsen* Ger.
93 E3 Bergen Norway
100 B2 Bergen op Zoom Neth.
104 C3 Bergerac France
100 C2 Bergheim (Erft) Ger.
100 C2 Bergisch Gladbach Ger.
122 A1 Bergland Namibia
92 H2 Bergsviken Sweden

83 M3 Beringa, Ostrov *i.* Rus. Fed.
100 B2 Beringen Belgium
124 C3 Bering Sea N. Pacific Ocean
83 N2 Bering Strait Rus. Fed./U.S.A.
135 B3 Berkeley U.S.A.
100 B1 Berkhout Neth.
55 Q2 Berkner Island Antarctica
110 B2 Berkovitsa Bulg.
92 I1 Berlevåg Norway
101 F1 Berlin Ger.
141 E2 Berlin U.S.A.
101 E2 Berlingerode Ger.
53 D3 Bermagui Austr.
144 B2 Bermejillo Mex.
152 B3 Bermejo Bol.
131 D1 Bermen, Lac *l.* Can.
125 K4 Bermuda *terr.* N. Atlantic Ocean
105 D2 Bern Switz.
101 E2 Bernburg (Saale) Ger.
127 F2 Bernier Bay Can.
100 C3 Bernkastel-Kues Ger.
121 D3 Beroroha Madag.
52 B2 Berri Austr.
107 D2 Berrouaghia Alg.
146 C2 Berry Islands Bahamas
100 C1 Bersenbrück Ger.
90 B2 Bershad' Ukr.
131 D1 Berté, Lac *l.* Can.
118 B2 Bertoua Cameroon
150 B2 Beruri Brazil
98 B1 Berwick-upon-Tweed U.K.
91 C2 Beryslav Ukr.
121 D2 Besalampy Madag.
105 D2 Besançon France
129 D2 Besnard Lake Can.
142 C2 Bessemer U.S.A.
76 B2 Besshoky, Gora *h.* Kazakh.
106 B1 Betanzos Spain
118 B2 Bétaré Oya Cameroon
122 A2 Bethanie Namibia
123 C2 Bethlehem S. Africa
141 D2 Bethlehem U.S.A.
121 D3 Betioky Madag.
77 D2 Betpak-Dala *plain* Kazakh.
121 D3 Betroka Madag.
131 D2 Betsiamites Can.
121 D2 Betsiboka *r.* Madag.
137 E2 Bettendorf U.S.A.
75 C2 Bettiah India
75 B2 Betul India
75 B2 Betwa *r.* India
98 B2 Betws-y-coed U.K.
98 C2 Beverley U.K.
101 D2 Beverungen Ger.
100 B1 Beverwijk Neth.
99 D3 Bexhill U.K.
111 C3 Beykoz Turkey
114 B4 Beyla Guinea
76 B2 Beyneu Kazakh.
80 B1 Beypazarı Turkey
Beyrouth Lebanon *see* Beirut
80 B2 Beyşehir Turkey
80 B2 Beyşehir Gölü *l.* Turkey
91 D2 Beysug *r.* Rus. Fed.
88 C2 Bezhanitsy Rus. Fed.
89 E2 Bezhetsk Rus. Fed.
105 C3 Béziers France
75 C2 Bhadrak India
73 B3 Bhadravati India
75 C2 Bhagalpur India
74 A2 Bhairi Hol *mt.* Pak.
74 B1 Bhakkar Pak.
62 A1 Bhamo Myanmar
75 C3 Bhanjanagar India
74 B2 Bharatpur India
74 B2 Bharuch India

74 B2 Bhavnagar India
75 C3 Bhawanipatna India
123 D2 Bhekuzulu S. Africa
74 B2 Bhilwara India
73 B3 Bhima *r.* India
123 C3 Bhisho S. Africa
74 B2 Bhiwani India
123 C3 Bhongweni S. Africa
74 B2 Bhopal India
75 C2 Bhubaneshwar India
74 A2 Bhuj India
74 B2 Bhusawal India
75 D2 Bhutan *country* Asia
62 B2 Bia, Phou *mt.* Laos
59 D3 Biak Indon.
59 D3 Biak *i.* Indon.
103 E1 Biała Podlaska Pol.
103 D1 Białogard Pol.
103 E1 Białystok Pol.
109 C3 Bianco Italy
104 B3 Biarritz France
105 D2 Biasca Switz.
66 D2 Bibai Japan
120 A2 Bibala Angola
102 B2 Biberach an der Riß Ger.
115 C4 Bida Nigeria
141 E2 Biddeford U.S.A.
99 A3 Bideford U.K.
101 D2 Biedenkopf Ger.
105 D2 Biel Switz.
101 D1 Bielefeld Ger.
108 A1 Biella Italy
103 D1 Bielsko-Biała Pol.
63 B2 Biên Hoa Vietnam
130 C1 Bienville, Lac *l.* Can.
100 B3 Bièvre Belgium
118 B3 Bifoun Gabon
111 C2 Biga Turkey
123 D2 Big Bend Swaziland
129 D2 Biggar Can.
96 C3 Biggar U.K.
134 D1 Big Hole *r.* U.S.A.
136 B1 Bighorn *r.* U.S.A.
136 B2 Bighorn Mountains U.S.A.
139 C2 Big Lake U.S.A.
140 B2 Big Rapids U.S.A.
129 D2 Big River Can.
129 E2 Big Sand Lake Can.
137 D2 Big Sioux *r.* U.S.A.
139 C2 Big Spring U.S.A.
134 E1 Big Timber U.S.A.
130 B1 Big Trout Lake Can.
130 A1 Big Trout Lake Can.
109 C2 Bihać Bos.-Herz.
75 C2 Bihar Sharif India
110 B1 Bihor, Vârful *mt.* Romania
114 A3 Bijagós, Arquipélago dos *is* Guinea-Bissau
81 C2 Bījār Iran
109 C2 Bijeljina Bos.-Herz.
109 C2 Bijelo Polje Montenegro
71 A3 Bijie China
74 B2 Bikaner India
69 E1 Bikin Rus. Fed.
118 B3 Bikoro Dem. Rep. Congo
79 C2 Bilād Banī Bū 'Alī Oman
75 C2 Bilaspur India
90 C2 Bila Tserkva Ukr.
63 A2 Bilauktaung Range *mts* Myanmar/Thai.
106 C1 Bilbao Spain
111 C2 Bilecik Turkey
111 C2 Biłgoraj Pol.
90 C2 Bilhorod-Dnistrovs'kyy Ukr.
119 C2 Bili Dem. Rep. Congo
83 M2 Bilibino Rus. Fed.
134 E1 Billings U.S.A.

99 B3 **Bill of Portland** hd U.K.
115 D3 Bilma Niger
115 D3 Bilma, Grand Erg de des. Niger
51 E2 Biloela Austr.
91 C2 Bilohirs'k Ukr.
90 B1 Bilohir"ya Ukr.
91 C1 Bilopillya Ukr.
91 D2 Bilovods'k Ukr.
142 C2 Biloxi U.S.A.
51 C2 Bilpa Morea Claypan salt flat Austr.
101 E2 Bilshausen Ger.
115 E3 Biltine Chad
90 C2 Bilyayivka Ukr.
143 E3 Bimini Islands Bahamas
75 B2 Bina-Etawa India
59 C3 Binaija, Gunung mt. Indon.
118 B3 Bindu Dem. Rep. Congo
121 C2 Bindura Zimbabwe
107 D1 Binefar Spain
53 D1 Bingara Austr.
100 C3 Bingen am Rhein Ger.
141 F1 Bingham U.S.A.
141 D2 Binghamton U.S.A.
81 C2 Bingöl Turkey
60 A1 Binjai Indon.
60 B2 Bintuhan Indon.
61 C1 Bintulu Sarawak Malaysia
70 B2 Binzhou China
109 C2 Biograd na Moru Croatia
118 A2 Bioko i. Equat. Guinea
118 C1 Birao C.A.R.
75 C2 Biratnagar Nepal
128 C2 Birch Mountains Can.
51 C2 Birdsville Austr.
80 B2 Birecik Turkey
60 A1 Bireun Indon.
75 C2 Birganj Nepal
117 B3 Birhan mt. Eth.
154 B2 Birigüi Brazil
76 B3 Birjand Iran
98 B2 Birkenhead U.K.
99 C2 Birmingham U.K.
142 C2 Birmingham U.S.A.
114 A2 Bir Mogreïn Maur.
115 C3 Birnin-Kebbi Nigeria
115 C3 Birnin Konni Niger
69 E1 Birobidzhan Rus. Fed.
97 C2 Birr Ireland
96 C1 Birsay U.K.
78 A2 Bi'r Shalatayn Egypt
88 B2 Biržai Lith.
75 B2 Bisalpur India
138 B2 Bisbee U.S.A.
104 A2 Biscay, Bay of sea France/Spain
102 C2 Bischofshofen Austria
130 B2 Biscotasi Lake Can.
77 D2 Bishkek Kyrg.
135 C3 Bishop U.S.A.
69 E1 Bishui China
150 B1 Bisinaca Col.
115 C1 Biskra Alg.
136 C1 Bismarck U.S.A.
48 D3 Bismarck Sea sea P.N.G.
107 D3 Bissa, Djebel mt. Alg.
114 A3 Bissau Guinea-Bissau
129 E2 Bissett Can.
128 C2 Bistcho Lake Can.
110 B1 Bistriţa Romania
110 C1 Bistriţa r. Romania
100 C3 Bitburg Ger.
105 D2 Bitche France
115 D3 Bitkine Chad
109 D2 Bitola Macedonia
109 C2 Bitonto Italy

122 A3 Bitterfontein S. Africa
134 D1 Bitterroot r. U.S.A.
134 C1 Bitterroot Range mts U.S.A.
91 D1 Bityug r. Rus. Fed.
115 D3 Biu Nigeria
67 C3 Biwa-ko l. Japan
68 B1 Biysk Rus. Fed.
115 C1 Bizerte Tunisia
92 A2 Bjargtangar hd Iceland
92 G3 Bjästa Sweden
92 G2 Bjerkvik Norway
82 C2 Bjørnøya i. Arctic Ocean
114 B3 Bla Mali
137 E3 Black r. U.S.A.
51 D2 Blackall Austr.
98 B2 Blackburn U.K.
134 D2 Blackfoot U.S.A.
102 B2 Black Forest mts Ger.
136 C2 Black Hills U.S.A.
96 B2 Black Isle pen. U.K.
129 D2 Black Lake Can.
129 D2 Black Lake Can.
99 B3 Black Mountains hills U.K.
98 B2 Blackpool U.K.
62 B1 Black River r. Vietnam
140 A2 Black River Falls U.S.A.
140 C3 Blacksburg U.S.A.
80 B1 Black Sea Asia/Europe
97 A1 Blacksod Bay Ireland
97 C2 Blackstairs Mountains hills Ireland
114 B4 Black Volta r. Africa
97 C2 Blackwater r. Ireland
128 B1 Blackwater Lake Can.
50 A3 Blackwood r. Austr.
76 A2 Blagodarnyy Rus. Fed.
110 B2 Blagoevgrad Bulg.
69 E1 Blagoveshchensk Rus. Fed.
129 D2 Blaine Lake Can.
137 D2 Blair U.S.A.
96 C2 Blair Atholl U.K.
96 C2 Blairgowrie U.K.
143 D2 Blakely U.S.A.
105 D2 Blanc, Mont mt. France/Italy
153 B4 Blanca, Bahía b. Arg.
152 A1 Blanca, Laguna imp. l. Austr.
152 B2 Blanco r. Bol.
131 E1 Blanc-Sablon Can.
92 A2 Blanda r. Iceland
99 B3 Blandford Forum U.K.
135 E3 Blanding U.S.A.
107 D1 Blanes Spain
60 A1 Blangkejeren Indon.
100 C2 Blankenheim Ger.
100 C2 Blankenrath Ger.
103 D2 Blansko Czech Rep.
121 C2 Blantyre Malawi
98 C1 Blaydon U.K.
53 C2 Blayney Austr.
54 B2 Blenheim N.Z.
115 C1 Blida Alg.
130 B2 Blind River Can.
123 C2 Bloemfontein S. Africa
123 C2 Bloemhof S. Africa
123 C2 Bloemhof Dam S. Africa
92 A2 Blönduós Iceland
97 B1 Bloody Foreland pt Ireland
138 B1 Bloomfield U.S.A.
140 B2 Bloomington IL U.S.A.
140 B3 Bloomington IN U.S.A.
140 C3 Bluefield U.S.A.
146 B3 Bluefields Nic.
53 C2 Blue Mountains Austr.
134 C1 Blue Mountains U.S.A.
116 B3 Blue Nile r. Eth./Sudan
126 D2 Bluenose Lake Can.
140 C3 Blue Ridge mts U.S.A.

97 B1 Blue Stack Mountains hills Ireland
54 A3 Bluff N.Z.
135 E3 Bluff U.S.A.
152 D3 Blumenau Brazil
52 A2 Blyth Austr.
98 C1 Blyth U.K.
135 D4 Blythe U.S.A.
142 C1 Blytheville U.S.A.
114 A4 Bo Sierra Leone
64 B1 Boac Phil.
151 D2 Boa Esperança, Açude resr Brazil
150 B1 Boa Vista Brazil
53 C2 Bobadah Austr.
71 B3 Bobai China
121 D2 Bobaomby, Tanjona c. Madag.
114 B3 Bobo-Dioulasso Burkina
89 F3 Bobrov Rus. Fed.
91 C1 Bobrovytsya Ukr.
91 C2 Bobrynets' Ukr.
121 D3 Boby mt. Madag.
150 B2 Boca do Acre Brazil
155 C1 Bocaiúva Brazil
118 B2 Bocaranga C.A.R.
103 E2 Bochnia Pol.
100 C2 Bocholt Ger.
100 C2 Bochum Ger.
101 E1 Bockenem Ger.
118 B2 Boda C.A.R.
83 I3 Bodaybo Rus. Fed.
115 D3 Bodélé reg. Chad
92 H2 Boden Sweden
99 A3 Bodmin U.K.
99 A3 Bodmin Moor moorland U.K.
92 F2 Bodø Norway
111 C3 Bodrum Turkey
118 C3 Boende Dem. Rep. Congo
142 C2 Bogalusa U.S.A.
114 B3 Bogandé Burkina
68 B2 Bogda Shan mts China
53 D1 Boggabilla Austr.
97 B2 Boggeragh Mountains hills Ireland
100 B3 Bogny-sur-Meuse France
97 C2 Bog of Allen reg. Ireland
53 C3 Bogong, Mount Austr.
60 B2 Bogor Indon.
89 E3 Bogoroditsk Rus. Fed.
150 A1 Bogotá Col.
82 G3 Bogotol Rus. Fed.
83 H3 Boguchany Rus. Fed.
91 E2 Boguchar Rus. Fed.
70 B2 Bo Hai g. China
100 A3 Bohain-en-Vermandois France
70 B2 Bohai Wan b. China
123 C2 Bohlokong S. Africa
102 C2 Böhmer Wald mts Ger.
91 D1 Bohodukhiv Ukr.
64 B2 Bohol i. Phil.
64 B2 Bohol Sea Phil.
70 A2 Bohu China
155 C2 Boi, Ponta do pt Brazil
154 B1 Bois r. Brazil
126 C2 Bois, Lac des l. Can.
134 C2 Boise U.S.A.
139 C1 Boise City U.S.A.
123 C2 Boitumelong S. Africa
101 E1 Boizenburg Ger.
76 B3 Bojnūrd Iran
118 B3 Bokatola Dem. Rep. Congo
114 A3 Boké Guinea
118 C3 Bokele Dem. Rep. Congo
93 E4 Boknafjorden sea chan. Norway
115 D3 Bokoro Chad

63 A2 Bokpyin Myanmar
89 D2 Boksitogorsk Rus. Fed.
122 B2 Bokspits Botswana
114 A3 Bolama Guinea-Bissau
75 D2 Bolangir India
63 B2 Bolavén, Phouphiang *plat.* Laos
104 C2 Bolbec France
77 E2 Bole China
118 B3 Boleko Dem. Rep. Congo
114 B3 Bolgatanga Ghana
90 B2 Bolhrad Ukr.
66 B1 Boli China
110 C2 Bolintin-Vale Romania
137 E3 Bolívar U.S.A.
150 A1 Bolívar, Pico *mt.* Venez.
152 B2 Bolivia *country* S. America
89 E3 Bolkhov Rus. Fed.
105 C3 Bollène France
93 G3 Bollnäs Sweden
53 D1 Bollon Austr.
101 E2 Bollstedt Ger.
93 F4 Bolmen *l.* Sweden
118 B3 Bolobo Dem. Rep. Congo
108 B2 Bologna Italy
89 D2 Bologoye Rus. Fed.
89 D2 Bologovo Rus. Fed.
118 B3 Bolomba Dem. Rep. Congo
83 H1 Bol'shevik, Ostrov *i.* Rus. Fed.
86 E2 Bol'shezemel'skaya Tundra *lowland* Rus. Fed.
66 B2 Bol'shoy Kamen' Rus. Fed.
Bol'shoy Kavkaz *mts* Asia/Europe *see* Caucasus
83 K2 Bol'shoy Lyakhovskiy, Ostrov *i.* Rus. Fed.
144 B2 Bolsón de Mapimí *des.* Mex.
100 B1 Bolsward Neth.
98 B2 Bolton U.K.
80 B1 Bolu Turkey
92 A2 Bolungarvík Iceland
108 B1 Bolzano Italy
118 B3 Boma Dem. Rep. Congo
53 D2 Bomaderry Austr.
53 C3 Bombala Austr.
Bombay India *see* Mumbai
155 C1 Bom Despacho Brazil
75 C1 Bomdila India
151 D3 Bom Jesus da Lapa Brazil
155 D2 Bom Jesus do Itabapoana Brazil
115 A2 Bon, Cap *c.* Tunisia
147 D3 Bonaire *i.* Neth. Antilles
50 B1 Bonaparte Archipelago *is* Austr.
131 E2 Bonavista Can.
131 E2 Bonavista Bay Can.
118 C2 Bondo Dem. Rep. Congo
114 B4 Bondoukou Côte d'Ivoire
58 C3 Bonerate, Kepulauan *is* Indon.
155 C1 Bonfinópolis de Minas Brazil
117 B4 Bonga Eth.
75 D2 Bongaigaon India
118 C3 Bongandanga Dem. Rep. Congo
118 C2 Bongo, Massif des *mts* C.A.R.
115 D3 Bongor Chad
114 B4 Bongouanou Côte d'Ivoire
63 B2 Bông Sơn Vietnam
140 B1 Bonham U.S.A.
105 D3 Bonifacio Corse France
108 A2 Bonifacio, Strait of France/Italy
100 C2 Bonn Ger.
134 C1 Bonners Ferry U.S.A.
53 A3 Bonnie Rock Austr.
129 C2 Bonnyville Can.

108 A2 Bonorva *Sardegna* Italy
61 C1 Bontang Indon.
64 B1 Bontoc Phil.
58 B3 Bontosunggu Indon.
123 C3 Bontrug S. Africa
52 B2 Booligal Austr.
53 C1 Boomi Austr.
53 D1 Boonah Austr.
137 E2 Boone U.S.A.
142 C2 Booneville U.S.A.
137 E3 Boonville U.S.A.
53 C2 Boorowa Austr.
126 F2 Boothia, Gulf of Can.
126 E2 Boothia Peninsula Can.
100 C2 Boppard Ger.
144 B2 Boquilla, Presa de la *resr* Mex.
109 D2 Bor Serbia
117 B4 Bor Sudan
80 B2 Bor Turkey
121 E2 Boraha, Nosy *i.* Madag.
93 F4 Borås Sweden
79 C2 Borāzjān Iran
150 C2 Borba Brazil
104 B3 Bordeaux France
127 F2 Borden Peninsula Can.
52 B3 Bordertown Austr.
107 D2 Bordj Bou Arréridj Alg.
107 D2 Bordj Bounaama Alg.
115 C1 Bordj Messaouda Alg.
115 C2 Bordj Omer Driss Alg.
94 B1 Borðoy *i.* Faroe Is
92 A3 Borgarnes Iceland
108 A1 Borgosesia Italy
87 D3 Borisoglebsk Rus. Fed.
89 E2 Borisoglebskiy Rus. Fed.
91 D1 Borisovka Rus. Fed.
100 C2 Borken Ger.
92 G2 Borkenes Norway
100 C1 Borkum Ger.
100 C1 Borkum *i.* Ger.
93 G3 Borlänge Sweden
101 F2 Borna Ger.
61 C1 Borneo *i.* Asia
93 F4 Bornholm *i.* Denmark
111 C3 Bornova Turkey
90 B1 Borodyanka Ukr.
89 D2 Borovichi Rus. Fed.
89 E2 Borovsk Rus. Fed.
51 C1 Borroloola Austr.
110 B1 Borşa Romania
90 B2 Borshchiv Ukr.
69 D1 Borshchovochnyy Khrebet *mts* Rus. Fed.
101 E1 Börßum Ger.
81 C2 Borüjerd Iran
90 A2 Boryslav Ukr.
90 C1 Boryspil' Ukr.
91 C1 Borzna Ukr.
69 D1 Borzya Rus. Fed.
109 C1 Bosanska Dubica Bos.-Herz.
109 C1 Bosanska Gradiška Bos.-Herz.
109 C2 Bosanska Krupa Bos.-Herz.
109 C1 Bosanski Novi Bos.-Herz.
109 C2 Bosansko Grahovo Bos.-Herz.
71 A3 Bose China
123 C2 Boshof S. Africa
109 C2 Bosnia-Herzegovina *country* Europe
118 B2 Bosobolo Dem. Rep. Congo
110 C2 Bosporus *str.* Turkey
118 B2 Bossangoa C.A.R.
118 B2 Bossembélé C.A.R.
68 B2 Bosten Hu *l.* China
98 C2 Boston U.K.
141 E2 Boston U.S.A.
142 B1 Boston Mountains U.S.A.

53 D2 Botany Bay Austr.
110 B2 Botev *mt.* Bulg.
93 G3 Bothnia, Gulf of Fin./Sweden
110 C1 Botoşani Romania
123 C2 Botshabelo S. Africa
120 B3 Botswana *country* Africa
109 C3 Botte Donato, Monte *mt.* Italy
136 C1 Bottineau U.S.A.
100 C2 Bottrop Ger.
154 C2 Botucatu Brazil
114 B4 Bouaké Côte d'Ivoire
118 B2 Bouar C.A.R.
114 B1 Bouârfa Morocco
131 D2 Bouctouche Can.
107 E2 Bougaa Alg.
114 B3 Bougouni Mali
100 B3 Bouillon Belgium
107 D2 Bouira Alg.
114 A2 Boujdour Western Sahara
136 B2 Boulder U.S.A.
135 D3 Boulder City U.S.A.
51 C2 Boulia Austr.
104 C2 Boulogne-Billancourt France
99 D3 Boulogne-sur-Mer France
118 B3 Boumango Gabon
118 B2 Boumba *r.* Cameroon
107 D2 Boumerdes Alg.
114 B4 Bouna Côte d'Ivoire
114 B4 Boundiali Côte d'Ivoire
134 D2 Bountiful U.S.A.
114 B3 Bourem Mali
104 C2 Bourganeuf France
105 D2 Bourg-en-Bresse France
104 C2 Bourges France
53 C2 Bourke Austr.
99 C3 Bournemouth U.K.
115 C1 Bou Saâda Alg.
115 D3 Bousso Chad
114 A3 Boutilimit Maur.
129 C3 Bow *r.* Can.
51 D2 Bowen Austr.
129 C3 Bow Island Can.
140 B3 Bowling Green *KY* U.S.A.
140 C2 Bowling Green *OH* U.S.A.
136 C1 Bowman U.S.A.
101 D3 Boxberg Ger.
100 B2 Boxtel Neth.
80 B1 Boyabat Turkey
Boyang China *see* Poyang
97 B3 Boyle Ireland
97 C2 Boyne *r.* Ireland
136 B2 Boysen Reservoir U.S.A.
152 B3 Boyuibe Bol.
111 C3 Bozburun Turkey
111 C3 Bozcaada *i.* Turkey
111 C3 Bozdağ *mt.* Turkey
111 C3 Boz Dağları *mts* Turkey
111 C3 Bozdoğan Turkey
134 D1 Bozeman U.S.A.
118 B2 Bozoum C.A.R.
111 D3 Bozüyük Turkey
109 C2 Brač *i.* Croatia
130 C2 Bracebridge Can.
99 C3 Bracknell U.K.
109 C2 Bradano *r.* Italy
143 D3 Bradenton U.S.A.
98 C2 Bradford U.K.
141 D2 Bradford U.S.A.
139 D2 Brady U.S.A.
96 C2 Braemar U.K.
106 B1 Braga Port.
151 D2 Bragança Brazil
106 B1 Bragança Port.
155 C2 Bragança Paulista Brazil
89 D3 Brahin Belarus
73 C3 Brahmapur India
62 A1 Brahmaputra *r.* China/India

110 C1 Brăila Romania
137 E1 Brainerd U.S.A.
99 D3 Braintree U.K.
100 B2 Braives Belgium
101 D1 Brake (Unterweser) Ger.
100 D1 Bramsche Ger.
150 B2 Branco r. Brazil
101 F1 Brandenburg Ger.
129 E3 Brandon Can.
97 A2 Brandon Mountain h. Ireland
122 B3 Brandvlei S. Africa
103 D1 Braniewo Pol.
130 B2 Brantford Can.
131 D2 Bras d'Or Lake Can.
155 D1 Brasil, Planalto do plat. Brazil
154 C1 Brasilândia Brazil
154 C1 Brasília Brazil
155 D1 Brasília de Minas Brazil
88 C2 Braslaw Belarus
110 C1 Braşov Romania
103 D2 Bratislava Slovakia
83 H3 Bratsk Rus. Fed.
102 C2 Braunau am Inn Austria
101 E1 Braunschweig Ger.
92 A2 Brautarholt Iceland
Bravo del Norte, Río r.
Mex./U.S.A. see Rio Grande
135 C4 Brawley U.S.A.
97 C2 Bray Ireland
150 C2 Brazil country S. America
139 D3 Brazos r. U.S.A.
118 B3 Brazzaville Congo
109 C2 Brčko Bos.-Herz.
96 C2 Brechin U.K.
100 B2 Brecht Belgium
139 D2 Breckenridge U.S.A.
103 D2 Břeclav Czech Rep.
99 B3 Brecon U.K.
99 B3 Brecon Beacons reg. U.K.
100 B2 Breda Neth.
122 B3 Bredasdorp S. Africa
102 B2 Bregenz Austria
92 H1 Breivikbotn Norway
92 E3 Brekstad Norway
101 D1 Bremen Ger.
134 B1 Bremerton U.S.A.
101 D1 Bremerhaven Ger.
101 D1 Bremervörde Ger.
139 D2 Brenham U.S.A.
108 B1 Brennero Italy
102 C2 Brenner Pass Austria/Italy
99 D3 Brentwood U.K.
108 B1 Brescia Italy
108 B1 Bressanone Italy
96 □ Bressay i. U.K.
104 B2 Bressuire France
88 B3 Brest Belarus
104 B2 Brest France
142 C3 Breton Sound b. U.S.A.
151 C2 Breves Brazil
53 C1 Brewarrina Austr.
134 C1 Brewster U.S.A.
89 E2 Breytovo Rus. Fed.
109 C1 Brezovo Polje plain Croatia
118 C2 Bria C.A.R.
105 D3 Briançon France
90 B2 Briceni Moldova
99 B3 Bridgend U.K.
141 E2 Bridgeport CT U.S.A.
136 C2 Bridgeport NE U.S.A.
147 E3 Bridgetown Barbados
131 D2 Bridgewater Can.
99 B3 Bridgwater U.K.
98 C1 Bridlington U.K.
98 C1 Bridlington Bay U.K.
105 D2 Brig Switz.
134 D2 Brigham City U.S.A.

54 B3 Brighton N.Z.
99 C3 Brighton U.K.
105 D3 Brignoles France
101 D2 Brilon Ger.
109 C2 Brindisi Italy
53 D1 Brisbane Austr.
99 B3 Bristol U.K.
143 D1 Bristol U.S.A.
99 A3 Bristol Channel est. U.K.
128 B2 British Columbia prov. Can.
56 G7 British Indian Ocean
Territory terr. Indian Ocean
95 B2 British Isles is Europe
123 C2 Brits S. Africa
122 B3 Britstown S. Africa
104 C2 Brive-la-Gaillarde France
106 C1 Briviesca Spain
103 D2 Brno Czech Rep.
143 D2 Broad r. U.S.A.
130 C1 Broadback r. Can.
96 C3 Broad Law h. U.K.
136 B1 Broadus U.S.A.
129 D2 Brochet Can.
129 D2 Brochet, Lac l. Can.
131 D2 Brochet, Lac au l. Can.
101 E1 Bröckel Ger.
126 D1 Brock Island Can.
130 C2 Brockville Can.
127 F2 Brodeur Peninsula Can.
96 B3 Brodick U.K.
103 D1 Brodnica Pol.
90 B1 Brody Ukr.
139 D1 Broken Arrow U.S.A.
137 D2 Broken Bow U.S.A.
52 B2 Broken Hill Austr.
99 B2 Bromsgrove U.K.
93 E4 Brønderslev Denmark
92 F2 Brønnøysund Norway
64 A2 Brooke's Point Phil.
142 B2 Brookhaven U.S.A.
134 B2 Brookings OR U.S.A.
137 D2 Brookings SD U.S.A.
129 C2 Brooks Can.
126 B2 Brooks Range mts U.S.A.
143 D3 Brooksville U.S.A.
96 B2 Broom, Loch inlet U.K.
50 B1 Broome Austr.
134 B2 Brothers U.S.A.
Broughton Island Can. see
Qikiqtarjuaq
90 C1 Brovary Ukr.
139 C1 Brownfield U.S.A.
128 C3 Browning U.S.A.
142 C1 Brownsville TN U.S.A.
139 D3 Brownsville TX U.S.A.
139 D2 Brownwood U.S.A.
92 A2 Brú Iceland
104 C1 Bruay-la-Bussière France
140 B1 Bruce Crossing U.S.A.
103 D2 Bruck an der Mur Austria
Bruges Belgium see Brugge
100 A2 Brugge Belgium
128 C2 Brûlé Can.
151 D3 Brumado Brazil
93 F3 Brumunddal Norway
61 C1 Brunei country Asia
102 C2 Brunico Italy
101 D1 Brunsbüttel Ger.
143 D2 Brunswick GA U.S.A.
141 F2 Brunswick ME U.S.A.
53 D1 Brunswick Heads Austr.
136 C2 Brush U.S.A.
100 B2 Brussels Belgium
Bruxelles Belgium see
Brussels
139 D2 Bryan U.S.A.
89 D3 Bryansk Rus. Fed.

91 D2 Bryn'kovskaya Rus. Fed.
91 D2 Bryukhovetskaya Rus. Fed.
103 D1 Brzeg Pol.
114 A3 Buba Guinea-Bissau
80 B2 Bucak Turkey
150 A1 Bucaramanga Col.
53 C3 Buchan Austr.
114 A4 Buchanan Liberia
110 C2 Bucharest Romania
101 D1 Bucholz in der Nordheide
Ger.
110 C1 Bucin, Pasul pass Romania
101 D1 Bückeburg Ger.
138 A2 Buckeye U.S.A.
96 C2 Buckhaven U.K.
96 C2 Buckie U.K.
51 C1 Buckingham Bay Austr.
51 D2 Buckland Tableland reg. Austr.
52 A2 Buckleboo Austr.
141 F2 Bucksport U.S.A.
Bucureşti Romania see
Bucharest
89 D3 Buda-Kashalyova Belarus
103 D2 Budapest Hungary
75 B2 Budaun India
108 A2 Buddusò Sardegna Italy
99 A3 Bude U.K.
87 D4 Budennovsk Rus. Fed.
89 D2 Budogoshch' Rus. Fed.
108 A2 Budoni Sardegna Italy
118 A2 Buea Cameroon
144 B2 Buenaventura Mex.
106 C1 Buendia, Embalse de resr
Spain
155 D1 Buenópolis Brazil
153 C4 Buenos Aires Arg.
153 A5 Buenos Aires, Lago l.
Arg./Chile
141 D2 Buffalo NY U.S.A.
136 C1 Buffalo SD U.S.A.
136 B2 Buffalo WY U.S.A.
129 D2 Buffalo Narrows Can.
110 C2 Buftea Romania
103 E1 Bug r. Pol.
61 C2 Bugel, Tanjung pt Indon.
109 C2 Bugojno Bos.-Herz.
64 A2 Bugsuk i. Phil.
87 E3 Buguruslan Rus. Fed.
110 C1 Buhuşi Romania
99 B2 Builth Wells U.K.
69 D1 Buir Nur l. Mongolia
120 A3 Buitepos Namibia
109 D2 Bujanovac Serbia
119 C3 Bujumbura Burundi
69 D1 Bukachacha Rus. Fed.
119 C3 Bukavu Dem. Rep. Congo
119 D3 Bukittinggi Indon.
119 D3 Bukoba Tanz.
53 D2 Bulahdelah Austr.
121 B3 Bulawayo Zimbabwe
111 C3 Buldan Turkey
123 D2 Bulembu Swaziland
69 C1 Bulgan Mongolia
110 C2 Bulgaria country Europe
54 B2 Buller r. N.Z.
52 B1 Bulloo Downs Austr.
122 A1 Büllsport Namibia
58 C3 Bulukumba Indon.
118 B3 Bulungu Dem. Rep. Congo
118 C2 Bumba Dem. Rep. Congo
62 A1 Bumhkang Myanmar
118 B3 Buna Dem. Rep. Congo
50 A3 Bunbury Austr.
97 C1 Buncrana Ireland
119 D3 Bunda Tanz.
51 E2 Bundaberg Austr.

53 D2 Bundarra Austr.
74 B2 Bundi India
97 B1 Bundoran Ireland
53 C3 Bungendore Austr.
67 B4 Bungo-suidō *sea chan.* Japan
119 D2 Bunia Dem. Rep. Congo
118 C3 Bunianga Dem. Rep. Congo
63 B2 Buôn Ma Thuột Vietnam
119 D3 Bura Kenya
78 B2 Buraydah Saudi Arabia
100 D2 Burbach Ger.
117 C4 Burco Somalia
100 B1 Burdaard Neth.
80 B2 Burdur Turkey
117 B3 Burë Eth.
99 D2 Bure *r.* U.K.
74 B1 Burewala Pak.
110 C2 Burgas Bulg.
101 E1 Burg bei Magdeburg Ger.
101 E1 Burgdorf *Niedersachsen* Ger.
101 E1 Burgdorf *Niedersachsen* Ger.
131 E2 Burgeo Can.
117 B3 Burgersfort S. Africa
100 A2 Burgh-Haamstede Neth.
145 C2 Burgos Mex.
106 C1 Burgos Spain
111 C3 Burhaniye Turkey
74 B2 Burhanpur India
101 D1 Burhave (Butjadingen) Ger.
131 C2 Burin Can.
154 B2 Buriti Bravo Brazil
155 C1 Buritis Brazil
51 C3 Burketown Austr.
114 B3 Burkina *country* Africa
134 B2 Burley U.S.A.
136 C3 Burlington CO U.S.A.
137 E2 Burlington IA U.S.A.
143 E1 Burlington NC U.S.A.
141 E2 Burlington VT U.S.A.
Burma *country* Asia *see*
Myanmar
134 B2 Burney U.S.A.
51 D4 Burnie Austr.
98 B2 Burnley U.K.
134 C2 Burns U.S.A.
128 B2 Burns Lake Can.
70 A2 Burqin China
52 A2 Burra Austr.
97 B2 Burrel Albania
109 D2 Burren *reg.* Ireland
53 C2 Burrendong, Lake *resr* Austr.
53 C2 Burren Junction Austr.
107 C2 Burriana Spain
53 C2 Burrinjuck Reservoir Austr.
144 B2 Burro, Serranías del *mts* Mex.
111 C2 Bursa Turkey
116 B2 Bûr Safājah Egypt
Bûr Sa'îd Egypt *see* Port Said
130 C1 Burton, Lac *l.* Can.
99 C3 Burton upon Trent U.K.
59 C3 Buru *i.* Indon.
119 C3 Burundi *country* Africa
119 C3 Bururi Burundi
91 C1 Buryn' Ukr.
99 D2 Bury St Edmunds U.K.
118 C3 Busanga Dem. Rep. Congo
79 C2 Büsheher Iran
119 D3 Bushenyi Uganda
118 C3 Businga Dem. Rep. Congo
50 A3 Busselton Austr.
139 C3 Bustamante Mex.
64 A1 Busuanga Phil.
118 C2 Buta Dem. Rep. Congo
119 C3 Butare Rwanda
123 C3 Butha-Buthe Lesotho
140 D2 Butler U.S.A.

59 C3 Buton *i.* Indon.
134 C1 Butte U.S.A.
60 B1 Butterworth Malaysia
96 A1 Butt of Lewis *hd* U.K.
129 E2 Button Bay Can.
64 B2 Butuan Phil.
91 E1 Buturlinovka Rus. Fed.
75 C2 Butwal Nepal
101 D2 Butzbach Ger.
117 C4 Buulobarde Somalia
117 C5 Buur Gaabo Somalia
117 C4 Buurhabaka Somalia
76 C3 Buxoro Uzbek.
101 D1 Buxtehude Ger.
89 F2 Buy Rus. Fed.
87 D4 Buynaksk Rus. Fed.
111 C3 Büyükmenderes *r.* Turkey
110 C1 Buzău Romania
121 C2 Búzi Moz.
87 E3 Buzuluk Rus. Fed.
110 C2 Byala Bulg.
88 C3 Byalynichy Belarus
88 D3 Byarezina *r.* Belarus
88 B3 Byaroza Belarus
103 D1 Bydgoszcz Pol.
88 C3 Byerazino Belarus
88 C3 Byeshankovichy Belarus
89 D3 Bykhaw Belarus
127 F2 Bylot Island Can.
53 C2 Byrock Austr.
53 D1 Byron Bay Austr.
83 J2 Bytantay *r.* Rus. Fed.
103 D1 Bytom Pol.
103 D1 Bytów Pol.

C

154 B2 Caarapó Brazil
64 B1 Cabanatuan Phil.
117 C3 Cabdul Qaadir Somalia
106 B2 Cabeza del Buey Spain
152 B2 Cabezas Bol.
150 A1 Cabimas Venez.
120 A1 Cabinda Angola
118 B3 Cabinda *prov.* Angola
155 D2 Cabo Frio Brazil
155 D2 Cabo Frio, Ilha do *i.* Brazil
130 C2 Cabonga, Réservoir *resr* Can.
51 E2 Caboolture Austr.
150 A2 Cabo Pantoja Peru
144 A1 Caborca Mex.
131 D2 Cabot Strait Can.
155 D1 Cabral, Serra do *mts* Brazil
107 D2 Cabrera, Illa de *i.* Spain
106 B1 Cabrera, Sierra de *mts*
Spain
129 D2 Cabri Can.
107 C2 Cabriel *r.* Spain
152 C3 Caçador Brazil
109 D2 Čačak Serbia
108 A2 Caccia, Capo *c. Sardegna* Italy
151 C3 Cáceres Brazil
106 B2 Cáceres Spain
128 B2 Cache Creek Can.
114 A3 Cacheu Guinea-Bissau
151 C2 Cachimbo, Serra do *hills*
Brazil
154 B1 Cachoeira Alta Brazil
155 D2 Cachoeiro de Itapemirim
Brazil
114 A3 Cacine Guinea-Bissau
120 A2 Cacolo Angola
154 B1 Caçu Brazil
103 D2 Čadca Slovakia
101 D1 Cadenberge Ger.

145 B2 Cadereyta Mex.
140 B2 Cadillac U.S.A.
106 B2 Cádiz Spain
106 B2 Cádiz, Golfo de *g.* Spain
128 C2 Cadotte Lake Can.
104 B2 Caen France
98 A2 Caernarfon U.K.
98 A2 Caernarfon Bay U.K.
152 B3 Cafayate Arg.
64 B2 Cagayan de Oro Phil.
64 A2 Cagayan de Tawi-Tawi *i.* Phil.
108 B2 Cagli Italy
108 A3 Cagliari *Sardegna* Italy
108 A3 Cagliari, Golfo di *b. Sardegna*
Italy
76 B2 Çagyl Turkm.
97 B3 Caha Mountains *hills* Ireland
97 A3 Cahermore Ireland
97 C2 Cahir Ireland
97 A3 Cahirsiveen Ireland
97 C2 Cahore Point Ireland
104 C3 Cahors France
90 B2 Cahul Moldova
121 C2 Caia Moz.
151 C3 Caiabis, Serra dos *hills* Brazil
120 B2 Caianda Angola
154 B1 Caiapó, Serra do *mts* Brazil
154 B1 Caiapônia Brazil
147 C2 Caicos Islands Turks and
Caicos Is
96 C2 Cairngorm Mountains U.K.
98 A1 Cairnryan U.K.
51 D1 Cairns Austr.
116 B1 Cairo Egypt
98 C2 Caistor U.K.
120 A2 Caiundo Angola
150 A2 Cajamarca Peru
109 C1 Čakovec Croatia
123 C3 Cala S. Africa
150 B1 Calabozo Venez.
110 B2 Calafat Romania
153 A6 Calafate Arg.
107 C1 Calahorra Spain
104 C1 Calais France
141 F1 Calais U.S.A.
152 B3 Calama Chile
64 A1 Calamian Group *is* Phil.
107 C1 Calamocha Spain
120 A1 Calandula Angola
60 A1 Calang Indon.
110 C2 Calapan Romania
107 C1 Călărași Romania
64 B1 Calayan *i.* Phil.
64 B1 Calbayog Phil.
151 E2 Calcanhar, Ponta do *pt* Brazil
151 C1 Calçoene Brazil
Calcutta India *see* Kolkata
106 B2 Caldas da Rainha Port.
154 C1 Caldas Novas Brazil
152 A3 Caldera Chile
134 C2 Caldwell U.S.A.
123 C3 Caledon *r.* Lesotho/S. Africa
122 A3 Caledon S. Africa
153 B5 Caleta Olivia Arg.
98 A1 Calf of Man *i.* Isle of Man
128 C2 Calgary Can.
150 A1 Cali Col.
Calicut India *see* Kozhikode
135 D3 Caliente U.S.A.
135 B2 California *state* U.S.A.
144 A1 California, Gulf of Mex.
135 B3 California Aqueduct *canal*
U.S.A.
122 B3 Calitzdorp S. Africa
145 C2 Calkiní Mex.
52 B1 Callabonna, Lake *imp. l.* Austr.

Callander

96 B2 Callander U.K.
150 A3 Callao Peru
108 B3 Caltagirone *Sicilia* Italy
108 B3 Caltanissetta *Sicilia* Italy
120 A2 Caluquembe Angola
117 D3 Caluula Somalia
105 D3 Calvi *Corse* France
107 D2 Calvia Spain
144 B2 Calvillo Mex.
122 A3 Calvinia S. Africa
109 C2 Calvo, Monte *mt.* Italy
144 B2 Camacho Mex.
120 A2 Camacupa Angola
146 C2 Camagüey Cuba
150 A3 Camana Peru
154 B1 Camapuã Brazil
145 C2 Camargo Mex.
63 B3 Ca Mau Vietnam
63 B3 Ca Mau, Mui *c.* Vietnam
63 B2 Cambodia *country* Asia
99 A3 Camborne U.K.
105 C1 Cambrai France
99 B2 Cambrian Mountains *hills* U.K.
54 C1 Cambridge N.Z.
99 D2 Cambridge U.K.
141 E2 Cambridge MA U.S.A.
141 D3 Cambridge MD U.S.A.
137 E1 Cambridge MN U.S.A.
140 C2 Cambridge OH U.S.A.
131 D1 Cambrien, Lac *l.* Can.
53 D2 Camden Austr.
142 B2 Camden AR U.S.A.
141 F2 Camden ME U.S.A.
118 B2 Cameroon *country* Africa
118 B2 Cameroon Highlands *slope* Cameroon/Nigeria
151 D2 Cametá Brazil
64 B1 Camiguin *i.* Phil.
152 B3 Camiri Bol.
151 D2 Camocim Brazil
51 C1 Camooweal Austr.
63 A3 Camorta *i.* India
153 A5 Campana, Isla *i.* Chile
122 B3 Campbell S. Africa
54 C1 Campbell, Cape N.Z.
48 F6 Campbell Island N.Z.
128 B2 Campbell River Can.
140 B3 Campbellsville U.S.A.
131 D2 Campbellton Can.
96 B3 Campbeltown U.K.
145 C3 Campeche Mex.
145 C3 Campeche, Bahía de *g.* Mex.
52 B3 Camperdown Austr.
110 C1 Câmpina Romania
151 E2 Campina Grande Brazil
154 C2 Campinas Brazil
154 C1 Campina Verde Brazil
108 B2 Campobasso Italy
155 C2 Campo Belo Brazil
154 C1 Campo Florido Brazil
152 B3 Campo Gallo Arg.
154 B2 Campo Grande Brazil
151 D2 Campo Maior Brazil
106 C2 Campo Maior Port.
154 B2 Campo Mourão Brazil
155 D2 Campos Brazil
155 C1 Campos Altos Brazil
154 C2 Campos do Jordão Brazil
110 C1 Câmpulung Romania
138 A2 Camp Verde U.S.A.
128 C2 Camrose Can.
129 D2 Camsell Portage Can.
111 C2 Çan Turkey
126 F2 Canada *country* N. America
139 C1 Canadian U.S.A.
139 D1 Canadian *r.* U.S.A.

111 C2 Çanakkale Turkey
144 A1 Cananea Mex.
154 C2 Cananéia Brazil
Canarias, Islas *terr.* N. Atlantic Ocean *see* Canary Islands
114 A2 Canary Islands *terr.* N. Atlantic Ocean
155 C1 Canastra, Serra da *mts* Brazil
144 B2 Canatlán Mex.
143 D3 Canaveral, Cape U.S.A.
155 E1 Canavieiras Brazil
53 C2 Canberra Austr.
145 D2 Cancún Mex.
111 C3 Çandarlı Turkey
145 C3 Candelaria Mex.
129 D2 Candle Lake Can.
120 A2 Cangamba Angola
106 B1 Cangas del Narcea Spain
152 C4 Canguçu Brazil
70 B2 Cangzhou China
131 D1 Caniapiscau Can.
131 D1 Caniapiscau *r.* Can.
131 C1 Caniapiscau, Réservoir de *resr* Can.
108 B3 Canicattì *Sicilia* Italy
151 E2 Canindé Brazil
144 B2 Cañitas de Felipe Pescador Mex.
80 B3 Çankırı Turkey
128 C2 Canmore Can.
96 A2 Canna *i.* U.K.
105 D3 Cannes France
99 B3 Cannock U.K.
53 C3 Cann River Austr.
Cannanore India *see* Kannur
152 C3 Canoas Brazil
129 D2 Canoe Lake Can.
154 B3 Canoinhas Brazil
136 B3 Canon City U.S.A.
129 D2 Canora Can.
53 C2 Canowindra Austr.
106 C1 Cantábrica, Cordillera *mts* Spain
106 B1 Cantábrico, Mar *sea* Spain
99 D3 Canterbury U.K.
54 B2 Canterbury Bight *b.* N.Z.
54 B2 Canterbury Plains N.Z.
63 B2 Cân Thơ Vietnam
151 D2 Canto do Buriti Brazil
Canton China *see* Guangzhou
142 C2 Canton MS U.S.A.
140 C2 Canton OH U.S.A.
139 C1 Canyon U.S.A.
134 D1 Canyon Ferry Lake U.S.A.
62 B1 Cao Bằng Vietnam
154 C2 Capão Bonito Brazil
155 D2 Caparaó, Serra do *mts* Brazil
51 D4 Cape Barren Island Austr.
52 A3 Cape Borda Austr.
131 D2 Cape Breton Island Can.
114 B4 Cape Coast Ghana
141 E2 Cape Cod Bay U.S.A.
127 F2 Cape Dorset Can.
143 E2 Cape Fear *r.* U.S.A.
137 F3 Cape Girardeau U.S.A.
155 D1 Capelinha Brazil
100 B2 Capelle aan de IJssel Neth.
120 A1 Capenda-Camulemba Angola
122 A3 Cape Town S. Africa
112 C5 Cape Verde *country* N. Atlantic Ocean
51 D1 Cape York Peninsula Austr.
147 C3 Cap-Haïtien Haiti
151 D2 Capim *r.* Brazil
58 D1 Capitol Hill N. Mariana Is
109 C2 Čapljina Bos.-Herz.
109 B3 Capo d'Orlando *Sicilia* Italy

108 A2 Capraia, Isola di *i.* Italy
108 A2 Caprara, Punta *pt* Sardegna Italy
108 B2 Capri, Isola di *i.* Italy
120 B2 Caprivi Strip *reg.* Namibia
150 B2 Caquetá *r.* Col.
110 B2 Caracal Romania
150 B1 Caracas Venez.
151 D2 Caracol Brazil
155 C2 Caraguatatuba Brazil
153 A4 Carahue Chile
155 D1 Caraí Brazil
155 D2 Carangola Brazil
110 B1 Caransebeș Romania
131 D2 Caraquet Can.
146 B3 Caratasca, Laguna de *lag.* Hond.
155 D1 Caratinga Brazil
150 B2 Carauari Brazil
107 C2 Caravaca de la Cruz Spain
155 E1 Caravelas Brazil
129 E3 Carberry Can.
144 A2 Carbó Mex.
107 C2 Carbon, Cap *c.* Alg.
153 B5 Carbón, Laguna del *l.* Arg.
108 A3 Carbonara, Capo *c.* Sardegna Italy
136 B3 Carbondale CO U.S.A.
140 B3 Carbondale IL U.S.A.
131 E2 Carbonear Can.
155 D1 Carbonita Brazil
107 C2 Carcaixent Spain
104 C3 Carcassonne France
128 A1 Carcross Can.
145 C3 Cárdenas Mex.
99 B3 Cardiff U.K.
99 A2 Cardigan U.K.
99 A2 Cardigan Bay U.K.
128 C3 Cardston Can.
110 B1 Carei Romania
104 B2 Carentan France
50 B2 Carey, Lake *imp. l.* Austr.
155 D2 Cariacica Brazil
146 B3 Caribbean Sea N. Atlantic Ocean
141 F1 Caribou U.S.A.
130 B1 Caribou Lake Can.
128 C2 Caribou Mountains Can.
144 B2 Carichic Mex.
100 B3 Carignan France
53 C2 Carinda Austr.
107 C1 Cariñena Spain
130 C2 Carleton Place Can.
123 C2 Carletonville S. Africa
97 C1 Carlingford Lough *inlet* Ireland/U.K.
98 B1 Carlisle U.K.
141 D2 Carlisle U.S.A.
155 D1 Carlos Chagas Brazil
97 C2 Carlow Ireland
135 C4 Carlsbad CA U.S.A.
138 C2 Carlsbad NM U.S.A.
129 D3 Carlyle Can.
128 A1 Carmacks Can.
129 E3 Carman Can.
99 A3 Carmarthen U.K.
99 A3 Carmarthen Bay U.K.
104 C3 Carmaux France
145 C3 Carmelita Guat.
144 A2 Carmen, Isla *i.* Mex.
104 B2 Carnac France
122 B3 Carnarvon S. Africa
97 C1 Carndonagh Ireland
50 B2 Carnegie, Lake *imp. l.* Austr.
96 B2 Carn Eige *mt.* U.K.
63 A3 Car Nicobar *i.* India
118 B2 Carnot C.A.R.

52 A2 Carnot, Cape Austr.
97 C2 Carnsore Point Ireland
151 D2 Carolina Brazil
48 D2 Caroline Islands *is* N. Pacific Ocean
59 D2 Caroline Islands N. Pacific Ocean
103 D2 Carpathian Mountains Europe
Carpaţii Meridionali *mts* Romania *see* Transylvanian Alps
51 C1 Carpentaria, Gulf of Austr.
105 D3 Carpentras France
97 B3 Carrantuohill *mt.* Ireland
105 E3 Carrara Italy
97 B2 Carrickmacross Ireland
97 C2 Carrick-on-Shannon Ireland
97 C2 Carrick-on-Suir Ireland
137 D1 Carrington U.S.A.
139 D3 Carrizo Springs U.S.A.
138 B2 Carrizozo U.S.A.
137 E2 Carroll U.S.A.
143 C2 Carrollton U.S.A.
129 D2 Carson River Can.
135 C3 Carson City U.S.A.
106 A1 Cartagena Col.
107 C4 Cartagena Spain
136 B4 Cartago Costa Rica
137 E3 Carthage MO U.S.A.
139 D2 Carthage TX U.S.A.
131 E1 Cartwright Can.
114 B1 Casablanca Morocco
154 C2 Casa Branca Brazil
144 B2 Casa de Janos Mex.
138 A1 Casa Grande U.S.A.
108 A2 Casale Monferrato Italy
109 C2 Casarano Italy
134 C2 Cascade U.S.A.
134 B2 Cascade Range *mts* Can./U.S.A.
106 B1 Cascais Port.
154 C2 Cascavel Brazil
108 B2 Caserta Italy
97 C2 Cashel Ireland
53 D1 Casino Austr.
107 C1 Caspe Spain
136 B2 Casper U.S.A.
76 A2 Caspian Lowland Kazakh./Rus. Fed.
81 C1 Caspian Sea Asia/Europe
154 C2 Cássia Brazil
128 B2 Cassiar Can.
128 A2 Cassiar Mountains Can.
154 B1 Cassilândia Brazil
108 B2 Cassino Italy
96 B2 Cassley *r.* U.K.
152 B4 Castanhal Brazil
104 C3 Castaño *r.* Arg.
144 B2 Castaños Mex.
104 C3 Casteljaloux France
107 C2 Castellón de la Plana Spain
106 B2 Castelo Branco Port.
108 B3 Casterton Austr.
108 B2 Castiglione della Pescaia Italy
97 B2 Castlebar Ireland
96 A2 Castlebay U.K.
97 C1 Castleblayney Ireland
97 C1 Castlederg U.K.
96 C3 Castle Douglas U.K.
128 C3 Castlegar Can.
97 B2 Castleisland Ireland
52 B3 Castlemaine Austr.
97 B3 Castlerea Ireland
53 C2 Castlereagh *r.* Austr.
136 C3 Castle Rock U.S.A.

129 C2 Castor Can.
104 C3 Castres France
100 B1 Castricum Neth.
147 D3 Castries *St* Lucia
154 C2 Castro Brazil
153 A5 Castro Chile
106 B2 Castro Verde Port.
109 C3 Castrovillari Italy
150 A2 Catacaos Peru
155 C2 Cataguases Brazil
154 C1 Catalão Brazil
152 B3 Catamarca Arg.
64 C1 Catanduanes *i.* Phil.
154 C2 Catanduva Brazil
154 B3 Catanduvas Brazil
109 C3 Catania *Sicilia* Italy
109 C3 Catanzaro Italy
64 B1 Catarman Phil.
64 B1 Catbalogan Phil.
145 C3 Catemaco Mex.
147 C2 Cat Island Bahamas
130 A1 Cat Lake Can.
145 D2 Catoche, Cabo *c.* Mex.
141 E2 Catskill Mountains U.S.A.
64 B2 Cauayan Phil.
150 A1 Cauca *r.* Col.
151 E2 Caucaia Brazil
81 C1 Caucasus *mts* Asia/Europe
100 A2 Caudry France
109 C3 Caulonia Italy
131 D2 Causapscal Can.
105 D3 Cavaillon France
151 D3 Cavalcante Brazil
97 C2 Cavan Ireland
154 B3 Cavernoso, Serra do *mts* Brazil
151 D2 Caxias Brazil
152 C3 Caxias do Sul Brazil
120 A1 Caxito Angola
151 C1 Cayenne Fr. Guiana
146 B3 Cayman Islands *terr.* West Indies
117 C4 Caynabo Somalia
120 B2 Cazombo Angola
144 B2 Ceballos Mex.
64 B1 Cebu Phil.
64 B1 Cebu *i.* Phil.
108 B2 Cecina Italy
137 F2 Cedar *r.* U.S.A.
135 D3 Cedar City U.S.A.
137 E2 Cedar Falls U.S.A.
129 D2 Cedar Lake Can.
137 E2 Cedar Rapids U.S.A.
144 A2 Cedros, Isla *i.* Mex.
51 C3 Ceduna Austr.
117 C4 Ceeldheere Somalia
117 C3 Ceerigaabo Somalia
108 B3 Cefalù *Sicilia* Italy
145 B2 Celaya Mex.
58 C3 Celebes *i.* Indon.
156 B5 Celebes Sea Indon./Phil.
145 C2 Celestún Mex.
101 E1 Celle Ger.
95 B3 Celtic Sea Ireland/U.K.
59 D3 Cenderawasih, Teluk *b.* Indon.
150 A1 Central, Cordillera *mts* Col.
150 A3 Central, Cordillera *mts* Peru
64 B1 Central, Cordillera *mts* Phil.
118 C2 Central African Republic country Africa
74 A2 Central Brahui Range *mts* Pak.
137 D2 Central City U.S.A.
140 B3 Centralia *IL* U.S.A.
134 B1 Centralia *WA* U.S.A.
74 A2 Central Makran Range *mts* Pak.

59 D3 Central Range *mts* P.N.G.
89 E3 Central Russian Upland *hills* Rus. Fed.
83 I2 Central Siberian Plateau Rus. Fed.
111 B3 Cephalonia *i.* Greece
Ceram Sea Indon. *see* Seram, Laut
152 B3 Ceres Arg.
154 C1 Ceres Brazil
122 A3 Ceres S. Africa
104 C3 Céret France
106 C1 Cerezo de Abajo Spain
109 C2 Cerignola Italy
110 C2 Cernavodă Romania
145 C2 Cerralvo Mex.
144 B2 Cerralvo, Isla *i.* Mex.
145 B2 Cerritos Mex.
154 C2 Cerro Azul Brazil
145 C2 Cerro Azul Mex.
150 A3 Cerro de Pasco Peru
105 D3 Cervione *Corse* France
106 B1 Cervo Spain
108 B2 Cesena Italy
88 C2 Cēsis Latvia
102 C2 České Budějovice Czech Rep.
101 F3 Český les *mts* Czech Rep.
111 C3 Çeşme Turkey
53 D2 Cessnock Austr.
109 C2 Cetinje Montenegro
109 C3 Cetraro Italy
106 B2 Ceuta N. Africa
105 C3 Cévennes *mts* France
Ceylon *country* Asia *see* Sri Lanka
79 D2 Chābahār Iran
75 C1 Chabyêr Caka *salt l.* China
150 A2 Chachapoyas Peru
89 D3 Chachersk Belarus
63 B2 Chachoengsao Thai.
115 D3 Chad *country* Africa
115 D3 Chad, Lake Africa
69 C1 Chadaasan Mongolia
68 C1 Chadan Rus. Fed.
123 C1 Chadibe Botswana
136 C2 Chadron U.S.A.
65 B2 Chaeryŏng N. Korea
74 A2 Chagai Pak.
77 C3 Chaghcharān Afgh.
89 E2 Chagoda Rus. Fed.
75 C2 Chaibasa India
63 B2 Chainat Thai.
63 B2 Chaiyaphum Thai.
152 C4 Chajari Arg.
131 D1 Chakonipau, Lac *l.* Can.
150 A3 Chala Peru
74 A1 Chalap Dalan *mts* Afgh.
131 D2 Chaleur Bay *inlet* Can.
74 B2 Chalisgaon India
111 C3 Chalki *i.* Greece
111 B3 Chalkida Greece
104 B2 Challans France
134 D2 Challis U.S.A.
105 C2 Châlons-en-Champagne France
105 C2 Chalon-sur-Saône France
138 B3 Chama U.S.A.
121 C2 Chama Zambia
74 A1 Chaman Pak.
74 B1 Chamba India
74 B2 Chamba *r.* India
137 D2 Chamberlain U.S.A.
141 D3 Chambersburg U.S.A.
105 D2 Chambéry France
121 C2 Chambeshi Zambia
140 B2 Champaign U.S.A.
141 E2 Champlain, Lake Can./U.S.A.

145	C3	**Champotón** Mex.
152	A3	**Chañaral** Chile
126	B2	**Chandalar** r. U.S.A.
142	C3	**Chandeleur Islands** U.S.A.
74	B1	**Chandigarh** India
138	A2	**Chandler** U.S.A.
75	B3	**Chandrapur** India
63	B2	**Chang, Ko** i. Thai.
		Chang'an China see **Rong'an**
		Yangtze
121	C2	**Changane** r. Moz.
121	C2	**Changara** Moz.
65	B1	**Changbai** China
65	B1	**Changbai Shan** mts China/
		N. Korea
69	E2	**Changchun** China
71	B3	**Changde** China
65	B2	**Ch'angdo** N. Korea
71	C3	**Changhua** Taiwan
65	B3	**Changhŭng** S. Korea
		Chang Jiang r. China see
		Yangtze
65	B1	**Changjin** N. Korea
65	B1	**Changjin-gang** r. N. Korea
71	B3	**Changsha** China
65	B2	**Changsŏng** S. Korea
71	B3	**Changting** China
65	B2	**Ch'angwŏn** S. Korea
70	B2	**Changyuan** China
70	B2	**Changzhi** China
70	B2	**Changzhou** China
111	B3	**Chania** Greece
95	C4	**Channel Islands** English
		Chan.
135	C4	**Channel Islands** U.S.A.
131	E2	**Channel-Port-aux-Basques**
		Can.
63	B2	**Chanthaburi** Thai.
104	C2	**Chantilly** France
137	D3	**Chanute** U.S.A.
82	G3	**Chany, Ozero** salt l. Rus. Fed.
71	B3	**Chaoyang** China
		Chaoyang China see
		Huinan
71	B3	**Chaozhou** China
144	B2	**Chapala, Laguna de** l. Mex.
76	B1	**Chapayevo** Kazakh.
152	C3	**Chapecó** Brazil
143	E1	**Chapel Hill** U.S.A.
130	B2	**Chapleau** Can.
89	E2	**Chaplygin** Rus. Fed.
91	C2	**Chaplynka** Ukr.
145	B2	**Charcas** Mex.
99	B3	**Chard** U.K.
104	B2	**Charente** r. France
77	C3	**Chārīkār** Afgh.
86	E2	**Charkayuvom** Rus. Fed.
100	B2	**Charleroi** Belgium
141	D3	**Charles, Cape** U.S.A.
137	E2	**Charles City** U.S.A.
140	B3	**Charleston** IL U.S.A.
143	E2	**Charleston** SC U.S.A.
140	C3	**Charleston** WV U.S.A.
135	C3	**Charleston Peak** U.S.A.
51	D2	**Charleville** Austr.
105	C2	**Charleville-Mézières** France
143	D1	**Charlotte** U.S.A.
143	D3	**Charlotte Harbor** b. U.S.A.
141	D3	**Charlottesville** U.S.A.
131	D2	**Charlottetown** Can.
52	B3	**Charlton** Austr.
130	C1	**Charlton Island** Can.
51	D2	**Charters Towers** Austr.
104	C2	**Chartres** France
128	C2	**Chase** Can.
88	C3	**Chashniki** Belarus
54	A3	**Chaslands Mistake** c. N.Z.
65	B1	**Chasŏng** N. Korea
104	B2	**Chassiron, Pointe de** pt
		France
104	B2	**Châteaubriant** France
104	C2	**Château-du-Loir** France
104	C2	**Châteaudun** France
104	B2	**Châteaulin** France
105	D3	**Châteauneuf-les-Martigues**
		France
104	C2	**Châteauneuf-sur-Loire** France
105	C2	**Château-Thierry** France
128	C2	**Chateh** Can.
100	B2	**Châtelet** Belgium
104	C2	**Châtellerault** France
140	C2	**Chatham** Ont. Can.
49	G5	**Chatham Islands** is N.Z.
105	C2	**Châtillon-sur-Seine** France
143	D2	**Chattahoochee** r. U.S.A.
143	C1	**Chattanooga** U.S.A.
63	B2	**Châu Đốc** Vietnam
62	A1	**Chauk** Myanmar
105	D2	**Chaumont** France
151	D2	**Chauny** France
106	B1	**Chaves** Brazil
106	B1	**Chaves** Port.
130	C1	**Chavigny, Lac** l. Can.
89	D3	**Chavusy** Belarus
89	E2	**Chayevo** Rus. Fed.
86	E3	**Chaykovskiy** Rus. Fed.
102	C1	**Cheb** Czech Rep.
87	D3	**Cheboksary** Rus. Fed.
140	C1	**Cheboygan** U.S.A.
65	B2	**Chech'ŏn** S. Korea
114	B2	**Chegga** Maur.
134	B1	**Chehalis** U.S.A.
65	B3	**Cheju** S. Korea
65	B3	**Cheju-do** i. S. Korea
65	B3	**Cheju-haehyŏp** sea chan.
		S. Korea
89	E2	**Chekhov** Rus. Fed.
134	B1	**Chelan, Lake** U.S.A.
103	E1	**Chełm** Pol.
99	D3	**Chelmer** r. U.K.
103	D1	**Chełmno** Pol.
99	D3	**Chelmsford** U.K.
99	B3	**Cheltenham** U.K.
87	F3	**Chelyabinsk** Rus. Fed.
101	F2	**Chemnitz** Ger.
114	B2	**Chenachane** Alg.
70	B1	**Chengde** China
70	A2	**Chengdu** China
71	B4	**Chengmai** China
		Chengshou China see
		Yingshan
70	A2	**Chengxian** China
		Chengyang China see **Juxian**
73	C3	**Chennai** India
71	B3	**Chenzhou** China
99	B3	**Chepstow** U.K.
104	B2	**Cherbourg** France
89	E3	**Cheremisinovo** Rus. Fed.
69	C1	**Cheremkhovo** Rus. Fed.
89	E2	**Cherepovets** Rus. Fed.
91	C2	**Cherkasy** Ukr.
87	D4	**Cherkessk** Rus. Fed.
91	C1	**Chernihiv** Ukr.
91	D2	**Cherninivka** Ukr.
90	B2	**Chernivtsi** Ukr.
91	B1	**Chernyakhiv** Ukr.
88	B3	**Chernyakhovsk** Rus. Fed.
89	E3	**Chernyanka** Rus. Fed.
83	I2	**Chernyshevskiy** Rus. Fed.
137	D2	**Cherokee** U.S.A.
83	K2	**Cherskogo, Khrebet** mts
		Rus. Fed.
91	E2	**Chertkovo** Rus. Fed.
90	A1	**Chervonohrad** Ukr.
88	C3	**Chervyen'** Belarus
89	D3	**Cherykaw** Belarus
141	D3	**Chesapeake Bay** U.S.A.
86	D2	**Cheshskaya Guba** b. Rus. Fed.
98	B2	**Chester** U.K.
140	B3	**Chester** IL U.S.A.
143	D2	**Chester** SC U.S.A.
98	C2	**Chesterfield** U.K.
129	E1	**Chesterfield Inlet** Can.
129	E1	**Chesterfield Inlet** Can.
141	F1	**Chesuncook Lake** U.S.A.
131	D2	**Chéticamp** Can.
145	D3	**Chetumal** Mex.
128	B2	**Chetwynd** Can.
98	B1	**Cheviot Hills** U.K.
136	C2	**Cheyenne** U.S.A.
136	C2	**Cheyenne** r. U.S.A.
136	C3	**Cheyenne Wells** U.S.A.
75	C2	**Chhapra** India
75	B2	**Chhatarpur** India
71	C3	**Chiai** Taiwan
62	A2	**Chiang Dao** Thai.
62	A2	**Chiang Mai** Thai.
62	A2	**Chiang Rai** Thai.
108	A1	**Chiavenna** Italy
70	B3	**Chibi** China
121	C3	**Chiboma** Moz.
130	C2	**Chibougamau** Can.
123	D1	**Chibuto** Moz.
140	B2	**Chicago** U.S.A.
128	A2	**Chichagof Island** U.S.A.
99	C3	**Chichester** U.K.
50	A2	**Chichester Range** mts Austr.
139	D1	**Chickasha** U.S.A.
150	A2	**Chiclayo** Peru
153	B5	**Chico** r. Arg.
135	B3	**Chico** U.S.A.
131	C2	**Chicoutimi** Can.
108	B2	**Chieti** Italy
145	C3	**Chietla** Mex.
69	D2	**Chifeng** China
155	D1	**Chifre, Serra do** mts Brazil
77	D2	**Chiganak** Kazakh.
145	C3	**Chignahuapán** Mex.
121	C3	**Chigubo** Moz.
144	B2	**Chihuahua** Mex.
88	C2	**Chikhachevo** Rus. Fed.
67	C3	**Chikuma-gawa** r. Japan
128	B2	**Chilanko** r. Can.
74	B1	**Chilas** Pak.
139	C2	**Childress** U.S.A.
153	A4	**Chile** country S. America
152	B3	**Chilecito** Arg.
75	C3	**Chilika Lake** India
121	B2	**Chililabombwe** Zambia
128	B2	**Chilko** r. Can.
128	B2	**Chilko Lake** Can.
153	A4	**Chillán** Chile
137	E3	**Chillicothe** MO U.S.A.
140	C3	**Chillicothe** OH U.S.A.
128	B3	**Chilliwack** Can.
153	A5	**Chiloé, Isla de** i. Chile
145	C3	**Chilpancingo** Mex.
53	C3	**Chiltern** Austr.
71	C3	**Chilung** Taiwan
119	D3	**Chimala** Tanz.
152	B4	**Chimbas** Arg.
150	A2	**Chimborazo** mt. Ecuador
150	A2	**Chimbote** Peru
87	E4	**Chimboy** Uzbek.
		Chimkent Kazakh. see
		Shymkent
121	C2	**Chimoio** Moz.
77	C3	**Chimtargha, Qullai** mt. Tajik.
68	C2	**China** country Asia
145	C2	**China** Mex.
150	A3	**Chincha Alta** Peru
128	C2	**Chinchaga** r. Can.

145	D3	Chinchorro, Banco Mex.
121	C2	Chinde Moz.
65	B3	Chindo S. Korea
65	B3	Chin-do i. S. Korea
68	C2	Chindu China
62	A1	Chindwin r. Myanmar
65	B2	Chinghwa N. Korea
120	B2	Chingola Zambia
120	A2	Chinguar Angola
65	B2	Chinhae S. Korea
121	C2	Chinhoyi Zimbabwe
74	B1	Chiniot Pak.
144	B2	Chinipas Mex.
65	B2	Chinju S. Korea
118	C2	Chinko r. C.A.R.
138	B1	Chinle U.S.A.
71	B3	Chinmen Taiwan
67	C3	Chino Japan
104	C2	Chinon France
138	A2	Chino Valley U.S.A.
120	B2	Chinsali Zambia
108	B1	Chioggia Italy
111	C3	Chios Greece
111	C3	Chios i. Greece
120	A2	Chipindo Angola
121	C3	Chipinge Zimbabwe
73	B3	Chiplun India
99	B3	Chippenham U.K.
99	C3	Chipping Norton U.K.
77	C2	Chirchiq Uzbek.
121	C3	Chiredzi Zimbabwe
138	B2	Chiricahua Peak U.S.A.
146	B4	Chiriquí, Golfo de b. Panama
65	B2	Chiri-san mt. S. Korea
146	B4	Chirripó mt. Costa Rica
121	B2	Chirundu Zimbabwe
130	C1	Chisasibi Can.
137	E1	Chisholm U.S.A.
90	B2	Chişinău Moldova
87	E3	Chistopol' Rus. Fed.
69	D1	Chita Rus. Fed.
120	A2	Chitado Angola
121	C2	Chitambo Zambia
120	B1	Chitato Angola
121	C1	Chitipa Malawi
73	B3	Chitradurga India
74	B1	Chitral Pak.
146	B4	Chitré Panama
75	D2	Chittagong Bangl.
74	B2	Chittaurgarh India
121	C3	Chitungwiza Zimbabwe
120	B2	Chiume Angola
121	C2	Chivhu Zimbabwe
70	C1	Chizhou China
114	C1	Chlef Alg.
107	D2	Chlef, Oued r. Alg.
153	B4	Choele Choel Arg.
144	B2	Choix Mex.
103	D1	Chojnice Pol.
117	B3	Ch'ok'ē Mountains Eth.
83	K2	Chokurdakh Rus. Fed.
121	C3	Chókwé Moz.
102	C1	Cholet France
102	C1	Chomutov Czech Rep.
83	I2	Chona r. Rus. Fed.
150	A2	Chone Ecuador
65	B2	Ch'ŏnan S. Korea
65	B2	Ch'ŏngjin N. Korea
65	B2	Ch'ŏngju S. Korea
65	B2	Chŏngp'yŏng N. Korea
70	A3	Chongqing China
70	A2	Chongqing mun. China
71	A3	Chongzuo China
65	B2	Chŏnju S. Korea
153	A5	Chonos, Archipiélago de los is Chile

154	B3	Chopimzinho Brazil
111	B3	Chora Sfakion Greece
98	B2	Chorley U.K.
91	C2	Chornomors'ke Ukr.
90	B2	Chortkiv Ukr.
65	B2	Ch'ŏrwŏn S. Korea
65	B1	Ch'osan N. Korea
67	D3	Chōshi Japan
103	D1	Choszczno Pol.
114	A2	Choûm Maur.
69	D1	Choybalsan Mongolia
69	D1	Choyr Mongolia
54	B2	Christchurch N.Z.
99	C3	Christchurch U.K.
127	G2	Christian, Cape Can.
123	C2	Christiana S. Africa
54	A2	Christina, Mount N.Z.
153	B5	Chubut r. Arg.
90	B1	Chudniv Ukr.
89	D2	Chudovo Rus. Fed.
		Chudskoye Ozero l. Estonia/Rus. Fed. see Peipus, Lake
126	B3	Chugach Mountains U.S.A.
67	B4	Chūgoku-sanchi mts Japan
66	B2	Chuguyevka Rus. Fed.
91	D2	Chuhuyiv Ukr.
160	J3	Chukchi Sea Rus. Fed./U.S.A.
83	N2	Chukotskiy Poluostrov pen. Rus. Fed.
135	C4	Chula Vista U.S.A.
82	G3	Chulym Rus. Fed.
152	B3	Chumbicha Arg.
83	K3	Chumikan Rus. Fed.
63	A2	Chumphon Thai.
65	B2	Ch'unch'ŏn S. Korea
		Chungking China see Chongqing
83	H2	Chunya r. Rus. Fed.
150	A3	Chuquibamba Peru
152	B3	Chuquicamata Chile
105	D2	Chur Switz.
62	A1	Churachandpur India
129	E2	Churchill Can.
129	E2	Churchill r. Man. Can.
131	D1	Churchill r. Nfld. and Lab. Can.
129	E2	Churchill, Cape Can.
131	D1	Churchill Falls Can.
129	D2	Churchill Lake Can.
74	B2	Churu India
131	C2	Chute-des-Passes Can.
62	B1	Chuxiong China
90	B2	Ciadîr-Lunga Moldova
61	B2	Ciamis Indon.
60	B2	Cianjur Indon.
154	B2	Cianorte Brazil
103	E1	Ciechanów Pol.
146	C2	Ciego de Ávila Cuba
146	B2	Cienfuegos Cuba
107	C2	Cieza Spain
106	C2	Cigüela r. Spain
80	B2	Cihanbeyli Turkey
144	B3	Cihuatlán Mex.
106	C2	Cíjara, Embalse de resr Spain
61	B2	Cilacap Indon.
139	C1	Cimarron r. U.S.A.
90	B2	Cimişlia Moldova
108	B2	Cimone, Monte mt. Italy
140	C3	Cincinnati U.S.A.
111	C3	Çine Turkey
100	B2	Ciney Belgium
145	C3	Cintalapa Mex.
71	B3	Ciping China
126	B2	Circle AK U.S.A.
136	B1	Circle MT U.S.A.
58	B3	Cirebon Indon.

99	C3	Cirencester U.K.
108	A1	Ciriè Italy
109	C3	Cirò Marina Italy
109	C2	Čitluk Bos.-Herz.
122	A3	Citrusdal S. Africa
145	B2	Ciudad Acuña Mex.
145	B3	Ciudad Altamirano Mex.
150	B1	Ciudad Bolívar Venez.
144	B2	Ciudad Camargo Mex.
144	A2	Ciudad Constitución Mex.
145	C3	Ciudad del Carmen Mex.
144	B2	Ciudad Delicias Mex.
145	C2	Ciudad de Valles Mex.
150	B1	Ciudad Guayana Venez.
138	B3	Ciudad Guerrero Mex.
144	B3	Ciudad Guzmán Mex.
145	C3	Ciudad Hidalgo Mex.
145	C3	Ciudad Ixtepec Mex.
144	B1	Ciudad Juárez Mex.
145	C2	Ciudad Mante Mex.
145	C2	Ciudad Mier Mex.
144	B2	Ciudad Obregón Mex.
106	C2	Ciudad Real Spain
145	C2	Ciudad Río Bravo Mex.
106	B1	Ciudad Rodrigo Spain
145	C2	Ciudad Victoria Mex.
107	D1	Ciutadella Spain
111	C3	Civan Dağ mt. Turkey
108	B1	Cividale del Friuli Italy
108	B2	Civitanova Marche Italy
108	B2	Civitavecchia Italy
104	C2	Civray France
111	C3	Çivril Turkey
70	C2	Cixi China
99	D3	Clacton-on-Sea U.K.
128	C2	Claire, Lake Can.
105	C2	Clamecy France
122	A3	Clanwilliam S. Africa
52	A2	Clare Austr.
97	A2	Clare Island Ireland
141	E2	Claremont U.S.A.
97	B2	Claremorris Ireland
54	B2	Clarence N.Z.
131	E2	Clarenville Can.
128	C2	Claresholm Can.
137	D2	Clarinda U.S.A.
123	C3	Clarkebury S. Africa
134	C1	Clark Fork r. U.S.A.
143	D2	Clark Hill Reservoir U.S.A.
140	C3	Clarksburg U.S.A.
142	B2	Clarksdale U.S.A.
142	B1	Clarksville AR U.S.A.
142	C1	Clarksville TN U.S.A.
154	B1	Claro r. Brazil
139	C1	Clayton U.S.A.
97	B3	Clear, Cape Ireland
137	E2	Clear Lake U.S.A.
135	B3	Clear Lake U.S.A.
128	C2	Clearwater Can.
129	C2	Clearwater r. Can.
143	D3	Clearwater U.S.A.
134	C1	Clearwater r. U.S.A.
139	D2	Cleburne U.S.A.
51	D2	Clermont Austr.
105	C2	Clermont-Ferrand France
52	A2	Cleve Austr.
142	B2	Cleveland MS U.S.A.
140	C2	Cleveland OH U.S.A.
143	D1	Cleveland TN U.S.A.
134	D1	Cleveland, Mount U.S.A.
143	D3	Clewiston U.S.A.
97	A2	Clifden Ireland
53	D1	Clifton Austr.
138	B2	Clifton U.S.A.
128	B2	Clinton Can.
137	E2	Clinton IA U.S.A.
137	E3	Clinton MO U.S.A.

139 D1 Clinton *OK* U.S.A.
96 A2 Clisham *h.* U.K.
98 B2 Clitheroe U.K.
97 B3 Clonakilty Ireland
51 D2 Cloncurry Austr.
97 C1 Clones Ireland
97 C2 Clonmel Ireland
100 D1 Cloppenburg Ger.
136 B2 Cloud Peak U.S.A.
139 C2 Clovis U.S.A.
129 D2 Cluff Lake Mine Can.
110 B1 Cluj-Napoca Romania
51 C2 Cluny Austr.
105 D2 Cluses France
54 A3 Clutha *r.* N.Z.
96 A3 Clyde *r.* U.K.
96 B3 Clyde, Firth of *est.* U.K.
96 B3 Clydebank U.K.
127 G2 Clyde River Can.
144 B3 Coalcomán Mex.
135 C3 Coaldale U.S.A.
128 B2 Coal River Can.
150 B2 Coari Brazil
150 B2 Coari *r.* Brazil
142 B2 Coastal Plain U.S.A.
128 B2 Coast Mountains Can.
135 B2 Coast Ranges *mts* U.S.A.
96 B3 Coatbridge U.K.
127 F2 Coats Island Can.
55 R2 Coats Land *reg.* Antarctica
145 C3 Coatzacoalcos Mex.
146 A3 Cobán Guat.
53 C2 Cobar Austr.
97 B3 Cobh Ireland
152 B2 Cobija Bol.
141 D2 Cobourg Can.
50 C1 Cobourg Peninsula Austr.
53 C3 Cobram Austr.
101 E2 Coburg Ger.
152 B2 Cochabamba Bol.
100 C2 Cochem Ger.
Cochin India *see* Kochi
128 C2 Cochrane *Alta* Can.
130 B2 Cochrane *Ont.* Can.
153 A5 Cochrane Chile
52 B2 Cockburn Austr.
Cockburn Town Turks and Caicos Is *see* Grand Turk
98 B1 Cockermouth U.K.
122 B3 Cockscomb *mt.* S. Africa
146 B3 Coco *r.* Hond./Nic.
144 B3 Cocula Mex.
150 A1 Cocuy, Sierra Nevada del *mt.* Col.
141 E2 Cod, Cape U.S.A.
108 B2 Codigoro Italy
131 D1 Cod Island Can.
151 D2 Codó Brazil
136 B2 Cody U.S.A.
51 D1 Coen Austr.
100 C2 Coesfeld Ger.
134 C1 Coeur d'Alene U.S.A.
123 C3 Coffee Bay S. Africa
137 D3 Coffeyville U.S.A.
53 D2 Coffs Harbour Austr.
104 B2 Cognac France
118 A2 Cogo Equat. Guinea
52 B3 Cohuna Austr.
146 B4 Coiba, Isla de *i.* Panama
153 A5 Coihaique Chile
73 B3 Coimbatore India
106 B1 Coimbra Port.
53 C3 Colac Austr.
155 D1 Colatina Brazil
136 C3 Colby U.S.A.
99 D3 Colchester U.K.
129 C2 Cold Lake Can.

96 C3 Coldstream U.K.
139 D2 Coleman U.S.A.
52 B3 Coleraine Austr.
97 C1 Coleraine U.K.
123 C2 Colesberg S. Africa
144 B3 Colima Mex.
144 B3 Colima, Nevado de *vol.* Mex.
96 A2 Coll *i.* U.K.
53 C1 Collarenebri Austr.
50 B1 Collier Bay Austr.
54 B2 Collingwood N.Z.
97 B1 Collooney Ireland
105 D2 Colmar France
100 C2 Cologne Ger.
154 C2 Colômbia Brazil
150 A1 Colombia *country* S. America
73 B4 Colombo Sri Lanka
104 C3 Colomiers France
152 C4 Colón Arg.
146 C4 Colón Panama
109 C3 Colonna, Capo *c.* Italy
96 A2 Colonsay *i.* U.K.
153 B4 Colorado *r.* Arg.
138 A2 Colorado *r.* Mex./U.S.A.
139 D3 Colorado *r.* U.S.A.
136 B3 Colorado *state* U.S.A.
135 E3 Colorado Plateau U.S.A.
136 C3 Colorado Springs U.S.A.
144 B2 Colotlán Mex.
136 B1 Colstrip U.S.A.
137 E3 Columbia *MO* U.S.A.
143 D2 Columbia *SC* U.S.A.
142 C1 Columbia *TN* U.S.A.
134 B1 Columbia *r.* U.S.A.
128 C2 Columbia, Mount Can.
134 D1 Columbia Falls U.S.A.
128 B2 Columbia Mountains Can.
134 C1 Columbia Plateau U.S.A.
143 D2 Columbus *GA* U.S.A.
140 B3 Columbus *IN* U.S.A.
142 C2 Columbus *MS* U.S.A.
137 D2 Columbus *NE* U.S.A.
138 B2 Columbus *NM* U.S.A.
140 C3 Columbus *OH* U.S.A.
134 C1 Colville U.S.A.
126 A2 Colville *r.* U.S.A.
128 B2 Colville Lake Can.
98 B2 Colwyn Bay U.K.
108 B2 Comacchio Italy
145 C3 Comalcalco Mex.
110 C1 Comănești Romania
130 C1 Comencho, Lac *l.* Can.
97 C2 Comeragh Mountains *hills* Ireland
75 D2 Comilla Bangl.
108 A2 Comino, Capo *c. Sardegna* Italy
145 C3 Comitán de Domínguez Mex.
104 C2 Commentry France
139 D2 Commerce U.S.A.
127 F2 Committee Bay Can.
108 A1 Como Italy
153 B5 Comodoro Rivadavia Arg.
121 D2 Comoros *country* Africa
104 C2 Compiègne France
144 B2 Compostela Mex.
90 B2 Comrat Moldova
114 A4 Conakry Guinea
155 E1 Conceição da Barra Brazil
151 D2 Conceição do Araguaia Brazil
155 D1 Conceição do Mato Dentro Brazil
152 B3 Concepción Arg.
153 A4 Concepción Chile
144 B2 Concepción Mex.
135 B4 Conception, Point U.S.A.
154 C2 Conchas Brazil

138 C1 Conchas Lake U.S.A.
144 B2 Conchos *r. Chihuahua* Mex.
145 C2 Conchos *r. Nuevo León/Tamaulipas* Mex.
135 B3 Concord *CA* U.S.A.
141 E2 Concord *NH* U.S.A.
152 C4 Concordia Arg.
122 A2 Concordia S. Africa
137 D3 Concordia U.S.A.
53 C2 Condobolin Austr.
104 C3 Condom France
134 B1 Condon U.S.A.
108 B1 Conegliano Italy
104 C2 Confolens France
75 C2 Congdü China
118 B3 Congo *country* Africa
118 B3 Congo *r.* Congo/Dem. Rep. Congo
118 C3 Congo, Democratic Republic of the *country* Africa
129 C2 Conklin Can.
97 B1 Conn, Lough *l.* Ireland
97 B2 Connaught *reg.* Ireland
141 E2 Connecticut *r.* U.S.A.
141 E2 Connecticut *state* U.S.A.
97 B2 Connemara *reg.* Ireland
134 D1 Conrad U.S.A.
139 D2 Conroe U.S.A.
155 D2 Conselheiro Lafaiete Brazil
155 D1 Conselheiro Pena Brazil
98 C1 Consett U.K.
63 B3 Côn Sơn, Đao *i.* Vietnam
110 C2 Constanţa Romania
106 B2 Constantina Spain
115 C1 Constantine Alg.
134 D2 Contact U.S.A.
150 A2 Contamana Peru
153 A6 Contreras, Isla *i.* Chile
126 D2 Contwoyto Lake Can.
142 B1 Conway *AR* U.S.A.
141 E2 Conway *NH* U.S.A.
51 C2 Coober Pedy Austr.
Cook, Mount *mt.* N.Z. *see* Aoraki
143 C1 Cookeville U.S.A.
49 H4 Cook Islands S. Pacific Ocean
131 E1 Cook's Harbour Can.
97 C1 Cookstown U.K.
54 B2 Cook Strait N.Z.
51 D1 Cooktown Austr.
53 C2 Coolabah Austr.
53 C2 Coolamon Austr.
53 D1 Coolangatta Austr.
50 B3 Coolgardie Austr.
53 C3 Cooma Austr.
52 B2 Coombah Austr.
53 C2 Coonabarabran Austr.
52 A3 Coonalpyn Austr.
53 C2 Coonamble Austr.
52 A1 Cooper Creek *watercourse* Austr.
53 D2 Coos Bay U.S.A.
53 C2 Cootamundra Austr.
145 C3 Copainalá Mex.
145 C3 Copala Mex.
93 F4 Copenhagen Denmark
109 C2 Copertino Italy
152 A3 Copiapó Chile
140 B1 Copper Harbor U.S.A.
Coppermine Can. *see* Kugluktuk
126 D2 Coppermine *r.* Can.
122 B2 Copperton S. Africa
152 A3 Coquimbo Chile
110 B2 Corabia Romania
155 D1 Coração de Jesus Brazil
150 A3 Coracora Peru

53 D1 Coraki Austr.
50 A2 Coral Bay Austr.
127 F2 Coral Harbour Can.
156 D7 Coral Sea S. Pacific Ocean
48 D4 Coral Sea Islands Territory Austr.
52 B3 Corangamite, Lake Austr.
99 C2 Corby U.K.
153 A5 Corcovado, Golfo de sea chan. Chile
143 D2 Cordele U.S.A.
64 B1 Cordilleras Range mts Phil.
152 B4 Córdoba Arg.
145 C3 Córdoba Mex.
106 C2 Córdoba Spain
153 B4 Córdoba, Sierras de mts Arg.
111 A3 Corfu i. Greece
106 B2 Coria Spain
111 B3 Corinth Greece
142 C2 Corinth U.S.A.
155 D1 Corinto Brazil
97 B3 Cork Ireland
111 C2 Çorlu Turkey
154 B2 Cornélio Procópio Brazil
131 E2 Corner Brook Can.
53 C3 Corner Inlet b. Austr.
135 B3 Corning CA U.S.A.
141 D2 Corning NY U.S.A.
Corn Islands is Nic. see Maíz, Islas del
108 B2 Corno, Monte mt. Italy
130 C2 Cornwall Can.
126 E1 Cornwallis Island Can.
150 B1 Coro Venez.
154 C1 Coromandel Brazil
54 C1 Coromandel Peninsula N.Z.
129 C2 Coronation Can.
126 D2 Coronation Gulf Can.
152 C3 Coronel Oviedo Para.
53 B4 Coronel Suárez Arg.
109 D3 Çorovodë Albania
137 D3 Corpus Christi U.S.A.
152 B2 Corque Bol.
151 D3 Corrente Brazil
154 B1 Correntes Brazil
151 D3 Correntina Brazil
97 B2 Corrib, Lough l. Ireland
152 C3 Corrientes Arg.
144 D2 Corrientes, Cabo c. Mex.
53 C3 Corryong Austr.
Corse i. France see Corsica
105 D3 Corse, Cap c. Corse France
105 D3 Corsica i. France
139 D2 Corsicana U.S.A.
105 D3 Corte Corse France
106 B3 Cortegana Spain
136 B3 Cortez U.S.A.
108 B1 Cortina d'Ampezzo Italy
141 D2 Cortland U.S.A.
108 B2 Cortona Italy
106 B2 Coruche Port.
Çoruh Turkey see Artvin
80 B1 Çorum Turkey
152 C2 Corumbá Brazil
154 B1 Corumbá r. Brazil
134 B2 Corvallis U.S.A.
98 B2 Corwen U.K.
144 B2 Cosalá Mex.
145 C3 Cosamaloapan Mex.
108 B2 Cosenza Italy
105 C2 Cosne-Cours-sur-Loire France
107 C2 Costa Blanca coastal area Spain
107 D1 Costa Brava coastal area Spain
106 B2 Costa del Sol coastal area Spain

146 B3 Costa de Mosquitos coastal area Nic.
154 B1 Costa Rica Brazil
146 B3 Costa Rica country Central America
144 B2 Costa Rica Mex.
110 B2 Costeşti Romania
64 B2 Cotabato Phil.
114 B4 Côte d'Ivoire country Africa
150 A2 Cotopaxi, Volcán vol. Ecuador
99 B3 Cotswold Hills U.K.
134 B2 Cottage Grove U.S.A.
102 C1 Cottbus Ger.
104 B2 Coubre, Pointe de la pt France
52 A3 Couedic, Cape du Austr.
137 D2 Council Bluffs U.S.A.
88 B2 Courland Lagoon b. Lith./ Rus. Fed.
128 B3 Courtenay Can.
104 B2 Coutances France
104 B2 Coutras France
100 B2 Couvin Belgium
99 C2 Coventry U.K.
140 C3 Covington U.S.A.
50 B3 Cowan, Lake imp. l. Austr.
96 C2 Cowdenbeath U.K.
53 C3 Cowes Austr.
134 B1 Cowlitz r. U.S.A.
53 C2 Cowra Austr.
154 B1 Coxim Brazil
75 D2 Cox's Bazar Bangl.
145 B3 Coyuca de Benitez Mex.
145 C2 Cozumel Mex.
145 D2 Cozumel, Isla de i. Mex.
123 C3 Cradock S. Africa
136 B2 Craig U.S.A.
102 C2 Crailsheim Ger.
110 B2 Craiova Romania
129 D2 Cranberry Portage Can.
53 C3 Cranbourne Austr.
128 C3 Cranbrook Can.
151 D2 Crateús Brazil
151 E2 Crato Brazil
136 C2 Crawford U.S.A.
140 B2 Crawfordsville U.S.A.
99 C3 Crawley U.K.
134 D1 Crazy Mountains U.S.A.
129 D2 Cree r. Can.
144 B2 Creel Mex.
129 D2 Cree Lake Can.
100 B1 Creil Neth.
105 D2 Crema Italy
108 B1 Cremona Italy
108 B2 Cres i. Croatia
134 B2 Crescent City U.S.A.
128 C3 Creston Can.
137 E2 Creston U.S.A.
142 C2 Crestview U.S.A.
111 B3 Crete i. Greece
107 D1 Creus, Cap de c. Spain
98 B2 Crewe U.K.
96 B2 Crianlarich U.K.
152 D3 Criciúma Brazil
96 C2 Crieff U.K.
108 B1 Crikvenica Croatia
91 C2 Crimea pen. Ukr.
101 F2 Crimmitschau Ger.
154 C1 Cristalina Brazil
101 E1 Crivitz Ger.
Crna Gora country Europe see Montenegro
109 D2 Crni Vrh h. Serbia
109 C1 Črnomelj Slovenia
97 B2 Croagh Patrick h. Ireland
109 C1 Croatia country Europe
61 C1 Crocker, Banjaran mts Malaysia

139 D2 Crockett U.S.A.
59 C3 Croker Island Austr.
99 D2 Cromer U.K.
54 A3 Cromwell N.Z.
137 D1 Crookston U.S.A.
53 C2 Crookwell Austr.
136 C1 Crosby U.S.A.
143 D3 Cross City U.S.A.
142 B2 Crossett U.S.A.
98 B1 Cross Fell h. U.K.
129 E2 Cross Lake Can.
143 C1 Crossville U.S.A.
108 B3 Crotone Italy
99 D3 Crowborough U.K.
142 B2 Crowley U.S.A.
128 C3 Crowsnest Pass Can.
146 C3 Cruz, Cabo c. Cuba
152 C3 Cruz Alta Brazil
152 B4 Cruz del Eje Arg.
155 D2 Cruzeiro Brazil
150 A2 Cruzeiro do Sul Brazil
52 A2 Crystal Brook Austr.
139 D3 Crystal City U.S.A.
140 B1 Crystal Falls U.S.A.
103 E2 Csongrád Hungary
120 B2 Cuando r. Angola/Zambia
120 A2 Cuangar Angola
118 B3 Cuango r. Angola/Dem. Rep. Congo
120 A1 Cuanza r. Angola
139 C3 Cuatro Ciénegas Mex.
144 B2 Cuauhtémoc Mex.
145 C3 Cuautla Mex.
146 B2 Cuba country West Indies
120 A2 Cubal Angola
120 B2 Cubango r. Angola/Namibia
150 A1 Cúcuta Col.
73 B3 Cuddalore India
73 B3 Cuddapah India
106 C1 Cuéllar Spain
120 A2 Cuemba Angola
150 A2 Cuenca Ecuador
107 C1 Cuenca Spain
107 C1 Cuenca, Serranía de mts Spain
145 C3 Cuernavaca Mex.
139 D3 Cuero U.S.A.
151 C3 Cuiabá Brazil
151 C3 Cuiabá r. Brazil
96 A2 Cuillin Sound sea chan. U.K.
120 A1 Cuilo Angola
120 B2 Cuito r. Angola
120 A2 Cuito Cuanavale Angola
60 B1 Cukai Malaysia
53 C3 Culcairn Austr.
53 C1 Culgoa r. Austr.
144 B2 Culiacán Mex.
64 A1 Culion i. Phil.
107 C2 Cullera Spain
142 C2 Cullman U.S.A.
97 C1 Cullybackey U.K.
151 C3 Culuene r. Brazil
150 B1 Cumaná Venez.
141 D3 Cumberland U.S.A.
140 B3 Cumberland r. U.S.A.
129 D2 Cumberland Lake Can.
127 G2 Cumberland Peninsula Can.
142 C1 Cumberland Plateau U.S.A.
127 G2 Cumberland Sound sea chan. Can.
96 C3 Cumbernauld U.K.
135 B3 Cummings U.S.A.
96 B3 Cumnock U.K.
144 B1 Cumpas Mex.
145 C3 Cunduacán Mex.
120 A2 Cunene r. Angola
108 A2 Cuneo Italy
53 C1 Cunnamulla Austr.

Cuorgnè

108 A1 **Cuorgnè** Italy
96 C2 **Cupar** U.K.
147 D3 **Curaçao** i. Neth. Antilles
150 A2 **Curaray** r. Ecuador
153 A4 **Curicó** Chile
154 C3 **Curitiba** Brazil
52 A2 **Curnamona** Austr.
51 D3 **Currie** Austr.
51 E2 **Curtis Island** Austr.
151 C2 **Curuá** r. Brazil
60 B2 **Curup** Indon.
151 D2 **Cururupu** Brazil
155 D1 **Curvelo** Brazil
150 A3 **Cusco** Peru
139 D1 **Cushing** U.S.A.
134 D1 **Cut Bank** U.S.A.
75 C2 **Cuttack** India
101 D1 **Cuxhaven** Ger.
64 B1 **Cuyo Islands** Phil.
　　Cuzco Peru see **Cusco**
119 C3 **Cyangugu** Rwanda
111 B3 **Cyclades** is Greece
129 C3 **Cypress Hills** Can.
80 B2 **Cyprus** country Asia
102 C2 **Czech Republic** country
　　Europe
103 D1 **Czersk** Pol.
103 D1 **Częstochowa** Pol.

D

　　Đa, Sông r. Vietnam see
　　Black River
69 D2 **Daban** China
114 A3 **Dabola** Guinea
　　Dacca Bangl. see **Dhaka**
102 C2 **Dachau** Ger.
74 A2 **Dadu** Pak.
64 B1 **Daet** Phil.
114 A3 **Dagana** Senegal
64 B1 **Dagupan** Phil.
74 B3 **Dahanu** India
69 D2 **Da Hinggan Ling** mts China
116 C3 **Dahlak Archipelago** is Eritrea
100 C2 **Dahlem** Ger.
78 B3 **Dahm, Ramlat** des. Saudi
　　Arabia/Yemen
60 B2 **Daik** Indon.
106 C2 **Daimiel** Spain
51 C2 **Dajarra** Austr.
114 A3 **Dakar** Senegal
116 A2 **Dākhilah, Wāḥāt ad** oasis
　　Egypt
　　Dakhla Oasis Egypt see
　　Dākhilah, Wāḥāt ad
63 A3 **Dakoank** India
88 C3 **Dakol'ka** r. Belarus
　　Đakovica Kosovo see **Gjakovë**
109 C1 **Đakovo** Croatia
120 B2 **Dala** Angola
68 C2 **Dalain Hob** China
93 G3 **Dalälven** r. Sweden
111 C3 **Dalaman** Turkey
111 C3 **Dalaman** r. Turkey
69 C2 **Dalandzadgad** Mongolia
63 B2 **Đa Lat** Vietnam
74 A2 **Dalbandin** Pak.
96 C3 **Dalbeattie** U.K.
51 E2 **Dalby** Austr.
143 C1 **Dale Hollow Lake** U.S.A.
53 C3 **Dalgety** Austr.
139 C1 **Dalhart** U.S.A.
131 D2 **Dalhousie** Can.
62 B1 **Dali** China
70 C2 **Dalian** China

96 C3 **Dalkeith** U.K.
139 D2 **Dallas** U.S.A.
128 A2 **Dall Island** U.S.A.
109 C2 **Dalmatia** reg. Bos.-Herz./
　　Croatia
66 C2 **Dal'negorsk** Rus. Fed.
66 B1 **Dal'nerechensk** Rus. Fed.
114 B4 **Daloa** Côte d'Ivoire
51 D2 **Dalrymple, Mount** Austr.
92 A3 **Dalsmynni** Iceland
75 C2 **Daltenganj** India
143 D2 **Dalton** U.S.A.
60 B1 **Daludalu** Indon.
92 B2 **Dalvík** Iceland
50 C1 **Daly** r. Austr.
51 C1 **Daly Waters** Austr.
74 B2 **Daman** India
80 B2 **Damanhūr** Egypt
59 C3 **Damar** i. Indon.
80 B2 **Damascus** Syria
115 D3 **Damaturu** Nigeria
76 B3 **Damāvand, Qolleh-ye** mt. Iran
81 D2 **Damghan** Iran
79 C2 **Dammam** Saudi Arabia
101 D1 **Damme** Ger.
75 C2 **Damoh** India
114 B4 **Damongo** Ghana
59 C3 **Dampir, Selat** sea chan. Indon.
75 D1 **Damxung** China
114 B4 **Danané** Côte d'Ivoire
63 B2 **Đa Năng** Vietnam
141 E2 **Danbury** U.S.A.
65 A1 **Dandong** China
146 B3 **Dangriga** Belize
70 B2 **Dangshan** China
89 F2 **Danilov** Rus. Fed.
89 E3 **Danilovskaya Vozvyshennost'**
　　hills Rus. Fed.
70 B2 **Danjiangkou** China
89 E3 **Dankov** Rus. Fed.
146 B3 **Danlí** Hond.
101 E1 **Dannenberg (Elbe)** Ger.
54 C2 **Dannevirke** N.Z.
62 B2 **Dan Sai** Thai.
　　Dantu China see **Zhenjiang**
110 A1 **Danube** r. Europe
110 C1 **Danube Delta** Romania/Ukr.
140 B2 **Danville** IL U.S.A.
140 C3 **Danville** KY U.S.A.
141 D3 **Danville** VA U.S.A.
71 A4 **Danxian** China
71 B3 **Daoxian** China
114 C3 **Dapaong** Togo
64 B2 **Dapitan** Phil.
68 C2 **Da Qaidam Zhen** China
69 E1 **Daqing** China
80 B2 **Dar'ā** Syria
79 C2 **Dārāb** Iran
115 D1 **Daraj** Libya
81 D3 **Daran** Iran
69 D1 **Darhan** Mongolia
150 A1 **Darién, Golfo del** g. Col.
75 C2 **Darjiling** India
62 C2 **Darlag** China
52 B2 **Darling** r. Austr.
53 C1 **Darling Downs** hills Austr.
50 A3 **Darling Range** hills Austr.
98 C1 **Darlington** U.K.
53 C2 **Darlington Point** Austr.
103 D1 **Darłowo** Pol.
101 D3 **Darmstadt** Ger.

115 E1 **Darnah** Libya
52 B2 **Darnick** Austr.
107 C1 **Daroca** Spain
99 D3 **Dartford** U.K.
99 A3 **Dartmoor** hills U.K.
131 D2 **Dartmouth** Can.
99 B3 **Dartmouth** U.K.
59 D3 **Daru** P.N.G.
50 C1 **Darwin** Austr.
74 A2 **Dasht** r. Pak.
76 B2 **Daşoguz** Turkm.
61 C1 **Datadian** Indon.
111 C3 **Datça** Turkey
70 B1 **Datong** China
64 B2 **Datu Piang** Phil.
74 B1 **Daud Khel** Pak.
88 B2 **Daugava** r. Latvia
88 C2 **Daugavpils** Latvia
100 C2 **Daun** Ger.
129 D2 **Dauphin** Can.
129 E2 **Dauphin Lake** Can.
73 B3 **Davangere** India
64 B2 **Davao** Phil.
64 B2 **Davao Gulf** Phil.
137 E2 **Davenport** U.S.A.
99 C2 **Daventry** U.K.
123 C2 **Daveyton** S. Africa
146 B4 **David** Panama
129 D2 **Davidson** Can.
126 E3 **Davidson Lake** Can.
135 B3 **Davis** U.S.A.
131 D1 **Davis Inlet (abandoned)** Can
159 F3 **Davis Sea** Antarctica
160 P3 **Davis Strait** Can./Greenland
105 D2 **Davos** Switz.
78 A2 **Dawmat al Jandal** Saudi
　　Arabia
79 C3 **Dawqah** Oman
126 B2 **Dawson** r. Austr.
143 D2 **Dawson** U.S.A.
128 B2 **Dawson Creek** Can.
128 B2 **Dawsons Landing** Can.
68 C2 **Dawu** China
　　Dawukou China see
　　Shizuishan
104 B3 **Dax** France
62 B1 **Da Xueshan** mts China
80 C2 **Dayr az Zawr** Syria
140 C3 **Dayton** U.S.A.
143 D3 **Daytona Beach** U.S.A.
70 A2 **Dazhou** China
122 B3 **De Aar** S. Africa
80 B2 **Dead Sea** salt l. Asia
71 B3 **De'an** China
152 B4 **Deán Funes** Arg.
128 B2 **Dease Lake** Can.
126 D2 **Dease Strait** Can.
135 C3 **Death Valley** depr. U.S.A.
104 C2 **Deauville** France
61 C1 **Debak** Sarawak Malaysia
109 D2 **Debar** Macedonia
117 B3 **Debre Birhan** Eth.
117 B3 **Debrecen** Hungary
117 B3 **Debre Markos** Eth.
117 B3 **Debre Tabor** Eth.
117 B4 **Debre Zeyit** Eth.
142 C2 **Decatur** AL U.S.A.
140 B3 **Decatur** IL U.S.A.
73 B3 **Deccan** plat. India
102 C1 **Děčín** Czech Rep.
137 E2 **Decorah** U.S.A.
88 C2 **Dedovichi** Rus. Fed.
121 C2 **Dedza** Malawi
98 B2 **Dee** r. England/Wales U.K.
96 C2 **Dee** r. Scotland U.K.
53 D1 **Deepwater** Austr.
131 E2 **Deer Lake** Can.
134 D1 **Deer Lodge** U.S.A.

40 C2 **Defiance** U.S.A.
68 C2 **Dêgê** China
47 C2 **Degeh Bur** Eth.
02 C2 **Deggendorf** Ger.
91 E2 **Degtevo** Rus. Fed.
75 C2 **Dehra Dun** India
75 C2 **Dehri** India
69 E2 **Dehui** China
00 A2 **Deinze** Belgium
40 B1 **Dej** Romania
40 B2 **De Kalb** U.S.A.
78 A3 **Dekemhare** Eritrea
18 C3 **Dekese** Dem. Rep. Congo
35 C3 **Delano** U.S.A.
35 D3 **Delano Peak** U.S.A.
74 A1 **Delārām** Afgh.
23 C2 **Delareyville** S. Africa
29 D2 **Delaronde Lake** Can.
41 C2 **Delaware** U.S.A.
41 D2 **Delaware** r. U.S.A.
41 D3 **Delaware** state U.S.A.
41 D3 **Delaware Bay** U.S.A.
53 C3 **Delegate** Austr.
53 D2 **Delémont** Switz.
00 B1 **Delft** Neth.
00 C1 **Delfzijl** Neth.
21 D2 **Delgado, Cabo** c. Moz.
69 C1 **Delgerhaan** Mongolia
75 B2 **Delhi** India
26 C2 **Déline** Can.
12 F2 **Delitzsch** Ger.
07 D2 **Dellys** Alg.
01 D1 **Delmenhorst** Ger.
09 B1 **Delnice** Croatia
83 L1 **De-Longa, Ostrova** is Rus. Fed.
29 D3 **Deloraine** Can.
11 B3 **Delphi** tourist site Greece
39 C3 **Del Rio** U.S.A.
36 B3 **Delta** CO U.S.A.
35 D3 **Delta** UT U.S.A.
26 C2 **Delta Junction** U.S.A.
09 D2 **Delvinë** Albania
06 C1 **Demanda, Sierra de la** mts Spain
18 C3 **Demba** Dem. Rep. Congo
17 B4 **Dembi Dolo** Eth.
89 D2 **Demidov** Rus. Fed.
38 B2 **Deming** U.S.A.
13 C3 **Demirci** Turkey
11 C2 **Demirköy** Turkey
02 C1 **Demmin** Ger.
24 C2 **Demopolis** U.S.A.
60 B2 **Dempo, Gunung** vol. Indon.
89 D2 **Demyansk** Rus. Fed.
22 B3 **De Naawte** S. Africa
17 C3 **Denakil** reg. Africa
00 B1 **Den Burg** Neth.
00 B2 **Dendermonde** Belgium
70 B1 **Dengkou** China
70 B2 **Dengzhou** China
Den Haag Neth. see **The Hague**
50 A2 **Denham** Austr.
00 B1 **Den Helder** Neth.
52 B3 **Deniliquin** Austr.
34 C2 **Denio** U.S.A.
37 D2 **Denison** IA U.S.A.
39 D2 **Denison** TX U.S.A.
11 C3 **Denizli** Turkey
53 D2 **Denman** Austr.
50 A3 **Denmark** Austr.
93 E4 **Denmark** country Europe
60 Q2 **Denmark Strait** Greenland/Iceland
61 C2 **Denpasar** Indon.

139 D2 **Denton** U.S.A.
50 A3 **D'Entrecasteaux, Point** Austr.
136 B3 **Denver** U.S.A.
75 C2 **Deogarh** Orissa India
74 B2 **Deogarh** Rajasthan India
75 C2 **Deoghar** India
83 K2 **Deputatskiy** Rus. Fed.
68 C3 **Dêqên** China
142 B2 **De Queen** U.S.A.
74 A2 **Dera Bugti** Pak.
74 B1 **Dera Ghazi Khan** Pak.
74 B1 **Dera Ismail Khan** Pak.
87 D4 **Derbent** Rus. Fed.
50 B1 **Derby** Austr.
99 C2 **Derby** U.K.
99 D2 **Dereham** U.K.
97 B2 **Derg, Lough** l. Ireland
91 D1 **Derhachi** Ukr.
142 B2 **De Ridder** U.S.A.
91 D2 **Derkul** r. Rus. Fed./Ukr.
75 B1 **Dêrub** China
116 B3 **Derudeb** Sudan
122 B3 **De Rust** S. Africa
109 C2 **Derventa** Bos.-Herz.
98 C2 **Derwent** r. U.K.
98 B1 **Derwent Water** l. U.K.
77 C1 **Derzhavinsk** Kazakh.
152 B2 **Desaguadero** r. Bol.
129 D2 **Deschambault Lake** Can.
134 B1 **Deschutes** r. U.S.A.
117 B3 **Desē** Eth.
153 B5 **Deseado** Arg.
153 B5 **Deseado** r. Arg.
137 E2 **Des Moines** U.S.A.
137 E2 **Des Moines** r. U.S.A.
91 C1 **Desna** r. Rus. Fed./Ukr.
89 D3 **Desnogorsk** Rus. Fed.
101 F2 **Dessau** Ger.
126 B2 **Destruction Bay** Can.
149 C3 **Desventuradas, Islas** is S. Pacific Ocean
128 C1 **Detah** Can.
101 D2 **Detmold** Ger.
140 C2 **Detroit** U.S.A.
137 D1 **Detroit Lakes** U.S.A.
100 B2 **Deurne** Neth.
110 B1 **Deva** Romania
100 C1 **Deventer** Neth.
96 C2 **Deveron** r. U.K.
103 D2 **Devét Skal** h. Czech Rep.
137 D1 **Devil's Lake** U.S.A.
128 A2 **Devil's Paw** mt. U.S.A.
99 C3 **Devizes** U.K.
74 B2 **Devli** India
110 C2 **Devnya** Bulg.
128 C2 **Devon** Can.
126 E1 **Devon Island** Can.
51 D4 **Devonport** Austr.
74 B2 **Dewas** India
137 F3 **Dexter** U.S.A.
70 A2 **Deyang** China
59 D3 **Deyong, Tanjung** pt Indon.
81 C2 **Dezful** Iran
70 B2 **Dezhou** China
79 C2 **Dhahran** Saudi Arabia
75 D2 **Dhaka** Bangl.
78 B3 **Dhamār** Yemen
75 C2 **Dhamtari** India
75 C2 **Dhanbad** India
75 C2 **Dhankuta** Nepal
62 A1 **Dharmanagar** India
75 C2 **Dharmjaygarh** India
73 B3 **Dharwad** India
74 B2 **Dhasa** India
78 B3 **Dhubāb** Yemen
74 B2 **Dhule** India
144 A1 **Diablo, Picacho del** mt. Mex.

51 C2 **Diamantina** watercourse Austr.
155 D1 **Diamantina** Brazil
151 D3 **Diamantina, Chapada** plat. Brazil
151 C3 **Diamantino** Brazil
71 B3 **Dianbai** China
155 D2 **Dianópolis** Brazil
114 B4 **Dianra** Côte d'Ivoire
114 C3 **Diapaga** Burkina
79 C2 **Dibā al Ḥiṣn** U.A.E.
118 C3 **Dibaya** Dem. Rep. Congo
62 A1 **Dibrugarh** India
136 C1 **Dickinson** U.S.A.
142 C1 **Dickson** U.S.A.
Dicle r. Turkey see **Tigris**
105 D3 **Die** France
129 D2 **Diefenbaker, Lake** Can.
114 B3 **Diéma** Mali
62 B2 **Diên Châu** Vietnam
101 D1 **Diepholz** Ger.
104 C2 **Dieppe** France
115 D3 **Diffa** Niger
131 D2 **Digby** Can.
105 D3 **Digne-les-Bains** France
105 C2 **Digoin** France
64 B2 **Digos** Phil.
59 D3 **Digul** r. Indon.
Dihang r. China/India see **Yarlung Zangbo**
Dihang r. China/India see **Brahmaputra**
105 D2 **Dijon** France
117 C3 **Dikhil** Djibouti
111 C3 **Dikili** Turkey
100 A2 **Diksmuide** Belgium
115 D3 **Dikwa** Nigeria
117 B4 **Dīla** Eth.
59 C3 **Dili** East Timor
101 D2 **Dillenburg** Ger.
134 D1 **Dillon** U.S.A.
118 C4 **Dilolo** Dem. Rep. Congo
62 A1 **Dimapur** India
Dimashq Syria see **Damascus**
52 B3 **Dimboola** Austr.
110 C2 **Dimitrovgrad** Bulg.
87 D3 **Dimitrovgrad** Rus. Fed.
64 B1 **Dinagat** i. Phil.
104 B2 **Dinan** France
100 B2 **Dinant** Belgium
111 D3 **Dinar** Turkey
81 D2 **Dinār, Kūh-e** mt. Iran
73 B3 **Dindigul** India
123 D1 **Dindiza** Moz.
101 E2 **Dingelstädt** Ger.
97 A2 **Dingle Bay** Ireland
96 B2 **Dingwall** U.K.
70 A2 **Dingxi** China
75 C2 **Dinngyê** China
154 B3 **Dionisio Cerqueira** Brazil
114 A3 **Diourbel** Senegal
74 B1 **Dir** Pak.
51 D1 **Direction, Cape** Austr.
117 C4 **Dirē Dawa** Eth.
120 B2 **Dirico** Angola
50 A2 **Dirk Hartog Island** Austr.
53 C1 **Dirranbandi** Austr.
78 B3 **Dirs** Saudi Arabia
50 B2 **Disappointment, Lake** imp. l. Austr.
52 B3 **Discovery Bay** Austr.
143 E1 **Dismal Swamp** U.S.A.
99 D2 **Diss** U.K.
108 B3 **Dittaino** r. Sicilia Italy
74 B2 **Diu** India
155 D2 **Divinópolis** Brazil
87 D4 **Divnoye** Rus. Fed.
114 B4 **Divo** Côte d'Ivoire

80 B2 Divriği Turkey
140 B2 Dixon U.S.A.
128 A2 Dixon Entrance *sea chan.* Can./U.S.A.
80 C2 Diyarbakır Turkey
74 A2 Diz Pak.
115 D2 Djado Niger
115 D2 Djado, Plateau du Niger
118 B3 Djambala Congo
115 C2 Djanet Alg.
115 C1 Djelfa Alg.
119 C2 Djéma C.A.R.
114 B3 Djenné Mali
114 B3 Djibo Burkina
117 C3 Djibouti *country* Africa
117 C3 Djibouti Djibouti
114 C4 Djougou Benin
92 C3 Djúpivogur Iceland
91 E1 Dmitriyevka Rus. Fed.
89 E3 Dmitriyev-L'govskiy Rus. Fed.
89 E2 Dmitrov Rus. Fed.
Dnepr *r. Ukr. see* Dnieper
91 C2 Dnieper *r.* Ukr.
90 B2 Dniester *r.* Ukr.
Dnipro *r. Ukr. see* Dnieper
91 C2 Dniprodzerzhyns'k Ukr.
91 D2 Dnipropetrovs'k Ukr.
91 C2 Dniprorudne Ukr.
Dnister *r. Ukr. see* Dniester
88 C2 Dno Rus. Fed.
115 D4 Doba Chad
88 B2 Dobele Latvia
101 F2 Döbeln Ger.
59 C3 Doberai, Jazirah *pen.* Indon.
59 C3 Dobo Indon.
109 C2 Doboj Bos.-Herz.
110 C2 Dobrich Bulg.
89 F3 Dobrinka Rus. Fed.
89 E3 Dobroye Rus. Fed.
89 D3 Dobrush Belarus
155 E1 Doce *r.* Brazil
145 B2 Doctor Arroyo Mex.
144 B2 Doctor Belisario Domínguez Mex.
111 C3 Dodecanese *is* Greece
Dodekanisos *is* Greece *see* Dodecanese
136 C3 Dodge City U.S.A.
119 D3 Dodoma Tanz.
100 C2 Doetinchem Neth.
59 C3 Dofa Indon.
75 C1 Dogai Coring *salt l.* China
128 B2 Dog Creek Can.
67 B3 Dōgo *i.* Japan
115 C3 Dogondoutchi Niger
81 C2 Doğubeyazıt Turkey
79 C2 Doha Qatar
62 A2 Doi Saket Thai.
100 B1 Dokkum Neth.
88 C3 Dokshytsy Belarus
91 D2 Dokuchayevs'k Ukr.
131 C2 Dolbeau-Mistassini Can.
104 B2 Dol-de-Bretagne France
105 D2 Dole France
99 B2 Dolgellau U.K.
89 E3 Dolgorukovo Rus. Fed.
89 E3 Dolgoye Rus. Fed.
Dolisie Congo *see* Loubomo
59 D3 Dolok, Pulau *i.* Indon.
108 B1 Dolomites *mts* Italy
117 C4 Dolo Odo Eth.
126 D2 Dolphin and Union Strait Can.
90 A2 Dolyna Ukr.
102 C2 Domažlice Czech Rep.
93 E3 Dombås Norway
103 D2 Dombóvár Hungary

128 B2 Dome Creek Can.
147 D3 Dominica *country* West Indies
147 C3 Dominican Republic *country* West Indies
89 E2 Domodedovo Rus. Fed.
111 B3 Domokos Greece
61 C2 Dompu Indon.
89 E3 Don *r.* Rus. Fed.
96 C2 Don *r.* U.K.
97 D1 Donaghadee U.K.
52 B3 Donald Austr.
Donau *r. Austria/Ger. see* Danube
102 C2 Donauwörth Ger.
106 B2 Don Benito Spain
98 C2 Doncaster U.K.
120 A1 Dondo Angola
121 C2 Dondo Moz.
73 C4 Dondra Head Sri Lanka
97 B1 Donegal Ireland
97 B1 Donegal Bay Ireland
91 D2 Donets'k Ukr.
91 D2 Donets'kyy Kryazh *hills* Rus. Fed./Ukr.
50 A2 Dongara Austr.
62 B1 Dongchuan China
71 A4 Dongfang China
66 B1 Dongfanghong China
58 B3 Donggala Indon.
65 A2 Donggang China
71 B3 Dongguan China
62 B2 Đông Ha Vietnam
Dong Hai *sea N. Pacific Ocean see* East China Sea
62 B2 Đông Hơi Vietnam
118 B2 Dongou Congo
71 B3 Dongshan China
70 C2 Dongtai China
71 B3 Dongting Hu *l.* China
Dongxing Qi China *see* Uliastai
70 B2 Dongying China
54 B1 Donnellys Crossing N.Z.
107 C1 Donostia-San Sebastián Spain
117 C4 Dooxo Nugaaleed *val.* Somalia
99 D3 Dorchester U.K.
122 A1 Dordabis Namibia
104 B2 Dordogne *r.* France
100 B2 Dordrecht Neth.
123 C3 Dordrecht S. Africa
129 D2 Doré Lake Can.
101 D1 Dorfmark Ger.
114 B3 Dori Burkina
122 A3 Doring *r.* S. Africa
96 B2 Dornoch U.K.
96 B2 Dornoch Firth *est.* U.K.
89 D3 Dorogobuzh Rus. Fed.
90 B2 Dorohoi Romania
68 C1 Döröö Nuur *salt l.* Mongolia
92 G3 Dorotea Sweden
50 A2 Dorre Island Austr.
53 D2 Dorrigo Austr.
100 C2 Dortmund Ger.
100 C2 Dortmund-Ems-Kanal *canal* Ger.
153 B5 Dos Bahías, Cabo *c.* Arg.
101 F1 Dosse *r.* Ger.
114 C3 Dosso Niger
143 C2 Dothan U.S.A.
101 D1 Dötlingen Ger.
105 C1 Douai France
118 A2 Douala Cameroon
104 B2 Douarnenez France
114 B3 Douentza Mali
98 A1 Douglas Isle of Man
122 B2 Douglas S. Africa
128 A2 Douglas AK U.S.A.

138 B2 Douglas AZ U.S.A.
143 D2 Douglas GA U.S.A.
136 B2 Douglas WY U.S.A.
104 C1 Doullens France
154 B1 Dourada, Serra *hills* Brazil
154 B2 Dourados Brazil
154 B2 Dourados, Serra dos *hills* Brazil
106 B1 Douro *r.* Port.
99 D3 Dover U.K.
141 D3 Dover U.S.A.
95 D3 Dover, Strait of France/U.K.
141 F1 Dover-Foxcroft U.S.A.
79 C2 Dowlatābād *Būshehr* Iran
79 C2 Dowlatābād *Kermān* Iran
97 D1 Downpatrick U.K.
77 C3 Dowshī Afgh.
67 B3 Dōzen *is* Japan
130 C2 Dozois, Réservoir *resr* Can.
114 B2 Drâa, Hamada du *plat.* Alg.
154 B2 Dracena Brazil
100 C1 Drachten Neth.
110 B2 Drăgănești-Olt Romania
110 B2 Drăgășani Romania
88 C3 Drahichyn Belarus
123 C2 Drakensberg *mts* Lesotho/ S. Africa
123 C2 Drakensberg *mts* S. Africa
158 B8 Drake Passage S. Atlantic Ocean
111 B2 Drama Greece
93 F4 Drammen Norway
109 C1 Drava *r.* Europe
128 C2 Drayton Valley Can.
101 D2 Dreieich Ger.
102 C1 Dresden Ger.
104 C2 Dreux France
100 B1 Driemond Neth.
109 C2 Drina *r.* Bos.-Herz./Serbia
109 C2 Drniš Croatia
110 B2 Drobeta-Turnu Severin Romania
101 D1 Drochtersen Ger.
97 C2 Drogheda Ireland
90 A2 Drohobych Ukr.
97 C1 Dromore U.K.
74 B1 Drosh Pak.
53 C3 Drouin Austr.
128 C2 Drumheller Can.
140 C1 Drummond Island U.S.A.
131 C2 Drummondville Can.
88 B3 Druskininkai Lith.
91 D2 Druzhkivka Ukr.
88 D2 Druzhnaya Gorka Rus. Fed.
130 A2 Dryden Can.
50 B1 Drysdale *r.* Austr.
78 A2 Duba Saudi Arabia
79 C2 Dubai U.A.E.
129 D1 Dubawnt Lake Can.
78 A2 Dubayy U.A.E. *see* Dubai
78 A2 Dubbagh, Jabal ad *mt.* Saudi Arabia
53 C2 Dubbo Austr.
97 C2 Dublin Ireland
143 D2 Dublin U.S.A.
90 B1 Dubno Ukr.
141 D2 Du Bois U.S.A.
114 A4 Dubréka Guinea
109 C2 Dubrovnik Croatia
90 B1 Dubrovytsya Ukr.
89 D3 Dubrowna Belarus
137 E2 Dubuque U.S.A.
129 D2 Duck Bay Can.
101 E2 Duderstadt Ger.
82 G2 Dudinka Rus. Fed.
99 B2 Dudley U.K.
106 B1 Duero *r.* Spain

31 C1 Duffreboy, Lac l. Can.
96 C2 Dufftown U.K.
09 C2 Dugi Rat Croatia
23 D1 Duisburg Ger.
60 B1 Duiwelskloof S. Africa
23 C3 Dukathole S. Africa
79 C2 Dukhan Qatar
89 D2 Dukhovshchina Rus. Fed.
Dukou China *see* Panzhihua
88 C2 Dūkštas Lith.
68 C2 Dulan China
52 B4 Dulce r. Arg.
00 C2 Dülmen Ger.
10 C2 Dulovo Bulg.
37 E1 Duluth U.S.A.
64 B2 Dumaguete Phil.
64 B1 Dumai Indon.
64 B1 Dumaran i. Phil.
42 B2 Dumas AR U.S.A.
39 C1 Dumas TX U.S.A.
96 B3 Dumbarton U.K.
03 D2 Ďumbier mt. Slovakia
96 C3 Dumfries U.K.
55 J3 Dumont d'Urville Sea
       Antarctica
16 B1 Dumyât Egypt
       Duna r. Hungary *see* Danube
       Dunaj r. Slovakia *see* Danube
03 D2 Dunakeszi Hungary
       Dunărea r. Romania *see*
       Danube
03 D2 Dunaújváros Hungary
       Dunav r. Serbia *see* Danube
90 B1 Dunayivtsi Ukr.
96 C3 Dunbar U.K.
96 C1 Dunbeath U.K.
28 B3 Duncan Can.
39 D2 Duncan U.S.A.
96 C1 Duncansby Head U.K.
97 C1 Dundalk Ireland
97 C2 Dundalk Bay Ireland
27 G1 Dundas Greenland
23 C2 Dundee S. Africa
96 C2 Dundee U.K.
54 B3 Dundrum Bay U.K.
54 B3 Dunedin N.Z.
97 C1 Dunfermline U.K.
97 C1 Dungannon U.K.
74 B2 Dungarpur India
97 C2 Dungarvan Ireland
99 D3 Dungeness hd U.K.
97 C1 Dungiven U.K.
53 D2 Dungog Austr.
19 C2 Dungu Dem. Rep. Congo
60 B1 Dungun Malaysia
16 B2 Dungunab Sudan
69 E2 Dunhua China
68 C2 Dunhuang China
       Dunkerque France *see*
       Dunkirk
04 D2 Dunkirk France
41 D2 Dunkirk U.S.A.
97 C2 Dún Laoghaire Ireland
97 C1 Dunmurry U.K.
96 C1 Dunnet Head U.K.
96 C3 Duns U.K.
99 C3 Dunstable U.K.
10 B2 Dupnitsa Bulg.
36 C1 Dupree U.S.A.
50 B1 Durack r. Austr.
44 B2 Durango Mex.
06 C1 Durango Spain
36 B3 Durango U.S.A.
39 D2 Durant U.S.A.
53 C4 Durazno Uru.
23 D2 Durban S. Africa
04 C3 Durban-Corbières France

122 A3 Durbanville S. Africa
100 B2 Durbuy Belgium
100 B2 Düren Ger.
73 C2 Durg India
98 C1 Durham U.K.
143 E1 Durham U.S.A.
60 B1 Duri Indon.
109 C2 Durmitor mt. Montenegro
96 B1 Durness U.K.
109 C2 Durrës Albania
97 A3 Dursey Island Ireland
111 C3 Dursunbey Turkey
59 C3 D'Urville, Tanjung pt Indon.
54 B2 D'Urville Island N.Z.
71 A3 Dushan China
77 C3 Dushanbe Tajik.
100 C2 Düsseldorf Ger.
71 A3 Duyun China
91 D2 Dvorichna Ukr.
74 A2 Dwarka India
123 C1 Dwarsberg S. Africa
134 C1 Dworshak Reservoir U.S.A.
89 D3 Dyat'kovo Rus. Fed.
96 C2 Dyce U.K.
127 G2 Dyer, Cape U.S.A.
142 C1 Dyersburg U.S.A.
103 D2 Dyje r. Austria/Czech Rep.
103 D1 Dylewska Góra h. Pol.
91 D2 Dymytrov Ukr.
123 C3 Dyoki S. Africa
87 E3 Dyurtyuli Rus. Fed.
69 D2 Dzamïn Üüd Mongolia
120 D2 Dzaoudzi Mayotte
       Dzhambul Kazakh. *see* Taraz
76 B2 Dzhangala Kazakh.
91 C2 Dzhankoy Ukr.
91 D3 Dzhubga Rus. Fed.
83 K3 Dzhugdzhur, Khrebet mts
       Rus. Fed.
77 D2 Dzhungarskiy Alatau, Khrebet
       mts China/Kazakh.
76 C2 Dzhusaly Kazakh.
103 E1 Działdowo Pol.
69 D1 Dzuunmod Mongolia
88 C3 Dzyarzhynsk Belarus
88 C3 Dzyatlavichy Belarus

E

131 E1 Eagle r. Can.
134 C1 Eagle Cap mt. U.S.A.
130 A2 Eagle Lake Can.
134 B2 Eagle Lake U.S.A.
139 C3 Eagle Pass U.S.A.
126 B2 Eagle Plain Can.
130 A1 Ear Falls Can.
99 D3 Eastbourne U.K.
156 C3 East China Sea N. Pacific
       Ocean
54 B1 East Coast Bays N.Z.
129 D3 Eastend Can.
123 C3 Eastern Cape prov. S. Africa
116 B2 Eastern Desert Egypt
73 B3 Eastern Ghats mts India
129 E2 Easterville Can.
153 C6 East Falkland i. Falkland Is
100 C1 East Frisian Islands Ger.
96 B3 East Kilbride U.K.
99 C3 Eastleigh U.K.
140 C2 East Liverpool U.S.A.
123 C3 East London S. Africa
130 C1 Eastmain Can.
130 C1 Eastmain r. Can.
143 D2 Eastman U.S.A.
140 A3 East St Louis U.S.A.

       East Sea N. Pacific Ocean *see*
       Japan, Sea of
83 K2 East Siberian Sea Rus. Fed.
59 C3 East Timor country Asia
140 A2 Eau Claire U.S.A.
130 C1 Eau Claire, Lac à l' l. Can.
59 D2 Eauripik atoll Micronesia
145 C3 Ebano Mex.
99 B3 Ebbw Vale U.K.
102 C1 Eberswalde-Finow Ger.
108 B2 Eboli Italy
118 B2 Ebolowa Cameroon
107 C1 Ebro r. Spain
144 A2 Echeverria, Pico mt. Mex.
129 E2 Echoing r. Can.
100 C3 Echternach Lux.
52 B3 Echuca Austr.
106 B2 Écija Spain
102 B1 Eckernförde Ger.
127 F2 Eclipse Sound sea chan. Can.
150 A2 Ecuador country S. America
116 C3 Ed Eritrea
117 A3 Ed Da'ein Sudan
117 B3 Ed Damazin Sudan
116 B3 Ed Damer Sudan
116 B3 Ed Debba Sudan
116 B3 Ed Dueim Sudan
51 D4 Eddystone Point Austr.
100 B1 Ede Neth.
118 B2 Edéa Cameroon
154 C1 Edéia Brazil
53 C3 Eden Austr.
98 B1 Eden r. U.K.
123 C2 Edenburg S. Africa
97 C2 Edenderry Ireland
52 B3 Edenhope Austr.
111 B2 Edessa Greece
82 C1 Edgeøya i. Svalbard
139 D3 Edinburg U.S.A.
96 C3 Edinburgh U.K.
110 C2 Edirne Turkey
128 C2 Edmonton Can.
131 D2 Edmundston Can.
111 C3 Edremit Turkey
111 C3 Edremit Körfezi b. Turkey
128 C2 Edson Can.
119 C3 Edward, Lake Dem. Rep.
       Congo/Uganda
139 C2 Edwards Plateau TX U.S.A.
100 C1 Eenrum Neth.
48 F4 Éfaté i. Vanuatu
140 B3 Effingham U.S.A.
135 C3 Egan Range mts U.S.A.
103 E2 Eger Hungary
93 E4 Egersund Norway
92 C2 Egilsstaðir Iceland
80 B2 Eğirdir Turkey
80 B2 Eğirdir Gölü l. Turkey
104 C2 Égletons France
       Egmont, Mount vol. N.Z. *see*
       Taranaki, Mount
83 M2 Egvekinot Rus. Fed.
116 A2 Egypt country Africa
68 C2 Ehen Hudag China
100 C1 Eibergen Neth.
100 C2 Eifel hills Ger.
96 A2 Eigg i. U.K.
73 B4 Eight Degree Channel
       India/Maldives
50 B1 Eighty Mile Beach Austr.
80 B2 Eilat Israel
101 F2 Eilenburg Ger.
100 D1 Einbeck Ger.
100 B2 Eindhoven Neth.
150 B2 Eirunepé Brazil
120 B2 Eiseb watercourse Namibia
101 E2 Eisenach Ger.

Eisenhüttenstadt

102 C1 Eisenhüttenstadt Ger.
103 D2 Eisenstadt Austria
101 E2 Eisleben Lutherstadt Ger.
Eivissa Spain *see* Ibiza
Eivissa *i.* Spain *see* Ibiza
107 C1 Ejea de los Caballeros Spain
121 D3 Ejeda Madag.
Ejin Qi China *see* Dalain Hob
93 H4 Ekenäs Fin.
77 D1 Ekibastuz Kazakh.
92 J2 Ekostrovskaya Imandra, Ozero *l.* Rus. Fed.
93 F4 Eksjö Sweden
122 A2 Eksteenfontein S. Africa
130 B1 Ekwan *r.* Can.
62 A2 Ela Myanmar
123 C2 Elandsdoorn S. Africa
111 B3 Elassona Greece
80 B2 Elazığ Turkey
108 B2 Elba, Isola d' *i.* Italy
150 A1 El Banco Col.
138 B2 El Barreal *salt l.* Mex.
109 D2 Elbasan Albania
150 B1 El Baúl Venez.
114 C1 El Bayadh Alg.
101 D1 Elbe *r.* Ger.
136 B3 Elbert, Mount U.S.A.
143 D2 Elberton U.S.A.
104 C2 Elbeuf France
80 B2 Elbistan Turkey
103 D1 Elbląg Pol.
150 B1 El'brus *mt.* Rus. Fed.
81 C2 Elburz Mountains Iran
150 B1 El Callao Venez.
139 D3 El Campo U.S.A.
135 C4 El Centro U.S.A.
152 B2 El Cerro Bol.
107 C2 Elche-Elx Spain
107 C2 Elda Spain
137 E3 Eldon U.S.A.
144 B2 El Dorado U.S.A.
142 B2 El Dorado *AR* U.S.A.
137 D3 El Dorado *KS* U.S.A.
114 B2 El Eglab *plat.* Alg.
106 C2 El Ejido Spain
89 E2 Elektrostal' Rus. Fed.
150 A2 El Encanto Col.
146 C2 Eleuthera *i.* Bahamas
117 A3 El Fasher Sudan
144 B2 El Fuerte Mex.
117 A3 El Geneina Sudan
116 B3 El Geteina Sudan
96 C2 Elgin U.K.
140 B2 Elgin U.S.A.
115 C1 El Goléa Alg.
144 A1 El Golfo de Santa Clara Mex.
119 D3 Elgon, Mount Kenya/Uganda
114 A2 El Hammâmi *reg.* Maur.
114 A2 El Hierro *i.* Islas Canarias
145 C2 El Higo Mex.
114 C2 El Homr Alg.
87 D4 Elista Rus. Fed.
141 E2 Elizabeth U.S.A.
143 E1 Elizabeth City U.S.A.
140 B3 Elizabethtown U.S.A.
114 B1 El Jadida Morocco
103 E1 Ełk Pol.
139 D1 Elk City U.S.A.
128 C2 Elkford U.S.A.
140 B2 Elkhart U.S.A.
El Khartum Sudan *see* Khartoum
110 C2 Elkhovo Bulg.
140 D3 Elkins U.S.A.
128 C3 Elko Can.
134 C2 Elko U.S.A.
129 C2 Elk Point Can.

126 E1 Ellef Ringnes Island Can.
137 D1 Ellendale U.S.A.
134 B1 Ellensburg U.S.A.
54 B2 Ellesmere, Lake N.Z.
127 F1 Ellesmere Island Can.
98 B2 Ellesmere Port U.K.
126 E2 Ellice *r.* Can.
Ellice Islands *country* S. Pacific Ocean *see* Tuvalu
123 C3 Elliotdale S. Africa
96 C2 Ellon U.K.
141 F2 Ellsworth U.S.A.
55 O2 Ellsworth Mountains Antarctica
111 C3 Elmalı Turkey
115 C1 El Meghaïer Alg.
141 D2 Elmira U.S.A.
107 C2 El Moral Spain
101 D1 Elmshorn Ger.
117 A3 El Muglad Sudan
64 A1 El Nido Phil.
117 B3 El Obeid Sudan
144 B2 El Oro Mex.
115 C1 El Oued Alg.
138 A2 Eloy U.S.A.
138 B2 El Paso U.S.A.
144 B1 El Porvenir Mex.
107 D1 El Prat de Llobregat Spain
139 D1 El Reno U.S.A.
145 B2 El Salado Mex.
144 B2 El Salto Mex.
146 B3 El Salvador *country* Central America
145 B2 El Salvador Mex.
138 B3 El Sauz Mex.
144 A1 El Socorro Mex.
145 C2 El Temascal Mex.
150 B1 El Tigre Venez.
147 D4 El Tocuyo Venez.
88 C2 Elva Estonia
106 B2 Elvas Port.
93 F3 Elverum Norway
119 E2 El Wak Kenya
99 D2 Ely U.K.
137 E1 Ely *MN* U.S.A.
135 D3 Ely *NV* U.S.A.
81 D2 Emämrüd Iran
93 G4 Emån *r.* Sweden
76 B2 Emba Kazakh.
76 B2 Emba *r.* Kazakh.
123 C2 Embalenhle S. Africa
154 C1 Emborcação, Represa de *resr* Brazil
119 D3 Embu Kenya
100 C1 Emden Ger.
51 D2 Emerald Austr.
129 E3 Emerson Can.
111 C3 Emet Turkey
123 C3 eMgwenya S. Africa
115 D3 Emi Koussi *mt.* Chad
110 C2 Emine, Nos *pt* Bulg.
80 B2 Emirdağ Turkey
123 C2 eMjindini S. Africa
88 B2 Emmaste Estonia
100 B1 Emmeloord Neth.
100 C2 Emmelshausen Ger.
100 C1 Emmen Neth.
139 C3 Emory Peak U.S.A.
144 A2 Empalme Mex.
123 D2 Empangeni S. Africa
108 B2 Empoli Italy
137 D3 Emporia *KS* U.S.A.
141 D3 Emporia *VA* U.S.A.
Empty Quarter *des.* Saudi Arabia *see* Rub' al Khālī
100 C1 Ems *r.* Ger.
100 C1 Emsdetten Ger.

123 C2 eMzinoni S. Africa
59 D3 Enarotali Indon.
144 B2 Encarnación Mex.
152 C3 Encarnación Para.
155 D1 Encruzilhada Brazil
58 C3 Ende Indon.
126 A2 Endicott Mountains U.S.A.
91 C2 Enerhodar Ukr.
87 D3 Engel's Rus. Fed.
60 B2 Enggano *i.* Indon.
98 C2 England *admin. div.* U.K.
130 A1 English *r.* Can.
95 C4 English Channel France/U.K.
139 D1 Enid U.S.A.
100 B1 Enkhuizen Neth.
93 G4 Enköping Sweden
108 B3 Enna *Sicilia* Italy
129 D1 Ennadai Lake Can.
117 A3 En Nahud Sudan
115 E3 Ennedi, Massif *mts* Chad
53 C1 Enngonia Austr.
97 B2 Ennis Ireland
139 D2 Ennis U.S.A.
97 C2 Enniscorthy Ireland
97 C1 Enniskillen U.K.
97 B2 Ennistymon Ireland
102 C2 Enns *r.* Austria
92 H2 Enontekiö Fin.
53 C3 Ensay Austr.
100 C1 Enschede Neth.
144 A1 Ensenada Mex.
70 A2 Enshi China
128 C1 Enterprise Can.
142 C2 Enterprise *AL* U.S.A.
134 C1 Enterprise *OR* U.S.A.
152 B3 Entre Ríos Bol.
106 B2 Entroncamento Port.
115 C4 Enugu Nigeria
150 A2 Envira Brazil
135 D3 Ephraim U.S.A.
134 C1 Ephrata U.S.A.
105 D2 Épinal France
99 C3 Epsom U.K.
118 A2 Equatorial Guinea *country* Africa
101 F3 Erbendorf Ger.
100 C3 Erbeskopf *h.* Ger.
81 C2 Erciş Turkey
65 B1 Erdao Jiang *r.* China
111 C2 Erdek Turkey
80 B2 Erdemli Turkey
152 C3 Erechim Brazil
69 D1 Ereentsav Mongolia
80 B2 Ereğli *Konya* Turkey
80 B1 Ereğli *Zonguldak* Turkey
69 D2 Erenhot China
Erevan Armenia *see* Yerevan
101 E2 Erfurt Ger.
80 B2 Ergani Turkey
114 B2 'Erg Chech *des.* Alg./Mali
111 C2 Ergene *r.* Turkey
140 C2 Erie U.S.A.
140 C2 Erie, Lake Can./U.S.A.
66 D2 Erimo-misaki *c.* Japan
116 B3 Eritrea *country* Africa
101 E3 Erlangen Ger.
50 C2 Erldunda Austr.
123 C2 Ermelo S. Africa
80 B2 Ermenek Turkey
111 B3 Ermoupoli Greece
73 B4 Ernakulam India
73 B3 Erode India
100 B2 Erp Neth.
114 B1 Er Rachidia Morocco
117 B3 Er Rahad Sudan
97 B1 Errigal *h.* Ireland
97 A1 Erris Head Ireland

109 D2 Ersekë Albania
91 E1 Ertil' Rus. Fed.
101 D2 Erwitte Ger.
102 C1 Erzgebirge mts Czech Rep./
Ger.
80 B2 Erzincan Turkey
81 C2 Erzurum Turkey
93 E4 Esbjerg Denmark
135 D3 Escalante U.S.A.
144 B2 Escalón Mex.
140 B1 Escanaba U.S.A.
145 C3 Escárcega Mex.
107 C1 Escatrón Spain
100 A2 Escaut r. Belgium/France
101 E1 Eschede Ger.
100 B3 Esch-sur-Alzette Lux.
101 E2 Eschwege Ger.
100 C2 Eschweiler Ger.
135 C4 Escondido U.S.A.
144 B2 Escuinapa Mex.
111 C3 Eşen Turkey
81 D2 Eşfahān Iran
123 D2 Esikhawini S. Africa
98 B1 Esk r. U.K.
131 D1 Esker Can.
92 C2 Eskifjörður Iceland
93 G4 Eskilstuna Sweden
Eskimo Point Can. see Arviat
80 B2 Eskişehir Turkey
81 C2 Eslāmābād-e Gharb Iran
111 C3 Esler Dağı mt. Turkey
111 C3 Eşme Turkey
150 A1 Esmeraldas Ecuador
79 D2 Espakeh Iran
104 C3 Espalion France
130 B2 Espanola Can.
138 B1 Espanola U.S.A.
50 B3 Esperance Austr.
144 B2 Esperanza Mex.
106 B2 Espichel, Cabo c. Port.
155 D1 Espinhaço, Serra do mts Brazil
151 D3 Espinosa Brazil
48 F4 Espíritu Santo i. Vanuatu
144 A2 Espíritu Santo, Isla i. Mex.
93 H3 Espoo Fin.
153 A5 Esquel Arg.
114 B1 Esquimalt Can.
114 A2 Es Semara Western Sahara
100 C2 Essen Ger.
150 C1 Essequibo r. Guyana
83 L3 Esso Rus. Fed.
79 C2 Eştahbān Iran
151 E3 Estância Brazil
123 C2 Estcourt S. Africa
107 C1 Estella Spain
106 B2 Estepona Spain
106 C1 Esteras de Medinaceli Spain
129 D2 Esterhazy Can.
152 B3 Esteros Para.
136 B2 Estes Park U.S.A.
129 D3 Estevan Can.
137 E2 Estherville U.S.A.
129 D2 Eston Can.
88 C2 Estonia country Europe
106 B1 Estrela, Serra da mts Port.
106 B2 Estremoz Port.
52 A1 Etadunna Austr.
104 C2 Étampes France
104 C1 Étaples France
75 B2 Etawah India
123 D2 Ethandakukhanya S. Africa
117 B4 Ethiopia country Africa
109 C3 Etna, Mount vol. Sicilia Italy
128 A2 Etolin Island U.S.A.
120 A2 Etosha Pan salt pan Namibia
100 C3 Ettelbruck Lux.
100 B2 Etten-Leur Neth.

107 C1 Etxarri-Aranatz Spain
99 D3 Eu France
53 C2 Euabalong Austr.
Euboea i. Greece see Evvoia
50 B3 Eucla Austr.
143 D2 Eufaula U.S.A.
139 D1 Eufaula Lake resr U.S.A.
134 B2 Eugene U.S.A.
144 A2 Eugenia, Punta pt Mex.
53 C1 Eulo Austr.
53 C2 Eumungerie Austr.
139 C2 Eunice U.S.A.
80 C2 Euphrates r. Asia
134 B2 Eureka CA U.S.A.
134 C1 Eureka MT U.S.A.
135 D3 Eureka NV U.S.A.
52 B2 Euriowie Austr.
53 C3 Euroa Austr.
106 B2 Europa Point Gibraltar
128 B2 Eutsuk Lake Can.
130 C1 Evans, Lac l. Can.
53 D1 Evans Head Austr.
127 F2 Evans Strait Can.
136 A2 Evanston U.S.A.
140 B3 Evansville U.S.A.
123 C2 Evaton S. Africa
79 C2 Evaz Iran
83 L2 Evensk Rus. Fed.
50 C2 Everard Range hills Austr.
75 C2 Everest, Mount China/Nepal
134 B1 Everett U.S.A.
100 A2 Evergem Belgium
143 D3 Everglades swamp U.S.A.
118 B2 Evinayong Equat. Guinea
93 E4 Evje Norway
106 B2 Évora Port.
104 C2 Évreux France
111 C2 Evros r. Greece/Turkey
111 B3 Evrotas r. Greece
80 B2 Evrychou Cyprus
111 B3 Evvoia i. Greece
119 E2 Ewaso Ngiro r. Kenya
152 B2 Exaltación Bol.
99 B3 Exe r. U.K.
99 B3 Exeter U.K.
99 B3 Exmoor hills U.K.
50 A2 Exmouth Austr.
99 B3 Exmouth U.K.
146 C2 Exuma Cays is Bahamas
117 C4 Eyl Somalia
52 A1 Eyre (North), Lake imp. l.
Austr.
51 C3 Eyre Peninsula Austr.
94 B1 Eysturoy i. Faroe Is
123 D2 Ezakheni S. Africa
123 C2 Ezenzeleni S. Africa
70 B2 Ezhou China
86 E2 Ezhva Rus. Fed.
111 C3 Ezine Turkey

F

138 B2 Fabens U.S.A.
108 B2 Fabriano Italy
115 D3 Fachi Niger
114 C3 Fada-N'Gourma Burkina
108 B2 Faenza Italy
59 C3 Fanlap Indon.
110 B1 Făgăraş Romania
49 G3 Fagatogo American Samoa
93 E3 Fagernes Norway
93 G4 Fagersta Sweden
153 B6 Fagnano, Lago l. Arg./Chile
114 B3 Faguibine, Lac l. Mali
92 B3 Fagurhólsmýri Iceland

126 B2 Fairbanks U.S.A.
137 D2 Fairbury U.S.A.
135 B3 Fairfield U.S.A.
96 □ Fair Isle i. U.K.
137 E2 Fairmont MN U.S.A.
140 C3 Fairmont WV U.S.A.
128 C2 Fairview Can.
59 D2 Fais i. Micronesia
74 B1 Faisalabad Pak.
136 C1 Faith U.S.A.
75 C2 Faizabad India
59 C3 Fakfak Indon.
70 B1 Faku China
114 A4 Falaba Sierra Leone
139 D3 Falcon Lake Mex./U.S.A.
139 D3 Falfurrias U.S.A.
128 C2 Falher Can.
101 F2 Falkenberg Ger.
93 F4 Falkenberg Sweden
101 F1 Falkensee Ger.
96 C3 Falkirk U.K.
153 C6 Falkland Islands terr.
S. Atlantic Ocean
93 F4 Falköping Sweden
135 C3 Fallon U.S.A.
141 E2 Fall River U.S.A.
137 D2 Falls City U.S.A.
99 A3 Falmouth U.K.
122 A3 False Bay S. Africa
93 F4 Falster i. Denmark
110 C1 Fălticeni Romania
93 G3 Falun Sweden
71 A3 Fangcheng(gang) China
71 C3 Fangshan Taiwan
69 E1 Fangzheng China
108 B2 Fano Italy
119 C2 Faradje Dem. Rep. Congo
121 D3 Farafangana Madag.
116 A2 Farāfirah, Wāḥāt al oasis
Egypt
76 C3 Farāh Afgh.
114 A3 Faranah Guinea
78 B3 Farasān, Jazā'ir is Saudi Arabia
127 J3 Farewell, Cape Greenland
54 B2 Farewell, Cape N.Z.
137 D1 Fargo U.S.A.
77 D2 Farg'ona Uzbek.
137 E2 Faribault U.S.A.
141 E2 Farmington ME U.S.A.
138 B1 Farmington NM U.S.A.
141 D3 Farmville U.S.A.
99 C3 Farnborough U.K.
128 C2 Farnham, Mount Can.
128 A1 Faro Can.
106 B2 Faro Port.
88 A2 Fårö i. Sweden
94 B1 Faroe Islands terr. N. Atlantic
Ocean
79 C2 Farrāshband Iran
139 C2 Farwell U.S.A.
79 C2 Fāryāb Iran
79 C2 Fasā Iran
109 C2 Fasano Italy
90 B1 Fastiv Ukr.
75 B2 Fatehgarh India
75 C2 Fatehpur India
92 G2 Fauske Norway
92 A3 Faxaflói b. Iceland
92 G3 Faxälven r. Sweden
115 D3 Faya Chad
142 B1 Fayetteville AR U.S.A.
143 E1 Fayetteville NC U.S.A.
142 C1 Fayetteville TN U.S.A.
77 D3 Fayzābād Afgh.
74 B1 Fāzilka India
114 A2 Fdérik Maur.
143 E2 Fear, Cape U.S.A.

Featherston

54 C2 Featherston N.Z.
104 C2 Fécamp France
102 C1 Fehmarn *i.* Ger.
101 F1 Fehrbellin Ger.
155 D2 Feia, Lagoa *lag.* Brazil
150 A2 Feijó Brazil
54 C2 Feilding N.Z.
151 E3 Feira de Santana Brazil
107 D2 Felanitx Spain
145 D3 Felipe C. Puerto Mex.
155 D1 Felixlândia Brazil
99 D3 Felixstowe U.K.
101 E2 Felsberg Ger.
108 B1 Feltre Italy
93 F3 Femunden *l.* Norway
71 B3 Fengcheng *Jiangxi* China
65 A1 Fengcheng *Liaoning* China
62 A1 Fengqing China
70 B2 Fengxian China
Fengxiang China *see* Lincang
71 C3 Fengyüan Taiwan
70 B1 Fengzhen China
105 D3 Feno, Capo di *c.* Corse France
121 D2 Feonoarivo Atsinanana Madag.
91 D2 Feodosiya Ukr.
108 A3 Fer, Cap de *c.* Alg.
137 D3 Fergus Falls U.S.A.
109 D2 Ferizaj Kosovo
108 B4 Ferkessédougou Côte d'Ivoire
108 B2 Fermo Italy
131 D1 Fermont Can.
106 B1 Fermoselle Spain
97 B2 Fermoy Ireland
143 D2 Fernandina Beach U.S.A.
154 B2 Fernandópolis Brazil
128 C3 Fernie Can.
108 B2 Ferrara Italy
154 B2 Ferreiros Brazil
108 A2 Ferro, Capo *c.* Sardegna Italy
106 B1 Ferrol Spain
100 B1 Ferwert Neth.
114 B1 Fès Morocco
118 B3 Feshi Dem. Rep. Congo
137 E3 Festus U.S.A.
111 C3 Fethiye Turkey
96 □ Fetlar *i.* U.K.
130 C1 Feuilles, Rivière aux *r.* Can.
Fez Morocco *see* Fès
121 D3 Fianarantsoa Madag.
117 B4 Fichê Eth.
109 C4 Fier Albania
96 C2 Fife Ness *pt* U.K.
104 C3 Figeac France
106 B1 Figueira da Foz Port.
107 D1 Figueres Spain
114 B1 Figuig Morocco
48 F3 Fiji *country* S. Pacific Ocean
152 B3 Filadelfia Para.
55 Q2 Filchner Ice Shelf Antarctica
98 C1 Filey U.K.
111 B3 Filippiada Greece
93 F4 Filipstad Sweden
96 C2 Findhorn *r.* U.K.
140 C2 Findlay U.S.A.
51 D4 Fingal Austr.
141 D2 Finger Lakes U.S.A.
106 B1 Finisterre, Cape Spain
92 I3 Finland *country* Europe
93 H4 Finland, Gulf of Europe
128 B2 Finlay *r.* Can.
53 C3 Finley Austr.
101 E2 Finne *ridge* Ger.
92 H2 Finnmarksvidda *reg.* Norway
92 G2 Finnsnes Norway
93 G4 Finspång Sweden
96 A2 Fionnphort U.K.
Firat *r.* Turkey *see* Euphrates

Firenze Italy *see* Florence
105 C2 Firminy France
75 B2 Firozabad India
74 B1 Firozpur India
79 C2 Firūzābād Iran
122 A2 Fish *watercourse* Namibia
122 B3 Fish *r.* S. Africa
99 A3 Fishguard U.K.
105 C2 Fismes France
Fisterra, Cabo *c.* Spain *see*
Finisterre, Cape
141 E2 Fitchburg U.S.A.
129 C2 Fitzgerald Can.
50 B1 Fitzroy Crossing Austr.
108 B2 Fivizzano Italy
119 C3 Fizi Dem. Rep. Congo
92 G3 Fjällsjöälven *r.* Sweden
123 C3 Flagstaff S. Africa
138 A1 Flagstaff U.S.A.
130 C1 Flaherty Island Can.
98 C1 Flamborough Head U.K.
101 F1 Fläming *hills* Ger.
136 B2 Flaming Gorge Reservoir
U.S.A.
134 D1 Flathead *r.* U.S.A.
134 D1 Flathead Lake U.S.A.
51 D1 Flattery, Cape Austr.
134 B1 Flattery, Cape U.S.A.
98 B2 Fleetwood U.K.
93 E4 Flekkefjord Norway
102 B1 Flensburg Ger.
104 B2 Flers France
51 D1 Flinders *r.* Austr.
50 A3 Flinders Bay Austr.
51 D3 Flinders Island Austr.
52 A2 Flinders Ranges *mts* Austr.
129 D2 Flin Flon Can.
140 C2 Flint U.S.A.
107 D1 Florac France
108 B2 Florence Italy
142 C2 Florence AL U.S.A.
138 A2 Florence AZ U.S.A.
134 B2 Florence OR U.S.A.
143 E2 Florence SC U.S.A.
150 A1 Florencia Col.
146 B3 Flores Guat.
58 C3 Flores *i.* Indon.
58 B3 Flores *i.* Indon.
Flores, Laut *sea* Indon. *see*
Flores Sea
Flores Sea Indon. *sea*
Flores, Laut
151 E3 Floresta Brazil
139 D3 Floresville U.S.A.
151 D2 Floriano Brazil
152 D3 Florianópolis Brazil
153 C4 Florida Uru.
143 D2 Florida *state* U.S.A.
143 D4 Florida, Straits of N. Atlantic
Ocean
143 D4 Florida Keys *is* U.S.A.
111 B2 Florina Greece
93 E3 Florø Norway
129 D2 Foam Lake Can.
109 C2 Foča Bos.-Herz.
110 C1 Focşani Romania
71 B3 Fogang China
108 C2 Foggia Italy
131 E2 Fogo Island Can.
104 C3 Foix France
89 D3 Fokino Rus. Fed.
130 B2 Foleyet Can.
108 B2 Foligno Italy
99 D3 Folkestone U.K.
143 D2 Folkston U.S.A.
108 B2 Follonica Italy
129 D2 Fond-du-Lac Can.
129 C2 Fond du Lac *r.* Can.
140 B2 Fond du Lac U.S.A.

106 B1 Fondevila Spain
108 B2 Fondi Italy
146 B3 Fonseca, Golfo de *b.*
Central America
150 B2 Fonte Boa Brazil
104 B2 Fontenay-le-Comte France
92 C2 Fontur *pt* Iceland
53 C2 Forbes Austr.
101 E3 Forchheim Ger.
93 E3 Førde Norway
53 C1 Fords Bridge Austr.
142 B2 Fordyce U.S.A.
142 C2 Forest U.S.A.
53 C3 Forest Hill Austr.
131 D2 Forestville Can.
72 C2 Forfar U.K.
134 B1 Forks U.S.A.
108 B2 Forlì Italy
107 D2 Formentera *i.* Spain
107 D2 Formentor, Cap de *c.* Spain
155 D2 Formiga Brazil
152 C3 Formosa Arg.
Formosa *country* Asia *see*
Taiwan
154 C1 Formosa Brazil
96 C2 Forres U.K.
50 B3 Forrest Austr.
142 B1 Forrest City U.S.A.
51 D1 Forsayth Austr.
93 H3 Forssa Fin.
53 D2 Forster Austr.
136 B1 Forsyth U.S.A.
74 B2 Fort Abbas Pak.
130 B1 Fort Albany Can.
151 E2 Fortaleza Brazil
128 C2 Fort Assiniboine Can.
96 B2 Fort Augustus U.K.
134 D1 Fort Benton U.S.A.
135 B3 Fort Bragg U.S.A.
Fort Chimo Can. *see* Kuujjuaq
129 C2 Fort Chipewyan Can.
136 B2 Fort Collins U.S.A.
147 D3 Fort-de-France Martinique
137 E2 Fort Dodge U.S.A.
130 A2 Fort Frances Can.
Fort Franklin Can. *see* Déline
Fort George Can. *see* Chisasibi
126 C2 Fort Good Hope Can.
96 C2 Forth *r.* U.K.
96 C2 Forth, Firth of *est.* U.K.
152 C3 Fortín Madrejón Para.
143 D3 Fort Lauderdale U.S.A.
128 B1 Fort Liard Can.
129 C2 Fort Mackay Can.
129 C2 Fort McMurray Can.
126 C2 Fort McPherson Can.
136 C2 Fort Morgan U.S.A.
143 D3 Fort Myers U.S.A.
128 B2 Fort Nelson Can.
128 B2 Fort Nelson *r.* Can.
142 C2 Fort Payne U.S.A.
136 B1 Fort Peck U.S.A.
136 B1 Fort Peck Reservoir U.S.A.
143 D3 Fort Pierce U.S.A.
128 C1 Fort Providence Can.
129 D2 Fort Qu'Appelle Can.
128 C1 Fort Resolution Can.
Fort Rupert Can. *see*
Waskaganish
128 B2 Fort St James Can.
128 B2 Fort St John Can.
128 C2 Fort Saskatchewan Can.
137 E3 Fort Scott U.S.A.
130 B1 Fort Severn Can.
76 B2 Fort-Shevchenko Kazakh.
128 B1 Fort Simpson Can.
129 C1 Fort Smith Can.

42 B1 Fort Smith U.S.A.
39 C2 Fort Stockton U.S.A.
28 C2 Fort Sumner U.S.A.
48 C2 Fort Vermilion Can.
42 C2 Fort Walton Beach U.S.A.
40 B2 Fort Wayne U.S.A.
91 B6 Fort William U.K.
89 D2 Fort Worth U.S.A.
26 B2 Fort Yukon U.S.A.
71 B3 Foshan China
92 F3 Fosna pen. Norway
93 E2 Fosnavåg Norway
92 B3 Foss Iceland
92 A2 Fossá Iceland
08 A2 Fossano Italy
53 C2 Foster Austr.
04 B2 Fougères France
96 □ Foula i. U.K.
11 C3 Fournoi i. Greece
54 A3 Fouta Djallon reg. Guinea
54 A3 Foveaux Strait N.Z.
36 C3 Fowler U.S.A.
50 C3 Fowlers Bay Austr.
28 C2 Fox Creek Can.
27 F2 Foxe Basin g. Can.
27 F2 Foxe Channel Can.
27 F2 Foxe Peninsula Can.
28 C2 Fox Glacier N.Z.
28 C2 Fox Lake Can.
14 A3 Fox Mountain Can.
54 C2 Foxton N.Z.
29 D2 Fox Valley Can.
97 C1 Foyle, Lough b. Ireland/U.K.
54 B3 Foz de Areia, Represa de resr
       Brazil
20 A2 Foz do Cunene Angola
80 B3 Foz do Iguaçu Brazil
07 D2 Fraga Spain
54 C2 Franca Brazil
09 C2 Francavilla Fontana Italy
04 C2 France country Europe
18 B3 Franceville Gabon
37 D2 Francis Case, Lake l. U.S.A.
20 B3 Francistown Botswana
28 B3 François Lake Can.
01 D2 Frankenberg (Eder) Ger.
01 D3 Frankenthal (Pfalz) Ger.
01 E2 Frankenwald mts Ger.
40 C3 Frankfort U.S.A.
01 D2 Frankfurt am Main Ger.
02 C1 Frankfurt an der Oder Ger.
02 C2 Fränkische Alb hills Ger.
01 E3 Fränkische Schweiz reg. Ger.
41 D2 Franklin U.S.A.
26 C2 Franklin Bay Can.
34 C1 Franklin D. Roosevelt Lake
       U.S.A.
28 B1 Franklin Mountains Can.
26 E2 Franklin Strait Can.
82 E1 Frantsa-Iosifa, Zemlya is
       Rus. Fed.
54 C2 Franz Josef Glacier N.Z.
       Franz Josef Land is Rus. Fed.
       see Frantsa-Iosifa, Zemlya
08 A3 Frasca, Capo della c. Sardegna
       Italy
28 B3 Fraser r. B.C. Can.
31 D1 Fraser r. Nfld. and Lab. Can.
22 B3 Fraserburg S. Africa
96 C2 Fraserburgh U.K.
30 B2 Fraserdale Can.
51 E2 Fraser Island Austr.
28 B2 Fraser Lake Can.
53 C4 Fray Bentos Uru.
93 E4 Fredericia Denmark
39 D2 Frederick U.S.A.

139 D2 Fredericksburg TX U.S.A.
141 D3 Fredericksburg VA U.S.A.
128 A2 Frederick Sound sea chan.
       U.S.A.
131 D2 Fredericton Can.
93 F4 Frederikshavn Denmark
       Frederikshamn Fin. see
       Hamina
93 F4 Fredrikstad Norway
140 B2 Freeport IL U.S.A.
139 D3 Freeport TX U.S.A.
146 C2 Freeport City Bahamas
139 D3 Freer U.S.A.
123 C2 Free State prov. S. Africa
114 A4 Freetown Sierra Leone
106 B2 Fregenal de la Sierra Spain
104 B2 Fréhel, Cap c. France
102 B2 Freiburg im Breisgau Ger.
102 C2 Freising Ger.
102 C2 Freistadt Austria
105 D3 Fréjus France
50 A3 Fremantle Austr.
137 D2 Fremont NE U.S.A.
140 C2 Fremont OH U.S.A.
151 C1 French Guiana terr. S. America
134 E1 Frenchman r. U.S.A.
49 I4 French Polynesia terr.
       S. Pacific Ocean
144 B2 Fresnillo Mex.
135 C3 Fresno U.S.A.
107 D2 Freu, Cap des c. Spain
105 D2 Freyming-Merlebach France
114 A3 Fria Guinea
152 B3 Frías Arg.
102 B2 Friedrichshafen Ger.
101 F1 Friesack Ger.
100 C1 Friesoythe Ger.
127 G2 Frobisher Bay Can. see Iqaluit
101 F2 Frobisher Bay Can.
87 D4 Frolovo Rus. Fed.
52 A2 Frome, Lake imp. l. Austr.
52 A2 Frome Downs Austr.
100 C2 Fröndenberg Ger.
145 C3 Frontera Mex.
144 B1 Fronteras Mex.
108 B2 Frosinone Italy
92 E3 Frøya i. Norway
       Frunze Kyrg. see Bishkek
105 D2 Frutigen Switz.
103 D2 Frýdek-Místek Czech Rep.
71 B3 Fu'an China
106 C1 Fuenlabrada Spain
152 C3 Fuerte Olimpo Para.
114 A2 Fuerteventura i. Islas Canarias
64 B1 Fuga i. Phil.
79 C2 Fujairah U.A.E.
67 C3 Fuji Japan
71 B3 Fujian prov. China
67 C3 Fujinomiya Japan
67 C3 Fuji-san vol. Japan
67 C3 Fukui Japan
67 B4 Fukuoka Japan
67 D3 Fukushima Japan
101 D2 Fulda Ger.
101 D2 Fulda r. Ger.
70 A3 Fuling China
137 E1 Fulton U.S.A.
105 C2 Fumay France
49 F3 Funafuti atoll Tuvalu
114 A1 Funchal Arquipélago da
       Madeira
106 B1 Fundão Port.
131 D2 Fundy, Bay of g. Can.
70 B2 Funing Jiangsu China
71 A3 Funing Yunnan China
115 C3 Funtua Nigeria

79 C2 Fürgun, Küh-e mt. Iran
89 F2 Furmanov Rus. Fed.
155 C2 Furnas, Represa resr Brazil
51 D4 Furneaux Group is Austr.
100 C1 Fürstenau Ger.
101 E3 Fürth Ger.
66 D3 Furukawa Japan
127 F2 Fury and Hecla Strait Can.
65 A1 Fushun China
65 B1 Fusong China
79 C2 Fuwayriţ Qatar
70 B2 Fuyang China
69 E1 Fuyu China
68 B1 Fuyun China
71 B3 Fuzhou Fujian China
71 B3 Fuzhou Jiangxi China
93 F4 Fyn i. Denmark
       F.Y.R.O.M. country Europe see
       Macedonia

G

117 C4 Gaalkacyo Somalia
120 A2 Gabela Angola
115 D1 Gabès Tunisia
115 D1 Gabès, Golfe de g. Tunisia
118 B3 Gabon country Africa
123 C1 Gaborone Botswana
110 C2 Gabrovo Bulg.
114 A3 Gabú Guinea-Bissau
73 B3 Gadag India
75 C2 Gadchiroli India
101 E1 Gadebusch Ger.
142 C2 Gadsden U.S.A.
110 C2 Găeşti Romania
108 B2 Gaeta Italy
143 D1 Gaffney U.S.A.
115 C1 Gafsa Tunisia
89 E2 Gagarin Rus. Fed.
114 B4 Gagnoa Côte d'Ivoire
131 D1 Gagnon Can.
81 C1 Gagra Georgia
122 A2 Gaiab watercourse Namibia
111 C3 Gaïdouronisi i. Greece
104 C3 Gaillac France
143 D3 Gainesville FL U.S.A.
143 D2 Gainesville GA U.S.A.
139 D2 Gainesville TX U.S.A.
98 C2 Gainsborough U.K.
52 A2 Gairdner, Lake imp. l. Austr.
96 B2 Gairloch U.K.
119 E3 Galana r. Kenya
103 D2 Galanta Slovakia
148 B3 Galapagos Islands Ecuador
96 C3 Galashiels U.K.
110 C1 Galaţi Romania
93 E3 Galdhøpiggen mt. Norway
145 B2 Galeana Mex.
140 A2 Galena Bay Can.
140 A2 Galesburg U.S.A.
122 B2 Galeshewe S. Africa
86 D3 Galich Rus. Fed.
116 B1 Galilee, Sea of l. Israel
142 C1 Gallatin U.S.A.
73 C4 Galle Sri Lanka
150 A1 Gallinas, Punta pt Col.
109 C2 Gallipoli Italy
111 C2 Gallipoli Turkey
92 H2 Gällivare Sweden
138 B1 Gallup U.S.A.
114 A2 Galtat Zemmour Western
       Sahara
97 B2 Galtymore h. Ireland
139 E3 Galveston U.S.A.
139 E3 Galveston Bay U.S.A.

97 B2	Galway Ireland	
97 B2	Galway Bay Ireland	
154 C1	Gamá Brazil	
123 D3	Gamalakhe S. Africa	
114 A3	Gambia, The country Africa	
52 A3	Gambier Islands Austr.	
131 E2	Gambo Can.	
118 B3	Gamboma Congo	
128 C1	Gamêtî Can.	
138 B1	Ganado U.S.A.	
81 C1	Gäncä Azer.	
	Gand Belgium see Ghent	
61 C2	Gandadiwata, Bukit mt. Indon.	
118 C3	Gandajika Dem. Rep. Congo	
131 E2	Gander Can.	
131 E2	Gander r. Can.	
101 D1	Ganderkesee Ger.	
107 D1	Gandesa Spain	
74 B2	Gandhidham India	
74 B2	Gandhinagar India	
74 B2	Gandhi Sagar resr India	
107 C2	Gandia Spain	
	Ganga r. Bangl./India see Ganges	
153 B5	Gangán Arg.	
74 B1	Ganganagar India	
68 C2	Gangca China	
75 C1	Gangdisê Shan mts China	
75 C2	Ganges r. Bangl./India	
105 C3	Ganges France	
75 C2	Ganges, Mouths of the Bangl./India	
75 C2	Gangtok India	
105 C2	Gannat France	
136 B2	Gannett Peak U.S.A.	
122 A3	Gansbaai S. Africa	
70 A1	Gansu prov. China	
70 B2	Ganzhou China	
114 B3	Gao Mali	
97 B1	Gaoth Dobhair Ireland	
114 A3	Gaoual Guinea	
70 B2	Gaoyou China	
70 B2	Gaoyou Hu l. China	
105 D3	Gap France	
75 C1	Gar China	
76 B2	Garabogaz Turkm.	
76 B2	Garabogazköl Turkm.	
76 B2	Garabogazköl Aylagy b. Turkm.	
53 C1	Garah Austr.	
151 E2	Garanhuns Brazil	
135 E2	Garberville U.S.A.	
101 D1	Garbsen Ger.	
154 C2	Garça Brazil	
101 E1	Gardelegen Ger.	
136 C3	Garden City U.S.A.	
129 E2	Garden Hill Can.	
77 C3	Gardêz Afgh.	
88 B2	Gargždai Lith.	
123 C3	Gariep Dam dam S. Africa	
122 A3	Garies S. Africa	
119 D3	Garissa Kenya	
102 C2	Garmisch-Partenkirchen Ger.	
52 B2	Garnpung Lake imp. l. Austr.	
104 B3	Garonne r. France	
117 C4	Garoowe Somalia	
74 B2	Garoth India	
118 B2	Garoua Cameroon	
96 B2	Garry r. U.K.	
126 E2	Garry Lake Can.	
119 E3	Garsen Kenya	
61 B2	Garut Indon.	
140 B2	Gary U.S.A.	
145 B2	Garza García Mex.	
68 C2	Garzê China	
104 B2	Gascony, Gulf of France	
50 A2	Gascoyne r. Austr.	
115 D3	Gashua Nigeria	
131 D2	Gaspé Can.	
131 D2	Gaspésie, Péninsule de la pen. Can.	
143 E1	Gaston, Lake U.S.A.	
143 D1	Gastonia U.S.A.	
107 C2	Gata, Cabo de c. Spain	
88 D2	Gatchina Rus. Fed.	
98 C1	Gateshead U.K.	
139 D2	Gatesville U.S.A.	
130 C2	Gatineau r. Can.	
53 D1	Gatton Austr.	
129 E2	Gauer Lake Can.	
93 E4	Gausta mt. Norway	
123 C2	Gauteng prov. S. Africa	
79 C2	Gāvbandī Iran	
111 B3	Gavdos i. Greece	
93 G3	Gävle Sweden	
89 F2	Gavrilov Posad Rus. Fed.	
89 E2	Gavrilov-Yam Rus. Fed.	
62 A1	Gawai Myanmar	
52 A2	Gawler Austr.	
52 A2	Gawler Ranges hills Austr.	
75 C2	Gaya India	
114 C3	Gaya Niger	
140 C1	Gaylord U.S.A.	
86 E2	Gayny Rus. Fed.	
80 B2	Gaza terr. Asia	
80 B2	Gaza terr. Asia	
76 C2	Gazojak Turkm.	
114 B4	Gbarnga Liberia	
103 D1	Gdańsk Pol.	
88 A3	Gdańsk, Gulf of Pol./Rus. Fed.	
88 C2	Gdov Rus. Fed.	
103 D1	Gdynia Pol.	
116 B3	Gedaref Sudan	
101 D2	Gedern Ger.	
111 C3	Gediz r. Turkey	
102 C1	Gedser Denmark	
100 B2	Geel Belgium	
52 B3	Geelong Austr.	
101 E1	Geesthacht Ger.	
75 C1	Gê'gyai China	
129 D2	Geikie r. Can.	
93 E3	Geilo Norway	
62 B1	Gejiu China	
108 B3	Gela Sicilia Italy	
91 D3	Gelendzhik Rus. Fed.	
	Gelibolu Turkey see Gallipoli	
100 C2	Gelsenkirchen Ger.	
118 B2	Gemena Dem. Rep. Congo	
111 C2	Gemlik Turkey	
117 C4	Genalē Wenz r. Eth.	
81 D3	Genāveh Iran	
153 B4	General Acha Arg.	
153 B4	General Alvear Arg.	
153 C4	General Belgrano Arg.	
144 B2	General Cepeda Mex.	
153 B4	General Pico Arg.	
153 B4	General Roca Arg.	
64 B2	General Santos Phil.	
141 D2	Genesee r. U.S.A.	
141 D2	Geneseo U.S.A.	
105 D2	Geneva Switz.	
141 D2	Geneva U.S.A.	
105 D2	Geneva, Lake France/Switz.	
	Genève Switz. see Geneva	
106 B2	Genil r. Spain	
100 B2	Genk Belgium	
108 A2	Genoa Italy	
	Genova Italy see Genoa	
101 F1	Genthin Ger.	
50 A2	Geographe Bay Austr.	
131 D1	George r. Can.	
122 B3	George S. Africa	
143 D3	George, Lake FL U.S.A.	
141 E2	George, Lake NY U.S.A.	
114 A3	Georgetown Gambia	
151 C1	Georgetown Guyana	
60 B1	Georgetown Malaysia	
143 E2	Georgetown SC U.S.A.	
139 D2	Georgetown TX U.S.A.	
55 I2	George V Land reg. Antarctica	
81 C1	Georgia country Asia	
143 D2	Georgia state U.S.A.	
130 B2	Georgian Bay Can.	
51 C2	Georgina watercourse Austr.	
77 E2	Georgiyevka Kazakh.	
87 D4	Georgiyevsk Rus. Fed.	
101 F2	Gera Ger.	
151 D3	Geral de Goiás, Serra hills Brazil	
54 B2	Geraldine N.Z.	
50 A2	Geraldton Austr.	
80 B1	Gerede Turkey	
74 A1	Gereshk Afgh.	
135 C2	Gerlach U.S.A.	
103 E2	Gerlachovský štít mt. Slovak.	
102 C1	Germany country Europe	
100 C2	Gerolstein Ger.	
101 E3	Gerolzhofen Ger.	
101 D2	Gersfeld (Rhön) Ger.	
75 C1	Gêrzê China	
141 D3	Gestro, Wabē r. Eth.	
141 D3	Gettysburg PA U.S.A.	
136 D1	Gettysburg SD U.S.A.	
109 D2	Gevgelija Macedonia	
111 C3	Geyikli Turkey	
122 B2	Ghaap Plateau S. Africa	
115 C1	Ghadāmis Libya	
75 C2	Ghaghara r. India	
114 B4	Ghana country Africa	
120 B3	Ghanzi Botswana	
115 C1	Ghardaïa Alg.	
115 D1	Gharyān Libya	
75 C2	Ghatal India	
75 B2	Ghaziabad India	
75 C2	Ghazipur India	
77 C3	Ghaznī Afgh.	
100 A2	Ghent Belgium	
110 B1	Gherla Romania	
105 D3	Ghisonaccia Corse France	
74 B2	Ghotaru India	
74 A2	Ghotki Pak.	
91 E3	Giaginskaya Rus. Fed.	
97 C1	Giant's Causeway lava field U.K.	
61 C2	Gianyar Indon.	
109 C3	Giarre Sicilia Italy	
108 A1	Giaveno Italy	
122 A2	Gibeon Namibia	
106 B2	Gibraltar Gibraltar	
106 B2	Gibraltar, Strait of Morocco/Spain	
50 B2	Gibson Desert Austr.	
68 C1	Gichgeniyn Nuruu mts Mongolia	
117 B4	Gīdolē Eth.	
104 C2	Gien France	
101 D2	Gießen Ger.	
101 E1	Gifhorn Ger.	
128 C2	Gift Lake Can.	
67 C3	Gifu Japan	
96 B3	Gigha i. U.K.	
106 B1	Gijón-Xixón Spain	
138 A2	Gila r. U.S.A.	
138 A2	Gila Bend U.S.A.	
51 D1	Gilbert r. Austr.	
49 F2	Gilbert Islands is Kiribati	
134 D1	Gildford U.S.A.	
53 C2	Gilgandra Austr.	
74 B1	Gilgit Pak.	

4 B1 Gilgit r. Pak.
3 C2 Gilgunnia Austr.
9 E2 Gillam Can.
6 B2 Gillette U.S.A.
9 E2 Gillingham U.K.
9 E2 Gimli Can.
7 C4 Ginir Eth.
9 C2 Ginosa Italy
3 C3 Gippsland reg. Austr.
4 A2 Girdar Dhor r. Pak.
7 D1 Giresun Turkey
7 D1 Girona Spain
3 B3 Girvan U.K.
4 C1 Gisborne N.Z.
3 F4 Gislaved Sweden
9 C3 Gitarama Rwanda
8 B2 Giulianova Italy
8 C2 Giurgiu Romania
0 C1 Giuvala, Pasul pass Romania
5 C2 Givors France
3 C3 Giyani S. Africa
6 B2 Giza Egypt
9 D2 Gjakovë Kosovo
9 D2 Gjilan Kosovo
9 D2 Gjirokastër Albania
6 E2 Gjoa Haven Can.
3 F3 Gjøvik Norway
1 C2 Glace Bay Can.
4 B1 Glacier Peak vol. U.S.A.
9 E2 Gladstone Austr.
2 A3 Gláma mts Iceland
9 C2 Glamoč Bos.-Herz.
0 C3 Glan r. Ger.
7 B2 Glanaruddery Mountains hills Ireland
6 B3 Glasgow U.K.
0 F3 Glasgow KY U.S.A.
6 B1 Glasgow MT U.S.A.
9 B3 Glastonbury U.K.
1 F2 Glauchau Ger.
6 E3 Glazov Rus. Fed.
8 E3 Glazunovka Rus. Fed.
9 E3 Glen Coe val. U.K.
8 A2 Glendale U.S.A.
3 D2 Glen Davis Austr.
6 C1 Glendive U.S.A.
2 B3 Glenelg r. Austr.
3 D1 Glen Innes Austr.
6 B2 Glennallen U.S.A.
6 C2 Glenrothes U.K.
1 E2 Glens Falls U.S.A.
9 E4 Glen Shee val. U.K.
7 B2 Glenties Ireland
3 C1 Glenwood U.S.A.
6 B3 Glenwood Springs U.S.A.
.03 D1 Gliwice Pol.
8 A2 Globe U.S.A.
3 D1 Głogów Pol.
2 F3 Glomfjord Norway
3 F3 Glomma r. Norway
3 D2 Gloucester Austr.
9 B3 Gloucester U.K.
.01 F1 Glöwen Ger.
7 E1 Glubokoye Kazakh.
01 D1 Glückstadt Ger.
03 C2 Gmünd Austria
02 C2 Gmunden Austria
01 D1 Gnarrenburg Ger.
01 D1 Gniezno Pol.
Gnjilane Kosovo see Gjilan
5 D2 Goalpara India
6 B3 Goat Fell h. U.K.
17 C4 Goba Eth.
20 A3 Gobabis Namibia
53 A6 Gobernador Gregores Arg.
9 D2 Gobi des. China/Mongolia
00 C2 Goch Ger.

122 A1 Gochas Namibia
74 B3 Godavari r. India
73 C3 Godavari, Mouths of the India
130 B2 Goderich Can.
74 B2 Godhra India
129 E2 Gods r. Can.
129 E2 Gods Lake Can.
Godthåb Greenland see Nuuk
Godwin-Austen, Mount China/Pakistan see K2
130 C2 Goéland, Lac au l. Can.
131 D1 Goélands, Lac aux l. Can.
100 A2 Goes Neth.
154 C1 Goiandira Brazil
154 C1 Goiânia Brazil
154 B1 Goiás Brazil
154 B2 Goio-Erê Brazil
111 C2 Gökçeada i. Turkey
111 C3 Gökçedağ Turkey
121 B2 Gokwe Zimbabwe
93 E3 Gol Norway
62 A1 Golaghat India
111 C2 Gölcük Turkey
103 E1 Goldap Pol.
101 F1 Goldberg Ger.
53 D1 Gold Coast Austr.
114 B4 Gold Coast Ghana
128 C2 Golden Can.
54 B2 Golden Bay N.Z.
128 B3 Golden Hinde mt. Can.
97 B2 Golden Vale lowland Ireland
135 C3 Goldfield U.S.A.
128 B3 Gold River Can.
143 E1 Goldsboro U.S.A.
135 C4 Goleta U.S.A.
68 C2 Golmud China
81 D2 Golpāyegān Iran
96 C2 Golspie U.K.
119 C3 Goma Dem. Rep. Congo
75 C2 Gomati r. India
115 D3 Gombe Nigeria
115 D3 Gombi Nigeria
Gomel' Belarus see Homyel'
144 B2 Gómez Palacio Mex.
147 C3 Gonaïves Haiti
147 C3 Gonâve, Île de la i. Haiti
81 D2 Gonbad-e Kavus Iran
117 B3 Gonder Eth.
75 C2 Gondia India
111 C2 Gönen Turkey
115 D4 Gongola r. Nigeria
53 C2 Gongolgon Austr.
145 C2 Gonzáles Mex.
139 D3 Gonzales U.S.A.
122 A3 Good Hope, Cape of S. Africa
134 D2 Gooding U.S.A.
136 C3 Goodland U.S.A.
53 C1 Goodooga Austr.
98 C2 Goole U.K.
53 C2 Goolgowi Austr.
52 A3 Goolwa Austr.
53 D1 Goondiwindi Austr.
134 B2 Goose Lake U.S.A.
102 B2 Göppingen Ger.
75 C2 Gorakhpur India
109 C2 Goražde Bos.-Herz.
111 C3 Gördes Turkey
89 D3 Gordeyevka Rus. Fed.
51 D4 Gordon, Lake Austr.
115 D4 Goré Chad
117 B4 Gorē Eth.
54 A3 Gore N.Z.
81 C1 Gorey Ireland
81 D2 Gorgān Iran
81 C1 Gori Georgia
108 B1 Gorizia Italy

Gor'kiy Rus. Fed. see Nizhniy Novgorod
103 E2 Gorlice Pol.
103 C1 Görlitz Ger.
109 D2 Gornji Milanovac Serbia
109 C2 Gornji Vakuf Bos.-Herz.
77 E1 Gorno-Altaysk Rus. Fed.
110 C2 Gornotrakiyska Nizina lowland Bulg.
77 E1 Gornyak Rus. Fed.
59 D3 Goroka P.N.G.
114 B3 Gorom Gorom Burkina
59 C2 Gorontalo Indon.
89 E3 Gorshechnoye Rus. Fed.
97 B2 Gorumna Island Ireland
91 D3 Goryachiy Klyuch Rus. Fed.
103 D1 Gorzów Wielkopolski Pol.
53 D2 Gosford Austr.
66 D2 Goshogawara Japan
101 E2 Goslar Ger.
109 C2 Gospić Croatia
99 C3 Gosport U.K.
109 D2 Gostivar Macedonia
Göteborg Sweden see Gothenburg
101 E2 Gotha Ger.
93 F4 Gothenburg Sweden
136 C2 Gothenburg U.S.A.
93 G4 Gotland i. Sweden
111 B2 Gotse Delchev Bulg.
93 G4 Gotska Sandön i. Sweden
67 B4 Gōtsu Japan
101 D2 Göttingen Ger.
128 B2 Gott Peak Can.
100 B1 Gouda Neth.
114 A3 Goudiri Senegal
115 D3 Goudoumaria Niger
130 C2 Gouin, Réservoir resr Can.
53 C2 Goulburn Austr.
53 B3 Goulburn r. N.S.W. Austr.
53 B3 Goulburn r. Vic. Austr.
114 B3 Goundam Mali
107 D2 Gouraya Alg.
104 C3 Gourdon France
115 D3 Gouré Niger
122 B3 Gourits r. S. Africa
114 B3 Gourma-Rharous Mali
53 C3 Gourock Range mts Austr.
155 D1 Governador Valadares Brazil
143 E3 Governor's Harbour Bahamas
68 C2 Govĭ Altayn Nuruu mts Mongolia
75 C2 Govind Ballash Pant Sagar resr India
99 A3 Gower pen. U.K.
152 C3 Goya Arg.
81 C1 Göyçay Azer.
75 C1 Gozha Co salt l. China
122 B3 Graaff-Reinet S. Africa
101 E1 Grabow Ger.
109 C2 Gračac Croatia
87 E3 Grachevka Rus. Fed.
101 F2 Gräfenhainichen Ger.
53 D1 Grafton Austr.
137 D1 Grafton U.S.A.
139 D2 Graham U.S.A.
128 A2 Graham Island Can.
55 P3 Graham Land pen. Antarctica
123 C3 Grahamstown S. Africa
151 D2 Grajaú Brazil
111 B2 Grammos mt. Greece
96 B2 Grampian Mountains U.K.
146 B3 Granada Nic.
106 C2 Granada Spain
141 E1 Granby Can.
114 A2 Gran Canaria i. Islas Canarias
152 B3 Gran Chaco reg. Arg./Para.

Grand

136 C1 **Grand** r. U.S.A.
146 C2 **Grand Bahama** i. Bahamas
131 E2 **Grand Bank** Can.
158 C2 **Grand Banks of Newfoundland** N. Atlantic Ocean
138 A1 **Grand Canyon** U.S.A.
138 A1 **Grand Canyon** gorge U.S.A.
146 B3 **Grand Cayman** i. Cayman Is
129 C2 **Grand Centre** Can.
134 C1 **Grand Coulee** U.S.A.
152 B2 **Grande** r. Bol.
154 B2 **Grande** r. Brazil
153 B6 **Grande, Bahía** b. Arg.
155 D2 **Grande, Ilha** i. Brazil
128 C2 **Grande Cache** Can.
Grand Canal canal China see *Jinghang Yunhe*
128 C2 **Grande Prairie** Can.
114 B2 **Grand Erg Occidental** des. Alg.
115 C2 **Grand Erg Oriental** des. Alg.
131 D2 **Grande-Rivière** Can.
152 B4 **Grandes, Salinas** salt flat Arg.
131 D2 **Grand Falls** N.B. Can.
131 E2 **Grand Falls-Windsor** Nfld. and Lab. Can.
128 C2 **Grand Forks** Can.
137 D1 **Grand Forks** U.S.A.
128 C1 **Grandin, Lac** l. Can.
137 D2 **Grand Island** U.S.A.
142 B3 **Grand Isle** U.S.A.
136 B3 **Grand Junction** U.S.A.
114 B4 **Grand-Lahou** Côte d'Ivoire
131 D2 **Grand Lake** N.B. Can.
131 E2 **Grand Lake** Nfld. and Lab. Can.
137 E1 **Grand Marais** Can.
106 B2 **Grândola** Port.
129 E2 **Grand Rapids** Can.
140 B2 **Grand Rapids** MI U.S.A.
137 E1 **Grand Rapids** MN U.S.A.
136 A2 **Grand Teton** mt. U.S.A.
147 C2 **Grand Turk** Turks and Caicos Is
134 C1 **Grangeville** U.S.A.
128 B2 **Granisle** Can.
134 E1 **Granite Peak** U.S.A.
108 B3 **Granitola, Capo** c. Sicilia Italy
93 F4 **Gränna** Sweden
101 F1 **Gransee** Ger.
99 C2 **Grantham** U.K.
96 C2 **Grantown-on-Spey** U.K.
138 B1 **Grants** U.S.A.
134 B2 **Grants Pass** U.S.A.
104 B2 **Granville** France
129 C2 **Granville Lake** Can.
155 D1 **Grão Mogol** Brazil
123 C3 **Graskop** S. Africa
105 D3 **Grasse** France
107 D1 **Graus** Spain
92 F1 **Gravdal** Norway
104 B2 **Grave, Pointe de** pt France
129 D3 **Gravelbourg** Can.
130 C2 **Gravenhurst** Can.
53 D1 **Gravesend** Austr.
99 D3 **Gravesend** U.K.
105 D2 **Gray** France
103 D2 **Graz** Austria
146 C2 **Great Abaco** i. Bahamas
50 B3 **Great Australian Bight** g. Austr.
54 C1 **Great Barrier Island** N.Z.
51 D1 **Great Barrier Reef** Austr.
135 C3 **Great Basin** U.S.A.
126 D2 **Great Bear Lake** Can.
93 F4 **Great Belt** sea chan. Denmark
137 D3 **Great Bend** U.S.A.

63 A2 **Great Coco Island** Cocos Is
53 B3 **Great Dividing Range** mts Austr.
146 B2 **Greater Antilles** is Caribbean Sea
60 A3 **Greater Sunda Islands** is Indon.
134 D1 **Great Falls** U.S.A.
123 C3 **Great Fish** r. S. Africa
123 C3 **Great Fish Point** S. Africa
147 C2 **Great Inagua** i. Bahamas
122 B3 **Great Karoo** plat. S. Africa
123 C3 **Great Kei** r. S. Africa
99 B2 **Great Malvern** U.K.
122 A2 **Great Namaqualand** reg. Namibia
63 A3 **Great Nicobar** i. India
99 D2 **Great Ouse** r. U.K.
119 D3 **Great Rift Valley** Africa
119 D3 **Great Ruaha** r. Tanz.
134 D2 **Great Salt Lake** U.S.A.
135 D2 **Great Salt Lake Desert** U.S.A.
116 A2 **Great Sand Sea** des. Egypt/Libya
128 C1 **Great Slave Lake** Can.
143 D1 **Great Smoky Mountains** U.S.A.
50 B2 **Great Victoria Desert** Austr.
70 B1 **Great Wall** tourist site China
99 D3 **Great Yarmouth** U.K.
106 B1 **Gredos, Sierra de** mts Spain
111 B3 **Greece** country Europe
136 C2 **Greeley** U.S.A.
82 F1 **Greem-Bell, Ostrov** i. Rus. Fed.
140 B3 **Green** r. KY U.S.A.
136 B3 **Green** r. WY U.S.A.
140 B1 **Green Bay** U.S.A.
140 B1 **Green Bay** b. U.S.A.
140 C3 **Greenbrier** r. U.S.A.
140 B3 **Greencastle** U.S.A.
143 D1 **Greeneville** U.S.A.
141 E2 **Greenfield** U.S.A.
129 D2 **Green Lake** Can.
127 I2 **Greenland** terr. N. America
160 R2 **Greenland Sea** Greenland/Svalbard
96 B3 **Greenock** U.K.
135 D3 **Green River** UT U.S.A.
136 B2 **Green River** WY U.S.A.
140 B3 **Greensburg** IN U.S.A.
141 D2 **Greensburg** PA U.S.A.
143 E2 **Green Swamp** U.S.A.
138 A2 **Green Valley** U.S.A.
114 B4 **Greenville** Liberia
142 C2 **Greenville** AL U.S.A.
142 B2 **Greenville** MS U.S.A.
143 E1 **Greenville** NC U.S.A.
143 D2 **Greenville** SC U.S.A.
139 D2 **Greenville** TX U.S.A.
53 D2 **Greenwell Point** Austr.
143 D2 **Greenwood** U.S.A.
50 B2 **Gregory, Lake** imp. l. Austr.
51 D1 **Gregory Range** hills Austr.
102 C1 **Greifswald** Ger.
101 F2 **Greiz** Ger.
93 F4 **Grenaa** Denmark
147 D3 **Grenada** country West Indies
104 C3 **Grenade** France
53 C2 **Grenfell** Austr.
129 D2 **Grenfell** Can.
105 D2 **Grenoble** France
51 D1 **Grenville, Cape** Austr.
134 B1 **Gresham** U.S.A.
100 C1 **Greven** Ger.

111 B2 **Grevena** Greece
100 C2 **Grevenbroich** Ger.
101 E1 **Grevesmühlen** Ger.
136 B2 **Greybull** U.S.A.
128 A1 **Grey Hunter Peak** Can.
54 B2 **Greymouth** N.Z.
52 B1 **Grey Range** hills Austr.
97 C2 **Greystones** Ireland
143 D2 **Griffin** U.S.A.
53 C2 **Griffith** Austr.
101 F2 **Grimma** Ger.
102 C1 **Grimmen** Ger.
98 C2 **Grimsby** U.K.
128 C2 **Grimshaw** Can.
92 B2 **Grímsstaðir** Iceland
93 E4 **Grimstad** Norway
137 E2 **Grinnell** U.S.A.
123 C3 **Griqualand East** reg. S. Afr
122 B2 **Griqualand West** reg. S. Africa
127 F1 **Grise Fiord** Can.
96 C1 **Gritley** U.K.
123 C2 **Groblersdal** S. Africa
122 B2 **Groblershoop** S. Africa
Grodno Belarus see *Hrodna*
104 B2 **Groix, Île de** i. France
100 C1 **Gronau (Westfalen)** Ger.
92 F3 **Grong** Norway
100 C1 **Groningen** Neth.
122 B2 **Grootdrink** S. Africa
51 C1 **Groote Eylandt** i. Austr.
120 A2 **Grootfontein** Namibia
122 A2 **Groot Karas Berg** plat. Namibia
122 B3 **Groot Swartberge** mts S. Af
123 C3 **Groot Winterberg** mt. S. Af
101 E2 **Großenlüder** Ger.
102 C2 **Großer Rachel** mt. Ger.
103 C2 **Grosser Speikkogel** mt. Austria
108 B2 **Grosseto** Italy
101 D3 **Groß-Gerau** Ger.
102 C2 **Großglockner** mt. Austria
100 C1 **Groß-Hesepe** Ger.
101 E2 **Großlohra** Ger.
122 A1 **Gross Ums** Namibia
131 E1 **Groswater Bay** Can.
130 B2 **Groundhog** r. Can.
49 I4 **Groupe Actéon** is Fr. Polyn.
135 B3 **Grover Beach** U.S.A.
141 E2 **Groveton** U.S.A.
87 D4 **Groznyy** Rus. Fed.
109 C1 **Grubišno Polje** Croatia
103 D1 **Grudziądz** Pol.
122 A2 **Grünau** Namibia
92 A3 **Grundarfjörður** Iceland
89 E3 **Gryazi** Rus. Fed.
89 F2 **Gryazovets** Rus. Fed.
103 D1 **Gryfice** Pol.
102 C1 **Gryfino** Pol.
146 C2 **Guacanayabo, Golfo de** b. Cuba
144 B2 **Guadalajara** Mex.
106 C1 **Guadalajara** Spain
49 E3 **Guadalcanal** i. Solomon Is
107 C1 **Guadalope** r. Spain
106 B2 **Guadalquivir** r. Spain
132 B4 **Guadalupe** i. Mex.
106 B2 **Guadalupe, Sierra de** mts Spain
138 C2 **Guadalupe Peak** U.S.A.
144 B2 **Guadalupe Victoria** Mex.
144 B2 **Guadalupe y Calvo** Mex.
106 C1 **Guadarrama, Sierra de** mts Spain
147 D3 **Guadeloupe** terr. West Indie

106 B2	Guadiana r. Port./Spain	
106 C2	Guadix Spain	
154 B2	Guaíra Brazil	
147 C3	Guajira, Península de la pen. Col.	
150 A2	Gualaceo Ecuador	
59 D2	Guam terr. N. Pacific Ocean	
144 B2	Guamúchil Mex.	
144 B2	Guanacevi Mex.	
151 D3	Guanambi Brazil	
150 B1	Guanare Venez.	
146 B2	Guane Cuba	
70 A2	Guang'an China	
71 B3	Guangchang China	
71 B3	Guangdong prov. China	
71 A3	Guangxi Zhuangzu Zizhiqu aut. reg. China	

Guansuo China see Guanling

70 A2	Guangyuan China
71 B3	Guangzhou China
155 D1	Guanhães Brazil
70 A2	Guanipa r. Venez.
71 A3	Guanling China
65 A1	Guanshui China
147 C2	Guantánamo Cuba
150 B3	Guaporé r. Bol./Brazil
154 C3	Guarapuava Brazil
154 C3	Guaraqueçaba Brazil
155 C2	Guaratinguetá Brazil
106 B1	Guarda Port.
154 C1	Guarda Mor Brazil
106 C1	Guardo Spain
152 B2	Guarujá Brazil
144 B2	Guasave Mex.
146 A3	Guatemala country Central America
146 A3	Guatemala City Guat.
150 B1	Guaviare r. Col.
155 C2	Guaxupé Brazil
150 A2	Guayaquil Ecuador
150 B3	Guayaramerín Bol.
144 A2	Guaymas Mex.
68 C2	Guazhou China
117 B3	Guba Eth.
86 E1	Guba Dolgaya Rus. Fed.
89 E3	Gubkin Rus. Fed.
115 C1	Guelma Alg.
130 C2	Guelmine Morocco
130 B2	Guelph Can.
145 C2	Guémez Mex.
104 C2	Guéret France
95 C4	Guernsey terr. Channel Is
144 A2	Guerrero Negro Mex.
131 D1	Guers, Lac l. Can.
118 B2	Guider Cameroon
108 B2	Guidonia-Montecelio Italy
71 A3	Guigang China
104 B2	Guignicourt France
123 D1	Guija Moz.
99 C3	Guildford U.K.
71 B3	Guilin China
130 C1	Guillaume-Delisle, Lac l. Can.
106 B1	Guimarães Port.
114 A3	Guinea country Africa
113 F6	Guinea, Gulf of Africa
114 A3	Guinea-Bissau country Africa
104 B2	Guingamp France
104 B2	Guipavas France
154 B2	Guiratinga Brazil
150 B1	Güiria Venez.
100 A3	Guise France
150 B1	Guiuan Phil.
71 A3	Guiyang China
71 A3	Guizhou prov. China
74 B1	Gujranwala Pak.
74 B1	Gujrat Pak.

91 D2	Gukovo Rus. Fed.	
53 C2	Gulargambone Austr.	
73 B3	Gulbarga India	
88 C2	Gulbene Latvia	
79 C2	Gulf, The Asia	
111 B3	Gulf of Corinth sea chan. Greece	
142 D2	Gulfport U.S.A.	
69 E1	Gulian China	
77 C2	Guliston Uzbek.	

Gulja China see Yining

129 D2	Gull Lake Can.
111 C3	Güllük Turkey
119 D2	Gulu Uganda
76 B3	Gumare Botswana
120 B2	Gumdag Turkm.
75 C2	Gumla India
100 C2	Gummersbach Ger.
74 B2	Guna India
53 C3	Gundagai Austr.
111 C3	Güney Turkey
118 B3	Gungu Dem. Rep. Congo
129 E2	Guninao r. Can.
53 D2	Gunnedah Austr.
136 B3	Gunnison CO U.S.A.
135 D3	Gunnison UT U.S.A.
136 B3	Gunnison r. U.S.A.
73 B3	Guntakal India
74 B2	Guru Sikhar mt. India

Gur'yev Kazakh. see Atyrau

115 C3	Gusau Nigeria
65 A2	Gushan China
70 B2	Gushi China
83 I3	Gusinoozersk Rus. Fed.
89 F2	Gus'-Khrustal'nyy Rus. Fed.
108 A3	Guspini Sardegna Italy
128 A2	Gustavus U.S.A.
101 F1	Güstrow Ger.
101 D2	Gütersloh Ger.
121 C2	Gutu Zimbabwe
75 D2	Guwahati India
150 C1	Guyana country S. America

Guyi China see Sanjiang

139 C1	Guymon U.S.A.
53 C1	Guyra Austr.
70 A2	Guyuan China
144 B1	Guzmán Mex.
74 A2	Gwadar Pak.
75 B2	Gwalior India
121 B3	Gwanda Zimbabwe
117 D3	Gwardafuy, Gees c. Somalia
97 B1	Gweebarra Bay Ireland
121 B2	Gweru Zimbabwe
115 D3	Gwoza Nigeria
53 D2	Gwydir r. Austr.
75 C2	Gyangzê China
75 C1	Gyaring Co l. China
68 C2	Gyaring Hu l. China
86 G1	Gydan Peninsula Rus. Fed.

Gydanskiy Poluostrov pen. Rus. Fed. see Gydan Peninsula

Gyêgu China see Yushu

68 C3	Gyigang China
51 E2	Gympie Austr.
103 D2	Gyöngyös Hungary
103 D2	Győr Hungary
129 E2	Gypsumville Can.

| 103 E2 | Gyula Hungary |
| 81 C1 | Gyumri Armenia |

H

88 B2	Haapsalu Estonia	
100 B1	Haarlem Neth.	
101 C2	Haarstrang ridge Ger.	
54 A2	Haast N.Z.	
78 B3	Habban Yemen	
81 C2	Ḩabbānīyah, Hawr al l. Iraq	
67 C4	Hachijō-jima i. Japan	
66 D2	Hachinohe Japan	
121 C3	Hacufera Moz.	
79 C2	Ḩadd, Ra's al pt Oman	
96 C3	Haddington U.K.	
115 D3	Hadejia Nigeria	
93 E4	Haderslev Denmark	
65 B2	Hadyach Ukr.	
65 B2	Haeju N. Korea	
65 B2	Haeju-man b. N. Korea	
65 B3	Haenam S. Korea	
78 B3	Ḩafar al Bāţin Saudi Arabia	
62 A1	Haflong India	
92 A3	Hafnarfjörður Iceland	
78 A3	Hagar Nish Plateau Eritrea/Sudan	
48 D2	Hagåtña Guam	
100 C2	Hagen Ger.	
101 E1	Hagenow Ger.	
128 B2	Hagensborg Can.	
141 D3	Hagerstown U.S.A.	
93 F3	Hagfors Sweden	
67 B4	Hagi Japan	
62 B1	Ha Giang Vietnam	
97 B2	Hag's Head Ireland	
104 B2	Hague, Cap de la c. France	
119 D3	Hai Tanz.	
62 B1	Hai Dương Vietnam	
80 B2	Haifa Israel	
71 B3	Haifeng China	
71 B3	Haikou China	
78 B2	Ḩā'il Saudi Arabia	
92 H2	Hailuoto i. Fin.	
69 D3	Hainan i. China	
71 A4	Hainan prov. China	
128 A2	Haines U.S.A.	
128 A1	Haines Junction Can.	
101 C2	Hainich ridge Ger.	
101 E2	Hainleite ridge Ger.	
62 B1	Hai Phong Vietnam	
147 C3	Haiti country West Indies	
116 B3	Haiya Sudan	
103 E2	Hajdúböszörmény Hungary	
78 B3	Hajjah Yemen	
79 C2	Ḩājjīābād Iran	
62 A1	Haka Myanmar	
81 C2	Hakkârı Turkey	
66 D2	Hakodate Japan	

Ḩalab Syria see Aleppo

78 B2	Halabān Saudi Arabia
81 C2	Ḩalabja Iraq
116 B2	Halaib Sudan
78 A2	Halaib Triangle terr. Egypt/Sudan
79 C3	Ḩalānīyāt, Juzur al is Oman
78 A2	Ḩālat 'Ammār Saudi Arabia
101 E2	Halberstadt Ger.
93 F4	Halcon, Mount Phil.
93 E4	Halden Norway
101 E1	Haldensleben Ger.
75 B2	Haldwani India
79 C2	Ḩāleh Iran
54 A2	Halfmoon Bay N.Z.
131 D2	Halifax Can.

98 C2 Halifax U.K.
141 D3 Halifax U.S.A.
65 B3 Halla-san mt. S. Korea
127 F2 Hall Beach Can.
100 B2 Halle Belgium
101 E2 Halle (Saale) Ger.
102 C2 Hallein Austria
137 D2 Hallock U.S.A.
127 G2 Hall Peninsula Can.
50 B1 Halls Creek Austr.
59 C2 Halmahera i. Indon.
93 F4 Halmstad Sweden
62 B1 Ha Long Vietnam
67 B4 Hamada Japan
81 C2 Hamadān Iran
80 B2 Hamāh Syria
67 C4 Hamamatsu Japan
93 F3 Hamar Norway
116 B2 Ḥamāţah, Jabal mt. Egypt
73 C4 Hambantota Sri Lanka
101 D1 Hamburg Ger.
78 A2 Ḩanīs̲h, Wādī al watercourse
      Saudi Arabia
78 B3 Ḩamdah Saudi Arabia
93 H3 Hämeenlinna Fin.
101 D1 Hameln Ger.
50 A2 Hamersley Range mts Austr.
65 B2 Hamhŭng N. Korea
68 C2 Hami China
116 B2 Hamid Sudan
52 B3 Hamilton Austr.
130 C2 Hamilton Can.
54 C1 Hamilton N.Z.
96 B3 Hamilton U.K.
142 C2 Hamilton AL U.S.A.
134 D1 Hamilton MT U.S.A.
140 C3 Hamilton OH U.S.A.
93 I3 Hamina Fin.
100 C2 Hamm Ger.
81 C2 Ḩammār, Hawr al imp. l. Iraq
101 D2 Hammelburg Ger.
92 G3 Hammerdal Sweden
92 H1 Hammerfest Norway
142 B2 Hammond U.S.A.
141 E3 Hammonton U.S.A.
115 D2 Ḩamrā', Al Ḩamādah al plat.
      Libya
78 A2 Ḩanak Saudi Arabia
66 D3 Hanamaki Japan
101 D2 Hanau Ger.
69 D2 Hanbogd Mongolia
70 B2 Hancheng China
140 B1 Hancock U.S.A.
70 B2 Handan China
135 C3 Hanford U.S.A.
68 C1 Hangayn Nuruu mts
      Mongolia
      Hanggin Houqi China see
      Xamba
      Hangö Fin. see Hanko
70 C2 Hangzhou China
70 C2 Hangzhou Wan b. China
      Hanjia China see Pengshui
      Hanjiang China see Yangzhou
93 H4 Hanko Fin.
135 D3 Hanksville U.S.A.
54 B2 Hanmer Springs N.Z.
129 C2 Hanna Can.
137 E3 Hannibal U.S.A.
101 D1 Hannover Ger.
101 D2 Hannoversch Münden Ger.
93 F4 Hanöbukten b. Sweden
62 B1 Ha Nôi Vietnam
      Hanoi Vietnam see Ha Nôi
130 B2 Hanover Can.
122 B3 Hanover S. Africa
93 E4 Hanstholm Denmark

88 C3 Hantsavichy Belarus
75 C2 Hanumana India
74 B2 Hanumangarh India
70 A2 Hanzhong China
92 H2 Haparanda Sweden
100 B2 Hapert Neth.
131 D1 Happy Valley-Goose Bay Can.
78 A2 Ḩaql Saudi Arabia
79 B2 Ḩaradh Saudi Arabia
88 C2 Haradok Belarus
78 B3 Ḩarajā' Saudi Arabia
121 C2 Harare Zimbabwe
79 C3 Ḩarāsis, Jiddat al des. Oman
69 D1 Har-Ayrag Mongolia
69 E1 Harbin China
131 E1 Harbour Breton Can.
74 B2 Harda India
      Hardangerfjorden sea chan.
      Norway
100 C1 Hardenberg Neth.
100 B1 Harderwijk Neth.
122 A3 Hardeveld mts S. Africa
134 E1 Hardin U.S.A.
128 C1 Hardisty Lake Can.
100 C1 Haren (Ems) Ger.
117 C4 Härer Eth.
117 C4 Hargeysa Somalia
110 C1 Harghita-Mădăraş, Vârful mt.
      Romania
68 C2 Har Hu l. China
74 B1 Haripur Pak.
74 A1 Hari Rūd r. Afgh./Iran
100 B1 Harlingen Neth.
139 D3 Harlingen U.S.A.
99 C3 Harlow U.K.
134 E1 Harlowton U.S.A.
134 C2 Harney Basin U.S.A.
134 C2 Harney Lake U.S.A.
93 G3 Härnösand Sweden
69 E1 Har Nur China
68 C1 Har Nuur l. Mongolia
114 B4 Harper Liberia
101 D1 Harpstedt Ger.
130 C1 Harricana, Rivière d' r. Can.
53 D2 Harrington Austr.
131 E1 Harrington Harbour Can.
96 A2 Harris, Sound of sea chan.
      U.K.
140 B3 Harrisburg IL U.S.A.
141 D2 Harrisburg PA U.S.A.
123 C2 Harrismith S. Africa
142 B1 Harrison U.S.A.
131 E1 Harrison, Cape Can.
126 A2 Harrison Bay U.S.A.
141 D3 Harrisonburg U.S.A.
137 E3 Harrisonville U.S.A.
98 C2 Harrogate U.K.
110 C2 Hârşova Romania
92 G2 Harstad Norway
122 B2 Hartbees watercourse S. Africa
103 D2 Hartberg Austria
141 E2 Hartford U.S.A.
99 A3 Hartland Point U.K.
98 C1 Hartlepool U.K.
128 B2 Hartley Bay Can.
123 B2 Harts r. S. Africa
143 D2 Hartwell Reservoir U.S.A.
68 C1 Har Us Nuur l. Mongolia
136 C1 Harvey U.S.A.
99 D3 Harwich U.K.
101 E2 Harz hills Ger.
73 B3 Hassan India
100 B2 Hasselt Belgium
115 C1 Hassi Messaoud Alg.
93 F4 Hässleholm Sweden
100 B2 Hastière-Lavaux Belgium
53 C3 Hastings Austr.

54 C1 Hastings N.Z.
99 D3 Hastings U.K.
137 E2 Hastings MN U.S.A.
137 D2 Hastings NE U.S.A.
      Hatay Turkey see Antakya
129 D2 Hatchet Lake Can.
52 B2 Hatfield Austr.
68 C1 Hatgal Mongolia
62 B2 Ha Tinh Vietnam
143 E1 Hatteras, Cape U.S.A.
142 C2 Hattiesburg U.S.A.
100 C2 Hattingen Ger.
63 B3 Hat Yai Thai.
117 C4 Haud reg. Eth.
93 E4 Haugesund Norway
93 E4 Haukeligrend Norway
92 I2 Haukipudas Fin.
54 C1 Hauraki Gulf N.Z.
114 B1 Haut Atlas mts Morocco
131 D2 Hauterive Can.
114 B2 Hauts Plateaux Alg.
146 B2 Havana Cuba
99 C3 Havant U.K.
101 E1 Havel r. Ger.
101 F1 Havelberg Ger.
54 B2 Havelock N.Z.
54 C1 Havelock North N.Z.
99 A3 Haverfordwest U.K.
103 D2 Havlíčkův Brod Czech Rep.
92 H1 Havøysund Norway
111 C3 Havran Turkey
134 E1 Havre U.S.A.
131 D2 Havre-Aubert Can.
131 D1 Havre-St-Pierre Can.
124 E5 Hawai'i i. U.S.A.
124 E5 Hawai'ian Islands N. Pacific
      Ocean
98 B2 Hawes U.K.
54 A2 Hawea, Lake N.Z.
54 B1 Hawera N.Z.
98 B1 Hawes U.K.
96 C3 Hawick U.K.
54 C1 Hawke Bay N.Z.
52 A2 Hawker Austr.
52 B1 Hawkers Gate Austr.
135 C3 Hawthorne U.S.A.
52 B2 Hay Austr.
128 C1 Hay r. Can.
134 C1 Hayden U.S.A.
129 E2 Hayes r. Man. Can.
126 E2 Hayes r. Nunavut Can.
79 C3 Haymā' Oman
77 C2 Hayotboshi tog'i mt. Uzbek.
111 C2 Hayrabolu Turkey
128 C1 Hay River Can.
137 D3 Hays U.S.A.
78 B3 Ḩays Yemen
90 B2 Haysyn Ukr.
99 C3 Haywards Heath U.K.
81 D2 Hazar Turkm.
74 A1 Hazarajat reg. Afgh.
140 C3 Hazard U.S.A.
75 C2 Hazaribagh India
75 C2 Hazaribagh Range mts India
128 B2 Hazelton Can.
141 D2 Hazleton U.S.A.
53 C3 Healesville Austr.
130 B2 Hearst Can.
70 B2 Hebi China
53 C1 Hebel Austr.
142 B1 Heber Springs U.S.A.
70 B2 Hebi China
131 D1 Hebron Can.
128 A2 Hecate Strait Can.
71 A3 Hechi China
93 F3 Hede Sweden
100 B1 Heerenveen Neth.

100 B1 Heerhugowaard Neth.
100 B2 Heerlen Neth.
Hefa Israel see Haifa
70 B2 Hefei China
70 B3 Hefeng China
69 E1 Hegang China
102 B1 Heide Ger.
122 A1 Heide Namibia
102 B2 Heidelberg Ger.
122 B3 Heidelberg S. Africa
102 B2 Heilbronn Ger.
69 E1 Heilong Jiang r. China
93 I3 Heinola Fin.
92 F3 Helagsfjället mt. Sweden
142 B2 Helena AR U.S.A.
134 D1 Helena MT U.S.A.
96 B2 Helensburgh U.K.
102 B1 Helgoland i. Ger.
102 B1 Helgoländer Bucht g. Ger.
Helixi China see Ningguo
92 A3 Hella Iceland
100 B2 Hellevoetsluis Neth.
107 C2 Hellín Spain
76 C3 Helmand r. Afgh.
101 E2 Helmbrechts Ger.
122 A2 Helmeringhausen Namibia
100 B2 Helmond Neth.
96 C1 Helmsdale U.K.
96 C1 Helmsdale r. U.K.
101 E1 Helmstedt Ger.
65 B1 Helong China
93 F4 Helsingborg Sweden
Helsingfors Fin. see Helsinki
93 F4 Helsingør Denmark
93 H3 Helsinki Fin.
97 C2 Helvick Head Ireland
99 C3 Hemel Hempstead U.K.
101 D1 Hemmoor Ger.
92 F2 Hemnesberget Norway
70 B2 Henan prov. China
140 B3 Henderson KY U.S.A.
143 E1 Henderson NC U.S.A.
135 D3 Henderson NV U.S.A.
139 E2 Henderson TX U.S.A.
143 D1 Hendersonville U.S.A.
99 C3 Hendon U.K.
62 A1 Hengduan Shan mts China
100 C1 Hengelo Neth.
Hengnan China see Hengyang
70 B2 Hengshui China
71 A3 Hengxian China
71 B3 Hengyang China
Hengzhou China see Hengxian
91 C2 Heniches'k Ukr.
.00 C2 Hennef (Sieg) Ger.
.30 E1 Henrietta Maria, Cape Can.
.39 D1 Henryetta U.S.A.
.27 G2 Henry Kater, Cape Can.
.01 D1 Henstedt-Ulzburg Ger.
.20 A3 Hentiesbaai Namibia
71 A3 Hepu China
76 C3 Herāt Afgh.
29 D2 Herbert Can.
01 D2 Herbstein Ger.
98 B2 Hereford U.K.
39 C2 Hereford U.S.A.
01 D1 Herford Ger.
00 C2 Herkenbosch Neth.
96 □ Herma Ness hd U.K.
22 A3 Hermanus S. Africa
53 C2 Hermidale Austr.
34 C1 Hermiston U.S.A.
59 D3 Hermit Islands P.N.G.
44 B2 Hermosillo Mex.
54 B3 Hernandarias Para.
00 C2 Herne Ger.

93 E4 Herning Denmark
99 C3 Hertford U.K.
123 C2 Hertzogville S. Africa
51 E2 Herwey Bay Austr.
101 F2 Herzberg Ger.
101 E3 Herzogenaurach Ger.
71 A3 Heshan China
128 A1 Hess r. Can.
101 D2 Hessisch Lichtenau Ger.
136 C1 Hettinger U.S.A.
101 E2 Hettstedt Ger.
98 B1 Hexham U.K.
71 B3 Heyuan China
52 B3 Heywood Austr.
70 B2 Heze China
71 B3 Hezhou China
137 D3 Hiawatha U.S.A.
137 E1 Hibbing U.S.A.
54 C1 Hicks Bay N.Z.
66 D2 Hidaka-sanmyaku mts Japan
145 C2 Hidalgo Mex.
144 B2 Hidalgo del Parral Mex.
154 C1 Hidrolândia Brazil
High Atlas mts Morocco see
Haut Atlas
134 B2 High Desert U.S.A.
128 C2 High Level Can.
143 E1 High Point U.S.A.
128 C2 High Prairie Can.
128 C2 High River Can.
129 D2 Highrock Lake Can.
99 C3 High Wycombe U.K.
78 A2 Hijaz reg. Saudi Arabia
54 C1 Hikurangi mt. N.Z.
101 E2 Hildburghausen Ger.
100 C2 Hilders Ger.
101 D1 Hildesheim Ger.
81 C2 Hillah Iraq
100 C2 Hillesheim Ger.
140 C3 Hillsboro OH U.S.A.
139 D2 Hillsboro TX U.S.A.
53 C2 Hillston Austr.
143 D2 Hilton Head Island U.S.A.
100 B1 Hilversum Neth.
68 B1 Himalaya mts Asia
67 B4 Himeji Japan
123 C2 Himeville S. Africa
51 D1 Hinchinbrook Island Austr.
74 A1 Hindu Kush mts Afgh./Pak.
143 D2 Hinesville U.S.A.
75 B2 Hinganghat India
81 C2 Hınıs Turkey
92 G2 Hinnøya i. Norway
106 C2 Hinojosa del Duque Spain
62 A2 Hinthada Myanmar
128 C2 Hinton Can.
75 C2 Hirakud Reservoir India
66 D2 Hirosaki Japan
67 B4 Hiroshima Japan
101 E3 Hirschaid Ger.
101 E2 Hirschberg Ger.
105 C2 Hirson France
93 E4 Hirtshals Denmark
74 B2 Hisar India
147 C2 Hispaniola i. Caribbean Sea
81 C2 Hīt Iraq
67 D3 Hitachi Japan
67 D3 Hitachinaka Japan
92 E3 Hitra i. Norway
49 I3 Hiva Oa i. Fr. Polynesia
92 F3 Hjälmaren l. Sweden
129 D1 Hjalmar Lake Can.
93 F4 Hjørring Denmark
123 D2 Hlabisa S. Africa
92 B2 Hlíð Iceland
91 C2 Hlobyne Ukr.

123 C2 Hlohlowane S. Africa
123 C2 Hlotse Lesotho
91 C1 Hlukhiv Ukr.
88 C3 Hlybokaye Belarus
114 C4 Ho Ghana
62 B2 Hoa Binh Vietnam
122 A1 Hoachanas Namibia
51 D4 Hobart Austr.
139 D1 Hobart U.S.A.
139 C2 Hobbs U.S.A.
93 E4 Hobro Denmark
117 C4 Hobyo Somalia
63 B2 Ho Chi Minh City Vietnam
114 B3 Hôd reg. Maur.
78 B3 Hodeidah Yemen
103 E2 Hódmezővásárhely Hungary
Hoek van Holland Neth. see
Hook of Holland
65 B2 Hoeyang N. Korea
101 E2 Hof Ger.
101 E2 Hofheim in Unterfranken
Ger.
92 B3 Höfn Austurland Iceland
92 A2 Höfn Vestfirðir Iceland
92 B3 Hofsjökull Iceland
67 B4 Hōfu Japan
115 C2 Hoggar plat. Alg.
93 G4 Högsby Sweden
101 D2 Hohe Rhön mts Ger.
100 C2 Hohe Venn moorland Belgium
70 B1 Hohhot China
75 C1 Hoh Xil Shan mts China
63 B2 Hôi An Vietnam
62 A1 Hojai India
54 B2 Hokitika N.Z.
66 D2 Hokkaidō i. Japan
128 B2 Holberg Can.
138 A2 Holbrook U.S.A.
137 D2 Holdrege U.S.A.
146 C2 Holguín Cuba
92 B2 Hóll Iceland
Holland country Europe see
Netherlands
140 B2 Holland U.S.A.
100 B1 Hollum Neth.
142 C2 Holly Springs U.S.A.
134 C4 Hollywood U.S.A.
143 D3 Hollywood U.S.A.
92 F2 Holm Norway
92 H3 Holmsund Sweden
122 A2 Holoog Namibia
93 E4 Holstebro Denmark
143 D1 Holston r. U.S.A.
98 A2 Holyhead U.K.
98 C1 Holy Island England U.K.
98 A2 Holy Island Wales U.K.
136 C2 Holyoke U.S.A.
101 D2 Holzminden Ger.
62 A1 Homalin Myanmar
101 D2 Homberg (Efze) Ger.
114 B3 Hombori Mali
127 G2 Home Bay Can.
143 D2 Homestead U.S.A.
92 F3 Hommelvik Norway
80 B2 Homs Syria
89 D3 Homyel' Belarus
122 A3 Hondeklipbaai S. Africa
145 D3 Hondo r. Belize/Mex.
139 D3 Hondo U.S.A.
146 B3 Honduras country Central
America
93 F3 Hønefoss Norway
135 B2 Honey Lake U.S.A.
104 B2 Honfleur France
70 B3 Honghu China
71 A3 Hongjiang China
69 D3 Hong Kong China

71 B3	Hong Kong *aut. reg.* China	
65 B1	Hongwŏn N. Korea	
70 B2	Hongze Hu *l.* China	
49 E3	Honiara Solomon Is	
66 D3	Honjō Japan	
92 I1	Honningsvåg Norway	
67 B3	Honshū *i.* Japan	
134 B1	Hood, Mount *vol.* U.S.A.	
50 A3	Hood Point U.S.A.	
134 B1	Hood River U.S.A.	
100 C1	Hoogeveen Neth.	
100 C1	Hoogezand-Sappemeer Neth.	
100 C2	Hoog-Keppel Neth.	
100 B2	Hook of Holland Neth.	
128 A2	Hoonah U.S.A.	
100 B1	Hoorn Neth.	
128 B3	Hope Can.	
142 B2	Hope U.S.A.	
83 N2	Hope, Point U.S.A.	
131 D1	Hopedale Can.	
131 D1	Hope Mountains Can.	
52 B3	Hopetoun Austr.	
122 B2	Hopetown S. Africa	
141 D3	Hopewell U.S.A.	
130 C1	Hopewell Islands Can.	
50 B2	Hopkins, Lake *imp. l.* Austr.	
140 B3	Hopkinsville U.S.A.	
134 B1	Hoquiam U.S.A.	
81 C1	Horasan Turkey	
93 F4	Hörby Sweden	
89 D3	Horki Belarus	
91 D2	Horlivka Ukr.	
79 D2	Hormak Iran	
79 C2	Hormuz, Strait of Iran/Oman	
103 D2	Horn Austria	
92 A2	Horn *c.* Iceland	
153 B6	Horn, Cape Chile	
141 D2	Hornell U.S.A.	
130 B2	Hornepayne Can.	
98 C2	Hornsea U.K.	
90 B2	Horodenka Ukr.	
91 C1	Horodnya Ukr.	
90 B2	Horodok *Khmel'nyts'ka Oblast'* Ukr.	
90 A2	Horodok *L'vivs'ka Oblast'* Ukr.	
90 A1	Horodyshche Ukr.	
	Horqin Youyi Qianqi China *see* Ulanhot	
131 E1	Horse Islands Can.	
52 B3	Horsham Austr.	
126 C2	Horton *r.* Can.	
117 B4	Hosa'ina Eth.	
74 A2	Hoshab Pak.	
74 B1	Hoshiarpur India	
77 E3	Hotan China	
122 B2	Hotazel S. Africa	
142 B2	Hot Springs AR U.S.A.	
136 C2	Hot Springs SD U.S.A.	
128 C1	Hottah Lake Can.	
62 B1	Houayxay Laos	
100 B2	Houffalize Belgium	
70 B2	Houma China	
142 B3	Houma U.S.A.	
128 B2	Houston Can.	
139 D3	Houston U.S.A.	
122 B3	Houwater S. Africa	
68 C1	Hovd Mongolia	
99 C3	Hove U.K.	
68 C1	Hövsgöl Nuur *l.* Mongolia	
116 A3	Howar, Wadi *watercourse* Sudan	
53 C3	Howe, Cape Austr.	
49 G2	Howland Island N. Pacific Ocean	
53 C3	Howlong Austr.	
101 D2	Höxter Ger.	
96 C1	Hoy *i.* U.K.	
93 E3	Høyanger Norway	
102 C1	Hoyerswerda Ger.	
62 A2	Hpapun Myanmar	
103 D1	Hradec Králové Czech Rep.	
109 C2	Hrasnica Bos.-Herz.	
91 C1	Hrebinka Ukr.	
88 B3	Hrodna Belarus	
62 A1	Hsi-hseng Myanmar	
71 C3	Hsinchu Taiwan	
71 C3	Hsinying Taiwan	
62 A1	Hsipaw Myanmar	
70 A2	Huachi China	
150 A3	Huacho Peru	
69 D2	Huade China	
65 B1	Huadian China	
70 B2	Huai'an China	
70 B2	Huaibei China	
71 A3	Huaihua China	
70 B2	Huainan China	
70 B2	Huaiyang China	
145 C3	Huajuápan de León Mex.	
59 C3	Huaki Indon.	
71 C3	Hualien Taiwan	
150 A2	Huallaga *r.* Peru	
120 A2	Huambo Angola	
150 A3	Huancayo Peru	
	Huancgaoba China *see* Xingyi	
70 B2	Huangchuan China	
	Huang Hai *sea* N. Pacific Ocean *see* Yellow Sea	
	Huang He *r.* China *see* Yellow River	
71 A4	Huangliu China	
70 B2	Huangshan China	
70 B2	Huangshi China	
70 A2	Huangtu Gaoyuan *plat.* China	
71 C3	Huangyan China	
65 B1	Huanren China	
150 A2	Huánuco Peru	
152 B2	Huanuni Bol.	
150 A2	Huaráz Peru	
150 A3	Huarmey Peru	
152 A3	Huasco Chile	
152 A3	Huasco *r.* Chile	
144 B2	Huatabampo Mex.	
145 C3	Huatusco Mex.	
71 A3	Huayuan China	
70 B2	Hubei *prov.* China	
73 B3	Hubli India	
100 C2	Hückelhoven Ger.	
98 C2	Hucknall U.K.	
98 C2	Huddersfield U.K.	
93 G3	Hudiksvall Sweden	
141 E2	Hudson *r.* U.S.A.	
129 D2	Hudson Bay Can.	
127 F3	Hudson Bay *sea* Can.	
128 B2	Hudson's Hope Can.	
127 G2	Hudson Strait Can.	
63 B2	Huê Vietnam	
146 A3	Huehuetenango Guat.	
144 B2	Huehueto, Cerro *mt.* Mex.	
145 C2	Huejutla Mex.	
106 B2	Huelva Spain	
107 C2	Huércal-Overa Spain	
107 C1	Huesca Spain	
106 C2	Huéscar Spain	
50 B3	Hughes (abandoned) Austr.	
139 D2	Hugo U.S.A.	
122 B2	Huhudi S. Africa	
122 A2	Huib-Hoch Plateau Namibia	
71 B3	Huichang China	
65 B1	Huich'ŏn N. Korea	
120 A2	Huila, Planalto da Angola	
71 B3	Huilai China	
62 B1	Huili China	
65 B1	Huinan China	
93 H3	Huittinen Fin.	
145 C3	Huixtla Mex.	
	Huiyang China *see* Huizhou	
62 B1	Huize China	
71 B3	Huizhou China	
78 B2	Hujr Saudi Arabia	
122 B1	Hukuntsi Botswana	
78 B2	Hulayfah Saudi Arabia	
66 B1	Hulin China	
130 C2	Hull Can.	
	Hull U.K. *see* Hulun Buir	
69 D1	Hulun Buir China	
69 D1	Hulun Nur *l.* China	
91 D2	Hulyaypole Ukr.	
69 E1	Huma China	
150 B2	Humaitá Brazil	
122 B3	Humansdorp S. Africa	
98 C2	Humber *est.* U.K.	
126 D3	Humboldt Can.	
142 C1	Humboldt U.S.A.	
135 C2	Humboldt *r.* U.S.A.	
103 E2	Humenné Slovakia	
53 C3	Hume Reservoir Austr.	
138 A1	Humphreys Peak U.S.A.	
92 A2	Húnaflói *b.* Iceland	
71 B3	Hunan *prov.* China	
65 C1	Hunchun China	
110 B1	Hunedoara Romania	
101 D2	Hünfeld Ger.	
103 D2	Hungary *country* Europe	
52 B1	Hungerford Austr.	
65 B2	Hŭngnam N. Korea	
65 A1	Hun He *r.* China	
99 D2	Hunstanton U.K.	
101 D1	Hunte *r.* Ger.	
51 D4	Hunter Islands Austr.	
99 C2	Huntingdon U.K.	
140 B2	Huntington IN U.S.A.	
140 C3	Huntington WV U.S.A.	
54 C1	Huntly N.Z.	
96 C2	Huntly U.K.	
130 C2	Huntsville Can.	
142 C2	Huntsville AL U.S.A.	
139 D2	Huntsville TX U.S.A.	
59 D3	Huon Peninsula P.N.G.	
70 B2	Huozhou China	
137 D2	Huron U.S.A.	
140 C2	Huron, Lake Can./U.S.A.	
135 D3	Hurricane U.S.A.	
92 B2	Húsavík Iceland	
110 C1	Huşi Romania	
126 A2	Huslia U.S.A.	
78 B3	Ḥuṣn Al 'Abr Yemen	
102 B1	Husum Ger.	
69 C1	Hutag-Öndör Mongolia	
60 A1	Hutanopan Indon.	
137 D3	Hutchinson U.S.A.	
70 C2	Huzhou China	
92 C3	Hvalnes Iceland	
92 B3	Hvannadalshnúkur *vol.* Iceland	
109 C2	Hvar *i.* Croatia	
120 B2	Hwange Zimbabwe	
136 C2	Hyannis U.S.A.	
68 C1	Hyargas Nuur *salt l.* Mongolia	
50 A3	Hyden Austr.	
73 B3	Hyderabad India	
74 A2	Hyderabad Pak.	
105 D3	Hyères France	
105 D3	Hyères, Îles d' *is* France	
65 B1	Hyesan N. Korea	
128 B2	Hyland Post Can.	
67 B3	Hyōno-sen *mt.* Japan	

99 D3 **Hythe** U.K.
93 H3 **Hyvinkää** Fin.

I

150 B2 **Iaco** r. Brazil
110 C1 **Ialomiţa** r. Romania
110 C1 **Ianca** Romania
110 C1 **Iaşi** Romania
64 A1 **Iba** Phil.
115 C4 **Ibadan** Nigeria
150 A1 **Ibagué** Col.
150 A1 **Ibarra** Ecuador
78 B3 **Ibb** Yemen
100 C1 **Ibbenbüren** Ger.
115 C4 **Ibi** Nigeria
155 C1 **Ibiá** Brazil
155 D1 **Ibiraçu** Brazil
107 D2 **Ibiza** Spain
107 D2 **Ibiza** i. Spain
151 D3 **Ibotirama** Brazil
79 C2 **Ibrā'** Oman
79 C2 **Ibrī** Oman
150 A3 **Ica** Peru
92 B2 **Iceland** country Europe
66 D3 **Ichinoseki** Japan
91 C1 **Ichnya** Ukr.
65 B2 **Ich'ŏn** N. Korea
139 E2 **Idabel** U.S.A.
134 D2 **Idaho** state U.S.A.
134 D2 **Idaho Falls** U.S.A.
100 C3 **Idar-Oberstein** Ger.
116 B2 **Idfu** Egypt
118 B3 **Idiofa** Dem. Rep. Congo
80 B2 **Idlib** Syria
154 B2 **Iepê** Brazil
100 A2 **Ieper** Belgium
119 D3 **Ifakara** Tanz.
121 D3 **Ifanadiana** Madag.
115 C4 **Ife** Nigeria
114 C3 **Ifôghas, Adrar des** hills Mali
61 C1 **Igan** Sarawak Malaysia
154 C2 **Igarapava** Brazil
82 G2 **Igarka** Rus. Fed.
74 B3 **Igatpuri** India
81 C1 **Iğdır** Turkey
108 A3 **Iglesias** Sardegna Italy
127 F2 **Igloolik** Can.
Igluligaarjuk Can. see
Chesterfield Inlet
130 A2 **Ignace** Can.
88 C2 **Ignalina** Lith.
110 C2 **İğneada** Turkey
111 B3 **Igoumenitsa** Greece
86 E3 **Igra** Rus. Fed.
86 F2 **Igrim** Rus. Fed.
54 B3 **Iguaçu** r. Brazil
154 C3 **Iguaçu Falls** Arg./Brazil
145 C3 **Iguala** Mex.
107 D1 **Igualada** Spain
154 C2 **Iguape** Brazil
154 B2 **Iguatemi** Brazil
154 B2 **Iguatemi** r. Brazil
151 E2 **Iguatu** Brazil
118 A3 **Iguéla** Gabon
119 D3 **Igunga** Tanz.
121 D2 **Ihosy** Madag.
92 I3 **Iisalmi** Fin.
115 C4 **Ijebu-Ode** Nigeria
100 B1 **IJmuiden** Neth.
100 B1 **IJssel** r. Neth.
100 B1 **IJsselmeer** l. Neth.
123 C3 **Ikageng** S. Africa
111 C3 **Ikaria** i. Greece
118 C3 **Ikela** Dem. Rep. Congo

110 B2 **Ikhtiman** Bulg.
67 A4 **Iki-shima** i. Japan
121 D3 **Ikongo** Madag.
65 B2 **Iksan** S. Korea
64 B1 **Ilagan** Phil.
81 C2 **Īlām** Iran
75 C2 **Ilam** Nepal
103 D1 **Iława** Pol.
79 C2 **Ilazārān, Kūh-e** mt. Iran
129 D2 **Île-à-la-Crosse** Can.
129 D2 **Île-à-la-Crosse, Lac** l. Can.
118 C3 **Ilebo** Dem. Rep. Congo
124 H6 **Île Clipperton** terr. N. Pacific
Ocean
119 D2 **Ileret** Kenya
113 K11 **Îles Crozet** is Indian Ocean
49 I3 **Îles du Désappointement** is Fr.
Polynesia
49 I4 **Îles Gambier** is Fr. Polynesia
99 A3 **Ilford** U.K.
99 A3 **Ilfracombe** U.K.
155 D2 **Ilha Grande, Baía de** b. Brazil
154 B2 **Ilha Grande, Represa** resr
Brazil
154 B2 **Ilha Solteira, Represa** resr
Brazil
106 B1 **Ílhavo** Port.
151 E3 **Ilhéus** Brazil
64 B2 **Iligan** Phil.
152 A4 **Illapel** Chile
90 F2 **Illichivs'k** Ukr.
140 A3 **Illinois** r. U.S.A.
140 B3 **Illinois** state U.S.A.
90 B2 **Illintsi** Ukr.
115 C2 **Illizi** Alg.
89 D2 **Il'men', Ozero** l. Rus. Fed.
101 E2 **Ilmenau** Ger.
150 A3 **Ilo** Peru
64 B1 **Iloilo** Phil.
92 J3 **Ilomantsi** Fin.
115 C4 **Ilorin** Nigeria
53 D1 **Iluka** Austr.
127 H2 **Ilulissat** Greenland
67 A4 **Imari** Japan
117 C4 **Īmī** Eth.
108 B2 **Imola** Italy
151 D2 **Imperatriz** Brazil
136 C2 **Imperial** U.S.A.
118 B2 **Impfondo** Congo
62 A1 **Imphal** India
111 C2 **İmroz** Turkey
150 B3 **Inambari** r. Peru
115 C3 **In Aménas** Alg.
59 C3 **Inanwatan** Indon.
92 I2 **Inari** Fin.
92 I2 **Inarijärvi** l. Fin.
67 D3 **Inawashiro-ko** l. Japan
80 B1 **İnce Burun** pt Turkey
65 B2 **Inch'ŏn** S. Korea
123 D2 **Incomati** r. Moz.
78 A3 **Inda Silasē** Eth.
144 B2 **Indé** Mex.
135 C2 **Independence** CA U.S.A.
137 E2 **Independence** IA U.S.A.
137 D3 **Independence** KS U.S.A.
137 E3 **Independence** MO U.S.A.
134 C2 **Independence Mountains**
U.S.A.
76 B2 **Inderborskiy** Kazakh.
72 B2 **India** country Asia
141 D2 **Indiana** U.S.A.
140 B2 **Indiana** state U.S.A.
140 B3 **Indianapolis** U.S.A.
129 D2 **Indian Head** Can.
159 **Indian Ocean** World
137 D2 **Indianola** IA U.S.A.
142 B2 **Indianola** MS U.S.A.

135 C3 **Indian Springs** U.S.A.
86 D2 **Indiga** Rus. Fed.
83 K2 **Indigirka** r. Rus. Fed.
109 D1 **Indija** Serbia
135 C4 **Indio** U.S.A.
58 B3 **Indonesia** country Asia
74 B2 **Indore** India
61 B2 **Indramayu, Tanjung** pt Indon.
104 C2 **Indre** r. France
74 A2 **Indus** r. China/Pak.
74 A2 **Indus, Mouths of the** Pak.
80 B1 **Inebolu** Turkey
111 C2 **İnegöl** Turkey
144 B3 **Infiernillo, Presa** resr Mex.
53 D1 **Inglewood** Austr.
102 C2 **Ingolstadt** Ger.
75 C2 **Ingraj Bazar** India
123 D2 **Inhaca** Moz.
121 C3 **Inhambane** Moz.
97 A2 **Inishbofin** i. Ireland
97 B2 **Inishmore** i. Ireland
97 C1 **Inishowen** pen. Ireland
54 B2 **Inland Kaikoura Range** mts
N.Z.
102 C2 **Inn** r. Europe
127 G1 **Innaanganeq** c. Greenland
96 B2 **Inner Sound** sea chan. U.K.
51 D1 **Innisfail** Austr.
102 C2 **Innsbruck** Austria
154 B1 **Inocência** Brazil
118 B3 **Inongo** Dem. Rep. Congo
103 D1 **Inowrocław** Pol.
114 C2 **In Salah** Alg.
62 A2 **Insein** Myanmar
86 F2 **Inta** Rus. Fed.
137 E1 **International Falls** U.S.A.
130 C1 **Inukjuak** Can.
126 C2 **Inuvik** Can.
96 B2 **Inveraray** U.K.
54 A3 **Invercargill** N.Z.
53 D1 **Inverell** Austr.
96 B2 **Invergordon** U.K.
128 C2 **Invermere** Can.
131 D2 **Inverness** Can.
96 B2 **Inverness** U.K.
96 C2 **Inverurie** U.K.
52 A3 **Investigator Strait** Austr.
71 **Inya** Rus. Fed.
119 D3 **Inyonga** Tanz.
87 D3 **Inza** Rus. Fed.
111 B3 **Ioannina** Greece
137 D3 **Iola** U.S.A.
96 A2 **Iona** i. U.K.
111 B3 **Ionian Islands** Greece
109 C3 **Ionian Sea** Greece/Italy
Ionioi Nisoi is Greece see
Ionian Islands
111 C3 **Ios** i. Greece
137 E2 **Iowa** state U.S.A.
137 E2 **Iowa City** U.S.A.
154 C1 **Ipameri** Brazil
155 D1 **Ipatinga** Brazil
123 C2 **Ipatovo** Rus. Fed.
123 C2 **Ipelegeng** S. Africa
150 A1 **Ipiales** Col.
154 B3 **Ipiranga** Brazil
60 B1 **Ipoh** Malaysia
154 B1 **Iporá** Brazil
118 C2 **Ippy** C.A.R.
111 C2 **Ipsala** Turkey
53 D1 **Ipswich** Austr.
99 D2 **Ipswich** U.K.
127 G2 **Iqaluit** Can.
152 A3 **Iquique** Chile
150 A2 **Iquitos** Peru
Irakleio Greece see **Iraklion**
111 C3 **Iraklion** Greece

Iran

76 B3 **Iran** *country* Asia
61 C1 **Iran, Pegunungan** *mts* Indon.
79 D2 **Īrānshahr** Iran
144 B2 **Irapuato** Mex.
81 C2 **Iraq** *country* Asia
154 B3 **Irati** Brazil
80 B2 **Irbid** Jordan
86 F3 **Irbit** Rus. Fed.
151 D3 **Irecê** Brazil
97 C2 **Ireland** *country* Europe
118 C3 **Irema** Dem. Rep. Congo
76 C2 **Irgiz** Kazakh.
114 B3 **Irigui** *reg.* Mali/Maur.
119 D3 **Iringa** Tanz.
154 C2 **Iriri** *r.* Brazil
95 B3 **Irish Sea** Ireland/U.K.
69 C1 **Irkutsk** Rus. Fed.
52 A2 **Iron Knob** Austr.
140 B1 **Iron Mountain** U.S.A.
140 A1 **Ironwood** U.S.A.
64 B1 **Irosin** Phil.
67 C4 **Irō-zaki** *pt* Japan
90 C1 **Irpin'** Ukr.
62 A2 **Irrawaddy** *r.* Myanmar
63 A2 **Irrawaddy, Mouths of the Myanmar**
86 F2 **Irtysh** *r.* Kazakh./Rus. Fed.
107 C1 **Irun** Spain
96 B3 **Irvine** U.K.
64 B2 **Isabela** Phil.
146 B3 **Isabela, Cordillera** *mts* Nic.
92 A2 **Ísafjörður** Iceland
67 B4 **Isahaya** Japan
105 E2 **Isar** *r.* Ger.
96 □ **Isbister** U.K.
108 B2 **Ischia, Isola d'** *i.* Italy
67 C4 **Ise** Japan
118 C2 **Isengi** Dem. Rep. Congo
100 C2 **Iserlohn** Ger.
101 D1 **Isernhagen** Ger.
67 C4 **Ise-wan** *b.* Japan
114 C4 **Iseyin** Nigeria
Isfahan Iran *see* **Eşfahān**
66 D2 **Ishikari-wan** *b.* Japan
77 D1 **Ishim** *r.* Kazakh./Rus. Fed.
66 D3 **Ishinomaki** Japan
67 D3 **Ishioka** Japan
140 B1 **Ishpeming** U.S.A.
111 C2 **Işıklar Dağı** *mts* Turkey
111 C3 **Işıklı** Turkey
123 D2 **Isipingo** S. Africa
119 C2 **Isiro** Dem. Rep. Congo
80 B2 **İskenderun** Turkey
82 G3 **Iskitim** Rus. Fed.
110 B2 **Iskūr** *r.* Bulg.
128 A2 **Iskut** *r.* Can.
74 B1 **Islamabad** Pak.
52 A2 **Island Lagoon** *imp. l.* Austr.
129 E2 **Island Lake** Can.
54 B1 **Islands, Bay of** N.Z.
96 A3 **Islay** *i.* U.K.
98 A1 **Isle of Man** *i.* Irish Sea
77 D3 **Ismoili Somoní, Qullai** *mt.* Tajik.
109 C3 **Isola di Capo Rizzuto** Italy
110 C2 **Isperikh** Bulg.
80 B2 **Israel** *country* Asia
105 C2 **Issoire** France
111 C2 **İstanbul** Turkey
İstanbul Boğazı *str.* Turkey *see* **Bosporus**
111 B3 **Istiaia** Greece
105 C3 **Istres** France
108 B1 **Istria** *pen.* Croatia
151 D3 **Itaberaba** Brazil
155 D1 **Itabira** Brazil
155 D2 **Itabirito** Brazil
151 E3 **Itabuna** Brazil
150 C2 **Itacoatiara** Brazil
154 B2 **Itaguajé** Brazil
154 C2 **Itaí** Brazil
154 B3 **Itaipu, Represa de** *resr* Brazil
151 C2 **Itaituba** Brazil
152 D3 **Itajaí** Brazil
155 D2 **Itajubá** Brazil
108 B2 **Italy** *country* Europe
155 D1 **Itamarandiba** Brazil
155 D1 **Itambacuri** Brazil
155 D1 **Itambé, Pico de** *mt.* Brazil
62 A1 **Itanagar** India
154 C2 **Itanhaém** Brazil
155 D1 **Itanhém** Brazil
155 D1 **Itaobím** Brazil
154 C1 **Itapajipe** Brazil
155 E1 **Itapebi** Brazil
155 D2 **Itapemirim** Brazil
155 D2 **Itaperuna** Brazil
155 D1 **Itapetinga** Brazil
154 C2 **Itapetininga** Brazil
154 C2 **Itapeva** Brazil
151 E3 **Itapicuru** *r.* Brazil
151 D2 **Itapicuru Mirim** Brazil
154 C1 **Itapuranga** Brazil
154 C2 **Itararé** Brazil
75 B2 **Itarsi** India
154 B1 **Itarumã** Brazil
155 D2 **Itaúna** Brazil
71 C3 **Itbayat** *i.* Phil.
141 D2 **Ithaca** U.S.A.
101 D1 **Ith Hils** *ridge* Ger.
118 C2 **Itimbiri** *r.* Dem. Rep. Congo
155 D1 **Itinga** Brazil
154 B1 **Itiquira** Brazil
154 B1 **Itiquira** *r.* Brazil
67 C4 **Itō** Japan
67 C4 **Itu** Brazil
150 A2 **Itui** *r.* Brazil
119 C3 **Ituiutaba** Brazil
118 C3 **Itula** Dem. Rep. Congo
154 C1 **Itumbiara** Brazil
154 B1 **Iturama** Brazil
101 D1 **Itzehoe** Ger.
83 N2 **Iul'tin** Rus. Fed.
154 B2 **Ivaí** *r.* Brazil
92 I2 **Ivalo** Fin.
88 C3 **Ivanava** Belarus
52 B2 **Ivanhoe** Austr.
90 B1 **Ivankiv** Ukr.
90 A2 **Ivano-Frankivs'k** Ukr.
89 F2 **Ivanovo** Rus. Fed.
88 C3 **Ivatsevichy** Belarus
111 C2 **Ivaylovgrad** Bulg.
86 F2 **Ivdel'** Rus. Fed.
154 B2 **Ivinheima** Brazil
154 B2 **Ivinheima** *r.* Brazil
127 H2 **Ivittuut** Greenland
Ivory Coast *country* Africa *see* **Côte d'Ivoire**
108 A1 **Ivrea** Italy
111 C3 **İvrindi** Turkey
127 H2 **Ivujivik** Can.
67 D3 **Iwaki** Japan
67 B4 **Iwakuni** Japan
66 D2 **Iwamizawa** Japan
66 D2 **Iwanai** Japan
88 C3 **Iwye** Belarus
123 D3 **Ixopo** S. Africa
144 B2 **Ixtlán** Mex.
145 D2 **Izamal** Mex.
81 C1 **Izberbash** Rus. Fed.
86 E3 **Izhevsk** Rus. Fed.
86 E2 **Izhma** Rus. Fed.
89 E3 **Izmalkovo** Rus. Fed.
90 B2 **Izmayil** Ukr.
111 C3 **İzmir** Turkey
111 C2 **İznik Gölü** *l.* Turkey
152 B2 **Izozog, Bañados del** *swamp* Bol.
67 B3 **Izumo** Japan
90 B1 **Izyaslav** Ukr.
91 D2 **Izyum** Ukr.

J

106 C2 **Jabal, Bahr el** *r.* Sudan/Uganda *see* **White Nile**
75 B2 **Jabalón** *r.* Spain
50 C1 **Jabalpur** India
109 C1 **Jabiru** Austr.
151 E2 **Jablanica** Bos.-Herz.
Jaboatão dos Guararapes Brazil
154 C2 **Jaboticabal** Brazil
107 C1 **Jaca** Spain
145 C2 **Jacala** Mex.
151 C2 **Jacareacanga** Brazil
155 C2 **Jacareí** Brazil
155 D1 **Jacinto** Brazil
141 E1 **Jackman** U.S.A.
142 C2 **Jackson** *AL* U.S.A.
140 C2 **Jackson** *MI* U.S.A.
142 B2 **Jackson** *MS* U.S.A.
142 C1 **Jackson** *TN* U.S.A.
136 A2 **Jackson** *WY* U.S.A.
54 A2 **Jackson Head** N.Z.
143 D2 **Jacksonville** *AR* U.S.A.
140 A3 **Jacksonville** *FL* U.S.A.
143 E2 **Jacksonville** *NC* U.S.A.
139 D2 **Jacksonville** *TX* U.S.A.
147 C3 **Jacmel** Haiti
74 A2 **Jacobabad** Pak.
151 D3 **Jacobina** Brazil
131 D2 **Jacques-Cartier, Mont** *mt.* Can.
151 D2 **Jacunda** Brazil
154 C2 **Jacupiranga** Brazil
109 C2 **Jadovnik** *mt.* Bos.-Herz.
150 A2 **Jaén** Peru
106 C2 **Jaén** Spain
52 A3 **Jaffa, Cape** Austr.
73 B4 **Jaffna** Sri Lanka
73 C3 **Jagdalpur** India
123 C2 **Jagersfontein** S. Africa
79 C2 **Jaghin** Iran
154 C2 **Jaguariaíva** Brazil
79 C2 **Jahrom** Iran
74 B2 **Jaipur** India
74 B2 **Jaisalmer** India
75 C2 **Jajarkot** Nepal
109 C2 **Jajce** Bos.-Herz.
60 B2 **Jakarta** Indon.
128 A1 **Jakes Corner** Can.
92 G2 **Jäkkvik** Sweden
92 H3 **Jakobstad** Fin.
77 D3 **Jalalabad** Afgh.
77 D2 **Jalal-Abad** Kyrg.
74 B1 **Jalandhar** India
145 C3 **Jalapa** Mex.
154 B2 **Jales** Brazil
74 B2 **Jalgaon** India
115 D4 **Jalingo** Nigeria
74 B3 **Jalna** India
144 B2 **Jalpa** Mex.
75 C2 **Jalpaiguri** India
145 C2 **Jalpan** Mex.
115 E2 **Jālū** Libya
146 C3 **Jamaica** *country* West Indies

146	C3	Jamaica Channel Haiti/Jamaica
75	C3	Jamalpur Bangl.
60	B2	Jambi Indon.
137	D2	James r. N. Dakota/S. Dakota U.S.A.
141	D3	James r. VA U.S.A.
130	B1	James Bay Can.
52	A2	Jamestown Austr.
137	D1	Jamestown ND U.S.A.
141	D2	Jamestown NY U.S.A.
74	B1	Jammu India
74	B1	Jammu and Kashmir terr. Asia
74	B2	Jamnagar India
93	I3	Jämsä Fin.
75	C2	Jamshedpur India
75	C2	Jamuna r. Brazil
75	C2	Janakpur Nepal
155	D1	Janaúba Brazil
81	D2	Jandaq Iran
140	B2	Janesville U.S.A.
84	F1	Jan Mayen terr. Arctic Ocean
81	D1	Jañña Turkm.
122	B3	Jansenville S. Africa
155	D1	Januária Brazil
74	B2	Jaora India
67	C3	Japan country Asia
156	C3	Japan, Sea of N. Pacific Ocean
150	B2	Japurá r. Brazil
154	C1	Jaraguá Brazil
154	B2	Jaraguari Brazil
152	C3	Jardim Brazil
103	D1	Jarocin Pol.
103	E1	Jarosław Pol.
92	F3	Järpen Sweden
70	A2	Jartai China
150	B3	Jarú Brazil
		Jarud China see Lubei
49	H3	Jarvis Island S. Pacific Ocean
79	C2	Jāsk Iran
103	E2	Jasło Pol.
128	C2	Jasper Can.
140	B3	Jasper IN U.S.A.
139	E2	Jasper TX U.S.A.
103	D2	Jastrzębie-Zdrój Pol.
103	D2	Jászberény Hungary
154	B1	Jataí Brazil
74	A2	Jati Pak.
154	C2	Jaú Brazil
150	B2	Jaú r. Brazil
145	C2	Jaumave Mex.
75	C2	Jaunpur India
154	B1	Jauru Brazil
61	B2	Java i. Indon.
		Java Sea Indon. see Jawa, Laut
		Jawa i. Indon. see Java
159	D4	Jawa, Laut sea Indon.
117	C4	Jawhar Somalia
103	D1	Jawor Pol.
103	D1	Jaworzno Pol.
59	D3	Jaya, Puncak mt. Indon.
59	D3	Jayapura Indon.
79	C2	Jaz Mūrīān, Hāmūn-e imp. l. Iran
128	B1	Jean Marie River Can.
131	D1	Jeannin, Lac l. Can.
116	A3	Jebel Abyad Plateau Sudan
96	C3	Jedburgh U.K.
78	A2	Jeddah Saudi Arabia
101	E1	Jeetze r. Ger.
135	C3	Jefferson, Mount U.S.A.
137	E3	Jefferson City U.S.A.
88	C2	Jēkabpils Latvia
103	D1	Jelenia Góra Pol.
88	B2	Jelgava Latvia
61	C2	Jember Indon.
101	E2	Jena Ger.
80	B2	Jengish Chokusu mt. China/Kyrg. see Pobeda Peak
80	B2	Jenīn West Bank
142	B2	Jennings U.S.A.
151	D3	Jequié Brazil
155	D1	Jequitaí Brazil
155	D1	Jequitinhonha Brazil
155	E1	Jequitinhonha r. Brazil
147	C3	Jérémie Haiti
144	B2	Jerez Mex.
106	B2	Jerez de la Frontera Spain
109	D3	Jergucat Albania
115	C1	Jerid, Chott el salt l. Tunisia
134	D2	Jerome U.S.A.
95	C4	Jersey terr. Channel Is
151	D2	Jerumenha Brazil
80	B2	Jerusalem Israel/West Bank
53	D3	Jervis Bay Territory admin. div. Austr.
108	B1	Jesenice Slovenia
108	B2	Jesi Italy
101	F2	Jessen Ger.
75	C2	Jessore Bangl.
143	D2	Jesup U.S.A.
145	C3	Jesús Carranza Mex.
74	B2	Jhalawar India
74	B1	Jhang Pak.
75	C2	Jhansi India
75	C2	Jharsuguda India
74	B1	Jhelum Pak.
70	C2	Jiading China
69	E1	Jiamusi China
71	B3	Ji'an Jiangxi China
65	B1	Ji'an Jilin China
62	A1	Jianchuan China
		Jiandaoyu China see Guojiaba
70	B2	Jiangsu prov. China
71	B3	Jiangxi prov. China
70	A2	Jiangyou China
70	B3	Jianli China
70	B2	Jianqiao China
71	B3	Jianyang Fujian China
70	A2	Jianyang Sichuan China
70	C2	Jiaohe China
70	C2	Jiaozhou China
70	B2	Jiaozuo China
70	C2	Jiaxing China
68	C2	Jiayuguan China
		Jiddah Saudi Arabia see Jeddah
92	G2	Jiehkkevárri mt. Norway
71	B3	Jiexiu China
68	C2	Jigzhi China
103	D2	Jihlava Czech Rep.
117	C4	Jijiga Somalia
116	A2	Jilf al Kabīr, Haḍabat al plat. Egypt
117	C4	Jilib Somalia
69	E2	Jilin China
65	B1	Jilin prov. China
65	A1	Jilin Hada Ling mts China
117	B4	Jīma Eth.
144	B2	Jiménez Chihuahua Mex.
145	C2	Jiménez Tamaulipas Mex.
70	B2	Jinan China
70	B2	Jincheng China
53	D3	Jindabyne Austr.
103	D2	Jindřichův Hradec Czech Rep.
71	B3	Jingdezhen China
70	B2	Jinghang Yunhe canal China
62	B1	Jinghong China
70	B2	Jingmen China
70	A2	Jingning China
70	A2	Jingtai China
71	A3	Jingxi China
65	B1	Jingyu China
70	A2	Jingyuan China
70	B2	Jingzhou China
70	B2	Jingzhou China
71	B3	Jinhua China
70	B1	Jining Nei Mongol China
70	B2	Jining Shandong China
119	D2	Jinja Uganda
117	B4	Jinka Eth.
146	B3	Jinotepe Nic.
71	A3	Jinping China
		Jinsha Jiang r. China see Yangtze
70	B3	Jinshi China
70	B2	Jinzhong China
70	C1	Jinzhou China
150	B2	Jiparaná r. Brazil
75	C1	Jirang China
79	C2	Jiroft Iran
71	A3	Jishou China
110	B2	Jiu r. Romania
70	A2	Jiuding Shan mt. China
70	A2	Jiujiang China
66	B1	Jixi China
78	B3	Jīzān Saudi Arabia
77	C2	Jizzax Uzbek.
151	E2	João Pessoa Brazil
155	C1	João Pinheiro Brazil
74	B2	Jodhpur India
92	I3	Joensuu Fin.
67	C3	Jōetsu Japan
121	C3	Jofane Moz.
88	C2	Jõgeva Estonia
123	C2	Johannesburg S. Africa
134	C2	John Day U.S.A.
134	B1	John Day r. U.S.A.
128	C2	John D'Or Prairie Can.
143	E1	John H. Kerr Reservoir U.S.A.
96	C1	John o'Groats U.K.
143	D1	Johnson City U.S.A.
128	A1	Johnson's Crossing Can.
49	H1	Johnston Atoll N. Pacific Ocean
96	B3	Johnstone U.K.
141	D2	Johnstown U.S.A.
60	B1	Johor Bahru Malaysia
88	C2	Jõhvi Estonia
154	C3	Joinville Brazil
105	D2	Joinville France
92	G2	Jokkmokk Sweden
92	B3	Jökulsá á Fjöllum r. Iceland
140	B2	Joliet U.S.A.
130	C2	Joliette Can.
64	B2	Jolo Phil.
64	B2	Jolo i. Phil.
61	C2	Jombang Indon.
75	C2	Jomsom Nepal
88	B2	Jonava Lith.
142	B1	Jonesboro AR U.S.A.
142	B2	Jonesboro LA U.S.A.
127	F1	Jones Sound sea chan. Can.
93	F4	Jönköping Sweden
131	C2	Jonquière Can.
145	C3	Jonuta Mex.
137	E3	Joplin U.S.A.
80	B2	Jordan country Asia
80	B2	Jordan r. Asia
136	B1	Jordan U.S.A.
134	C2	Jordan Valley U.S.A.
62	A1	Jorhat India
93	E4	Jørpeland Norway
115	C4	Jos Nigeria
145	C3	José Cardel Mex.
131	D1	Joseph, Lac l. Can.
50	B1	Joseph Bonaparte Gulf Austr.
115	C4	Jos Plateau Nigeria
93	E3	Jotunheimen mts Norway
122	B3	Joubertina S. Africa
123	C2	Jouberton S. Africa
93	I3	Joutseno Fin.

Juan de Fuca Strait

134	B1	Juan de Fuca Strait Can./U.S.A.
		Juanshui China *see* **Tongcheng**
145	D2	Juaréz Mex.
151	D2	Juazeiro Brazil
151	E2	Juazeiro do Norte Brazil
117	B4	Juba Sudan
117	C5	Jubba *r.* Somalia
78	B2	Jubbah Saudi Arabia
145	C3	Juchitán Mex.
102	C2	Judenburg Austria
101	D2	Jühnde Ger.
146	B3	Juigalpa Nic.
100	C1	Juist *i.* Ger.
155	D2	Juiz de Fora Brazil
150	A3	Juliaca Peru
75	C2	Jumla Nepal
74	B2	Junagadh India
139	D2	Junction U.S.A.
137	D3	Junction City U.S.A.
154	C2	Jundiaí Brazil
128	A2	Juneau U.S.A.
53	C2	Junee Austr.
105	D2	Jungfrau *mt.* Switz.
141	D2	Juniata *r.* U.S.A.
92	G3	Junsele Sweden
134	C2	Juntura U.S.A.
154	C2	Juquiá Brazil
117	A4	Jur *r.* Sudan
105	D2	Jura *mts* France/Switz.
96	B2	Jura *i.* U.K.
96	B3	Jura, Sound of *sea chan.* U.K.
88	B2	Jurbarkas Lith.
88	B2	Jūrmala Latvia
150	B2	Juruá *r.* Brazil
150	C2	Juruena *r.* Brazil
150	B2	Jutaí *r.* Brazil
101	F2	Jüterbog Ger.
146	B2	Juventud, Isla de la *i.* Cuba
70	B2	Jūyom Iran
79	C2	Jūyom Iran
122	B1	Jwaneng Botswana
93	I3	Jyväskylä Fin.

K

74	B1	K2 *mt.* China/Pakistan
119	C3	Kabalo Dem. Rep. Congo
119	C3	Kabare Dem. Rep. Congo
130	B2	Kabinakagami Lake Can.
118	C3	Kabinda Dem. Rep. Congo
118	B2	Kabo C.A.R.
120	B2	Kabompo Zambia
119	C3	Kabongo Dem. Rep. Congo
77	C3	Kābul Afgh.
64	B2	Kaburuang *i.* Indon.
121	B2	Kabwe Zambia
74	A2	Kachchh, Gulf of India
74	B2	Kachchh, Rann of *marsh* India
83	I3	Kachug Rus. Fed.
81	C1	Kaçkar Dağı *mt.* Turkey
111	C2	Kadıköy Turkey
114	B3	Kadiolo Mali
73	B3	Kadmat *atoll* India
121	B2	Kadoma Zimbabwe
63	A2	Kadonkani Myanmar
114	A3	Kadugli Sudan
115	C3	Kaduna Nigeria
89	E2	Kaduy Rus. Fed.
86	E2	Kadzherom Rus. Fed.
114	A3	Kaédi Maur.
118	B1	Kaélé Cameroon
65	B2	Kaesŏng N. Korea
114	A3	Kaffrine Senegal
121	B2	Kafue Zambia
120	B2	Kafue *r.* Zambia
118	B2	Kaga Bandoro C.A.R.
91	E2	Kagal'nitskaya Rus. Fed.
67	B4	Kagoshima Japan
90	C2	Kaharlyk Ukr.
61	C2	Kahayan *r.* Indon.
118	B3	Kahemba Dem. Rep. Congo
101	E2	Kahla Ger.
79	C2	Kahnūj Iran
92	H2	Kahperusvaarat *mts* Fin.
80	B2	Kahramanmaraş Turkey
79	C2	Kahūrak Iran
59	C3	Kai, Kepulauan *is* Indon.
115	C4	Kaiama Nigeria
54	B2	Kaiapoi N.Z.
59	C3	Kai Besar *i.* Indon.
70	B2	Kaifeng China
		Kaihua China *see* **Wenshan**
122	B2	Kaiingveld *reg.* S. Africa
59	C3	Kai Kecil *i.* Indon.
54	B2	Kaikoura N.Z.
114	A4	Kailahun Sierra Leone
71	A3	Kaili China
59	C3	Kaimana Indon.
54	C1	Kaimanawa Mountains N.Z.
67	C4	Kainan Japan
115	C3	Kainji Reservoir Nigeria
54	B1	Kaipara Harbour N.Z.
74	B2	Kairana India
115	D1	Kairouan Tunisia
54	B1	Kaitaia N.Z.
54	C1	Kaitawa N.Z.
		Kaitong China *see* **Tongyu**
59	C3	Kaiwatu Indon.
65	A1	Kaiyuan *Liaoning* China
62	B1	Kaiyuan *Yunnan* China
92	I3	Kajaani Fin.
51	D2	Kajabbi Austr.
122	B2	Kakamas S. Africa
119	D2	Kakamega Kenya
91	C2	Kakhovka Ukr.
91	C2	Kakhovs'ke Vodoskhovyshche *resr* Ukr.
73	C3	Kakinada India
128	C1	Kakisa Can.
119	C3	Kakoswa Dem. Rep. Congo
126	B2	Kaktovik U.S.A.
		Kalaallit Nunaat *terr.* N. America *see* **Greenland**
59	C3	Kalabahi Indon.
120	B2	Kalabo Zambia
91	E1	Kalach Rus. Fed.
119	D2	Kalacha Dida Kenya
62	A1	Kaladan *r.* India/Myanmar
120	B3	Kalahari Desert Africa
92	H3	Kalajoki Fin.
111	B2	Kalamaria Greece
111	B3	Kalamata Greece
140	B2	Kalamazoo U.S.A.
111	B3	Kalampaka Greece
91	C2	Kalanchak Ukr.
115	E1	Kalanshiyū ar Ramlī al Kabīr, Sarīr *des.* Libya
63	B2	Kalasin Thai.
74	A1	Kalāt Afgh.
79	C2	Kalāt Iran
74	A2	Kalat Pak.
50	A2	Kalbarri Austr.
111	C3	Kale Turkey
80	B1	Kalecik Turkey
118	C3	Kalema Dem. Rep. Congo
119	C3	Kalemie Dem. Rep. Congo
62	A1	Kalemyo Myanmar
		Kalgan China *see* **Zhangjiakou**
50	B3	Kalgoorlie Austr.
109	C2	Kali Croatia
110	C2	Kaliakra, Nos *pt* Bulg.
119	C3	Kalima Dem. Rep. Congo
61	C2	Kalimantan *reg.* Indon.
88	B3	Kaliningrad Rus. Fed.
91	D2	Kalininskaya Rus. Fed.
88	C3	Kalinkavichy Belarus
134	D1	Kalispell U.S.A.
103	D1	Kalisz Pol.
91	E2	Kalitva *r.* Rus. Fed.
92	H2	Kalix Sweden
92	H2	Kalixälven *r.* Sweden
111	C3	Kalkan Turkey
120	A3	Kalkfeld Namibia
92	I3	Kallavesi *l.* Fin.
92	F3	Kallsjön *l.* Sweden
93	G4	Kalmar Sweden
93	G4	Kalmarsund *sea chan.* Sweden
120	B2	Kalomo Zambia
128	B2	Kalone Peak Can.
75	B1	Kalpa India
73	B3	Kalpeni *atoll* India
75	B2	Kalpi India
101	D1	Kaltenkirchen Ger.
89	E3	Kaluga Rus. Fed.
93	F4	Kalundborg Denmark
90	A2	Kalush Ukr.
73	B3	Kalyan India
89	E2	Kalyazin Rus. Fed.
111	C3	Kalymnos *i.* Greece
119	C3	Kama Dem. Rep. Congo
62	A2	Kama Myanmar
86	E3	Kama *r.* Rus. Fed.
66	D3	Kamaishi Japan
80	B2	Kaman Turkey
120	A2	Kamanjab Namibia
78	B3	Kamarān *i.* Yemen
74	A2	Kamarod Pak.
50	B3	Kambalda Austr.
119	C4	Kambove Dem. Rep. Congo
183	L3	Kamchatka Peninsula Rus. Fed.
110	C2	Kamchiya *r.* Bulg.
110	B2	Kamenitsa *mt.* Bulg.
108	B2	Kamenjak, Rt *pt* Croatia
76	B1	Kamenka Kazakh.
91	D1	Kamenka Rus. Fed.
91	E2	Kamennomorni Rus. Fed.
83	M2	Kamenskoye Rus. Fed.
91	E2	Kamensk-Shakhtinskiy Rus. Fed.
86	F3	Kamensk-Ural'skiy Rus. Fed.
122	A3	Kamiesberge *mts* S. Africa
122	A3	Kamieskroon S. Africa
129	D1	Kamilukuak Lake Can.
119	C3	Kamina Dem. Rep. Congo
129	E1	Kaminak Lake Can.
90	A1	Kamin'-Kashyrs'kyy Ukr.
128	B2	Kamloops Can.
118	C3	Kamonia Dem. Rep. Congo
119	D2	Kampala Uganda
60	B1	Kampar *r.* Indon.
60	B1	Kampar Malaysia
100	B1	Kampen Neth.
119	C3	Kampene Dem. Rep. Congo
63	A2	Kamphaeng Phet Thai.
63	B2	Kâmpóng Cham Cambodia
63	B2	Kâmpóng Chhnăng Cambodia
		Kâmpóng Saôm Cambodia *see* **Sihanoukville**
63	B2	Kâmpóng Spœ Cambodia
63	B2	Kâmpôt Cambodia
129	D2	Kamsack Can.
86	E3	Kamskoye Vodokhranilishche *resr* Rus. Fed.
117	C4	Kamsuuma Somalia
90	B2	Kam''yanets'-Podil's'kyy Ukr.

90 A1 **Kam"yanka-Buz'ka** Ukr.
88 B3 **Kamyanyets** Belarus
91 D2 **Kamyshevatskaya** Rus. Fed.
87 D3 **Kamyshin** Rus. Fed.
135 D3 **Kanab** U.S.A.
118 C3 **Kananga** Dem. Rep. Congo
87 D3 **Kanash** Rus. Fed.
140 C3 **Kanawha** r. U.S.A.
67 C3 **Kanazawa** Japan
62 A1 **Kanbalu** Myanmar
63 C2 **Kanchanaburi** Thai.
73 B3 **Kanchipuram** India
68 C2 **Kandahār** Afgh.
86 C2 **Kandalaksha** Rus. Fed.
61 C2 **Kandangan** Indon.
74 A2 **Kandh Kot** Pak.
114 C3 **Kandi** Benin
74 B2 **Kandla** India
53 C2 **Kandos** Austr.
121 D2 **Kandreho** Madag.
73 C4 **Kandy** Sri Lanka
76 B2 **Kandyagash** Kazakh.
127 G1 **Kane Bassin** b. Greenland
91 D2 **Kanevskaya** Rus. Fed.
122 B1 **Kang** Botswana
127 H2 **Kangaatsiaq** Greenland
114 B3 **Kangaba** Mali
80 B2 **Kangal** Turkey
79 C2 **Kangān** Iran
60 B1 **Kangar** Malaysia
52 A3 **Kangaroo Island** Austr.
75 C2 **Kangchenjunga** mt. India/Nepal
65 B2 **Kangdong** N. Korea
61 C2 **Kangean, Kepulauan** is Indon.
127 I2 **Kangeq** c. Greenland
127 H2 **Kangersuatsiaq** Greenland
127 H2 **Kangerlussuaq** inlet Greenland
127 I2 **Kangerlussuaq** inlet Greenland
65 B1 **Kanggye** N. Korea
131 D1 **Kangiqsualujjuaq** Can.
127 G2 **Kangiqsujuaq** Can.
127 G2 **Kangirsuk** Can.
75 C2 **Kangmar** China
65 B2 **Kangnŭng** S. Korea
65 A1 **Kangping** China
72 D2 **Kangto** mt. China/India
62 A1 **Kani** Myanmar
86 D2 **Kanin, Poluostrov** pen. Rus. Fed.
86 D2 **Kanin Nos** Rus. Fed.
91 C2 **Kaniv** Ukr.
93 H3 **Kankaanpää** Fin.
140 B2 **Kankakee** U.S.A.
114 B3 **Kankan** Guinea
75 C2 **Kanker** India
73 B3 **Kannur** India
115 C3 **Kano** Nigeria
122 B3 **Kanonpunt** pt S. Africa
67 B4 **Kanoya** Japan
75 C2 **Kanpur** India
136 C3 **Kansas** r. U.S.A.
137 D3 **Kansas** state U.S.A.
137 E3 **Kansas City** U.S.A.
83 H3 **Kansk** Rus. Fed.
114 C3 **Kantchari** Burkina
91 D2 **Kantemirovka** Rus. Fed.
97 B2 **Kanturk** Ireland
123 D2 **Kanyamazane** S. Africa
123 C1 **Kanye** Botswana
71 C3 **Kaohsiung** Taiwan
120 A2 **Kaokoveld** plat. Namibia
114 A3 **Kaolack** Senegal
119 C2 **Kaoma** Zambia
118 C3 **Kapanga** Dem. Rep. Congo
77 D2 **Kapchagay** Kazakh.

77 D2 **Kapchagayskoye Vodokhranilishche** resr Kazakh.
100 B2 **Kapellen** Belgium
121 B2 **Kapiri Mposhi** Zambia
127 H2 **Kapisillit** Greenland
130 B1 **Kapiskau** r. Can.
61 C1 **Kapit** Sarawak Malaysia
63 A3 **Kapoe** Thai.
117 B4 **Kapoeta** Sudan
103 D2 **Kaposvár** Hungary
61 B2 **Kapuas** r. Indon.
52 A2 **Kapunda** Austr.
130 B2 **Kapuskasing** Can.
103 D2 **Kapuvár** Hungary
88 C3 **Kapyl'** Belarus
114 C4 **Kara** Togo
111 C3 **Kara Ada** i. Turkey
76 C1 **Karabalyk** Kazakh.
80 B1 **Karabük** Turkey
76 C2 **Karabutak** Kazakh.
110 C2 **Karacaköy** Turkey
89 D3 **Karachev** Rus. Fed.
74 A2 **Karachi** Pak.
Kara Deniz sea Asia/Europe see **Black Sea**
77 D2 **Karaganda** Kazakh.
77 D2 **Karagayly** Kazakh.
83 L3 **Karaginskiy Zaliv** b. Rus. Fed.
81 D2 **Karaj** Iran
64 B2 **Karakelong** i. Indon.
77 D2 **Kara-Köl** Kyrg.
77 D2 **Karakol** Kyrg.
74 B1 **Karakoram Range** mts Asia
Karakum, Peski des. Kazakh. see **Karakum Desert**
76 B2 **Karakum Desert** Kazakh.
76 C3 **Karakum Desert** Turkm.
Karakumy, Peski des. Turkm. see **Karakum Desert**
80 B2 **Karaman** Turkey
77 E2 **Karamay** China
54 B2 **Karamea** N.Z.
54 B2 **Karamea Bight** b. N.Z.
80 B2 **Karapınar** Turkey
122 A2 **Karasburg** Namibia
86 F1 **Kara Sea** Rus. Fed.
92 I2 **Karasjok** Norway
82 G3 **Karasuk** Rus. Fed.
77 D2 **Karatau** Kazakh.
77 C2 **Karatau, Khrebet** mts Kazakh.
86 F2 **Karatayka** Rus. Fed.
67 A4 **Karatsu** Japan
60 B2 **Karawang** Indon.
81 C2 **Karbalā'** Iraq
103 E2 **Karcag** Hungary
111 B3 **Karditsa** Greece
88 B2 **Kärdla** Estonia
122 B3 **Kareeberge** mts S. Africa
75 B2 **Kareli** India
74 B1 **Kargil** India
121 B2 **Kariba** Zimbabwe
121 B2 **Kariba, Lake** resr Zambia/Zimbabwe
61 B2 **Karimata, Pulau-pulau** is Indon.
61 B2 **Karimata, Selat** str. Indon.
73 B3 **Karimnagar** India
61 C2 **Karimunjawa, Pulau-pulau** is Indon.
91 C2 **Karkinits'ka Zatoka** g. Ukr.
91 D2 **Karlivka** Ukr.
109 C1 **Karlovac** Croatia
102 F1 **Karlovy Vary** Czech Rep.
93 F4 **Karlshamn** Sweden
93 G4 **Karlskrona** Sweden
102 B2 **Karlsruhe** Ger.
93 F4 **Karlstad** Sweden

101 D3 **Karlstadt** Ger.
89 D3 **Karma** Belarus
93 E4 **Karmøy** i. Norway
75 D2 **Karnafuli Reservoir** Bangl.
74 B2 **Karnal** India
110 C2 **Karnobat** Bulg.
74 A2 **Karodi** Pak.
121 B2 **Karoi** Zimbabwe
121 C1 **Karonga** Malawi
116 B3 **Karora** Eritrea
111 C3 **Karpathos** i. Greece
111 B3 **Karpenisi** Greece
86 D2 **Karpogory** Rus. Fed.
50 A2 **Karratha** Austr.
81 C1 **Kars** Turkey
88 C2 **Kārsava** Latvia
86 E2 **Karskiye Vorota, Proliv** str. Rus. Fed.
Karskoye More sea Rus. Fed. see **Kara Sea**
101 C2 **Karstädt** Ger.
111 C2 **Kartal** Turkey
87 F3 **Kartaly** Rus. Fed.
73 B3 **Karwar** India
83 I3 **Karymskoye** Rus. Fed.
111 B3 **Karystos** Greece
80 A2 **Kaş** Turkey
130 B1 **Kasabonika Lake** Can.
118 C4 **Kasaji** Dem. Rep. Congo
121 C2 **Kasama** Zambia
120 B2 **Kasane** Botswana
118 B3 **Kasangulu** Dem. Rep. Congo
73 B3 **Kasaragod** India
129 C1 **Kasba Lake** Can.
120 B2 **Kasempa** Zambia
118 C4 **Kasenga** Dem. Rep. Congo
119 C3 **Kasese** Dem. Rep. Congo
119 D2 **Kasese** Uganda
81 D2 **Kāshān** Iran
77 D3 **Kashi** China
67 D3 **Kashima-nada** b. Japan
89 E2 **Kashin** Rus. Fed.
89 E3 **Kashira** Rus. Fed.
89 E3 **Kashirskoye** Rus. Fed.
67 C3 **Kashiwazaki** Japan
76 B3 **Kāshmar** Iran
74 A2 **Kashmore** Pak.
119 C3 **Kashyukulu** Dem. Rep. Congo
87 D3 **Kasimov** Rus. Fed.
93 H3 **Kaskinen** Fin.
119 C3 **Kasongo** Dem. Rep. Congo
118 B3 **Kasongo-Lunda** Dem. Rep. Congo
111 C3 **Kasos** i. Greece
Kaspiyskoye More l. Asia/Europe see **Caspian Sea**
116 B3 **Kassala** Sudan
101 D2 **Kassel** Ger.
80 B1 **Kastamonu** Turkey
111 B2 **Kastoria** Greece
89 D3 **Kastsyukovichy** Belarus
119 D3 **Kasulu** Tanz.
121 C2 **Kasungu** Malawi
141 F1 **Katahdin, Mount** U.S.A.
118 C3 **Katako-Kombe** Dem. Rep. Congo
50 A2 **Katanning** Austr.
63 A3 **Katchall** i. India
128 A2 **Kate's Needle** mt. Can./U.S.A.
121 C2 **Katete** Zambia
62 A1 **Katha** Myanmar
50 C1 **Katherine** r. Austr.
74 B2 **Kathiawar** pen. India
75 C2 **Kathmandu** Nepal
122 B2 **Kathu** S. Africa

74 B1 **Kathua** India
114 B3 **Kati** Mali
75 C2 **Katihar** India
54 C1 **Katikati** N.Z.
123 C3 **Katikati** S. Africa
120 B2 **Katima Mulilo** Namibia
123 C2 **Katiehong** S. Africa
111 B3 **Kato Achaïa** Greece
53 D2 **Katoomba** Austr.
103 D1 **Katowice** Pol.
78 A2 **Kātrīna, Jabal** *mt.* Egypt
93 G4 **Katrineholm** Sweden
115 C3 **Katsina** Nigeria
115 C4 **Katsina-Ala** Nigeria
77 C3 **Kattaqo'rg'on** Uzbek.
93 F4 **Kattegat** *str.* Denmark/Sweden
100 B1 **Katwijk aan Zee** Neth.
124 E5 **Kaua'i** *i.* U.S.A.
93 H3 **Kauhajoki** Fin.
88 B3 **Kaunas** Lith.
115 C3 **Kaura-Namoda** Nigeria
92 H2 **Kautokeino** Norway
111 B2 **Kavala** Greece
66 C2 **Kavalerovo** Rus. Fed.
73 C3 **Kavali** India
73 B3 **Kavaratti** *atoll* India
110 C2 **Kavarna** Bulg.
81 D2 **Kavīr, Dasht-e** *des.* Iran
67 C3 **Kawagoe** Japan
54 B1 **Kawakawa** N.Z.
67 C3 **Kawanishi** Japan
130 C2 **Kawartha Lakes** Can.
67 C3 **Kawasaki** Japan
54 C1 **Kawerau** N.Z.
62 A1 **Kawkareik** Myanmar
62 A1 **Kawlin** Myanmar
63 A2 **Kawmapyin** Myanmar
63 A2 **Kawthaung** Myanmar
77 D3 **Kaxgar He** *r.* China
114 B3 **Kaya** Burkina
61 C1 **Kaya** *r.* Indon.
136 B2 **Kaycee** U.S.A.
138 A1 **Kayenta** U.S.A.
114 A3 **Kayes** Mali
77 D2 **Kaynar** Kazakh.
80 B2 **Kayseri** Turkey
77 D1 **Kazakhskiy Melkosopochnik**
     plain Kazakh.
81 C1 **Kazakhskiy Zaliv** *b.* Kazakh.
76 C2 **Kazakhstan** *country* Asia
87 D3 **Kazan'** Rus. Fed.
80 A1 **Kazanlŭk** Bulg.
76 A2 **Kazbek** *mt.* Georgia/Rus. Fed.
81 D3 **Kāzerūn** Iran
103 E2 **Kazincbarcika** Hungary
86 F2 **Kazatayskoy** Rus. Fed.
111 B3 **Kea** *i.* Greece
97 C1 **Keady** U.K.
137 D2 **Kearney** U.S.A.
138 A2 **Kearny** U.S.A.
116 A3 **Kebkabiya** Sudan
92 G2 **Kebnekaise** *mt.* Sweden
117 C4 **K'ebrī Dehar** Eth.
61 B2 **Kebumen** Indon.
128 B2 **Kechika** *r.* Can.
103 D2 **Kecskemét** Hungary
88 B2 **Kėdainiai** Lith.
114 A3 **Kédougou** Senegal
103 D1 **Kędzierzyn-Koźle** Pol.
128 B1 **Keele** *r.* Can.
128 A1 **Keele Peak** Can.
     Keelung Taiwan *see* **Chilung**
141 E2 **Keene** U.S.A.
122 A2 **Keetmanshoop** Namibia
129 E3 **Keewatin** Can.
     Kefallonia *i.* Greece *see*
     Cephalonia

59 C3 **Kefamenanu** Indon.
92 A3 **Keflavík** Iceland
77 D2 **Kegen** Kazakh.
128 C2 **Keg River** Can.
62 A1 **Kehsi Mansam** Myanmar
98 C2 **Keighley** U.K.
88 B2 **Keila** Estonia
122 B2 **Keimoes** S. Africa
92 I3 **Keitele** *i.* Fin.
52 B3 **Keith** Austr.
103 E2 **Kékes** *mt.* Hungary
92 J2 **Keles-Uayv, Gora** *h.* Rus. Fed.
102 C2 **Kelheim** Ger.
80 B1 **Kelkit** *r.* Turkey
128 B1 **Keller Lake** Can.
134 C1 **Kellogg** U.S.A.
92 I2 **Kelloselkä** Fin.
97 C2 **Kells** Ireland
88 B2 **Kelmė** Lith.
115 D4 **Kélo** Chad
128 C3 **Kelowna** Can.
96 C3 **Kelso** U.K.
134 B1 **Kelso** U.S.A.
60 B1 **Keluang** Malaysia
129 D2 **Kelvington** Can.
86 C2 **Kem'** Rus. Fed.
128 B2 **Kemano (abandoned)** Can.
111 C3 **Kemer** Turkey
82 G3 **Kemerovo** Rus. Fed.
92 H2 **Kemi** Fin.
92 I2 **Kemijärvi** Fin.
92 I2 **Kemijoki** *r.* Fin.
136 A2 **Kemmerer** U.S.A.
92 I3 **Kempele** Fin.
53 D2 **Kempsey** Austr.
130 C2 **Kempt, Lac** *l.* Can.
102 C2 **Kempten (Allgäu)** Ger.
123 C3 **Kempton Park** S. Africa
61 C2 **Kemujan** *i.* Indon.
129 D2 **Kenaston** Can.
98 B1 **Kendal** U.K.
59 C3 **Kendari** Indon.
61 C2 **Kendawangan** Indon.
115 D3 **Kendégué** Chad
114 A4 **Kenema** Sierra Leone
118 B3 **Kenge** Dem. Rep. Congo
62 A1 **Kengtung** Myanmar
122 B2 **Kenhardt** S. Africa
114 B1 **Kenitra** Morocco
97 B3 **Kenmare** Ireland
136 C1 **Kenmare** U.S.A.
97 A3 **Kenmare River** *inlet* Ireland
100 C3 **Kenn** Ger.
137 E3 **Kennett** U.S.A.
134 C1 **Kennewick** U.S.A.
129 E3 **Kenora** Can.
140 B2 **Kenosha** U.S.A.
138 C2 **Kent** U.S.A.
77 C2 **Kentau** Kazakh.
140 B3 **Kentucky** *r.* U.S.A.
140 C3 **Kentucky** *state* U.S.A.
140 B3 **Kentucky Lake** U.S.A.
119 D2 **Kenya** *country* Africa
119 D3 **Kenya, Mount** Kenya
137 E2 **Keokuk** U.S.A.
75 C2 **Keonjhar** India
111 C3 **Kepsut** Turkey
52 B3 **Kerang** Austr.
91 D2 **Kerch'** Ukr.
59 D3 **Kerema** P.N.G.
128 C3 **Keremeos** Can.
116 B3 **Keren** Eritrea
81 C2 **Kerend** Iran
159 C7 **Kerguelen Plateau** Indian
     Ocean
119 D3 **Kericho** Kenya
54 B1 **Kerikeri** N.Z.

60 B2 **Kerinci, Gunung** *vol.* Indon.
111 A3 **Kerkyra** Greece
     Kerkyra *i.* Greece *see* **Corfu**
116 B3 **Kerma** Sudan
49 G4 **Kermadec Islands** S. Pacific
     Ocean
79 C1 **Kermān** Iran
81 C2 **Kermānshāh** Iran
139 C2 **Kermit** U.S.A.
135 C3 **Kern** *r.* U.S.A.
100 C2 **Kerpen** Ger.
129 D2 **Kerrobert** Can.
139 D2 **Kerrville** U.S.A.
     Keryneia Cyprus *see* **Kyrenia**
130 B1 **Kesagami Lake** Can.
111 C2 **Keşan** Turkey
66 D3 **Kesennuma** Japan
74 B2 **Keshod** India
100 C2 **Kessel** Neth.
98 B1 **Keswick** U.K.
103 D2 **Keszthely** Hungary
82 G3 **Ket'** *r.* Rus. Fed.
61 C2 **Ketapang** Indon.
128 A2 **Ketchikan** U.S.A.
134 D2 **Ketchum** U.S.A.
99 C2 **Kettering** U.K.
93 H3 **Keuruu** Fin.
100 C2 **Kevelaer** Ger.
140 B2 **Kewanee** U.S.A.
140 B1 **Keweenaw Bay** U.S.A.
140 B1 **Keweenaw Peninsula** U.S.A.
143 D3 **Key Largo** U.S.A.
141 D3 **Keyser** U.S.A.
143 D4 **Key West** U.S.A.
123 C2 **Kgotsong** S. Africa
69 E1 **Khabarovsk** Rus. Fed.
80 B1 **Khadyzhensk** Rus. Fed.
62 A1 **Khagrachari** Bangl.
74 A2 **Khairpur** Pak.
122 B1 **Khakhea** Botswana
68 C1 **Khamar-Daban, Khrebet** *mts*
     Rus. Fed.
74 B2 **Khambhat** India
73 B3 **Khambhat, Gulf of** India
74 B2 **Khamgaon** India
78 B3 **Khamir** Yemen
78 B3 **Khamis Mushayṭ** Saudi Arabia
77 C3 **Khānābād** Afgh.
74 B2 **Khandwa** India
83 K2 **Khandyga** Rus. Fed.
74 B1 **Khanewal** Pak.
66 B2 **Khanka, Lake** China/Rus. Fed.
74 B2 **Khanpur** Pak.
77 D2 **Khantau** Kazakh.
83 H2 **Khantayskoye, Ozero** *l.*
     Rus. Fed.
86 F2 **Khanty-Mansiysk** Rus. Fed.
63 A3 **Khao Chum Thong** Thai.
63 A2 **Khao Laem, Ang Kep Nam**
     Thai.
87 D4 **Kharabali** Rus. Fed.
75 C2 **Kharagpur** India
79 C2 **Khārān** *r.* Iran
116 B2 **Khārijah, Wāḩāt al** *oasis* Egypt
91 D2 **Kharkiv** Ukr.
     Khar'kov Ukr. *see* **Kharkiv**
110 C2 **Kharmanli** Bulg.
86 D3 **Kharovsk** Rus. Fed.
116 B3 **Khartoum** Sudan
87 D4 **Khasavyurt** Rus. Fed.
79 D2 **Khāsh** Iran
78 A3 **Khashm el Girba** Sudan
78 A3 **Khashm el Girba Dam** Sudan
74 D2 **Khasi Hills** India
110 C2 **Khaskovo** Bulg.
123 C3 **Khayamnandi** S. Africa
78 A2 **Khaybar** Saudi Arabia

122 A3 Khayelitsha S. Africa
107 D2 Khemis Miliana Alg.
63 B2 Khemmarat Thai.
115 C1 Khenchela Alg.
81 D3 Kherāmeh Iran
91 C2 Kherson Ukr.
83 H2 Kheta r. Rus. Fed.
69 D1 Khilok Rus. Fed.
89 E2 Khimki Rus. Fed.
74 A2 Khipro Pak.
89 E3 Khlevnoye Rus. Fed.
90 B2 Khmel'nyts'kyy Ukr.
76 B1 Khobda Kazakh.
89 E3 Khokhol'skiy Rus. Fed.
74 B2 Khokhropar Pak.
89 D2 Kholm Rus. Fed.
89 D2 Kholm-Zhirkovskiy Rus. Fed.
79 C2 Khonj Iran
63 B2 Khon Kaen Thai.
62 A1 Khonsa India
83 K2 Khonuu Rus. Fed.
86 E2 Khoreyver Rus. Fed.
69 D1 Khorinsk Rus. Fed.
91 C2 Khorol Ukr.
81 C2 Khorramābād Iran
81 C2 Khorramshahr Iran
77 D3 Khorugh Tajik.
74 A1 Khōst Afgh.
62 A1 Khreum Myanmar
76 B1 Khromtau Kazakh.
90 B2 Khrystynivka Ukr.
77 C2 Khŭjand Tajik.
63 B2 Khu Khan Thai.
78 A2 Khulays Saudi Arabia
75 C2 Khulna Bangl.
81 D2 Khunsar Iran
79 B2 Khuraybah Saudi Arabia
74 B1 Khushab Pak.
90 A2 Khust Ukr.
123 C2 Khutsong S. Africa
74 A2 Khuzdar Pak.
79 C2 Khvormūj Iran
81 C2 Khvoy Iran
77 D3 Khvoynaya Rus. Fed.
77 D3 Khyber Pass Afgh./Pak.
53 D2 Kiama Austr.
119 C3 Kiambi Dem. Rep. Congo
119 D3 Kibiti Tanz.
109 D2 Kičevo Macedonia
114 C3 Kidal Mali
99 B2 Kidderminster U.K.
114 A3 Kidira Senegal
54 C1 Kidnappers, Cape N.Z.
102 C1 Kiel Ger.
103 E1 Kielce Pol.
98 B1 Kielder Water U.K.
90 C1 Kiev Ukr.
114 A3 Kiffa Maur.
119 D3 Kigali Rwanda
119 C3 Kigoma Tanz.
88 B2 Kihnu i. Estonia
92 I2 Kiiminki Fin.
67 B4 Kii-suidō sea chan. Japan
109 D1 Kikinda Serbia
119 C3 Kikondja Dem. Rep. Congo
59 D3 Kikori P.N.G.
59 D3 Kikori r. P.N.G.
118 B3 Kikwit Dem. Rep. Congo
65 B1 Kilchu N. Korea
118 B3 Kilembe Dem. Rep. Congo
139 E2 Kilgore U.S.A.
119 D3 Kilimanjaro vol. Tanz.
80 B2 Kilis Turkey
90 B2 Kiliya Ukr.
97 B2 Kilkee Ireland
97 D1 Kilkeel U.K.
97 C2 Kilkenny Ireland

111 B2 Kilkis Greece
97 B1 Killala Bay Ireland
97 B2 Killaloe Ireland
129 C2 Killam Can.
97 B2 Killarney Ireland
139 D2 Killeen U.S.A.
96 B2 Killin U.K.
97 B1 Killybegs Ireland
96 B3 Kilmarnock U.K.
53 B3 Kilmore Austr.
119 D3 Kilosa Tanz.
97 B2 Kilrush Ireland
119 C3 Kilwa Dem. Rep. Congo
119 D3 Kilwa Masoko Tanz.
119 D3 Kimambi Tanz.
52 A2 Kimba Austr.
136 C2 Kimball U.S.A.
128 C3 Kimberley Can.
122 B2 Kimberley S. Africa
50 B1 Kimberley Plateau Austr.
65 B1 Kimch'aek N. Korea
65 B2 Kimch'ŏn S. Korea
127 G2 Kimmirut Can.
89 E3 Kimovsk Rus. Fed.
118 B3 Kimpese Dem. Rep. Congo
89 E2 Kimry Rus. Fed.
61 C1 Kinabalu, Gunung mt. Sabah Malaysia
128 C2 Kinbasket Lake Can.
130 B2 Kincardine Can.
62 A1 Kinchang Myanmar
119 C3 Kinda Dem. Rep. Congo
98 C2 Kinder Scout h. U.K.
129 D2 Kindersley Can.
114 A3 Kindia Guinea
119 C3 Kindu Dem. Rep. Congo
86 D3 Kineshma Rus. Fed.
51 E2 Kingaroy Austr.
135 B3 King City U.S.A.
130 C1 King George Islands Can.
88 C2 Kingisepp Rus. Fed.
51 D3 King Island Austr.
50 B1 King Leopold Ranges hills Austr.
138 A1 Kingman U.S.A.
135 B3 Kings r. U.S.A.
52 A3 Kingscote Austr.
99 D2 King's Lynn U.K.
48 F3 Kingsmill Group is Kiribati
50 B1 King Sound b. Austr.
134 D2 Kings Peak U.S.A.
143 D1 Kingsport U.S.A.
130 C2 Kingston Can.
146 C3 Kingston Jamaica
141 E2 Kingston U.S.A.
52 A3 Kingston South East Austr.
98 C2 Kingston upon Hull U.K.
147 D3 Kingstown St Vincent
139 D3 Kingsville U.S.A.
99 B3 Kingswood U.K.
96 B2 Kingussie U.K.
126 E2 King William Island Can.
123 C3 King William's Town S. Africa
67 D3 Kinka-san i. Japan
93 F4 Kinna Sweden
97 B3 Kinsale Ireland
118 B3 Kinshasa Dem. Rep. Congo
143 E1 Kinston U.S.A.
88 B2 Kintai Lith.
114 B4 Kintampo Ghana
96 B3 Kintyre pen. U.K.
62 A1 Kin-U Myanmar
130 C2 Kipawa, Lac l. Can.
83 I3 Kirensk Rus. Fed.
89 E3 Kireyevsk Rus. Fed.
       Kirghizia country Asia see Kyrgyzstan

49 G3 Kiribati country Pacific Ocean
80 B2 Kırıkkale Turkey
89 E2 Kirillov Rus. Fed.
       Kirin China see Jilin
       Kirinyaga mt. Kenya see Kenya, Mount
89 D2 Kirishi Rus. Fed.
49 H2 Kiritimati atoll Kiribati
111 C3 Kırkağaç Turkey
96 C2 Kirkcaldy U.K.
96 B3 Kirkcudbright U.K.
92 J2 Kirkenes Norway
130 B2 Kirkland Lake Can.
137 E2 Kirksville U.S.A.
81 C2 Kirkūk Iraq
96 C1 Kirkwall U.K.
89 D3 Kirov Kaluzhskaya Oblast' Rus. Fed.
86 D3 Kirov Rus. Fed.
       Kirovabad Azer. see Gäncä
86 E3 Kirovo-Chepetsk Rus. Fed.
91 C2 Kirovohrad Ukr.
86 C2 Kirovsk Rus. Fed.
91 D2 Kirovs'ke Ukr.
96 C2 Kirriemuir U.K.
86 E3 Kirs Rus. Fed.
74 A2 Kirthar Range mts Pak.
92 H2 Kiruna Sweden
67 C3 Kiryū Japan
89 E2 Kirzhach Rus. Fed.
119 C2 Kisangani Dem. Rep. Congo
118 B3 Kisantu Dem. Rep. Congo
60 A1 Kisaran Indon.
82 G3 Kiselevsk Rus. Fed.
75 C2 Kishanganj India
115 C4 Kishi Nigeria
       Kishinev Moldova see Chişinău
77 D1 Kishkenekol' Kazakh.
74 B1 Kishtwar India
119 D3 Kisii Kenya
103 D2 Kiskunfélegyháza Hungary
103 D2 Kiskunhalas Hungary
87 D4 Kislovodsk Rus. Fed.
117 C5 Kismaayo Somalia
119 C3 Kisoro Uganda
111 B3 Kissamos Greece
114 A4 Kissidougou Guinea
143 D3 Kissimmee U.S.A.
143 D3 Kissimmee, Lake U.S.A.
129 D2 Kississing Lake Can.
119 D3 Kisumu Kenya
114 B3 Kita Mali
66 D3 Kitakami Japan
66 D3 Kitakami-gawa r. Japan
67 B4 Kita-Kyūshū Japan
119 D2 Kitale Kenya
66 D2 Kitami Japan
130 B2 Kitchener Can.
93 J3 Kitee Fin.
119 D2 Kitgum Uganda
128 B2 Kitimat Can.
118 B3 Kitona Dem. Rep. Congo
119 D3 Kitunda Tanz.
128 B2 Kitwanga Can.
121 B2 Kitwe Zambia
101 E3 Kitzingen Ger.
92 I3 Kiuruvesi Fin.
119 C3 Kivu, Lake Dem. Rep. Congo/Rwanda
110 C2 Kıyıköy Turkey
86 E3 Kizel Rus. Fed.
111 C3 Kızılca Dağ mt. Turkey
92 H1 Kizlyar Rus. Fed.
92 H1 Kjøllefjord Norway
92 H1 Kjøpsvik Norway
102 C1 Kladno Czech Rep.

Klagenfurt

102 C2 **Klagenfurt** Austria
88 B2 **Klaipėda** Lith.
94 B1 **Klaksvík** Faroe Is
134 B2 **Klamath** r. U.S.A.
134 B2 **Klamath Falls** U.S.A.
134 B2 **Klamath Mountains** U.S.A.
60 B1 **Klang** Malaysia
102 C2 **Klatovy** Czech Rep.
122 A3 **Klawer** S. Africa
128 A2 **Klawock** U.S.A.
128 B2 **Kleena Kleene** Can.
122 B2 **Kleinbegin** S. Africa
122 A2 **Kleinsee** S. Africa
123 C2 **Klerksdorp** S. Africa
89 D3 **Kletnya** Rus. Fed.
100 C2 **Kleve** Ger.
89 D3 **Klimavichy** Belarus
89 D3 **Klimovo** Rus. Fed.
89 E2 **Klimovsk** Rus. Fed.
89 E2 **Klin** Rus. Fed.
101 F2 **Klínovec** mt. Czech Rep.
93 G4 **Klintehamn** Sweden
89 D3 **Klintsy** Rus. Fed.
109 C2 **Ključ** Bos.-Herz.
103 D1 **Kłodzko** Pol.
100 C1 **Kloosterhaar** Neth.
103 D2 **Klosterneuburg** Austria
101 E1 **Klötze (Altmark)** Ger.
103 D1 **Kluczbork** Pol.
128 A2 **Klukwan** U.S.A.
88 C3 **Klyetsk** Belarus
98 C1 **Knaresborough** U.K.
93 F3 **Knästen** h. Sweden
129 E2 **Knee Lake** Can.
101 E1 **Knesebeck** Ger.
101 E3 **Knetzgau** Ger.
109 C2 **Knin** Croatia
103 C2 **Knittelfeld** Austria
109 D2 **Knjaževac** Serbia
100 A2 **Knokke-Heist** Belgium
143 D1 **Knoxville** U.S.A.
122 B3 **Knysna** S. Africa
67 C4 **Kōbe** Japan
        København Denmark see
        Copenhagen
100 C2 **Koblenz** Ger.
59 C3 **Kobroör** i. Indon.
88 B3 **Kobryn** Belarus
109 D2 **Kočani** Macedonia
111 C2 **Kocasu** r. Turkey
75 C2 **Koch Bihar** India
73 B4 **Kochi** India
67 B4 **Kōchi** Japan
87 D4 **Kochubey** Rus. Fed.
75 C2 **Kodarma** India
117 B4 **Kodok** Sudan
90 B2 **Kodyma** Ukr.
111 C2 **Kodzhaele** mt. Bulg./Greece
122 A2 **Koës** Namibia
122 C2 **Koffiefontein** S. Africa
114 B4 **Koforidua** Ghana
67 C3 **Kōfu** Japan
131 D1 **Kogaluk** r. Can.
74 B1 **Kohat** Pak.
62 A1 **Kohima** India
88 C2 **Kohtla-Järve** Estonia
92 H3 **Kokkola** Fin.
140 B2 **Kokomo** U.S.A.
77 E2 **Kokpekti** Kazakh.
77 C1 **Kokshetau** Kazakh.
131 D1 **Koksoak** r. Can.
123 C3 **Kokstad** S. Africa
        Koktokay China see **Fuyun**
58 C3 **Kolaka** Indon.
86 C2 **Kola Peninsula** Rus. Fed.
92 H2 **Kolari** Fin.
114 A3 **Kolda** Senegal
93 E4 **Kolding** Denmark
107 D2 **Koléa** Alg.
86 D2 **Kolguyev, Ostrov** i. Rus. Fed.
73 B3 **Kolhapur** India
88 B2 **Kolkasrags** pt Latvia
75 C2 **Kolkata** India
73 B4 **Kollam** India
        Köln Ger. see **Cologne**
103 D1 **Kołobrzeg** Pol.
114 B3 **Kolokani** Mali
89 E2 **Kolomna** Rus. Fed.
90 B2 **Kolomyya** Ukr.
122 B2 **Kolonkwaneng** Botswana
82 G3 **Kolpashevo** Rus. Fed.
89 E3 **Kolpny** Rus. Fed.
        Kol'skiy Poluostrov pen.
        Rus. Fed. see **Kola Peninsula**
78 B3 **Koluli** Eritrea
119 C4 **Kolwezi** Dem. Rep. Congo
83 L2 **Kolyma** r. Rus. Fed.
83 L2 **Kolymskaya Nizmennost'**
        lowland Rus. Fed.
83 M2 **Kolymskiy, Khrebet** mts
        Rus. Fed.
67 C3 **Komaki** Japan
83 M3 **Komandorskiye Ostrova** is
        Rus. Fed.
103 D2 **Komárno** Slovakia
123 D2 **Komati** r. S. Africa/Swaziland
67 C3 **Komatsu** Japan
119 C3 **Kombe** Dem. Rep. Congo
90 C2 **Kominternivs'ke** Ukr.
109 C2 **Komiža** Croatia
103 D2 **Komló** Hungary
118 B3 **Komono** Congo
111 C2 **Komotini** Greece
122 B3 **Komsberg** mts S. Africa
83 H1 **Komsomolets, Ostrov** i.
        Rus. Fed.
89 F2 **Komsomol'sk** Rus. Fed.
91 C2 **Komsomol's'k** Ukr.
87 D4 **Komsomol'skiy** Rus. Fed.
69 E1 **Komsomol'sk-na-Amure**
        Rus. Fed.
89 E2 **Konakovo** Rus. Fed.
75 C3 **Kondagaon** India
86 F2 **Kondinskoye** Rus. Fed.
119 D3 **Kondoa** Tanz.
86 C2 **Kondopoga** Rus. Fed.
89 E3 **Kondrovo** Rus. Fed.
127 I2 **Kong Christian IX Land** reg.
        Greenland
127 I2 **Kong Frederik VI Kyst** coastal
        area Greenland
65 B2 **Kongju** S. Korea
119 C3 **Kongolo** Dem. Rep. Congo
93 E3 **Kongsberg** Norway
93 F3 **Kongsvinger** Norway
77 D3 **Kongur Shan** mt. China
100 C2 **Königswinter** Ger.
103 D1 **Konin** Pol.
109 C2 **Konjic** Bos.-Herz.
122 A2 **Konkiep** watercourse Namibia
91 C1 **Konotop** Ukr.
102 B2 **Konstanz** Ger.
115 C3 **Kontagora** Nigeria
63 B2 **Kon Tum** Vietnam
63 B2 **Kon Tum, Cao Nguyên** plat.
        Vietnam
80 B2 **Konya** Turkey
100 C3 **Konz** Ger.
86 E3 **Konzhakovskiy Kamen', Gora**
        mt. Rus. Fed.
134 C1 **Kooskia** U.S.A.
128 C3 **Kootenay Lake** Can.
122 B3 **Kootjieskolk** S. Africa
92 B2 **Kópasker** Iceland
108 B1 **Koper** Slovenia
93 G4 **Kopparberg** Sweden
109 C1 **Koprivnica** Croatia
89 F3 **Korablino** Rus. Fed.
73 C3 **Koraput** India
101 D2 **Korbach** Ger.
109 D2 **Korçë** Albania
109 C2 **Korčula** Croatia
109 C2 **Korčula** i. Croatia
70 C2 **Korea Bay** g. China/N. Korea
65 B1 **Korea, North** country Asia
65 B2 **Korea, South** country Asia
65 B3 **Korea Strait** Japan/S. Korea
91 D2 **Korenovsk** Rus. Fed.
90 B1 **Korets'** Ukr.
111 C2 **Körfez** Turkey
114 B4 **Korhogo** Côte d'Ivoire
        Korinthos Greece see **Corinth**
103 D2 **Kőris-hegy** h. Hungary
109 D2 **Koritnik** mt. Albania/Kosovo
67 D3 **Kōriyama** Japan
80 B2 **Korkuteli** Turkey
68 B2 **Korla** China
103 D2 **Körmend** Hungary
114 B3 **Koro** Mali
131 D1 **Koroc** r. Can.
91 D1 **Korocha** Rus. Fed.
119 D3 **Korogwe** Tanz.
59 C2 **Koror** Palau
90 B1 **Korosten'** Ukr.
90 B1 **Korostyshiv** Ukr.
115 D3 **Koro Toro** Chad
91 C2 **Korsun'-Shevchenkivs'kyy**
        Ukr.
103 E1 **Korsze** Pol.
100 A2 **Kortrijk** Belgium
83 L3 **Koryakskaya, Sopka** vol.
        Rus. Fed.
83 M2 **Koryakskoye Nagor'ye** mts
        Rus. Fed.
86 D2 **Koryazhma** Rus. Fed.
65 B2 **Koryŏng** S. Korea
91 C1 **Koryukivka** Ukr.
111 C3 **Kos** Greece
111 C3 **Kos** i. Greece
65 B2 **Kosan** N. Korea
103 D1 **Kościan** Pol.
53 C3 **Kosciuszko, Mount** Austr.
68 B1 **Kosh-Agach** Rus. Fed.
103 E2 **Košice** Slovakia
92 H2 **Koskullskulle** Sweden
65 B2 **Kosŏng** N. Korea
109 D2 **Kosovo** country Europe
        Kosovska Mitrovica Kosovo
        see **Mitrovicë**
48 E2 **Kosrae** atoll Micronesia
114 B4 **Kossou, Lac de** l. Côte d'Ivoire
76 C1 **Kostanay** Kazakh.
110 B2 **Kostenets** Bulg.
123 C2 **Koster** S. Africa
117 B3 **Kosti** Sudan
86 C2 **Kostomuksha** Rus. Fed.
90 B1 **Kostopil'** Ukr.
89 F2 **Kostroma** Rus. Fed.
89 F2 **Kostroma** r. Rus. Fed.
102 C1 **Kostrzyn** Pol.
103 D1 **Koszalin** Pol.
103 D2 **Kőszeg** Hungary
74 B2 **Kota** India
60 B2 **Kotaagung** Indon.
61 C2 **Kotabaru** Indon.
60 B1 **Kota Belud** Sabah Malaysia
60 B1 **Kota Bharu** Malaysia
60 B2 **Kotabumi** Indon.
61 C1 **Kota Kinabalu** Sabah Malaysia
61 C1 **Kota Samarahan** Sarawak
        Malaysia

86 D3	**Kotel'nich** Rus. Fed.	
87 D4	**Kotel'nikovo** Rus. Fed.	
83 K1	**Kotel'nyy, Ostrov** *i.* Rus. Fed.	
101 E2	**Köthen (Anhalt)** Ger.	
93 I3	**Kotka** Fin.	
86 D2	**Kotlas** Rus. Fed.	
109 C2	**Kotor Varoš** Bos.-Herz.	
87 D3	**Kotovo** Rus. Fed.	
91 E1	**Kotovsk** Rus. Fed.	
90 B2	**Kotovs'k** Ukr.	
83 H2	**Kotuy** *r.* Rus. Fed.	
100 A2	**Koudekerke** Neth.	
114 B3	**Koudougou** Burkina	
122 B3	**Kougaberge** *mts* S. Africa	
118 B3	**Koulamoutou** Gabon	
114 B3	**Koulikoro** Mali	
114 A3	**Koundâra** Guinea	
151 C1	**Kourou** Fr. Guiana	
114 B3	**Kouroussa** Guinea	
115 C3	**Kousséri** Cameroon	
114 B3	**Koutiala** Mali	
93 I3	**Kouvola** Fin.	
92 J2	**Kovdor** Rus. Fed.	
90 A1	**Kovel'** Ukr.	
89 F2	**Kovrov** Rus. Fed.	
54 B2	**Kowhitirangi** N.Z.	
111 C3	**Köyceğiz** Turkey	
83 K2	**Koyda** Rus. Fed.	
126 A2	**Koyukuk** *r.* U.S.A.	
111 B2	**Kozani** Greece	
90 C1	**Kozelets'** Ukr.	
89 E3	**Kozel'sk** Rus. Fed.	
73 B3	**Kozhikode** India	
90 B2	**Kozyatyn** Ukr.	
63 A3	**Krabi** Thai.	
63 A2	**Kra Buri** Thai.	
63 B2	**Krâchéh** Cambodia	
93 E4	**Kragerø** Norway	
100 B1	**Kraggenburg** Neth.	
109 D2	**Kragujevac** Serbia	
60 B2	**Krakatau** *i.* Indon.	
103 D1	**Kraków** Pol.	
91 C2	**Kramators'k** Ukr.	
93 G3	**Kramfors** Sweden	
111 B3	**Kranidi** Greece	
86 E3	**Krasino** Rus. Fed.	
88 C2	**Krāslava** Latvia	
101 F2	**Kraslice** Czech Rep.	
89 D3	**Krasnapollye** Belarus	
89 D3	**Krasnaya Gora** Rus. Fed.	
87 D3	**Krasnoarmeysk** Rus. Fed.	
91 C2	**Krasnoarmiys'k** Ukr.	
86 D2	**Krasnoborsk** Rus. Fed.	
91 D2	**Krasnodar** Rus. Fed.	
91 D2	**Krasnodon** Ukr.	
88 C2	**Krasnogorodskoye** Rus. Fed.	
91 D1	**Krasnogvardeyskoye** Rus. Fed.	
91 D2	**Krasnohrad** Ukr.	
91 C2	**Krasnohvardiys'ke** Ukr.	
86 E3	**Krasnokamsk** Rus. Fed.	
89 D2	**Krasnomayskiy** Rus. Fed.	
91 C2	**Krasnoperekops'k** Ukr.	
87 D3	**Krasnoslobodsk** Rus. Fed.	
86 E3	**Krasnoufimsk** Rus. Fed.	
83 H3	**Krasnoyarsk** Rus. Fed.	
89 F2	**Krasnoye-na-Volge** Rus. Fed.	
89 D3	**Krasnyy** Rus. Fed.	
89 E2	**Krasnyy Kholm** Rus. Fed.	
87 C4	**Krasnyy Luch** Ukr.	
91 E2	**Krasnyy Sulin** Rus. Fed.	
90 B2	**Krasyliv** Ukr.	
100 C2	**Krefeld** Ger.	
91 C2	**Kremenchuk** Ukr.	
91 C2	**Kremenchuts'ke Vodoskhovyshche** *resr* Ukr.	
103 D2	**Křemešník** *h.* Czech Rep.	
91 D2	**Kreminna** Ukr.	
103 D2	**Krems an der Donau** Austria	
89 D2	**Kresttsy** Rus. Fed.	
88 B2	**Kretinga** Lith.	
100 C2	**Kreuzau** Ger.	
100 C2	**Kreuztal** Ger.	
118 A2	**Kribi** Cameroon	
111 B3	**Krikellos** Greece	
66 D1	**Kril'on, Mys** *c.* Rus. Fed.	
73 C3	**Krishna** *r.* India	
73 C3	**Krishna, Mouths of the** India	
73 C2	**Krishnanagar** India	
93 E4	**Kristiansand** Norway	
93 F4	**Kristianstad** Sweden	
92 E3	**Kristiansund** Norway	
93 F4	**Kristinehamn** Sweden	
	Kriti *i.* Greece *see* Crete	
111 C3	**Kritiko Pelagos** *sea* Greece	
	Krivoy Rog Ukr. *see* Kryvyy Rih	
109 C1	**Križevci** Croatia	
108 B1	**Krk** *i.* Croatia	
92 F3	**Krokom** Sweden	
91 C1	**Krolevets'** Ukr.	
101 E2	**Kronach** Ger.	
63 B2	**Krŏng Kaôh Kŏng** Cambodia	
127 I2	**Kronprins Frederik Bjerge** *nunataks* Greenland	
123 C2	**Kroonstad** S. Africa	
87 D4	**Kropotkin** Rus. Fed.	
103 E2	**Krosno** Pol.	
103 D1	**Krotoszyn** Pol.	
60 B2	**Krui** Indon.	
109 C2	**Krujë** Albania	
111 C2	**Krumovgrad** Bulg.	
	Krung Thep Thai. *see* Bangkok	
88 C3	**Krupki** Belarus	
109 D2	**Kruševac** Serbia	
101 F2	**Krušné hory** *mts* Czech Rep.	
128 A2	**Kruzof Island** U.S.A.	
89 D3	**Krychaw** Belarus	
91 D3	**Krymsk** Rus. Fed.	
91 C2	**Kryvyy Rih** Ukr.	
114 B2	**Ksabi** Alg.	
107 D2	**Ksar el Boukhari** Alg.	
114 B1	**Ksar el Kebir** Morocco	
89 E3	**Kshenskiy** Rus. Fed.	
78 B2	**Kū', Jabal al** *h.* Saudi Arabia	
61 C1	**Kuala Belait** Brunei	
60 B1	**Kuala Kerai** Malaysia	
60 B1	**Kuala Lipis** Malaysia	
60 B1	**Kuala Lumpur** Malaysia	
61 C2	**Kualapembuang** Indon.	
60 B1	**Kuala Terengganu** Malaysia	
60 B2	**Kualatungal** Indon.	
61 C1	**Kuamut** *Sabah* Malaysia	
65 A1	**Kuandian** China	
61 C1	**Kuantan** Malaysia	
91 D2	**Kuban'** *r.* Rus. Fed.	
89 E2	**Kubenskoye, Ozero** *l.* Rus. Fed.	
110 C2	**Kubrat** Bulg.	
61 C1	**Kubuang** Indon.	
61 C1	**Kuching** *Sarawak* Malaysia	
109 C2	**Kuçovë** Albania	
61 C1	**Kudat** *Sabah* Malaysia	
61 C2	**Kudus** Indon.	
102 C2	**Kufstein** Austria	
127 F2	**Kugaaruk** Can.	
126 D2	**Kugluktuk** Can.	
92 I3	**Kuhmo** Fin.	
79 C2	**Kührān, Küh-e** *mt.* Iran	
	Kuitin China *see* Kuytun	
120 A2	**Kuito** Angola	
92 I2	**Kuivaniemi** Fin.	
65 B2	**Kujang** N. Korea	
109 D2	**Kukës** Albania	
111 C3	**Kula** Turkey	
75 D2	**Kula Kangri** *mt.* Bhutan/China	
76 B2	**Kulandy** Kazakh.	
88 C2	**Kuldīga** Latvia	
122 B1	**Kule** Botswana	
101 E2	**Kulmbach** Ger.	
77 C3	**Kŭlob** Tajik.	
76 B2	**Kul'sary** Kazakh.	
77 D1	**Kulunda** Rus. Fed.	
127 I2	**Kulusuk** Greenland	
67 C3	**Kumagaya** Japan	
67 B4	**Kumamoto** Japan	
109 D2	**Kumanovo** Macedonia	
114 B4	**Kumasi** Ghana	
118 A2	**Kumba** Cameroon	
78 B2	**Kumdah** Saudi Arabia	
87 E3	**Kumertau** Rus. Fed.	
65 B2	**Kumi** S. Korea	
93 G4	**Kumla** Sweden	
115 D3	**Kumo** Nigeria	
62 A1	**Kumon Range** *mts* Myanmar	
62 B2	**Kumphawapi** Thai.	
	Kumul China *see* Hami	
66 D2	**Kunashir, Ostrov** *i.* Rus. Fed.	
120 A2	**Kunene** *r.* Angola/Namibia	
77 D2	**Kungei Alatau** *mts* Kazakh./Kyrg.	
93 F4	**Kungsbacka** Sweden	
118 B2	**Kungu** Dem. Rep. Congo	
86 E3	**Kungur** Rus. Fed.	
62 A1	**Kunhing** Myanmar	
77 D3	**Kunlun Shan** *mts* China	
62 B1	**Kunming** China	
65 B2	**Kunsan** S. Korea	
50 B1	**Kununurra** Austr.	
92 I3	**Kuopio** Fin.	
109 C1	**Kupa** *r.* Croatia/Slovenia	
59 C3	**Kupang** Indon.	
88 B2	**Kupiškis** Lith.	
111 C2	**Küplü** Turkey	
128 A2	**Kupreanof Island** U.S.A.	
91 D2	**Kup"yans'k** Ukr.	
71 E2	**Kuqa** China	
67 B4	**Kurashiki** Japan	
67 B3	**Kurayoshi** Japan	
89 E3	**Kurchatov** Rus. Fed.	
110 C2	**Kürdzhali** Bulg.	
67 B4	**Kure** Japan	
88 B2	**Kuressaare** Estonia	
86 F3	**Kurgan** Rus. Fed.	
93 H3	**Kurikka** Fin.	
156 C3	**Kuril Trench** N. Pacific Ocean	
89 E3	**Kurkino** Rus. Fed.	
117 B3	**Kurmuk** Sudan	
73 B3	**Kurnool** India	
67 D3	**Kuroiso** Japan	
67 D2	**Kurri Kurri** Austr.	
89 E3	**Kursk** Rus. Fed.	
122 B2	**Kuruman** S. Africa	
122 B2	**Kuruman** *watercourse* S. Africa	
67 B4	**Kurume** Japan	
83 I3	**Kurumkan** Rus. Fed.	
73 C4	**Kurunegala** Sri Lanka	
111 C3	**Kuşadası** Turkey	
111 C3	**Kuşadası Körfezi** *b.* Turkey	
111 C3	**Kuş Gölü** *l.* Turkey	
91 D2	**Kushchevskaya** Rus. Fed.	
66 D2	**Kushiro** Japan	
76 C1	**Kushmurun** Kazakh.	
75 C2	**Kushtia** Bangl.	
66 D2	**Kussharo-ko** *l.* Japan	
111 C3	**Kütahya** Turkey	
81 C1	**K'ut'aisi** Georgia	
109 C1	**Kutjevo** Croatia	
103 D1	**Kutno** Pol.	
118 B3	**Kutu** Dem. Rep. Congo	
126 D2	**Kuujjua** *r.* Can.	

131 D1 **Kuujjuaq** Can.
130 C1 **Kuujjuarapik** Can.
92 I2 **Kuusamo** Fin.
120 A2 **Kuvango** Angola
89 D2 **Kuvshinovo** Rus. Fed.
78 B2 **Kuwait** *country* Asia
79 B2 **Kuwait** Kuwait
Kuybyshev Rus. Fed. *see*
Samara
91 D2 **Kuybysheve** Ukr.
87 D3 **Kuybyshevskoye**
Vodokhranilishche *resr*
Rus. Fed.
77 E2 **Kuytun** China
111 C3 **Kuyucak** Turkey
87 D3 **Kuznetsk** Rus. Fed.
90 B1 **Kuznetsovs'k** Ukr.
92 H1 **Kvalsund** Norway
123 D2 **KwaMashu** S. Africa
65 B2 **Kwangju** S. Korea
65 B1 **Kwanmo-bong** *mt.* N. Korea
123 B3 **Kwanobuhle** S. Africa
122 B3 **KwaNonzame** S. Africa
123 C3 **Kwatinidubu** S. Africa
123 C2 **KwaZamokuhle** S. Africa
123 D2 **KwaZulu-Natal** *prov.* S. Africa
121 B2 **Kwekwe** Zimbabwe
118 B3 **Kwenge** *r.* Dem. Rep. Congo
103 D1 **Kwidzyn** Pol.
118 B3 **Kwilu** *r.* Angola/Dem. Rep.
Congo
59 C3 **Kwoka** *mt.* Indon.
53 C3 **Kyabram** Austr.
62 A2 **Kyaikto** Myanmar
69 D1 **Kyakhta** Rus. Fed.
52 A2 **Kyancutta** Austr.
62 A1 **Kyaukpadaung** Myanmar
62 A2 **Kyaukpyu** Myanmar
88 B3 **Kybartai** Lith.
62 A2 **Kyebogyi** Myanmar
62 A2 **Kyeintali** Myanmar
74 B1 **Kyelang** India
Kyiv Ukr. *see* **Kiev**
90 C1 **Kyiv's'ke Vodoskhovyshche** *resr*
Ukr.
Kyklades *is* Greece *see*
Cyclades
129 D2 **Kyle** Can.
96 B2 **Kyle of Lochalsh** U.K.
100 C3 **Kyll** *r.* Ger.
111 B3 **Kyllini** *mt.* Greece
111 B3 **Kymi** Greece
52 B3 **Kyneton** Austr.
119 D2 **Kyoga, Lake** Uganda
53 D1 **Kyogle** Austr.
65 A2 **Kyŏnggi-man** *b.* S. Korea
65 B2 **Kyŏngju** S. Korea
67 C4 **Kyōto** Japan
111 B3 **Kyparissia** Greece
77 C1 **Kypshak, Ozero** *salt l.* Kazakh.
111 B3 **Kyra Panagia** *i.* Greece
111 B3 **Kyrenia** Cyprus
80 B2 **Kyrgyzstan** *country* Asia
101 F1 **Kyritz** Ger.
92 H3 **Kyrönjoki** *r.* Fin.
86 E2 **Kyrta** Rus. Fed.
86 D2 **Kyssa** Rus. Fed.
111 B3 **Kythira** *i.* Greece
111 B3 **Kythnos** *i.* Greece
128 B2 **Kyuquot** Can.
67 B4 **Kyūshū** *i.* Japan
110 D2 **Kyustendil** Bulg.
92 H3 **Kyyjärvi** Fin.
68 C1 **Kyzyl** Rus. Fed.
76 C2 **Kyzyl Kum** Desert
Kazakh./Uzbek.
77 C2 **Kyzylorda** Kazakh.

L

145 C3 **La Angostura, Presa de** *resr*
Mex.
117 C4 **Laascaanood** Somalia
150 B1 **La Asunción** Venez.
114 A2 **Laâyoune** Western Sahara
87 D4 **Laba** *r.* Rus. Fed.
144 B2 **La Babia** Mex.
146 B3 **La Bahía, Islas de** *is* Hond.
152 B3 **La Banda** Arg.
104 B2 **La Baule-Escoublac** France
114 A3 **Labé** Guinea
128 A1 **Laberge, Lake** Can.
129 C2 **La Biche, Lac** *l.* Can.
87 D4 **Labinsk** Rus. Fed.
64 C1 **Labo** Phil.
104 B3 **Labouheyre** France
131 D1 **Labrador** *reg.* Can.
131 D1 **Labrador City** Can.
158 C1 **Labrador Sea** Can./Greenland
150 B2 **Lábrea** Brazil
61 C1 **Labuan** Malaysia
60 B1 **Labuhanbilik** Indon.
61 C2 **Labuna** Indon.
63 A2 **Labutta** Myanmar
86 F2 **Labytnangi** Rus. Fed.
109 C2 **Laç** Albania
105 C2 **La Capelle** France
73 B3 **Laccadive Islands** India
129 E2 **Lac du Bonnet** Can.
146 B4 **La Ceiba** Hond.
53 B2 **Lachlan** *r.* Austr.
141 E1 **Lachute** Can.
105 D3 **La Ciotat** France
129 C2 **Lac La Biche** Can.
Lac La Martre Can. *see*
Whati
141 E1 **Lac-Mégantic** Can.
128 C2 **Lacombe** Can.
146 B4 **La Concepción** Panama
145 C3 **La Concordia** Mex.
108 A3 **Laconi** *Sardegna* Italy
141 E2 **Laconia** U.S.A.
128 C2 **La Crete** Can.
140 A2 **La Crosse** U.S.A.
144 B2 **La Cruz** Mex.
144 B2 **La Cuesta** Mex.
75 B1 **Ladakh Range** *mts* India/Pak.
122 B3 **Ladismith** S. Africa
79 D2 **Lādīz** Iran
86 C2 **Ladoga, Lake** Rus. Fed.
Ladozhskoye Ozero *l.*
Rus. Fed. *see* **Ladoga, Lake**
128 B3 **Ladysmith** Can.
123 C2 **Ladysmith** S. Africa
59 D3 **Lae** P.N.G.
152 B3 **La Esmeralda** Bol.
93 F4 **Læsø** *i.* Denmark
143 C2 **La Fayette** U.S.A.
140 B2 **Lafayette** *IN* U.S.A.
142 B2 **Lafayette** *LA* U.S.A.
115 C4 **Lafia** Nigeria
104 B2 **La Flèche** France
143 D1 **La Follette** U.S.A.
131 C1 **Laforge** Can.
79 C2 **Lāft** Iran
108 A3 **La Galite** *i.* Tunisia
81 C1 **Lagan'** Rus. Fed.
118 B2 **Lagdo, Lac de** *l.* Cameroon
115 C1 **Laghouat** Alg.
154 C1 **Lagoa Santa** Brazil
114 A2 **Lagos** *i.* Islas Canarias
115 C4 **Lagos** Nigeria
106 B2 **Lagos** Port.
134 C1 **La Grande** U.S.A.

130 C1 **La Grande 3, Réservoir** *resr*
Can.
131 C1 **La Grande 4, Réservoir** *resr*
Can.
50 B1 **La Grange** Austr.
143 C2 **La Grange** U.S.A.
150 B1 **La Gran Sabana** *plat.* Venez.
152 D3 **Laguna** Brazil
144 A2 **Laguna, Picacho de la** *mt.*
Mex.
150 A2 **Lagunas** Peru
La Habana Cuba *see* **Havana**
61 C1 **Lahad Datu** *Sabah* Malaysia
60 B2 **Lahat** Indon.
78 B3 **Labij** Yemen
81 C2 **Lāhījān** Iran
100 C2 **Lahnstein** Ger.
74 B1 **Lahore** Pak.
74 A2 **Lahri** Pak.
93 I3 **Lahti** Fin.
115 D4 **Laï** Chad
53 C1 **Laidley** Austr.
104 C2 **L'Aigle** France
111 B3 **Laimos, Akrotirio** *pt* Greece
122 B3 **Laingsburg** S. Africa
92 H2 **Lainioälven** *r.* Sweden
96 B2 **Lairg** U.K.
108 B1 **Laives** Italy
70 B2 **Laiwu** China
70 C2 **Laiyang** China
70 B2 **Laizhou** China
70 B2 **Laizhou Wan** *b.* China
50 C1 **Lajamanu** Austr.
152 C3 **Lajes** Brazil
144 B2 **La Junta** Mex.
136 C3 **La Junta** U.S.A.
121 C2 **Lake Cabora Bassa** *resr* Moz.
53 C2 **Lake Cargelligo** Austr.
53 D2 **Lake Cathie** Austr.
142 B2 **Lake Charles** U.S.A.
143 D2 **Lake City** *FL* U.S.A.
143 E2 **Lake City** *SC* U.S.A.
128 A1 **Lake Como** Italy
128 B3 **Lake Cowichan** Can.
108 B1 **Lake Garda** Italy
138 A2 **Lake Havasu City** U.S.A.
143 D3 **Lakeland** U.S.A.
128 C2 **Lake Louise** Can.
143 D2 **Lake Oswego** U.S.A.
54 A2 **Lake Paringa** N.Z.
142 B2 **Lake Providence** U.S.A.
54 B2 **Lake Pukaki** N.Z.
53 C2 **Lakes Entrance** Austr.
134 B2 **Lakeview** U.S.A.
136 B3 **Lakewood** *CO* U.S.A.
141 E2 **Lakewood** *NJ* U.S.A.
143 D3 **Lake Worth** U.S.A.
74 A2 **Lakhpat** India
111 B3 **Lakki Marwat** Pak.
111 B3 **Lakonikos Kolpos** *b.* Greece
92 H1 **Lakselv** Norway
107 C1 **L'Alcora** Spain
145 C3 **La Libertad** Guat.
106 B1 **Lalín** Spain
75 B2 **Lalitpur** India
129 D2 **La Loche** Can.
100 B2 **La Louvière** Belgium
108 A2 **La Maddalena** *Sardegna* Italy
61 C1 **Lamag** *Sabah* Malaysia
La Manche *str.* France/U.K. *see*
English Channel
136 C3 **Lamar** U.S.A.
79 C2 **Lamard** Iran
108 A3 **La Marmora, Punta** *mt.*
Sardegna Italy
128 C1 **La Martre, Lac** *l.* Can.
118 B3 **Lambaréné** Gabon

122 A3 Lambert's Bay S. Africa
92 A2 Lambeyri Iceland
106 D2 Lamego Port.
150 A3 La Merced Peru
52 B3 Lameroo Austr.
139 C2 Lamesa U.S.A.
111 B3 Lamia Greece
137 E2 Lamoni U.S.A.
62 A2 Lampang Thai.
139 D2 Lampasas U.S.A.
145 B2 Lampazos Mex.
99 A2 Lampeter U.K.
62 A2 Lamphun Thai.
119 E3 Lamu Kenya
96 C3 Lanark U.K.
63 A2 Lanbi Kyun i. Myanmar
Lancang Jiang r. China see
Mekong
98 B3 Lancaster U.K.
135 C4 Lancaster CA U.S.A.
140 C3 Lancaster OH U.S.A.
141 D2 Lancaster PA U.S.A.
143 D2 Lancaster SC U.S.A.
127 F2 Lancaster Sound str. Can.
Lanchow China see Lanzhou
102 C2 Landeck Austria
136 B2 Lander U.S.A.
99 A3 Land's End pt U.K.
102 C2 Landshut Ger.
93 F4 Landskrona Sweden
143 C2 Lanett U.S.A.
122 B2 Langberg mts S. Africa
137 D1 Langdon U.S.A.
93 F4 Langeland i. Denmark
101 D1 Langen Ger.
100 C1 Langeoog Ger.
100 C1 Langeoog i. Ger.
92 A3 Langjökull Iceland
105 C3 Langogne France
104 B3 Langon France
105 D2 Langres France
60 A1 Langsa Indon.
62 B1 Lang Sơn Vietnam
101 D1 Langwedel Ger.
129 D2 Lanigan Can.
153 A4 Lanín, Volcán vol. Arg./Chile
81 C2 Länkäran Azer.
104 B2 Lannion France
140 C2 Lansing U.S.A.
71 B3 Lanxi China
117 B3 Lanya Sudan
114 A2 Lanzarote i. Islas Canarias
70 A2 Lanzhou China
64 B1 Laoag Phil.
62 B1 Lao Cai Vietnam
62 B2 Laohekou China
68 C2 Laojunmiao China
65 B1 Laoling China
65 B1 Lao Ling mts China
105 C2 Laon France
62 B2 Laos country Asia
65 B1 Laotougou China
154 C3 Lapa Brazil
114 A2 La Palma i. Islas Canarias
146 C4 La Palma Panama
150 B1 La Paragua Venez.
152 B2 La Paz Bol.
144 A2 La Paz Mex.
150 B2 La Pedrera Col.
66 D1 La Pérouse Strait Japan/
Rus. Fed.
145 C2 La Pesca Mex.
144 B2 La Piedad Mex.
153 C4 La Plata Arg.
153 C4 La Plata, Río de sea chan.
Arg./Uru.

93 I3 Lappeenranta Fin.
92 G2 Lappland reg. Europe
111 C2 Lâpseki Turkey
83 J1 Laptev Sea Rus. Fed.
Lapteyikh, More sea Rus. Fed.
see Laptev Sea
92 H3 Lapua Fin.
152 B3 La Quiaca Arg.
79 C2 Lār Iran
114 B1 Larache Morocco
136 B2 Laramie U.S.A.
136 B2 Laramie Mountains U.S.A.
154 B3 Laranjeiras do Sul Brazil
59 C3 Larantuka Indon.
59 C3 Larat i. Indon.
107 D2 Larba Alg.
106 C1 Laredo Spain
139 D3 Laredo U.S.A.
96 B3 Largs U.K.
152 B3 La Rioja Arg.
111 B3 Larisa Greece
74 A2 Larkana Pak.
80 B2 Larnaca Cyprus
97 D1 Larne U.K.
100 B2 La Roche-en-Ardenne
Belgium
104 B2 La Rochelle France
104 B2 La Roche-sur-Yon France
107 C2 La Roda Spain
147 D3 La Romana Dom. Rep.
129 D2 La Ronge Can.
129 D2 La Ronge, Lac l. Can.
50 C1 Larrimah Austr.
55 P3 Larsen Ice Shelf Antarctica
93 F4 Larvik Norway
130 C2 La Sarre Can.
138 B2 Las Cruces U.S.A.
153 C4 Las Flores Arg.
153 B4 Las Heras Arg.
62 A1 Lashio Myanmar
74 A1 Lashkar Gāh Afgh.
109 C3 La Sila reg. Italy
152 B3 Las Lomitas Arg.
144 B2 Las Nieves Mex.
114 A2 Las Palmas de Gran Canaria
Islas Canarias
108 A2 La Spezia Italy
153 B5 Las Plumas Arg.
129 D2 Last Mountain Lake Can.
152 B3 Las Tórtolas, Cerro mt.
Arg./Chile
118 B3 Lastoursville Gabon
109 C2 Lastovo i. Croatia
144 A2 Las Tres Vírgenes, Volcán vol.
Mex.
146 C2 Las Tunas Cuba
144 B2 Las Varas Chihuahua Mex.
144 B2 Las Varas Nayarit Mex.
138 B1 Las Vegas NM U.S.A.
135 C3 Las Vegas NV U.S.A.
131 E1 La Tabatière Can.
80 B2 Latakia Syria
104 B3 La Teste-de-Buch France
108 B2 Latina Italy
147 D3 La Tortuga, Isla i. Venez.
64 B1 La Trinidad Phil.
89 E2 Latskoye Rus. Fed.
131 C2 La Tuque Can.
88 B2 Latvia country Europe
102 C1 Lauchhammer Ger.
101 E3 Lauf an der Pegnitz Ger.
105 D2 Laufen Switz.
51 D4 Launceston Austr.
99 A3 Launceston U.K.
62 A1 Launggyaung Myanmar
51 D1 Laura Austr.
142 C2 Laurel MS U.S.A.

134 E1 Laurel MT U.S.A.
109 C2 Lauria Italy
143 E2 Laurinburg U.S.A.
105 D2 Lausanne Switz.
61 C2 Laut i. Indon.
61 C2 Laut Bali sea Indon.
101 D2 Lautersbach (Hessen) Ger.
61 C2 Laut Kecil, Kepulauan is
Indon.
100 C1 Lauwersmeer l. Neth.
104 B2 Laval France
107 C2 La Vall d'Uixó Spain
52 B2 Laverton Austr.
155 D2 Lavras Brazil
123 D2 Lavumisa Swaziland
61 C1 Lawas Sarawak Malaysia
62 A1 Lawksawk Myanmar
114 B3 Lawra Ghana
137 D3 Lawrence U.S.A.
142 C1 Lawrenceburg U.S.A.
139 D2 Lawton U.S.A.
78 A2 Lawz, Jabal al mt. Saudi Arabia
93 F4 Laxå Sweden
74 B1 Layyah Pak.
109 D2 Lazarevac Serbia
144 A1 Lázaro Cárdenas Baja
California Mex.
144 B3 Lázaro Cárdenas Michoacán
Mex.
88 B3 Lazdijai Lith.
136 C2 Lead U.S.A.
129 D2 Leader Can.
136 B3 Leadville U.S.A.
Leaf Bay Can. see Tasiujaq
129 D2 Leaf Rapids Can.
97 B2 Leane, Lough l. Ireland
137 E3 Leavenworth U.S.A.
80 B2 Lebanon MO U.S.A.
137 E3 Lebanon MO U.S.A.
141 E2 Lebanon NH U.S.A.
134 B2 Lebanon OR U.S.A.
141 D2 Lebanon PA U.S.A.
89 E3 Lebedyan' Rus. Fed.
91 C1 Lebedyn Ukr.
104 C2 Le Blanc France
103 D1 Lębork Pol.
123 C1 Lebowakgomo S. Africa
106 B2 Lebrija Spain
153 A4 Lebu Chile
104 C3 Le Bugue France
109 C2 Lecce Italy
108 A1 Lecco Italy
102 C2 Lech r. Austria/Ger.
111 B3 Lechaina Greece
71 B3 Lechang China
102 B1 Leck Ger.
104 C3 Lectoure France
106 B1 Ledesma Spain
104 C2 Le Dorat France
128 C2 Leduc Can.
137 E1 Leech Lake U.S.A.
62 C2 Leeds U.K.
98 B2 Leek U.K.
100 C1 Leer (Ostfriesland) Ger.
143 D3 Leesburg U.S.A.
142 B2 Leesville U.S.A.
53 C2 Leeton Austr.
122 B3 Leeu-Gamka S. Africa
100 B1 Leeuwarden Neth.
50 A3 Leeuwin, Cape Austr.
147 D3 Leeward Islands Caribbean
Sea
111 B3 Lefkada Greece
111 B3 Lefkada i. Greece
Lefkosia Cyprus see Nicosia
64 B1 Legaspi Phil.
108 B1 Legnago Italy

103 D1 **Legnica** Pol.
75 B1 **Leh** India
104 C2 **Le Havre** France
122 B1 **Lehututu** Botswana
103 D2 **Leibnitz** Austria
99 C2 **Leicester** U.K.
51 C1 **Leichhardt** r. Austr.
100 B1 **Leiden** Neth.
100 A2 **Leie** r. Belgium
52 A2 **Leigh Creek** Austr.
93 E3 **Leikanger** Norway
101 D1 **Leine** r. Ger.
97 C2 **Leinster** reg. Ireland
101 F2 **Leipzig** Ger.
92 F2 **Leiranger** Norway
106 B2 **Leiria** Port.
93 E4 **Leirvik** Norway
97 C2 **Leixlip** Ireland
71 B3 **Leizhou** China
71 B3 **Leizhou Bandao** pen. China
118 B3 **Lékana** Congo
100 B1 **Lelystad** Neth.
153 B6 **Le Maire, Estrecho de** sea chan. Arg.
         Léman, Lac l. France/Switz. see Geneva, Lake
104 C2 **Le Mans** France
137 D2 **Le Mars** U.S.A.
154 C2 **Leme** Brazil
         Lemesos Cyprus see Limassol
101 D1 **Lemförde** Ger.
127 G2 **Lemieux Islands** Can.
136 C1 **Lemmon** U.S.A.
135 C3 **Lemoore** U.S.A.
131 D1 **Le Moyne, Lac** l. Can.
62 A1 **Lemro** r. Myanmar
109 C2 **La Murge** hills Italy
83 J2 **Lena** r. Rus. Fed.
100 C1 **Lengerich** Ger.
71 B3 **Lengshuijiang** China
71 B3 **Lengshuitan** China
91 D2 **Lenine** Ukr.
         Leningrad Rus. Fed. see St Petersburg
91 D2 **Leningradskaya** Rus. Fed.
77 D3 **Lenin Peak** Kyrg./Tajik.
         Leninsk Kazakh. see Baykonyr
89 E3 **Leninskiy** Rus. Fed.
100 A1 **Lens** Belgium
104 C1 **Lens** France
83 I2 **Lensk** Rus. Fed.
103 D2 **Lenti** Hungary
109 C3 **Lentini** Sicilia Italy
114 B3 **Léo** Burkina
103 D2 **Leoben** Austria
99 B2 **Leominster** U.K.
144 B2 **León** Mex.
146 B3 **León** Nic.
106 B1 **León** Spain
122 A1 **Leonardville** Namibia
50 B2 **Leonora** Austr.
155 D2 **Leopoldina** Brazil
123 C1 **Lephalale** S. Africa
123 C1 **Lephepe** Botswana
123 C3 **Lephoi** S. Africa
71 B3 **Leping** China
105 C2 **Le Puy-en-Velay** France
150 A2 **Lérida** Col.
106 C1 **Lerma** Spain
111 C3 **Leros** i. Greece
130 C1 **Le Roy, Lac** l. Can.
93 F4 **Lerum** Sweden
96 □ **Lerwick** U.K.
111 C3 **Lesbos** i. Greece
147 C3 **Les Cayes** Haiti
69 C3 **Leshan** China
86 D2 **Leshukonskoye** Rus. Fed.
109 D2 **Leskovac** Serbia
104 B2 **Lesneven** France
89 E2 **Lesnoye** Rus. Fed.
83 H3 **Lesosibirsk** Rus. Fed.
123 C2 **Lesotho** country Africa
66 B1 **Lesozavodsk** Rus. Fed.
104 B2 **Les Sables-d'Olonne** France
147 D3 **Lesser Antilles** is Caribbean Sea
81 C1 **Lesser Caucasus** mts Asia
128 C2 **Lesser Slave Lake** Can.
58 B3 **Lesser Sunda Islands** is Indon.
105 C3 **Les Vans** France
         Lesvos i. Greece see Lesbos
103 D1 **Leszno** Pol.
99 C3 **Letchworth Garden City** U.K.
128 C3 **Lethbridge** Can.
150 C1 **Lethem** Guyana
59 C3 **Leti, Kepulauan** is Indon.
150 B2 **Leticia** Col.
123 C1 **Lethakeng** Botswana
104 C1 **Le Touquet-Paris-Plage** France
63 A2 **Le Tréport** France
123 C2 **Letsok-aw Kyun** i. Myanmar
97 C1 **Letsopa** S. Africa
105 C3 **Leucate, Étang de** l. France
60 A1 **Leuser, Gunung** mt. Indon.
100 B2 **Leuven** Belgium
92 F3 **Levanger** Norway
139 C2 **Levelland** U.S.A.
50 B1 **Lévêque, Cape** Austr.
100 C2 **Leverkusen** Ger.
103 D2 **Levice** Slovakia
54 C2 **Levin** N.Z.
131 C2 **Lévis** Can.
89 E3 **Lev Tolstoy** Rus. Fed.
99 D3 **Lewes** U.K.
96 A1 **Lewis, Isle of** i. U.K.
140 C3 **Lewisburg** U.S.A.
134 D1 **Lewis Range** mts U.S.A.
134 C1 **Lewiston** ID U.S.A.
141 E2 **Lewiston** ME U.S.A.
134 E1 **Lewistown** U.S.A.
140 C3 **Lexington** KY U.S.A.
136 D2 **Lexington** NE U.S.A.
141 D3 **Lexington** VA U.S.A.
64 B1 **Leyte** i. Phil.
109 C2 **Lezhë** Albania
89 F2 **Lezhnevo** Rus. Fed.
89 E3 **L'gov** Rus. Fed.
75 C2 **Lhagoi Kangri** mt. China
68 C2 **Lharigarbo** China
75 D2 **Lhasa** China
75 C2 **Lhazê** China
60 A1 **Lhokseumawe** Indon.
111 B3 **Liakoura** mt. Greece
67 B3 **Liancourt Rocks** i. N. Pacific Ocean
71 B3 **Lianhua** China
71 B3 **Lianjiang** China
70 C2 **Lianshan** China
70 B2 **Lianyungang** China
71 B3 **Lianzhou** China
70 B2 **Liaocheng** China
70 C1 **Liaodong Bandao** pen. China
70 C1 **Liaodong Wan** b. China
65 A1 **Liao He** r. China
70 C1 **Liaoning** prov. China
65 A1 **Liaoyang** China
65 B1 **Liaoyuan** China
128 B1 **Liard** r. Can.
134 C1 **Libby** U.S.A.
118 B2 **Libenge** Dem. Rep. Congo
136 C3 **Liberal** U.S.A.
103 D1 **Liberec** Czech Rep.
114 B4 **Liberia** country Africa
146 B3 **Liberia** Costa Rica
150 B1 **Libertad** Venez.
100 B3 **Libin** Belgium
104 B3 **Libourne** France
118 A2 **Libreville** Gabon
115 E2 **Libya** country Africa
115 E2 **Libyan Desert** Egypt/Libya
116 A1 **Libyan Plateau** Egypt/Libya
108 B3 **Licata** Sicilia Italy
         Licheng China see **Lipu**
121 C2 **Lichinga** Moz.
101 E2 **Lichte** Ger.
123 C2 **Lichtenburg** S. Africa
101 E2 **Lichtenfels** Ger.
88 C3 **Lida** Belarus
93 F4 **Lidköping** Sweden
50 C2 **Liebig, Mount** Austr.
105 D2 **Liechtenstein** country Europe
100 B2 **Liège** Belgium
92 J3 **Lieksa** Fin.
119 C2 **Lienart** Dem. Rep. Congo
63 B2 **Liên Nghia** Vietnam
102 C2 **Lienz** Austria
88 B2 **Liepāja** Latvia
102 C2 **Liezen** Austria
97 C2 **Liffey** r. Ireland
97 C1 **Lifford** Ireland
53 C1 **Lightning Ridge** Austr.
121 C2 **Ligonha** r. Moz.
105 D3 **Ligurian Sea** France/Italy
119 C4 **Likasi** Dem. Rep. Congo
128 B2 **Likely** Can.
89 E2 **Likhoslavl'** Rus. Fed.
61 B1 **Liku** China
105 D3 **L'Île-Rousse** Corse France
71 B3 **Liling** China
93 F4 **Lilla Edet** Sweden
100 B2 **Lille** Belgium
105 C1 **Lille** France
         Lille Bælt sea chan. Denmark see **Little Belt**
93 F3 **Lillehammer** Norway
93 F4 **Lillestrøm** Norway
128 B2 **Lillooet** Can.
121 C2 **Lilongwe** Malawi
64 B2 **Liloy** Phil.
150 A3 **Lima** Peru
140 C2 **Lima** U.S.A.
80 B2 **Limassol** Cyprus
97 C1 **Limavady** U.K.
153 B4 **Limay** r. Arg.
101 F2 **Limbach-Oberfrohna** Ger.
88 B2 **Limbaži** Latvia
118 A2 **Limbe** Cameroon
100 D2 **Limburg an der Lahn** Ger.
122 B2 **Lime Acres** S. Africa
154 C2 **Limeira** Brazil
97 B2 **Limerick** Ireland
93 E4 **Limfjorden** sea chan. Denmark
111 C3 **Limnos** i. Greece
104 C2 **Limoges** France
136 C3 **Limon** U.S.A.
104 C3 **Limoux** France
123 C1 **Limpopo** prov. S. Africa
121 C3 **Limpopo** r. S. Africa/Zimbabwe
64 A1 **Linapacan** i. Phil.
153 A4 **Linares** Chile
145 C2 **Linares** Mex.
106 C2 **Linares** Spain
62 B1 **Lincang** China
         Linchuan Jiangxi China see **Fuzhou**
98 C2 **Lincoln** U.K.

140 B2 Lincoln *IL* U.S.A.
141 F1 Lincoln *ME* U.S.A.
137 D2 Lincoln *NE* U.S.A.
151 C1 Linden Guyana
142 C1 Linden U.S.A.
119 C2 Lindi *r.* Dem. Rep. Congo
119 D3 Lindi Tanz.
Lindisfarne *i.* U.K. *see*
Holy Island
80 A2 Lindos Greece
141 D2 Lindsay Can.
49 H2 Line Islands Kiribati
70 B2 Linfen China
64 B1 Lingayen Phil.
70 B2 Lingbao China
123 C3 Lingelethu S. Africa
123 C3 Lingelihle S. Africa
100 C1 Lingen (Ems) Ger.
60 B2 Lingga, Kepulauan *is* Indon.
71 A3 Lingshan China
71 A4 Lingshui China
114 A3 Linguère Senegal
155 D1 Linhares Brazil
70 A1 Linhe China
93 G4 Linköping Sweden
66 B1 Linkou China
70 B2 Linqing China
154 C2 Lins Brazil
136 C1 Linton U.S.A.
69 D2 Linxi China
69 C2 Linxia China
70 B2 Linyi *Shandong* China
70 B2 Linyi *Shandong* China
70 B2 Linying China
102 C2 Linz Austria
105 C3 Lion, Golfe du *g.* France
109 B3 Lipari Italy
108 B3 Lipari, Isole *is* Italy
89 E3 Lipetsk Rus. Fed.
110 B1 Lipova Romania
71 B3 Lipu China
76 C1 Lisakovsk Kazakh.
118 C2 Lisala Dem. Rep. Congo
Lisboa Port. *see* Lisbon
106 B2 Lisbon Port.
97 C1 Lisburn U.K.
97 B2 Liscannor Bay Ireland
104 C2 Lisieux France
99 A3 Liskeard U.K.
89 E3 Liski Rus. Fed.
53 D1 Lismore Austr.
97 C1 Lisnaskea U.K.
97 B2 Listowel Ireland
71 A3 Litang *Guangxi* China
68 C2 Litang *Sichuan* China
140 B3 Litchfield *IL* U.S.A.
137 E1 Litchfield *MN* U.S.A.
53 D2 Lithgow Austr.
111 B3 Lithino, Akrotirio *pt* Greece
88 B2 Lithuania *country* Europe
102 C1 Litoměřice Czech Rep.
146 C2 Little Abaco *i.* Bahamas
73 D3 Little Andaman *i.* India
93 E4 Little Belt *sea chan.* Denmark
137 E1 Little Falls U.S.A.
139 C2 Littlefield U.S.A.
99 C3 Littlehampton U.K.
122 A2 Little Karas Berg *plat.*
Namibia
122 B3 Little Karoo *plat.* S. Africa
96 A2 Little Minch *sea chan.* U.K.
136 C1 Little Missouri *r.* U.S.A.
63 A3 Little Nicobar *i.* India
138 B2 Little Rock U.S.A.
141 E2 Littleton U.S.A.
70 B2 Liujiachang China

71 A3 Liuzhou China
111 B3 Livadeia Greece
88 C2 Līvāni Latvia
50 B1 Liveringa Austr.
138 C2 Livermore, Mount U.S.A.
131 D2 Liverpool Can.
98 B2 Liverpool U.K.
127 F2 Liverpool, Cape Can.
53 C2 Liverpool Range *mts* Austr.
134 D1 Livingston *MT* U.S.A.
139 E2 Livingston *TX* U.S.A.
139 D2 Livingston, Lake U.S.A.
120 B2 Livingstone Zambia
109 C2 Livno Bos.-Herz.
89 E3 Livny Rus. Fed.
140 C2 Livonia U.S.A.
108 B2 Livorno Italy
119 D3 Liwale Tanz.
70 B2 Liyang China
99 A4 Lizard Point U.K.
108 B1 Ljubljana Slovenia
93 G3 Ljungan *r.* Sweden
93 F3 Ljungby Sweden
93 G3 Ljusdal Sweden
93 G3 Ljusnan *r.* Sweden
99 B3 Llandeilo U.K.
99 B3 Llandovery U.K.
99 B2 Llandrindod Wells U.K.
98 B2 Llandudno U.K.
99 A3 Llanelli U.K.
98 A2 Llangefni U.K.
139 C2 Llano Estacado *plain* U.S.A.
150 B1 Llanos *plain* Col./Venez.
107 D1 Lleida Spain
99 A2 Lleyn Peninsula U.K.
107 C2 Lliria Spain
106 C1 Llodio Spain
128 B2 Lloyd George, Mount Can.
129 D2 Lloyd Lake Can.
129 C2 Lloydminster Can.
152 B3 Llullaillaco, Volcán *vol.* Chile
123 C2 Lobatse Botswana
120 A2 Lobito Angola
101 F1 Loburg Ger.
96 B2 Lochaber *reg.* U.K.
104 C2 Loches France
96 B2 Lochgilphead U.K.
96 B1 Lochinver U.K.
96 A2 Lochmaddy U.K.
96 C2 Lochnagar *mt.* U.K.
52 A2 Lock Austr.
96 C3 Lockerbie U.K.
139 D3 Lockhart U.S.A.
141 D2 Lock Haven U.S.A.
141 D2 Lockport U.S.A.
63 B2 Lộc Ninh Vietnam
105 C3 Lodève France
86 C2 Lodeynoye Pole Rus. Fed.
92 F2 Lødingen Norway
119 D2 Lodwar Kenya
103 D1 Łódź Pol.
62 B2 Loei Thai.
122 A3 Loeriesfontein S. Africa
92 F2 Lofoten *is* Norway
134 D2 Logan U.S.A.
126 B2 Logan, Mount Can.
140 B2 Logansport U.S.A.
108 B1 Logatec Slovenia
106 C1 Logroño Spain
101 D1 Löhne Ger.
101 D1 Lohne (Oldenburg) Ger.
62 A1 Loikaw Myanmar
62 A2 Loi Lan *mt.* Myanmar/Thai.
104 B2 Loire *r.* France
150 A2 Loja Ecuador
106 C2 Loja Spain
92 I2 Lokan tekojärvi *resr* Fin.

100 B2 Lokeren Belgium
122 B1 Lokgwabe Botswana
119 D2 Lokichar Kenya
119 D2 Lokichokio Kenya
89 D2 Loknya Rus. Fed.
115 C4 Lokoja Nigeria
89 D3 Lokot' Rus. Fed.
88 C2 Loksa Estonia
127 G2 Loks Land *i.* Can.
93 F4 Lolland *i.* Denmark
119 D3 Lolondo Tanz.
122 B2 Lolwane S. Africa
110 B2 Lom Bulg.
93 E3 Lom Norway
119 C2 Lomami *r.* Dem. Rep. Congo
153 C4 Lomas de Zamora Arg.
61 C2 Lombok *i.* Indon.
61 C2 Lombok, Selat *sea chan.*
Indon.
114 C4 Lomé Togo
118 C3 Lomela *r.* Dem. Rep. Congo
100 B2 Lommel Belgium
96 B2 Lomond, Loch *l.* U.K.
88 C2 Lomonosov Rus. Fed.
135 B4 Lompoc U.S.A.
63 B2 Lom Sak Thai.
103 E1 Łomża Pol.
130 B2 London Can.
99 C3 London U.K.
140 C3 London U.S.A.
97 C1 Londonderry U.K.
50 B1 Londonderry, Cape Austr.
154 B2 Londrina Brazil
83 M2 Longa, Proliv *sea chan.*
Rus. Fed.
61 C1 Long Akah *Sarawak* Malaysia
143 E2 Long Bay U.S.A.
135 C4 Long Beach U.S.A.
97 C2 Longford Ireland
61 C2 Longiram Indon.
147 C2 Long Island Bahamas
130 C1 Long Island Can.
59 D3 Long Island P.N.G.
141 E2 Long Island U.S.A.
130 B2 Longlac Can.
130 B2 Long Lake Can.
136 B2 Longmont U.S.A.
70 A2 Longnan China
140 C2 Long Point Can.
71 B3 Longquan China
131 E2 Long Range Mountains Can.
51 D2 Longreach Austr.
99 D2 Long Stratton U.K.
98 B1 Longtown U.K.
105 D2 Longuyon France
139 E2 Longview *TX* U.S.A.
134 B1 Longview *WA* U.S.A.
70 A2 Longxi China
71 B3 Longxi Shan *mt.* China
63 B2 Long Xuyên Vietnam
71 B3 Longyan China
82 C1 Longyearbyen Svalbard
102 B2 Lons-le-Saunier France
143 E2 Lookout, Cape U.S.A.
97 B2 Loop Head Ireland
63 B2 Lop Buri Thai.
64 B1 Lopez Phil.
68 C2 Lop Nur *salt flat* China
118 C2 Lopori *r.* Dem. Rep. Congo
74 A2 Lora, Hamun-i- *dry lake*
Afgh./Pak.
106 B2 Lora del Río Spain
140 C2 Lorain U.S.A.
74 A1 Loralai Pak.
107 C2 Lorca Spain
48 E5 Lord Howe Island Austr.
138 B2 Lordsburg U.S.A.

Lorena

92	G3	Lycksele Sweden
88	C3	Lyel'chytsy Belarus
88	C3	Lyepyel' Belarus
99	B3	Lyme Bay U.K.
141	E4	Lynchburg U.S.A.
129	D2	Lynn Lake Can.
129	D1	Lynx Lake Can.
105	C2	Lyon France
89	D2	Lyozna Belarus
86	E3	Lys'va Rus. Fed.
91	E2	Lysi Cyprus
98	B2	Lysychans'k Ukr.
98	B2	Lytham St Anne's U.K.
88	C2	Lyuban' Belarus
89	E2	Lyubertsy Rus. Fed.
90	B1	Lyubeshiv Ukr.
89	F2	Lyubim Rus. Fed.
91	D2	Lyubotyn Ukr.
89	D2	Lyubytino Rus. Fed.
89	D3	Lyudinovo Rus. Fed.

M

80	B2	Ma'ān Jordan
88	C2	Maardu Estonia
100	B2	Maas r. Neth.
100	B2	Maaseik Belgium
64	B1	Maasin Phil.
100	B2	Maastricht Neth.
121	C3	Mabalane Moz.
150	C1	Mabaruma Guyana
121	C3	Mabote Moz.
122	B1	Mabule Botswana
122	B1	Mabutsane Botswana
155	D2	Macaé Brazil
121	C2	Macaloge Moz.
71	B3	MacAlpine Lake Can.
150	A2	Macapá Brazil
155	C3	Macará Ecuador
155	D1	Macarani Brazil
151	E2	Macau Brazil
123	D1	Maccaretane Moz.
98	B2	Macclesfield U.K.
50	B2	Macdonald, Lake imp. l. Austr.
50	C2	Macdonnell Ranges mts Austr.
130	A1	McDowell Lake Can.
106	B1	Macedo de Cavaleiros Port.
52	B3	Macedon mt. Austr.
109	D2	Macedonia country Europe
151	E2	Maceió Brazil
108	B2	Macerata Italy
52	A2	Macfarlane, Lake imp. l. Austr.
97	B2	MacGillycuddy's Reeks mts Ireland
74	A2	Mach Pak.
155	C3	Machado Brazil
121	C3	Machaila Moz.
119	D3	Machakos Kenya
150	A2	Machala Ecuador
121	C3	Machanga Moz.
70	B2	Macheng China
142	C2	Machias U.S.A.
150	A1	Machiques Venez.
150	A3	Machu Picchu tourist site Peru
123	D2	Macia Moz.
110	C1	Măcin Romania
114	B3	Macina Mali
51	D2	Macintyre r. Austr.
51	D1	Mackay Austr.
50	B2	Mackay, Lake imp. l. Austr.
129	C1	MacKay Lake Can.
128	B2	Mackenzie r. Can.
126	B2	Mackenzie Bay Can.
126	D1	Mackenzie King Island Can.

128	A1	Mackenzie Mountains Can.
129	D2	Macklin Can.
53	D2	Macksville Austr.
53	D1	Maclean Austr.
50	A2	MacLeod, Lake dry lake Austr.
140	A2	Macomb U.S.A.
108	A2	Macomer Sardegna Italy
105	C2	Mâcon France
143	D2	Macon GA U.S.A.
137	E3	Macon MO U.S.A.
53	C2	Macquarie r. Austr.
48	E6	Macquarie Island S. Pacific Ocean
53	C2	Macquarie Marshes Austr.
97	B3	Macroom Ireland
52	A1	Macumba watercourse Austr.
145	C3	Macuspana Mex.
144	B2	Macuzari, Presa resr Mex.
123	D2	Madadeni S. Africa
121	D3	Madagascar country Africa
115	D2	Madama Niger
111	B2	Madan Bulg.
59	D3	Madang P.N.G.
150	C2	Madeira r. Brazil
114	A1	Madeira terr. N. Atlantic Ocean
131	D2	Madeleine, Îles de la is Can.
144	B2	Madera Mex.
135	B3	Madera U.S.A.
73	B3	Madgaon India
118	B3	Madingou Congo
140	B3	Madison IN U.S.A.
137	D2	Madison SD U.S.A.
140	B2	Madison WI U.S.A.
140	C3	Madison WV U.S.A.
134	D1	Madison r. U.S.A.
140	B3	Madisonville U.S.A.
61	C2	Madiun Indon.
119	D2	Mado Gashi Kenya
68	C2	Madoi China
88	C2	Madona Latvia
78	A2	Madrakah Saudi Arabia
		Madras India see Chennai
134	B2	Madras U.S.A.
145	C2	Madre, Laguna lag. Mex.
145	B3	Madre del Sur, Sierra mts Mex.
144	B2	Madre Occidental, Sierra mts Mex.
145	B2	Madre Oriental, Sierra mts Mex.
106	C1	Madrid Spain
106	C2	Madridejos Spain
61	C2	Madura i. Indon.
61	C2	Madura, Selat sea chan. Indon.
73	B4	Madurai India
67	C3	Maebashi Japan
62	A2	Mae Hong Son Thai.
62	A1	Mae Sai Thai.
62	A2	Mae Sariang Thai.
62	A2	Mae Suai Thai.
123	C2	Mafeteng Lesotho
119	D3	Mafia Island Tanz.
123	C2	Mafikeng S. Africa
119	D3	Mafinga Tanz.
154	C3	Mafra Brazil
83	L3	Magadan Rus. Fed.
147	C4	Magangue Col.
144	A1	Magdalena Mex.
138	B2	Magdalena U.S.A.
144	A2	Magdalena, Bahía b. Mex.
101	E1	Magdeburg Ger.
153	A6	Magellan, Strait of Chile
97	C1	Magherafelt U.K.
87	E3	Magnitogorsk Rus. Fed.
142	B2	Magnolia U.S.A.
131	D1	Magpie, Lac l. Can.

114	A3	Magta' Lahjar Maur.
151	D2	Maguarinho, Cabo c. Brazil
123	D2	Magude Moz.
62	A1	Magwe Myanmar
81	C2	Mahābād Iran
74	B2	Mahajan India
121	D2	Mahajanga Madag.
61	C2	Mahakam r. Indon.
121	D2	Mahalapye Botswana
121	D2	Mahalevona Madag.
75	C2	Mahanadi r. India
121	D2	Mahanoro Madag.
63	B2	Maha Sarakham Thai.
121	D2	Mahavavy r. Madag.
78	B2	Mahd adh Dhahab Saudi Arabia
150	C1	Mahdia Guyana
113	K7	Mahé i. Seychelles
74	B2	Mahesana India
74	B2	Mahi r. India
54	C1	Mahia Peninsula N.Z.
89	D3	Mahilyow Belarus
107	D2	Mahón Spain
74	B2	Mahuva India
110	C2	Mahya Dağı mt. Turkey
74	A1	Maidan Shahr Afgh.
129	D2	Maidstone Can.
99	D3	Maidstone U.K.
115	D3	Maiduguri Nigeria
75	C2	Mailani India
101	D2	Main r. Ger.
118	B3	Mai-Ndombe, Lac l. Dem. Rep. Congo
101	E3	Main-Donau-Kanal canal Ger.
141	F1	Maine state U.S.A.
62	A1	Maingkwan Myanmar
96	C1	Mainland i. Scotland U.K.
96	□	Mainland i. Scotland U.K.
121	D2	Maintirano Madag.
101	D2	Mainz Ger.
150	B1	Maiquetía Venez.
53	D2	Maitland N.S.W. Austr.
52	A2	Maitland S.A. Austr.
146	B3	Maíz, Islas del is Nic.
67	C3	Maizuru Japan
109	C2	Maja Jezercë mt. Albania
61	C2	Majene Indon.
107	D2	Majorca i. Spain
48	F2	Majuro atoll Marshall Is
123	C2	Majwemasweu S. Africa
118	B3	Makabana Congo
58	B3	Makale Indon.
77	E2	Makanchi Kazakh.
109	C2	Makarska Croatia
58	B3	Makassar Indon.
61	C2	Makassar, Selat str. Indon.
		Makassar Strait Indon. see Makassar, Selat
76	B2	Makat Kazakh.
123	D2	Makatini Flats lowland S. Africa
114	A4	Makeni Sierra Leone
120	B3	Makgadikgadi depr. Botswana
87	D4	Makhachkala Rus. Fed.
76	B2	Makhambet Kazakh.
119	D3	Makindu Kenya
77	D1	Makinsk Kazakh.
91	D2	Makiyivka Ukr.
		Makkah Saudi Arabia see Mecca
131	E1	Makkovik Can.
103	E2	Makó Hungary
118	B2	Makokou Gabon
119	D3	Makongolosi Tanz.
122	B2	Makopong Botswana
79	D2	Makran reg. Iran/Pak.
74	A2	Makran Coast Range mts Pak.

Maksatikha

89 E2 **Maksatikha** Rus. Fed.
81 C2 **Mākū** Iran
62 A1 **Makum** India
67 B4 **Makurazaki** Japan
115 C4 **Makurdi** Nigeria
92 G2 **Malå** Sweden
146 B4 **Mala, Punta** pt Panama
118 A2 **Malabo** Equat. Guinea
60 A1 **Malacca, Strait of** Indon./Malaysia
134 D2 **Malad City** U.S.A.
88 C3 **Maladzyechna** Belarus
106 C2 **Málaga** Spain
97 B1 **Málainn Mhóir** Ireland
48 E3 **Malaita** i. Solomon Is
117 B4 **Malakal** Sudan
48 F4 **Malakula** i. Vanuatu
61 C2 **Malang** Indon.
120 A1 **Malanje** Angola
93 G4 **Mälaren** l. Sweden
153 B4 **Malargüe** Arg.
80 B2 **Malatya** Turkey
121 C2 **Malawi** country Africa
Malawi, Lake Africa see **Nyasa, Lake**
89 D2 **Malaya Vishera** Rus. Fed.
64 B2 **Malaybalay** Phil.
81 C2 **Malāyer** Iran
60 B1 **Malaysia** country Asia
81 C2 **Malazgirt** Turkey
103 D1 **Malbork** Pol.
101 F1 **Malchin** Ger.
100 A2 **Maldegem** Belgium
49 H3 **Malden Island** Kiribati
56 G6 **Maldives** country Indian Ocean
153 C4 **Maldonado** Uru.
56 G6 **Male** Maldives
111 B3 **Maleas, Akrotirio** pt Greece
103 D2 **Malé Karpaty** hills Slovakia
134 C2 **Malheur Lake** U.S.A.
114 B3 **Mali** country Africa
114 A3 **Mali** Guinea
58 C3 **Malili** Indon.
119 E3 **Malindi** Kenya
97 C1 **Malin Head** Ireland
111 C2 **Malkara** Turkey
88 C3 **Mal'kavichy** Belarus
110 C2 **Malko Tŭrnovo** Bulg.
53 C3 **Mallacoota** Austr.
53 C3 **Mallacoota Inlet** b. Austr.
96 B2 **Mallaig** U.K.
129 E1 **Mallery Lake** Can.
Mallorca i. Spain see **Majorca**
97 B2 **Mallow** Ireland
92 H2 **Malmberget** Sweden
100 C2 **Malmédy** Belgium
122 A3 **Malmesbury** S. Africa
93 F4 **Malmö** Sweden
62 B1 **Malong** China
118 C4 **Malonga** Dem. Rep. Congo
93 E3 **Måløy** Norway
89 E2 **Maloyaroslavets** Rus. Fed.
89 E2 **Maloye Borisovo** Rus. Fed.
85 H5 **Malta** country Europe
88 C2 **Malta** Latvia
134 E1 **Malta** U.S.A.
122 A1 **Maltahöhe** Namibia
98 C1 **Malton** U.K.
Maluku is Indon. see **Moluccas**
59 C3 **Maluku, Laut** sea Indon.
93 F3 **Malung** Sweden
123 C2 **Maluti Mountains** Lesotho
73 B3 **Malvan** India
142 B2 **Malvern** U.S.A.
90 B1 **Malyn** Ukr.
83 L2 **Malyy Anyuy** r. Rus. Fed.

83 K2 **Malyy Lyakhovskiy, Ostrov** i. Rus. Fed.
123 C2 **Mamafubedu** S. Africa
119 C2 **Mambasa** Dem. Rep. Congo
118 B2 **Mambéré** r. C.A.R.
123 C2 **Mamelodi** S. Africa
150 B3 **Mamoré** r. Bol./Brazil
114 A3 **Mamou** Guinea
61 C2 **Mamuju** Indon.
114 B4 **Man** Côte d'Ivoire
98 A1 **Man, Isle of** i. Irish Sea
150 B2 **Manacapuru** Brazil
107 D2 **Manacor** Spain
59 C2 **Manado** Indon.
146 B3 **Managua** Nic.
121 D3 **Manakara** Madag.
78 B3 **Manākhah** Yemen
79 C2 **Manama** Bahrain
59 D3 **Manam Island** P.N.G.
121 D3 **Mananara** r. Madag.
121 D2 **Mananara Avaratra** Madag.
121 D3 **Mananjary** Madag.
114 A3 **Manantali, Lac de** l. Mali
77 E2 **Manas Hu** l. China
59 C3 **Manatuto** East Timor
62 A2 **Man-aung Kyun** i. Myanmar
150 B2 **Manaus** Brazil
80 B2 **Manavgat** Turkey
98 B2 **Manchester** U.K.
141 E2 **Manchester** U.S.A.
121 D3 **Mandabe** Madag.
93 E4 **Mandal** Norway
59 D3 **Mandala, Puncak** mt. Indon.
62 A1 **Mandalay** Myanmar
69 D1 **Mandalgovĭ** Mongolia
136 C1 **Mandan** U.S.A.
118 B1 **Mandara Mountains** Cameroon/Nigeria
108 A3 **Mandas** Sardegna Italy
100 C2 **Manderscheid** Ger.
74 B2 **Mandi** India
114 B3 **Mandiana** Guinea
75 C2 **Mandla** India
121 D2 **Mandritsara** Madag.
74 B2 **Mandsaur** India
50 A3 **Mandurah** Austr.
73 B3 **Mandya** India
108 B1 **Manerbio** Italy
90 B1 **Manevychi** Ukr.
109 C2 **Manfredonia** Italy
114 B3 **Manga** Burkina
118 B3 **Mangai** Dem. Rep. Congo
54 C1 **Mangakino** N.Z.
110 C2 **Mangalia** Romania
73 B3 **Mangalore** India
123 C2 **Manguang** S. Africa
61 B2 **Manggar** Indon.
68 C2 **Mangnai** China
121 C2 **Mangochi** Malawi
59 C3 **Mangole** i. Indon.
154 B3 **Mangueirinha** Brazil
69 E1 **Mangui** China
137 D3 **Manhattan** U.S.A.
121 C3 **Manhica** Moz.
155 D2 **Manhuaçu** Brazil
121 D2 **Mania** r. Madag.
108 B1 **Maniago** Italy
150 B2 **Manicoré** Brazil
131 D1 **Manicouagan** r. Can.
131 D1 **Manicouagan, Petit Lac** l. Can.
131 D1 **Manicouagan, Réservoir** resr Can.
79 B2 **Manifah** Saudi Arabia
64 B1 **Manila** Phil.
53 D2 **Manilla** Austr.
111 C3 **Manisa** Turkey

140 B2 **Manistee** U.S.A.
129 E2 **Manitoba** prov. Can.
129 E2 **Manitoba, Lake** Can.
140 B1 **Manitou Islands** U.S.A.
130 B2 **Manitoulin Island** Can.
140 B2 **Manitowoc** U.S.A.
130 C2 **Maniwaki** Can.
150 A1 **Manizales** Col.
137 E2 **Mankato** U.S.A.
114 B4 **Mankono** Côte d'Ivoire
129 D3 **Mankota** Can.
73 C4 **Mankulam** Sri Lanka
74 B2 **Manmad** India
73 B4 **Mannar, Gulf of** India/Sri Lanka
101 D3 **Mannheim** Ger.
128 C2 **Manning** Can.
52 A2 **Mannum** Austr.
129 C2 **Mannville** Can.
59 C3 **Manokwari** Indon.
119 C3 **Manono** Dem. Rep. Congo
63 A2 **Manoron** Myanmar
105 D3 **Manosque** France
131 C1 **Manouane, Lac** l. Can.
107 D1 **Manresa** Spain
121 B2 **Mansa** Zambia
127 F2 **Mansel Island** Can.
92 I2 **Mansel'k'ya** ridge Fin./Rus. Fed.
53 C3 **Mansfield** Austr.
98 C2 **Mansfield** U.K.
142 B2 **Mansfield** LA U.S.A.
140 C2 **Mansfield** OH U.S.A.
141 D2 **Mansfield** PA U.S.A.
150 A2 **Manta** Ecuador
143 E1 **Manteo** U.S.A.
104 C2 **Mantes-la-Jolie** France
155 C2 **Mantiqueira, Serra de** mts Brazil
Mantova Italy see **Mantua**
108 B1 **Mantua** Italy
151 C2 **Manuelzinho** Brazil
59 C3 **Manui** i. Indon.
54 B1 **Manukau** N.Z.
142 B2 **Many** U.S.A.
87 D4 **Manych-Gudilo, Ozero** l. Rus. Fed.
119 D3 **Manyoni** Tanz.
106 C2 **Manzanares** Spain
144 B3 **Manzanillo** Mex.
69 D1 **Manzhouli** China
123 D2 **Manzini** Swaziland
115 D3 **Mao** Chad
59 D3 **Maoke, Pegunungan** mts Indon.
123 C2 **Maokeng** S. Africa
65 A1 **Maokui Shan** mt. China
71 B3 **Maoming** China
121 C3 **Mapai** Moz.
75 C1 **Mapam Yumco** l. China
145 C3 **Mapastepec** Mex.
144 B2 **Mapimí** Mex.
151 C2 **Mapinhane** Moz.
129 D3 **Maple Creek** Can.
121 C3 **Maputo** Moz.
121 D2 **Maputo** r. Moz./S. Africa
75 C2 **Maquan He** r. China
120 A1 **Maquela do Zombo** Angola
153 B5 **Maquinchao** Arg.
137 E2 **Maquoketa** U.S.A.
150 B2 **Maraã** Brazil
151 D2 **Marabá** Brazil
151 C1 **Maracá, Ilha de** i. Brazil
150 A1 **Maracaibo** Venez.
150 A1 **Maracaibo, Lake** Venez.
152 C3 **Maracaju, Serra de** hills Brazil
154 A2 **Maracaju, Serra de** hills Brazil
150 B1 **Maracay** Venez.

115 D2 Marādah Libya
115 C3 Marādī Niger
81 C3 Marāgheh Iran
151 D2 Marajó, Baía de est. Brazil
151 C2 Marajó, Ilha de i. Brazil
79 C2 Marākī Iran
119 D2 Maralal Kenya
50 C3 Maralinga Austr.
81 C2 Marand Iran
150 A2 Marañón r. Peru
130 B2 Marathon Can.
143 D4 Marathon U.S.A.
106 C2 Marbella Spain
50 A2 Marble Bar Austr.
123 C1 Marble Hall S. Africa
123 D3 Marburg S. Africa
101 D2 Marburg an der Lahn Ger.
99 D2 March U.K.
100 B2 Marche-en-Famenne Belgium
106 B2 Marchena Spain
152 B4 Mar Chiquita, Laguna l. Arg.
141 E2 Marcy, Mount U.S.A.
74 B1 Mardan Pak.
153 C4 Mar del Plata Arg.
81 C2 Mardin Turkey
96 B2 Maree, Loch l. U.K.
108 B3 Marettimo, Isola i. Sicilia Italy
89 D2 Marevo Rus. Fed.
138 C2 Marfa U.S.A.
50 A3 Margaret River Austr.
147 D3 Margarita, Isla de i. Venez.
123 D3 Margate S. Africa
99 D3 Margate U.K.
119 C2 Margherita Peak Dem. Rep.
       Congo/Uganda
76 C3 Mārgow, Dasht-e des. Afgh.
91 C2 Marhanets' Ukr.
62 A1 Mari Myanmar
152 B3 María Elena Chile
156 C1 Mariana Trench N. Pacific
       Ocean
142 B2 Marianna AR U.S.A.
143 C2 Marianna FL U.S.A.
102 C2 Mariánské Lázně Czech Rep.
144 B2 Marías, Islas is Mex.
78 B3 Ma'rib Yemen
109 C1 Maribor Slovenia
117 A4 Maridi watercourse Sudan
55 M2 Marie Byrd Land reg.
       Antarctica
147 D3 Marie-Galante i. Guadeloupe
93 G3 Mariehamn Fin.
122 A1 Mariental Namibia
93 F4 Mariestad Sweden
143 D2 Marietta GA U.S.A.
140 C3 Marietta OH U.S.A.
105 D3 Marignane France
83 K3 Marii, Mys pt Rus. Fed.
88 B3 Marijampolė Lith.
154 C2 Marília Brazil
106 B1 Marín Spain
109 C3 Marina di Gioiosa Ionica Italy
88 C3 Mar"ina Horka Belarus
141 B1 Marinette U.S.A.
154 B2 Maringá Brazil
106 B2 Marinha Grande Port.
140 B2 Marion IN U.S.A.
140 C2 Marion OH U.S.A.
143 E2 Marion SC U.S.A.
140 C3 Marion VA U.S.A.
143 D2 Marion, Lake U.S.A.
52 A3 Marion Bay Austr.
152 B3 Mariscal José Félix
       Estigarribia Para.
110 C2 Maritsa r. Bulg.
91 D2 Mariupol' Ukr.
117 C4 Marka Somalia

123 C1 Marken S. Africa
100 B1 Markermeer l. Neth.
83 I2 Markha r. Rus. Fed.
91 D2 Markivka Ukr.
142 B2 Marksville U.S.A.
101 D3 Marktheidenfeld Ger.
101 F2 Marktredwitz Ger.
100 C2 Marl Ger.
100 A3 Marle France
139 D2 Marlin U.S.A.
104 C3 Marmande France
111 C2 Marmara, Sea of g. Turkey
       Marmara Denizi g. Turkey see
       Marmara, Sea of
111 C3 Marmaris Turkey
104 C2 Marne-la-Vallée France
121 D2 Maroantsetra Madag.
101 E2 Maroldsweisach Ger.
121 D2 Maromokotro mt. Madag.
121 C2 Marondera Zimbabwe
151 C1 Maroni r. Fr. Guiana
118 B1 Maroua Cameroon
121 D2 Marovoay Madag.
49 I3 Marquesas Islands is Fr.
       Polynesia
140 B1 Marquette U.S.A.
117 A3 Marra, Jebel mt. Sudan
117 A3 Marra, Jebel plat. Sudan
123 D2 Marracuene Moz.
114 B1 Marrakech Morocco
52 A1 Marree Austr.
86 F2 Marresale Rus. Fed.
121 C2 Marromeu Moz.
121 C2 Marrupa Moz.
116 B2 Marsá al 'Alam Egypt
115 D1 Marsa al Burayqah Libya
119 D2 Marsabit Kenya
108 B3 Marsala Sicilia Italy
116 A1 Marsá Maṭrūḥ Egypt
101 D2 Marsberg Ger.
108 B2 Marsciano Italy
53 C2 Marsden Austr.
105 D3 Marseille France
137 D2 Marshall MN U.S.A.
137 E3 Marshall MO U.S.A.
139 E2 Marshall TX U.S.A.
48 F2 Marshall Islands country
       N. Pacific Ocean
137 E2 Marshalltown U.S.A.
140 A2 Marshfield U.S.A.
143 E3 Marsh Harbour Bahamas
142 B3 Marsh Island U.S.A.
88 A2 Märsta Sweden
61 C2 Martapura Kalimantan Selatan
       Indon.
60 B2 Martapura Sumatera Selatan
       Indon.
141 E2 Martha's Vineyard i. U.S.A.
105 D2 Martigny Switz.
103 D2 Martin Slovakia
136 C2 Martin U.S.A.
145 C2 Martínez Mex.
147 D3 Martinique terr. West Indies
141 D3 Martinsburg U.S.A.
140 D3 Martinsville U.S.A.
54 C2 Marton N.Z.
107 D1 Martorell Spain
106 C2 Martos Spain
76 B1 Martuk Kazakh.
105 C3 Marvejols France
76 C3 Mary Turkm.
51 E2 Maryborough Austr.
122 B2 Marydale S. Africa
141 D3 Maryland state U.S.A.
137 D3 Marysville U.S.A.
137 E2 Maryville MO U.S.A.
143 D1 Maryville TN U.S.A.

119 D3 Masai Steppe plain Tanz.
119 D3 Masaka Uganda
65 B2 Masan S. Korea
119 D4 Masasi Tanz.
64 B1 Masbate Phil.
64 B1 Masbate i. Phil.
123 C2 Maseru Lesotho
76 B3 Mashhad Iran
123 D2 Mashishing S. Africa
74 A2 Mashkel, Hamun-i- salt flat
       Pak.
123 C3 Masibambane S. Africa
79 C3 Masilah, Wādī al watercourse
       Yemen
123 C2 Masilo S. Africa
119 D2 Masindi Uganda
79 C2 Maşirah, Jazirat i. Oman
79 C3 Maşirah, Khalij b. Oman
81 C2 Masjed Soleymān Iran
97 B2 Mask, Lough l. Ireland
121 E2 Masoala, Tanjona c. Madag.
137 E2 Mason City U.S.A.
       Masqaṭ Oman see Muscat
108 B2 Massa Italy
141 E2 Massachusetts state U.S.A.
141 E2 Massachusetts Bay U.S.A.
121 C3 Massangena Moz.
120 A1 Massango Angola
116 B3 Massawa Eritrea
141 E2 Massena U.S.A.
128 A2 Masset Can.
105 C2 Massif Central mts France
140 C2 Massillon U.S.A.
121 C3 Massinga Moz.
123 D1 Massingir Moz.
78 A2 Mastābah Saudi Arabia
54 C2 Masterton N.Z.
74 A2 Mastung Pak.
78 A2 Mastūrah Saudi Arabia
88 B3 Masty Belarus
67 B4 Masuda Japan
       Masuku Gabon see Franceville
121 C3 Masvingo Zimbabwe
69 D1 Matad Mongolia
118 B3 Matadi Dem. Rep. Congo
89 E3 Matagalpa Nic.
130 C2 Matagami Can.
130 C2 Matagami, Lac l. Can.
139 D3 Matagorda Island U.S.A.
120 A2 Matala Angola
114 A3 Matam Senegal
144 B2 Matamoros Coahuila Mex.
145 C2 Matamoros Tamaulipas Mex.
119 D3 Matandu r. Tanz.
131 D2 Matane Can.
146 B2 Matanzas Cuba
73 C4 Matara Sri Lanka
61 C2 Mataram Indon.
50 C1 Mataranka Austr.
107 D1 Mataró Spain
123 C3 Matatiele S. Africa
54 A3 Mataura N.Z.
49 G3 Mata'utu Wallis and Futuna Is
54 C1 Matawai N.Z.
152 B2 Mategua Bol.
145 B2 Matehuala Mex.
109 C2 Matera Italy
139 D3 Mathis U.S.A.
75 B2 Mathura India
64 B2 Mati Phil.
98 C2 Matlock U.K.
150 C3 Mato Grosso Brazil
154 B1 Mato Grosso, Planalto do plat.
       Brazil
123 D2 Matola Moz.
       Matou China see Pingguo
67 B3 Matsue Japan

66 D2 **Matsumae** Japan
67 C4 **Matsusaka** Japan
71 C3 **Matsu Tao** *i.* Taiwan
67 B4 **Matsuyama** Japan
130 B1 **Mattagami** *r.* Can.
105 D2 **Matterhorn** *mt.* Italy/Switz.
134 C2 **Matterhorn** *mt.* U.S.A.
140 B3 **Mattoon** U.S.A.
150 B1 **Maturín** Venez.
123 C2 **Matwabeng** S. Africa
100 A2 **Maubeuge** France
104 C3 **Maubourguet** France
124 E5 **Maui** *i.* U.S.A.
140 C2 **Maumee** *r.* U.S.A.
120 B2 **Maun** Botswana
62 A1 **Maungdaw** Myanmar
50 C2 **Maurice, Lake** *imp. l.* Austr.
114 A3 **Mauritania** *country* Africa
113 K9 **Mauritius** *country* Indian
        Ocean
78 B2 **Māwān, Khashm** *mt.*
        Saudi Arabia
118 B3 **Mawanga** Dem. Rep. Congo
71 B3 **Mawei** China
62 A1 **Mawkmai** Myanmar
62 A1 **Mawlaik** Myanmar
63 A2 **Mawlamyaing** Myanmar
78 B2 **Mawqaq** Saudi Arabia
78 B3 **Mawza** Yemen
108 A3 **Maxia, Punta** *mt. Sardegna*
        Italy
83 J2 **Maya** *r.* Rus. Fed.
147 C2 **Mayaguana** *i.* Bahamas
96 B3 **Maybole** U.K.
104 B2 **Mayenne** France
104 B2 **Mayenne** *r.* France
128 C2 **Mayerthorpe** Can.
140 B3 **Mayfield** U.S.A.
87 H4 **Maykop** Rus. Fed.
76 C3 **Maymanah** Afgh.
126 B2 **Mayo** Can.
118 B3 **Mayoko** Congo
121 D2 **Mayotte** *terr.* Africa
83 J3 **Mayskiy** Rus. Fed.
140 C3 **Maysville** U.S.A.
118 B3 **Mayumba** Gabon
137 D1 **Mayville** U.S.A.
151 C2 **Mazagão** Brazil
104 C3 **Mazamet** France
77 D3 **Mazar** China
108 B3 **Mazara del Vallo** *Sicilia* Italy
77 C3 **Mazār-e Sharīf** Afgh.
146 A2 **Mazatán** Mex.
146 A3 **Mazatenango** Guat.
144 B2 **Mazatlán** Mex.
88 B2 **Mazeikiai** Lith.
88 B2 **Mazirbe** Latvia
121 B3 **Mazunga** Zimbabwe
88 C3 **Mazyr** Belarus
123 D2 **Mbabane** Swaziland
118 B2 **Mbaïki** C.A.R.
121 C1 **Mbala** Zambia
118 D2 **Mbale** Uganda
118 B2 **Mbalmayo** Cameroon
118 B3 **Mbandaka** Dem. Rep. Congo
118 A2 **Mbanga** Cameroon
120 A1 **M'banza Congo** Angola
119 D3 **Mbeya** Tanz.
118 D3 **Mbinga** Tanz.
118 B2 **Mbomo** Congo
118 B2 **Mbouda** Cameroon
114 A3 **Mbour** Senegal
114 A3 **Mbout** Maur.
118 C3 **Mbuji-Mayi** Dem. Rep. Congo
119 D3 **Mbuyuni** Tanz.
139 D2 **McAlester** U.S.A.
139 D3 **McAllen** U.S.A.

128 B2 **McBride** Can.
134 C2 **McCall** U.S.A.
126 E2 **McClintock Channel** Can.
126 E2 **McClure Strait** Can.
142 B2 **McComb** U.S.A.
136 C3 **McConaughy, Lake** U.S.A.
136 C2 **McCook** U.S.A.
134 C2 **McDermitt** U.S.A.
134 D1 **McDonald Peak** U.S.A.
134 D1 **McGuire, Mount** U.S.A.
128 C2 **McLennan** Can.
128 B2 **McLeod Lake** Can.
134 B1 **McMinnville** *OR* U.S.A.
142 C1 **McMinnville** *TN* U.S.A.
137 D3 **McPherson** U.S.A.
123 C3 **Mdantsane** S. Africa
135 D3 **Mead, Lake** *resr* U.S.A.
129 D2 **Meadow Lake** Can.
140 C2 **Meadville** U.S.A.
66 D2 **Meaken-dake** *vol.* Japan
106 B1 **Mealhada** Port.
131 E1 **Mealy Mountains** Can.
78 A2 **Meander River** Can.
100 B2 **Mecca** Saudi Arabia
100 B2 **Mechelen** Belgium
100 B2 **Mechelen** Neth.
100 C2 **Mechernich** Ger.
100 C2 **Meckenheim** Ger.
106 B1 **Meda** Port.
60 A1 **Medan** Indon.
153 B5 **Medanosa, Punta** *pt* Arg.
73 C4 **Medawachchiya** Sri Lanka
107 D2 **Médéa** Alg.
150 A1 **Medellín** Col.
115 D1 **Medenine** Tunisia
134 B2 **Medford** U.S.A.
110 C2 **Medgidia** Romania
110 B1 **Medias** Romania
136 B2 **Medicine Bow Mountains**
        U.S.A.
136 B2 **Medicine Bow Peak** U.S.A.
129 C2 **Medicine Hat** Can.
137 D3 **Medicine Lodge** U.S.A.
155 D1 **Medina** Brazil
78 A2 **Medina** Saudi Arabia
106 C1 **Medinaceli** Spain
106 C1 **Medina del Campo** Spain
106 B1 **Medina de Rioseco** Spain
84 G5 **Mediterranean Sea**
129 C2 **Medley** Can.
87 E3 **Mednogorsk** Rus. Fed.
83 L2 **Medvezh'i, Ostrova** *is*
        Rus. Fed.
86 C2 **Medvezh'yegorsk** Rus. Fed.
50 A2 **Meekatharra** Austr.
136 B2 **Meeker** U.S.A.
75 B2 **Meerut** India
100 A2 **Meetkerke** Belgium
111 B3 **Megalopoli** Greece
75 C2 **Meghasani** *mt.* India
80 A2 **Megisti** *i.* Greece
92 I1 **Mehamn** Norway
50 A2 **Meharry, Mount** Austr.
79 C2 **Mehrān** *watercourse* Iran
74 B1 **Mehtar Lām** Afgh.
154 C1 **Meia Ponte** *r.* Brazil
118 B2 **Meiganga** Cameroon
65 B1 **Meihekou** China
        Meijiang China *see*
        Ningdu
62 A1 **Meiktila** Myanmar
101 E2 **Meiningen** Ger.
102 C1 **Meißen** Ger.
71 B3 **Meizhou** China
152 B3 **Mejicana** *mt.* Arg.
152 A3 **Mejillones** Chile
117 B3 **Mek'elē** Eth.

114 C2 **Mekerrhane, Sebkha** *salt pan*
        Alg.
114 B1 **Meknès** Morocco
63 B2 **Mekong** *r.* Asia
63 B3 **Mekong, Mouths of the**
        Vietnam
60 B1 **Melaka** Malaysia
53 B3 **Melbourne** Austr.
143 D3 **Melbourne** U.S.A.
108 A2 **Mele, Capo c.** Italy
131 C1 **Mélèzes, Rivière aux** *r.* Can.
115 D3 **Melfi** Chad
109 C2 **Melfi** Italy
129 D2 **Melfort** Can.
92 F3 **Melhus** Norway
106 B1 **Melide** Spain
114 B1 **Melilla** N. Africa
91 D2 **Melitopol'** Ukr.
101 D1 **Melle** Ger.
93 F4 **Mellerud** Sweden
101 E2 **Mellrichstadt** Ger.
100 C1 **Mellum** *i.* Ger.
146 Uru.
115 C1 **Melrhir, Chott** *salt l.* Alg.
99 C2 **Melton Mowbray** U.K.
104 C2 **Melun** France
129 D2 **Melville** Can.
51 D1 **Melville, Cape** Austr.
131 E1 **Melville, Lake** Can.
50 C1 **Melville Island** Austr.
126 D1 **Melville Island** Can.
127 F2 **Melville Peninsula** Can.
102 C2 **Memmingen** Ger.
61 B1 **Mempawah** Indon.
80 B3 **Memphis** *tourist site* Egypt
142 B1 **Memphis** *TN* U.S.A.
139 C2 **Memphis** *TX* U.S.A.
91 C1 **Mena** Ukr.
142 B2 **Mena** U.S.A.
114 C3 **Ménaka** Mali
        Mènam Khong *r.* Laos/Thai.
        see Mekong
105 C3 **Mende** France
116 B3 **Mendefera** Eritrea
145 C2 **Méndez** Mex.
119 D2 **Mendi** Eth.
59 D3 **Mendi** P.N.G.
99 B3 **Mendip Hills** U.K.
153 B4 **Mendoza** Arg.
111 C3 **Menemen** Turkey
60 B2 **Menggala** Indon.
62 B1 **Mengzi** China
131 D1 **Menihek** Can.
52 B3 **Menindee** Austr.
52 B2 **Menindee Lake** Austr.
52 A3 **Meningie** Austr.
104 C2 **Mennecy** France
140 B1 **Menominee** U.S.A.
120 A2 **Menongue** Angola
        Menorca *i.* Spain *see* Minorca
60 A2 **Mentawai, Kepulauan** *is*
        Indon.
60 B2 **Mentok** Indon.
50 C2 **Menzies** Austr.
100 C1 **Meppel** Neth.
100 C1 **Meppen** Ger.
123 D1 **Mepuze** Moz.
123 C2 **Meqheleng** S. Africa
108 B1 **Merano** Italy
59 D3 **Merauke** Indon.
52 B2 **Merbein** Austr.
135 B3 **Merced** U.S.A.
152 C3 **Mercedes** Arg.
127 G2 **Mercy, Cape** Can.
139 C1 **Meredith, Lake** U.S.A.
91 D2 **Merefa** Ukr.
116 A3 **Merga Oasis** Sudan

63 A2 **Mergui Archipelago** *is* Myanmar
10 C2 **Meriç** *r.* Greece/Turkey
45 D2 **Mérida** Mex.
06 C2 **Mérida** Spain
50 A1 **Mérida** Venez.
42 C2 **Meridian** U.S.A.
53 C2 **Merimbula** Austr.
16 B3 **Merowe** Sudan
50 A3 **Merredin** Austr.
96 B3 **Merrick** *h.* U.K.
40 B1 **Merrill** U.S.A.
28 B2 **Merritt** Can.
52 C2 **Merrygoen** Austr.
16 C3 **Mersa Fatma** Eritrea
00 C3 **Mersch** Lux.
01 C2 **Merseburg (Saale)** Ger.
98 B2 **Mersey** *r.* U.K.
80 B2 **Mersin** Turkey
60 B1 **Mersing** Malaysia
99 D5 **Mers-les-Bains** France
74 B2 **Merta** India
99 B3 **Merthyr Tydfil** U.K.
06 B2 **Mértola** Port.
76 B2 **Mertvyy Kultuk, Sor** *dry lake* Kazakh.
19 D3 **Meru** *vol.* Tanz.
00 C3 **Merzig** Ger.
38 A2 **Mesa** U.S.A.
09 C2 **Mesagne** Italy
28 C2 **Meschede** Ger.
89 E3 **Meshchovsk** Rus. Fed.
91 E2 **Meshkovskaya** Rus. Fed.
11 B2 **Mesimeri** Greece
11 B3 **Mesolongi** Greece
21 D2 **Messalo** *r.* Moz.
09 C3 **Messina** *Sicilia* Italy
09 C3 **Messina, Strait of** Italy
16 D2 **Messiniakos Kolpos** *g.* Greece
10 B2 **Mesta** *r.* Bulg.
50 B1 **Meta** *r.* Col./Venez.
27 C2 **Meta Incognita Peninsula** Can.
44 B3 **Metán** Arg.
11 B3 **Methoni** Greece
09 C2 **Metković** Croatia
60 B2 **Metro** Indon.
17 B4 **Metu** Eth.
05 D2 **Metz** France
00 D2 **Meuse** *r.* Belgium/France
39 D2 **Mexia** U.S.A.
44 A1 **Mexicali** Mex.
44 B2 **Mexico** *country* Central America
37 E3 **Mexico** U.S.A.
25 I5 **Mexico, Gulf of** Mex./U.S.A.
45 C3 **Mexico City** Mex.
01 C2 **Meyenburg** Ger.
86 D2 **Mezen'** Rus. Fed.
86 D2 **Mezen'** *r.* Rus. Fed.
86 E2 **Mezhdusharskiy, Ostrov** *i.* Rus. Fed.
03 E2 **Mezőtúr** Hungary
44 B2 **Mezquitic** Mex.
88 C2 **Mežvidi** Latvia
21 C2 **Mfuwe** Zambia
23 D2 **Mhlume** Swaziland
74 B2 **Mhow** India
45 C3 **Miahuatlán** Mex.
06 B2 **Miajadas** Spain
43 D3 **Miami** *FL* U.S.A.
39 E1 **Miami** *OK* U.S.A.
43 D3 **Miami Beach** U.S.A.
81 C2 **Miāndowāb** Iran
21 D2 **Miandrivazo** Madag.
81 C2 **Miāneh** Iran

74 B1 **Mianwali** Pak.
70 A2 **Mianyang** China
121 D2 **Miarinarivo** Madag.
87 F3 **Miass** Rus. Fed.
128 C2 **Mica Creek** Can.
103 E2 **Michalovce** Slovakia
140 B1 **Michigan** *state* U.S.A.
140 B2 **Michigan, Lake** U.S.A.
140 B2 **Michigan City** U.S.A.
130 B2 **Michipicoten Island** Can.
130 B2 **Michipicoten River** Can.
89 F3 **Michurinsk** Rus. Fed.
48 D2 **Micronesia, Federated States of** *country* N. Pacific Ocean
100 A2 **Middelburg** Neth.
123 C3 **Middelburg** *E. Cape* S. Africa
123 C2 **Middelburg** *Mpumalanga* S. Africa
100 B2 **Middelharnis** Neth.
134 B2 **Middle Alkali Lake** U.S.A.
73 D3 **Middle Andaman** *i.* India
136 D2 **Middle Loup** *r.* U.S.A.
140 C3 **Middlesboro** U.S.A.
98 C1 **Middlesbrough** U.K.
141 E2 **Middletown** *NY* U.S.A.
140 C3 **Middletown** *OH* U.S.A.
78 B3 **Midi** Yemen
130 C2 **Midland** Can.
140 C2 **Midland** *MI* U.S.A.
139 C2 **Midland** *TX* U.S.A.
97 B3 **Midleton** Ireland
94 B1 **Miðvágur** Faroe Is
109 D2 **Midzhur** *mt.* Bulg./S.M.
103 E1 **Mielec** Pol.
110 C1 **Miercurea-Ciuc** Romania
106 B1 **Mieres** Spain
101 E1 **Mieste** Ger.
75 D1 **Migriggyangzham Co** *l.* China
145 C3 **Miguel Alemán, Presa** *resr* Mex.
144 B2 **Miguel Auza** Mex.
144 B2 **Miguel Hidalgo, Presa** *resr* Mex.
63 A2 **Migyaunglaung** Myanmar
89 E3 **Mikhaylov** Rus. Fed.
Mikhaylovgrad Bulg. *see* Montana
66 B2 **Mikhaylovka** Rus. Fed.
77 D1 **Mikhaylovskiy** Rus. Fed.
93 I3 **Mikkeli** Fin.
86 E2 **Mikun'** Rus. Fed.
67 C3 **Mikuni-sanmyaku** *mts* Japan
108 A1 **Milan** Italy
121 C2 **Milange** Moz.
Milano Italy *see* Milan
111 C3 **Milas** Turkey
137 D1 **Milbank** U.S.A.
99 D2 **Mildenhall** U.K.
52 B2 **Mildura** Austr.
62 B1 **Mile** China
136 B1 **Miles City** U.S.A.
141 D3 **Milford** *DE* U.S.A.
135 D3 **Milford** *UT* U.S.A.
99 A3 **Milford Haven** U.K.
54 A2 **Milford Sound** N.Z.
107 D2 **Miliana** Alg.
116 B3 **Milk, Wadi el** *watercourse* Sudan
83 L3 **Mil'kovo** Rus. Fed.
129 C3 **Milk River** Can.
105 C3 **Millau** France
143 D2 **Milledgeville** U.S.A.
137 E1 **Mille Lacs** *lakes* U.S.A.
130 A2 **Mille Lacs, Lac des** *l.* Can.
137 D2 **Miller** U.S.A.
91 E2 **Millerovo** Rus. Fed.
52 A2 **Millers Creek** Austr.

52 B3 **Millicent** Austr.
141 F1 **Millinocket** U.S.A.
53 D1 **Millmerran** Austr.
98 B1 **Millom** U.K.
128 C1 **Mills Lake** Can.
111 B3 **Milos** *i.* Greece
89 E3 **Miloslavskoye** Rus. Fed.
91 E2 **Milove** Ukr.
52 B1 **Milparinka** Austr.
54 A3 **Milton** N.Z.
99 C2 **Milton Keynes** U.K.
140 B2 **Milwaukee** U.S.A.
104 B3 **Mimizan** France
118 B3 **Mimongo** Gabon
79 C2 **Mīnāb** Iran
58 C2 **Minahasa, Semenanjung** *pen.* Indon.
79 C2 **Mina Jebel Ali** U.A.E.
60 B1 **Minas** Indon.
153 C4 **Minas** Uru.
155 D1 **Minas Novas** Brazil
145 C3 **Minatitlán** Mex.
62 A1 **Minbu** Myanmar
64 B2 **Mindanao** *i.* Phil.
101 D1 **Minden** Ger.
142 B2 **Minden** *LA* U.S.A.
137 D2 **Minden** *NE* U.S.A.
64 B1 **Mindoro** *i.* Phil.
64 A1 **Mindoro Strait** Phil.
118 B3 **Mindouli** Congo
99 B3 **Minehead** U.K.
154 B1 **Mineiros** Brazil
139 D2 **Mineral Wells** U.S.A.
77 E3 **Minfeng** China
119 C4 **Minga** Dem. Rep. Congo
81 C1 **Mingäçevir** Azer.
131 D1 **Mingan** Can.
52 B2 **Mingary** Austr.
70 B2 **Mingguang** China
62 A1 **Mingin** Myanmar
107 C2 **Minglanilla** Spain
119 D4 **Mingoyo** Tanz.
69 E1 **Mingshui** China
71 B3 **Mingxi** China
73 B4 **Minicoy** *atoll* India
50 A2 **Minilya** Austr.
131 D1 **Minipi Lake** Can.
130 A1 **Miniss Lake** Can.
115 C4 **Minna** Nigeria
137 E2 **Minneapolis** U.S.A.
129 E2 **Minnedosa** Can.
137 E2 **Minnesota** *r.* U.S.A.
137 E1 **Minnesota** *state* U.S.A.
106 B1 **Miño** *r.* Port./Spain
107 D1 **Minorca** *i.* Spain
136 C1 **Minot** U.S.A.
88 C3 **Minsk** Belarus
103 E1 **Mińsk Mazowiecki** Pol.
131 D2 **Minto** Can.
130 C1 **Minto, Lac** *l.* Can.
70 A2 **Minxian** China
155 D1 **Mirabela** Brazil
155 D1 **Miralta** Brazil
131 D2 **Miramichi** *N.B.* Can.
111 C3 **Mirampellou, Kolpos** *b.* Greece
152 C3 **Miranda** Brazil
152 C2 **Miranda** *r.* Brazil
106 C1 **Miranda de Ebro** Spain
106 B1 **Mirandela** Port.
154 B2 **Mirandópolis** Brazil
79 C3 **Mirbāţ** Oman
153 C4 **Miri** *Sarawak* Malaysia
153 C4 **Mirim, Lagoa** *l.* Brazil/Uru.
79 D2 **Mirjäveh** Iran
83 I2 **Mirnyy** Rus. Fed.
101 F1 **Mirow** Ger.

74 A2 **Mirpur Khas** Pak.
111 B3 **Mirtoö Pelagos** sea Greece
65 C1 **Miryang** S. Korea
75 C2 **Mirzapur** India
66 B1 **Mishan** China
146 B3 **Miskitos, Cayos** is Nic.
103 E2 **Miskolc** Hungary
59 C3 **Misoöl** i. Indon.
115 D1 **Miṣrātah** Libya
130 B1 **Missinaibi** r. Can.
130 B2 **Missinaibi Lake** Can.
128 B3 **Mission** Can.
130 B1 **Missisa Lake** Can.
142 C3 **Mississippi** r. U.S.A.
142 C2 **Mississippi** state U.S.A.
142 C3 **Mississippi Delta** U.S.A.
134 D1 **Missoula** U.S.A.
137 E3 **Missouri** r. U.S.A.
137 E3 **Missouri** state U.S.A.
131 C2 **Mistassibi** r. Can.
130 C1 **Mistassini, Lac** l. Can.
131 D1 **Mistastin Lake** Can.
103 D2 **Mistelbach** Austria
131 D1 **Mistinibi, Lac** l. Can.
130 C1 **Mistissini** Can.
51 D2 **Mitchell** Austr.
51 D1 **Mitchell** r. Austr.
137 D2 **Mitchell** U.S.A.
97 B2 **Mitchelstown** Ireland
74 A2 **Mithi** Pak.
67 B3 **Mito** Japan
119 D3 **Mitole** Tanz.
109 D3 **Mitrovicë** Kosovo
53 D2 **Mittagong** Austr.
101 E2 **Mittelhausen** Ger.
101 D1 **Mittellandkanal** canal Ger.
101 F3 **Mitterteich** Ger.
150 A1 **Mitú** Col.
119 C4 **Mitumba, Chaîne des** mts
Dem. Rep. Congo
119 C3 **Mitumba, Monts** mts Dem.
Rep. Congo
118 B2 **Mitzic** Gabon
78 B2 **Miyah, Wādi al** watercourse
Saudi Arabia
67 C4 **Miyake-jima** i. Japan
66 D3 **Miyako** Japan
67 B4 **Miyakonojō** Japan
76 B2 **Miyaly** Kazakh.
Miyang China see Mile
67 B4 **Miyazaki** Japan
115 D1 **Mizdah** Libya
97 B3 **Mizen Head** Ireland
90 A2 **Mizhhirr''ya** Ukr.
93 G4 **Mjölby** Sweden
93 F3 **Mjøsa** l. Norway
119 D3 **Mkomazi** Tanz.
103 C1 **Mladá Boleslav** Czech Rep.
109 D2 **Mladenovac** Serbia
103 E1 **Mława** Pol.
123 C3 **Mlungisi** S. Africa
90 B1 **Mlyniv** Ukr.
123 C2 **Mmabatho** S. Africa
123 C2 **Mmathethe** Botswana
135 E3 **Moab** U.S.A.
123 D2 **Moamba** Moz.
119 C3 **Moba** Dem. Rep. Congo
118 C2 **Mobayi-Mbongo** Dem. Rep.
Congo
137 E3 **Moberly** U.S.A.
142 C2 **Mobile** U.S.A.
142 C2 **Mobile Bay** U.S.A.
136 C1 **Mobridge** U.S.A.
121 D2 **Moçambique** Moz.
62 B1 **Mộc Châu** Vietnam
78 B3 **Mocha** Yemen
123 C1 **Mochudi** Botswana

121 D2 **Mocimboa da Praia** Moz.
150 A1 **Mocoa** Col.
154 C2 **Mococa** Brazil
144 B2 **Mocorito** Mex.
144 B1 **Moctezuma** Chihuahua Mex.
145 B2 **Moctezuma** San Luis Potosí
Mex.
144 B2 **Moctezuma** Sonora Mex.
121 C2 **Mocuba** Moz.
105 D2 **Modane** France
122 B2 **Modder** r. S. Africa
108 B2 **Modena** Italy
135 B3 **Modesto** U.S.A.
123 C1 **Modimolle** S. Africa
53 C3 **Moe** Austr.
100 C2 **Moers** Ger.
96 C3 **Moffat** U.K.
117 C4 **Mogadishu** Somalia
123 C1 **Mogalakwena** r. S. Africa
62 A1 **Mogaung** Myanmar
Mogilev Belarus see **Mahilyow**
154 C2 **Mogi-Mirim** Brazil
83 I3 **Mogocha** Rus. Fed.
62 A1 **Mogok** Myanmar
103 D2 **Mohács** Hungary
123 C2 **Mohale's Hoek** Lesotho
107 D2 **Mohammadia** Alg.
141 E2 **Mohawk** r. U.S.A.
119 D3 **Mohoro** Tanz.
90 B2 **Mohyliv-Podil's'kyy** Ukr.
110 C1 **Moinești** Romania
92 F2 **Mo i Rana** Norway
104 C3 **Moissac** France
135 C3 **Mojave** U.S.A.
135 C3 **Mojave Desert** U.S.A.
62 B1 **Mojiang** China
155 C2 **Moji das Cruzes** Brazil
154 C2 **Moji-Guaçu** r. Brazil
54 B1 **Mokau** N.Z.
123 C2 **Mokhotlong** Lesotho
123 C1 **Mokopane** S. Africa
65 B3 **Mokp'o** S. Korea
145 C2 **Molango** Mex.
Moldavia country Europe see
Moldova
92 E3 **Molde** Norway
90 B2 **Moldova** country Europe
110 B1 **Moldoveanu, Vârful** mt.
Romania
90 B2 **Moldovei Centrale, Podișul**
plat. Moldova
123 C1 **Molepolole** Botswana
88 C2 **Molėtai** Lith.
109 C2 **Molfetta** Italy
107 C1 **Molina de Aragón** Spain
150 A3 **Mollendo** Peru
53 C2 **Molong** Austr.
122 B2 **Molopo** watercourse
Botswana/S. Africa
118 B2 **Moloundou** Cameroon
59 C3 **Moluccas** is Indon.
Molucca Sea Indon. see
Maluku, Laut
52 B2 **Momba** Austr.
119 D3 **Mombasa** Kenya
154 B1 **Mombuca, Serra da** hills Brazil
93 F4 **Møn** i. Denmark
105 D3 **Monaco** country Europe
96 B2 **Monadhliath Mountains** U.K.
97 C1 **Monaghan** Ireland
89 D3 **Monastyrshchina** Rus. Fed.
90 B2 **Monastyryshche** Ukr.
66 D2 **Monbetsu** Japan
108 A1 **Moncalieri** Italy
86 C2 **Monchegorsk** Rus. Fed.
100 C2 **Mönchengladbach** Ger.
144 B2 **Monclova** Mex.

131 D2 **Moncton** Can.
106 B1 **Mondego** r. Port.
123 D2 **Mondlo** S. Africa
108 A2 **Mondovì** Italy
111 B3 **Monemvasia** Greece
66 D1 **Moneron, Ostrov** i. Rus. Fed.
137 E3 **Monett** U.S.A.
108 B1 **Monfalcone** Italy
106 B1 **Monforte de Lemos** Spain
62 B1 **Mông Cai** Vietnam
68 C1 **Mongolia** country Asia
62 A1 **Mong Lin** Myanmar
62 A1 **Mong Pawk** Myanmar
62 A1 **Mong Ping** Myanmar
120 B2 **Mongu** Zambia
135 C3 **Monitor Range** mts U.S.A.
114 C4 **Mono** r. Benin/Togo
135 C3 **Mono Lake** U.S.A.
109 C2 **Monopoli** Italy
107 C1 **Monreal del Campo** Spain
142 B2 **Monroe** LA U.S.A.
140 B2 **Monroe** WI U.S.A.
142 C2 **Monroeville** U.S.A.
114 A4 **Monrovia** Liberia
100 A2 **Mons** Belgium
122 B3 **Montagu** S. Africa
109 C3 **Montalto** mt. Italy
110 B2 **Montana** Bulg.
134 E1 **Montana** state U.S.A.
104 C2 **Montargis** France
104 C3 **Montauban** France
141 E2 **Montauk Point** U.S.A.
123 C2 **Mont-aux-Sources** mt.
Lesotho
105 C2 **Montbard** France
105 C2 **Montbrison** France
100 B3 **Montcornet** France
104 B3 **Mont-de-Marsan** France
104 C2 **Montdidier** France
151 C2 **Monte Alegre** Brazil
105 D3 **Monte-Carlo** Monaco
152 C4 **Monte Caseros** Arg.
146 C3 **Montego Bay** Jamaica
105 C3 **Montélimar** France
145 C2 **Montemorelos** Mex.
104 B2 **Montendre** France
109 C2 **Montenegro** country Europe
121 C2 **Montepuez** Moz.
108 B2 **Montepulciano** Italy
135 B3 **Monterey** U.S.A.
135 B3 **Monterey Bay** U.S.A.
150 A1 **Montería** Col.
152 B2 **Montero** Bol.
145 B2 **Monterrey** Mex.
109 C2 **Montesano sulla Marcellana**
Italy
109 C2 **Monte Sant'Angelo** Italy
151 E3 **Monte Santo** Brazil
108 A2 **Monte Santu, Capo di** c.
Sardegna Italy
155 D1 **Montes Claros** Brazil
153 C4 **Montevideo** Uru.
137 D2 **Montevideo** U.S.A.
136 B3 **Monte Vista** U.S.A.
142 C2 **Montgomery** U.S.A.
105 D2 **Monthey** Switz.
142 B2 **Monticello** AR U.S.A.
135 E3 **Monticello** UT U.S.A.
104 C2 **Montignac** France
105 D2 **Montigny-le-Roi** France
106 C2 **Montilla** Spain
131 D2 **Mont-Joli** Can.
130 C2 **Mont-Laurier** Can.
104 C2 **Montluçon** France
131 C2 **Montmagny** Can.
104 C2 **Montmorillon** France

51 E2 Monto Austr.
34 D2 Montpelier *ID* U.S.A.
41 E2 Montpelier *VT* U.S.A.
05 C3 Montpellier France
30 C2 Montréal Can.
29 D2 Montreal Lake Can.
29 D2 Montreal Lake Can.
99 D3 Montreuil France
05 D2 Montreux Switz.
26 C2 Montrose U.K.
36 B3 Montrose U.S.A.
47 D3 Montserrat *terr.* West Indies
62 A1 Monywa Myanmar
08 A1 Monza Italy
07 D1 Monzón Spain
23 C1 Mookane Botswana
53 D1 Moonie Austr.
53 C1 Moonie *r.* Austr.
52 A2 Moonta Austr.
50 A2 Moore, Lake *imp. l.* Austr.
51 C1 Moorhead U.S.A.
53 C3 Mooroopna Austr.
22 A3 Moorreesburg S. Africa
30 B1 Moose *r.* Can.
30 B1 Moose Factory Can.
41 F1 Moosehead Lake U.S.A.
30 C2 Moose Jaw Can.
37 E1 Moose Lake U.S.A.
29 D1 Moosomin Can.
30 B2 Moosonee Can.
52 B2 Mootwingee Austr.
23 C1 Mopane S. Africa
14 B3 Mopti Mali
50 A3 Moquegua Peru
93 F3 Mora Sweden
51 E4 Mora U.S.A.
75 B2 Moradabad India
22 D1 Moramanga Madag.
03 D2 Morava *r.* Europe
96 B2 Moray Firth *b.* U.K.
00 C3 Morbach Ger.
74 B2 Morbi India
04 B3 Morcenx France
69 E1 Mordaga China
29 E3 Morden Can.
91 E1 Mordovo Rus. Fed.
98 B1 Morecambe U.K.
98 B1 Morecambe Bay U.K.
53 C1 Moree Austr.
59 D4 Morehead P.N.G.
34 C3 Morehead U.S.A.
43 E2 Morehead City U.S.A.
06 B3 Morelia Mex.
07 C1 Morella Spain
06 B2 Morena, Sierra *mts* Spain
10 C2 Moreni Romania
28 A2 Moresby, Mount Can.
28 A2 Moresby Island Can.
42 B3 Morgan City U.S.A.
34 C3 Morganton U.S.A.
43 D1 Morgantown U.S.A.
05 D2 Morges Switz.
76 B3 Morghāb Afgh.
77 C3 Morghāb *r.* Afgh.
66 D2 Mori Japan
28 B2 Morice Lake Can.
66 D3 Morioka Japan
53 D2 Morisset Austr.
04 B2 Morlaix France
51 C1 Mornington Island Austr.
59 D3 Morobe P.N.G.
15 C4 Morocco *country* Africa
19 D3 Morogoro Tanz.
64 B3 Moro Gulf Phil.
22 B2 Morokweng S. Africa
21 D3 Morombe Madag.
68 C1 Mörön Mongolia

121 D3 Morondava Madag.
121 D2 Moroni Comoros
59 C2 Morotai *i.* Indon.
119 D2 Moroto Uganda
98 C1 Morpeth U.K.
154 C1 Morrinhos Brazil
129 E3 Morris Can.
137 D1 Morris U.S.A.
143 D1 Morristown U.S.A.
87 D3 Morshanska Rus. Fed.
154 B1 Mortes, Rio das *r.* Brazil
52 B3 Mortlake Austr.
53 D3 Moruya Austr.
96 B2 Morvern *reg.* U.K.
53 C3 Morwell Austr.
102 B2 Mosbach Ger.
89 E2 Moscow Rus. Fed.
134 C1 Moscow U.S.A.
100 C2 Mosel *r.* Ger.
105 D2 Moselle *r.* France
134 C1 Moses Lake U.S.A.
92 A3 Mosfellsbær Iceland
54 B3 Mosgiel N.Z.
89 D2 Moshenskoye Rus. Fed.
119 D3 Moshi Tanz.
92 F2 Mosjøen Norway
Moskva Rus. Fed. *see* Moscow
103 D2 Mosonmagyaróvár Hungary
146 B4 Mosquitos, Golfo de los *b.* Panama
93 F4 Moss Norway
122 B3 Mossel Bay S. Africa
122 B3 Mossel Bay S. Africa
118 B3 Mossendjo Congo
52 B2 Mossgiel Austr.
51 D1 Mossman Austr.
151 E2 Mossoró Brazil
53 D2 Moss Vale Austr.
102 C1 Most Czech Rep.
114 C1 Mostaganem Alg.
109 C2 Mostar Bos.-Herz.
152 C4 Mostardas Brazil
81 C2 Mosul Iraq
93 G4 Motala Sweden
96 C3 Motherwell U.K.
107 C2 Motilla del Palancar Spain
122 B1 Motokwe Botswana
106 C2 Motril Spain
110 B2 Motru Romania
62 A2 Mottama, Gulf of Myanmar
145 D2 Motul Mex.
111 C3 Moudros Greece
118 B3 Mouila Gabon
52 B3 Moulamein Austr.
105 C2 Moulins France
143 D2 Moultrie U.S.A.
143 E2 Moultrie, Lake U.S.A.
140 B3 Mound City U.S.A.
115 D4 Moundou Chad
137 E3 Mountain Grove U.S.A.
142 B1 Mountain Home *AR* U.S.A.
134 C2 Mountain Home *ID* U.S.A.
143 D1 Mount Airy U.S.A.
52 A3 Mount Barker Austr.
53 C3 Mount Beauty Austr.
121 C2 Mount Darwin Zimbabwe
141 F2 Mount Desert Island U.S.A.
123 C3 Mount Fletcher S. Africa
123 C3 Mount Frere S. Africa
52 B3 Mount Gambier Austr.
59 D3 Mount Hagen P.N.G.
53 C2 Mount Hope Austr.
51 C2 Mount Isa Austr.
50 A2 Mount Magnet Austr.
52 B2 Mount Manara Austr.
54 C1 Mount Maunganui N.Z.
111 B2 Mount Olympus Greece

137 E2 Mount Pleasant *IA* U.S.A.
140 C2 Mount Pleasant *MI* U.S.A.
139 D2 Mount Pleasant *TX* U.S.A.
99 A3 Mount's Bay U.K.
134 B2 Mount Shasta U.S.A.
140 B3 Mount Vernon *IL* U.S.A.
140 C2 Mount Vernon *OH* U.S.A.
134 B1 Mount Vernon *WA* U.S.A.
51 D2 Moura Austr.
115 E3 Mourdi, Dépression du *depr.* Chad
97 C1 Mourne Mountains *hills* U.K.
100 A2 Mouscron Belgium
115 D3 Moussoro Chad
58 C2 Moutong Indon.
115 C2 Mouydir, Monts du *plat.* Alg.
100 B3 Mouzon France
97 B1 Moy *r.* Ireland
117 B4 Moyale Eth.
123 C3 Moyeni Lesotho
76 B2 Mo'ynoq Uzbek.
77 D2 Moyynty Kazakh.
121 C3 Mozambique *country* Africa
113 I9 Mozambique Channel Africa
89 E2 Mozhaysk Rus. Fed.
119 D3 Mpanda Tanz.
121 C2 Mpika Zambia
121 C1 Mporokoso Zambia
123 C2 Mpumalanga *prov.* S. Africa
62 A1 Mrauk-U Myanmar
88 C2 Mshinskaya Rus. Fed.
107 D2 M'Sila Alg.
89 D2 Msta *r.* Rus. Fed.
89 D2 Mstinskiy Most Rus. Fed.
89 D3 Mstsislaw Belarus
89 E3 Mtsensk Rus. Fed.
119 E4 Mtwara Tanz.
118 B3 Muanda Dem. Rep. Congo
63 B2 Muang Khong Laos
62 B1 Muang Ngoy Laos
62 B2 Muang Pakbeng Laos
62 B1 Muang Sing Laos
62 B2 Muang Vangviang Laos
60 B1 Muar Malaysia
60 B2 Muarabungo Indon.
61 C2 Muaradua Indon.
60 A2 Muarasiberut Indon.
60 B2 Muaratembesi Indon.
61 C2 Muarateweh Indon.
119 D2 Mubende Uganda
115 D3 Mubi Nigeria
120 B2 Muconda Angola
155 E1 Mucuri Brazil
155 E1 Mucuri *r.* Brazil
66 A2 Mudanjiang China
66 A1 Mudan Jiang *r.* China
111 C2 Mudanya Turkey
101 E1 Müden (Örtze) Ger.
53 C2 Mudgee Austr.
63 A2 Mudon Myanmar
80 B1 Mudurnu Turkey
121 C2 Mueda Moz.
121 B2 Mufulira Zambia
120 B2 Mufumbwe Zambia
111 C3 Muğla Turkey
116 B2 Muhammad Qol Sudan
101 F2 Mühlberg Ger.
101 E2 Mühlhausen (Thüringen) Ger.
121 C2 Muite Moz.
65 B2 Muju S. Korea
90 A2 Mukacheve Ukr.
61 C1 Mukah *Sarawak* Malaysia
79 B3 Mukalla Yemen
63 B2 Mukdahan Thai.
50 A3 Mukinbudin Austr.
60 B2 Mukomuko Indon.

121 C2 **Mulanje, Mount** Malawi
101 F2 **Mulde** r. Ger.
144 A2 **Mulegé** Mex.
139 C2 **Muleshoe** U.S.A.
106 C2 **Mulhacén** mt. Spain
100 C2 **Mülheim an der Ruhr** Ger.
105 D2 **Mulhouse** France
66 B2 **Muling** China
66 B1 **Muling He** r. China
96 B2 **Mull** i. U.K.
53 C2 **Mullaley** Austr.
136 C2 **Mullen** U.S.A.
61 C1 **Muller, Pegunungan** mts Indon.
50 A2 **Mullewa** Austr.
97 C2 **Mullingar** Ireland
96 B3 **Mull of Galloway** c. U.K.
96 B3 **Mull of Kintyre** hd U.K.
96 A3 **Mull of Oa** hd U.K.
120 B2 **Mulobezi** Zambia
74 B1 **Multan** Pak.
73 B3 **Mumbai** India
120 B2 **Mumbwa** Zambia
145 D2 **Muna** Mex.
101 E2 **Münchberg** Ger.
München Ger. see Munich
140 B2 **Muncie** U.S.A.
50 B3 **Mundrabilla** Austr.
119 C2 **Mungbere** Dem. Rep. Congo
75 C2 **Munger** India
52 A1 **Mungeranie** Austr.
53 C1 **Mungindi** Austr.
102 C2 **Munich** Ger.
155 D2 **Muniz Freire** Brazil
101 E1 **Münster** Niedersachsen Ger.
100 C2 **Münster** Nordrhein-Westfalen Ger.
97 C2 **Munster** reg. Ireland
100 C2 **Münsterland** reg. Ger.
62 B1 **Mường Nhe** Vietnam
92 H2 **Muonio** Fin.
92 H2 **Muonioälven** r. Fin./Sweden
Muqdisho Somalia see Mogadishu
103 D2 **Mur** r. Austria
119 D3 **Muramvya** Burundi
119 D3 **Murang'a** Kenya
81 D2 **Murat** r. Turkey
111 C2 **Muratlı** Turkey
50 A2 **Murchison** watercourse Austr.
107 C2 **Murcia** Spain
111 C2 **Mürefte** Turkey
110 B1 **Mureşul** r. Romania
104 C3 **Muret** France
142 C1 **Murfreesboro** U.S.A.
77 D3 **Murghob** Tajik.
155 D2 **Muriaé** Brazil
120 B1 **Muriege** Angola
101 F1 **Müritz** l. Ger.
86 C2 **Murmansk** Rus. Fed.
87 D3 **Murom** Rus. Fed.
66 D2 **Muroran** Japan
106 B1 **Muros** Spain
67 B4 **Muroto** Japan
67 B4 **Muroto-zaki** pt Japan
143 D1 **Murphy** U.S.A.
53 C2 **Murra Murra** Austr.
52 A3 **Murray** r. Austr.
128 B2 **Murray** r. Can.
140 B3 **Murray** U.S.A.
143 D2 **Murray, Lake** U.S.A.
52 A3 **Murray Bridge** Austr.
122 B3 **Murraysburg** S. Africa
52 B3 **Murrayville** Austr.
52 B2 **Murrumbidgee** r. Austr.
121 C2 **Murrupula** Moz.
53 D2 **Murrurundi** Austr.

109 C1 **Murska Sobota** Slovenia
54 C1 **Murupara** N.Z.
49 I4 **Mururoa** atoll Fr. Polynesia
75 C2 **Murwara** India
53 D1 **Murwillumbah** Austr.
115 D2 **Murzūq** Libya
115 D2 **Murzūq, Idhān** des. Libya
81 C2 **Muş** Turkey
110 B2 **Musala** mt. Bulg.
65 B1 **Musan** N. Korea
78 B3 **Musaymir** Yemen
79 C2 **Muscat** Oman
137 E2 **Muscatine** U.S.A.
50 C2 **Musgrave Ranges** mts Austr.
118 B3 **Mushie** Dem. Rep. Congo
60 B2 **Musi** r. Indon.
123 D1 **Musina** S. Africa
140 B2 **Muskegon** U.S.A.
139 D1 **Muskogee** U.S.A.
128 B2 **Muskwa** r. Can.
74 A1 **Muslimbagh** Pak.
78 A3 **Musmar** Sudan
119 D3 **Musoma** Tanz.
96 C3 **Musselburgh** U.K.
88 B2 **Mustjala** Estonia
53 D2 **Muswellbrook** Austr.
116 A2 **Mūt** Egypt
121 C2 **Mutare** Zimbabwe
66 D2 **Mutsu** Japan
121 C2 **Mutuali** Moz.
91 I2 **Muurola** Fin.
70 A2 **Mu Us Shamo** des. China
120 A1 **Muxaluando** Angola
86 C2 **Muyezerskiy** Rus. Fed.
119 D3 **Muyinga** Burundi
74 B1 **Muzaffargarh** Pak.
75 C2 **Muzaffarpur** India
144 B2 **Múzquiz** Mex.
75 C1 **Muztag** mt. China
119 C3 **Mwanza** Dem. Rep. Congo
119 D3 **Mwanza** Tanz.
118 C3 **Mweka** Dem. Rep. Congo
121 B2 **Mwenda** Zambia
118 C3 **Mwene-Ditu** Dem. Rep. Congo
121 C3 **Mwenezi** Zimbabwe
119 C3 **Mweru, Lake** Dem. Rep. Congo/Zambia
118 C3 **Mwimba** Dem. Rep. Congo
120 B2 **Mwinilunga** Zambia
88 C3 **Myadzyel** Belarus
62 A2 **Myanaung** Myanmar
62 A1 **Myanmar** country Asia
63 A2 **Myaungmya** Myanmar
63 A2 **Myeik** Myanmar
Myeik Kyunzu is Myanmar see Mergui Archipelago
62 A1 **Myingyan** Myanmar
62 A1 **Myitkyina** Myanmar
91 C2 **Mykolayiv** Ukr.
111 C3 **Mykonos** Greece
111 C3 **Mykonos** i. Greece
86 E2 **Myla** Rus. Fed.
75 D2 **Mymensingh** Bangl.
65 B1 **Myŏnggan** N. Korea
88 C2 **Myory** Belarus
92 B3 **Mýrdalsjökull** Iceland
91 C2 **Myrhorod** Ukr.
90 C2 **Myronivka** Ukr.
143 E2 **Myrtle Beach** U.S.A.
53 C3 **Myrtleford** Austr.
142 D3 **Myrtle Point** U.S.A.
89 E2 **Myshkin** Rus. Fed.
103 C1 **Myślibórz** Pol.
73 B3 **Mysore** India
83 N2 **Mys Shmidta** Rus. Fed.
63 B2 **My Tho** Vietnam

111 C3 **Mytilini** Greece
89 E3 **Mytishchi** Rus. Fed.
123 C3 **Mzamomhle** S. Africa
121 C2 **Mzimba** Malawi
121 C2 **Mzuzu** Malawi

N

97 C2 **Naas** Ireland
122 A2 **Nababeep** S. Africa
87 E3 **Naberezhnyye Chelny** Rus. Fed.
59 D3 **Nabire** Indon.
80 B2 **Näblus** West Bank
123 C1 **Naboomspruit** S. Africa
121 D2 **Nacala** Moz.
63 A2 **Nachuge** India
139 E2 **Nacogdoches** U.S.A.
144 B1 **Nacozari de García** Mex.
74 B2 **Nadiad** India
90 A2 **Nadvirna** Ukr.
86 C2 **Nadvoitsy** Rus. Fed.
86 G2 **Nadym** Rus. Fed.
93 F4 **Næstved** Denmark
111 B3 **Nafpaktos** Greece
111 B3 **Nafplio** Greece
115 D1 **Nafüsah, Jabal** hills Libya
78 B2 **Nafy** Saudi Arabia
64 B1 **Naga** Phil.
130 B1 **Nagagami** r. Can.
67 C3 **Nagano** Japan
67 C3 **Nagaoka** Japan
75 D2 **Nagaon** India
74 B1 **Nagar** India
74 B2 **Nagar Parkar** Pak.
A4 **Nagasaki** Japan
67 B4 **Nagato** Japan
73 B4 **Nagercoil** India
74 A2 **Nagha Kalat** Pak.
75 B2 **Nagina** India
67 C3 **Nagoya** Japan
75 B2 **Nagpur** India
68 C2 **Nagqu** China
103 D2 **Nagyatád** Hungary
103 D2 **Nagykanizsa** Hungary
128 B1 **Nahanni Butte** Can.
76 A3 **Nahävand** Iran
101 E1 **Nahrendorf** Ger.
153 A5 **Nahuel Huapi, Lago** l. Arg.
131 D1 **Nain** Can.
81 D2 **Nā'īn** Iran
96 C2 **Nairn** U.K.
119 D3 **Nairobi** Kenya
119 D3 **Naivasha** Kenya
81 D2 **Najafābād** Iran
78 B2 **Najd** reg. Saudi Arabia
106 C1 **Nájera** Spain
65 C1 **Najin** N. Korea
78 B3 **Najrān** Saudi Arabia
Nakambé r. Burkina/Ghana see White Volta
67 C3 **Nakatsugawa** Japan
78 A3 **Nakfa** Eritrea
66 B2 **Nakhodka** Rus. Fed.
63 B2 **Nakhon Pathom** Thai.
63 B2 **Nakhon Ratchasima** Thai.
63 B2 **Nakhon Sawan** Thai.
63 A3 **Nakhon Si Thammarat** Thai.
130 B1 **Nakina** Can.
121 C2 **Nakonde** Zambia
93 F4 **Nakskov** Denmark
119 D3 **Nakuru** Kenya
128 C2 **Nakusp** Can.
75 D2 **Nalbari** India

87 D4	Nal'chik Rus. Fed.	
115 D1	Nālūt Libya	
123 C2	Namahadi S. Africa	
77 C2	Namangan Uzbek.	
122 A2	Namaqualand reg. S. Africa	
51 E2	Nambour Austr.	
53 C2	Nambucca Heads Austr.	
75 B1	Nam Co salt l. China	
62 B1	Nam Đinh Vietnam	
120 A1	Namib Desert Namibia	
120 A1	Namibe Angola	
120 A3	Namibia country Africa	
72 D2	Namjagbarwa Feng mt. China	
59 C3	Namlea Indon.	
53 C2	Namoi r. Austr.	
134 C2	Nampa U.S.A.	
114 B3	Nampala Mali	
65 B2	Namp'o N. Korea	
121 C2	Nampula Moz.	
62 A1	Namrup India	
62 A1	Namsang Myanmar	
92 F3	Namsos Norway	
63 A2	Nam Tok Thai.	
83 J2	Namtsy Rus. Fed.	
62 A1	Namtu Myanmar	
100 B2	Namur Belgium	
120 B2	Namwala Zambia	
65 B2	Namwŏn S. Korea	
62 A1	Namya Ra Myanmar	
128 B3	Nan Thai.	
71 B3	Nanaimo Can.	
122 A1	Nananib Plateau Namibia	
67 C3	Nanao Japan	
71 B3	Nanchang Jiangxi China	
71 B3	Nanchang Jiangxi China	
70 A2	Nanchong China	
63 A2	Nancowry i. India	
105 D2	Nancy France	
75 C1	Nanda Devi mt. India	
71 A3	Nandan China	
73 B3	Nanded India	
73 B2	Nandurbar India	
73 B3	Nandyal India	
118 B2	Nanfeng China	
61 C2	Nanga Eboko Cameroon	
74 B1	Nangahpinoh Indon.	
74 B1	Nanga Parbat mt. Pak.	
61 C2	Nangatayap Indon.	
119 D3	Nangulangwa Tanz.	
70 C2	Nanhui China	
70 B2	Nanjing China	
	Nanking China see Nanjing	
120 A2	Nankova Angola	
71 B3	Nan Ling mts China	
71 A3	Nanning China	
127 H2	Nanortalik Greenland	
71 A3	Nanpan Jiang r. China	
75 C2	Nanpara India	
71 B3	Nanping China	
	Nansei-shotō is japan see Ryukyu Islands	
104 B2	Nantes France	
71 B3	Nantong China	
141 F2	Nantucket Island U.S.A.	
155 D1	Nanuque Brazil	
64 B2	Nanusa, Kepulauan is Indon.	
71 B3	Nanxiong China	
70 B2	Nanyang China	
70 B2	Nanzhang China	
107 D2	Nao, Cabo de la c. Spain	
131 C3	Naococane, Lac l. Can.	
135 B3	Napa U.S.A.	
126 D2	Napaktulik Lake Can.	
127 H2	Napasoq Greenland	
54 C1	Napier N.Z.	
108 B2	Naples Italy	
143 D3	Naples U.S.A.	
150 A2	Napo r. Ecuador/Peru	
	Napoli Italy see Naples	
114 B3	Nara Mali	
93 I4	Narach Belarus	
52 B3	Naracoorte Austr.	
145 C2	Naranjos Mex.	
63 B3	Narathiwat Thai.	
105 C3	Narbonne France	
63 A2	Narcondam Island India	
127 G1	Nares Strait Can./Greenland	
122 A1	Narib Namibia	
67 D2	Narita Japan	
74 B2	Narmada r. India	
74 B2	Narnaul India	
108 B2	Narni Italy	
90 B1	Narodychi Ukr.	
89 E2	Naro-Fominsk Rus. Fed.	
53 D2	Narooma Austr.	
88 C3	Narowlya Belarus	
53 C2	Narrabri Austr.	
53 C2	Narrandera Austr.	
53 C2	Narromine Austr.	
88 C2	Narva Estonia	
88 C2	Narva Bay Estonia/Rus. Fed.	
92 G2	Narvik Norway	
88 C2	Narvskoye Vodokhranilishche resr Estonia/Rus. Fed.	
86 E2	Nar'yan-Mar Rus. Fed.	
77 D2	Naryn Kyrg.	
74 B2	Nashik India	
141 E2	Nashua U.S.A.	
142 C1	Nashville U.S.A.	
117 B4	Nasir Sudan	
128 B2	Nass r. Can.	
146 C2	Nassau Bahamas	
116 B2	Nasser, Lake resr Egypt	
93 F4	Nässjö Sweden	
130 C1	Nastapoca r. Can.	
130 C1	Nastapoka Islands Can.	
120 B3	Nata Botswana	
151 E2	Natal Brazil	
131 D1	Natashquan Can.	
131 D1	Natashquan r. Can.	
142 B2	Natchez U.S.A.	
142 B2	Natchitoches U.S.A.	
53 C3	Nathalia Austr.	
107 D1	Nati, Punta pt Spain	
114 C3	Natitingou Benin	
151 D3	Natividade Brazil	
67 D3	Natori Japan	
131 D1	Natuashish Can.	
61 B1	Natuna, Kepulauan is Indon.	
61 B1	Natuna Besar i. Indon.	
120 A3	Nauchas Namibia	
101 F1	Nauen Ger.	
88 B2	Naujoji Akmenė Lith.	
74 A2	Naukot Pak.	
101 E2	Naumburg (Saale) Ger.	
48 E3	Nauru country S. Pacific Ocean	
145 C2	Nautla Mex.	
88 C2	Navahrudak Belarus	
106 B2	Navalmoral de la Mata Spain	
106 B2	Navalvillar de Pela Spain	
97 C2	Navan Ireland	
88 C2	Navapolatsk Belarus	
83 M2	Navarin, Mys c. Rus. Fed.	
153 B6	Navarino, Isla i. Chile	
96 B1	Naver r. U.K.	
73 B3	Navi Mumbai India	
89 D3	Navlya Rus. Fed.	
110 C2	Năvodari Romania	
77 C2	Navoiy Uzbek.	
144 B2	Navojoa Mex.	
144 B2	Navolato Mex.	
74 A2	Nawabshah Pak.	
62 A1	Nawnghkio Myanmar	
62 A1	Nawngleng Myanmar	
81 C2	Naxçıvan Azer.	
111 C3	Naxos i. Greece	
144 B2	Nayar Mex.	
66 D2	Nayoro Japan	
144 B2	Nazas Mex.	
144 B2	Nazas r. Mex.	
150 A3	Nazca Peru	
80 B2	Nazerat Israel	
111 C3	Nazilli Turkey	
117 B4	Nazrēt Eth.	
79 C2	Nazwá Oman	
121 B1	Nchelenge Zambia	
122 B1	Ncojane Botswana	
120 A1	N'dalatando Angola	
118 C2	Ndélé C.A.R.	
118 B3	Ndendé Gabon	
115 D3	Ndjamena Chad	
121 B2	Ndola Zambia	
97 C1	Neagh, Lough l. U.K.	
50 C1	Neale, Lake imp. l. Austr.	
111 B2	Nea Roda Greece	
98 B1	Neath U.K.	
53 C1	Nebine Creek r. Austr.	
150 B1	Neblina, Pico da mt. Brazil	
89 D2	Nebolchi Rus. Fed.	
136 C2	Nebraska state U.S.A.	
137 D2	Nebraska City U.S.A.	
108 B3	Nebrodi, Monti mts Sicilia Italy	
131 C4	Necochea Arg.	
131 C4	Nedluc, Lac l. Can.	
135 D4	Needles U.S.A.	
74 B2	Neemuch India	
129 E2	Neepawa Can.	
87 E3	Neftekamsk Rus. Fed.	
82 F2	Nefteyugansk Rus. Fed.	
120 A1	Negage Angola	
118 B4	Negēlē Eth.	
150 A2	Negra, Punta pt Peru	
63 A2	Negrais, Cape Myanmar	
153 B5	Negro r. Arg.	
150 C2	Negro r. S. America	
152 C4	Negro r. Uru.	
106 B2	Negro, Cabo c. Morocco	
64 B2	Negros i. Phil.	
69 E1	Nehe China	
70 A3	Neijiang China	
129 D2	Neilburg Can.	
150 A1	Neiva Col.	
129 E2	Nejanilini Lake Can.	
117 B4	Nek'emtē Eth.	
89 F2	Nekrasovskoye Rus. Fed.	
82 G2	Nelidovo Rus. Fed.	
73 B3	Nellore India	
128 C3	Nelson Can.	
129 E2	Nelson r. Can.	
54 B2	Nelson N.Z.	
52 B3	Nelson, Cape Austr.	
53 D2	Nelson Bay Austr.	
129 E2	Nelson House Can.	
134 E1	Nelson Reservoir U.S.A.	
123 D2	Nelspruit S. Africa	
114 B3	Néma Maur.	
88 B2	Neman Rus. Fed.	
104 C2	Nemours France	
66 D2	Nemuro Japan	
90 B2	Nemyriv Ukr.	
97 B2	Nenagh Ireland	
99 D2	Nene r. U.K.	
69 E1	Nenjiang China	
137 E3	Neosho U.S.A.	
75 C2	Nepal country Asia	
75 C2	Nepalganj Nepal	
135 D3	Nephi U.S.A.	

97	B1	**Nephin** h. Ireland	
97	B1	**Nephin Beg Range** hills Ireland	
131	D2	**Nepisiguit** r. Can.	
119	C2	**Nepoko** r. Dem. Rep. Congo	
104	C3	**Nérac** France	
53	D1	**Nerang** Austr.	
69	D1	**Nerchinsk** Rus. Fed.	
89	F2	**Nerekhta** Rus. Fed.	
109	C2	**Neretva** r. Bos.-Herz./Croatia	
120	B2	**Neriquinha** Angola	
88	B3	**Neris** r. Lith.	
89	E2	**Nerl'** r. Rus. Fed.	
86	F2	**Nerokhi** Rus. Fed.	
154	C1	**Nerópolis** Brazil	
83	J3	**Neryungri** Rus. Fed.	
92	C2	**Neskaupstaður** Iceland	
96	B2	**Ness, Loch** l. U.K.	
136	D3	**Ness City** U.S.A.	
111	B2	**Nestos** r. Greece	
100	B1	**Netherlands** country Europe	
147	B3	**Netherlands Antilles** terr. West Indies	
127	G2	**Nettilling Lake** Can.	
101	F1	**Neubrandenburg** Ger.	
105	D2	**Neuchâtel** Switz.	
105	D2	**Neuchâtel** Ger.	
100	B3	**Neufchâteau** Belgium	
105	D2	**Neufchâteau** France	
104	C2	**Neufchâtel-en-Bray** France	
101	D2	**Neuhof** Ger.	
102	B1	**Neumünster** Ger.	
102	B2	**Neunkirchen** Ger.	
153	B4	**Neuquén** Arg.	
153	B4	**Neuquén** r. Arg.	
101	F1	**Neuruppin** Ger.	
100	C2	**Neuss** Ger.	
101	D1	**Neustadt am Rübenberge** Ger.	
101	E3	**Neustadt an der Aisch** Ger.	
101	F1	**Neustrelitz** Ger.	
100	C2	**Neuwied** Ger.	
137	E3	**Nevada** U.S.A.	
135	C3	**Nevada** state U.S.A.	
106	C2	**Nevada, Sierra** mts Spain	
135	B2	**Nevada, Sierra** mts U.S.A.	
88	C2	**Nevel'** Rus. Fed.	
105	C2	**Nevers** France	
53	C2	**Nevertire** Austr.	
109	C2	**Nevesinje** Bos.-Herz.	
87	D4	**Nevinnomyssk** Rus. Fed.	
128	B2	**New Aiyansh** Can.	
140	B3	**New Albany** U.S.A.	
151	C1	**New Amsterdam** Guyana	
141	E2	**Newark** NJ U.S.A.	
140	C2	**Newark** OH U.S.A.	
98	C2	**Newark-on-Trent** U.K.	
141	E2	**New Bedford** U.S.A.	
143	E1	**New Bern** U.S.A.	
143	D2	**Newberry** U.S.A.	
139	E2	**New Boston** U.S.A.	
139	D3	**New Braunfels** U.S.A.	
97	C2	**Newbridge** Ireland	
48	E3	**New Britain** i. P.N.G.	
131	D2	**New Brunswick** prov. Can.	
99	C3	**Newbury** U.K.	
48	E4	**New Caledonia** terr. S. Pacific Ocean	
53	D2	**Newcastle** Austr.	
123	C2	**Newcastle** S. Africa	
97	D1	**Newcastle** U.K.	
140	C2	**New Castle** U.S.A.	
136	C2	**Newcastle** U.S.A.	
98	B2	**Newcastle-under-Lyme** U.K.	
98	C1	**Newcastle upon Tyne** U.K.	
97	B2	**Newcastle West** Ireland	
74	B2	**New Delhi** India	
128	C3	**New Denver** Can.	
53	D2	**New England Range** mts Austr.	
131	E2	**Newfoundland** i. Can.	
131	E1	**Newfoundland and Labrador** prov. Can.	
131	D2	**New Glasgow** Can.	
59	D3	**New Guinea** i. Indon./P.N.G.	
141	E2	**New Hampshire** state U.S.A.	
141	E2	**New Haven** U.S.A.	
128	B2	**New Hazelton** Can.	
		New Hebrides country S. Pacific Ocean see Vanuatu	
142	B2	**New Iberia** U.S.A.	
48	E3	**New Ireland** i. P.N.G.	
141	E3	**New Jersey** state U.S.A.	
130	C2	**New Liskeard** Can.	
50	A2	**Newman** Austr.	
138	B2	**New Mexico** state U.S.A.	
142	B3	**New Orleans** U.S.A.	
140	C2	**New Philadelphia** U.S.A.	
54	B1	**New Plymouth** N.Z.	
99	C3	**Newport** England U.K.	
99	B3	**Newport** Wales U.K.	
142	B1	**Newport** AR U.S.A.	
134	B2	**Newport** OR U.S.A.	
141	E2	**Newport** RI U.S.A.	
141	E2	**Newport** VT U.S.A.	
134	C1	**Newport** WA U.S.A.	
141	D3	**Newport News** U.S.A.	
143	E3	**New Providence** i. Bahamas	
99	A3	**Newquay** U.K.	
142	B2	**New Roads** U.S.A.	
97	C2	**New Ross** Ireland	
97	C1	**Newry** U.K.	
83	K1	**New Siberia Islands** Rus. Fed.	
52	B2	**New South Wales** state Austr.	
137	E2	**Newton** IA U.S.A.	
137	D3	**Newton** KS U.S.A.	
99	B3	**Newton Abbot** U.K.	
96	B3	**Newton Stewart** U.K.	
97	B2	**Newtown** Ireland	
99	B2	**Newtown** U.K.	
136	C1	**New Town** U.S.A.	
97	D1	**Newtownabbey** U.K.	
97	D1	**Newtownards** U.K.	
96	C3	**Newtown St Boswells** U.K.	
97	C1	**Newtownstewart** U.K.	
137	E2	**New Ulm** U.S.A.	
141	E2	**New York** U.S.A.	
141	D2	**New York** state U.S.A.	
54	B2	**New Zealand** country Oceania	
79	C2	**Neyrīz** Iran	
76	B3	**Neyshābūr** Iran	
145	C3	**Nezahualcóyotl** Mex.	
145	C3	**Nezahualcóyotl, Presa** resr Mex.	
61	B1	**Ngabang** Indon.	
75	C2	**Ngamring** China	
75	C1	**Ngangla Ringco** salt l. China	
75	C1	**Nganglong Kangri** mts China	
75	C1	**Ngangzê Co** salt l. China	
62	A2	**Ngao** Thai.	
118	B2	**Ngaoundéré** Cameroon	
54	C1	**Ngaruawahia** N.Z.	
62	A2	**Ngathaingyaung** Myanmar	
118	B3	**Ngo** Congo	
63	B2	**Ngok Linh** mt. Vietnam	
115	C4	**Ngol Bembo** Nigeria	
68	C2	**Ngoring Hu** l. China	
115	D3	**Ngourti** Niger	
115	D3	**Nguigmi** Niger	
59	D2	**Ngulu** atoll Micronesia	
115	D3	**Nguru** Nigeria	
123	D2	**Ngwelezana** S. Africa	
121	C2	**Nhamalabué** Moz.	
63	B2	**Nha Trang** Vietnam	
52	B3	**Nhill** Austr.	
123	D2	**Nhlangano** Swaziland	
51	C1	**Nhulunbuy** Austr.	
141	D2	**Niagara Falls** Can.	
114	C3	**Niamey** Niger	
119	C2	**Niangara** Dem. Rep. Congo	
114	B3	**Niangay, Lac** l. Mali	
60	A1	**Nias** i. Indon.	
146	B3	**Nicaragua** country Central America	
146	B3	**Nicaragua, Lake** Nic.	
105	D3	**Nice** France	
73	D4	**Nicobar Islands** India	
80	B2	**Nicosia** Cyprus	
146	B4	**Nicoya, Golfo de** b. Costa Rica	
88	B2	**Nida** Lith.	
103	E1	**Nidzica** Pol.	
102	B1	**Niebüll** Ger.	
101	D2	**Niederaula** Ger.	
118	B2	**Niefang** Equat. Guinea	
101	F1	**Niemegk** Ger.	
101	D1	**Nienburg (Weser)** Ger.	
100	B1	**Nieuwe-Niedorp** Neth.	
151	C1	**Nieuw Nickerie** Suriname	
122	A3	**Nieuwoudtville** S. Africa	
100	A2	**Nieuwpoort** Belgium	
80	B2	**Niğde** Turkey	
115	C3	**Niger** country Africa	
115	C4	**Niger** r. Africa	
115	C4	**Niger, Mouths of the** Nigeria	
115	C4	**Nigeria** country Africa	
130	B2	**Nighthawk Lake** Can.	
111	B2	**Nigrita** Greece	
67	C3	**Niigata** Japan	
67	B4	**Niihama** Japan	
67	C4	**Nii-jima** i. Japan	
67	C3	**Niitsu** Japan	
100	B2	**Nijmegen** Neth.	
100	C1	**Nijverdal** Neth.	
92	J2	**Nikel'** Rus. Fed.	
83	M3	**Nikol'skoye** Rus. Fed.	
91	C2	**Nikopol'** Ukr.	
80	B1	**Niksar** Turkey	
79	D2	**Nikshahr** Iran	
109	C2	**Nikšić** Montenegro	
116	B1	**Nile** r. Africa	
140	B2	**Niles** U.S.A.	
74	A1	**Nīlī** Afgh.	
105	C3	**Nîmes** France	
53	C3	**Nimmitabel** Austr.	
117	B4	**Nimule** Sudan	
53	C1	**Nindigully** Austr.	
73	B4	**Nine Degree Channel** India	
53	C3	**Ninety Mile Beach** Austr.	
54	B1	**Ninety Mile Beach** N.Z.	
70	C3	**Ningbo** China	
71	B3	**Ningde** China	
71	B3	**Ningdu** China	
70	B2	**Ningguo** China	
71	C3	**Ninghai** China	
		Ningjiang China see Songyuan	
68	C2	**Ningjing Shan** mts China	
70	A2	**Ningxia Huizu Zizhiqu** aut. reg. China	
70	B2	**Ningyang** China	
62	B1	**Ninh Binh** Vietnam	
63	B2	**Ninh Hoa** Vietnam	
66	D2	**Ninohe** Japan	
137	D2	**Niobrara** r. U.S.A.	
114	B3	**Niono** Mali	
114	B3	**Nioro** Mali	
104	B2	**Niort** France	
129	C2	**Nipawin** Can.	
130	B2	**Nipigon** Can.	
130	B2	**Nipigon, Lake** Can.	
131	D1	**Nipishish Lake** Can.	

130	C2	**Nipissing, Lake** Can.
135	C3	**Nipton** U.S.A.
151	E3	**Niquelândia** Brazil
73	B3	**Nirmal** India
109	D2	**Niš** Serbia
109	D2	**Nišava** r. Serbia
108	B3	**Niscemi** Sicilia Italy
67	B4	**Nishino-omote** Japan
155	D2	**Niterói** Brazil
96	C3	**Nith** r. U.K.
103	D2	**Nitra** Slovakia
49	G4	**Niue** terr. S. Pacific Ocean
92	H3	**Nivala** Fin.
100	D2	**Nivelles** Belgium
72	H3	**Nizamabad** India
87	E3	**Nizhnekamsk** Rus. Fed.
83	H3	**Nizhneudinsk** Rus. Fed.
82	G2	**Nizhnevartovsk** Rus. Fed.
89	F3	**Nizhniy Kislyay** Rus. Fed.
87	D3	**Nizhniy Lomov** Rus. Fed.
87	D3	**Nizhniy Novgorod** Rus. Fed.
86	E2	**Nizhniy Odes** Rus. Fed.
86	E3	**Nizhniy Tagil** Rus. Fed.
83	G2	**Nizhnyaya Tunguska** r. Rus. Fed.
91	C1	**Nizhyn** Ukr.
121	D3	**Njazidja** i. Comoros
119	D3	**Njinjo** Tanz.
119	D3	**Njombe** Tanz.
121	C2	**Nkhotakota** Malawi
118	A2	**Nkongsamba** Cameroon
123	C3	**Nkululeko** S. Africa
123	C3	**Nkwenkwezi** S. Africa
67	B4	**Nobeoka** Japan
52	B1	**Noccundra** Austr.
144	A1	**Nogales** Mex.
138	A2	**Nogales** U.S.A.
104	C2	**Nogent-le-Rotrou** France
87	D2	**Noginsk** Rus. Fed.
74	B2	**Nohar** India
100	C2	**Nohfelden** Ger.
104	B2	**Noirmoutier, Île de** i. France
104	B2	**Noirmoutier-en-l'Île** France
67	C4	**Nojima-zaki** c. Japan
74	B2	**Nokha** India
93	H3	**Nokia** Fin.
74	A2	**Nok Kundi** Pak.
118	B2	**Nola** C.A.R.
86	D3	**Nolinsk** Rus. Fed.
123	C3	**Nomonde** S. Africa
123	D2	**Nondweni** S. Africa
65	B2	**Nong Khai** Thai.
52	A2	**Nonning** Austr.
144	B2	**Nonoava** Mex.
65	B2	**Nonsan** S. Korea
63	B2	**Nonthaburi** Thai.
122	B3	**Nonzwakazi** S. Africa
77	C3	**Norak** Tajik.
82	C1	**Nordaustlandet** i. Svalbard
128	C2	**Nordegg** Can.
100	C2	**Norden** Ger.
83	H1	**Nordenshel'da, Arkhipelag** is Rus. Fed.
100	C1	**Norderney** Ger.
100	C1	**Norderney** i. Ger.
101	E1	**Norderstedt** Ger.
92	F3	**Nordfjordeid** Norway
101	E2	**Nordhausen** Ger.
101	D1	**Nordholz** Ger.
100	C1	**Nordhorn** Ger.
		Nordkapp c. Norway see **North Cape**
92	F3	**Nordli** Norway
102	C2	**Nördlingen** Ger.
92	G3	**Nordmaling** Sweden
94	B1	**Norðoyar** is Faroe Is
97	C2	**Nore** r. Ireland
137	D2	**Norfolk** NE U.S.A.
141	D3	**Norfolk** VA U.S.A.
48	F4	**Norfolk Island** terr. S. Pacific Ocean
93	E3	**Norheimsund** Norway
82	G2	**Noril'sk** Rus. Fed.
75	C2	**Norkyung** China
139	D1	**Norman** U.S.A.
		Normandes, Îles is English Chan. see **Channel Islands**
51	D1	**Normanton** Austr.
93	G4	**Norrköping** Sweden
93	G4	**Norrtälje** Sweden
50	B3	**Norseman** Austr.
92	G3	**Norsjö** Sweden
54	I1	**Northallerton** U.K.
50	A2	**Northampton** Austr.
99	C2	**Northampton** U.K.
73	D3	**North Andaman** i. India
129	D2	**North Battleford** Can.
130	C2	**North Bay** Can.
130	C1	**North Belcher Islands** Can.
96	C2	**North Berwick** U.K.
92	I1	**North Cape** Norway
54	B1	**North Cape** N.Z.
130	A1	**North Caribou Lake** Can.
143	E1	**North Carolina** state U.S.A.
130	B2	**North Channel** lake channel Can.
96	A3	**North Channel** U.K.
128	B3	**North Cowichan** Can.
136	C1	**North Dakota** state U.S.A.
99	C3	**North Downs** hills U.K.
143	E3	**Northeast Providence Channel** Bahamas
101	D2	**Northeim** Ger.
122	A2	**Northern Cape** prov. S. Africa
129	E2	**Northern Indian Lake** Can.
97	C1	**Northern Ireland** prov. U.K.
48	D1	**Northern Mariana Islands** terr. N. Pacific Ocean
50	C1	**Northern Territory** admin. div. Austr.
96	C2	**North Esk** r. U.K.
137	E2	**Northfield** U.S.A.
99	D3	**North Foreland** c. U.K.
54	B1	**North Fork Lake** Can.
129	E2	**North Knife Lake** Can.
65	B2	**North Korea** country Asia
62	A1	**North Lakhimpur** India
128	B1	**North Nahanni** r. Can.
136	C2	**North Platte** U.S.A.
136	C2	**North Platte** r. U.S.A.
96	C1	**North Ronaldsay** i. U.K.
94	□2	**North Sea** Europe
130	A1	**North Spirit Lake** Can.
53	D1	**North Stradbroke Island** Austr.
54	B1	**North Taranaki Bight** b. N.Z.
130	C1	**North Twin Island** Can.
98	B1	**North Tyne** r. U.K.
96	A2	**North Uist** i. U.K.
131	D2	**Northumberland Strait** Can.
122	C2	**North West** prov. S. Africa
50	A2	**North West Cape** Austr.
143	E3	**Northwest Providence Channel** Bahamas
131	E1	**North West River** Can.
128	B1	**Northwest Territories** admin. div. Can.
98	C1	**North York Moors** moorland U.K.
140	C3	**Norton** U.S.A.
121	C2	**Norton** Zimbabwe
140	C2	**Norwalk** U.S.A.
93	F3	**Norway** country Europe
129	E2	**Norway House** Can.
160	A3	**Norwegian Sea** N. Atlantic Ocean
99	D2	**Norwich** U.K.
141	E2	**Norwich** CT U.S.A.
141	D2	**Norwich** NY U.S.A.
66	D2	**Noshiro** Japan
91	C1	**Nosivka** Ukr.
122	B2	**Nosop** watercourse Africa
86	E2	**Nosovaya** Rus. Fed.
79	C2	**Noşratābād** Iran
		Nossob watercourse Africa see **Nosop**
103	D1	**Noteć** r. Pol.
93	E4	**Notodden** Norway
67	C3	**Noto-hantō** pen. Japan
131	D2	**Notre-Dame, Monts** mts Can.
131	E2	**Notre Dame Bay** Can.
130	C1	**Nottaway** r. Can.
99	C2	**Nottingham** U.K.
114	A2	**Nouâdhibou** Maur.
114	A3	**Nouakchott** Maur.
114	A3	**Nouâmghâr** Maur.
48	F4	**Nouméa** New Caledonia
114	B3	**Nouna** Burkina
154	B2	**Nova Esperança** Brazil
155	D2	**Nova Friburgo** Brazil
109	C1	**Nova Gradiška** Croatia
154	C2	**Nova Granada** Brazil
154	C2	**Nova Iguaçu** Brazil
154	C2	**Nova Kakhovka** Ukr.
155	D1	**Nova Lima** Brazil
154	B2	**Nova Londrina** Brazil
91	C2	**Nova Odesa** Ukr.
150	B1	**Nova Paraíso** Brazil
131	D2	**Nova Scotia** prov. Can.
155	D1	**Nova Venécia** Brazil
83	K1	**Novaya Sibir', Ostrov** i. Rus. Fed.
86	E1	**Novaya Zemlya** is Rus. Fed.
103	D2	**Nové Zámky** Slovakia
91	C1	**Novhorod-Sivers'kyy** Ukr.
110	B2	**Novi Iskŭr** Bulg.
108	A2	**Novi Ligure** Italy
109	D2	**Novi Pazar** Serbia
109	D1	**Novi Sad** Serbia
87	D3	**Novoanninskiy** Rus. Fed.
150	B2	**Novo Aripuanã** Brazil
91	D2	**Novoazovs'k** Ukr.
91	E2	**Novocherkassk** Rus. Fed.
86	D2	**Novodvinsk** Rus. Fed.
152	C3	**Novo Hamburgo** Brazil
154	C2	**Novo Horizonte** Brazil
90	B1	**Novohrad-Volyns'kyy** Ukr.
103	D2	**Novo Mesto** Slovenia
91	D3	**Novomikhaylovskiy** Rus. Fed.
89	E3	**Novomoskovsk** Rus. Fed.
91	D2	**Novomoskovs'k** Ukr.
91	C2	**Novomyrhorod** Ukr.
91	C2	**Novooleksiyivka** Ukr.
91	D2	**Novopskov** Ukr.
91	D3	**Novorossiysk** Rus. Fed.
88	C2	**Novorzhev** Rus. Fed.
87	E3	**Novosergiyevka** Rus. Fed.
91	D2	**Novoshakhtinsk** Rus. Fed.
82	G3	**Novosibirsk** Rus. Fed.
		Novosibirskiye Ostrova is Rus. Fed. see **New Siberia Islands**
89	E3	**Novosil'** Rus. Fed.
89	D2	**Novosokol'niki** Rus. Fed.
91	C2	**Novotroyits'ke** Ukr.
91	C2	**Novoukrayinka** Ukr.
90	A1	**Novovolyns'k** Ukr.
91	D1	**Novozybkov** Rus. Fed.
103	D2	**Nový Jičín** Czech Rep.
86	E2	**Novyy Bor** Rus. Fed.
91	D1	**Novyy Oskol** Rus. Fed.

86 G2	**Novyy Port** Rus. Fed.
82 G2	**Novyy Urengoy** Rus. Fed.
69 E1	**Novyy Urgal** Rus. Fed.
103 D1	**Nowogard** Pol.
53 D2	**Nowra** Austr.
81 D2	**Nowshahr** Iran
74 B1	**Nowshera** Pak.
103 E2	**Nowy Sącz** Pol.
103 E2	**Nowy Targ** Pol.
87 G2	**Noyabr'sk** Rus. Fed.
105 C2	**Noyon** France
68 C2	**Noyon** Mongolia
121 C2	**Nsanje** Malawi
118 B3	**Ntandembele** Dem. Rep. Congo
111 B3	**Ntoro, Kavo** *pt* Greece
119 D3	**Ntungamo** Uganda
79 C2	**Nu'aym** *reg.* Oman
116 B2	**Nubian Desert** Sudan
150 A3	**Nudo Coropuna** *mt.* Peru
129 E1	**Nueltin Lake** Can.
153 A5	**Nueva Lubecka** Arg.
145 B2	**Nueva Rosita** Mex.
144 B1	**Nuevo Casas Grandes** Mex.
144 B2	**Nuevo Ideal** Mex.
145 C2	**Nuevo Laredo** Mex.
117 C4	**Nugaal** *watercourse* Somalia
105 C2	**Nuits-St-Georges** France
	Nu Jiang *r.* China/Myanmar *see* Salween
49 G4	**Nuku'alofa** Tonga
49 I3	**Nuku Hiva** *i.* Fr. Polynesia
76 B2	**Nukus** Uzbek.
50 B2	**Nullagine** Austr.
50 B3	**Nullarbor Plain** Austr.
115 D4	**Numan** Nigeria
67 C3	**Numazu** Japan
93 E3	**Numedal** *val.* Norway
59 C3	**Numfoor** *i.* Indon.
53 C3	**Numurkah** Austr.
	Nunap Isua *c.* Greenland *see* Farewell, Cape
127 G3	**Nunavik** *reg.* Can.
129 E1	**Nunavut** *admin. div.* Can.
99 C2	**Nuneaton** U.K.
106 B1	**Nuñomoral** Spain
108 A2	**Nuoro** *Sardegna* Italy
78 B2	**Nuqrah** Saudi Arabia
101 E3	**Nuremberg** Ger.
74 B1	**Nürestän** Afgh.
52 A2	**Nuriootpa** Austr.
92 I3	**Nurmes** Fin.
	Nürnberg Ger. *see* **Nuremberg**
62 A1	**Nu Shan** *mts* China
74 A2	**Nushki** Pak.
127 H2	**Nuuk** Greenland
127 H2	**Nuussuaq** Greenland
127 H2	**Nuussuaq** *pen.* Greenland
78 A2	**Nuwaybi' al Muzayyinah** Egypt
122 B3	**Nuweveldberge** *mts* S. Africa
86 F2	**Nyagan'** Rus. Fed.
75 D1	**Nyainqêntanglha Feng** *mt.* China
75 D2	**Nyainqêntanglha Shan** *mts* China
117 A3	**Nyala** Sudan
86 D2	**Nyandoma** Rus. Fed.
118 B3	**Nyanga** *r.* Gabon
121 C2	**Nyanga** Zimbabwe
121 C1	**Nyasa, Lake** Africa
93 F4	**Nyborg** Denmark
92 I1	**Nyborg** Norway
93 G4	**Nybro** Sweden
119 D3	**Nyeri** Kenya
75 C1	**Nyima** China
68 C3	**Nyingchi** China

103 E2	**Nyíregyháza** Hungary
93 F4	**Nykøbing** Denmark
93 G4	**Nyköping** Sweden
53 C2	**Nymagee** Austr.
93 G4	**Nynäshamn** Sweden
53 C2	**Nyngan** Austr.
88 B3	**Nyoman** *r.* Belarus/Lith.
105 D3	**Nyons** France
86 E2	**Nyrob** Rus. Fed.
134 C2	**Nyssa** U.S.A.
119 C3	**Nyunzu** Dem. Rep. Congo
91 C2	**Nyzhn'ohirs'kyy** Ukr.
119 D3	**Nzega** Tanz.
114 B4	**Nzérékoré** Guinea
120 A1	**N'zeto** Angola

O

136 C2	**Oahe, Lake** U.S.A.
124 E5	**O'ahu** *i.* U.S.A.
52 B2	**Oakbank** Austr.
142 B2	**Oakdale** U.S.A.
53 D1	**Oakey** Austr.
134 B1	**Oak Harbor** U.S.A.
140 C3	**Oak Hill** U.S.A.
135 B3	**Oakland** U.S.A.
50 B2	**Oakover** *r.* Austr.
134 B2	**Oakridge** U.S.A.
143 D1	**Oak Ridge** U.S.A.
54 B3	**Oamaru** N.Z.
64 B1	**Oas** Phil.
145 C3	**Oaxaca** Mex.
86 F2	**Ob'** *r.* Rus. Fed.
118 B2	**Obala** Cameroon
96 B2	**Oban** U.K.
106 B1	**O Barco** Spain
53 C2	**Oberon** Austr.
101 F3	**Oberpfälzer Wald** *mts* Ger.
101 F3	**Oberviechtach** Ger.
59 C3	**Obi** *i.* Indon.
151 C2	**Óbidos** Brazil
66 D2	**Obihiro** Japan
69 E1	**Obluch'ye** Rus. Fed.
89 E2	**Obninsk** Rus. Fed.
119 C2	**Obo** C.A.R.
117 C3	**Obock** Djibouti
118 B3	**Obouya** Congo
89 E3	**Oboyan'** Rus. Fed.
144 B2	**Obregón, Presa** *resr* Mex.
109 D2	**Obrenovac** Serbia
87 E3	**Obshchiy Syrt** *hills* Kazakh./Rus. Fed.
86 D2	**Obskaya Guba** *sea chan.* Rus. Fed.
114 B4	**Obuasi** Ghana
90 C1	**Obukhiv** Ukr.
86 D2	**Ob'yachevo** Rus. Fed.
143 D3	**Ocala** U.S.A.
144 B2	**Ocampo** Mex.
106 C2	**Ocaña** Spain
150 A1	**Occidental, Cordillera** *mts* Col.
150 A3	**Occidental, Cordillera** *mts* Peru
141 D3	**Ocean City** U.S.A.
128 B3	**Ocean Falls** Can.
135 C4	**Oceanside** U.S.A.
91 C2	**Ochakiv** Ukr.
86 E3	**Ocher** Rus. Fed.
101 E3	**Ochsenfurt** Ger.
143 D2	**Oconee** *r.* U.S.A.
145 C3	**Ocosingo** Mex.
58 C3	**Ocussi** *enclave* East Timor
116 B2	**Oda, Jebel** *mt.* Sudan
66 D2	**Ōdate** Japan

67 C3	**Odawara** Japan
93 E3	**Odda** Norway
106 B2	**Odemira** Port.
111 C3	**Ödemiş** Turkey
93 F4	**Odense** Denmark
101 D3	**Odenwald** *reg.* Ger.
102 C1	**Oderbucht** *b.* Ger.
	Odesa Ukr. *see* **Odessa**
90 C2	**Odessa** Ukr.
139 C2	**Odessa** U.S.A.
114 B4	**Odienné** Côte d'Ivoire
103 D2	**Odra** *r.* Ger./Pol.
151 D2	**Oeiras** Brazil
100 D2	**Oelde** Ger.
136 C2	**Oelrichs** U.S.A.
101 F2	**Oelsnitz** Ger.
100 B1	**Oenkerk** Neth.
109 C2	**Ofanto** *r.* Italy
101 D2	**Offenbach am Main** Ger.
101 C2	**Offenburg** Ger.
117 C4	**Ogadēn** *reg.* Eth.
66 C3	**Oga-hantō** *pen.* Japan
67 C3	**Ōgaki** Japan
136 C2	**Ogallala** U.S.A.
115 C4	**Ogbomosho** Nigeria
134 D2	**Ogden** U.S.A.
141 D2	**Ogdensburg** U.S.A.
126 B2	**Ogilvie** *r.* Can.
126 B2	**Ogilvie Mountains** Can.
143 D2	**Oglethorpe, Mount** U.S.A.
130 B1	**Ogoki** *r.* Can.
130 B1	**Ogoki Reservoir** Can.
88 B2	**Ogre** Latvia
109 C1	**Ogulin** Croatia
140 C3	**Ohio** *r.* U.S.A.
140 C2	**Ohio** *state* U.S.A.
101 E2	**Ohrdruf** Ger.
109 D2	**Ohrid** Macedonia
151 C1	**Oiapoque** Brazil
141 D2	**Oil City** U.S.A.
100 A3	**Oise** *r.* France
67 B4	**Ōita** Japan
144 B2	**Ojinaga** Mex.
152 B3	**Ojos del Salado, Nevado** *mt.* Arg./Chile
89 H5	**Oka** *r.* Rus. Fed.
120 A3	**Okahandja** Namibia
120 A3	**Okakarara** Namibia
128 C3	**Okanagan Falls** Can.
128 C3	**Okanagan Lake** Can.
134 C1	**Okanogan** U.S.A.
134 C1	**Okanogan** *r.* U.S.A.
74 B1	**Okara** Pak.
120 B2	**Okavango** *r.* Africa
120 B2	**Okavango Delta** *swamp* Botswana
67 C3	**Okaya** Japan
67 B4	**Okayama** Japan
67 C4	**Okazaki** Japan
143 D3	**Okeechobee, Lake** U.S.A.
143 D2	**Okefenokee Swamp** U.S.A.
99 A3	**Okehampton** U.K.
74 A2	**Okha** India
83 K3	**Okha** Rus. Fed.
75 C2	**Okhaldhunga** Nepal
83 K3	**Okhotka** *r.* Rus. Fed.
83 K3	**Okhotsk** Rus. Fed.
156 C2	**Okhotsk, Sea of** Japan/Rus. Fed.
91 C1	**Okhtyrka** Ukr.
69 E3	**Okinawa** *i.* Japan
67 B3	**Oki-shotō** *is* Japan
139 D1	**Oklahoma** *state* U.S.A.
139 D1	**Oklahoma City** U.S.A.
139 D1	**Okmulgee** U.S.A.
78 A2	**Oko, Wadi** *watercourse* Sudan
118 B3	**Okondja** Gabon

28 C2 Okotoks Can.
89 D3 Okovskiy Les *for.* Rus. Fed.
18 A3 Okoyo Congo
92 H1 Øksfjord Norway
62 A2 Oktwin Myanmar
86 D2 Oktyabr'skiy *Arkhangel'skaya Oblast'* Rus. Fed.
83 L3 Oktyabr'skiy *Kamchatskiy Kray* Rus. Fed.
87 E3 Oktyabr'skiy *Respublika Bashkortostan* Rus. Fed.
86 F2 Oktyabr'skoye Rus. Fed.
83 H1 Oktyabr'skoy Revolyutsii, Ostrov *i.* Rus. Fed.
87 D2 Okulovka Rus. Fed.
66 C2 Okushiri-tō *i.* Japan
93 A3 Ólafsvík Iceland
93 G4 Öland *i.* Sweden
52 B2 Olary Austr.
153 B4 Olavarría Arg.
103 D1 Oława Pol.
108 A2 Olbia *Sardegna* Italy
126 B2 Old Crow Can.
101 D1 Oldenburg Ger.
102 C1 Oldenburg in Holstein Ger.
100 C1 Oldenzaal Neth.
97 D3 Old Head of Kinsale Ireland
128 C2 Olds Can.
129 D2 Old Wives Lake Can.
141 D2 Olean U.S.A.
103 E1 Olecko Pol.
83 J2 Olekminsk Rus. Fed.
91 C2 Oleksandriya Ukr.
86 C2 Olenegorsk Rus. Fed.
83 I2 Olenek Rus. Fed.
83 I2 Olenek *r.* Rus. Fed.
89 D2 Olenino Rus. Fed.
90 B1 Olevs'k Ukr.
106 B2 Olhão Port.
122 A2 Olifants *watercourse* Namibia
123 D1 Olifants S. Africa
123 D1 Olifants *r. Northern* S. Africa
122 A3 Olifants *r. W. Cape* S. Africa
154 C2 Olifantshoek S. Africa
154 C2 Olímpia Brazil
123 B1 Olinda Brazil
123 E1 Oliphants Drift Botswana
107 C2 Oliva Spain
155 B2 Oliveira Brazil
106 B2 Olivenza Spain
152 B3 Ollagüe Chile
150 A2 Olmos Peru
140 B3 Olney U.S.A.
103 D2 Olomouc Czech Rep.
64 B1 Olongapo Phil.
104 B3 Oloron-Ste-Marie France
107 D1 Olot Spain
69 D1 Olovyannaya Rus. Fed.
83 L2 Oloy *r.* Rus. Fed.
100 C2 Olpe Ger.
103 E1 Olsztyn Pol.
110 E2 Olt *r.* Romania
81 C1 Oltu Turkey
111 B3 Olympia *tourist site* Greece
134 B1 Olympia U.S.A.
134 B1 Olympus, Mount U.S.A.
83 M3 Olyutorskiy, Mys *c.* Rus. Fed.
97 C1 Omagh U.K.
137 D2 Omaha U.S.A.
79 C2 Oman *country* Asia
79 C2 Oman, Gulf of Asia
120 A3 Omaruru Namibia
120 A2 Omatako *watercourse* Namibia
116 B3 Omdurman Sudan
53 C3 Omeo Austr.
145 C3 Ometepec Mex.

78 A3 Om Hajèr Eritrea
128 B2 Omineca Mountains Can.
100 C1 Ommen Neth.
83 L2 Omolon *r.* Rus. Fed.
100 B3 Omont France
82 F3 Omsk Rus. Fed.
86 C2 Omsukchan Rus. Fed.
67 A4 Ōmura Japan
141 D3 Onancock U.S.A.
140 C1 Onaping Lake Can.
131 C2 Onatchiway, Lac *l.* Can.
120 A2 Oncócua Angola
122 B3 Onderstedorings S. Africa
120 A2 Ondjiva Angola
86 C2 Onega Rus. Fed.
86 C2 Onega *r.* Rus. Fed.
Onega, Lake *l.* Rus. Fed. *see*
Onezhskoye Ozero
141 D2 Oneida Lake U.S.A.
137 D2 O'Neill U.S.A.
141 D2 Oneonta U.S.A.
110 C1 Oneşti Romania
86 C2 Onezhskoye Ozero *l.* Rus. Fed.
122 B3 Ongers *watercourse* S. Africa
65 B2 Ongjin N. Korea
73 C3 Ongole India
121 D3 Onilahy *r.* Madag.
115 C4 Onitsha Nigeria
122 A2 Onseepkans S. Africa
50 A2 Onslow Austr.
143 E2 Onslow Bay U.S.A.
130 A1 Ontario *prov.* Can.
134 C2 Ontario U.S.A.
141 D2 Ontario, Lake Can./U.S.A.
51 C2 Oodnadatta Austr.
Oostende Belgium *see* Ostend
100 B2 Oosterhout Neth.
100 A2 Oosterschelde *est.* Neth.
100 B1 Oost-Vlieland Neth.
128 B2 Ootsa Lake Can.
128 B2 Ootsa Lake *l.* Can.
118 C3 Opala Dem. Rep. Congo
130 C1 Opataca, Lac *l.* Can.
103 D2 Opava Czech Rep.
143 C2 Opelika U.S.A.
142 B2 Opelousas U.S.A.
130 C1 Opinaca, Réservoir *resr* Can.
131 D1 Opiscotéo, Lac *l.* Can.
88 C2 Opochka Rus. Fed.
144 A2 Opodepe Mex.
103 D1 Opole Pol.
106 B1 Oporto Port.
54 C1 Opotiki N.Z.
93 E3 Oppdal Norway
54 B1 Opunake N.Z.
120 A2 Opuwo Namibia
110 B1 Oradea Romania
Orahovac Kosovo *see*
Rahovec
114 B1 Oran Alg.
152 B3 Oran Arg.
65 B1 Ŏrang N. Korea
53 C2 Orange Austr.
105 C3 Orange France
122 A2 Orange *r.* Namibia/S. Africa
139 E2 Orange U.S.A.
143 D2 Orangeburg U.S.A.
140 C2 Orangeville Can.
101 F1 Oranienburg Ger.
122 A2 Oranjemund Namibia
120 B3 Orapa Botswana
110 B1 Orăştie Romania
108 B2 Orbetello Italy
53 C3 Orbost Austr.
50 B1 Ord, Mount *h.* Austr.

106 B1 Ordes Spain
70 B2 Ordos China
80 B1 Ordu Turkey
Ordzhonikidze Rus. Fed. *see*
Vladikavkaz
91 C2 Ordzhonikidze Ukr.
93 G4 Örebro Sweden
134 B2 Oregon *state* U.S.A.
134 B1 Oregon City U.S.A.
87 C3 Orekhovo-Zuyevo Rus. Fed.
89 E3 Orel Rus. Fed.
83 K3 Orel', Ozero *l.* Rus. Fed.
135 D3 Orem U.S.A.
111 C3 Ören Turkey
87 E3 Orenburg Rus. Fed.
54 A3 Orepuki N.Z.
93 F4 Öresund *str.*
Denmark/Sweden
99 D3 Orford Ness *hd* U.K.
111 C3 Orhaneli Turkey
111 C3 Orhangazi Turkey
83 I3 Orhon Gol *r.* Mongolia
152 B2 Oriental, Cordillera *mts* Bol.
150 A1 Oriental, Cordillera *mts* Col.
150 A3 Oriental, Cordillera *mts* Peru
107 C2 Orihuela Spain
91 D2 Orikhiv Ukr.
130 C2 Orillia Can.
150 B1 Orinoco *r.* Col./Venez.
150 B1 Orinoco Delta Venez.
93 H4 Orissaare Estonia
108 A3 Oristano *Sardegna* Italy
93 I3 Orivesi *l.* Fin.
151 C2 Oriximiná Brazil
145 C3 Orizaba Mex.
145 C3 Orizaba, Pico de *vol.* Mex.
92 E3 Orkanger Norway
93 F4 Örkelljunga Sweden
92 E3 Orkla *r.* Norway
96 C1 Orkney Islands U.K.
154 C2 Orlândia Brazil
141 D3 Orlando U.S.A.
104 C2 Orléans France
74 A2 Ormara Pak.
64 B1 Ormoc Phil.
98 B2 Ormskirk U.K.
92 G3 Örnsköldsvik Sweden
114 B3 Orodara Burkina
134 C1 Orofino U.S.A.
Oroqen Zizhiqi China *see*
Alihe
64 B2 Oroquieta Phil.
108 A2 Orosei *Sardegna* Italy
108 A2 Orosei, Golfo di *b. Sardegna* Italy
103 E2 Orosháza Hungary
135 B3 Oroville U.S.A.
52 A2 Orroroo Austr.
89 D3 Orsha Belarus
87 E3 Orsk Rus. Fed.
93 E3 Ørsta Norway
106 B1 Ortegal, Cabo *c.* Spain
104 B3 Orthez France
106 B1 Ortigueira Spain
137 D1 Ortonville U.S.A.
83 J2 Orulgan, Khrebet *mts* Rus. Fed.
Orūmīyeh, Daryācheh-ye *salt l.* Iran *see* Urmia, Lake
152 B2 Oruro Bol.
108 B2 Orvieto Italy
146 B4 Osa, Península de *pen.* Costa Rica
137 E3 Osage *r.* U.S.A.
67 C4 Osaka Japan
101 E1 Oschersleben (Bode) Ger.
108 A2 Oschiri *Sardegna* Italy

89 E3 Osetr r. Rus. Fed.
77 D2 Osh Kyrg.
120 A2 Oshakati Namibia
130 C2 Oshawa Can.
66 C2 Ō-shima i. Japan
67 C4 Ō-shima i. Japan
140 B2 Oshkosh U.S.A.
81 C2 Oshnoviyeh Iran
115 C4 Oshogbo Nigeria
118 B3 Oshwe Dem. Rep. Congo
109 C1 Osijek Croatia
128 B2 Osilinka r. Can.
108 B2 Osimo Italy
123 D2 Osizweni S. Africa
137 E2 Oskaloosa U.S.A.
93 G4 Oskarshamn Sweden
89 E3 Oskol r. Rus. Fed.
93 F4 Oslo Norway
93 F4 Oslofjorden sea chan. Norway
80 B1 Osmancık Turkey
111 C2 Osmaneli Turkey
80 B2 Osmaniye Turkey
88 C2 Os'mino Rus. Fed.
100 D1 Osnabrück Ger.
153 A5 Osorno Chile
106 C1 Osorno Spain
128 C3 Osoyoos Can.
100 B2 Oss Neth.
51 D4 Ossa, Mount Austr.
83 L3 Ossora Rus. Fed.
89 D2 Ostashkov Rus. Fed.
101 D1 Oste r. Ger.
100 A2 Ostend Belgium
101 E1 Osterburg (Altmark) Ger.
93 F3 Österdalälven r. Sweden
101 D1 Osterholz-Scharmbeck Ger.
101 E2 Osterode am Harz Ger.
92 F3 Östersund Sweden
Ostfriesische Inseln is Ger. see East Frisian Islands
100 C1 Ostfriesland reg. Ger.
93 G3 Östhammar Sweden
103 D2 Ostrava Czech Rep.
103 D1 Ostróda Pol.
89 E3 Ostrogozhsk Rus. Fed.
103 E1 Ostrołęka Pol.
101 F2 Ostrov Czech Rep.
88 C2 Ostrov Rus. Fed.
103 E1 Ostrowiec Świętokrzyski Pol.
103 E1 Ostrów Mazowiecka Pol.
103 D1 Ostrów Wielkopolski Pol.
110 B2 Osüm r. Bulg.
67 B4 Ōsumi-kaikyō sea chan. Japan
67 B4 Ōsumi-shotō is Japan
106 B2 Osuna Spain
141 D2 Oswego U.S.A.
99 B2 Oswestry U.K.
67 C3 Ōta Japan
54 B3 Otago Peninsula N.Z.
54 C2 Otaki N.Z.
66 D2 Otaru Japan
120 A2 Otavi Namibia
134 C1 Othello U.S.A.
120 A3 Otjiwarongo Namibia
117 B3 Otoro, Jebel mt. Sudan
93 E4 Otra r. Norway
109 C2 Otranto, Strait of Albania/Italy
67 C3 Ōtsu Japan
93 E3 Otta Norway
130 C2 Ottawa Can.
130 C2 Ottawa r. Can.
140 B2 Ottawa IL U.S.A.
137 D3 Ottawa KS U.S.A.
130 B1 Otter Rapids Can.
100 B2 Ottignies Belgium

137 E2 Ottumwa U.S.A.
150 A2 Otuzco Peru
52 B3 Otway, Cape Austr.
142 B2 Ouachita r. U.S.A.
142 B2 Ouachita, Lake U.S.A.
142 B2 Ouachita Mountains U.S.A.
118 C2 Ouadda C.A.R.
115 D3 Ouaddaï reg. Chad
114 B3 Ouagadougou Burkina
114 B3 Ouahigouya Burkina
118 A3 Oualâta Maur.
118 C2 Ouanda-Djalé C.A.R.
114 B2 Ouarâne reg. Maur.
115 C1 Ouargla Alg.
114 B1 Ouarzazate Morocco
100 A2 Oudenaarde Belgium
122 B3 Oudtshoorn S. Africa
107 C2 Oued Tlélat Alg.
104 A2 Ouessant, Île d' i. France
118 B2 Ouesso Congo
114 B1 Oujda Morocco
107 D2 Ouled Farès Alg.
92 I2 Oulu Fin.
92 I3 Oulujärvi l. Fin.
108 A1 Oulx Italy
115 E3 Oum-Chalouba Chad
115 D3 Oum-Hadjer Chad
115 E3 Ounianga Kébir Chad
100 B2 Oupeye Belgium
106 B1 Ourense Spain
154 C2 Ourinhos Brazil
151 D3 Ouro Preto Brazil
100 B2 Ourthe r. Belgium
98 C2 Ouse r. U.K.
131 D2 Outardes, Rivière aux r. Can.
131 D1 Outardes Quatre, Réservoir resr Can.
96 A2 Outer Hebrides is U.K.
120 A3 Outjo Namibia
129 D2 Outlook Can.
92 I3 Outokumpu Fin.
52 B3 Ouyen Austr.
106 B1 Ovar Port.
92 H2 Överkalix Sweden
135 D3 Overton U.S.A.
92 H2 Övertorneå Sweden
106 B1 Oviedo Spain
93 E3 Øvre Årdal Norway
93 F3 Øvre Rendal Norway
90 B1 Ovruch Ukr.
118 B3 Owando Congo
67 C4 Owase Japan
137 E2 Owatonna U.S.A.
140 B3 Owensboro U.S.A.
135 C3 Owens Lake U.S.A.
130 B2 Owen Sound Can.
115 C4 Owerri Nigeria
140 C2 Owosso U.S.A.
134 C2 Owyhee U.S.A.
134 C2 Owyhee r. U.S.A.
54 B2 Oxford N.Z.
99 C3 Oxford U.K.
142 C2 Oxford U.S.A.
129 E2 Oxford Lake Can.
52 A2 Oxley Austr.
97 B1 Ox Mountains hills Ireland
135 C4 Oxnard U.S.A.
67 C3 Oyama Japan
118 B2 Oyem Gabon
129 C2 Oyen Can.
105 D2 Oyonnax France
64 B2 Ozamiz Phil.
142 C2 Ozark U.S.A.
137 E3 Ozark Plateau U.S.A.
137 E3 Ozarks, Lake of the U.S.A.
83 L3 Ozernovskiy Rus. Fed.
88 B3 Ozersk Rus. Fed.

89 E3 Ozery Rus. Fed.
87 D3 Ozinki Rus. Fed.

P

127 H2 Paamiut Greenland
122 A3 Paarl S. Africa
103 D1 Pabianice Pol.
75 C2 Pabna Bangl.
74 A2 Pab Range mts Pak.
109 C3 Pachino Sicilia Italy
145 C3 Pachuca Mex.
156 Pacific Ocean
103 D1 Paczków Pol.
60 B2 Padang Indon.
60 B1 Padang Endau Malaysia
60 B2 Padangpanjang Indon.
60 A1 Padangsidimpuan Indon.
101 D2 Paderborn Ger.
Padova Italy see Padua
139 D3 Padre Island U.S.A.
52 B3 Padthaway Austr.
108 B1 Padua Italy
140 B3 Paducah KY U.S.A.
139 C2 Paducah TX U.S.A.
65 B1 Paegam N. Korea
65 A2 Paengnyŏng-do i. S. Korea
54 C1 Paeroa N.Z.
Pafos Cyprus see Paphos
109 C2 Pag Croatia
64 B2 Pagadian Phil.
60 B2 Pagai Selatan i. Indon.
60 B2 Pagai Utara i. Indon.
59 D1 Pagan i. N. Mariana Is
61 C2 Pagatan Indon.
138 A1 Page U.S.A.
88 B2 Pagegiai Lith.
136 B3 Pagosa Springs U.S.A.
88 C2 Paide Estonia
93 I3 Päijänne l. Fin.
75 C2 Paikü Co l. China
138 A1 Painted Desert U.S.A.
96 B3 Paisley U.K.
92 H2 Pajala Sweden
150 B1 Pakaraima Mountains S. America
150 C1 Pakaraima Mountains S. America
74 A2 Pakistan country Asia
62 A1 Pakokku Myanmar
88 B2 Pakruojis Lith.
103 D2 Paks Hungary
130 A1 Pakwash Lake Can.
62 B2 Pakxan Laos
63 B2 Pakxé Laos
115 D4 Pala Chad
60 B2 Palabuhanratu, Teluk b. Indon.
111 B3 Palaikastro Greece
111 B3 Palaiochora Greece
122 B1 Palamakoloi Botswana
107 D1 Palamós Spain
83 L3 Palana Rus. Fed.
64 B1 Palanan Phil.
61 C2 Palangkaraya Indon.
74 B2 Palanpur India
120 B3 Palapye Botswana
83 L2 Palatka Rus. Fed.
143 D3 Palatka U.S.A.
59 C2 Palau country N. Pacific Ocean
63 A2 Palaw Myanmar
64 A2 Palawan i. Phil.
93 H4 Paldiski Estonia
60 B2 Palembang Indon.
106 C1 Palencia Spain

145 C3 **Palenque** Mex.
108 B3 **Palermo** *Sicilia* Italy
139 D2 **Palestine** U.S.A.
62 A1 **Paletwa** Myanmar
74 B2 **Pali** India
48 E2 **Palikir** Micronesia
109 C2 **Palinuro, Capo** c. Italy
111 B3 **Paliouri, Akrotirio** pt Greece
100 B3 **Paliseul** Belgium
92 I3 **Paljakka** h. Fin.
88 C2 **Palkino** Rus. Fed.
73 B4 **Palk Strait** India/Sri Lanka
54 C2 **Palliser, Cape** N.Z.
49 I3 **Palliser, Îles** is Fr. Polynesia
106 B2 **Palma del Río** Spain
107 D2 **Palma de Mallorca** Spain
154 B3 **Palmas** Brazil
151 D1 **Palmas** Brazil
114 B4 **Palmas, Cape** Liberia
154 C3 **Palmeira** Brazil
151 D2 **Palmeirais** Brazil
55 P2 **Palmer Land** reg. Antarctica
54 C2 **Palmerston North** N.Z.
109 C3 **Palmi** Italy
145 C2 **Palmillas** Mex.
150 A1 **Palmira** Col.
135 C4 **Palm Springs** U.S.A.
49 H2 **Palmyra Atoll** N. Pacific Ocean
117 B3 **Paloich** Sudan
145 C3 **Palomares** Mex.
107 C2 **Palos, Cabo de** c. Spain
92 I3 **Paltamo** Fin.
58 B3 **Palu** Indon.
83 M2 **Palyavaam** r. Rus. Fed.
104 C3 **Pamiers** France
77 D3 **Pamir** mts Asia
143 E1 **Pamlico Sound** sea chan. U.S.A.
152 B4 **Pampa Grande** Bol.
154 B4 **Pampas** reg. Arg.
150 A1 **Pamplona** Col.
107 D1 **Pamplona** Spain
111 D2 **Pamukova** Turkey
60 B2 **Panaitan** i. Indon.
73 B3 **Panaji** India
84 B4 **Panama** country Central America
146 C4 **Panamá, Canal de** Panama
146 C4 **Panama, Gulf of** Panama
146 C4 **Panama City** Panama
142 C2 **Panama City** U.S.A.
135 C3 **Panamint Range** mts U.S.A.
61 B1 **Panarik** Indon.
64 B2 **Panay** i. Phil.
109 C2 **Pančevo** Serbia
64 B3 **Pandan** Phil.
75 C2 **Pandaria** India
73 B3 **Pandharpur** India
88 B2 **Panevėžys** Lith.
61 C2 **Pangkalanbuun** Indon.
60 A1 **Pangkalansusu** Indon.
60 B2 **Pangkalpinang** Indon.
127 G2 **Pangnirtung** Can.
86 C2 **Pangody** Rus. Fed.
89 F3 **Panino** Rus. Fed.
74 B2 **Panipat** India
74 A2 **Panjgur** Pak.
65 C1 **Pan Ling** mts China
75 C2 **Panna** India
50 A2 **Pannawonica** Austr.
154 B2 **Panorama** Brazil
65 B1 **Panshi** China
45 C2 **Pánuco** Mex.
71 A3 **Panxian** China
62 B1 **Panzhihua** China
109 C3 **Paola** Italy

63 B2 **Paôy Pêt** Cambodia
103 D2 **Pápa** Hungary
54 B1 **Papakura** N.Z.
145 C2 **Papantla** Mex.
49 I4 **Papeete** Fr. Polynesia
100 C1 **Papenburg** Ger.
80 B2 **Paphos** Cyprus
59 D3 **Papua, Gulf of** P.N.G.
59 D3 **Papua New Guinea** country Oceania
50 **Paraburdoo** Austr.
154 C1 **Paracatu** Brazil
155 C1 **Paracatu** r. Brazil
52 A2 **Parachilna** Austr.
109 D2 **Paraćin** Serbia
155 D1 **Pará de Minas** Brazil
135 B3 **Paradise** U.S.A.
142 B3 **Paragould** U.S.A.
151 C3 **Paraguai** r. Brazil
152 C3 **Paraguay** r. Arg./Para.
152 C3 **Paraguay** country S. America
154 B1 **Paraíba do Sul** r. Brazil
154 B1 **Paraíso** Brazil
145 C3 **Paraíso** Mex.
114 C4 **Parakou** Benin
151 C1 **Paramaribo** Suriname
83 L3 **Paramushir, Ostrov** i. Rus. Fed.
152 B4 **Paraná** Arg.
154 A3 **Paraná** r. S. America
154 C3 **Paranaguá** Brazil
154 B1 **Paranaíba** Brazil
154 B2 **Paranaíba** r. Brazil
154 B2 **Paranapanema** r. Brazil
154 B2 **Paranapiacaba, Serra** mts Brazil
154 B2 **Paranavaí** Brazil
54 B2 **Paraparaumu** N.Z.
155 D2 **Parati** Brazil
154 B1 **Paraúna** Brazil
105 C2 **Paray-le-Monial** France
73 B3 **Parbhani** India
101 E1 **Parchim** Ger.
155 E1 **Pardo** r. *Bahia* Brazil
154 B2 **Pardo** r. *Mato Grosso do Sul* Brazil
154 C2 **Pardo** r. *São Paulo* Brazil
103 D1 **Pardubice** Czech Rep.
150 B3 **Parecis, Serra dos** hills Brazil
130 C2 **Parent, Lac** l. Can.
58 B3 **Parepare** Indon.
89 D2 **Parfino** Rus. Fed.
111 B3 **Parga** Greece
109 C3 **Parghelia** Italy
147 D3 **Paria, Gulf of** Trin. and Tob./Venez.
150 B1 **Parima, Serra** mts Brazil
151 C2 **Parintins** Brazil
104 C2 **Paris** France
142 C1 **Paris** TN U.S.A.
139 D2 **Paris** TX U.S.A.
93 H3 **Parkano** Fin.
138 A2 **Parker** U.S.A.
140 C3 **Parkersburg** U.S.A.
53 C2 **Parkes** Austr.
140 A1 **Park Falls** U.S.A.
137 D1 **Park Rapids** U.S.A.
108 B2 **Parma** Italy
151 D2 **Parnaíba** Brazil
151 D2 **Parnaíba** r. Brazil
54 B2 **Parnassus** N.Z.
111 B3 **Parnonas** mts Greece
88 B2 **Pärnu** Estonia
65 B2 **P'aro-ho** l. S. Korea
52 B2 **Paroo** watercourse Austr.
111 C3 **Paros** i. Greece
144 B2 **Parras** Mex.

126 C2 **Parry, Cape** Can.
126 D1 **Parry Islands** Can.
130 B2 **Parry Sound** Can.
137 D3 **Parsons** U.S.A.
101 D2 **Partenstein** Ger.
104 B2 **Parthenay** France
97 B2 **Partry Mountains** hills Ireland
151 C2 **Paru** r. Brazil
135 C4 **Pasadena** U.S.A.
62 A2 **Pasawng** Myanmar
142 C2 **Pascagoula** U.S.A.
110 C1 **Pașcani** Romania
134 C1 **Pasco** U.S.A.
102 C2 **Pasewalk** Ger.
129 D2 **Pasfield Lake** Can.
60 B1 **Pasir Putih** Malaysia
74 A2 **Pasni** Pak.
153 A5 **Paso Río Mayo** Arg.
135 B3 **Paso Robles** U.S.A.
155 D2 **Passa Tempo** Brazil
102 C2 **Passau** Ger.
152 C3 **Passo Fundo** Brazil
155 C2 **Passos** Brazil
88 C2 **Pastavy** Belarus
150 A2 **Pastaza** r. Peru
150 A1 **Pasto** Col.
61 C2 **Pasuruan** Indon.
88 B2 **Pasvalys** Lith.
153 A6 **Patagonia** reg. Arg.
75 C2 **Patan** Nepal
54 B1 **Patea** N.Z.
141 E2 **Paterson** U.S.A.
Pathein Myanmar see **Bassein**
136 B2 **Pathfinder Reservoir** U.S.A.
61 C2 **Pati** Indon.
62 A1 **Patkai Bum** mts India/Myanmar
111 C3 **Patmos** i. Greece
75 C2 **Patna** India
81 C2 **Patnos** Turkey
154 B3 **Pato Branco** Brazil
152 C4 **Patos, Lagoa dos** l. Brazil
155 C1 **Patos de Minas** Brazil
152 B4 **Patquía** Arg.
111 B3 **Patras** Greece
154 C1 **Patrocínio** Brazil
63 B3 **Pattani** Thai.
63 B2 **Pattaya** Thai.
128 B2 **Pattullo, Mount** Can.
129 D2 **Patuanak** Can.
144 B3 **Pátzcuaro** Mex.
104 B3 **Pau** France
104 B2 **Pauillac** France
62 A1 **Pauk** Myanmar
151 D2 **Paulistana** Brazil
151 E2 **Paulo Afonso** Brazil
123 D2 **Paulpietersburg** S. Africa
139 D1 **Pauls Valley** U.S.A.
62 A2 **Paungde** Myanmar
155 C3 **Pavão** Brazil
108 A1 **Pavia** Italy
88 B2 **Pāvilosta** Latvia
110 C2 **Pavlikeni** Bulg.
77 D1 **Pavlodar** Kazakh.
91 D2 **Pavlohrad** Ukr.
91 E1 **Pavlovsk** Rus. Fed.
91 D2 **Pavlovskaya** Rus. Fed.
60 B2 **Payakumbuh** Indon.
134 C2 **Payette** U.S.A.
134 C2 **Payette** r. U.S.A.
86 F2 **Pay-Khoy, Khrebet** hills Rus. Fed.
152 C4 **Paysandú** Uru.
81 C1 **Pazar** Turkey
110 B2 **Pazardzhik** Bulg.
111 C3 **Pazarköy** Turkey

Pazin

108 B1 Pazin Croatia
63 A2 Pe Myanmar
128 C2 Peace r. Can.
128 C2 Peace River Can.
135 E3 Peale, Mount U.S.A.
142 C2 Pearl r. U.S.A.
139 D3 Pearsall U.S.A.
121 C2 Pebane Moz.
Peć Kosovo see Pejë
155 D1 Peçanha Brazil
86 E2 Pechora Rus. Fed.
86 E2 Pechora r. Rus. Fed.
88 C2 Pechory Rus. Fed.
139 C2 Pecos U.S.A.
139 C3 Pecos r. U.S.A.
103 D2 Pécs Hungary
155 D1 Pedra Azul Brazil
154 C2 Pedregulho Brazil
151 D2 Pedreiras Brazil
73 C4 Pedro, Point Sri Lanka
151 D2 Pedro Afonso Brazil
154 B1 Pedro Gomes Brazil
152 C3 Pedro Juan Caballero Para.
96 C3 Peebles U.K.
143 E2 Pee Dee r. U.S.A.
126 C2 Peel r. Can.
98 A1 Peel Isle of Man
128 C2 Peerless Lake Can.
54 B2 Pegasus Bay N.Z.
101 E3 Pegnitz Ger.
62 A2 Pegu Myanmar
62 A2 Pegu Yoma mts Myanmar
153 B4 Pehuajó Arg.
101 E1 Peine Ger.
88 C2 Peipus, Lake Estonia/Rus. Fed.
154 B2 Peixe r. Brazil
109 D2 Pejë Kosovo
61 B2 Pekalongan Indon.
60 B1 Pekan Malaysia
60 B1 Pekanbaru Indon.
Peking China see Beijing
130 B2 Pelee Island Can.
59 C3 Peleng i. Indon.
92 I2 Pelkosenniemi Fin.
122 A2 Pella S. Africa
59 D3 Pelleluhu Islands P.N.G.
92 H2 Pello Fin.
128 A1 Pelly r. Can.
128 A1 Pelly Mountains Can.
152 C4 Pelotas Brazil
152 C3 Pelotas, Rio das r. Brazil
141 F1 Pemadumcook Lake U.S.A.
61 B1 Pemangkat Indon.
60 A1 Pematangsiantar Indon.
121 D2 Pemba Moz.
120 B2 Pemba Zambia
119 D3 Pemba Island Tanz.
137 D1 Pembina r. Can./U.S.A.
130 C2 Pembroke Can.
99 A3 Pembroke U.K.
145 C2 Peña Nevada, Cerro mt. Mex.
154 B2 Penápolis Brazil
106 B1 Peñaranda de Bracamonte Spain
107 C1 Peñarroya mt. Spain
106 B2 Peñarroya-Pueblonuevo Spain
106 B1 Peñas, Cabo de c. Spain
153 A5 Penas, Golfo de g. Chile
134 C1 Pendleton U.S.A.
128 B2 Pendleton Bay Can.
134 C1 Pend Oreille Lake U.S.A.
74 B3 Penganga r. India
123 D1 Penge S. Africa
70 C2 Penglai China
71 A3 Pengshui China
106 B2 Peniche Port.

98 B1 Penicuik U.K.
108 B2 Penne Italy
98 B1 Pennines hills U.K.
141 D2 Pennsylvania state U.S.A.
127 G2 Penny Icecap Can.
141 F2 Penobscot r. U.S.A.
52 B3 Penola Austr.
50 C3 Penong Austr.
49 H3 Penrhyn atoll Cook Is
98 B1 Penrith U.K.
142 C2 Pensacola U.S.A.
55 Q1 Pensacola Mountains Antarctica
61 C1 Pensiangan Sabah Malaysia
128 C3 Penticton Can.
96 C1 Pentland Firth sea chan. U.K.
99 B2 Penygadair h. U.K.
87 D3 Penza Rus. Fed.
99 A3 Penzance U.K.
140 B2 Peoria U.S.A.
107 C1 Perales del Alfambra Spain
51 E2 Percy Isles Austr.
86 F2 Peregrebnoye Rus. Fed.
150 A1 Pereira Col.
154 B2 Pereira Barreto Brazil
90 A2 Peremyshlyany Ukr.
89 E2 Pereslavl'-Zalesskiy Rus. Fed.
91 C1 Pereyaslav-Khmel'nyts'kyy Ukr.
153 B4 Pergamino Arg.
92 H3 Perhonjoki r. Fin.
131 C1 Péribonka, Lac l. Can.
152 B3 Perico Arg.
144 B2 Pericos Mex.
104 C2 Périgueux France
147 C4 Perija, Sierra de mts Venez.
153 A5 Perito Moreno Arg.
101 E1 Perleberg Ger.
86 E3 Perm' Rus. Fed.
52 A2 Pernatty Lagoon imp. l. Austr.
105 C2 Péronne France
145 C3 Perote Mex.
104 C3 Perpignan France
99 A3 Perranporth U.K.
143 D2 Perry FL U.S.A.
143 D2 Perry GA U.S.A.
137 E2 Perry IA U.S.A.
139 C1 Perryton U.S.A.
137 F3 Perryville U.S.A.
99 B2 Pershore U.K.
91 D2 Pershotravens'k Ukr.
Persian Gulf Asia see The Gulf
50 A3 Perth Austr.
96 C2 Perth U.K.
105 D3 Pertuis France
108 A2 Pertusato, Capo c. Corse France
150 A2 Peru country S. America
157 H4 Peru-Chile Trench S. Pacific Ocean
108 B2 Perugia Italy
154 C2 Peruíbe Brazil
100 A2 Péruwelz Belgium
90 C2 Pervomays'k Ukr.
89 F3 Pervomayskiy Rus. Fed.
91 D2 Pervomays'kyy Ukr.
108 B2 Pesaro Italy
108 B2 Pescara Italy
108 B2 Pescara r. Italy
74 B1 Peshawar Pak.
109 D2 Peshkopi Albania
109 C1 Pesnica Slovenia
89 E2 Pestovo Rus. Fed.
144 B3 Petatlán Mex.
140 B2 Petenwell Lake U.S.A.
52 A2 Peterborough Austr.

130 C2 Peterborough Can.
99 C2 Peterborough U.K.
96 D2 Peterhead U.K.
50 B2 Petermann Ranges mts Austr.
129 D2 Peter Pond Lake Can.
128 A2 Petersburg AK U.S.A.
141 D3 Petersburg VA U.S.A.
101 D1 Petershagen Ger.
131 E1 Petit Mécatina r. Can.
145 E2 Peto Mex.
140 C1 Petoskey U.S.A.
80 B2 Petra tourist site Jordan
66 B2 Petra Velikogo, Zaliv b. Rus. Fed.
111 B2 Petrich Bulg.
151 D2 Petrolina Brazil
77 C1 Petropavlovsk Kazakh.
83 L3 Petropavlovsk-Kamchatskiy Rus. Fed.
110 B1 Petroşani Romania
89 F3 Petrovskoye Rus. Fed.
86 C2 Petrozavodsk Rus. Fed.
123 C2 Petrusburg S. Africa
123 C2 Petrus Steyn S. Africa
122 B3 Petrusville S. Africa
89 E2 Petushki Rus. Fed.
61 A1 Peureula Indon.
83 M2 Pevek Rus. Fed.
102 C2 Pforzheim Ger.
102 C2 Pfunds Austria
101 D3 Pfungstadt Ger.
123 C2 Phahameng S. Africa
123 D1 Phalaborwa S. Africa
74 B2 Phalodi India
63 B2 Phang Hoei, San Khao mts Thai.
63 A3 Phangnga Thai.
62 B1 Phăng Xi Păng mt. Vietnam
63 B1 Phan Rang-Thap Cham Vietnam
63 B2 Phan Thiết Vietnam
63 B3 Phatthalung Thai.
62 A2 Phayao Thai.
129 D2 Phelps Lake Can.
143 C2 Phenix City U.S.A.
63 A2 Phet Buri Thai.
63 B2 Phichit Thai.
141 D3 Philadelphia U.S.A.
136 C2 Philip U.S.A.
100 B2 Philippeville Belgium
100 A2 Philippine Neth.
64 B1 Philippines country Asia
64 B1 Philippine Sea N. Pacific Ocean
126 B2 Philip Smith Mountains U.S.A.
122 B3 Philipstown S. Africa
53 C3 Phillip Island Austr.
137 D3 Phillipsburg U.S.A.
123 C2 Phiritona S. Africa
63 B2 Phitsanulok Thai.
63 B2 Phnom Penh Cambodia
Phnum Pénh Cambodia see Phnom Penh
138 A2 Phoenix U.S.A.
49 G3 Phoenix Islands Kiribati
63 B2 Phon Thai.
62 B1 Phôngsali Laos
62 B2 Phônsavan Laos
62 B2 Phrae Thai.
63 A3 Phuket Thai.
62 A2 Phumiphon, Khuan Thai.
63 B2 Phumĭ Sâmraông Cambod.
123 C2 Phuthaditjhaba S. Africa
62 A2 Phyu Myanmar
108 A2 Piacenza Italy
110 C1 Piatra Neamţ Romania
151 D2 Piauí r. Brazil

08 B1 Piave r. Italy
17 B4 Pibor r. Sudan
17 B4 Pibor Post Sudan
42 C2 Picayune U.S.A.
52 B3 Pichanal Arg.
44 A2 Pichilingue Mex.
98 C1 Pickering U.K.
30 A1 Pickle Lake Can.
51 D2 Picos Brazil
53 B5 Pico Truncado Arg.
53 D2 Picton Austr.
50 B3 Piedras, Río de las r. Peru
45 C3 Piedras Negras Guat.
45 B2 Piedras Negras Mex.
45 I3 Pieksämäki Fin.
92 I3 Pielinen l. Fin.
36 C2 Pierre U.S.A.
05 C3 Pierrelatte France
23 D2 Pietermaritzburg S. Africa
10 B1 Pietrosa mt. Romania
28 C2 Pigeon Lake Can.
44 A3 Pigüé Arg.
92 I3 Pihtipudas Fin.
44 C2 Pijijiapan Mex.
36 C3 Pikes Peak U.S.A.
22 A3 Piketberg S. Africa
40 E3 Pikeville U.S.A.
03 D1 Piła Pol.
53 C4 Pilar Arg.
52 C2 Pilar Para.
53 C2 Pilliga Austr.
54 C1 Pilões, Serra dos mts Brazil
50 B3 Pimenta Bueno Brazil
44 A2 Pinamar Arg.
80 B2 Pınarbaşı Turkey
46 B2 Pinar del Río Cuba
03 E1 Pińczów Pol.
51 D2 Pindaré r. Brazil
    Pindos mts Greece see Pindus
    Mountains
11 B1 Pindus Mountains Greece
42 B2 Pine Bluff U.S.A.
50 C1 Pine Creek Austr.
36 B2 Pinedale U.S.A.
86 D2 Pinega Rus. Fed.
29 D2 Pinehouse Lake Can.
11 B3 Pineios r. Greece
23 C1 Pine Point (abandoned) Can.
36 C2 Pine Ridge U.S.A.
23 D2 Pinetown S. Africa
70 B2 Pingdingshan China
71 A3 Pingguo China
71 B3 Pingjiang China
71 C3 Pingliang China
71 C3 P'ingtung Taiwan
71 A3 Pingxiang Guangxi China
71 B3 Pingxiang Jiangxi China
70 B2 Pingyin China
51 D2 Pinheiro Brazil
01 D1 Pinneberg Ger.
45 C3 Pinotepa Nacional Mex.
88 C3 Pinsk Belarus
38 B3 Pioche U.S.A.
19 C3 Piodi Dem. Rep. Congo
03 E1 Pionki Pol.
03 D1 Piotrków Trybunalski Pol.
37 D2 Pipestone U.S.A.
31 C2 Pipmuacan, Réservoir resr
    Can.
54 C2 Piquiri r. Brazil
54 C1 Piracanjuba Brazil
55 C2 Piracicaba Brazil
55 D1 Piracicaba r. Brazil
54 C1 Piraçununga Brazil
11 B3 Piraeus Greece
54 C2 Piraí do Sul Brazil
54 C2 Pirajuí Brazil

154 B1 Piranhas Brazil
151 E2 Piranhas r. Brazil
155 D1 Pirapora Brazil
154 C1 Pires do Rio Brazil
151 D2 Piripiri Brazil
59 C3 Piru Indon.
108 B2 Pisa Italy
152 A2 Pisagua Chile
150 A3 Pisco Peru
102 C2 Písek Czech Rep.
79 D2 Pīshīn Iran
145 D2 Pisté Mex.
109 C2 Pisticci Italy
108 B2 Pistoia Italy
106 C1 Pisuerga r. Spain
134 B2 Pit r. U.S.A.
154 B2 Pitanga Brazil
155 D1 Pitangui Brazil
49 J4 Pitcairn Island i. Pitcairn Is
92 H2 Piteå Sweden
92 H2 Piteälven r. Sweden
110 B2 Piteşti Romania
75 C2 Pithoragarh India
96 C2 Pitlochry U.K.
128 B2 Pitt Island Can.
137 E3 Pittsburg U.S.A.
141 D2 Pittsburgh U.S.A.
141 E2 Pittsfield U.S.A.
53 D1 Pittsworth Austr.
155 C2 Piumhi Brazil
150 A2 Piura Peru
90 C2 Pivdennyy Buh r. Ukr.
131 E2 Placentia Can.
135 B3 Placerville U.S.A.
146 C2 Placetas Cuba
139 C2 Plainview U.S.A.
154 C1 Planaltina Brazil
142 B2 Plaquemine U.S.A.
106 B1 Plasencia Spain
147 C4 Plato Col.
137 D2 Platte r. U.S.A.
141 E2 Plattsburgh U.S.A.
101 F1 Plau Ger.
101 F2 Plauen Ger.
101 F1 Plauer See l. Ger.
89 E3 Plavsk Rus. Fed.
129 E2 Playgreen Lake Can.
63 B2 Plây Ku Vietnam
153 B4 Plaza Huincul Arg.
139 D3 Pleasanton U.S.A.
54 B2 Pleasant Point N.Z.
104 C2 Pleaux France
130 B1 Pledger Lake Can.
54 C1 Plenty, Bay of g. N.Z.
136 C1 Plentywood U.S.A.
86 D2 Plesetsk Rus. Fed.
131 C1 Plétipi, Lac l. Can.
100 C2 Plettenberg Ger.
122 B3 Plettenberg Bay S. Africa
110 B2 Pleven Bulg.
109 C2 Pljevlja Montenegro
109 C2 Ploče Croatia
103 D1 Płock Pol.
109 C2 Pločno mt. Bos.-Herz.
104 B2 Ploemeur France
110 C2 Ploieşti Romania
89 F2 Ploskoye Rus. Fed.
104 B2 Plouzané France
110 B2 Plovdiv Bulg.
88 B2 Plungė Lith.
88 C3 Plyeshchanitsy Belarus
99 A3 Plymouth U.K.
140 B2 Plymouth U.S.A.
147 D3 Plymouth (abandoned)
    Montserrat
88 C2 Plyussa Rus. Fed.
102 C2 Plzeň Czech Rep.

114 B3 Pô Burkina
108 B1 Po r. Italy
77 C2 Pobeda Peak China/Kyrg.
142 D3 Pocahontas U.S.A.
134 D2 Pocatello U.S.A.
90 B1 Pochayiv Ukr.
89 D3 Pochep Rus. Fed.
89 D3 Pochinok Rus. Fed.
145 C3 Pochutla Mex.
141 D3 Pocomoke City U.S.A.
155 C2 Poços de Caldas Brazil
89 D2 Poddor'ye Rus. Fed.
91 D1 Podgorenskiy Rus. Fed.
109 C2 Podgorica Montenegro
82 G3 Podgornoye Rus. Fed.
83 H2 Podkamennaya Tunguska r.
    Rus. Fed.
89 E2 Podol'sk Rus. Fed.
109 D2 Podujevë Kosovo
    Podujevo Kosovo see Podujevë
122 A2 Pofadder S. Africa
89 D3 Pogar Rus. Fed.
109 D2 Pogradec Albania
65 B2 P'ohang S. Korea
48 E2 Pohnpei atoll Micronesia
110 B2 Poiana Mare Romania
118 C3 Poie Dem. Rep. Congo
118 B3 Pointe-Noire Congo
126 D2 Point Lake Can.
140 C3 Point Pleasant U.S.A.
104 C2 Poitiers France
74 B2 Pokaran India
75 C2 Pokhara Nepal
83 J2 Pokrovsk Rus. Fed.
91 D2 Pokrovskoye Rus. Fed.
138 A1 Polacca U.S.A.
106 B1 Pola de Lena Spain
103 D1 Poland country Europe
88 C2 Polatsk Belarus
77 C3 Pol-e Khomri Afgh.
61 C2 Polewali Indon.
118 B2 Poli Cameroon
102 C1 Police Pol.
109 C2 Policoro Italy
105 D2 Poligny France
64 B1 Polillo Islands Phil.
90 B1 Polis'ke Ukr.
103 D1 Polkowice Pol.
109 C3 Pollino, Monte mt. Italy
91 D2 Polohy Ukr.
123 C1 Polokwane S. Africa
90 B1 Polonne Ukr.
134 D1 Polson U.S.A.
91 C2 Poltava Ukr.
66 B2 Poltavka Rus. Fed.
91 D2 Poltavskaya Rus. Fed.
88 C2 Põlva Estonia
111 B2 Polygyros Greece
106 B2 Pombal Port.
102 C1 Pomeranian Bay Ger./Pol.
108 B2 Pomezia Italy
92 I2 Pomokaira reg. Fin.
110 C2 Pomorie Bulg.
    Pomorska, Zatoka b. Ger./Pol.
    see Pomeranian Bay
155 D1 Pompéu Brazil
139 D1 Ponca City U.S.A.
147 D3 Ponce Puerto Rico
    Pondicherry India see
    Puducherry
127 F2 Pond Inlet Can.
106 B1 Ponferrada Spain
117 A4 Pongo watercourse Sudan
123 D2 Pongola r. S. Africa
128 C2 Ponoka Can.
84 D5 Ponta Delgada Arquipélago
    dos Açores

154	B3	**Ponta Grossa** Brazil
154	C1	**Pontalina** Brazil
105	D2	**Pont-à-Mousson** France
105	D2	**Pontarlier** France
102	B2	**Pontcharra** France
142	B2	**Pontchartrain, Lake** U.S.A.
106	B2	**Ponte de San** Port.
129	D3	**Ponteix** Can.
150	C3	**Pontes-e-Lacerda** Brazil
106	B1	**Pontevedra** Spain
140	B2	**Pontiac** IL U.S.A.
140	C2	**Pontiac** MI U.S.A.
61	B2	**Pontianak** Indon.
104	B2	**Pontivy** France
151	C1	**Pontoetoe** Suriname
129	E2	**Ponton** Can.
99	B3	**Pontypool** U.K.
108	B2	**Ponziane, Isole** is Italy
99	C3	**Poole** U.K.
		Poona India see **Pune**
52	B2	**Pooncarie** Austr.
152	B2	**Poopó, lago de** l. Bol.
150	A1	**Popayán** Col.
83	I2	**Popigay** r. Rus. Fed.
52	B2	**Popiltah** Austr.
129	E2	**Poplar** r. Can.
137	E3	**Poplar Bluff** U.S.A.
118	B3	**Popokabaka** Dem. Rep. Congo
110	C2	**Popovo** Bulg.
103	E2	**Poprad** Slovakia
151	D3	**Porangatu** Brazil
74	A2	**Porbandar** India
108	B1	**Porcupine** r. Can./U.S.A.
108	B1	**Poreč** Croatia
54	B2	**Porirua** N.Z.
88	C2	**Porkhov** Rus. Fed.
104	B2	**Pornic** France
83	K3	**Poronaysk** Rus. Fed.
111	B3	**Poros** Greece
93	E4	**Porsgrunn** Norway
97	C1	**Portadown** U.K.
97	D1	**Portaferry** U.K.
140	B2	**Portage** U.S.A.
129	E3	**Portage la Prairie** Can.
128	B3	**Port Alberni** Can.
106	B2	**Portalegre** Port.
139	C2	**Portales** U.S.A.
128	A2	**Port Alexander** U.S.A.
128	B2	**Port Alice** Can.
134	B1	**Port Angeles** U.S.A.
51	D4	**Port Arthur** Austr.
139	E3	**Port Arthur** U.S.A.
96	A3	**Port Askaig** U.K.
52	A2	**Port Augusta** Austr.
147	C3	**Port-au-Prince** Haiti
131	E1	**Port aux Choix** Can.
73	H4	**Port Blair** India
52	B3	**Port Campbell** Austr.
54	B3	**Port Chalmers** N.Z.
143	D3	**Port Charlotte** U.S.A.
147	C3	**Port-de-Paix** Haiti
128	A2	**Port Edward** Can.
155	D1	**Porteirinha** Brazil
151	C2	**Portel** Brazil
130	B2	**Port Elgin** Can.
123	C3	**Port Elizabeth** S. Africa
96	A3	**Port Ellen** U.K.
98	A1	**Port Erin** Isle of Man
122	A3	**Porterville** S. Africa
135	C3	**Porterville** U.S.A.
52	B3	**Port Fairy** Austr.
54	C1	**Port Fitzroy** N.Z.
118	A3	**Port-Gentil** Gabon
115	C4	**Port Harcourt** Nigeria
128	B2	**Port Hardy** Can.
		Port Harrison Can. see **Inukjuak**
131	D2	**Port Hawkesbury** Can.
50	A2	**Port Hedland** Austr.
99	A2	**Porthmadog** U.K.
131	E1	**Port Hope Simpson** Can.
140	C2	**Port Huron** U.S.A.
106	B2	**Portimão** Port.
53	C2	**Portland** N.S.W. Austr.
52	B3	**Portland** Vic. Austr.
141	E2	**Portland** ME U.S.A.
134	B1	**Portland** OR U.S.A.
128	A2	**Portland Canal** inlet Can.
97	C2	**Portlaoise** Ireland
139	D3	**Port Lavaca** U.S.A.
52	A2	**Port Lincoln** Austr.
114	A4	**Port Loko** Sierra Leone
113	K9	**Port Louis** Mauritius
53	D2	**Port Macquarie** Austr.
128	B2	**Port McNeill** Can.
131	D2	**Port-Menier** Can.
59	D3	**Port Moresby** P.N.G.
122	A2	**Port Nolloth** S. Africa
		Port-Nouveau-Québec Can. see **Kangiqsualujjuaq**
		Porto Port. see **Oporto**
150	B2	**Porto Acre** Brazil
152	C4	**Porto Alegre** Brazil
151	C3	**Porto Artur** Brazil
151	C3	**Porto dos Gaúchos Óbidos** Brazil
150	C3	**Porto Esperidião** Brazil
108	B2	**Portoferraio** Italy
96	A1	**Port of Ness** U.K.
151	D2	**Porto Franco** Brazil
147	D3	**Port of Spain** Trin. and Tob.
108	B1	**Portogruaro** Italy
108	B2	**Portomaggiore** Italy
154	B2	**Porto Mendes** Brazil
152	C3	**Porto Murtinho** Brazil
151	D3	**Porto Nacional** Brazil
114	C4	**Porto-Novo** Benin
154	B2	**Porto Primavera, Represa** resr Brazil
151	C2	**Porto Santana** Brazil
155	E1	**Porto Seguro** Brazil
108	B2	**Porto Tolle** Italy
108	A2	**Porto Torres** Sardegna Italy
105	D3	**Porto-Vecchio** Corse France
150	B2	**Porto-Velho** Brazil
150	A2	**Portoviejo** Ecuador
52	B3	**Port Phillip Bay** Austr.
52	A2	**Port Pirie** Austr.
96	A2	**Portree** U.K.
128	B3	**Port Renfrew** Can.
97	C1	**Portrush** U.K.
116	B3	**Port Said** Egypt
143	C3	**Port St Joe** U.S.A.
123	C3	**Port St Johns** S. Africa
123	C3	**Port Shepstone** S. Africa
99	C3	**Portsmouth** U.K.
141	E2	**Portsmouth** NH U.S.A.
140	C3	**Portsmouth** OH U.S.A.
141	D3	**Portsmouth** VA U.S.A.
97	C1	**Portstewart** U.K.
117	F3	**Port Sudan** Sudan
142	C3	**Port Sulphur** U.S.A.
99	B3	**Port Talbot** U.K.
106	B2	**Portugal** country Europe
97	B2	**Portumna** Ireland
105	C3	**Port-Vendres** France
48	F4	**Port Vila** Vanuatu
93	I3	**Porvoo** Fin.
65	B2	**Poryŏng** S. Korea
152	C3	**Posadas** Arg.
89	E2	**Poshekhon'ye** Rus. Fed.
92	I2	**Poso** Fin.
58	C2	**Poso** Indon.
151	D3	**Posse** Brazil
101	E2	**Pößneck** Ger.
139	C2	**Post** U.S.A.
		Poste-de-la-Baleine Can. see **Kuujjuarapik**
122	B2	**Postmasburg** S. Africa
109	C2	**Posušje** Bos.-Herz.
139	E1	**Poteau** U.S.A.
109	C2	**Potenza** Italy
151	D2	**Poti** r. Brazil
81	C1	**P'ot'i** Georgia
115	D3	**Potiskum** Nigeria
141	D3	**Potomac, South Branch** r. U.S.
152	B2	**Potosí** Bol.
64	B1	**Pototan** Phil.
138	C3	**Potrero del Llano** Mex.
101	F1	**Potsdam** Ger.
141	E2	**Potsdam** U.S.A.
141	D2	**Pottstown** U.S.A.
141	D2	**Pottsville** U.S.A.
131	E2	**Pouch Cove** Can.
141	E2	**Poughkeepsie** U.S.A.
98	B2	**Poulton-le-Fylde** U.K.
155	C2	**Pouso Alegre** Brazil
63	B2	**Poŭthĭsăt** Cambodia
103	D2	**Považská Bystrica** Slovakia
109	C2	**Povlen** mt. Serbia
106	B1	**Póvoa de Varzim** Port.
136	B2	**Powell** U.S.A.
135	D3	**Powell, Lake** resr U.S.A.
128	B3	**Powell River** Can.
154	B1	**Poxoréu** Brazil
71	B3	**Poyang** China
71	B3	**Poyang Hu** l. China
109	D2	**Požarevac** Serbia
145	C2	**Poza Rica** Mex.
109	C1	**Požega** Croatia
109	D2	**Požega** Serbia
79	D2	**Pozm Tīāb** Iran
103	D1	**Poznań** Pol.
106	C2	**Pozoblanco** Spain
108	B2	**Pozzuoli** Italy
60	B2	**Prabumulih** Indon.
102	C2	**Prachatice** Czech Rep.
63	A2	**Prachuap Khiri Khan** Thai.
155	E1	**Prado** Brazil
102	C2	**Prague** Czech Rep.
		Praha Czech Rep. see **Prague**
112	C5	**Praia** Cape Verde
139	C2	**Prairie Dog Town Fork** r. U.S.A.
140	A2	**Prairie du Chien** U.S.A.
60	A1	**Prapat** Indon.
154	C1	**Prata** Brazil
105	E3	**Prato** Italy
137	D3	**Pratt** U.S.A.
61	C2	**Praya** Indon.
63	B2	**Preăh Vihéar** Cambodia
89	F2	**Prechistoye** Rus. Fed.
129	D2	**Preeceville** Can.
88	C2	**Preiļi** Latvia
53	C2	**Premer** Austr.
105	C2	**Prémery** France
101	F1	**Premnitz** Ger.
102	C1	**Prenzlau** Ger.
63	A3	**Preparis Island** Cocos Is
63	A2	**Preparis North Channel** Cocos Is
63	A2	**Preparis South Channel** Cocos Is
103	D2	**Přerov** Czech Rep.
138	A2	**Prescott** U.S.A.
109	D2	**Preševo** Serbia
152	B3	**Presidencia Roque Sáenz Peña** Arg.
151	D2	**Presidente Dutra** Brazil
154	B2	**Presidente Epitácio** Brazil
154	B2	**Presidente Prudente** Brazil

88 C3 Presidio U.S.A.
03 E2 Prešov Slovakia
41 F1 Presque Isle U.S.A.
01 F2 Pressel Ger.
98 B2 Preston U.K.
34 D2 Preston U.S.A.
96 B3 Preston U.S.A.
84 C2 Prestwick U.K.
55 E2 Preto r. Brazil
23 C2 Pretoria S. Africa
11 B3 Preveza Greece
09 C2 Prey Vêng Cambodia
35 D3 Priboj Serbia
88 B3 Prienai Lith.
30 C2 Prieska S. Africa
03 D2 Prievidza Slovakia
09 C2 Prijedor Bos.-Herz.
Prikaspiyskaya Nizmennost'
lowland Kazakh./Rus. Fed. see
Caspian Lowland
09 D2 Prilep Macedonia
91 D2 Primorsko-Akhtarsk Rus. Fed.
29 D2 Primrose Lake Can.
29 D2 Prince Albert Can.
22 B3 Prince Albert S. Africa
26 D2 Prince Albert Peninsula Can.
22 B3 Prince Albert Road S. Africa
26 C2 Prince Alfred, Cape Can.
22 A3 Prince Alfred Hamlet S. Africa
27 F2 Prince Charles Island Can.
55 E2 Prince Charles Mountains
Antarctica
81 D2 Prince Edward Island prov.
Can.
13 I11 Prince Edward Islands Indian
Ocean
28 B2 Prince George Can.
26 D1 Prince of Wales Island Can.
28 A2 Prince of Wales Island U.S.A.
26 D2 Prince of Wales Strait Can.
26 D1 Prince Patrick Island Can.
26 E2 Prince Regent Inlet sea chan.
Can.
28 A2 Prince Rupert Can.
51 D1 Princess Charlotte Bay Austr.
28 B2 Princess Royal Island Can.
34 B2 Princeton Can.
34 B2 Prineville U.S.A.
90 B1 Pripet r. Belarus/Ukr.
90 A1 Pripet Marshes Belarus/Ukr.
09 D2 Prishtinë Kosovo
Priština Kosovo see Prishtinë
01 F1 Pritzwalk Ger.
09 C2 Privlaka Croatia
89 F2 Privolzhsk Rus. Fed.
09 D2 Prizren Kosovo
51 C1 Professor van Blommestein
Meer resr Suriname
45 D2 Progreso Mex.
91 D3 Prokhladnyy Rus. Fed.
09 D2 Prokuplje Serbia
26 C3 Prophet r. Can.
28 B2 Prophet River Can.
51 D2 Proserpine Austr.
86 E3 Protvino Rus. Fed.
10 C2 Provadiya Bulg.
41 E2 Providence U.S.A.
46 B3 Providencia, Isla de i.
Caribbean Sea
83 N2 Providentiya Rus. Fed.
35 D3 Provo U.S.A.
29 C2 Provost Can.
54 B3 Prudentópolis Brazil
26 C2 Prudhoe Bay U.S.A.
01 E2 Prüm Ger.
05 D2 Prunelli-di-Fiumorbo Corse
France

103 E1 Pruszków Pol.
110 C1 Prut r. Europe
91 C1 Pryluky Ukr.
91 D2 Prymors'k Ukr.
139 D1 Pryor U.S.A.
Prypyats' r. Belarus see Pripet
103 E2 Przemyśl Pol.
111 C3 Psara i. Greece
81 C1 Psebay Rus. Fed.
91 D3 Pshekha r. Rus. Fed.
88 C2 Pskov Rus. Fed.
88 C2 Pskov, Lake Estonia/Rus. Fed.
111 B3 Ptolemaïda Greece
109 C1 Ptuj Slovenia
150 A2 Pucallpa Peru
71 B3 Pucheng China
65 B2 Puch'ŏn S. Korea
103 D1 Puck Pol.
92 I2 Pudasjärvi Fin.
86 C2 Pudozh Rus. Fed.
73 B3 Puducherry India
145 C3 Puebla Mex.
136 C3 Pueblo U.S.A.
153 B4 Puelén Arg.
106 C2 Puente-Genil Spain
153 A5 Puerto Aisén Chile
152 B2 Puerto Alegre Bol.
145 C3 Puerto Ángel Mex.
146 B4 Puerto Armuelles Panama
150 B1 Puerto Ayacucho Venez.
146 B3 Puerto Cabezas Nic.
150 B1 Puerto Carreño Col.
153 A5 Puerto Cisnes Chile
144 A2 Puerto Cortés Mex.
145 C3 Puerto Escondido Mex.
152 B2 Puerto Frey Bol.
150 B1 Puerto Inírida Col.
152 C2 Puerto Isabel Bol.
150 A2 Puerto Leguizamo Col.
144 A2 Puerto Libertad Mex.
146 B3 Puerto Limón Costa Rica
106 C2 Puertollano Spain
153 B5 Puerto Madryn Arg.
150 B3 Puerto Maldonado Peru
153 A5 Puerto Montt Chile
153 A6 Puerto Natales Chile
150 B1 Puerto Nuevo Col.
144 A1 Puerto Peñasco Mex.
152 C3 Puerto Pinasco Para.
147 C3 Puerto Plata Dom. Rep.
150 A2 Puerto Portillo Peru
64 A2 Puerto Princesa Phil.
147 D3 Puerto Rico terr. West Indies
158 B3 Puerto Rico Trench Caribbean
Sea
146 A3 Puerto San José Guat.
153 B6 Puerto Santa Cruz Arg.
144 B2 Puerto Vallarta Mex.
87 D4 Pugachev Rus. Fed.
74 B2 Pugal India
54 B2 Pukaki, Lake N.Z.
129 D2 Pukatawagan Can.
65 B1 Pukchin N. Korea
65 B1 Pukch'ŏng N. Korea
54 B1 Pukekohe N.Z.
65 B1 Puksubaek-san mt. N. Korea
108 B2 Pula Croatia
108 A3 Pula Sardegna Italy
152 B3 Pulacayo Bol.
92 I3 Pulkkila Fin.
134 C1 Pullman U.S.A.
64 B1 Pulog, Mount Phil.
150 A2 Puná, Isla i. Ecuador
54 B2 Punakaiki N.Z.
123 D1 Punda Maria S. Africa
73 B3 Pune India
65 B1 P'ungsan N. Korea

121 C2 Púnguè r. Moz.
153 B4 Punta Alta Arg.
153 A6 Punta Arenas Chile
146 B3 Puntarenas Costa Rica
150 A1 Punto Fijo Venez.
92 I3 Puolanka Fin.
82 G2 Pur r. Rus. Fed.
75 C2 Puri India
100 B1 Purmerend Neth.
75 C2 Purnia India
75 C2 Puruliya India
150 B2 Purus r. Brazil/Peru
61 B2 Purwakarta Indon.
65 B1 Puryŏng N. Korea
65 B2 Pusan S. Korea
88 C2 Pushkinskiye Gory Rus. Fed.
88 C2 Pustoshka Rus. Fed.
62 A1 Putao Myanmar
71 B3 Putian China
Puting China see De'an
61 C2 Puting, Tanjung pt Indon.
101 F1 Putlitz Ger.
58 A1 Putrajaya Malaysia
102 C1 Puttgarden Ger.
150 A2 Putumayo r. Col.
61 C1 Putusibau Indon.
91 C1 Putyvl' Ukr.
127 F2 Puvirnituq Can.
70 B2 Puyang China
104 C3 Puylaurens France
99 A2 Pwllheli U.K.
63 A2 Pyapon Myanmar
82 G2 Pyasina r. Rus. Fed.
87 D4 Pyatigorsk Rus. Fed.
91 C2 P'yatykhatky Ukr.
62 A2 Pye Myanmar
88 C3 Pyetrykaw Belarus
93 H3 Pyhäjärvi l. Fin.
92 H3 Pyhäjoki r. Fin.
92 I3 Pyhäsalmi Fin.
62 A2 Pyinmana Myanmar
65 B2 Pyŏksŏng N. Korea
65 B2 P'yŏnggang N. Korea
65 B2 P'yŏngan N. Korea
65 B2 P'yŏngyang N. Korea
135 C2 Pyramid Lake U.S.A.
80 B3 Pyramids of Giza tourist site
Egypt
107 D1 Pyrenees mts Europe
111 B3 Pyrgos Greece
91 C1 Pyryatyn Ukr.
103 C1 Pyrzyce Pol.
88 C2 Pytalovo Rus. Fed.
111 B3 Pyxaria mt. Greece

Q

123 C3 Qaanaaq Greenland see Thule
69 D2 Qacha's Nek Lesotho
68 C2 Qagan Nur China
78 B2 Qaidam Pendi basin China
129 E1 Qal'at Bishah Saudi Arabia
Qamanirjuaq Lake Can.
Qamanittuaq Can. see
Baker Lake
79 C3 Qamar, Ghubbat al b. Yemen
78 B3 Qam Hadil Saudi Arabia
77 C2 Qarshi Uzbek.
78 B2 Qaryat al Ulyā Saudi Arabia
127 H2 Qasigiannguit Greenland
79 D2 Qaṣr-e Qand Iran
81 C2 Qaṣr-e Shīrīn Iran
127 H2 Qassimiut Greenland
78 B3 Qa'ṭabah Yemen
79 C2 Qatar country Asia

Qattara Depression

116 A2 **Qattara Depression** Egypt
81 C1 **Qazax** Azer.
81 C1 **Qazımämmäd** Azer.
81 C2 **Qazvin** Iran
127 H2 **Qeqertarsuaq** i. Greenland
127 H2 **Qeqertarsuatsiaat** Greenland
127 H2 **Qeqertarsuup Tunua** b. Greenland
79 C2 **Qeshm** Iran
70 A3 **Qianjiang** *Chongqing* China
70 B2 **Qianjiang** *Hubei* China
65 A1 **Qian Shan** mts China
70 C2 **Qidong** China
68 B2 **Qiemo** China
71 A3 **Qijiang** China
68 C2 **Qijiaojing** China
127 G2 **Qikiqtarjuaq** Can.
74 A2 **Qila Ladgasht** Pak.
68 C2 **Qilian Shan** mts China
127 I2 **Qillak** i. Greenland
70 B3 **Qimen** China
127 G1 **Qimusseriarsuaq** b. Greenland
116 B2 **Qina** Egypt
70 B2 **Qingdao** China
68 C2 **Qinghai Hu** salt l. China
68 C2 **Qinghai Nanshan** mts China
70 A2 **Qingyang** *Gansu* China
71 B3 **Qingyuan** *Guangdong* China
65 A1 **Qingyuan** *Liaoning* China
   Qingzang Gaoyuan plat. China *see* **Tibet, Plateau of**
70 B2 **Qingzhou** China
70 B2 **Qinhuangdao** China
70 A2 **Qin Ling** mts China
   Qinting China *see* **Lianhua**
70 B2 **Qinyang** China
71 A3 **Qinzhou** China
71 B4 **Qionghai** China
68 C2 **Qionglai Shan** mts China
71 B4 **Qiongshan** China
69 E1 **Qiqihar** China
79 C2 **Qir** Iran
66 B1 **Qitaihe** China
70 B2 **Qixian** China
   Qogir Feng mt. China/Pakistan *see* **K2**
81 D2 **Qom** Iran
   Qomolangma Feng mt. China/Nepal *see* **Everest, Mount**
76 B2 **Qo'ng'irot** Uzbek.
   Qoqek China *see* **Tacheng**
77 D2 **Qo'qon** Uzbek.
76 B2 **Qoraqalpog'iston** Uzbek.
100 C1 **Quakenbrück** Ger.
63 B2 **Quang Ngai** Vietnam
63 B2 **Quang Tri** Vietnam
71 B3 **Quanzhou** *Fujian* China
71 B3 **Quanzhou** *Guangxi* China
108 A3 **Quartu Sant'Elena** *Sardegna* Italy
138 A2 **Quartzsite** U.S.A.
81 C1 **Quba** Azer.
53 C3 **Queanbeyan** Austr.
131 C2 **Québec** Can.
130 C1 **Québec** prov. Can.
101 E2 **Quedlinburg** Ger.
128 A2 **Queen Charlotte** Can.
128 A2 **Queen Charlotte Islands** Can.
128 B2 **Queen Charlotte Sound** sea chan. Can.
128 B2 **Queen Charlotte Strait** Can.
126 D1 **Queen Elizabeth Islands** Can.
126 E2 **Queen Maud Gulf** Can.
55 B2 **Queen Maud Land** reg. Antarctica

55 N1 **Queen Maud Mountains** Antarctica
52 B1 **Queensland** state Austr.
51 D4 **Queenstown** Austr.
54 A3 **Queenstown** N.Z.
123 C3 **Queenstown** S. Africa
121 C2 **Quelimane** Moz.
138 B2 **Quemado** U.S.A.
154 B2 **Querência do Norte** Brazil
145 B2 **Querétaro** Mex.
101 E2 **Querfurt** Ger.
128 B2 **Quesnel** Can.
128 B2 **Quesnel Lake** Can.
74 A1 **Quetta** Pak.
64 A2 **Quezon** Phil.
64 B1 **Quezon City** Phil.
120 A2 **Quibala** Angola
150 A1 **Quibdó** Col.
104 B2 **Quiberon** France
104 C3 **Quillan** France
153 C4 **Quilmes** Arg.
   Quilon India *see* **Kollam**
51 D2 **Quilpie** Austr.
153 A4 **Quilpué** Chile
120 A1 **Quimbele** Angola
152 B3 **Quimili** Arg.
104 B2 **Quimper** France
104 B2 **Quimperlé** France
137 E3 **Quincy** *IL* U.S.A.
141 E2 **Quincy** *MA* U.S.A.
107 C1 **Quinto** Spain
121 D2 **Quionga** Moz.
53 D2 **Quirindi** Austr.
121 C3 **Quissico** Moz.
120 A2 **Quitapa** Angola
150 A2 **Quito** Ecuador
151 E2 **Quixadá** Brazil
71 A3 **Qujing** China
52 A2 **Quorn** Austr.
79 C2 **Qurayat** Oman
77 C3 **Qürghonteppa** Tajik.
63 B2 **Quy Nhơn** Vietnam
71 B3 **Quzhou** China

R

103 D2 **Raab** r. Austria
92 H3 **Raahe** Fin.
100 C1 **Raalte** Neth.
61 C2 **Raas** i. Indon.
61 C2 **Raba** Indon.
114 B1 **Rabat** Morocco
78 A2 **Räbigh** Saudi Arabia
131 E2 **Race, Cape** Can.
142 B3 **Raceland** U.S.A.
63 B3 **Rach Gia** Vietnam
140 B2 **Racine** U.S.A.
78 B3 **Radāʿ** Yemen
110 C1 **Rădăuți** Romania
140 B3 **Radcliff** U.S.A.
74 B2 **Radhanpur** India
130 C1 **Radisson** Can.
103 E1 **Radom** Pol.
103 D1 **Radomsko** Pol.
90 B1 **Radomyshl'** Ukr.
109 D2 **Radoviš** Macedonia
88 B2 **Radviliškis** Lith.
78 A2 **Radwá, Jabal** mt. Saudi Arabia
90 B1 **Radyvyliv** Ukr.
75 C2 **Rae Bareli** India
100 C2 **Raeren** Belgium
54 C1 **Raetihi** N.Z.
152 B4 **Rafaela** Arg.
118 C2 **Rafaï** C.A.R.

78 B2 **Rafha'** Saudi Arabia
79 C1 **Rafsanjän** Iran
64 D2 **Ragang, Mount** vol. Phil.
109 B3 **Ragusa** *Sicilia* Italy
59 C3 **Raha** Indon.
88 D3 **Rahachow** Belarus
74 B2 **Rahimyar Khan** Pak.
109 D2 **Rahovec** Kosovo
73 B3 **Raichur** India
75 C2 **Raigarh** India
128 C2 **Rainbow Lake** Can.
134 B1 **Rainier, Mount** vol. U.S.A.
130 A2 **Rainy Lake** Can./U.S.A.
129 E3 **Rainy River** Can.
75 C2 **Raipur** India
93 H3 **Raisio** Fin.
73 C3 **Rajahmundry** India
61 C1 **Rajang** r. *Sarawak* Malaysia
74 B2 **Rajanpur** Pak.
73 B4 **Rajapalaiyam** India
74 B2 **Rajasthan Canal** India
74 B2 **Rajgarh** India
74 B2 **Rajkot** India
74 B2 **Rajpur** India
75 C2 **Rajshahi** Bangl.
54 B2 **Rakaia** r. N.Z.
90 A2 **Rakhiv** Ukr.
91 D1 **Rakitnoye** Rus. Fed.
88 C2 **Rakke** Estonia
88 C2 **Rakvere** Estonia
143 E1 **Raleigh** U.S.A.
48 F2 **Ralik Chain** is Marshall Is
74 B2 **Ramgarh** India
81 C2 **Rämhormoz** Iran
   Ramlat Rabyānah des. Libya *see* **Rebiana Sand Sea**
110 C1 **Râmnicu Sărat** Romania
110 B1 **Râmnicu Vâlcea** Romania
89 E3 **Ramon'** Rus. Fed.
123 C1 **Ramotswa** Botswana
75 B2 **Rampur** India
62 A2 **Ramree Island** Myanmar
98 A1 **Ramsey** Isle of Man
99 D3 **Ramsgate** U.K.
75 C2 **Ranaghat** India
61 C1 **Ranau** *Sabah* Malaysia
153 A4 **Rancagua** Chile
75 C2 **Ranchi** India
93 F4 **Randers** Denmark
54 B2 **Rangiora** N.Z.
54 C1 **Rangitaiki** r. N.Z.
62 A2 **Rangoon** Myanmar
75 C2 **Rangpur** Bangl.
129 E1 **Rankin Inlet** Can.
53 C2 **Rankin's Springs** Austr.
96 B2 **Rannoch Moor** moorland U.K.
63 A3 **Ranong** Thai.
59 C3 **Ransiki** Indon.
61 C2 **Rantaupanjang** Indon.
60 A1 **Rantauprapat** Indon.
92 I2 **Ranua** Fin.
78 B2 **Ranyah, Wādī** watercourse Saudi Arabia
49 I4 **Rapa** i. Fr. Polynesia
136 C2 **Rapid City** U.S.A.
88 B2 **Rapla** Estonia
74 A2 **Rapur** India
49 H4 **Rarotonga** i. Cook Is
153 B5 **Rasa, Punta** pt Arg.
79 C2 **Ra's al Khaymah** U.A.E.
117 B3 **Ras Dejen** mt. Eth.
88 B2 **Raseiniai** Lith.
81 C2 **Rasht** Iran
74 A2 **Ras Koh** mt. Pak.
89 D3 **Rasony** Belarus
87 D3 **Rasskazovo** Rus. Fed.
79 C2 **Ras Tannūrah** Saudi Arabia

101 D1 Rastede Ger.
93 F3 Rätan Sweden
74 B2 Ratangarh India
63 A2 Rat Buri Thai.
62 A1 Rathedaung Myanmar
101 F1 Rathenow Ger.
97 C1 Rathlin Island U.K.
74 B2 Ratlam India
73 B3 Ratnagiri India
73 C4 Ratnapura Sri Lanka
91 A1 Ratne Ukr.
138 C1 Raton U.S.A.
74 B2 Rattray Head U.K.
101 E1 Ratzeburg Ger.
92 □A3 Raufarhöfn Iceland
54 C1 Raukumara Range mts N.Z.
74 H3 Rauma Fin.
61 C2 Raung, Gunung vol. Indon.
75 C2 Raurkela India
134 D1 Ravalli U.S.A.
81 C2 Ravänsar Iran
108 B2 Ravenna Italy
102 B2 Ravensburg Ger.
74 B1 Ravi r. Pak.
74 B1 Rawalpindi Pak.
103 D1 Rawicz Pol.
50 B3 Rawlinna Austr.
136 B2 Rawlins U.S.A.
153 B5 Rawson Arg.
73 C2 Rayagada India
69 E1 Raychikhinsk Rus. Fed.
78 B3 Raydah Yemen
87 E3 Rayevskiy Rus. Fed.
53 D2 Raymond U.S.A.
53 D2 Raymond Terrace Austr.
139 D3 Raymondville U.S.A.
145 C2 Rayón Mex.
63 B2 Rayong Thai.
78 A2 Rayyis Saudi Arabia
104 B2 Raz, Pointe du pt France
81 C2 Razāzah, Buhayrat ar l. Iraq
110 C2 Razgrad Bulg.
110 C2 Razim, Lacul lag. Romania
110 B2 Razlog Bulg.
104 B2 Ré, Île de i. France
99 C3 Reading U.K.
141 D2 Reading U.S.A.
115 E2 Rebiana Sand Sea des. Libya
66 D1 Rebun-tō i. Japan
50 B3 Recherche, Archipelago of the
        is Austr.
89 D3 Rechytsa Belarus
151 E2 Recife Brazil
123 C3 Recife, Cape S. Africa
100 C2 Recklinghausen Ger.
152 C3 Reconquista Arg.
142 B2 Red r. U.S.A.
131 E1 Red Bay Can.
134 B2 Red Bluff U.S.A.
98 C1 Redcar U.K.
129 C2 Redcliff Can.
52 B2 Red Cliffs Austr.
128 C2 Red Deer Can.
126 D3 Red Deer r. Can.
129 D2 Red Deer Lake Can.
134 B2 Redding U.S.A.
99 C2 Redditch U.K.
137 D2 Redfield U.S.A.
137 D2 Redfield U.S.A.
130 A1 Red Lake Can.
137 E1 Red Lakes U.S.A.
134 D1 Red Lodge U.S.A.
134 B2 Redmond U.S.A.
137 D2 Red Oak U.S.A.
106 B2 Redondo Port.
59 B2 Red Sea Africa/Asia
128 B2 Redstone r. Can.
100 B1 Reduzum Neth.

137 E2 Red Wing U.S.A.
137 D2 Redwood Falls U.S.A.
97 C2 Ree, Lough l. Ireland
134 B2 Reedsport U.S.A.
54 B2 Reefton N.Z.
102 C2 Regen Ger.
155 E1 Regência Brazil
102 C2 Regensburg Ger.
114 C2 Reggane Alg.
109 C3 Reggio di Calabria Italy
108 B2 Reggio nell'Emilia Italy
110 B1 Reghin Romania
129 D2 Regina Can.
122 A1 Rehoboth Namibia
101 F2 Reichenbach Ger.
143 E1 Reidsville U.S.A.
99 C3 Reigate U.K.
105 C2 Reims France
101 E1 Reinbek Ger.
129 D2 Reindeer r. Can.
129 E2 Reindeer Island Can.
129 D2 Reindeer Lake Can.
92 F2 Reine Norway
100 C3 Reinsfeld Ger.
123 C2 Reitz S. Africa
122 B2 Reivilo S. Africa
129 D1 Reliance Can.
107 D2 Relizane Alg.
79 C2 Remeshk Iran
105 D2 Remiremont France
100 C2 Remscheid Ger.
102 B1 Rendsburg Ger.
60 B2 Rengat Indon.
90 B2 Reni Ukr.
52 B2 Renmark Austr.
100 D2 Rennerod Ger.
104 B2 Rennes France
129 D1 Rennie Lake Can.
108 B2 Reno r. Italy
135 C3 Reno U.S.A.
70 A3 Renshou China
140 B2 Rensselaer U.S.A.
75 C2 Renukut India
54 B2 Renwick N.Z.
58 C3 Reo Indon.
136 D3 Republican r. U.S.A.
127 F2 Repulse Bay Can.
150 A2 Requena Peru
107 C2 Requena Spain
154 B2 Reserva Brazil
152 C3 Resistencia Arg.
110 B1 Reşiţa Romania
126 E2 Resolute Can.
127 G2 Resolution Island Can.
105 C2 Rethel France
111 B3 Rethymno Greece
113 K9 Réunion terr. Indian Ocean
107 D1 Reus Spain
102 B2 Reutlingen Ger.
128 C2 Revelstoke Can.
144 A3 Revillagigedo, Islas is Mex.
128 A2 Revillagigedo Island U.S.A.
75 C2 Rewa India
134 D2 Rexburg U.S.A.
92 A3 Reykjanestá pt Iceland
92 A3 Reykjavík Iceland
145 C2 Reynosa Mex.
88 C2 Rēzekne Latvia
        Rhein r. Ger. see Rhine
100 C1 Rheine Ger.
101 F1 Rheinsberg Ger.
        Rhin r. France see Rhine
100 C2 Rhine r. Europe
140 B1 Rhinelander U.S.A.
101 F1 Rhinluch marsh Ger.
101 F1 Rhinow Ger.

141 E2 Rhode Island state U.S.A.
111 C3 Rhodes Greece
111 C3 Rhodes i. Greece
110 B2 Rhodope Mountains
        Bulg./Greece
105 C3 Rhône r. France/Switz.
        Rhuthun U.K. see Ruthin
98 B2 Rhyl U.K.
154 C1 Rianópolis Brazil
60 B1 Riau, Kepulauan is Indon.
106 B1 Ribadeo Spain
106 B1 Ribadesella Spain
154 B2 Ribas do Rio Pardo Brazil
121 C2 Ribáuè Moz.
98 B2 Ribble r. U.K.
154 C2 Ribeira r. Brazil
154 C2 Ribeirão Preto Brazil
104 C2 Ribérac France
152 B2 Riberalta Bol.
90 B2 Rîbniţa Moldova
102 C1 Ribnitz-Damgarten Ger.
140 A1 Rice Lake U.S.A.
123 D2 Richards Bay S. Africa
126 B2 Richardson Mountains Can.
135 D3 Richfield U.S.A.
134 C1 Richland U.S.A.
140 A2 Richland Center U.S.A.
53 D2 Richmond N.S.W. Austr.
51 D2 Richmond Qld Austr.
54 B2 Richmond N.Z.
122 B3 Richmond S. Africa
98 C1 Richmond U.K.
140 C3 Richmond IN U.S.A.
140 C3 Richmond KY U.S.A.
141 D3 Richmond VA U.S.A.
130 C2 Rideau Lakes Can.
135 C3 Ridgecrest U.S.A.
102 C1 Riesa Ger.
100 D1 Rieste Ger.
123 B2 Riet r. S. Africa
101 D2 Rietberg Ger.
108 B2 Rieti Italy
136 B3 Rifle U.S.A.
88 B2 Rīga Latvia
88 B2 Riga, Gulf of Estonia/Latvia
79 C2 Rīgān Iran
134 D2 Rigby U.S.A.
131 E1 Rigolet Can.
93 H3 Riihimäki Fin.
108 B1 Rijeka Croatia
134 C2 Riley U.S.A.
78 B2 Rimah, Wādī al watercourse
        Saudi Arabia
103 D2 Rimavská Sobota Slovakia
128 C2 Rimbey Can.
108 B2 Rimini Italy
131 D2 Rimouski Can.
93 F3 Ringebu Norway
93 E4 Ringkøbing Denmark
92 G2 Ringvassøya i. Norway
101 D1 Rinteln Ger.
150 A2 Riobamba Ecuador
150 B3 Rio Branco Brazil
154 C3 Rio Branco do Sul Brazil
154 B2 Rio Brilhante Brazil
154 C2 Rio Claro Brazil
153 B4 Rio Colorado Arg.
153 B4 Rio Cuarto Arg.
155 D2 Rio de Janeiro Brazil
153 B6 Rio Gallegos Arg.
153 B6 Rio Grande Arg.
154 C2 Rio Grande Brazil
144 B2 Rio Grande Mex.
139 D3 Rio Grande r. Mex./U.S.A.
139 D3 Rio Grande City U.S.A.
150 A1 Riohacha Col.
150 A2 Rioja Peru

Río Lagartos

145 D2 Río Lagartos Mex.
105 C2 Riom France
152 B2 Río Mulatos Bol.
154 C3 Río Negro Brazil
155 D1 Río Pardo de Minas Brazil
138 B1 Rio Rancho U.S.A.
150 A2 Rio Tigre Ecuador
154 B1 Rio Verde Brazil
145 C2 Río Verde Mex.
154 B1 Rio Verde de Mato Grosso Brazil
90 C1 Ripky Ukr.
98 C2 Ripley U.K.
107 D1 Ripoll Spain
98 C1 Ripon U.K.
66 D1 Rishiri-tō i. Japan
93 E4 Risør Norway
122 B2 Ritchie S. Africa
63 A2 Ritchie's Archipelago is India
134 C1 Ritzville U.S.A.
152 B3 Rivadavia Arg.
108 B1 Riva del Garda Italy
146 B3 Rivas Nic.
152 C4 Rivera Uru.
129 D2 Riverhurst Can.
52 B2 Riverina reg. Austr.
122 B3 Riversdale S. Africa
135 C4 Riverside U.S.A.
136 B2 Riverton U.S.A.
131 D2 Riverview Can.
104 C3 Rivesaltes France
131 D2 Rivière-du-Loup Can.
90 B1 Rivne Ukr.
54 B2 Riwaka N.Z.
78 B2 Riyadh Saudi Arabia
81 C1 Rize Turkey
70 B2 Rizhao China
105 C2 Roanne France
141 D3 Roanoke U.S.A.
143 E1 Roanoke r. U.S.A.
143 E1 Roanoke Rapids U.S.A.
52 A3 Robe Austr.
101 F1 Röbel Ger.
130 C1 Robert-Bourassa, Réservoir resr Can.
92 H3 Robertsfors Sweden
122 A3 Robertson S. Africa
114 A4 Robertsport Liberia
131 C2 Roberval Can.
50 A2 Robinson Range hills Austr.
52 B2 Robinvale Austr.
129 D2 Roblin Can.
128 C2 Robson, Mount Can.
108 B3 Rocca Busambra mt. Sicilia Italy
153 C4 Rocha Uru.
98 B2 Rochdale U.K.
154 B1 Rochedo Brazil
100 B1 Rochefort Belgium
104 B2 Rochefort France
137 E2 Rochester MN U.S.A.
141 E2 Rochester NH U.S.A.
141 D2 Rochester NY U.S.A.
140 B2 Rockford U.S.A.
51 E2 Rockhampton Austr.
143 D2 Rock Hill U.S.A.
50 A3 Rockingham Austr.
140 A2 Rock Island U.S.A.
136 B1 Rock Springs MT U.S.A.
139 C3 Rocksprings U.S.A.
136 B2 Rock Springs WY U.S.A.
136 C3 Rocky Ford U.S.A.
143 E1 Rocky Mount U.S.A.
128 C2 Rocky Mountain House Can.
124 G3 Rocky Mountains Can./U.S.A.
100 B3 Rocroi France
102 C1 Rødbyhavn Denmark
131 E1 Roddickton Can.
104 C3 Rodez France
89 F2 Rodniki Rus. Fed.
Rodos Greece see Rhodes
Rodos i. Greece see Rhodes
50 A2 Roebourne Austr.
50 B1 Roebuck Bay Austr.
123 C1 Roedtan S. Africa
100 B2 Roermond Neth.
100 A2 Roeselare Belgium
127 F2 Roes Welcome Sound sea chan. Can.
142 B1 Rogers U.S.A.
122 B3 Roggeveldberge esc. S. Africa
92 G2 Rognan Norway
134 B2 Rogue r. U.S.A.
88 B2 Roja Latvia
60 B1 Rokan r. Indon.
88 C2 Rokiškis Lith.
90 B1 Rokytne Ukr.
154 B2 Rolândia Brazil
137 E3 Rolla U.S.A.
51 D2 Roma Austr.
Roma Italy see Rome
123 C2 Roma Lesotho
139 D3 Roma U.S.A.
143 E2 Romain, Cape U.S.A.
110 C1 Roman Romania
59 C3 Romang, Pulau i. Indon.
110 B1 Romania country Europe
91 C3 Roman-Kosh mt. Ukr.
69 D2 Romanovka Rus. Fed.
105 D2 Rombas France
64 B1 Romblon Phil.
108 B2 Rome Italy
143 C2 Rome GA U.S.A.
141 D2 Rome NY U.S.A.
99 D3 Romford U.K.
105 C2 Romilly-sur-Seine France
91 C1 Romny Ukr.
104 C2 Romorantin-Lanthenay France
99 C3 Romsey U.K.
96 □ Ronas Hill U.K.
151 C3 Roncador, Serra do hills Brazil
106 B2 Ronda Spain
154 B2 Rondon Brazil
154 B1 Rondonópolis Brazil
74 B1 Rondu Pak.
71 A3 Rong'an China
71 A3 Rongjiang China
62 A1 Rongklang Range mts Myanmar
Rongmei China see Hefeng
93 F4 Rønne Denmark
55 P2 Ronne Ice Shelf Antarctica
101 D1 Ronnenberg Ger.
100 A2 Ronse Belgium
75 C2 Roorkee India
100 B2 Roosendaal Neth.
135 E2 Roosevelt U.S.A.
128 B2 Roosevelt, Mount Can.
55 K2 Roosevelt Island Antarctica
104 B3 Roquefort France
150 B1 Roraima, Mount Guyana
93 F3 Røros Norway
153 B4 Rosario Arg.
144 A1 Rosario Baja California Mex.
144 B2 Rosario Sinaloa Mex.
144 B2 Rosario Sonora Mex.
151 C3 Rosário Oeste Brazil
144 A2 Rosarito Mex.
109 C3 Roscoff France
109 C2 Roscommon Ireland
97 C2 Roscrea Ireland
147 D3 Roseau Dominica
137 D1 Roseau U.S.A.
134 B2 Roseburg U.S.A.
139 D3 Rosenberg U.S.A.
101 D1 Rosengarten Ger.
102 C2 Rosenheim Ger.
129 D2 Rosetown Can.
122 A2 Rosh Pinah Namibia
110 C2 Roşiori de Vede Romania
93 F4 Roskilde Denmark
89 D3 Roslavl' Rus. Fed.
109 C3 Rossano Italy
97 B1 Rossan Point Ireland
55 K1 Ross Ice Shelf Antarctica
131 D2 Rossignol, Lake Can.
128 C3 Rossland Can.
97 C2 Rosslare Ireland
114 A3 Rosso Maur.
105 D3 Rosso, Capo c. Corse France
99 B3 Ross-on-Wye U.K.
91 D1 Rossosh' Rus. Fed.
128 A1 Ross River Can.
55 K2 Ross Sea Antarctica
92 F2 Røssvatnet l. Norway
79 C2 Rostāq Iran
129 D2 Rosthern Can.
102 C1 Rostock Ger.
89 E2 Rostov Rus. Fed.
91 D2 Rostov-na-Donu Rus. Fed.
92 H2 Rosvik Sweden
138 C2 Roswell U.S.A.
59 C3 Rota i. N. Mariana Is
59 C3 Rote i. Indon.
101 D1 Rotenburg (Wümme) Ger.
102 C2 Roth Ger.
98 C1 Rothbury U.K.
98 C2 Rotherham U.K.
96 B3 Rothesay U.K.
53 C1 Roto Austr.
105 D3 Rotondo, Monte mt. Corse France
54 C1 Rotorua N.Z.
54 C1 Rotorua, Lake N.Z.
101 E2 Rottenbach Ger.
102 C2 Rottenmann Austria
100 B2 Rotterdam Neth.
102 B2 Rottweil Ger.
49 F3 Rotuma i. Fiji
105 C1 Roubaix France
104 C2 Rouen France
Roulers Belgium see Roeselare
53 D2 Round Mountain Austr.
131 E2 Round Pond l. Can.
139 D2 Round Rock U.S.A.
134 E1 Roundup U.S.A.
96 C1 Rousay i. U.K.
130 C2 Rouyn-Noranda Can.
92 I2 Rovaniemi Fin.
91 D2 Roven'ki Rus. Fed.
91 D2 Roven'ky Ukr.
108 B1 Rovereto Italy
63 B2 Rôviĕng Tbong Cambodia
108 B1 Rovigo Italy
108 B1 Rovinj Croatia
53 C1 Rowena Austr.
64 B1 Roxas Capiz Phil.
64 B1 Roxas Oriental Mindoro Phil.
64 A1 Roxas Palawan Phil.
64 B2 Roxas Zamboanga del Norte Phil.
52 A2 Roxby Downs Austr.
138 C2 Roy U.S.A.
140 B1 Royale, Isle i. U.S.A.
104 B2 Royan France
99 C2 Royston U.K.
90 C2 Rozdil'na Ukr.
91 C2 Rozdol'ne Ukr.

100 B3 Rozoy-sur-Serre France
87 D3 Rtishchevo Rus. Fed.
54 C1 Ruapehu, Mount vol. N.Z.
54 A3 Ruapuke Island N.Z.
78 B3 Rub' al Khālī des. Saudi Arabia
71 D2 Rubizhne Ukr.
77 E1 Rubtsovsk Rus. Fed.
135 C2 Ruby Mountains U.S.A.
66 C2 Rudnaya Pristan' Rus. Fed.
87 D3 Rudnya Rus. Fed.
76 C1 Rudnyy Kazakh.
82 E1 Rudol'fa, Ostrov i. Rus. Fed.
101 E2 Rudolstadt Ger.
119 D2 Rufiji r. Tanz.
153 B4 Rufino Arg.
121 B2 Rufunsa Zambia
70 C2 Rugao China
99 C2 Rugby U.K.
132 C1 Rugby U.S.A.
102 E1 Rügen i. Ger.
62 E1 Ruhla Ger.
88 B2 Ruhnu i. Estonia
100 C2 Ruhr r. Ger.
71 C3 Rui'an China
138 B2 Ruidoso U.S.A.
144 B2 Ruiz Mex.
119 D3 Rukwa, Lake Tanz.
44 I.U.K.
109 C1 Rum i. U.K.
109 C1 Ruma Serbia
78 B2 Rumāh Saudi Arabia
117 A4 Rumbek Sudan
105 D2 Rumilly France
50 C1 Rum Jungle Austr.
54 B2 Runanga N.Z.
98 B2 Runcorn U.K.
120 A2 Rundu Namibia
68 B2 Ruoqiang China
62 C1 Rupert r. Can.
128 C1 Rupert Bay Can.
121 C2 Rusape Zimbabwe
110 C2 Ruse Bulg.
77 Rushon Tajik.
136 C2 Rushville U.S.A.
53 C3 Rushworth Austr.
54 B1 Russell N.Z.
142 C2 Russellville AL U.S.A.
142 B1 Russellville AR U.S.A.
142 B1 Russellville KY U.S.A.
101 D2 Rüsselsheim Ger.
82 F2 Russian Federation country
     Asia/Europe
123 C2 Rustenburg S. Africa
142 B2 Ruston U.S.A.
98 B2 Ruthin U.K.
141 E2 Rutland U.S.A.
119 D3 Ruvuma r. Moz./Tanz.
79 C2 Ruweis U.A.E.
77 C1 Ruzayevka Kazakh.
87 D3 Ruzayevka Rus. Fed.
119 C3 Rwanda country Africa
89 E3 Ryazan' Rus. Fed.
89 E3 Ryazhsk Rus. Fed.
86 C2 Rybachiy, Poluostrov pen.
     Rus. Fed.
89 E2 Rybinsk Rus. Fed.
89 E2 Rybinskoye
     Vodokhranilishche resr
     Rus. Fed.
103 D1 Rybnik Pol.
89 E3 Rybnoye Rus. Fed.
99 C3 Rye U.K.
67 D3 Ryl'sk Rus. Fed.
67 D3 Ryōtsu Japan
67 Ryukyu Islands Japan
103 E1 Rzeszów Pol.
89 D2 Rzhev Rus. Fed.

79 C2 Sa'ādatābād Iran
101 E2 Saale r. Ger.
101 E2 Saalfeld Ger.
102 B2 Saarbrücken Ger.
88 B2 Saaremaa i. Estonia
92 I2 Saarenkylä Fin.
93 I3 Saarijärvi Fin.
102 B2 Saarlouis Ger.
80 B2 Sab' Ābār Syria
107 D1 Sabadell Spain
61 C1 Sabah state Malaysia
61 C2 Sabalana i. Indon.
155 D1 Sabará Brazil
108 B2 Sabaudia Italy
115 D2 Sabhā Libya
123 D2 Sabie r. Moz./S. Africa
145 B2 Sabinas Mex.
145 B2 Sabinas Hidalgo Mex.
131 D2 Sable, Cape Can.
143 D3 Sable, Cape U.S.A.
131 E2 Sable Island Can.
106 B1 Sabugal Port.
78 B3 Şabyā Saudi Arabia
76 B3 Sabzevār Iran
120 A2 Sachanga Angola
130 B1 Sachigo Lake Can.
65 B3 Sach'on S. Korea
126 C2 Sachs Harbour Can.
135 B3 Sacramento U.S.A.
138 B2 Sacramento Mountains U.S.A.
135 B2 Sacramento Valley U.S.A.
123 C3 Sada S. Africa
107 C1 Sádaba Spain
78 B3 Şa'dah Yemen
62 A1 Sadiya India
67 C3 Sadoga-shima i. Japan
107 D2 Sa Dragonera i. Spain
93 F4 Säffle Sweden
138 B2 Safford U.S.A.
99 D2 Saffron Walden U.K.
114 B1 Safi Morocco
76 C3 Safīd Kūh mts Afgh.
86 D2 Safonovo Arkhangel'skaya
     Oblast' Rus. Fed.
89 D2 Safonovo Smolenskaya Oblast'
     Rus. Fed.
78 B2 Safrā' as Sark esc. Saudi
     Arabia
75 C2 Saga China
67 B4 Saga Japan
62 A1 Sagaing Myanmar
67 C3 Sagamihara Japan
75 B2 Sagar India
140 C2 Saginaw U.S.A.
140 C2 Saginaw Bay U.S.A.
106 B2 Sagres Port.
146 B2 Sagua la Grande Cuba
141 F1 Saguenay r. Can.
107 C2 Sagunto Spain
76 B2 Sagyndyk, Mys pt Kazakh.
106 B1 Sahagún Spain
114 C3 Sahara des. Africa
     Saharan Atlas mts Alg. see
     Atlas Saharien
75 B2 Saharanpur India
75 C2 Saharsa India
114 B3 Sahel reg. Africa
144 B2 Sahuayo Mex.
78 B2 Şāḥūq reg. Saudi Arabia
     Saïda Lebanon see Sidon
75 C2 Saidpur Bangl.
     Saigon Vietnam see Ho Chi
     Minh City
62 A1 Saiha India

69 D2 Saihan Tal China
67 B4 Saiki Japan
93 I3 Saimaa l. Fin.
144 B2 Sain Alto Mex.
96 C3 St Abb's Head U.K.
99 C3 St Albans U.K.
99 B3 St Aldhelm's Head U.K.
96 C2 St Andrews U.K.
131 E1 St Anthony Can.
134 D2 St Anthony U.S.A.
52 B3 St Arnaud Austr.
131 E1 St-Augustin Can.
131 E1 St-Augustin r. Can.
143 D3 St Augustine U.S.A.
99 A3 St Austell U.K.
104 C2 St-Avertin France
98 B1 St Bees Head U.K.
105 D3 St-Bonnet-en-Champsaur
     France
99 A3 St Bride's Bay U.K.
104 B2 St-Brieuc France
130 C2 St Catharines Can.
99 C3 St Catherine's Point U.K.
137 E3 St Charles U.S.A.
140 C2 St Clair, Lake Can./U.S.A.
105 D2 St-Claude France
137 E1 St Cloud U.S.A.
140 A1 St Croix r. U.S.A.
147 D3 St Croix i. Virgin Is (U.S.A.)
105 C2 St-Dizier France
131 D2 Ste-Anne-des-Monts Can.
105 D2 St-Égrève France
126 B2 St Elias Mountains Can.
131 D1 Ste-Marguerite r. Can.
129 E2 Sainte Rose du Lac Can.
104 B2 Saintes France
105 C2 St-Étienne France
108 A2 St-Florent Corse France
105 C2 St-Flour France
136 C3 St Francis U.S.A.
104 C3 St-Gaudens France
53 C1 St George Austr.
135 D3 St George U.S.A.
143 D3 St George Island U.S.A.
131 C2 St-Georges Can.
147 D3 St George's Grenada
97 C3 St George's Channel
     Ireland/U.K.
105 D2 St Gotthard Pass Switz.
113 E8 St Helena terr. S. Atlantic
     Ocean
122 A3 St Helena Bay S. Africa
122 A3 St Helena Bay S. Africa
98 B2 St Helens U.K.
134 B1 St Helens, Mount vol. U.S.A.
95 C4 St Helier Channel Is
100 B2 St-Hubert Belgium
141 E1 St-Hyacinthe Can.
140 C1 St Ignace U.S.A.
130 B2 St Ignace Island Can.
99 A3 St Ives U.K.
128 A2 St James, Cape Can.
131 C2 St-Jean, Lac l. Can.
104 B2 St-Jean-d'Angély France
104 B2 St-Jean-de-Monts France
130 C2 St-Jean-sur-Richelieu Can.
141 E1 St-Jérôme Can.
134 C1 St Joe r. U.S.A.
131 D2 Saint John Can.
141 F1 St John r. U.S.A.
147 D3 St John's Antigua
131 E2 St John's Can.
138 B2 St Johns U.S.A.
141 E2 St Johnsbury U.S.A.
137 E3 St Joseph U.S.A.
130 A1 St Joseph, Lake Can.
130 B2 St Joseph Island Can.

104 C2	St-Junien France	
94 B2	St Kilda *is* U.K.	
147 D3	St Kitts and Nevis *country*	
	West Indies	
	St-Laurent, Golfe du *g.* Can.	
	see St Lawrence, Gulf of	
151 C1	St-Laurent-du-Maroni	
	Fr. Guiana	
131 D2	St Lawrence *inlet* Can.	
131 D2	St Lawrence, Gulf of Can.	
83 N2	St Lawrence Island U.S.A.	
104 B2	St-Lô France	
114 A3	St-Louis Senegal	
137 E3	St Louis U.S.A.	
137 E1	St Louis *r.* U.S.A.	
147 D3	St Lucia *country* West Indies	
123 D2	St Lucia Estuary S. Africa	
104 B2	St-Malo France	
104 B2	St-Malo, Golfe de *g.* France	
122 A3	St Martin, Cape S. Africa	
141 D2	St Marys U.S.A.	
130 C2	St-Maurice *r.* Can.	
104 B2	St-Nazaire France	
104 C1	St-Omer France	
129 E2	St Paul Can.	
137 E2	St Paul U.S.A.	
137 E2	St Peter U.S.A.	
95 C4	St Peter Port Channel Is	
89 D2	St Petersburg Rus. Fed.	
143 D3	St Petersburg U.S.A.	
131 E2	St-Pierre St Pierre and	
	Miquelon	
131 E2	St Pierre and Miquelon *terr.*	
	N. America	
104 B2	St-Pierre-d'Oléron France	
105 C2	St-Pourçain-sur-Sioule France	
131 D2	St Quentin Can.	
105 C2	St-Quentin France	
131 D2	St-Siméon Can.	
129 E2	St Theresa Point Can.	
130 B2	St Thomas Can.	
105 D3	St-Tropez France	
105 D3	St-Tropez, Cap de *c.* France	
52 A3	St Vincent, Gulf Austr.	
147 D3	St Vincent and the	
	Grenadines *country* West	
	Indies	
100 C2	St-Vith Belgium	
129 D2	St Walburg Can.	
104 C2	St-Yrieix-la-Perche France	
59 D1	Saipan *i.* N. Mariana Is	
67 C3	Sajama Japan	
152 B2	Sajama, Nevado *mt.* Bol.	
122 B2	Sak *watercourse* S. Africa	
67 C4	Sakai Japan	
67 B4	Sakaide Japan	
78 B2	Sakākah Saudi Arabia	
136 C1	Sakakawea, Lake U.S.A.	
111 D2	Sakarya *r.* Turkey	
66 C3	Sakata Japan	
65 B1	Sakchu N. Korea	
83 K3	Sakhalin *i.* Rus. Fed.	
122 B3	Sakhile S. Africa	
81 C1	Şäki Azer.	
88 B3	Šakiai Lith.	
69 E3	Sakishima-shotō *is* Japan	
62 B2	Sakon Nakhon Thai.	
122 B3	Sakrivier S. Africa	
67 D3	Sakura Japan	
91 C2	Saky Ukr.	
93 G4	Sala Sweden	
130 C2	Salaberry-de-Valleyfield Can.	
88 B2	Salacgrīva Latvia	
109 C2	Sala Consilina Italy	
135 C4	Salada, Laguna *salt l.* Mex.	
152 B4	Salado *r.* Arg.	
145 C2	Salado *r.* Mex.	
114 B4	Salaga Ghana	
122 B1	Salajwe Botswana	
115 D3	Salal Chad	
78 A2	Salāla Sudan	
79 C3	Şalālah Oman	
145 B2	Salamanca Mex.	
106 C1	Salamanca Spain	
106 B1	Salas Spain	
63 B2	Salavan Laos	
59 C3	Salawati *i.* Indon.	
58 C3	Salayar *i.* Indon.	
104 C2	Salbris France	
88 C3	Šalčininkai Lith.	
106 C1	Saldaña Spain	
122 A3	Saldanha S. Africa	
88 B2	Saldus Latvia	
53 C3	Sale Austr.	
86 F2	Salekhard Rus. Fed.	
73 B3	Salem India	
137 E3	Salem MO U.S.A.	
134 B2	Salem OR U.S.A.	
96 B2	Salen U.K.	
109 B2	Salerno Italy	
98 B2	Salford U.K.	
151 E2	Salgado *r.* Brazil	
103 D2	Salgótarján Hungary	
151 E2	Salgueiro Brazil	
136 B3	Salida U.S.A.	
111 C3	Salihli Turkey	
88 C3	Salihorsk Belarus	
121 C2	Salima Malawi	
121 C2	Salima Moz.	
137 D3	Salina U.S.A.	
108 B3	Salina, Isola *i.* Italy	
145 C3	Salina Cruz Mex.	
155 D1	Salinas Brazil	
146 A2	Salinas Mex.	
135 B3	Salinas U.S.A.	
107 D2	Salines, Cap de ses *c.* Spain	
151 D2	Salinópolis Brazil	
99 C3	Salisbury U.K.	
141 D3	Salisbury MD U.S.A.	
143 D1	Salisbury NC U.S.A.	
99 B3	Salisbury Plain U.K.	
151 D2	Salitre *r.* Brazil	
92 I2	Salla Fin.	
127 F2	Salluit Can.	
75 C2	Sallyana Nepal	
81 C2	Salmās Iran	
134 D1	Salmon U.S.A.	
134 C1	Salmon *r.* U.S.A.	
128 C2	Salmon Arm Can.	
134 C2	Salmon River Mountains	
	U.S.A.	
100 C3	Salmtal Ger.	
93 H3	Salo Fin.	
87 D4	Sal'sk Rus. Fed.	
122 B3	Salt *watercourse* S. Africa	
138 A2	Salt *r.* U.S.A.	
152 B3	Salta Arg.	
145 B2	Saltillo Mex.	
134 D2	Salt Lake City U.S.A.	
154 C2	Salto Brazil	
152 C4	Salto Uru.	
155 E1	Salto da Divisa Brazil	
154 B2	Salto del Guairá Brazil	
135 C4	Salton Sea *salt l.* U.S.A.	
143 D2	Saluda U.S.A.	
108 A2	Saluzzo Italy	
151 E3	Salvador Brazil	
79 C2	Salwah Saudi Arabia	
62 A1	Salween *r.* China/Myanmar	
81 C2	Salyan Azer.	
102 C2	Salzburg Austria	
101 E1	Salzgitter Ger.	
101 D2	Salzkotten Ger.	
101 E1	Salzwedel Ger.	
144 B1	Samalayuca Mex.	
66 D2	Samani Japan	
64 B1	Samar *i.* Phil.	
87 E3	Samara Rus. Fed.	
61 C2	Samarinda Indon.	
77 C3	Samarqand Uzbek.	
81 C2	Sämarrä' Iraq	
81 C1	Şamaxı Azer.	
119 C3	Samba Dem. Rep. Congo	
61 C1	Sambaliung *mts* Indon.	
75 C2	Sambalpur India	
61 C2	Sambar, Tanjung *pt* Indon.	
61 B1	Sambas Indon.	
121 E2	Sambava Madag.	
90 A2	Sambir Ukr.	
153 C4	Samborombón, Bahía *b.* Arg.	
65 B2	Samch'ŏk S. Korea	
81 C2	Samdi Dag *mt.* Turkey	
119 D3	Same Tanz.	
78 B2	Samīrah Saudi Arabia	
65 B1	Samjiyŏn N. Korea	
49 G3	Samoa *country* S. Pacific	
	Ocean	
109 C1	Samobor Croatia	
111 C3	Samos *i.* Greece	
111 C2	Samothraki Greece	
111 C2	Samothraki *i.* Greece	
61 C2	Sampit Indon.	
119 C3	Sampwe Dem. Rep. Congo	
139 E2	Sam Rayburn Reservoir U.S.A.	
80 B1	Samsun Turkey	
81 C1	Samtredia Georgia	
63 B3	Samui, Ko *i.* Thai.	
63 B2	Samut Songkhram Thai.	
114 B3	San Mali	
78 B3	Şan'ā' Yemen	
118 A2	Sanaga *r.* Cameroon	
81 C2	Sanandaj Iran	
146 B3	San Andrés, Isla de *i.*	
	Caribbean Sea	
138 B2	San Andres Mountains U.S.A.	
145 C3	San Andrés Tuxtla Mex.	
139 C2	San Angelo U.S.A.	
139 D3	San Antonio U.S.A.	
135 C4	San Antonio, Mount U.S.A.	
152 B3	San Antonio de los Cobres	
	Arg.	
153 B5	San Antonio Oeste Arg.	
108 B2	San Benedetto del Tronto	
	Italy	
144 A3	San Benedicto, Isla *i.* Mex.	
135 C4	San Bernardino U.S.A.	
135 C4	San Bernardino Mountains	
	U.S.A.	
143 D3	San Blas, Cape U.S.A.	
152 B2	San Borja Bol.	
144 B2	San Buenaventura Mex.	
64 B1	San Carlos Phil.	
147 D4	San Carlos Venez.	
153 A5	San Carlos de Bariloche Arg.	
147 C4	San Carlos del Zulia Venez.	
135 C4	San Clemente Island U.S.A.	
104 C2	Sancoins France	
150 A1	San Cristóbal Venez.	
145 C3	San Cristóbal de las Casas	
	Mex.	
146 C2	Sancti Spíritus Cuba	
123 D1	Sand *r.* S. Africa	
61 C1	Sandakan *Sabah* Malaysia	
93 E3	Sandane Norway	
111 B2	Sandanski Bulg.	
96 C1	Sanday *i.* U.K.	
139 C2	Sanderson U.S.A.	
150 B3	Sandia Peru	
135 C4	San Diego U.S.A.	
80 B2	Sandıklı Turkey	
93 E4	Sandnes Norway	

92	F2	Sandnessjøen Norway
118	C3	Sandoa Dem. Rep. Congo
103	E1	Sandomierz Pol.
89	E2	Sandovo Rus. Fed.
94	B1	Sandoy i. Faroe Is
134	C1	Sandpoint U.S.A.
71	B3	Sandu China
94	B1	Sandur Faroe Is
140	C2	Sandusky U.S.A.
122	A3	Sandveld mts S. Africa
93	F4	Sandvika Norway
93	G3	Sandviken Sweden
131	E1	Sandwich Bay Can.
129	C2	Sandy Bay Can.
51	E2	Sandy Cape Austr.
130	A1	Sandy Lake Can.
130	A1	Sandy Lake Can.
144	A1	San Felipe Baja California Mex.
145	B2	San Felipe Guanajuato Mex.
150	B1	San Felipe Venez.
144	A1	San Fernando Baja California Mex.
145	C3	San Fernando Tamaulipas Mex.
64	B1	San Fernando La Union Phil.
64	B1	San Fernando Pampanga Phil.
106	B2	San Fernando Spain
147	D3	San Fernando Trin. and Tob.
150	B1	San Fernando de Apure Venez.
143	D3	Sanford FL U.S.A.
141	E2	Sanford ME U.S.A.
152	B4	San Francisco Arg.
135	B3	San Francisco U.S.A.
107	D2	San Francisco Javier Spain
74	B3	Sangamner India
83	J2	Sangar Rus. Fed.
108	A3	San Gavino Monreale Sardegna Italy
101	E2	Sangerhausen Ger.
61	C1	Sanggau Indon.
118	B3	Sangha r. Congo
109	C3	San Giovanni in Fiore Italy
64	B2	Sangir i. Indon.
59	C2	Sangir, Kepulauan is Indon.
65	B2	Sangju S. Korea
61	C1	Sangkulirang Indon.
73	B3	Sangli India
118	B2	Sangmélima Cameroon
121	C3	Sango Zimbabwe
136	B3	Sangre de Cristo Range mts U.S.A.
75	C2	Sangsang China
144	A2	San Hipólito, Punta pt Mex.
144	A2	San Ignacio Mex.
130	C1	Sanikiluaq Can.
71	A3	Sanjiang China
135	B3	San Joaquin r. U.S.A.
153	B5	San Jorge, Golfo de g. Arg.
146	B3	San José Costa Rica
64	B1	San Jose Nueva Ecija Phil.
64	B1	San Jose Occidental Mindoro Phil.
135	B3	San Jose U.S.A.
144	A2	San José, Isla i. Mex.
144	B2	San José de Bavicora Mex.
64	B1	San Jose de Buenavista Phil.
144	A2	San José de Comondú Mex.
144	A1	San José del Cabo Mex.
150	A1	San José del Guaviare Col.
152	B4	San Juan Arg.
146	B3	San Juan r. Costa Rica/Nic.
147	D3	San Juan Puerto Rico
135	D3	San Juan r. U.S.A.
145	C3	San Juan Bautista Tuxtepec Mex.
134	B1	San Juan Islands U.S.A.
144	B2	San Juanito Mex.
136	B3	San Juan Mountains U.S.A.
153	B5	San Julián Arg.
75	C2	Sankh r. India
105	D2	Sankt Gallen Switz.
105	D2	Sankt Moritz Switz.
		Sankt-Peterburg Rus. Fed. see St Petersburg
102	C2	Sankt Veit an der Glan Austria
100	C3	Sankt Wendel Ger.
80	B2	Şanlıurfa Turkey
138	B3	San Lorenzo Mex.
106	B2	Sanlúcar de Barrameda Spain
144	B2	San Lucas Mex.
153	B4	San Luis Arg.
145	B2	San Luis de la Paz Mex.
138	A2	San Luisito Mex.
135	B3	San Luis Obispo U.S.A.
145	B2	San Luis Potosí Mex.
144	A1	San Luis Río Colorado Mex.
139	D3	San Marcos U.S.A.
108	B2	San Marino country Europe
108	B2	San Marino San Marino
144	B2	San Martín de Bolaños Mex.
153	A5	San Martín de los Andes Arg.
70	B2	Sanmenxia China
146	B3	San Miguel El Salvador
152	B3	San Miguel de Tucumán Arg.
145	C3	San Miguel Sola de Vega Mex.
71	B3	Sanming China
153	B4	San Nicolás de los Arroyos Arg.
135	C4	San Nicolas Island U.S.A.
123	C2	Sannieshof S. Africa
103	E2	Sanok Pol.
64	B1	San Pablo Phil.
144	B2	San Pablo Balleza Mex.
152	B3	San Pedro Arg.
152	B2	San Pedro Bol.
114	B4	San-Pédro Côte d'Ivoire
144	A2	San Pedro Mex.
138	A2	San Pedro watercourse U.S.A.
106	B2	San Pedro, Sierra de mts Spain
144	B2	San Pedro de las Colonias Mex.
146	B3	San Pedro Sula Hond.
108	A3	San Pietro, Isola di i. Sardegna Italy
144	A1	San Quintín, Cabo c. Mex.
153	B4	San Rafael Arg.
108	A2	San Remo Italy
146	B3	San Salvador El Salvador
152	B3	San Salvador de Jujuy Arg.
109	C2	San Severo Italy
109	C2	Sanski Most Bos.-Herz.
152	B2	Santa Ana Bol.
146	B3	Santa Ana El Salvador
144	A1	Santa Ana Mex.
135	C4	Santa Ana U.S.A.
144	B2	Santa Bárbara Mex.
135	C4	Santa Barbara U.S.A.
154	B2	Santa Bárbara, Serra de hills Brazil
152	B3	Santa Catalina Chile
150	B2	Santa Clara Col.
146	C2	Santa Clara Cuba
135	C4	Santa Clarita U.S.A.
109	C3	Santa Croce, Capo c. Sicilia Italy
153	B6	Santa Cruz r. Arg.
152	B2	Santa Cruz Bol.
64	B1	Santa Cruz Phil.
135	B3	Santa Cruz U.S.A.
145	C3	Santa Cruz Barillas Guat.
155	E1	Santa Cruz Cabrália Brazil
107	C2	Santa Cruz de Moya Spain
114	A2	Santa Cruz de Tenerife Islas Canarias
135	C4	Santa Cruz Island U.S.A.
48	F3	Santa Cruz Islands Solomon Is
152	B4	Santa Fé Arg.
138	B1	Santa Fe U.S.A.
154	B1	Santa Helena de Goiás Brazil
153	B4	Santa Isabel Arg.
154	B1	Santa Luisa, Serra de hills Brazil
152	C3	Santa Maria Brazil
144	B1	Santa María r. Mex.
135	B4	Santa Maria U.S.A.
123	D2	Santa Maria, Cabo de c. Moz.
106	B2	Santa Maria, Cabo de c. Port.
151	D2	Santa Maria das Barreiras Brazil
109	C3	Santa Maria di Leuca, Capo c. Italy
150	A1	Santa Marta Col.
135	C4	Santa Monica U.S.A.
151	D3	Santana Brazil
106	C1	Santander Spain
108	A3	Sant'Antioco Sardegna Italy
108	A3	Sant'Antioco, Isola di i. Sardegna Italy
107	D2	Sant Antoni de Portmany Spain
151	C2	Santarém Brazil
106	B2	Santarém Port.
154	B1	Santa Rita do Araguaia Brazil
153	B4	Santa Rosa Arg.
152	C3	Santa Rosa Brazil
135	B3	Santa Rosa CA U.S.A.
138	C2	Santa Rosa NM U.S.A.
146	B3	Santa Rosa de Copán Hond.
135	B4	Santa Rosa Island U.S.A.
144	A2	Santa Rosalía Mex.
152	C3	Santiago Brazil
153	A4	Santiago Chile
147	C3	Santiago Dom. Rep.
144	B2	Santiago Mex.
146	B4	Santiago Panama
64	B1	Santiago Phil.
106	B1	Santiago de Compostela Spain
144	B2	Santiago Ixcuintla Mex.
144	B2	Santiago Papasquiaro Mex.
107	D2	Sant Joan de Labritja Spain
107	D1	Sant Jordi, Golf de g. Spain
155	D2	Santo Amaro de Campos Brazil
155	C2	Santo André Brazil
152	C3	Santo Angelo Brazil
154	B2	Santo Antônio da Platina Brazil
151	E3	Santo Antônio de Jesus Brazil
150	B2	Santo Antônio do Içá Brazil
155	C2	Santo Antônio do Monte Brazil
147	D3	Santo Domingo Dom. Rep.
138	B1	Santo Domingo Pueblo U.S.A.
111	C3	Santorini i. Greece
155	C2	Santos Brazil
152	C3	Santo Tomé Arg.
153	A5	San Valentín, Cerro mt. Chile
146	B3	San Vicente El Salvador
144	A1	San Vicente Mex.
150	A3	San Vicente de Cañete Peru
108	B2	San Vincenzo Italy
108	B3	San Vito, Capo c. Sicilia Italy

Sanya

71 A4 Sanya China
155 C2 São Bernardo do Campo Brazil
152 C3 São Borja Brazil
154 C2 São Carlos Brazil
151 C3 São Félix *Mato Grosso* Brazil
151 C2 São Félix *Pará* Brazil
155 D2 São Fidélis Brazil
155 D1 São Francisco Brazil
151 E3 São Francisco r. Brazil
154 C3 São Francisco, Ilha de i. Brazil
154 C3 São Francisco r. Brazil
152 C4 São Francisco do Sul Brazil
152 C4 São Gabriel Brazil
155 D2 São Gonçalo Brazil
155 C1 São Gotardo Brazil
155 D2 São João da Barra Brazil
155 C2 São João da Boa Vista Brazil
106 B1 São João da Madeira Port.
155 D1 São João do Paraíso Brazil
155 D2 São João Nepomuceno Brazil
154 C2 São Joaquim da Barra Brazil
155 C2 São José do Rio Preto Brazil
155 C3 São José dos Campos Brazil
154 C3 São José dos Pinhais Brazil
155 D2 São Lourenço Brazil
151 D2 São Luís Brazil
154 C1 São Manuel Brazil
154 C1 São Marcos r. Brazil
151 D2 São Marcos, Baía de b. Brazil
155 E1 São Mateus Brazil
155 C2 São Paulo Brazil
151 D2 São Raimundo Nonato Brazil
155 C1 São Romão Brazil
155 C2 São Sebastião, Ilha do i. Brazil
154 C2 São Sebastião do Paraíso Brazil
154 B1 São Simão Brazil
154 B1 São Simão, Barragem de resr Brazil
59 C2 Sao-Siu Indon.
113 F6 São Tomé São Tomé and Príncipe
155 D2 São Tomé, Cabo de c. Brazil
113 F6 São Tomé and Príncipe country Africa
155 C2 São Vicente Brazil
106 B2 São Vicente, Cabo de c. Port.
59 C3 Saparua Indon.
89 F3 Sapozhok Rus. Fed.
66 D2 Sapporo Japan
109 C2 Sapri Italy
81 C2 Saqqez Iran
81 C2 Sarāb Iran
63 B2 Sara Buri Thai.
109 C2 Sarajevo Bos.-Herz.
76 B1 Sarakhtash Rus. Fed.
141 E2 Saranac Lake U.S.A.
109 D3 Sarandë Albania
64 B2 Sarangani Islands Phil.
87 D3 Saransk Rus. Fed.
87 E3 Sarapul Rus. Fed.
143 D3 Sarasota U.S.A.
90 B2 Sarata Ukr.
136 B2 Saratoga U.S.A.
141 E2 Saratoga Springs U.S.A.
61 C1 Saratok Sarawak Malaysia
87 D3 Saratov Rus. Fed.
79 D2 Saravan Iran
61 C1 Sarawak state Malaysia
110 C2 Saray Turkey
111 C3 Sarayköy Turkey
79 D2 Sarbāz Iran
74 B2 Sardarshahr India
108 A2 Sardegna i. Italy see Sardinia
108 A2 Sardinia i. Italy
92 G2 Sarektjåkkå mt. Sweden
77 C3 Sar-e Pol Afgh.

158 B3 Sargasso Sea N. Atlantic Ocean
74 B1 Sargodha Pak.
115 D4 Sarh Chad
79 D2 Sarhad reg. Iran
81 D2 Sārī Iran
111 C3 Sarıgöl Turkey
81 C1 Sarıkamış Turkey
61 C1 Sarikei Sarawak Malaysia
51 D2 Sarina Austr.
115 D2 Sarīr Tibesti des. Libya
65 B2 Sariwŏn N. Korea
111 C2 Sarıyer Turkey
77 D2 Sarkand Kazakh.
111 C2 Şarköy Turkey
59 D3 Sarmi Indon.
140 C2 Sarnia Can.
90 B1 Sarny Ukr.
60 B2 Sarolangun Indon.
111 B3 Saronikos Kolpos g. Greece
111 C2 Saros Körfezi b. Turkey
87 D3 Sarova Rus. Fed.
105 D2 Sarrebourg France
106 B1 Sarria Spain
107 C1 Sarrión Spain
105 D3 Sartène Corse France
103 D2 Sárvár Hungary
76 B2 Sarykamyshskoye Ozero salt l. Turkm./Uzbek.
77 D2 Saryozek Kazakh.
82 F3 Sarysu watercourse Kazakh.
77 D3 Sary-Tash Kyrg.
75 C2 Sasaram India
67 A4 Sasebo Japan
129 D2 Saskatchewan prov. Can.
129 D2 Saskatchewan r. Can.
129 D2 Saskatoon Can.
83 I2 Saskylakh Rus. Fed.
123 C2 Sasolburg S. Africa
87 D3 Sasovo Rus. Fed.
114 B4 Sassandra Côte d'Ivoire
108 A2 Sassari Sardegna Italy
102 C1 Sassnitz Ger.
123 A3 Satadougou Mali
75 C2 Satara S. Africa
75 C2 Satna India
74 B2 Satpura Range mts India
63 B2 Sattahip Thai.
110 B1 Satu Mare Romania
63 B3 Satun Thai.
144 B2 Saucillo Mex.
93 E4 Sauda Norway
92 B2 Sauðárkrókur Iceland
78 B2 Saudi Arabia country Asia
105 C3 Saugues France
105 C2 Saulieu France
130 B2 Sault Sainte Marie Can.
140 C1 Sault Sainte Marie U.S.A.
77 C1 Saumalkol' Kazakh.
59 C3 Saumlakki Indon.
104 B2 Saumur France
120 B1 Saurimo Angola
109 C2 Sava r. Europe
49 G3 Savai'i i. Samoa
91 E1 Savala r. Rus. Fed.
143 D2 Savannah GA U.S.A.
142 C1 Savannah TN U.S.A.
143 D2 Savannah r. U.S.A.
63 B2 Savannakhét Laos
130 A1 Savant Lake Can.
111 C3 Savaştepe Turkey
89 F2 Savino Rus. Fed.
86 F2 Savinskiy Rus. Fed.
108 A2 Savona Italy
93 I3 Savonlinna Fin.
92 I2 Savukoski Fin.

74 B2 Savu Sea Indon. see Sawu, Savu
62 A2 Sawankhalok Thai.
136 B3 Sawatch Range mts U.S.A.
53 D2 Sawtell Austr.
59 C3 Sawu Indon.
79 C3 Saybūt Yemen
69 D2 Saynshand Mongolia
141 D2 Sayre U.S.A.
144 B3 Sayula Jalisco Mex.
145 C3 Sayula Veracruz Mex.
128 B2 Sayward Can.
89 E2 Sazonovo Rus. Fed.
114 B2 Sbaa Alg.
98 B1 Scafell Pike h. U.K.
109 C3 Scalea Italy
96 C1 Scapa Flow inlet U.K.
130 C2 Scarborough Can.
147 D3 Scarborough Trin. and Tob.
98 C1 Scarborough U.K.
64 A1 Scarborough Shoal sea feature S. China Sea
96 A2 Scarinish U.K.
Scarpanto i. Greece see Karpathos
105 D2 Schaffhausen Switz.
100 B1 Schagen Neth.
102 C2 Schärding Austria
100 A2 Scharendijke Neth.
101 D1 Scharhörn i. Ger.
101 D1 Scheeßel Ger.
131 D1 Schefferville Can.
135 D3 Schell Creek Range mts U.S.A.
141 E2 Schenectady U.S.A.
101 E3 Scheßlitz Ger.
100 C1 Schiermonnikoog i. Neth.
108 B1 Schio Italy
101 F2 Schkeuditz Ger.
101 E1 Schladen Ger.
101 E2 Schleiz Ger.
102 B1 Schleswig Ger.
101 D1 Schloss Holte-Stukenbrock Ger.
101 D2 Schlüchtern Ger.
101 E3 Schlüsselfeld Ger.
101 D2 Schmallenberg Ger.
101 D1 Schneverdingen Ger.
101 E1 Schönebeck (Elbe) Ger.
101 E1 Schöningen Ger.
100 B2 Schoonhoven Neth.
59 D3 Schouten Islands P.N.G.
102 B2 Schwäbische Alb mts Ger.
102 C2 Schwandorf Ger.
61 C2 Schwaner, Pegunungan mts Indon.
101 E1 Schwarzenbek Ger.
101 F2 Schwarzenberg Ger.
122 A2 Schwarzrand mts Namibia
Schwarzwald mts Ger. see Black Forest
102 C2 Schwaz Austria
102 C1 Schwedt an der Oder Ger.
101 E2 Schweinfurt Ger.
101 E1 Schwerin Ger.
101 E1 Schweriner See l. Ger.
105 D2 Schwyz Switz.
108 B3 Sciacca Sicilia Italy
95 B4 Scilly, Isles of U.K.
140 C3 Scioto r. U.S.A.
136 B1 Scobey U.S.A.
53 D2 Scone Austr.
55 R3 Scotia Ridge S. Atlantic Ocean
158 C8 Scotia Sea S. Atlantic Ocean
96 C2 Scotland admin. div. U.K.
128 B2 Scott, Cape Can.
123 D3 Scottburgh S. Africa

136 C3 Scott City U.S.A.
73 C2 Scottsbluff U.S.A.
142 C2 Scottsboro U.S.A.
96 B1 Scourie U.K.
141 D2 Scranton U.S.A.
98 C2 Scunthorpe U.K.
105 E2 Scuol Switz.
129 E2 Seal r. Can.
122 B3 Seal, Cape S. Africa
52 B3 Sea Lake Austr.
139 D3 Sealy U.S.A.
142 B1 Searcy U.S.A.
134 B1 Seascale U.K.
134 B1 Seattle U.S.A.
63 C2 Sebago Lake U.S.A.
144 A2 Sebastián Vizcaíno, Bahía b. Mex.
110 B1 Sebeş Romania
60 B2 Sebesi i. Indon.
88 C2 Sebezh Rus. Fed.
143 D3 Şebinkarahisar Turkey
128 B3 Sechelt Can.
150 A2 Sechura Peru
73 B3 Secunderabad India
137 E3 Sedalia U.S.A.
105 C2 Sedan France
54 B2 Seddon N.Z.
138 A2 Sedona U.S.A.
101 E2 Seeburg Ger.
101 E1 Seehausen (Altmark) Ger.
122 A2 Seeheim Namibia
104 C2 Sées France
101 E2 Seesen Ger.
101 E1 Seevetal Ger.
114 A4 Sefadu Sierra Leone
123 C1 Sefare Botswana
60 B1 Segamat Malaysia
86 C2 Segezha Rus. Fed.
114 B3 Ségou Mali
106 B1 Segovia Spain
115 D2 Séguédine Niger
114 B4 Séguéla Côte d'Ivoire
139 D3 Seguin U.S.A.
107 C2 Segura r. Spain
106 C2 Segura, Sierra de mts Spain
120 B3 Sehithwa Botswana
93 H3 Seinäjoki Fin.
104 C2 Seine r. France
104 B2 Seine, Baie de b. France
103 E1 Sejny Pol.
60 B2 Sekayu Indon.
114 B4 Sekondi Ghana
59 C3 Selaru i. Indon.
61 C2 Selatan, Tanjung pt Indon.
126 A2 Selawik U.S.A.
98 C2 Selby U.K.
120 B3 Selebi-Phikwe Botswana
105 D2 Sélestat France
92 A3 Selfoss Iceland
114 A3 Sélibabi Maur.
138 A1 Seligman U.S.A.
116 A2 Selîma Oasis Sudan
111 C3 Selimiye Turkey
114 B3 Sélingué, Lac de l. Mali
89 D2 Selizharovo Rus. Fed.
93 E4 Seljord Norway
129 E2 Selkirk Can.
96 C3 Selkirk U.K.
128 C2 Selkirk Mountains Can.
142 C2 Selma AL U.S.A.
135 C3 Selma CA U.S.A.
89 D3 Sel'tso Rus. Fed.
150 A2 Selvas reg. Brazil
129 D1 Selway r. U.S.A.
129 D1 Selwyn Lake l. Can.
128 A1 Selwyn Mountains Can.

51 C2 Selwyn Range hills Austr.
60 B2 Semangka, Teluk b. Indon.
61 C2 Semarang Indon.
61 B1 Sematan Sarawak Malaysia
118 B2 Sembé Congo
81 C2 Şemdinli Turkey
91 C1 Semenivka Ukr.
86 D3 Semenov Rus. Fed.
61 C2 Semeru, Gunung vol. Indon.
89 E3 Semiluki Rus. Fed.
136 B2 Seminoe Reservoir U.S.A.
139 D2 Seminole U.S.A.
143 D2 Seminole, Lake U.S.A.
77 E1 Semipalatinsk Kazakh.
61 C2 Semitau Indon.
81 D2 Semnān Iran
61 C1 Semporna Sabah Malaysia
105 C2 Semur-en-Auxois France
150 B2 Sena Madureira Brazil
120 B2 Senanga Zambia
67 B4 Sendai Kagoshima Japan
67 D3 Sendai Miyagi Japan
114 A3 Senegal country Africa
114 A3 Sénégal r. Maur./Senegal
102 C1 Senftenberg Ger.
119 D3 Sengerema Tanz.
151 D3 Senhor do Bonfim Brazil
108 B2 Senigallia Italy
109 B2 Senj Croatia
92 G2 Senja i. Norway
122 B2 Senlac S. Africa
104 C2 Senlis France
63 B2 Senmonorom Cambodia
117 B3 Sennar Sudan
130 C2 Senneterre Can.
123 C3 Senqu r. Lesotho
105 C2 Sens France
109 D1 Senta Serbia
128 B2 Sentinel Peak Can.
123 C2 Senwabarwana S. Africa
75 B2 Seoni India
65 B2 Seoul S. Korea
155 D2 Sepetiba, Baía de b. Brazil
59 D3 Sepik r. P.N.G.
61 C1 Sepinang Indon.
131 D1 Sept-Îles Can.
59 C3 Seram i. Indon.
59 C3 Seram, Laut sea Indon.
60 B2 Serang Indon.
109 D2 Serbia country Europe
76 B3 Serdar Turkm.
89 E3 Serebryanyye Prudy Rus. Fed.
60 B1 Seremban Malaysia
119 D3 Serengeti Plain Tanz.
87 D3 Sergach Rus. Fed.
89 E2 Sergiyev Posad Rus. Fed.
74 A1 Serhetabat Turkm.
61 C1 Seria Brunei
61 C1 Serian Sarawak Malaysia
111 B3 Serifos i. Greece
80 B2 Serik Turkey
59 C3 Sermata, Kepulauan is Indon.
86 F3 Serov Rus. Fed.
120 B3 Serowe Botswana
106 B2 Serpa Port.
89 E3 Serpukhov Rus. Fed.
151 D3 Serra da Mesa, Represa resr Brazil
154 B1 Serranópolis Brazil
100 A3 Serre r. France
111 B2 Serres Greece
151 E3 Serrinha Brazil
155 D1 Sêrro Brazil
154 C2 Sertãozinho Brazil
61 C2 Seruyan r. Indon.
68 C2 Sêrxü China
120 A2 Sesfontein Namibia

108 B2 Sessa Aurunca Italy
108 A2 Sestri Levante Italy
105 C3 Sète France
155 D1 Sete Lagoas Brazil
92 G2 Setermoen Norway
93 E4 Setesdal val. Norway
115 C1 Sétif Alg.
67 B4 Seto-naikai sea Japan
114 B1 Settat Morocco
98 B1 Settle U.K.
106 B2 Setúbal Port.
106 B2 Setúbal, Baía de b. Port.
130 A1 Seul, Lac l. Can.
76 A2 Sevan, Lake Armenia
Sevana Lich l. Armenia see
Sevan, Lake
91 C3 Sevastopol' Ukr.
105 C3 Sévérac-le-Château France
130 B1 Severn r. Can.
122 B2 Severn S. Africa
99 B3 Severn r. U.K.
86 D2 Severnaya Dvina r. Rus. Fed.
83 H1 Severnaya Zemlya is Rus. Fed.
86 D2 Severnyy Nenetskiy Avtonomnyy Okrug Rus. Fed.
86 F2 Severnyy Respublika Komi Rus. Fed.
86 C2 Severodvinsk Rus. Fed.
86 C2 Severomorsk Rus. Fed.
91 D3 Severskaya Rus. Fed.
135 D3 Sevier r. U.S.A.
135 D3 Sevier Lake U.S.A.
Sevilla Spain see Seville
106 B2 Seville Spain
128 A2 Sewall Inlet Can.
128 C2 Sexsmith Can.
144 B2 Sextín r. Mex.
86 G1 Seyakha Rus. Fed.
113 J7 Seychelles country Indian Ocean
92 C2 Seyðisfjörður Iceland
91 C1 Seym r. Rus. Fed./Ukr.
83 L2 Seymchan Rus. Fed.
53 C3 Seymour Austr.
140 B3 Seymour IN U.S.A.
139 D2 Seymour TX U.S.A.
105 C2 Sézanne France
110 C1 Sfântu Gheorghe Romania
115 D1 Sfax Tunisia
's-Gravenhage Neth. see The Hague
96 A2 Sgurr Alasdair h. U.K.
70 A2 Shaanxi prov. China
91 D2 Shabel'sk Rus. Fed.
77 D3 Shache China
55 R1 Shackleton Range mts Antarctica
99 B3 Shaftesbury U.K.
75 C2 Shahdol India
77 C3 Shah Fuladi mt. Afgh.
75 B2 Shahjahanpur India
81 D2 Shahr-e Kord Iran
81 D2 Shāhrezā Iran
77 C3 Shahrisabz Uzbek.
89 E2 Shakhovskaya Rus. Fed.
91 E2 Shakhty Rus. Fed.
86 D3 Shakhun'ya Rus. Fed.
66 D2 Shakotan-misaki c. Japan
76 B2 Shalkar Kazakh.
77 D3 Shaluli Shan mts China
129 E2 Shamattawa Can.
139 C1 Shamrock U.S.A.
68 C2 Shandan China
70 B2 Shandong prov. China
70 C2 Shandong Bandao pen. China
121 B2 Shangani r. Zimbabwe
70 C2 Shanghai China

70 C2 Shanghai *mun.* China
71 B3 Shanghang China
70 A2 Shangluo China
71 B3 Shangrao China
70 B2 Shangshui China
70 C2 Shangyu China
69 E1 Shangzhi China
97 C3 Shannon *r.* Ireland
97 B2 Shannon, Mouth of the
      Ireland
71 B3 Shantou China
70 B2 Shanxi *prov.* China
73 B3 Shaoguan China
71 B3 Shaowu China
70 C2 Shaoxing China
71 B3 Shaoyang China
116 C2 Shaqrā' Saudi Arabia
74 A1 Sharan Afgh.
90 B2 Sharbot Ukr.
79 C2 Sharjah U.A.E.
88 C2 Sharkawshchyna Belarus
50 A2 Shark Bay Austr.
78 A2 Sharm ash Shaykh Egypt
140 C2 Sharon U.S.A.
86 D3 Shar'ya Rus. Fed.
121 B3 Shashe *r.* Botswana/Zimbabwe
117 B4 Shashemenë Eth.
134 B2 Shasta, Mount *vol.* U.S.A.
134 B1 Shasta Lake U.S.A.
89 E2 Shatura Rus. Fed.
129 D3 Shaunavon Can.
140 B2 Shawano U.S.A.
131 C2 Shawinigan Can.
139 D1 Shawnee U.S.A.
50 B2 Shay Gap (abandoned) Austr.
89 E3 Shchekino Rus. Fed.
89 E2 Shchelkovo Rus. Fed.
89 E3 Shchigry Rus. Fed.
91 C1 Shchors Ukr.
88 B3 Shchuchyn Belarus
91 D1 Shebekino Rus. Fed.
117 C4 Shebelë Wenz, Wabë *r.*
      Ethiopia/Somalia
77 C3 Sheberghän Afgh.
140 B2 Sheboygan U.S.A.
91 D3 Shebsh *r.* Rus. Fed.
97 C2 Sheelin, Lough *l.* Ireland
98 C2 Sheffield U.K.
89 E2 Sheksna Rus. Fed.
89 E2 Sheksninskoye
      Vodokhranilishche *resr*
      Rus. Fed.
83 M2 Shelagskiy, Mys *pt* Rus. Fed.
131 D2 Shelburne Can.
134 D1 Shelby U.S.A.
140 B3 Shelbyville *IN* U.S.A.
142 C1 Shelbyville *TN* U.S.A.
83 L2 Shelikhova, Zaliv *g.* Rus. Fed.
129 D2 Shellbrook Can.
134 B1 Shelton U.S.A.
137 D2 Shenandoah U.S.A.
141 D3 Shenandoah *r.* U.S.A.
141 D3 Shenandoah Mountains
      U.S.A.
118 A2 Shendam Nigeria
86 D2 Shenkursk Rus. Fed.
65 A1 Shenyang China
71 B3 Shenzhen China
90 B1 Shepetivka Ukr.
53 C3 Shepparton Austr.
99 D3 Sheppey, Isle of *i.* U.K.
131 D2 Sherbrooke *N.S.* Can.
131 C2 Sherbrooke *Que.* Can.
116 B3 Shereiq Sudan
136 B2 Sheridan U.S.A.
139 D2 Sherman U.S.A.
100 B2 's-Hertogenbosch Neth.

96 □ Shetland Islands U.K.
76 B2 Shetpe Kazakh.
137 D1 Sheyenne *r.* U.S.A.
79 B3 Shibām Yemen
66 D2 Shibetsu Japan
71 B3 Shicheng China
96 B2 Shiel, Loch *l.* U.K.
77 E2 Shiezi China
      Shijiao China see Fogang
70 B2 Shijiazhuang China
74 A2 Shikarpur India
67 B4 Shikoku *i.* Japan
66 D2 Shikotsu-ko *l.* Japan
86 D2 Shilega Rus. Fed.
75 C2 Shiliguri India
75 D2 Shillong India
89 F3 Shilovo Rus. Fed.
117 C3 Shimbiris *mt.* Somalia
73 B3 Shimizu China
73 B3 Shimoga India
66 B4 Shimonoseki Japan
96 B1 Shin, Loch *l.* U.K.
67 C4 Shingū Japan
123 C1 Shingwedzi S. Africa
123 D1 Shingwedzi *r.* S. Africa
119 D3 Shinyanga Tanz.
67 C4 Shiono-misaki *c.* Japan
138 B1 Shiprock U.S.A.
71 A3 Shiqian China
70 A2 Shiquan China
      Shiquanhe China see Gar
      Shiquan He *r.* China/Pak. see
      Indus
67 C3 Shirane-san *mt.* Japan
81 D3 Shīrāz Iran
66 D2 Shiretoko-misaki *c.* Japan
66 D2 Shiriya-zaki *c.* Japan
74 B2 Shiv India
75 B2 Shivpuri India
70 B2 Shiyan China
70 A2 Shizuishan China
67 C4 Shizuoka Japan
89 D3 Shklow Belarus
109 C2 Shkodër Albania
83 H1 Shmidta, Ostrov *i.* Rus. Fed.
135 C3 Shoshone U.S.A.
135 C3 Shoshone Mountains U.S.A.
123 C1 Shoshong Botswana
91 C1 Shostka Ukr.
70 B2 Shouxian China
138 A2 Show Low U.S.A.
91 C2 Shpola Ukr.
142 B2 Shreveport U.S.A.
99 B2 Shrewsbury U.K.
62 A1 Shuangjiang China
87 E4 Shubarkuduk Kazakh.
116 B1 Shubrā al Khaymah Egypt
89 E2 Shugozero Rus. Fed.
120 B2 Shumba Zimbabwe
110 C2 Shumen Bulg.
88 C2 Shumilina Belarus
89 D3 Shumyachi Rus. Fed.
126 A2 Shungnak U.S.A.
78 B3 Shuqrah Yemen
89 F2 Shushkodom Rus. Fed.
81 C2 Shushtar Iran
128 C2 Shuswap Lake Can.
89 F2 Shuya Rus. Fed.
89 F2 Shuyskoye Rus. Fed.
62 A1 Shwebo Myanmar
62 A1 Shwedwin Myanmar
62 A2 Shwegyin Myanmar
77 C2 Shymkent Kazakh.
91 C2 Shyroke Ukr.
59 C3 Sia Indon.
74 A2 Siahan Range *mts* Pak.

74 B1 Sialkot Pak.
64 B2 Siargao *i.* Phil.
88 B2 Šiauliai Lith.
109 C2 Šibenik Croatia
83 I2 Siberia *reg.* Rus. Fed.
60 A2 Siberut *i.* Indon.
74 A2 Sibi Pak.
110 B1 Sibiu Romania
62 A1 Sibolga Indon.
62 A1 Sibsagar India
61 C1 Sibu Sarawak Malaysia
118 B2 Sibut C.A.R.
64 B1 Sibuyan *i.* Phil.
64 B1 Sibuyan Sea Phil.
128 C2 Sicamous Can.
63 A3 Sichon Thai.
70 A2 Sichuan *prov.* China
70 A3 Sichuan Pendi *basin* China
105 D3 Sicié, Cap *c.* France
      Sicilia *i.* Italy see Sicily
108 B3 Sicilian Channel Italy/Tunisia
108 B3 Sicily *i.* Italy
150 A3 Sicuani Peru
92 C3 Sideros, Akrotirio *pt* Greece
74 B2 Sidhpur India
107 D2 Sidi Aïssa Alg.
107 D2 Sidi Ali Alg.
114 B1 Sidi Bel Abbès Alg.
114 A2 Sidi Ifni Morocco
60 A1 Sidikalang Indon.
96 C2 Sidlaw Hills U.K.
96 B3 Sidmouth U.K.
134 B1 Sidney Can.
136 C1 Sidney *MT* U.S.A.
136 C2 Sidney *NE* U.S.A.
140 C2 Sidney *OH* U.S.A.
143 D2 Sidney Lanier, Lake U.S.A.
80 B2 Sidon Lebanon
154 B2 Sidrolândia Brazil
103 E1 Siedlce Pol.
100 C2 Sieg *r.* Ger.
100 D2 Siegen Ger.
63 B2 Siëmréab Cambodia
108 B2 Siena Italy
103 D1 Sieradz Pol.
153 B5 Sierra Grande Arg.
114 A4 Sierra Leone *country* Africa
144 B2 Sierra Mojada Mex.
138 A2 Sierra Vista U.S.A.
105 D2 Sierre Switz.
111 B3 Sifnos *i.* Greece
107 C2 Sig Alg.
127 H2 Sigguup Nunaa *pen.*
      Greenland
103 E2 Sighetu Marmaţiei Romania
110 B1 Sighişoara Romania
60 A1 Sigli Indon.
92 B2 Siglufjördur Iceland
102 B2 Sigmaringen Ger.
100 B3 Signy-l'Abbaye France
106 C1 Sigüenza Spain
114 B3 Siguiri Guinea
88 B2 Sigulda Latvia
63 B2 Sihanoukville Cambodia
92 I3 Siilinjärvi Fin.
81 C2 Siirt Turkey
60 B2 Sijunjung Indon.
74 B2 Sikar India
114 B3 Sikasso Mali
137 F3 Sikeston U.S.A.
66 B2 Sikhote-Alin' *mts* Rus. Fed.
111 C3 Sikinos *i.* Greece
144 B2 Silao Mex.
75 D2 Silchar India
77 D1 Siletiteniz, Ozero *salt l.*
      Kazakh.
75 C2 Silgarhi Nepal

80	B2	Silifke Turkey
75	C1	Siling Co salt l. China
110	C2	Silistra Bulg.
93	E4	Silivri Turkey
93	F3	Siljan l. Sweden
93	E4	Silkeborg Denmark
88	C2	Sillamäe Estonia
142	N1	Siloam Springs U.S.A.
123	D2	Silobela S. Africa
88	C2	Šiluté Lith.
81	C2	Silvan Turkey
138	B2	Silver City U.S.A.
136	B3	Silverton U.S.A.
62	B1	Simao China
131	D2	Simard, Lac l. Can.
111	C3	Simav Turkey
111	C3	Simav Dağları mts Turkey
118	C2	Simba Dem. Rep. Congo
132	C2	Simcoe, Lake Can.
60	A1	Simeulue i. Indon.
91	C2	Simferopol' Ukr.
110	B1	Şimleu Silvaniei Romania
100	C3	Simmern (Hunsrück) Ger.
129	D2	Simonhouse Can.
51	C2	Simpson Desert Austr.
93	F4	Simrishamn Sweden
60	A1	Sinabang Indon.
71	A3	Sinai pen. Egypt
65	B2	Sinan China
65	B1	Sinanju N. Korea
62	A1	Sinbo Myanmar
150	A1	Sincelejo Col.
111	C3	Sındırgı Turkey
86	E2	Sindor Rus. Fed.
111	C3	Sinekçi Turkey
106	B2	Sines Port.
106	B2	Sines, Cabo de c. Port.
63	B2	Singahi India
60	B1	Singapore country Asia
61	C2	Singaraja Indon.
119	D3	Singida Tanz.
62	A1	Singkaling Hkamti Myanmar
61	B1	Singkawang Indon.
61	B1	Singkil Indon.
53	D2	Singleton Austr.
62	A1	Singu Myanmar
108	A2	Siniscola Sardegna Italy
109	C2	Sinj Croatia
116	B3	Sinkat Sudan
		Sinkiang Uighur Autonomous
		Region aut. reg. China see
		Xinjiang Uygur Zizhiqu
80	B1	Sinop Turkey
65	B1	Sinp'o N. Korea
61	C1	Sintang Indon.
100	B2	Sint Anthonis Neth.
100	A2	Sint-Laureins Belgium
147	D3	Sint Maarten i. Neth. Antilles
100	B2	Sint-Niklaas Belgium
139	D3	Sinton U.S.A.
65	A1	Sinŭiju N. Korea
103	D2	Siófok Hungary
105	D2	Sion Switz.
137	D2	Sioux Center U.S.A.
137	D2	Sioux City U.S.A.
137	D2	Sioux Falls U.S.A.
130	A1	Sioux Lookout Can.
65	A1	Siping China
129	E2	Sipiwesk Lake Can.
60	A2	Sipura i. Indon.
93	E4	Sira r. Norway
		Siracusa Italy see Syracuse
51	C1	Sir Edward Pellew Group is
		Austr.
116	B1	Sirḥān, Wādī an watercourse
		Saudi Arabia
79	C2	Sīrīk Iran

62	B2	Siri Kit, Khuan Thai.
128	B1	Sir James MacBrien, Mount
		Can.
79	C2	Sīrjān Iran
81	C2	Şırnak Turkey
74	B2	Sirohi India
74	B2	Sirsa India
115	D1	Sirte Libya
115	D1	Sirte, Gulf of Libya
88	B2	Širvintos Lith.
145	C2	Sisal Mex.
122	B2	Sishen S. Africa
81	C2	Sisian Armenia
129	D2	Sisipuk Lake Can.
63	B2	Sisŏphŏn Cambodia
105	D3	Sisteron France
75	C2	Sitapur India
123	D2	Siteki Swaziland
128	A2	Sitka U.S.A.
100	B2	Sittard Neth.
62	A2	Sittaung r. Myanmar
62	A1	Sittwe Myanmar
61	C2	Situbondo Indon.
80	B2	Sivas Turkey
111	C3	Sivaslı Turkey
80	B2	Siverek Turkey
80	B2	Sivrihisar Turkey
116	A2	Siwah Egypt
74	B1	Siwalik Range mts
		India/Nepal
105	D3	Six-Fours-les-Plages France
70	B2	Sixian China
123	C2	Siyabuswa S. Africa
109	D2	Sjenica Serbia
92	G2	Sjøvegan Norway
91	C2	Skadovs'k Ukr.
93	F4	Skagen Denmark
93	E4	Skagerrak str.
		Denmark/Norway
134	B1	Skagit r. U.S.A.
128	A2	Skagway U.S.A.
74	B1	Skardu Pak.
103	E1	Skarżysko-Kamienna Pol.
103	D2	Skawina Pol.
128	B2	Skeena r. Can.
128	B2	Skeena Mountains Can.
98	D2	Skegness U.K.
92	H3	Skellefteå Sweden
92	H3	Skellefteälven r. Sweden
97	C2	Skerries Ireland
111	B3	Skiathos i. Greece
97	B3	Skibbereen Ireland
92	B3	Skíðadals-jökull glacier Iceland
98	B1	Skiddaw h. U.K.
93	E4	Skien Norway
103	E1	Skierniewice Pol.
115	C1	Skikda Alg.
52	B3	Skipton Austr.
98	B2	Skipton U.K.
93	E4	Skive Denmark
92	H1	Skjervøy Norway
111	B3	Skopelos i. Greece
89	E3	Skopin Rus. Fed.
109	D2	Skopje Macedonia
93	F4	Skövde Sweden
141	F2	Skowhegan U.S.A.
88	B2	Skrunda Latvia
128	A1	Skukum, Mount Can.
123	D1	Skukuza S. Africa
88	B2	Skuodas Lith.
96	A2	Skye i. U.K.
111	B3	Skyros Greece
111	B3	Skyros i. Greece
93	F4	Slagelse Denmark
97	C2	Slaney r. Ireland
88	C2	Slantsy Rus. Fed.
109	C1	Slatina Croatia

110	B2	Slatina Romania
129	C1	Slave r. Can.
114	C4	Slave Coast Africa
128	C2	Slave Lake Can.
82	G3	Slavgorod Rus. Fed.
109	C1	Slavonski Brod Croatia
90	B1	Slavuta Ukr.
90	C1	Slavutych Ukr.
91	D2	Slavyansk-na-Kubani
		Rus. Fed.
89	D3	Slawharad Belarus
103	D1	Sławno Pol.
97	A2	Slea Head Ireland
130	C1	Sleeper Islands Can.
97	D1	Slieve Donard h. U.K.
		Slieve Gamph hills Ireland see
		Ox Mountains
97	B1	Sligo Ireland
97	B1	Sligo Bay Ireland
93	G4	Slite Sweden
110	C2	Sliven Bulg.
110	C2	Slobozia Romania
128	C3	Slocan Can.
88	C3	Slonim Belarus
100	B1	Sloten Neth.
99	C3	Slough U.K.
103	D2	Slovakia country Europe
108	B1	Slovenia country Europe
91	D2	Slov"yans'k Ukr.
90	B1	Sluch r. Ukr.
103	D1	Słupsk Pol.
88	C3	Slutsk Belarus
97	A2	Slyne Head Ireland
131	D1	Smallwood Reservoir Can.
88	C3	Smalyavichy Belarus
88	C3	Smarhon' Belarus
129	D2	Smeaton Can.
109	D2	Smederevo Serbia
109	D2	Smederevska Palanka Serbia
91	C2	Smila Ukr.
88	C2	Smiltene Latvia
128	B2	Smithers Can.
143	E1	Smithfield U.S.A.
141	D3	Smith Mountain Lake U.S.A.
130	C2	Smiths Falls Can.
137	D3	Smoky Hills U.S.A.
92	E3	Smøla i. Norway
89	D3	Smolensk Rus. Fed.
110	B2	Smolyan Bulg.
130	B2	Smooth Rock Falls Can.
		Smyrna Turkey see İzmir
92	B3	Snæfell mt. Iceland
98	A1	Snaefell h. Isle of Man
132	B2	Snake r. U.S.A.
134	D2	Snake River Plain U.S.A.
100	B1	Sneek Neth.
97	B3	Sneem Ireland
122	B3	Sneeuberge mts S. Africa
108	B1	Snežnik mt. Slovenia
91	C2	Snihurivka Ukr.
93	E3	Snøhetta mt. Norway
129	D1	Snowbird Lake Can.
98	A2	Snowdon mt. U.K.
		Snowdrift Can. see Łutselk'e
129	C1	Snowdrift r. Can.
138	A2	Snowflake U.S.A.
129	D2	Snow Lake Can.
52	A2	Snowtown Austr.
53	C3	Snowy r. Austr.
53	C3	Snowy Mountains Austr.
139	C2	Snyder U.S.A.
121	□D2	Soalala Madag.
117	B4	Sobat r. Sudan
89	F2	Sobinka Rus. Fed.
151	D3	Sobradinho, Barragem de resr
		Brazil
151	D2	Sobral Brazil

Sochi

87 C4 **Sochi** Rus. Fed.
65 B2 **Sŏch'ŏn** S. Korea
49 H4 **Society Islands** Fr. Polynesia
150 A1 **Socorro** Col.
138 B2 **Socorro** U.S.A.
144 A3 **Socorro, Isla** i. Mex.
56 F6 **Socotra** i. Yemen
63 B3 **Soc Trăng** Vietnam
106 C2 **Soduéllamos** Spain
92 I2 **Sodankylä** Fin.
134 D2 **Soda Springs** U.S.A.
93 G3 **Söderhamn** Sweden
93 G4 **Södertälje** Sweden
116 A3 **Sodiri** Sudan
117 B4 **Sodo** Eth.
93 G3 **Södra Kvarken** str. Fin./Sweden
100 D2 **Soest** Ger.
110 B2 **Sofia** Bulg.
Sofiya Bulg. see **Sofia**
68 C1 **Sog** China
93 E3 **Sognefjorden** inlet Norway
111 D2 **Söğüt** Turkey
100 B2 **Soignies** Belgium
105 C2 **Soissons** France
90 A1 **Sokal'** Ukr.
111 C3 **Söke** Turkey
81 C1 **Sokhumi** Georgia
114 C4 **Sokodé** Togo
89 F2 **Sokol** Rus. Fed.
101 F2 **Sokolov** Czech Rep.
115 C3 **Sokoto** Nigeria
115 C3 **Sokoto** r. Nigeria
90 B2 **Sokyryany** Ukr.
73 B3 **Solapur** India
135 B3 **Soledad** U.S.A.
89 F2 **Soligalich** Rus. Fed.
99 C2 **Solihull** U.K.
86 E3 **Solikamsk** Rus. Fed.
87 E3 **Sol'-Iletsk** Rus. Fed.
100 C2 **Solingen** Ger.
92 G3 **Sollefteå** Sweden
93 G4 **Sollentuna** Sweden
101 D2 **Solling** hills Ger.
89 E2 **Solnechnogorsk** Rus. Fed.
60 B2 **Solok** Indon.
48 E3 **Solomon Islands** country S. Pacific Ocean
48 E3 **Solomon Sea** S. Pacific Ocean
105 D2 **Solothurn** Switz.
101 D1 **Soltau** Ger.
89 D1 **Sol'tsy** Rus. Fed.
96 C3 **Solway Firth** est. U.K.
120 B2 **Solwezi** Zambia
111 C3 **Soma** Turkey
117 C4 **Somalia** country Africa
120 B1 **Sombo** Angola
109 C1 **Sombor** Serbia
144 B2 **Sombrerete** Mex.
140 C3 **Somerset** U.S.A.
123 C3 **Somerset East** S. Africa
126 E2 **Somerset Island** Can.
122 A3 **Somerset West** S. Africa
101 E2 **Sömmerda** Ger.
75 C2 **Son** r. India
65 C1 **Sŏnbong** N. Korea
93 E4 **Sønderborg** Denmark
101 E2 **Sondershausen** Ger.
Søndre Strømfjord inlet Greenland see **Kangerlussuaq**
62 B1 **Sông Đa, Hô** resr Vietnam
119 D4 **Songea** Tanz.
65 B1 **Sŏnggan** N. Korea
65 B1 **Songhua Hu** resr China
Sŏngjin N. Korea see **Kimch'aek**

63 B3 **Songkhla** Thai.
65 B2 **Sŏngnam** S. Korea
65 B2 **Songnim** N. Korea
120 A1 **Songo** Angola
121 C2 **Songo** Moz.
69 E1 **Songyuan** China
Sonid Youqi China see **Saihan Tal**
89 E2 **Sonkovo** Rus. Fed.
62 B1 **Sơn La** Vietnam
74 A2 **Sonmiani** Pak.
101 E2 **Sonneberg** Ger.
138 A2 **Sonoita** Mex.
144 A2 **Sonora** r. Mex.
135 B3 **Sonora** CA U.S.A.
139 C2 **Sonora** TX U.S.A.
117 A4 **Sopo** watercourse Sudan
103 D2 **Sopron** Hungary
108 B2 **Sora** Italy
130 C2 **Sorel** Can.
51 D4 **Sorell** Austr.
106 C1 **Soria** Spain
90 B2 **Soroca** Moldova
154 C2 **Sorocaba** Brazil
87 E3 **Sorochinsk** Rus. Fed.
59 D2 **Sorol** atoll Micronesia
59 C3 **Sorong** Indon.
119 D2 **Soroti** Uganda
92 H1 **Sørøya** i. Norway
92 G2 **Sorsele** Sweden
64 B1 **Sorsogon** Phil.
86 C2 **Sortavala** Rus. Fed.
92 G2 **Sortland** Norway
65 B2 **Sŏsan** S. Korea
123 C2 **Soshanguve** S. Africa
89 E3 **Sosna** r. Rus. Fed.
153 B4 **Sosneado** mt. Arg.
86 E2 **Sosnogorsk** Rus. Fed.
86 D2 **Sosnovka** Rus. Fed.
88 C2 **Sosnovyy Bor** Rus. Fed.
103 D1 **Sosnowiec** Pol.
91 D2 **Sosyka** r. Rus. Fed.
145 C2 **Soto la Marina** Mex.
118 B2 **Souanké** Congo
104 C3 **Souillac** France
Soûl S. Korea see **Seoul**
104 B2 **Soulac-sur-Mer** France
104 B3 **Soulom** France
Soûr Lebanon see **Tyre**
107 D2 **Sour el Ghozlane** Alg.
129 D3 **Souris** Man. Can.
131 D2 **Souris** P.E.I. Can.
129 E3 **Souris** r. Can.
151 E2 **Sousa** Brazil
115 D1 **Sousse** Tunisia
104 B3 **Soustons** France
122 B3 **South Africa, Republic of** country Africa
99 C3 **Southampton** U.K.
127 F2 **Southampton Island** Can.
73 D3 **South Andaman** i. India
52 A1 **South Australia** state Austr.
130 B2 **South Baymouth** Can.
140 B2 **South Bend** U.S.A.
143 D2 **South Carolina** state U.S.A.
156 B4 **South China Sea** N. Pacific Ocean
136 C2 **South Dakota** state U.S.A.
99 C3 **South Downs** hills U.K.
129 D2 **Southend** Can.
99 D3 **Southend-on-Sea** U.K.
54 B2 **Southern Alps** mts N.Z.
50 A3 **Southern Cross** Austr.
129 E2 **Southern Indian Lake** Can.
159 **Southern Ocean**
143 E1 **Southern Pines** U.S.A.
96 B3 **Southern Uplands** hills U.K.

149 F6 **South Georgia and the South Sandwich Islands** terr. S. Atlantic Ocean
96 A2 **South Harris** pen. U.K.
129 E1 **South Henik Lake** Can.
54 B2 **South Island** N.Z.
65 B2 **South Korea** country Asia
135 B3 **South Lake Tahoe** U.S.A.
55 Q4 **South Orkney Islands** S. Atlantic Ocean
136 C2 **South Platte** r. U.S.A.
98 B2 **Southport** U.K.
143 E2 **Southport** U.S.A.
96 C1 **South Ronaldsay** i. U.K.
123 D3 **South Sand Bluff** pt S. Africa
129 D2 **South Saskatchewan** r. Can.
129 E2 **South Seal** r. Can.
55 P3 **South Shetland Islands** Antarctica
98 C1 **South Shields** U.K.
54 B1 **South Taranaki Bight** b. N.Z.
130 C1 **South Twin Island** Can.
96 A2 **South Uist** i. U.K.
53 D2 **South West Rocks** Austr.
99 D2 **Southwold** U.K.
109 C3 **Soverato** Italy
88 B2 **Sovetsk** Rus. Fed.
86 F2 **Sovetskiy** Rus. Fed.
91 C2 **Sovyets'kyy** Ukr.
123 C2 **Soweto** S. Africa
66 D1 **Sōya-misaki** c. Japan
90 C1 **Sozh** r. Belarus
110 C2 **Sozopol** Bulg.
106 C1 **Spain** country Europe
99 C2 **Spalding** U.K.
135 D2 **Spanish Fork** U.S.A.
97 B2 **Spanish Point** Ireland
108 B3 **Sparagio, Monte** mt. Sicilia Italy
135 C3 **Sparks** U.S.A.
140 A2 **Sparta** U.S.A.
143 D2 **Spartanburg** U.S.A.
111 B3 **Sparti** Greece
109 C3 **Spartivento, Capo** c. Italy
89 D3 **Spas-Demensk** Rus. Fed.
89 F2 **Spas-Klepiki** Rus. Fed.
66 B2 **Spassk-Dal'niy** Rus. Fed.
89 F3 **Spassk-Ryazanskiy** Rus. Fed.
111 B3 **Spatha, Akrotirio** pt Greece
136 C2 **Spearfish** U.S.A.
139 C1 **Spearman** U.S.A.
137 D2 **Spencer** U.S.A.
52 A2 **Spencer Gulf** est. Austr.
98 C1 **Spennymoor** U.K.
54 B2 **Spenser Mountains** N.Z.
101 D3 **Spessart** reg. Ger.
96 C2 **Spey** r. U.K.
102 B2 **Speyer** Ger.
100 C1 **Spiekeroog** i. Ger.
100 B2 **Spijkenisse** Neth.
128 C2 **Spirit River** Can.
103 E2 **Spišská Nová Ves** Slovakia
82 C1 **Spitsbergen** i. Svalbard
102 C2 **Spittal an der Drau** Austria
109 C2 **Split** Croatia
129 E2 **Split Lake** Can.
129 E2 **Split Lake** Can.
134 C1 **Spokane** U.S.A.
140 A1 **Spooner** U.S.A.
102 C1 **Spree** r. Ger.
122 A2 **Springbok** S. Africa
131 E2 **Springdale** Can.
142 B1 **Springdale** U.S.A.
101 D1 **Springe** Ger.
138 C1 **Springer** U.S.A.
138 B3 **Springerville** U.S.A.
136 C3 **Springfield** CO U.S.A.

140 B3 Springfield *IL* U.S.A.
141 E2 Springfield *MA* U.S.A.
137 E3 Springfield *MO* U.S.A.
140 C2 Springfield *OH* U.S.A.
134 B2 Springfield *OR* U.S.A.
123 C3 Springfontein S. Africa
131 D2 Springhill Can.
143 D3 Spring Hill U.S.A.
54 B2 Springs Junction N.Z.
98 D2 Spurn Head U.K.
128 B3 Squamish Can.
109 C3 Squillace, Golfo di *g.* Italy
Srbija *country* Europe *see*
Serbia
109 C2 Srebrenica Bos.-Herz.
110 C2 Sredets Bulg.
83 L3 Sredinnyy Khrebet *mts*
Rus. Fed.
83 L2 Srednekolymsk Rus. Fed.
Sredne-Russkaya
Vozvyshennost' *hills* Rus. Fed.
see Central Russian Upland
Sredne-Sibirskoye
Ploskogor'ye *plat.* Rus. Fed. *see*
Central Siberian Plateau
110 B2 Srednogorie Bulg.
69 D1 Sretensk Rus. Fed.
61 C1 Sri Aman *Sarawak* Malaysia
73 B4 Sri Jayewardenepura Kotte
Sri Lanka
73 C3 Srikakulam India
73 C4 Sri Lanka *country* Asia
68 C2 Srinagar India
74 B1 Srinagar India
73 B3 Srivardhan India
101 D1 Stade Ger.
58 C2 Stadensen Ger.
100 C1 Stadskanaal Neth.
101 D1 Stadtallendorf Ger.
101 D2 Stadthagen Ger.
72 E1 Staffelstein Ger.
99 B2 Stafford U.K.
99 C3 Staines U.K.
91 D2 Stakhanov Ukr.
Stalingrad Rus. Fed. *see*
Volgograd
103 E1 Stalowa Wola Pol.
99 C2 Stamford U.K.
141 E2 Stamford *CT* U.S.A.
139 D2 Stamford *TX* U.S.A.
122 A1 Stampriet Namibia
92 F2 Samsund Norway
123 C2 Standerton S. Africa
140 C2 Standish U.S.A.
123 D2 Stanger S. Africa
153 C6 Stanley Falkland Is
136 C1 Stanley U.S.A.
83 I3 Stanovoye Nagor'ye *mts*
Rus. Fed.
83 J3 Stanovoy Khrebet *mts* Rus. Fed.
54 C1 Stanthorpe Austr.
103 E1 Starachowice Pol.
Stara Planina *mts* Bulg./Serbia
see Balkan Mountains
89 D2 Staraya Russa Rus. Fed.
89 F2 Staraya Toropa Rus. Fed.
110 C2 Stara Zagora Bulg.
103 D1 Stargard Szczeciński Pol.
142 C2 Starkville U.S.A.
91 D2 Starobil's'k Ukr.
89 D3 Starodub Rus. Fed.
103 D1 Starogard Gdański Pol.
90 B2 Starokostyantyniv Ukr.
91 D2 Starominskaya Rus. Fed.
91 D2 Staroshcherbinovskaya
Rus. Fed.
91 D2 Starotitarovskaya Rus. Fed.

89 F3 Staroyur'yevo Rus. Fed.
99 B3 Start Point U.K.
88 C3 Staryya Darohi Belarus
89 E3 Staryy Oskol Rus. Fed.
101 E2 Staßfurt Ger.
141 D2 State College U.S.A.
143 D2 Statesboro U.S.A.
143 D1 Statesville U.S.A.
93 E4 Stavanger Norway
87 D4 Stavropol' Rus. Fed.
87 D4 Stavropol'skaya
Vozvyshennost' *hills* Rus. Fed.
52 B3 Stawell Austr.
123 C2 Steadville S. Africa
136 B2 Steamboat Springs U.S.A.
101 F2 Stedten Ger.
128 C2 Steen River Can.
134 C2 Steens Mountain U.S.A.
100 C1 Steenwijk Neth.
126 D2 Stefansson Island Can.
101 E3 Steigerwald *mts* Ger.
129 E3 Steinbach Can.
100 C1 Steinfurt Ger.
120 A3 Steinhausen Namibia
92 F3 Steinkjer Norway
122 A2 Steinkopf S. Africa
122 B2 Stella S. Africa
105 D2 Stenay France
101 E1 Stendal Ger.
Stepanakert Azer. *see*
Xankändi
131 E2 Stephenville Can.
139 D2 Stephenville U.S.A.
122 B3 Sterkstroom S. Africa
136 C2 Sterling *CO* U.S.A.
140 B2 Sterling *IL* U.S.A.
87 E3 Sterlitamak Rus. Fed.
101 E1 Sternberg Ger.
128 C2 Stettler Can.
140 C2 Steubenville U.S.A.
99 C3 Stevenage U.K.
129 E2 Stevenson Lake Can.
126 B2 Stevens Village U.S.A.
128 B2 Stewart Can.
126 B2 Stewart *r.* Can.
54 A3 Stewart Island N.Z.
127 F2 Stewart Lake Can.
102 C2 Steyr Austria
123 B3 Steytlerville S. Africa
128 A2 Stikine *r.* Can.
128 A2 Stikine Plateau Can.
122 B3 Stilbaai S. Africa
139 D1 Stillwater U.S.A.
109 D2 Štip Macedonia
96 C2 Stirling U.K.
92 F3 Stjørdalshalsen Norway
103 D2 Stockerau Austria
93 G4 Stockholm Sweden
98 B2 Stockport U.K.
135 B3 Stockton U.S.A.
98 C1 Stockton-on-Tees U.K.
63 B2 Stœng Trêng Cambodia
96 B1 Stoer, Point of U.K.
98 B2 Stoke-on-Trent U.K.
101 D2 Stol *mt.* Serbia
109 C2 Stolberg (Rheinland) Ger.
88 C3 Stolin Belarus
101 F2 Stollberg Ger.
101 D1 Stolzenau Ger.
96 C2 Stonehaven U.K.
129 E2 Stonewall Can.
129 D2 Stony Rapids Can.
92 G2 Storavan *l.* Sweden
Store Bælt *sea chan.* Denmark
see Great Belt
92 F3 Støren Norway

92 F2 Storforshei Norway
126 D2 Storkerson Peninsula Can.
137 D2 Storm Lake U.S.A.
93 E3 Stornosa *mt.* Norway
96 A1 Stornoway U.K.
86 E2 Storozhevsk Rus. Fed.
90 B2 Storozhynets' Ukr.
92 F3 Storsjön *l.* Sweden
92 H2 Storslett Norway
92 G2 Storuman Sweden
99 C2 Stour *r.* England U.K.
99 C3 Stour *r.* England U.K.
130 A1 Stout Lake Can.
88 C3 Stowbtsy Belarus
97 C1 Strabane U.K.
102 C2 Strakonice Czech Rep.
102 C1 Stralsund Ger.
122 A3 Strand S. Africa
93 E3 Stranda Norway
97 D1 Strangford Lough *inlet* U.K.
96 B3 Stranraer U.K.
105 D2 Strasbourg France
140 C2 Stratford Can.
54 B1 Stratford N.Z.
139 C1 Stratford U.S.A.
99 C2 Stratford-upon-Avon U.K.
128 C2 Strathmore Can.
96 C2 Strathspey *val.* U.K.
102 C2 Straubing Ger.
51 C3 Streaky Bay Austr.
140 B2 Streator U.S.A.
110 B2 Strehaia Romania
153 B5 Stroeder Arg.
101 D1 Ströhen Ger.
109 C3 Stromboli, Isola *i.* Italy
96 C1 Stromness U.K.
92 G3 Strömsund Sweden
96 C1 Stronsay *i.* U.K.
53 D2 Stroud Austr.
99 B3 Stroud U.K.
100 C1 Strücklingen (Saterland) Ger.
109 D2 Struga Macedonia
91 D1 Strugi-Krasnyye Rus. Fed.
122 B3 Struis Bay S. Africa
109 D2 Strumica Macedonia
122 B2 Strydenburg S. Africa
111 B2 Strymonas *r.* Greece
90 A2 Stryy Ukr.
128 B2 Stuart Lake Can.
130 A1 Stull Lake Can.
89 E3 Stupino Rus. Fed.
140 B2 Sturgeon Bay U.S.A.
130 C2 Sturgeon Falls Can.
130 A2 Sturgeon Lake Can.
140 B2 Sturgis *MI* U.S.A.
136 C2 Sturgis *SD* U.S.A.
50 B1 Sturt Creek *watercourse* Austr.
52 B1 Sturt Stony Desert Austr.
123 C3 Stutterheim S. Africa
102 B2 Stuttgart Ger.
142 B2 Stuttgart U.S.A.
92 A2 Stykkishólmur Iceland
90 B1 Styr *r.* Belarus/Ukr.
155 D1 Suaçui Grande *r.* Brazil
116 B3 Suakin Sudan
78 A3 Suara Eritrea
109 C1 Subotica Serbia
110 C1 Suceava Romania
97 B2 Suck *r.* Ireland
152 B2 Sucre Bolivia
154 B2 Sucuriú *r.* Brazil
89 E2 Suda Rus. Fed.
91 C2 Sudak Ukr.
117 A3 Sudan *country* Africa
130 B2 Sudbury Can.
117 A4 Sudd *swamp* Sudan
89 F2 Sudislavl' Rus. Fed.

89	F2	Sudogda Rus. Fed.
94	B1	Suðuroy i. Faroe Is
107	C2	Sueca Spain
116	B2	Suez Egypt
116	B2	Suez, Gulf of Egypt
80	B2	Suez Canal Egypt
141	D3	Suffolk U.S.A.
116	B2	Sūhāj Egypt
79	C2	Şuḩār Oman
69	D1	Sühbaatar Mongolia
101	E2	Suhl Ger.
109	C1	Suhopolje Croatia
70	B2	Suide China
66	B2	Suifenhe China
69	E1	Suihua China
70	A2	Suining China
70	B2	Suiping China
70	B2	Suiyang China
70	B2	Suizhou China
74	B1	Sujangarh India
74	A2	Sujanpur India
74	A2	Sujawal Pak.
60	B2	Sukabumi Indon.
61	B2	Sukadana Indon.
61	C2	Sukaraja Indon.
89	E3	Sukhinichi Rus. Fed.
89	F2	Sukhona r. Rus. Fed.
62	A2	Sukhothai Thai.
74	A2	Sukkur Pak.
89	E2	Sukromny Rus. Fed.
59	C3	Sula, Kepulauan is Indon.
74	A1	Sulaiman Range mts Pak.
		Sulawesi i. Indon. see Celebes
150	A1	Sullana Peru
137	E3	Sullivan U.S.A.
139	D2	Sulphur Springs U.S.A.
64	B2	Sulu Archipelago is Phil.
64	A2	Sulu Sea N. Pacific Ocean
101	E3	Sulzbach-Rosenberg Ger.
79	C2	Sumāil Oman
		Sumatera i. Indon. see Sumatra
60	A1	Sumatra i. Indon.
58	C3	Sumba i. Indon.
61	C2	Sumbawa i. Indon.
61	C2	Sumbawabesar Indon.
119	D3	Sumbawanga Tanz.
120	A2	Sumbe Angola
96	□	Sumburgh U.K.
96	□	Sumburgh Head U.K.
61	C2	Sumenep Indon.
67	D4	Sumisu-jima i. Japan
131	D2	Summerside Can.
140	C3	Summersville U.S.A.
128	B2	Summit Lake Can.
103	D2	Šumperk Czech Rep.
81	C1	Sumqayıt Azer.
143	D2	Sumter U.S.A.
91	C1	Sumy Ukr.
75	D2	Sunamganj Bangl.
65	B2	Sunan N. Korea
79	C2	Şunaynah Oman
52	B3	Sunbury Austr.
141	D2	Sunbury U.S.A.
65	B2	Sunch'ŏn N. Korea
65	B3	Sunch'ŏn S. Korea
123	C2	Sun City S. Africa
60	B2	Sunda, Selat str. Indon.
136	C2	Sundance U.S.A.
75	C2	Sundarbans coastal area Bangl./India
98	C1	Sunderland U.K.
128	C2	Sundre Can.
93	G3	Sundsvall Sweden
123	D2	Sundumbili S. Africa
60	B2	Sungailiat Indon.
60	B2	Sungaipenuh Indon.
60	B1	Sungai Petani Malaysia
80	B1	Sungurlu Turkey
93	E3	Sunndalsøra Norway
134	C1	Sunnyside U.S.A.
135	B3	Sunnyvale U.S.A.
83	I2	Suntar Rus. Fed.
74	A2	Suntsar Pak.
114	B4	Sunyani Ghana
82	D2	Suoyarvi Rus. Fed.
138	A2	Superior AZ U.S.A.
137	D2	Superior NE U.S.A.
140	A1	Superior WI U.S.A.
140	B1	Superior, Lake Can./U.S.A.
89	D3	Suponevo Rus. Fed.
81	C2	Sūq ash Shuyūkh Iraq
70	B2	Suqian China
78	A2	Sūq Suwayq Saudi Arabia
79	C2	Şūr Oman
74	A2	Surab Pak.
61	B2	Surabaya Indon.
61	C2	Surakarta Indon.
74	B2	Surat India
74	B2	Suratgarh India
63	A3	Surat Thani Thai.
89	D3	Surazh Rus. Fed.
109	D2	Surdulica Serbia
74	B2	Surendranagar India
82	F2	Surgut Rus. Fed.
64	B2	Surigao Phil.
63	B2	Surin Thai.
151	C1	Suriname country S. America
		Surt Libya see Sirte
		Surt, Khalīj g. Libya see Sirte, Gulf of
60	B2	Surulangun Indon.
89	F2	Susanino Rus. Fed.
135	B2	Susanville U.S.A.
80	B1	Suşehri Turkey
131	D2	Sussex Can.
101	D1	Süstedt Ger.
100	C1	Sustrum Ger.
83	J2	Susuman Rus. Fed.
111	C3	Susurluk Turkey
75	B1	Sutak India
122	B3	Sutherland S. Africa
99	C2	Sutton Coldfield U.K.
66	D2	Suttsu Japan
49	F4	Suva Fiji
89	E3	Suvorov Rus. Fed.
103	E1	Suwałki Pol.
63	B2	Suwannaphum Thai.
143	D2	Suwannee r. U.S.A.
		Suweis, Qanâ el canal Egypt see Suez Canal
65	B2	Suwŏn S. Korea
79	C2	Sūzā Iran
89	F2	Suzdal' Rus. Fed.
70	B2	Suzhou Anhui China
70	C2	Suzhou Jiangsu China
67	C3	Suzu Japan
67	C3	Suzu-misaki pt Japan
82	B1	Svalbard terr. Arctic Ocean
91	D2	Svatove Ukr.
63	B2	Svay Riĕng Cambodia
93	F3	Sveg Sweden
88	C2	Švenčionys Lith.
93	F4	Svendborg Denmark
		Sverdlovsk Rus. Fed. see Yekaterinburg
109	D2	Sveti Nikole Macedonia
88	B3	Svetlogorsk Rus. Fed.
88	B3	Svetlyy Rus. Fed.
93	I3	Svetogorsk Rus. Fed.
110	C2	Svilengrad Bulg.
110	B2	Svinecea Mare, Vârful mt. Romania
110	C2	Svishtov Bulg.
103	D2	Svitavy Czech Rep.
91	C2	Svitlovods'k Ukr.
69	E1	Svobodnyy Rus. Fed.
92	F2	Svolvær Norway
88	C3	Svyetlahorsk Belarus
143	D2	Swainsboro U.S.A.
120	A3	Swakopmund Namibia
52	B3	Swan Hill Austr.
128	C2	Swan Hills Can.
129	D2	Swan Lake Can.
129	D2	Swan River Can.
53	D2	Swansea Austr.
99	B3	Swansea U.K.
123	C2	Swartruggens S. Africa
		Swatow China see Shantou
123	D2	Swaziland country Africa
93	G3	Sweden country Europe
139	C2	Sweetwater U.S.A.
136	B2	Sweetwater r. U.S.A.
122	B3	Swellendam S. Africa
103	D1	Świdnica Pol.
103	D1	Świdwin Pol.
103	D1	Świebodzin Pol.
103	D1	Świecie Pol.
129	D2	Swift Current Can.
97	C1	Swilly, Lough inlet Ireland
99	C3	Swindon U.K.
102	C1	Świnoujście Pol.
105	D2	Switzerland country Europe
97	C2	Swords Ireland
88	C3	Syanno Belarus
89	D2	Sychevka Rus. Fed.
53	D2	Sydney Austr.
131	D2	Sydney Can.
131	D2	Sydney Mines Can.
91	D2	Syeverodonets'k Ukr.
86	E2	Syktyvkar Rus. Fed.
142	C2	Sylacauga U.S.A.
75	D2	Sylhet Bangl.
102	B1	Sylt i. Ger.
111	C3	Symi i. Greece
91	D2	Synel'nykove Ukr.
109	C3	Syracuse Sicilia Italy
136	C3	Syracuse KS U.S.A.
141	D2	Syracuse NY U.S.A.
77	C2	Syrdar'ya r. Asia
80	B2	Syria country Asia
80	B2	Syrian Desert Asia
111	B3	Syros i. Greece
87	D2	Syzran' Rus. Fed.
102	C1	Szczecin Pol.
103	D1	Szczecinek Pol.
103	E1	Szczytno Pol.
103	E2	Szeged Hungary
103	D2	Székesfehérvár Hungary
103	D2	Szekszárd Hungary
103	E2	Szentes Hungary
103	D2	Szentgotthárd Hungary
103	D2	Szigetvár Hungary
103	E2	Szolnok Hungary
103	D2	Szombathely Hungary

T

78	B2	Ṭābah Saudi Arabia
76	B3	Ṭabas Iran
150	B2	Tābask, Kūh-e mt. Iran
114	B2	Tabatinga Brazil
129	C3	Tabelbala Alg.
102	C2	Taber Can.
119	D3	Tábor Czech Rep.
114	B4	Tabora Tanz.
81	C2	Tabou Côte d'Ivoire
78	A2	Tabrīz Iran
		Tabūk Saudi Arabia

77	E2	Tacheng China
152	C2	Tachov Czech Rep.
64	B1	Tacloban Phil.
150	A3	Tacna Peru
134	B1	Tacoma U.S.A.
152	C4	Tacuarembó Uru.
138	B3	Tacupeto Mex.
117	C3	Tadjourah Djibouti
80	B2	Tadmur Syria
129	E2	Tadoule Lake Can.
65	B2	Taegu S. Korea
65	B3	Taejon S. Korea
65	B3	Taejŏng S. Korea
65	B3	T'aepaek S. Korea
107	C1	Tafalla Spain
152	B3	Tafí Viejo Arg.
79	D2	Taftān, Kūh-e mt. Iran
91	D2	Taganrog Rus. Fed.
91	D2	Taganrog, Gulf of Rus. Fed./Ukr.
62	A1	Tagaung Myanmar
64	B1	Tagaytay City Phil.
64	B1	Tagbilaran Phil.
64	B1	Tagudin Phil.
64	B2	Tagum Phil.
106	B2	Tagus r. Port./Spain
115	C2	Tahan, Gunung mt. Malaysia
115	C2	Tahat, Mont mt. Alg.
69	E1	Tahe China
49	I4	Tahiti i. Fr. Polynesia
139	E1	Tahlequah U.S.A.
135	B3	Tahoe, Lake U.S.A.
135	B3	Tahoe City U.S.A.
126	D2	Tahoe Lake Can.
115	C3	Tahoua Niger
79	C2	Tahrūd Iran
128	B3	Tahsis Can.
70	B2	Tai'an China
		Taibus Qi China see Baochang
71	C3	T'aichung Taiwan
54	C1	Taihape N.Z.
52	A3	Tai Hu l. China
52	A3	Tailem Bend Austr.
71	C3	T'ainan Taiwan
155	D1	Taiobeiras Brazil
71	C3	T'aipei Taiwan
60	B1	Taiping Malaysia
71	B3	Taishan China
153	A5	Taitao, Península de pen. Chile
71	C3	T'aitung Taiwan
92	I2	Taivalkoski Fin.
92	H2	Taivaskero h. Fin.
71	C3	Taiwan country Asia
71	B3	Taiwan Strait China/Taiwan
70	B2	Taiyuan China
70	B2	Taizhou Jiangsu China
71	B3	Taizhou Zhejiang China
78	B3	Ta'izz Yemen
77	D3	Tajikistan country Asia
		Taj Mahal tourist site India
		Tajo r. Port. see Tagus
58	A1	Tak Thai.
54	B2	Takaka N.Z.
67	B4	Takamatsu Japan
67	C3	Takaoka Japan
54	B2	Takapuna N.Z.
67	C3	Takasaki Japan
122	B1	Takatokwane Botswana
67	C3	Takayama Japan
67	C3	Takefu Japan
60	A1	Takengon Indon.
63	B2	Takêv Cambodia
63	B2	Ta Khmau Cambodia
66	D2	Takikawa Japan
128	B2	Takla Lake Can.
128	B2	Takla Landing Can.

77	E3	Taklimakan Desert China
		Taklimakan Shamo des. China see Taklimakan Desert
128	A2	Taku r. Can./U.S.A.
63	A3	Takua Pa Thai.
115	C4	Takum Nigeria
88	C3	Talachyn Belarus
74	B1	Talagang Pak.
150	A2	Talara Peru
59	C2	Talaud, Kepulauan is Indon.
106	C2	Talavera de la Reina Spain
153	A4	Talca Chile
153	A4	Talcahuano Chile
89	E2	Taldom Rus. Fed.
77	D2	Taldykorgan Kazakh.
59	C3	Taliabu i. Indon.
64	B1	Talisay Phil.
61	C2	Taliwang Indon.
81	C2	Tall 'Afar Iraq
143	D2	Tallahassee U.S.A.
88	B2	Tallinn Estonia
142	B2	Tallulah U.S.A.
104	B2	Talmont-St-Hilaire France
90	C2	Tal'ne Ukr.
117	B3	Talodi Sudan
91	E1	Talovaya Rus. Fed.
126	E2	Taloyoak Can.
88	B2	Talsi Latvia
152	A3	Taltal Chile
129	C1	Taltson r. Can.
60	A1	Talu Indon.
53	C1	Talwood Austr.
114	B4	Tamale Ghana
115	C2	Tamanrasset Alg.
99	A3	Tamar r. U.K.
145	C2	Tamazunchale Mex.
114	A3	Tambacounda Senegal
61	B1	Tambelan, Kepulauan is Indon.
91	E1	Tambov Rus. Fed.
145	C2	Tamiahua, Laguna de lag. Mex.
143	D3	Tampa U.S.A.
143	D3	Tampa Bay U.S.A.
93	H3	Tampere Fin.
145	C2	Tampico Mex.
69	D1	Tamsagbulag Mongolia
102	C2	Tamsweg Austria
53	D2	Tamworth Austr.
99	C2	Tamworth U.K.
119	E3	Tana r. Kenya
117	B3	Tana, Lake Eth.
67	C4	Tanabe Japan
92	I1	Tana Bru Norway
61	C2	Tanahgrogot Indon.
58	C3	Tanahjampea i. Indon.
50	C1	Tanami Desert Austr.
126	A2	Tanana U.S.A.
108	A1	Tanaro r. Italy
65	B1	Tanch'ŏn N. Korea
64	B2	Tandag Phil.
110	C2	Ţăndărei Romania
153	C4	Tandil Arg.
74	A2	Tando Adam Pak.
74	A2	Tando Muhammad Khan Pak.
114	B2	Tanezrouft reg. Alg./Mali
119	D3	Tanga Tanz.
119	C3	Tanganyika, Lake Africa
		Tanger Morocco see Tangier
101	E1	Tangermünde Ger.
75	C1	Tanggula Shan mts China
114	B1	Tangier Morocco
75	C1	Tangra Yumco salt l. China
70	B2	Tangshan China
68	C2	Taniantaweng Shan mts China
59	C3	Tanimbar, Kepulauan is Indon.

64	B2	Tanjay Phil.
60	A1	Tanjungbalai Indon.
61	B2	Tanjungpandan Indon.
60	B1	Tanjungpinang Indon.
61	C1	Tanjungredeb Indon.
61	C1	Tanjungselor Indon.
74	B1	Tank Pak.
115	C3	Tanout Niger
75	C2	Tansen Nepal
116	B1	Ţanţā Egypt
119	D3	Tanzania country Africa
69	E1	Taonan China
138	B1	Taos U.S.A.
114	B2	Taoudenni Mali
88	C2	Tapa Estonia
145	C3	Tapachula Mex.
151	C2	Tapajós r. Brazil
60	A1	Tapaktuan Indon.
145	C3	Tapanatepec Mex.
150	B2	Tapauá Brazil
114	B4	Tapeta Liberia
74	B2	Tapi r. India
141	D3	Tappahannock U.S.A.
150	B2	Tapurucuara Brazil
154	A1	Taquari r. Brazil
154	B1	Taquari, Serra do hills Brazil
154	C2	Taquaritinga Brazil
115	D4	Taraba r. Nigeria
		Ţarābulus Libya see Tripoli
61	C1	Tarakan Indon.
88	A3	Taran, Mys pt Rus. Fed.
54	B1	Taranaki, Mount vol. N.Z.
106	C1	Tarancón Spain
109	C2	Taranto Italy
109	C2	Taranto, Golfo di g. Italy
150	A2	Tarapoto Peru
91	E2	Tarasovskiy Rus. Fed.
150	B2	Tarauacá Brazil
150	B2	Tarauacá r. Brazil
48	F2	Tarawa atoll Kiribati
77	D2	Taraz Kazakh.
107	C1	Tarazona Spain
77	E2	Tarbagatay, Khrebet mts Kazakh.
96	A2	Tarbert Scotland U.K.
96	B3	Tarbert Scotland U.K.
104	C3	Tarbes France
96	B2	Tarbet U.K.
51	C3	Tarcoola Austr.
53	D2	Taree Austr.
110	C2	Târgoviște Romania
110	B1	Târgu Jiu Romania
110	B1	Târgu Mureş Romania
110	C1	Târgu Neamţ Romania
79	C2	Tarif U.A.E.
152	B3	Tarija Bol.
78	B3	Tarim Yemen
77	E2	Tarim Basin China
77	E2	Tarim He r. China
		Tarim Pendi basin China see Tarim Basin
59	D3	Taritatu r. Indon.
82	G2	Tarko-Sale Rus. Fed.
114	B4	Tarkwa Ghana
64	B1	Tarlac Phil.
92	G2	Tärnaby Sweden
77	C3	Tarnak r. Afgh.
110	B1	Târnăveni Romania
103	E1	Tarnobrzeg Pol.
103	E1	Tarnów Pol.
114	B1	Taroudant Morocco
108	B2	Tarquinia Italy
107	D1	Tarragona Spain
107	D1	Tàrrega Spain
80	B2	Tarsus Turkey
152	B3	Tartagal Arg.
104	B3	Tartas France

88	C2	Tartu Estonia
80	B2	Ţarţūs Syria
155	D1	Tarumirim Brazil
89	E3	Tarusa Rus. Fed.
108	B1	Tarvisio Italy
81	D3	Tashk, Daryācheh-ye l. Iran
		Tashkent Uzbek. see Toshkent
131	D1	Tasiujaq Can.
77	E2	Taskesken Kazakh.
54	B2	Tasman Bay N.Z.
51	D4	Tasmania state Austr.
54	B2	Tasman Mountains N.Z.
156	D8	Tasman Sea S. Pacific Ocean
115	C2	Tassili du Hoggar plat. Alg.
115	C2	Tassili n'Ajjer plat. Alg.
103	D2	Tatabánya Hungary
90	B2	Tatarbunary Ukr.
83	K3	Tatarskiy Proliv str. Rus. Fed.
67	C4	Tateyama Japan
128	C1	Tathlina Lake Can.
78	B3	Tathlīth Saudi Arabia
78	B2	Tathlīth, Wādī watercourse Saudi Arabia
53	C3	Tathra Austr.
62	A1	Tatkon Myanmar
128	B2	Tatla Lake Can.
103	D2	Tatra Mountains mts Pol./Slovakia
		Tatry mts Pol./Slovakia see Tatra Mountains
154	B2	Tatui Brazil
139	C2	Tatum U.S.A.
81	C2	Tatvan Turkey
151	D2	Taua Brazil
155	C2	Taubaté Brazil
101	D3	Tauberbischofsheim Ger.
54	C1	Taumarunui N.Z.
62	A1	Taunggyi Myanmar
62	A2	Taung-ngu Myanmar
62	A2	Taungup Myanmar
99	B3	Taunton U.K.
100	C2	Taunus hills Ger.
54	C1	Taupo N.Z.
54	C1	Taupo, Lake N.Z.
88	B2	Tauragė Lith.
54	C1	Tauranga N.Z.
80	B2	Taurus Mountains Turkey
111	C3	Tavas Turkey
86	F3	Tavda Rus. Fed.
106	B2	Tavira Port.
99	A3	Tavistock U.K.
63	A2	Tavoy Myanmar
111	C3	Tavşanlı Turkey
99	A3	Taw r. U.K.
140	C3	Tawas City U.S.A.
61	C1	Tawau Sabah Malaysia
64	C1	Tawi-Tawi i. Phil.
145	C3	Taxco Mex.
76	B2	Taxiatosh Uzbek.
77	D3	Taxkorgan China
96	C2	Tay r. U.K.
96	C2	Tay, Firth of est. U.K.
96	B2	Tay, Loch l. U.K.
128	B2	Taylor Can.
139	D2	Taylor U.S.A.
140	C3	Taylorville U.S.A.
78	A2	Taymā' Saudi Arabia
83	H2	Taymura r. Rus. Fed.
83	H2	Taymyr, Ozero l. Rus. Fed.
		Taymyr, Poluostrov pen. Rus. Fed. see Taymyr Peninsula
83	G2	Taymyr Peninsula Rus. Fed.
63	B2	Tây Ninh Vietnam
64	A1	Taytay Phil.
82	G2	Taz r. Rus. Fed.
114	B1	Taza Morocco
129	D2	Tazin Lake Can.
86	G2	Tazovskaya Guba sea chan. Rus. Fed.
81	C1	T'bilisi Georgia
91	E2	Tbilisskaya Rus. Fed.
118	B3	Tchibanga Gabon
118	B2	Tcholliré Cameroon
103	D1	Tczew Pol.
144	B2	Teacapán Mex.
54	A3	Te Anau N.Z.
54	A3	Te Anau, Lake N.Z.
145	C3	Teapa Mex.
54	C1	Te Awamutu N.Z.
115	C1	Tébessa Alg.
60	B2	Tebingtinggi Sumatera Selatan Indon.
60	A1	Tebingtinggi Sumatera Utara Indon.
114	B4	Techiman Ghana
144	B3	Tecomán Mex.
144	B2	Tecoripa Mex.
145	B3	Tecpan Mex.
144	B2	Tecuala Mex.
110	C1	Tecuci Romania
68	C1	Teeli Rus. Fed.
98	C1	Tees r. U.K.
111	C3	Tefenni Turkey
61	B2	Tegal Indon.
146	B3	Tegucigalpa Hond.
115	C3	Teguidda-n-Tessoumt Niger
114	B4	Téhini Côte d'Ivoire
81	D2	Tehrān Iran
145	C3	Tehuacán Mex.
145	C3	Tehuantepec, Gulf of Mex.
145	C3	Tehuantepec, Istmo de isth. Mex.
99	A2	Teifi r. U.K.
76	C3	Tejen Turkm.
76	C3	Tejen r. Turkm.
		Tejo r. Spain see Tagus
145	B3	Tejupilco Mex.
54	B2	Tekapo, Lake N.Z.
145	D2	Tekax Mex.
116	B3	Tekezē Wenz r. Eritrea/Eth.
111	C2	Tekirdağ Turkey
54	C1	Te Kuiti N.Z.
75	C2	Tel r. India
81	C1	T'elavi Georgia
80	B2	Tel Aviv-Yafo Israel
145	D2	Telchac Puerto Mex.
128	A2	Telegraph Creek Can.
154	B2	Telêmaco Borba Brazil
99	B2	Telford U.K.
60	A2	Telo Indon.
86	E2	Telpoziz, Gora mt. Rus. Fed.
88	B2	Telšiai Lith.
61	B1	Telukbatang Indon.
60	A1	Telukdalam Indon.
60	B1	Teluk Intan Malaysia
130	C2	Temagami Lake Can.
61	C2	Temanggung Indon.
123	C2	Temba S. Africa
60	B2	Tembilahan Indon.
120	A1	Tembo Aluma Angola
99	B2	Teme r. U.K.
60	B1	Temerluh Malaysia
77	D1	Temirtau Kazakh.
53	C2	Temora Austr.
139	D2	Temple U.S.A.
97	C2	Templemore Ireland
145	C2	Tempoal Mex.
91	D2	Temryuk Rus. Fed.
153	A4	Temuco Chile
54	B2	Temuka N.Z.
145	C2	Tenabo Mex.
73	C3	Tenali India
63	A2	Tenasserim Myanmar
99	A3	Tenby U.K.
117	C3	Tendaho Eth.
105	D3	Tende France
108	A2	Tende, Col de pass France/Italy
73	D4	Ten Degree Channel India
67	C3	Tendō Japan
114	B3	Ténenkou Mali
115	D3	Ténéré, Erg du des. Niger
115	D2	Ténéré du Tafassâsset des. Niger
114	A2	Tenerife i. Islas Canarias
107	D2	Ténès Alg.
61	C2	Tengah, Kepulauan is Indon.
62	A1	Tengchong China
61	C2	Tenggarong Indon.
70	A2	Tengger Shamo des. China
71	B3	Tengxian China
119	C4	Tenke Dem. Rep. Congo
114	B3	Tenkodogo Burkina
51	C1	Tennant Creek Austr.
142	C1	Tennessee r. U.S.A.
142	C1	Tennessee state U.S.A.
145	C3	Tenosique Mex.
53	D1	Tenterfield Austr.
154	B2	Teodoro Sampaio Brazil
155	D1	Teófilo Otôni Brazil
145	C3	Teopisca Mex.
144	B2	Tepache Mex.
54	B1	Te Paki N.Z.
144	B3	Tepalcatepec Mex.
144	B2	Tepatitlán Mex.
144	B2	Tepehuanes Mex.
109	D2	Tepelenë Albania
144	B2	Tepic Mex.
102	C1	Teplice Czech Rep.
89	E3	Teploye Rus. Fed.
144	B2	Tequila Mex.
108	B2	Teramo Italy
89	E3	Terbuny Rus. Fed.
90	B2	Terebovlya Ukr.
87	D4	Terek r. Rus. Fed.
151	D2	Teresina Brazil
155	D2	Teresópolis Brazil
63	A3	Teressa Island India
80	B1	Terme Turkey
108	B3	Termini Imerese Sicilia Italy
145	C3	Términos, Laguna de lag. Mex.
77	C3	Termiz Uzbek.
109	B2	Termoli Italy
59	C2	Ternate Indon.
100	A2	Terneuzen Neth.
108	B2	Terni Italy
90	B2	Ternopil' Ukr.
128	C2	Terrace Can.
130	B2	Terrace Bay Can.
122	B2	Terra Firma S. Africa
140	B3	Terre Haute U.S.A.
131	E2	Terrenceville Can.
100	B1	Terschelling i. Neth.
108	A3	Tertenia Sardegna Italy
107	C1	Teruel Spain
92	H2	Tervola Fin.
109	C2	Tešanj Bos.-Herz.
116	B3	Teseney Eritrea
66	D2	Teshio-gawa r. Japan
128	A1	Teslin Can.
128	A1	Teslin Lake Can.
154	B1	Tesouro Brazil
135	D3	Tessaoua Niger
121	C2	Tete Moz.
90	C1	Teteriv r. Ukr.
101	F1	Teterow Ger.
90	B2	Tetiyiv Ukr.
114	B1	Tétouan Morocco
109	D2	Tetovo Macedonia
152	B3	Teuco r. Arg.

144	B2	Teul de González Ortega Mex.
101	D1	Teutoburger Wald hills Ger.
		Tevere r. Italy see Tiber
54	A3	Teviot U.K.
51	E2	Tewantin Austr.
54	C2	Te Wharau N.Z.
139	E2	Texarkana U.S.A.
53	D1	Texas Austr.
139	C2	Texas state U.S.A.
139	E3	Texas City U.S.A.
100	B1	Texel i. Neth.
139	D2	Texoma, Lake U.S.A.
123	C2	Teyateyaneng Lesotho
89	F2	Teykovo Rus. Fed.
89	F2	Teza r. Rus. Fed.
75	D2	Tezpur India
62	A1	Tezu India
129	E1	Tha-anne r. Can.
123	C2	Thabana-Ntlenyana mt. Lesotho
123	C2	Thaba Putsoa mt. Lesotho
123	C1	Thabazimbi S. Africa
123	C2	Thabong S. Africa
63	A2	Thagyettaw Myanmar
62	B1	Thai Binh Vietnam
63	B2	Thailand country Asia
63	B2	Thailand, Gulf of Asia
62	B1	Thai Nguyên Vietnam
62	A3	Thakhèk Laos
63	A3	Thalang Thai.
74	B1	Thal Desert Pak.
101	E2	Thale (Harz) Ger.
62	B2	Tha Li Thai.
123	C1	Thamaga Botswana
116	C3	Thamar, Jabal mt. Yemen
79	C2	Thamarīt Oman
130	B2	Thames r. Can.
54	C1	Thames N.Z.
99	D3	Thames est. U.K.
99	D3	Thames r. U.K.
63	A2	Thanbyuzayat Myanmar
62	A2	Thandwè Myanmar
62	B2	Thanh Hoa Vietnam
73	B3	Thanjavur India
63	A2	Thanlyin Myanmar
74	A2	Thano Bula Khan Pak.
62	B1	Than Uyên Vietnam
74	A2	Thar Desert India/Pak.
52	B3	Thargomindah Austr.
81	C2	Tharthār, Buḩayrat ath l. Iraq
111	B3	Thasos i. Greece
62	B1	Thật Khê Vietnam
62	A2	Thaton Myanmar
74	A2	Thatta Pak.
62	A1	Thaungdut Myanmar
62	A2	Thayawadi Myanmar
62	A2	Thayetmyo Myanmar
62	A1	Thazi Myanmar
146	C2	The Bahamas country West Indies
98	B1	The Cheviot h. U.K.
134	C3	The Dalles U.S.A.
99	C2	The Fens reg. U.K.
114	A3	The Gambia country Africa
		The Great Oasis Egypt see Khārijah, Wāḩāt al
79	C2	The Gulf Asia
100	B1	The Hague Neth.
129	E1	Thelon r. Can.
101	E2	Themar Ger.
96	A1	The Minch sea chan. U.K.
150	B2	Theodore Roosevelt r. Brazil
129	D2	The Pas Can.
111	B2	Thermaïkos Kolpos g. Greece
136	B2	Thermopolis U.S.A.
53	C3	The Rock Austr.
130	B2	Thessalon Can.
111	B2	Thessaloniki Greece
99	D2	Thetford U.K.
131	C2	Thetford Mines Can.
62	A1	The Triangle mts Myanmar
131	D1	Thévenet, Lac l. Can.
99	D2	The Wash b. U.K.
139	D2	The Woodlands U.S.A.
142	B3	Thibodaux U.S.A.
129	E2	Thicket Portage Can.
137	D1	Thief River Falls U.S.A.
105	C2	Thiers France
119	D3	Thika Kenya
73	B4	Thiladhunmathi Atoll Maldives
75	C2	Thimphu Bhutan
105	D2	Thionville France
		Thira i. Greece see Santorini
98	C1	Thirsk U.K.
73	B4	Thiruvananthapuram India
93	E4	Thisted Denmark
129	E1	Thlewiaza r. Can.
62	A2	Thoen Thai.
123	D1	Thohoyandou S. Africa
97	C2	Thomastown Ireland
143	D2	Thomasville U.S.A.
100	C2	Thommen Belgium
129	E2	Thompson Can.
128	E3	Thompson r. U.S.A.
134	C1	Thompson Falls U.S.A.
128	B2	Thompson Sound Can.
96	C3	Thornhill U.K.
55	C2	Thorshavnheiane reg. Antarctica
104	B2	Thouars France
128	C2	Three Hills Can.
63	A2	Three Pagodas Pass Myanmar/Thai.
114	B4	Three Points, Cape Ghana
73	B3	Thrissur India
63	B2	Thu Dầu Một Vietnam
100	B2	Thuin Belgium
127	G1	Thule Greenland
121	B3	Thuli Zimbabwe
130	B2	Thunder Bay Can.
63	A3	Thung Song Thai.
101	E2	Thüringer Becken reg. Ger.
101	E2	Thüringer Wald mts Ger.
101	E2	Thüringer Wald mts Ger.
97	C2	Thurles Ireland
96	C1	Thurso U.K.
96	C1	Thurso r. U.K.
151	D2	Tianguá Brazil
70	B2	Tianjin China
70	B2	Tianjin mun. China
71	A3	Tianlin China
70	B2	Tianmen China
70	A2	Tianshui China
154	B2	Tibagi r. Brazil
118	B2	Tibati Cameroon
108	B2	Tiber r. Italy
		Tiberias, Lake Israel see Galilee, Sea of
115	D2	Tibesti mts Chad
		Tibet aut. reg. China see Xizang Zizhiqu
68	B2	Tibet, Plateau of China
		Tibet Autonomous Region aut. reg. China see Xizang Zizhiqu
52	B1	Tibooburra Austr.
144	A2	Tiburón, Isla i. Mex.
114	B3	Tichît Maur.
114	A2	Tichla Western Sahara
145	D2	Ticul Mex.
114	A3	Tidjikja Maur.
100	B2	Tiel Neth.
65	A1	Tieling China
100	A2	Tielt Belgium
100	B2	Tienen Belgium
68	B2	Tien Shan mts China/Kyrg.
		Tientsin China see Tianjin
93	G3	Tierp Sweden
145	C3	Tierra Blanca Mex.
145	C3	Tierra Colorada Mex.
153	B6	Tierra del Fuego, Isla Grande de i. Arg./Chile
154	C2	Tietê Brazil
		Tiflis Georgia see T'bilisi
143	D2	Tifton U.S.A.
90	B2	Tighina Moldova
131	D2	Tignish Can.
150	A2	Tigre r. Ecuador/Peru
81	C2	Tigris r. Asia
145	C2	Tihuatlán Mex.
144	A1	Tijuana Mex.
91	E2	Tikhoretsk Rus. Fed.
89	D2	Tikhvin Rus. Fed.
89	D2	Tikhvinskaya Gryada ridge Rus. Fed.
54	C1	Tikokino N.Z.
81	C2	Tikrīt Iraq
83	J2	Tiksi Rus. Fed.
100	B2	Tilburg Neth.
152	B3	Tilcara Arg.
52	B1	Tilcha (abandoned) Austr.
114	C3	Tillabéri Niger
134	B1	Tillamook U.S.A.
63	A3	Tillanchong Island India
111	C3	Tilos i. Greece
52	B2	Tilpa Austr.
86	F2	Til'tim Rus. Fed.
89	E3	Tim Rus. Fed.
86	D2	Timanskiy Kryazh ridge Rus. Fed.
54	B2	Timaru N.Z.
91	D2	Timashevsk Rus. Fed.
114	B3	Timbedgha Maur.
50	C1	Timber Creek Austr.
114	B3	Timbuktu Mali
114	C2	Timimoun Alg.
111	B2	Timiou Prodromou, Akrotirio pt Greece
110	B1	Timiş r. Romania
110	B1	Timişoara Romania
130	B2	Timmins Can.
89	E2	Timokhino Rus. Fed.
151	D2	Timon Brazil
59	C3	Timor i. East Timor/Indonesia
58	C3	Timor Sea Austr./Indon.
93	G3	Timrå Sweden
114	B2	Tindouf Alg.
75	C2	Tingri China
93	F4	Tingsryd Sweden
59	D2	Tinian i. N. Mariana Is
152	B3	Tinogasta Arg.
111	C3	Tinos Greece
111	C3	Tinos i. Greece
115	C2	Tinrhert, Hamada de Alg.
62	A1	Tinsukia India
107	D2	Tipasa Alg.
97	B2	Tipperary Ireland
109	C2	Tirana Albania
		Tiranë Albania see Tirana
108	B1	Tirano Italy
90	B2	Tiraspol Moldova
111	C3	Tire Turkey
96	A2	Tiree i. U.K.
74	B1	Tirich Mir mt. Pak.
73	B3	Tiruchchirappalli India
73	B4	Tirunelveli India
73	B3	Tirupati India
73	B3	Tiruppattur India
73	B3	Tiruppur India

109	D1	Tisa r. Serbia
129	C2	Tisdale Can.
107	D2	Tissemsilt Alg.
152	B2	Titicaca, Lake Bol./Peru
75	C2	Titlagarh India
110	C2	Titu Romania
143	D3	Titusville India
99	B3	Titusville U.S.A.
108	B2	Tiverton U.K.
79	C2	Tivoli Italy
145	D2	Tiwi Oman
107	D2	Tizimín Mex.
114	B2	Tizi Ouzou Alg.
117	D2	Tiznit Morocco
145	C3	Tlacotalpán Mex.
144	B2	Tlahualilo Mex.
145	C3	Tlapa Mex.
145	C3	Tlaxcala Mex.
145	C3	Tlaxiaco Mex.
114	B1	Tlemcen Alg.
123	C3	Tlokweng Botswana
128	B2	Toad River Can.
121	D2	Toamasina Madag.
60	A1	Toba, Danau l. Indon.
74	A1	Toba and Kakar Ranges mts Pak.
147	D3	Tobago i. Trin. and Tob.
59	C2	Tobelo Indon.
130	B2	Tobermory Can.
96	A2	Tobermory U.K.
129	D2	Tobin Lake Can.
60	D2	Toboali Indon.
76	C1	Tobol r. Kazakh./Rus. Fed.
86	F3	Tobol'sk Rus. Fed.
151	D2	Tocantinópolis Brazil
151	D2	Tocantins r. Brazil
143	D2	Toccoa U.S.A.
108	A1	Toce r. Italy
152	A3	Tocopilla Chile
53	C3	Tocumwal Austr.
144	A2	Todos Santos Mex.
128	B3	Tofino Can.
96	□	Toft U.K.
49	G4	Tofua i. Tonga
59	C2	Togian, Kepulauan is Indon.
114	C4	Togo country Africa
74	A2	Tohana India
126	B2	Tok U.S.A.
116	B3	Tokar Sudan
69	E3	Tokara-rettō is Japan
91	E1	Tokarevka Rus. Fed.
49	G3	Tokelau terr. S. Pacific Ocean
91	D2	Tokmak Ukr.
77	D2	Tokmok Kyrg.
54	C1	Tokoroa N.Z.
68	B2	Toksun China
67	B4	Tokushima Japan
67	C3	Tōkyō Japan
121	D3	Tôlañaro Madag.
154	B2	Toledo Brazil
106	C2	Toledo Spain
140	C2	Toledo U.S.A.
106	C2	Toledo, Montes de mts Spain
142	B2	Toledo Bend Reservoir U.S.A.
121	D3	Toliara Madag.
58	C2	Tolitoli Indon.
108	B1	Tolmezzo Italy
104	B3	Tolosa Spain
145	C3	Toluca Mex.
87	D3	Tol'yatti Rus. Fed.
140	A2	Tomah U.S.A.
66	D2	Tomakomai Japan
106	B2	Tomar Port.
103	E1	Tomaszów Lubelski Pol.
103	E1	Tomaszów Mazowiecki Pol.
144	B3	Tomatlán Mex.
142	C2	Tombigbee r. U.S.A.
155	D2	Tombos Brazil
		Tombouctou Mali see Timbuktu
120	A2	Tombua Angola
123	C1	Tom Burke S. Africa
53	C1	Tomingley Austr.
58	C3	Tomini, Teluk g. Indon.
109	C2	Tomislavgrad Bos.-Herz.
50	A2	Tom Price Austr.
82	G3	Tomsk Rus. Fed.
93	F4	Tomtabacken h. Sweden
145	C3	Tonalá Mex.
150	B2	Tonantins Brazil
59	C2	Tondano Indon.
49	G4	Tonga country S. Pacific Ocean
49	G4	Tongatapu Group is Tonga
71	B3	Tongcheng China
70	A2	Tongchuan China
71	A3	Tongdao China
65	B2	Tongduch'ŏn S. Korea
100	B2	Tongeren Belgium
65	B2	Tonghae S. Korea
62	B1	Tonghai China
65	B1	Tonghua China
65	B2	Tongjosŏn-man b. N. Korea
62	B1	Tongking, Gulf of China/Vietnam
69	E2	Tongliao China
70	B2	Tongling China
52	B2	Tongo Austr.
71	A3	Tongren China
		Tongshan China see Xuzhou
		Tongtian He r. China see Yangtze
96	B1	Tongue U.K.
65	B3	T'ongyŏng S. Korea
65	A1	Tongyu China
65	A1	Tongyuanpu China
74	B2	Tonk India
63	B2	Tonle Sap l. Cambodia
135	C3	Tonopah U.S.A.
93	F4	Tønsberg Norway
135	D2	Tooele U.S.A.
52	B3	Tooleybuc Austr.
53	D1	Toowoomba Austr.
137	D3	Topeka U.S.A.
144	B2	Topia Mex.
144	B2	Topolobampo Mex.
86	C2	Topozero, Ozero l. Rus. Fed.
134	B1	Toppenish U.S.A.
111	C3	Torbalı Turkey
76	B3	Torbat-e Heydarīyeh Iran
76	C3	Torbat-e Jām Iran
106	C1	Tordesillas Spain
107	C1	Tordesilos Spain
107	D1	Torelló Spain
101	F2	Torgau Ger.
100	A2	Torhout Belgium
		Torino Italy see Turin
154	B1	Torixoréu Brazil
106	B1	Tormes r. Spain
92	H2	Torneälven r. Sweden
127	G3	Torngat Mountains Can.
92	H2	Tornio Fin.
106	B1	Toro Spain
130	C2	Toronto Can.
119	D2	Tororo Uganda
		Toros Dağları mts Turkey see Taurus Mountains
99	B3	Torquay U.K.
106	B2	Torre mt. Spain
106	B1	Torre mt. Spain
107	D1	Torreblanca Spain
106	C1	Torrecerredo mt. Spain
106	B1	Torre de Moncorvo Port.
106	C2	Torrelavega Spain
106	C2	Torremolinos Spain
52	A2	Torrens, Lake imp. l. Austr.
107	C2	Torrent Spain
144	B2	Torreón Mex.
106	B2	Torres Novas Port.
106	B2	Torres Vedras Port.
107	C2	Torrevieja Spain
96	B2	Torridon U.K.
106	C2	Torrijos Spain
141	E2	Torrington CT U.S.A.
136	C2	Torrington WY U.S.A.
107	D1	Torroella de Montgrí Spain
94	B1	Tórshavn Faroe Is
108	A3	Tortolì Sardegna Italy
107	D1	Tortosa Spain
103	D1	Toruń Pol.
97	B1	Tory Island Ireland
89	D2	Torzhok Rus. Fed.
122	B2	Tosca S. Africa
108	B2	Toscana, Arcipelago is Italy
77	C2	Toshkent Uzbek.
89	D2	Tosno Rus. Fed.
152	B3	Tostado Arg.
101	D1	Tostedt Ger.
80	B1	Tosya Turkey
86	D3	Tot'ma Rus. Fed.
67	B3	Tottori Japan
114	B4	Touba Côte d'Ivoire
114	B1	Toubkal, Jbel mt. Morocco
114	B3	Tougan Burkina
115	C1	Touggourt Alg.
105	D2	Toul France
71	C3	Touliu Taiwan
105	D3	Toulon France
104	C3	Toulouse France
100	A2	Tournai Belgium
105	C2	Tournus France
151	E2	Touros Brazil
104	C2	Tours France
115	D2	Tousside, Pic mt. Chad
122	B3	Touwsrivier S. Africa
66	D2	Towada Japan
134	D1	Townsend U.S.A.
51	D1	Townsville Austr.
77	E2	Toxkan He r. China
66	D2	Tōya-ko l. Japan
67	C3	Toyama Japan
67	C3	Toyota Japan
115	C1	Tozeur Tunisia
81	C1	Tqvarch'eli Georgia
		Trâblous Lebanon see Tripoli
80	B1	Trabzon Turkey
106	B2	Trafalgar, Cabo c. Spain
128	C3	Trail Can.
88	B3	Trakai Lith.
97	B2	Tralee Ireland
97	C2	Tramore Ireland
63	A3	Trang Thai.
59	C3	Trangan i. Indon.
55	I2	Transantarctic Mountains Antarctica
110	B1	Transylvanian Alps mts Romania
108	B3	Trapani Sicilia Italy
53	C3	Traralgon Austr.
63	B2	Trat Thai.
102	C2	Traunstein Ger.
140	B2	Traverse City U.S.A.
103	D2	Třebíč Czech Rep.
109	C2	Trebinje Bos.-Herz.
103	E2	Trebišov Slovakia
109	C1	Trebnje Slovenia
153	C4	Treinta y Tres Uru.
153	B5	Trelew Arg.
93	F4	Trelleborg Sweden
130	C2	Tremblant, Mont h. Can.
109	C2	Tremiti, Isole is Italy
134	D2	Tremonton U.S.A.
107	D1	Tremp Spain

103 D2 Trenčín Slovakia
153 B4 Trenque Lauquén Arg.
98 C2 Trent r. U.K.
108 B1 Trento Italy
141 D2 Trenton Can.
137 E2 Trenton MO U.S.A.
141 E2 Trenton NJ U.S.A.
131 E2 Trepassey Can.
153 B4 Tres Arroyos Arg.
155 C2 Três Corações Brazil
154 B2 Três Lagoas Brazil
153 A5 Tres Lagos Arg.
155 C1 Três Marias, Represa resr Brazil
155 C2 Três Pontas Brazil
153 B5 Tres Puntas, Cabo c. Arg.
155 D2 Três Rios Brazil
101 F1 Treuenbrietzen Ger.
108 A1 Treviglio Italy
108 B1 Treviso Italy
99 A3 Trevose Head U.K.
109 C3 Tricase Italy
53 C2 Trida Austr.
100 C3 Trier Ger.
108 B1 Trieste Italy
108 B1 Triglav mt. Slovenia
59 D3 Trikora, Puncak mt. Indon.
97 C2 Trim Ireland
73 C4 Trincomalee Sri Lanka
154 C1 Trindade Brazil
152 B2 Trinidad Bol.
147 D3 Trinidad i. Trin. and Tob.
136 C3 Trinidad U.S.A.
147 D3 Trinidad and Tobago country West Indies
131 E2 Trinity Bay Can.
111 B3 Tripoli Greece
80 B2 Tripoli Lebanon
115 D1 Tripoli Libya
113 D10 Tristan da Cunha i. S. Atlantic Ocean
   Trivandrum India see Thiruvananthapuram
108 B2 Trivento Italy
103 D2 Trnava Slovakia
109 C2 Trogir Croatia
109 C2 Troia Italy
100 C2 Troisdorf Ger.
131 D2 Trois-Rivières Can.
86 E2 Troitsko-Pechorsk Rus. Fed.
151 F2 Trombetas r. Brazil
123 C3 Trompsburg S. Africa
92 F3 Tromsø Norway
92 F2 Trondheim Norway
128 C2 Trout Lake Can.
128 B1 Trout Lake N.W.T. Can.
130 A1 Trout Lake Ont. Can.
99 B3 Trowbridge U.K.
142 C2 Troy AL U.S.A.
141 E2 Troy NY U.S.A.
105 C2 Troyes France
109 D2 Trstenik Serbia
89 D3 Trubchevsk Rus. Fed.
106 B1 Truchas Spain
79 C2 Trucial Coast U.A.E.
146 B3 Trujillo Hond.
150 A2 Trujillo Peru
106 B2 Trujillo Spain
147 C4 Trujillo Venez.
142 B1 Trumann U.S.A.
131 D2 Truro Can.
99 A3 Truro U.K.
138 B2 Truth or Consequences U.S.A.
103 D1 Trutnov Czech Rep.
93 F3 Trysil Norway
103 D1 Trzebiatów Pol.
68 B1 Tsagaannuur Mongolia

121 D2 Tsaratanana, Massif du mts Madag.
110 C2 Tsarevo Bulg.
122 A2 Tses Namibia
122 B1 Tsetseng Botswana
68 C1 Tsetserleg Mongolia
68 C1 Tsetserleg Mongolia
122 B2 Tshabong Botswana
122 B1 Tshane Botswana
91 D2 Tschikskoye Vodokhranilishche resr Rus. Fed.
118 B3 Tshela Dem. Rep. Congo
118 C3 Tshikapa Dem. Rep. Congo
118 C3 Tshikapa r. Dem. Rep. Congo
123 D1 Tshipise S. Africa
118 C3 Tshitanzu Dem. Rep. Congo
118 C3 Tshuapa r. Dem. Rep. Congo
   Tshwane S. Africa see Pretoria
87 D4 Tsimlyanskoye Vodokhranilishche resr Rus. Fed.
   Tsingtao China see Qingdao
   Tsining China see Jining
121 D3 Tsiroanomandidy Madag.
123 C3 Tsomo S. Africa
67 C4 Tsu Japan
67 D3 Tsuchiura Japan
66 D2 Tsugarū-kaikyō str. Japan
120 A2 Tsumeb Namibia
122 A1 Tsumis Park Namibia
120 B2 Tsumkwe Namibia
67 C3 Tsuruga Japan
67 C3 Tsuruoka Japan
67 A4 Tsushima is Japan
   Tsushima-kaikyō str. Japan/ S. Korea see Korea Strait
67 B3 Tsuyama Japan
123 C2 Tswelelang S. Africa
91 C2 Tsyurupyns'k Ukr.
   T'thenaagoo Can. see Nahanni Butte
59 C3 Tual Indon.
97 B2 Tuam Ireland
91 D3 Tuapse Rus. Fed.
54 A3 Tuatapere N.Z.
96 A1 Tuath, Loch a' b. U.K.
138 A1 Tuba City U.S.A.
61 C2 Tuban Indon.
152 D3 Tubarão Brazil
102 B2 Tübingen Ger.
115 E1 Tubruq Libya
49 I4 Tubuai i. Fr. Polynesia
49 H4 Tubuai is Fr. Polynesia
144 A1 Tubutama Mex.
152 B2 Tucavaca Bol.
128 B1 Tuchitua Can.
138 A2 Tucson U.S.A.
139 C1 Tucumcari U.S.A.
150 B1 Tucupita Venez.
151 E2 Tucuruí Brazil
151 D2 Tucuruí, Represa resr Brazil
107 C1 Tudela Spain
106 B1 Tuela r. Port.
62 A1 Tuensang India
123 D2 Tugela r. S. Africa
64 B1 Tuguegarao Phil.
106 B1 Tui Spain
59 C3 Tukangbesi, Kepulauan is Indon.
126 C2 Tuktoyaktuk Can.
88 B2 Tukums Latvia
145 C2 Tula Mex.
89 E3 Tula Rus. Fed.
145 C2 Tulancingo Mex.
135 C3 Tulare U.S.A.
138 B2 Tularosa U.S.A.

110 C1 Tulcea Romania
90 B2 Tul'chyn Ukr.
129 E1 Tulemalu Lake Can.
139 C2 Tulia U.S.A.
142 C1 Tullahoma U.S.A.
97 C2 Tullamore Ireland
104 C2 Tulle France
51 D1 Tully Austr.
139 D1 Tulsa U.S.A.
150 A1 Tumaco Col.
123 C2 Tumahole S. Africa
93 G4 Tumba Sweden
118 B3 Tumba, Lac l. Dem. Rep. Congo
   Tumbarumba Austr.
53 C3 Tumbarumba Austr.
150 A2 Tumbes Peru
128 B2 Tumbler Ridge Can.
52 A2 Tumby Bay Austr.
65 B1 Tumen China
150 B1 Tumereng Guyana
64 A2 Tumindao i. Phil.
74 A2 Tump Pak.
151 C1 Tumucumaque, Serra hills Brazil
53 C3 Tumut Austr.
99 D3 Tunbridge Wells, Royal U.K.
80 B2 Tunceli Turkey
53 D2 Tuncurry Austr.
119 D4 Tunduru Tanz.
110 C2 Tundzha r. Bulg.
128 B2 Tungsten (abandoned) Can.
115 D1 Tunis Tunisia
115 C1 Tunisia country Africa
150 A1 Tunja Col.
92 F3 Tunnsjøen l. Norway
   Tunxi China see Huangshan
154 B2 Tupã Brazil
154 C1 Tupaciguara Brazil
142 C2 Tupelo U.S.A.
152 B3 Tupiza Bol.
83 H2 Tura Rus. Fed.
86 F3 Tura r. Rus. Fed.
78 B2 Turabah Saudi Arabia
83 I3 Turana, Khrebet mts Rus. Fed.
54 C1 Turangi N.Z.
76 B2 Turan Lowland Asia
78 A1 Turayf Saudi Arabia
88 B2 Turba Estonia
74 A2 Turbat Pak.
150 A1 Turbo Col.
110 B1 Turda Romania
   Turfan China see Turpan
76 C2 Turgay Kazakh.
111 C3 Turgutlu Turkey
80 B1 Turhal Turkey
107 C2 Tur r. Spain
108 A1 Turin Italy
86 F3 Turinsk Rus. Fed.
90 A1 Turiys'k Ukr.
119 D2 Turkana, Lake salt l. Eth./Kenya
77 C2 Turkestan Kazakh.
80 B2 Turkey country Asia/Europe
76 C3 Türkmenabat Turkm.
76 B2 Türkmenbaşy Turkm.
76 B2 Turkmenistan country Asia
147 C2 Turks and Caicos Islands terr. West Indies
93 H3 Turku Fin.
135 B3 Turlock U.S.A.
54 C2 Turnagain, Cape N.Z.
100 B2 Turnhout Belgium
129 D2 Turnor Lake Can.
110 B2 Turnu Măgurele Romania
68 B2 Turpan China
77 D2 Turugart Pass China/Kyrg.
142 C2 Tuscaloosa U.S.A.

Tuskegee

142 C2 Tuskegee U.S.A.
73 B4 Tuticorin India
120 B3 Tutume Botswana
49 F3 Tuvalu *country* S. Pacific Ocean
78 B2 Tuwayq, Jabal *hills* Saudi Arabia
78 B2 Tuwayq, Jabal *mts* Saudi Arabia
78 A2 Tuwwal Saudi Arabia
144 B2 Tuxpan *Nayarit* Mex.
145 C2 Tuxpan *Veracruz* Mex.
145 C3 Tuxtla Gutiérrez Mex.
62 B1 Tuyên Quang Vietnam
63 B2 Tuy Hoa Vietnam
80 B2 Tuz, Lake *salt l.* Turkey
       Tuz Gölü *salt l.* Turkey *see* Tuz, Lake
81 C2 Tuz Khurmātū Iraq
109 C2 Tuzla Bos.-Herz.
91 E2 Tuzlov r. Rus. Fed.
89 E2 Tver' Rus. Fed.
98 B1 Tweed r. U.K.
122 A2 Twee Rivier Namibia
135 C4 Twentynine Palms U.S.A.
131 E2 Twillingate Can.
134 D2 Twin Falls U.S.A.
137 E1 Two Harbors U.S.A.
129 C2 Two Hills Can.
139 D2 Tyler U.S.A.
83 J3 Tynda Rus. Fed.
93 F3 Tynset Norway
80 B2 Tyre Lebanon
111 B3 Tyrnavos Greece
52 B3 Tyrrell, Lake *dry lake* Austr.
108 B2 Tyrrhenian Sea France/Italy
76 B2 Tyub-Karagan, Mys *pt* Kazakh.
87 E3 Tyul'gan Rus. Fed.
86 F3 Tyumen' Rus. Fed.
83 J2 Tyung r. Rus. Fed.
99 A3 Tywi r. U.K.
123 D1 Tzaneen S. Africa

U

120 B2 Uamanda Angola
150 B2 Uaupés Brazil
155 D2 Ubá Brazil
155 D1 Ubaí Brazil
151 E3 Ubaitaba Brazil
118 B3 Ubangi r. C.A.R./Dem. Rep. Congo
67 B4 Ube Japan
106 C2 Úbeda Spain
154 C1 Uberaba Brazil
154 C1 Uberlândia Brazil
106 B1 Ubiña, Peña *mt.* Spain
123 D2 Ubombo S. Africa
63 B2 Ubon Ratchathani Thai.
119 C3 Ubundu Dem. Rep. Congo
150 A2 Ucayali r. Peru
74 B2 Uch Pak.
77 E2 Ucharal Kazakh.
66 D2 Uchiura-wan *b.* Japan
83 J3 Uchur r. Rus. Fed.
128 B3 Ucluelet Can.
74 B2 Udaipur India
91 C1 Uday r. Ukr.
93 F4 Uddevalla Sweden
92 G2 Uddjaure l. Sweden
100 B2 Uden Neth.
74 B1 Udhampur India
108 B1 Udine Italy
89 E2 Udomlya Rus. Fed.
62 B2 Udon Thani Thai.

73 B3 Udupi India
83 K3 Udyl', Ozero l. Rus. Fed.
67 C2 Ueda Japan
58 C3 Uekuli Indon.
118 C2 Uele r. Dem. Rep. Congo
101 E1 Uelzen Ger.
119 C2 Uere r. Dem. Rep. Congo
87 E3 Ufa Rus. Fed.
119 D3 Ugalla r. Tanz.
119 D2 Uganda *country* Africa
89 E2 Uglich Rus. Fed.
89 D3 Uglovka Rus. Fed.
89 D3 Ugra Rus. Fed.
103 D2 Uherské Hradiště Czech Rep.
101 E2 Uichteritz Ger.
96 A2 Uig U.K.
120 A1 Uíge Angola
65 B2 Ŭijŏngbu S. Korea
135 D2 Uinta Mountains U.S.A.
120 A3 Uis Mine Namibia
65 B2 Ŭisŏng S. Korea
123 C3 Uitenhage S. Africa
100 C1 Uithuizen Neth.
74 B2 Ujjain India
89 F3 Ukholovo Rus. Fed.
63 A1 Ukhrul India
86 E2 Ukhta Rus. Fed.
135 B3 Ukiah U.S.A.
127 H2 Ukkusissat Greenland
88 B2 Ukmergė Lith.
90 C2 Ukraine *country* Europe
       Ulaanbaatar Mongolia *see* Ulan Bator
68 C1 Ulaangom Mongolia
69 D1 Ulan Bator Mongolia
       Ulanhad China *see* Chifeng
69 E1 Ulanhot China
87 D4 Ulan-Khol Rus. Fed.
69 D1 Ulan-Ude Rus. Fed.
75 D1 Ulan Ul Hu l. China
65 B1 Ulchin S. Korea
       Uleåborg Fin. *see* Oulu
88 C2 Ülenurme Estonia
69 D1 Uliastai China
68 C1 Uliastay Mongolia
59 D2 Ulithi *atoll* Micronesia
53 D3 Ulladulla Austr.
96 B2 Ullapool U.K.
98 B1 Ullswater l. U.K.
65 C2 Ullŭng-do i. S. Korea
102 B2 Ulm Ger.
65 B2 Ulsan S. Korea
96 □ Ulsta U.K.
97 C1 Ulster *reg.* Ireland/U.K.
52 B3 Ultima Austr.
111 C3 Ulubey Turkey
111 C2 Uludağ *mt.* Turkey
126 D2 Ulukhaktok Can.
123 D2 Ulundi S. Africa
77 E2 Ulungur Hu l. China
50 C2 Uluru *h.* Austr.
98 B1 Ulverston U.K.
87 D3 Ul'yanovsk Rus. Fed.
136 C3 Ulysses U.S.A.
90 C2 Uman' Ukr.
86 C2 Umba Rus. Fed.
59 D3 Umboi i. P.N.G.
92 H3 Umeå Sweden
92 H3 Umeälven r. Sweden
127 I2 Umiiviip Kangertiva *inlet* Greenland
126 D2 Umingmaktok (abandoned) Can.
123 D2 Umlazi S. Africa
117 A3 Umm Keddada Sudan
78 A2 Umm Lajj Saudi Arabia

117 B3 Umm Ruwaba Sudan
115 E1 Umm Sa'ad Libya
134 B2 Umpqua r. U.S.A.
120 A2 Umpulo Angola
123 C3 Umtata S. Africa
154 B2 Umuarama Brazil
109 C1 Una r. Bos.-Herz./Croatia
155 E1 Una Brazil
154 C1 Unaí Brazil
78 B2 'Unayzah Saudi Arabia
136 C1 Underwood U.S.A.
89 D3 Unecha Rus. Fed.
53 C2 Ungarie Austr.
52 A2 Ungarra Austr.
127 G2 Ungava, Péninsule d' *pen.* Can.
127 G3 Ungava Bay Can.
90 B2 Ungheni Moldova
       Unguja i. Tanz. *see* Zanzibar Island
154 B3 União da Vitória Brazil
150 B2 Unini r. Brazil
142 C1 Union City U.S.A.
122 B3 Uniondale S. Africa
141 D3 Uniontown U.S.A.
79 C2 United Arab Emirates *country* Asia
95 C3 United Kingdom *country* Europe
132 D3 United States of America *country* N. America
129 D2 Unity Can.
96 □ Unst i. U.K.
101 E2 Unstrut r. Ger.
89 E3 Upa r. Rus. Fed.
119 C3 Upemba, Lac l. Dem. Rep. Congo
122 B2 Upington S. Africa
134 B2 Upper Alkali Lake U.S.A.
128 C2 Upper Arrow Lake Can.
134 B2 Upper Klamath Lake U.S.A.
128 B1 Upper Liard Can.
97 C1 Upper Lough Erne l. U.K.
93 G4 Uppsala Sweden
78 B2 'Uqlat aş Şuqūr Saudi Arabia
       Urad Qianqi China *see* Xishanzui
76 B2 Ural r. Kazakh./Rus. Fed.
53 D2 Uralla Austr.
87 E3 Ural Mountains Rus. Fed.
76 B1 Ural'sk Kazakh.
       Ural'skiy Khrebet *mts* Rus. Fed. *see* Ural Mountains
119 D3 Urambo Tanz.
53 C3 Urana Austr.
129 D2 Uranium City Can.
86 F2 Uray Rus. Fed.
98 C1 Ure r. U.K.
86 D3 Uren' Rus. Fed.
144 A2 Ures Mex.
76 C2 Urganch Uzbek.
100 B1 Urk Neth.
111 C3 Urla Turkey
81 C2 Urmia, Lake *salt l.* Iran
       Uroševac Kosovo *see* Ferizaj
144 B2 Uruáchic Mex.
151 D3 Uruaçu Brazil
144 B3 Uruapan Mex.
150 A3 Urubamba r. Peru
151 C2 Urucará Brazil
151 D2 Uruçuí Brazil
151 C2 Urucurituba Brazil
152 C3 Uruguaiana Brazil
153 C4 Uruguay *country* S. America
       Urumchi China *see* Ürümqi
68 C2 Ürümqi China
53 D2 Urunga Austr.

10 C2 Urziceni Romania
67 B4 Usa Japan
82 E2 Usa r. Rus. Fed.
11 C3 Uşak Turkey
82 G1 Ushakova, Ostrov i. Rus. Fed.
77 D2 Ushtobe Kazakh.
53 B6 Ushuaia Arg.
86 E2 Usinsk Rus. Fed.
88 C3 Uskhodni Belarus
89 E3 Usman' Rus. Fed.
104 C2 Usogorsk Rus. Fed.
104 C2 Ussel France
66 B2 Ussuriysk Rus. Fed.
108 B3 Ustica, Isola di i. Sicilia Italy
86 F2 Ust'-Ilimsk Rus. Fed.
86 E2 Ust'-Ilych Rus. Fed.
Ustka Pol.
83 L3 Ust'-Kamchatsk Rus. Fed.
77 E2 Ust'-Kamenogorsk Kazakh.
83 K2 Ust'-Kara Rus. Fed.
86 E2 Ust'-Kulom Rus. Fed.
83 L3 Ust'-Kut Rus. Fed.
91 D2 Ust'-Labinsk Rus. Fed.
86 E2 Ust'-Luga Rus. Fed.
83 K2 Ust'-Nem Rus. Fed.
83 K2 Ust'-Nera Rus. Fed.
83 K2 Ust'-Omchug Rus. Fed.
83 H3 Ust'-Ordynskiy Rus. Fed.
86 E2 Ust'-Tsil'ma Rus. Fed.
76 B2 Ustyurt Plateau
Kazakh./Uzbek.
89 E3 Ustyuzhna Rus. Fed.
89 D2 Usvyaty Rus. Fed.
135 D3 Utah state U.S.A.
135 D2 Utah Lake U.S.A.
93 I4 Utena Lith.
141 D2 Utica U.S.A.
107 C2 Utiel Spain
128 C2 Utikuma Lake Can.
100 B1 Utrecht Neth.
106 B2 Utrera Spain
93 I2 Utsjoki Fin.
67 C3 Utsunomiya Japan
87 D4 Utta Rus. Fed.
62 B2 Uttaradit Thai.
Uummannaq Greenland see
Dundas
127 Uummannaq Fjord inlet
Greenland
93 H3 Uusikaupunki Fin.
139 D3 Uvalde U.S.A.
119 D3 Uvinza Tanz.
72 Uvs Nuur salt l. Mongolia
67 B4 Uwajima Japan
74 'Uwayriḍ, Ḥarrat al lava field
Saudi Arabia
116 A2 Uweinat, Jebel mt. Sudan
83 H3 Uyar Rus. Fed.
115 C4 Uyo Nigeria
152 B3 Uyuni, Salar de salt flat Bol.
76 Uzbekistan country Asia
104 C2 Uzerche France
105 C3 Uzès France
91 C1 Uzh r. Ukr.
90 C1 Uzhhorod Ukr.
109 C2 Užice Serbia
89 D2 Uzlovaya Rus. Fed.
111 D3 Üzümlü Turkey
111 D3 Uzunköprü Turkey

V

123 B2 Vaal r. S. Africa
123 C2 Vaal Dam S. Africa

123 C1 Vaalwater S. Africa
92 H3 Vaasa Fin.
103 D2 Vác Hungary
152 C3 Vacaria Brazil
154 B2 Vacaria, Serra hills Brazil
135 B3 Vacaville U.S.A.
74 B2 Vadodara India
92 I1 Vadsø Norway
105 D2 Vaduz Liechtenstein
94 B1 Vágar i. Faroe Is
94 B1 Vágur Faroe Is
103 D2 Váh r. Slovakia
49 F3 Vaiaku Tuvalu
88 B2 Vaida Estonia
136 B3 Vail U.S.A.
79 C2 Vakīlābād Iran
108 B1 Valdagno Italy
89 D2 Valday Rus. Fed.
89 D2 Valdayskaya Vozvyshennost'
hills Rus. Fed.
106 B2 Valdecañas, Embalse de resr
Spain
93 G4 Valdemarsvik Sweden
106 C2 Valdepeñas Spain
153 B5 Valdés, Península pen. Arg.
153 A4 Valdivia Chile
130 C2 Val-d'Or Can.
143 D2 Valdosta U.S.A.
128 C2 Valemount Can.
105 C3 Valence France
107 C2 Valencia Spain
150 B1 Valencia Venez.
107 D2 Valencia, Golfo de g. Spain
100 A2 Valenciennes France
136 C2 Valentine U.S.A.
64 B1 Valenzuela Phil.
150 A1 Valera Venez.
109 C2 Valjevo Serbia
88 C2 Valka Latvia
93 H3 Valkeakoski Fin.
100 B2 Valkenswaard Neth.
91 D2 Valky Ukr.
55 D2 Valkyrie Dome Antarctica
145 D2 Valladolid Mex.
106 C1 Valladolid Spain
93 E4 Valle Norway
145 C2 Vallecillos Mex.
150 B1 Valle de la Pascua Venez.
150 A1 Valledupar Col.
145 C2 Valle Hermoso Mex.
135 B3 Vallejo U.S.A.
152 A3 Vallenar Chile
85 H5 Valletta Malta
137 D1 Valley City U.S.A.
134 D2 Valley Falls U.S.A.
128 C2 Valleyview Can.
107 D1 Valls Spain
129 D3 Val Marie Can.
88 C2 Valmiera Latvia
88 C3 Valozhyn Belarus
154 B2 Valparaíso Brazil
153 A4 Valparaíso Chile
105 C3 Valréas France
59 D3 Vals, Tanjung c. Indon.
74 B2 Valsad India
122 B2 Valspan S. Africa
91 D1 Valuyki Rus. Fed.
106 B2 Valverde del Camino Spain
81 C2 Van Turkey
81 C2 Van, Lake salt l. Turkey
141 F1 Van Buren U.S.A.
128 B3 Vancouver Can.
134 B1 Vancouver U.S.A.
128 B3 Vancouver Island Can.
140 B3 Vandalia U.S.A.
123 C2 Vanderbijlpark S. Africa
128 B2 Vanderhoof Can.

88 C2 Vändra Estonia
93 F4 Vänern l. Sweden
93 F4 Vänersborg Sweden
121 D3 Vangaindrano Madag.
Van Gölü salt l. Turkey see
Van, Lake
138 C2 Van Horn U.S.A.
59 D3 Vanimo P.N.G.
83 K3 Vanino Rus. Fed.
104 B2 Vannes France
59 D3 Van Rees, Pegunungan mts
Indon.
122 A3 Vanrhynsdorp S. Africa
93 H3 Vantaa Fin.
49 F4 Vanua Levu i. Fiji
48 E3 Vanuatu country S. Pacific
Ocean
140 C2 Van Wert U.S.A.
122 B3 Vanwyksvlei S. Africa
122 B2 Van Zylsrus S. Africa
75 C2 Varanasi India
92 I1 Varangerfjorden sea chan.
Norway
92 I1 Varangerhalvøya pen. Norway
109 C1 Varaždin Croatia
93 F4 Varberg Sweden
109 D2 Vardar r. Macedonia
93 E4 Varde Denmark
92 J1 Vardø Norway
100 D1 Varel Ger.
88 B3 Varėna Lith.
108 A1 Varese Italy
155 C2 Varginha Brazil
93 I3 Varkaus Fin.
110 C2 Varna Bulg.
93 F4 Värnamo Sweden
155 D1 Várzea da Palma Brazil
86 C2 Varzino Rus. Fed.
Vasa Fin. see Vaasa
88 C2 Vasknarva Estonia
110 C1 Vaslui Romania
93 G4 Västerås Sweden
93 G3 Västerdalälven r. Sweden
88 A2 Västerhaninge Sweden
93 G4 Västervik Sweden
108 B2 Vasto Italy
90 C1 Vasyl'kiv Ukr.
104 C2 Vatan France
108 B2 Vatican City Europe
92 B3 Vatnajökull Iceland
110 C1 Vatra Dornei Romania
93 F4 Vättern l. Sweden
138 B2 Vaughn U.S.A.
105 C3 Vauvert France
49 G4 Vava'u Group is Tonga
88 B3 Vawkavysk Belarus
93 F4 Växjö Sweden
86 E1 Vaygach, Ostrov i. Rus. Fed.
101 D1 Vechta Ger.
110 C2 Vedea r. Romania
100 C1 Veendam Neth.
100 B1 Veenendaal Neth.
129 C2 Vegreville Can.
106 B2 Vejer de la Frontera Spain
93 E4 Vejle Denmark
109 D2 Velbŭzhdki Prokhod pass
Bulg./Macedonia
100 B2 Veldhoven Neth.
109 B2 Velebit mts Croatia
100 C2 Velen Ger.
109 C1 Velenje Slovenia
109 D2 Veles Macedonia
106 C2 Vélez-Málaga Spain
155 D1 Velhas r. Brazil
109 D2 Velika Plana Serbia
88 C2 Velikaya r. Rus. Fed.
89 D2 Velikiye Luki Rus. Fed.

89	D2	Velikiy Novgorod Rus. Fed.
86	D2	Velikiy Ustyug Rus. Fed.
110	C2	Veliko Tŭrnovo Bulg.
108	B2	Veli Lošinj Croatia
89	D2	Velizh Rus. Fed.
86	D2	Vel'sk Rus. Fed.
101	F1	Velten Ger.
91	D1	Velykyy Burluk Ukr.
108	B2	Venafro Italy
154	C2	Venceslau Bráz Brazil
104	C2	Vendôme France
89	E3	Venev Rus. Fed.
		Venezia Italy see Venice
150	B1	Venezuela country S. America
150	A1	Venezuela, Golfo de g. Venez.
108	B1	Venice Italy
143	D3	Venice U.S.A.
108	B1	Venice, Gulf of Europe
100	C2	Venlo Neth.
100	B2	Venray Neth.
88	B2	Venta r. Latvia/Lith.
88	B2	Venta Lith.
123	C3	Venterstad S. Africa
99	C3	Ventnor Italy
88	B2	Ventspils Latvia
135	C4	Ventura U.S.A.
139	C3	Venustiano Carranza, Presa resr Mex.
107	C2	Vera Spain
145	C3	Veracruz Mex.
74	B2	Veraval India
108	A1	Verbania Italy
108	A1	Vercelli Italy
105	D3	Vercors reg. France
92	F3	Verdalsøra Norway
154	B2	Verde r. Goiás Brazil
154	B2	Verde r. Mato Grosso do Sul Brazil
144	B2	Verde r. Mex.
138	A2	Verde r. U.S.A.
155	D1	Verde Grande r. Brazil
101	D1	Verden (Aller) Ger.
144	B2	Verdinho, Serra do mts Brazil
105	D2	Verdon France
105	D2	Verdun France
123	C2	Vereeniging S. Africa
106	B1	Verín Spain
91	D3	Verkhnebakanskiy Rus. Fed.
92	J2	Verkhnetulomskiy Rus. Fed.
91	E1	Verkhniy Mamon Rus. Fed.
89	E3	Verkhov'ye Rus. Fed.
90	A2	Verkhovyna Ukr.
83	J2	Verkhoyanskiy Khrebet mts Rus. Fed.
129	C2	Vermilion Can.
137	D2	Vermillion U.S.A.
130	A2	Vermilion Bay Can.
141	E2	Vermont state U.S.A.
135	E2	Vernal U.S.A.
128	C2	Vernon Can.
139	D2	Vernon U.S.A.
143	D3	Vero Beach U.S.A.
111	B2	Veroia Greece
108	B1	Verona Italy
104	C2	Versailles France
104	B2	Vertou France
123	D2	Verulam S. Africa
100	B2	Verviers Belgium
105	C2	Vervins France
105	D3	Vescovato Corse France
87	E3	Veselaya, Gora mt. Rus. Fed.
91	C2	Vesele Ukr.
105	D2	Vesoul France
92	F2	Vesterålen is Norway
92	F2	Vestfjorden sea chan. Norway
94	B1	Vestmanna Faroe Is
93	E3	Vestnes Norway

108	B2	Vesuvius vol. Italy
89	E2	Ves'yegonsk Rus. Fed.
93	G4	Vetlanda Sweden
86	D3	Vetluga Rus. Fed.
100	A2	Veurne Belgium
105	D2	Vevey Switz.
91	D1	Veydelevka Rus. Fed.
80	B1	Vezirköprü Turkey
151	D2	Viana Brazil
106	B1	Viana do Castelo Port.
		Viangchan Laos see Vientiane
62	B1	Viangphoukha Laos
111	C3	Viannos Greece
154	C1	Vianópolis Brazil
108	B2	Viareggio Italy
93	E4	Viborg Denmark
109	C3	Vibo Valentia Italy
107	D1	Vic Spain
144	A1	Vicente Guerrero Mex.
108	B1	Vicenza Italy
105	C2	Vichy France
142	B2	Vicksburg U.S.A.
155	D2	Viçosa Brazil
52	A3	Victor Harbor Austr.
50	C1	Victoria r. Austr.
52	B3	Victoria state Austr.
128	B3	Victoria Can.
153	A4	Victoria Chile
113	K7	Victoria Seychelles
139	D3	Victoria U.S.A.
119	D3	Victoria, Lake Africa
52	B2	Victoria, Lake Austr.
62	A1	Victoria, Mount Myanmar
59	D3	Victoria, Mount P.N.G.
		Victoria Falls Zambia/Zimbabwe
126	D2	Victoria Island Can.
50	C1	Victoria River Downs Austr.
122	B3	Victoria West S. Africa
135	C4	Victorville U.S.A.
110	C2	Videle Romania
92	A2	Viðidalsá Iceland
153	B5	Viedma Arg.
153	A5	Viedma, Lago l. Arg.
100	B2	Vielsalm Belgium
101	E2	Vienenburg Ger.
103	D2	Vienna Austria
105	C2	Vienne France
104	C2	Vienne r. France
62	B2	Vientiane Laos
100	C2	Viersen Ger.
104	C2	Vierzon France
144	B2	Viesca Mex.
109	C2	Vieste Italy
62	B2	Vietnam country Asia
62	B1	Viêt Tri Vietnam
64	B1	Vigan Phil.
108	A1	Vigevano Italy
106	B1	Vigo Spain
73	C3	Vijayawada India
92	B3	Vík Iceland
129	C2	Viking Can.
106	B2	Vila Franca de Xira Port.
106	B1	Vilagarcía de Arousa Spain
106	B1	Vilalba Spain
106	B1	Vila Nova de Gaia Port.
107	D1	Vilanova i la Geltrú Spain
106	B1	Vila Real Port.
106	B1	Vilar Formoso Port.
155	D2	Vila Velha Brazil
150	A3	Vilcabamba, Cordillera mts Peru
92	G3	Vilhelmina Sweden
150	B3	Vilhena Brazil
88	C2	Viljandi Estonia
88	B3	Vilkaviškis Lith.

83	H1	Vil'kitskogo, Proliv str. Rus. Fed.
144	A2	Villa Ahumada Mex.
106	B1	Villablino Spain
102	C2	Villach Austria
144	B2	Villa de Cos Mex.
152	B4	Villa Dolores Arg.
145	C3	Villa Flores Mex.
145	C2	Villagrán Mex.
145	C3	Villahermosa Mex.
144	A2	Villa Insurgentes Mex.
152	B4	Villa María Arg.
152	B3	Villa Montes Bol.
144	B2	Villanueva Mex.
106	B2	Villanueva de la Serena Spain
106	C2	Villanueva de los Infantes Spain
152	B3	Villa Ocampo Arg.
108	A3	Villaputzu Sardegna Italy
152	C3	Villarrica Para.
106	C2	Villarrobledo Spain
152	B3	Villa Unión Arg.
144	B2	Villa Unión Durango Mex.
144	B2	Villa Unión Sinaloa Mex.
150	A1	Villavicencio Col.
152	B3	Villazón Bol.
107	C2	Villena Spain
104	C3	Villeneuve-sur-Lot France
142	C2	Ville Platte U.S.A.
105	C2	Villeurbanne France
102	B2	Villingen Ger.
88	C3	Vilnius Lith.
91	C2	Vil'nohirs'k Ukr.
91	D2	Vil'nyans'k Ukr.
100	B2	Vilvoorde Belgium
88	C3	Vilyeyka Belarus
83	J2	Vilyuy r. Rus. Fed.
93	G4	Vimmerby Sweden
153	A4	Viña del Mar Chile
107	D1	Vinaròs Spain
140	B3	Vincennes U.S.A.
55	G3	Vincennes Bay Antarctica
141	D3	Vineland U.S.A.
62	B2	Vinh Vietnam
63	B2	Vinh Long Vietnam
139	D1	Vinita U.S.A.
90	B2	Vinnytsya Ukr.
55	O2	Vinson Massif mt. Antarctica
93	E3	Vinstra Norway
108	B1	Vipiteno Italy
64	B1	Virac Phil.
129	D3	Virden Can.
104	B2	Vire France
120	A2	Virei Angola
155	D1	Virgem da Lapa Brazil
138	A1	Virgin r. U.S.A.
123	C2	Virginia S. Africa
137	E1	Virginia U.S.A.
141	D3	Virginia state U.S.A.
141	D3	Virginia Beach U.S.A.
135	C3	Virginia City U.S.A.
147	D3	Virgin Islands (U.K.) terr. West Indies
147	D3	Virgin Islands (U.S.A.) terr. West Indies
63	B2	Virôchey Cambodia
109	C1	Virovitica Croatia
100	B3	Virton Belgium
88	B2	Virtsu Estonia
109	C2	Vis i. Croatia
88	C2	Visaginas Lith.
135	C3	Visalia U.S.A.
74	B2	Visavadar India
64	B1	Visayan Sea Phil.
93	G4	Visby Sweden
126	D2	Viscount Melville Sound sea chan. Can.

151 D2 Viseu Brazil
106 B1 Viseu Port.
73 C3 Vishakhapatnam India
88 C2 Viški Latvia
103 D1 Vistula r. Pol.
108 B2 Viterbo Italy
49 F4 Viti Levu i. Fiji
83 I3 Vitim r. Rus. Fed.
155 D3 Vitória Brazil
153 D3 Vitória da Conquista Brazil
106 C1 Vitoria-Gasteiz Spain
104 B2 Vitré France
105 C2 Vitry-le-François France
89 D2 Vitsyebsk Belarus
105 D2 Vittel France
108 B3 Vittoria Sicilia Italy
108 B2 Vittorio Veneto Italy
106 B1 Viveiro Spain
144 A2 Vizcaíno, Sierra mts Mex.
110 C2 Vize Turkey
72 C2 Vizianagaram India
100 B2 Vlaardingen Neth.
87 F2 Vladikavkaz Rus. Fed.
62 C1 Vladimir Rus. Fed.
66 B2 Vladivostok Rus. Fed.
109 C2 Vlasotince Serbia
100 A2 Vlieland i. Neth.
100 A2 Vlissingen Neth.
109 C2 Vlorë Albania
102 C2 Vöcklabruck Austria
101 D2 Vogelsberg hills Ger.
91 D3 Voi Kenya
105 D2 Voiron France
109 C1 Voise's Bay Can.
92 J3 Vojvodina prov. Serbia

89 E2 Volga Rus. Fed.
87 F2 Volga r. Rus. Fed.
87 D4 Volgodonsk Rus. Fed.
87 D4 Volgograd Rus. Fed.
89 D2 Volkhov Rus. Fed.
89 D1 Volkhov r. Rus. Fed.
101 E2 Volkstedt Ger.
91 D2 Volnovakha Ukr.
90 B2 Volochys'k Ukr.
91 D2 Volodars'ke Ukr.
90 B1 Volodars'k-Volyns'kyy Ukr.
90 B1 Volodymyrets' Ukr.
89 A1 Volodymyr-Volyns'kyy Ukr.
89 E2 Vologda Rus. Fed.
91 D1 Volokonovka Rus. Fed.
111 B3 Volos Greece
88 C2 Volosovo Rus. Fed.
89 D2 Volot Rus. Fed.
89 E3 Volovo Rus. Fed.
87 D3 Vol'sk Rus. Fed.
114 C4 Volta, Lake resr Ghana
155 D3 Volta Redonda Brazil
87 D4 Volzhskiy Rus. Fed.
92 C2 Vopnafjörður Iceland
88 C3 Voranava Belarus
86 F2 Vorkuta Rus. Fed.
88 B2 Vormsi i. Estonia
89 E3 Voronezh Rus. Fed.
89 E1 Voronezh r. Rus. Fed.
89 E1 Vorontsovka Rus. Fed.
90 C1 Vorskla r. Rus. Fed.
88 C2 Võrtsjärv l. Estonia
88 C2 Võru Estonia
122 B3 Vosburg S. Africa
105 D2 Vosges mts France
89 E2 Voskresensk Rus. Fed.
93 E3 Voss Norway

83 H3 Vostochnyy Sayan mts Rus. Fed.
86 E3 Votkinsk Rus. Fed.
154 C2 Votuporanga Brazil
100 B3 Vouziers France
92 J2 Voynitsa Rus. Fed.
91 C2 Voznesens'k Ukr.
93 E4 Vrådal Norway
66 B2 Wrangel' Rus. Fed.
Wrangelya, Ostrov i. Rus. Fed. see Wrangel Island
109 D2 Vranje Serbia
110 C2 Vratnik pass Bulg.
110 B2 Vratsa Bulg.
109 C1 Vrbas r. Bos.-Herz.
109 C1 Vrbas Serbia
122 A3 Vredenburg S. Africa
122 A3 Vredendal S. Africa
100 B3 Vresse Belgium
109 D1 Vršac Serbia
122 B2 Vryburg S. Africa
123 D2 Vryheid S. Africa
89 D1 Vsevolozhsk Rus. Fed.
Vučitrn Kosovo see Vushtrri
109 C1 Vukovar Croatia
86 E2 Vuktyl' Rus. Fed.
123 C2 Vukuzakhe S. Africa
109 B3 Vulcano, Isola i. Italy
63 B2 Vung Tau Vietnam
109 D2 Vushtrri Kosovo
74 B2 Vyara India
89 D2 Vyatka Rus. Fed. see Kirov
93 I3 Vyaz'ma Rus. Fed.
88 C2 Vyerkhnyadzvinsk Belarus
87 D3 Vyksa Rus. Fed.
90 B2 Vylkove Ukr.
90 A2 Vynohradiv Ukr.
89 D2 Vypolzovo Rus. Fed.
89 D2 Vyritsa Rus. Fed.
91 D2 Vyselki Rus. Fed.
90 C1 Vyshhorod Ukr.
89 D2 Vyshniy-Volochek Rus. Fed.
103 D2 Vyškov Czech Rep.
86 C2 Vytegra Rus. Fed.

W

114 B3 Wa Ghana
100 B2 Waal r. Neth.
100 B2 Waalwijk Neth.
128 C2 Wabasca r. Can.
128 C2 Wabasca-Desmarais Can.
140 B3 Wabash r. U.S.A.
129 E2 Wabowden Can.
143 D3 Waccasassa Bay U.S.A.
101 D2 Wächtersbach Ger.
139 D2 Waco U.S.A.
115 D2 Waddān Libya
Waddeneilanden is Neth. see West Frisian Islands
100 B1 Waddenzee sea chan. Neth.
128 B2 Waddington, Mount Can.
100 B1 Waddinxveen Neth.
129 D2 Wadena Can.
137 D1 Wadena U.S.A.
74 A2 Wadh Pak.
116 B2 Wadi Halfa Sudan
116 B3 Wad Medani Sudan
70 C2 Wafangdian China
100 B2* Wageningen Neth.
127 F2 Wager Bay Can.
53 C3 Wagga Wagga Austr.
137 D2 Wahoo U.S.A.
137 D1 Wahpeton U.S.A.

54 B2 Waiau r. N.Z.
59 C3 Waigeo i. Indon.
58 B3 Waikabubak Indon.
52 A2 Waikerie Austr.
54 B2 Waimate Austr.
75 B3 Wainganga r. India
58 C3 Waingapu Indon.
129 C2 Wainwright Can.
54 C1 Waiouru N.Z.
54 B1 Waipara N.Z.
54 C1 Waipawa N.Z.
54 B2 Waipukurau N.Z.
54 C1 Wairau r. N.Z.
54 B1 Wairoa N.Z.
54 C1 Waitaki r. N.Z.
54 B1 Waitara N.Z.
54 B1 Waiuku N.Z.
119 E2 Wajir Kenya
67 C3 Wakasa-wan b. Japan
54 A3 Wakatipu, Lake N.Z.
129 D2 Wakaw Can.
67 C4 Wakayama Japan
136 D3 WaKeeney U.S.A.
54 B2 Wakefield N.Z.
98 C2 Wakefield U.K.
48 F1 Wake Island N. Pacific Ocean
66 D1 Wakkanai Japan
123 D2 Wakkerstroom S. Africa
103 D1 Walbrzych Pol.
53 D2 Walcha Austr.
100 C1 Walchum Ger.
103 D1 Walcz Pol.
99 B2 Wales admin. div. U.K.
53 C2 Walgett Austr.
119 C3 Walikale Dem. Rep. Congo
135 C3 Walker Lake U.S.A.
52 A2 Wallaroo Austr.
98 B2 Wallasey U.K.
134 C1 Walla Walla U.S.A.
101 D3 Walldürn Ger.
53 C2 Wallendbeen Austr.
49 G3 Wallis and Futuna Islands terr. S. Pacific Ocean
96 □ Walls U.K.
98 B1 Walney, Isle of i. U.K.
98 B2 Walsall U.K.
136 C3 Walsenburg U.S.A.
101 D1 Walsrode Ger.
143 D2 Walterboro U.S.A.
120 A3 Walvis Bay Namibia
119 C2 Wamba Dem. Rep. Congo
52 B1 Wanaaring Austr.
54 A2 Wanaka Austr.
54 A2 Wanaka, Lake N.Z.
130 B2 Wanapitei Lake Can.
154 B3 Wanda Arg.
66 B1 Wanda Shan mts China
62 C1 Wanding China
62 A1 Wanganui N.Z.
53 C3 Wangaratta Austr.
65 B3 Wangqing China
62 A1 Wan Hsa-la Myanmar
71 B4 Wanning China
100 B2 Wanroij Neth.
99 C3 Wantage U.K.
70 A2 Wanyuan China
70 A2 Wanzhou China
73 B3 Warangal India
101 D2 Warburg Ger.
50 B2 Warburton Austr.
52 A1 Warburton watercourse Austr.
75 B2 Wardha India
96 C1 Ward Hill U.K.
128 B2 Ware Can.
101 F1 Waren Ger.
100 C2 Warendorf Ger.
53 D1 Warialda Austr.
122 A2 Warmbad Namibia

135 C3 Warm Springs U.S.A.
134 C2 Warner Lakes U.S.A.
143 D2 Warner Robins U.S.A.
152 B2 Warnes Bol.
52 B3 Warracknabeal Austr.
53 C2 Warrego r. Austr.
53 C2 Warren Austr.
142 B2 Warren AR U.S.A.
140 C2 Warren OH U.S.A.
141 D2 Warren PA U.S.A.
97 C1 Warrenpoint U.K.
137 E3 Warrensburg U.S.A.
122 A2 Warrenton S. Africa
115 C4 Warri Nigeria
98 B2 Warrington U.K.
52 B3 Warrnambool Austr.
103 E1 Warsaw Pol.
Warszawa Pol. see Warsaw
103 C1 Warta r. Pol.
53 D1 Warwick Austr.
99 C2 Warwick U.K.
135 C3 Wasco U.S.A.
136 C1 Washburn U.S.A.
141 D3 Washington DC U.S.A.
137 E2 Washington IA U.S.A.
140 B3 Washington IN U.S.A.
137 E3 Washington MO U.S.A.
143 E1 Washington NC U.S.A.
140 C2 Washington PA U.S.A.
134 B1 Washington state U.S.A.
141 E2 Washington, Mount U.S.A.
140 C3 Washington Court House U.S.A.
74 A2 Washuk Pak.
130 C1 Waskaganish Can.
129 E2 Waskaiowaka Lake Can.
122 A2 Wasser Namibia
130 C2 Waswanipi, Lac l. Can.
58 C3 Watampone Indon.
141 E2 Waterbury U.S.A.
129 D2 Waterbury Lake Can.
97 C2 Waterford Ireland
97 C2 Waterford Harbour Ireland
137 E2 Waterloo U.S.A.
123 C1 Waterpoort S. Africa
141 D2 Watertown NY U.S.A.
137 D2 Watertown SD U.S.A.
140 B2 Watertown WI U.S.A.
141 F2 Waterville U.S.A.
99 C3 Watford U.K.
136 C1 Watford City U.S.A.
129 D2 Wathaman r. Can.
139 D1 Watonga U.S.A.
129 D2 Watrous Can.
119 C2 Watsa Dem. Rep. Congo
140 B2 Watseka U.S.A.
118 C3 Watsi Kengo Dem. Rep. Congo
128 B1 Watson Lake Can.
135 B3 Watsonville U.S.A.
59 C3 Watubela, Kepulauan is Indon.
59 D3 Wau P.N.G.
117 A4 Wau Sudan
53 D2 Wauchope Austr.
140 B2 Waukegan U.S.A.
139 D2 Waurika U.S.A.
140 B2 Wausau U.S.A.
99 D2 Waveney r. U.K.
137 E2 Waverly U.S.A.
143 D2 Waycross U.S.A.
137 D2 Wayne U.S.A.
143 D2 Waynesboro GA U.S.A.
141 D3 Waynesboro VA U.S.A.
143 D1 Waynesville U.S.A.
74 B1 Wazirabad Pak.
98 C1 Wear r. U.K.
139 D2 Weatherford U.S.A.

134 B2 Weaverville U.S.A.
130 B1 Webequie Can.
137 D1 Webster U.S.A.
137 E2 Webster City U.S.A.
55 Q2 Weddell Sea Antarctica
100 B2 Weert Neth.
53 C2 Wee Waa Austr.
100 C2 Wegberg Ger.
103 E1 Węgorzewo Pol.
101 F3 Weiden in der Oberpfalz Ger.
70 B2 Weifang China
70 C2 Weihai China
53 C1 Weilmoringle Austr.
101 E2 Weimar Ger.
70 A2 Weinan China
51 D1 Weipa Austr.
53 C1 Weir r. Austr.
140 C2 Weirton U.S.A.
62 B1 Weishan China
101 E2 Weißenfels Ger.
102 C2 Weißkugel mt. Austria/Italy
103 D1 Wejherowo Pol.
128 C1 Wekweètì Can.
140 C3 Welch U.S.A.
117 B3 Weldiya Eth.
123 C2 Welkom S. Africa
99 C2 Welland r. U.K.
51 C1 Wellesley Islands Austr.
53 C2 Wellington Austr.
122 A3 Wellington S. Africa
54 B2 Wellington N.Z.
123 C3 Wellington S. Africa
137 D3 Wellington U.S.A.
153 A5 Wellington, Isla i. Chile
53 C3 Wellington, Lake Austr.
128 B2 Wells Can.
99 B3 Wells U.K.
134 D2 Wells U.S.A.
50 B2 Wells, Lake imp. l. Austr.
54 B1 Wellsford N.Z.
98 D2 Wells-next-the-Sea U.K.
102 C2 Wels Austria
99 B2 Welshpool U.K.
123 C2 Wembesi S. Africa
130 C1 Wemindji Can.
134 B1 Wenatchee U.S.A.
71 B4 Wenchang China
114 B4 Wenchi Ghana
70 C2 Wendeng China
101 E1 Wendisch Evern Ger.
117 B4 Wendo Eth.
134 D2 Wendover U.S.A.
71 B3 Wengyuan China
71 C3 Wenling China
71 A3 Wenshan China
52 B2 Wentworth Austr.
71 C3 Wenzhou China
123 C2 Wepener S. Africa
122 B2 Werda Botswana
101 F2 Werdau Ger.
101 F1 Werder Ger.
101 F3 Wernberg-Köblitz Ger.
101 E2 Wernigerode Ger.
101 D2 Werra r. Ger.
53 D2 Werris Creek Austr.
101 D3 Wertheim Ger.
101 D3 Wesel Ger.
101 E1 Wesendorf Ger.
101 D1 Weser r. Ger.
101 D1 Weser sea chan. Ger.
51 C1 Wessel, Cape Austr.
51 C1 Wessel Islands Austr.
123 C2 Wesselton S. Africa
80 B2 West Bank terr. Asia
140 B2 West Bend U.S.A.
99 C2 West Bromwich U.K.
100 C2 Westerburg Ger.
100 C1 Westerholt Ger.

50 B2 Western Australia state Austr.
122 B3 Western Cape prov. S. Africa
116 A2 Western Desert Egypt
73 B3 Western Ghats mts India
114 A2 Western Sahara terr. Africa
100 A2 Westerschelde est. Neth.
100 C1 Westerstede Ger.
100 C2 Westerwald hills Ger.
142 B2 West Frankfort U.S.A.
100 B1 West Frisian Islands is Neth.
147 D2 West Indies is Caribbean Sea
96 A1 West Loch Roag b. U.K.
128 C2 Westlock Can.
100 A2 Westmalle Belgium
142 B1 West Memphis U.S.A.
140 C3 Weston U.S.A.
99 B3 Weston-super-Mare U.K.
143 D3 West Palm Beach U.S.A.
137 E3 West Plains U.S.A.
137 D2 West Point U.S.A.
54 B2 Westport N.Z.
97 B2 Westport Ireland
129 D2 Westray Can.
96 C1 Westray i. U.K.
100 B1 West-Terschelling Neth.
140 C3 West Virginia state U.S.A.
53 C2 West Wyalong Austr.
134 D2 West Yellowstone U.S.A.
59 C3 Wetar i. Indon.
128 C2 Wetaskiwin Can.
101 D2 Wetzlar Ger.
59 D3 Wewak P.N.G.
97 C2 Wexford Ireland
129 D2 Weyakwin Can.
129 D3 Weyburn Can.
101 D1 Weyhe Ger.
99 B3 Weymouth U.K.
54 C1 Whakatane N.Z.
129 E1 Whale Cove Can.
96 □ Whalsay i. U.K.
54 B1 Whangarei N.Z.
98 C2 Wharfe r. U.K.
129 D3 Wharton U.S.A.
128 C1 Whatì Can.
136 B2 Wheatland U.S.A.
138 B1 Wheeler Peak NM U.S.A.
135 D3 Wheeler Peak NV U.S.A.
140 C2 Wheeling U.S.A.
98 B1 Whernside h. U.K.
128 B2 Whistler Can.
98 C1 Whitby U.K.
142 B2 White r. U.S.A.
50 B2 White, Lake imp. l. Austr.
131 E2 White Bay Can.
136 C1 White Butte mt. U.S.A.
52 B2 White Cliffs Austr.
128 C2 Whitecourt Can.
98 B1 Whitefish U.S.A.
98 B1 Whitehaven U.K.
97 D1 Whitehead U.K.
128 A1 Whitehorse Can.
142 B3 White Lake U.S.A.
135 C3 White Mountain Peak U.S.A.
116 B3 White Nile r. Sudan/Uganda
86 C2 White Sea Rus. Fed.
134 D1 White Sulphur Springs U.S.A.
143 E2 Whiteville U.S.A.
114 B3 White Volta r. Burkina/Ghana
138 B2 Whitewater Baldy mt. U.S.A.
130 B1 Whitewater Lake Can.
122 B2 Whitewood Can.
96 B3 Whithorn U.K.
54 C1 Whitianga N.Z.
135 C3 Whitney, Mount U.S.A.
51 D2 Whitsunday Island Austr.
52 A2 Whyalla Austr.

00 A2 Wichelen Belgium
37 D3 Wichita U.S.A.
32 D2 Wichita Falls U.S.A.
96 C1 Wick U.K.
38 A2 Wickenburg U.S.A.
97 C3 Wicklow Ireland
97 D2 Wicklow Head Ireland
97 C3 Wicklow Mountains Ireland
98 B2 Widnes U.K.
01 D1 Wiehengebirge hills Ger.
02 C2 Wiehl Ger.
03 D1 Wieluń Pol.
Wien Austria see Vienna
03 D2 Wiener Neustadt Austria
00 B1 Wieringerwerf Neth.
00 C2 Wiesbaden Ger.
00 C1 Wiesmoor Ger.
03 D1 Wieżyca h. Pol.
99 C3 Wight, Isle of i. U.K.
96 B3 Wigtown U.K.
00 B2 Wijchen Neth.
52 B2 Wilcannia Austr.
23 C3 Wild Coast S. Africa
23 C2 Wilge r. S. Africa
00 C1 Wilhelmshaven Ger.
41 D2 Wilkes-Barre U.S.A.
55 H3 Wilkes Land reg. Antarctica
29 D2 Wilkie Can.
38 B2 Willcox U.S.A.
00 B2 Willebroek Belgium
47 L5 Willemstad Neth. Antilles
52 B3 William, Mount Austr.
52 A1 William Creek Austr.
38 A1 Williams U.S.A.
41 D3 Williamsburg U.S.A.
28 B2 Williams Lake Can.
40 C3 Williamson U.S.A.
41 D2 Williamsport U.S.A.
43 E1 Williamston U.S.A.
22 B3 Williston S. Africa
36 C1 Williston U.S.A.
28 C2 Williston Lake Can.
35 B3 Willits U.S.A.
37 D1 Willmar U.S.A.
22 B3 Willowmore S. Africa
23 C3 Willowvale S. Africa
50 B2 Wills, Lake imp. l. Austr.
52 A3 Willunga Austr.
52 A2 Wilmington Austr.
41 D3 Wilmington DE U.S.A.
43 E2 Wilmington NC U.S.A.
00 D2 Wilnsdorf Ger.
43 E2 Wilson U.S.A.
53 C3 Wilson's Promontory pen.
Austr.
00 B3 Wiltz Lux.
50 B2 Wiluna Austr.
99 C3 Winchester U.K.
40 C3 Winchester KY U.S.A.
41 D3 Winchester VA U.S.A.
98 B1 Windermere l. U.K.
20 A3 Windhoek Namibia
37 D2 Windom U.S.A.
51 D2 Windorah Austr.
36 B2 Wind River Range mts U.S.A.
53 D2 Windsor Austr.
30 B2 Windsor Can.
47 D3 Windward Islands Caribbean
Sea
47 D3 Windward Passage Cuba/Haiti
37 D3 Winfield U.S.A.
00 A2 Wingene Belgium
53 D2 Wingham Austr.
30 B1 Winisk r. Can.
30 B1 Winisk (abandoned) Can.
30 B1 Winisk Lake Can.
63 A2 Winkana Myanmar

129 E3 Winkler Can.
114 B4 Winneba Ghana
140 B2 Winnebago, Lake U.S.A.
134 C2 Winnemucca U.S.A.
136 C2 Winner U.S.A.
142 B2 Winnfield U.S.A.
137 E1 Winnibigoshish, Lake U.S.A.
129 E3 Winnipeg Can.
129 E2 Winnipeg r. Can.
129 E2 Winnipeg, Lake Can.
129 D2 Winnipegosis, Lake Can.
141 E2 Winnipesaukee, Lake U.S.A.
142 B2 Winnsboro U.S.A.
137 E2 Winona MN U.S.A.
142 C2 Winona MS U.S.A.
100 C1 Winschoten Neth.
101 D1 Winsen (Aller) Ger.
101 F1 Winsen (Luhe) Ger.
138 A1 Winslow U.S.A.
143 D1 Winston-Salem U.S.A.
101 D2 Winterberg Ger.
143 D3 Winter Haven U.S.A.
100 C1 Winterswijk Neth.
105 D2 Winterthur Switz.
51 D2 Winton Austr.
54 A3 Winton N.Z.
52 A2 Wirrabara Austr.
99 D2 Wisbech U.K.
140 A2 Wisconsin r. U.S.A.
140 B2 Wisconsin state U.S.A.
140 B2 Wisconsin Rapids U.S.A.
Wisła r. Pol. see Vistula
101 E1 Wismar Ger.
123 C2 Witbank S. Africa
98 C2 Withernsea U.K.
100 B1 Witmarsum Neth.
99 C3 Witney U.K.
123 D2 Witrivier S. Africa
101 F2 Wittenberg, Lutherstadt Ger.
101 E1 Wittenberge Ger.
101 E1 Wittenburg Ger.
101 E1 Wittingen Ger.
100 C3 Wittlich Ger.
100 C1 Wittmund Ger.
101 F1 Wittstock Ger.
120 A3 Witvlei Namibia
101 D2 Witzenhausen Ger.
103 D1 Władysławowo Pol.
103 D1 Włocławek Pol.
103 E1 Włodawa Pol.
101 E1 Wolbrom Pol.
101 E1 Wolfen Ger.
101 E1 Wolfenbüttel Ger.
136 B1 Wolf Point U.S.A.
101 E1 Wolfsberg Ger.
101 E1 Wolfsburg Ger.
100 C3 Wolfstein Ger.
131 D2 Wolfville Can.
102 C1 Wolgast Ger.
102 C1 Wolin Pol.
129 D2 Wollaston Lake Can.
129 D2 Wollaston Lake Can.
126 D2 Wollaston Peninsula Can.
53 D2 Wollongong Austr.
101 E2 Wolmirsleben Ger.
101 E1 Wolmirstedt Ger.
100 C1 Wolvega Neth.
99 B2 Wolverhampton U.K.
65 B3 Wŏnju S. Korea
128 B2 Wonowon Can.
65 B2 Wŏnsan N. Korea
53 C3 Wonthaggi Austr.
52 A2 Woocalla Austr.
51 C1 Woodah, Isle i. Austr.
99 D2 Woodbridge U.K.
136 B3 Woodland Park U.S.A.

50 C2 Woodroffe, Mount Austr.
51 C1 Woods, Lake imp. l. Austr.
129 E3 Woods, Lake of the
Can./U.S.A.
53 C3 Woods Point Austr.
131 D2 Woodstock N.B. Can.
140 C2 Woodstock Ont. Can.
54 C2 Woodville N.Z.
139 D1 Woodward U.S.A.
53 D2 Woolgoolga Austr.
52 A2 Woomera Austr.
140 C2 Wooster U.S.A.
122 A3 Worcester S. Africa
99 B2 Worcester U.K.
141 E2 Worcester U.S.A.
102 C2 Wörgl Austria
98 B1 Workington U.K.
98 C2 Worksop U.K.
136 B2 Worland U.S.A.
101 D3 Worms Ger.
99 C3 Worthing U.K.
137 D2 Worthington U.S.A.
58 C3 Wotu Indon.
59 C3 Wowoni i. Indon.
83 N2 Wrangel Island Rus. Fed.
128 A2 Wrangell U.S.A.
96 B1 Wrath, Cape U.K.
136 C2 Wray U.S.A.
122 A2 Wreck Point S. Africa
98 B2 Wrexham U.K.
63 A2 Wrightmyo India
128 B1 Wrigley Can.
103 D1 Wrocław Pol.
103 D1 Września Pol.
70 B2 Wu'an China
70 A2 Wuhai China
70 B2 Wuhan China
70 B2 Wuhu China
Wujin China see
Changzhou
115 C4 Wukari Nigeria
62 B1 Wuliang Shan mts China
59 C3 Wuliaru i. Indon.
71 A3 Wumeng Shan mts China
130 B1 Wunnummin Lake Can.
101 F2 Wunsiedel Ger.
101 D1 Wunstorf Ger.
62 A1 Wuntho Myanmar
100 C2 Wuppertal Ger.
122 A3 Wuppertal S. Africa
101 E2 Wurzbach Ger.
101 D3 Würzburg Ger.
101 F2 Wurzen Ger.
68 C2 Wuwei China
70 A2 Wuxi Chongqing China
70 C2 Wuxi Jiangsu China
Wuxing China see Huzhou
71 A3 Wuxuan China
Wuyang China see
Zhenyuan
69 E1 Wuying China
71 B3 Wuyishan China
71 B3 Wuyi Shan mts China
70 A1 Wuyuan China
71 A4 Wuzhishan China
70 A2 Wuzhong China
71 B3 Wuzhou China
53 C2 Wyangala Reservoir Austr.
52 B3 Wycheproof Austr.
99 B3 Wye r. U.K.
50 B1 Wyndham Austr.
142 B1 Wynne U.S.A.
129 D2 Wynyard Can.
136 B2 Wyoming state U.S.A.
103 E1 Wyszków Pol.
140 C3 Wytheville U.S.A.

X

117 D3 Xaafuun Somalia
62 B2 Xaignabouli Laos
121 C3 Xai-Xai Moz.
70 A1 Xamba China
62 B1 Xam Nua Laos
120 A2 Xangongo Angola
81 C2 Xankändi Azer.
111 B2 Xanthi Greece
150 B3 Xapuri Brazil
107 C2 Xàtiva Spain
Xiaguan China see Dali
71 B3 Xiamen China
70 A2 Xi'an China
70 A3 Xianfeng China
70 B2 Xiangfan China
62 A1 Xianggelila China
Xiangjiang China see Huichang
71 B3 Xiangtan China
Xiangyang China see Xiangfan
70 B2 Xiantao China
70 A2 Xianyang China
70 B2 Xiaogan China
69 E1 Xiao Hinggan Ling mts China
70 C2 Xiaoshan China
62 B1 Xichang China
145 D3 Xicoténcatl Mex.
71 A3 Xifeng Guizhou China
75 C2 Xigazê China
83 I4 Xilinhot China
70 C1 Xincai China
68 C2 Xinghai China
70 B2 Xinghua China
71 B3 Xingning China
70 B2 Xingping China
70 B2 Xingtai China
151 C2 Xingu r. Brazil
71 A3 Xingyi China
71 B3 Xinhua China
68 C2 Xining China
Xinjiang Uygur Autonomous Region aut. reg. China see Xinjiang Uygur Zizhiqu
75 C1 Xinjiang Uygur Zizhiqu aut. reg. China
Xinjing China see Jingxi
65 A1 Xinmin China
71 B3 Xinning China
70 B2 Xintai China
70 B2 Xinxiang China
70 B2 Xinyang China
70 B2 Xinyi China
71 B3 Xinyu China
69 D2 Xinzhou Shanxi China
70 B2 Xinzhou Shanxi China
106 B3 Xinzo de Limia Spain
Xiongshan China see Zhenghe
68 C2 Xiqing Shan mts China
151 D3 Xique Xique Brazil
70 A1 Xishanzui China
71 A3 Xiushan China
71 B3 Xiuying China
70 B2 Xixia China
68 B2 Xizang Zizhiqu aut. reg. China
76 B2 Xo'jayli Uzbek.
71 A3 Xuanwei China
70 B2 Xuchang China
Xucheng China see Xuwen
117 C4 Xuddur Somalia
Xujiang China see Guangchang
71 B3 Xun Jiang r. China
71 B3 Xunwu China

107 C2 Xúquer, Riu r. Spain
71 B3 Xuwen China
71 A3 Xuyong China
70 B2 Xuzhou China

Y

117 B4 Yabēlo Eth.
69 D1 Yablonovyy Khrebet mts Rus. Fed.
143 D1 Yadkin r. U.S.A.
75 C2 Yadong China
89 E2 Yagoda Rus. Fed.
118 B1 Yagoua Cameroon
128 C3 Yahk Can.
144 B2 Yahualica Mex.
80 B3 Yahyalı Turkey
67 C4 Yaizu Japan
134 B1 Yakima U.S.A.
114 B3 Yako Burkina
66 D2 Yakumo Japan
126 B3 Yakutat U.S.A.
83 J2 Yakutsk Rus. Fed.
91 D2 Yakymivka Ukr.
63 B3 Yala Thai.
53 C3 Yallourn Austr.
111 C2 Yalova Turkey
91 C3 Yalta Ukr.
65 A1 Yalu Jiang r. China/N. Korea
67 D3 Yamagata Japan
67 B4 Yamaguchi Japan
Yamal, Poluostrov pen. Rus. Fed. see Yamal Peninsula
86 F1 Yamal Peninsula Rus. Fed.
53 D1 Yamba Austr.
117 A4 Yambio Sudan
110 C2 Yambol Bulg.
86 G2 Yamburg Rus. Fed.
62 A1 Yamethin Myanmar
114 B4 Yamoussoukro Côte d'Ivoire
90 B2 Yampil' Ukr.
75 C2 Yamuna r. India
75 D2 Yamzho Yumco l. China
83 K2 Yana r. Rus. Fed.
70 A2 Yan'an China
150 A3 Yanaoca Peru
78 A2 Yanbu' al Baḥr Saudi Arabia
70 C2 Yancheng China
50 A3 Yanchep Austr.
71 B3 Yangchun China
65 B2 Yangdok N. Korea
71 B3 Yangjiang China
Yangôn Myanmar see Rangoon
70 B2 Yangquan China
71 B3 Yangshuo China
70 C3 Yangtze r. China
69 E2 Yangtze, Mouth of the China
70 B2 Yangzhou China
65 B1 Yanji China
137 D2 Yankton U.S.A.
83 K2 Yano-Indigirskaya Nizmennost' lowland Rus. Fed.
83 K2 Yanskiy Zaliv g. Rus. Fed.
53 C1 Yantabulla Austr.
70 C2 Yantai China
118 B2 Yaoundé Cameroon
59 D2 Yap i. Micronesia
59 D3 Yapen i. Indon.
59 D3 Yapen, Selat sea chan. Indon.
144 A2 Yaqui r. Mex.
51 D2 Yaraka Austr.
86 D3 Yaransk Rus. Fed.
48 F2 Yaren Nauru

78 B3 Yarīm Yemen
77 D3 Yarkant He r. China
75 B2 Yarlung Zangbo r. China
131 D2 Yarmouth Can.
86 F2 Yaronga Rus. Fed.
89 E2 Yaroslavl' Rus. Fed.
66 B2 Yaroslavskiy Rus. Fed.
53 C3 Yarram Austr.
89 D2 Yartsevo Rus. Fed.
89 E3 Yasnogorsk Rus. Fed.
63 B2 Yasothon Thai.
53 C2 Yass Austr.
111 C3 Yatağan Turkey
129 E1 Yathkyed Lake Can.
67 B4 Yatsushiro Japan
150 B2 Yavari r. Brazil/Peru
75 B2 Yavatmal India
90 A2 Yavoriv Ukr.
67 B4 Yawatahama Japan
81 D2 Yazd Iran
142 B2 Yazoo City U.S.A.
111 B3 Ydra i. Greece
63 A2 Ye Myanmar
77 D3 Yecheng China
144 B2 Yécora Mex.
89 E3 Yefremov Rus. Fed.
89 E3 Yegor'yevsk Rus. Fed.
117 B4 Yei Sudan
86 F3 Yekaterinburg Rus. Fed.
89 E3 Yelets Rus. Fed.
114 A3 Yélimané Mali
96 □ Yell i. U.K.
128 C1 Yellowknife Can.
70 B2 Yellow River r. China
69 E2 Yellow Sea N. Pacific Ocean
136 C1 Yellowstone r. U.S.A.
136 A2 Yellowstone Lake U.S.A.
88 D3 Yel'sk Belarus
78 B3 Yemen country Asia
86 E2 Yemva Rus. Fed.
91 D2 Yenakiyeve Ukr.
62 A1 Yenangyaung Myanmar
62 B2 Yên Bai Vietnam
114 B4 Yendi Ghana
111 C3 Yenice Turkey
111 C3 Yenifoça Turkey
68 C1 Yenisey r. Rus. Fed.
53 C3 Yeoval Austr.
99 B3 Yeovil U.K.
51 E2 Yeppoon Austr.
83 I2 Yerbogachen Rus. Fed.
81 C1 Yerevan Armenia
77 D1 Yereymentau Kazakh.
87 D3 Yershov Rus. Fed.
65 B2 Yesan S. Korea
77 C1 Yesil' Kazakh.
111 C3 Yeşilova Turkey
99 A3 Yes Tor h. U.K.
53 D1 Yetman Austr.
62 A1 Ye-U Myanmar
104 B2 Yeu, Île d' i. France
91 C2 Yevpatoriya Ukr.
91 D2 Yeya r. Rus. Fed.
91 D2 Yeysk Rus. Fed.
88 C2 Yeyyaryshcha Belarus
71 A3 Yibin China
71 B3 Yichang China
69 E1 Yichun Heilong. China
71 B3 Yichun Jiangxi China
110 C2 Yıldız Dağları mts Turkey
80 B2 Yıldızeli Turkey
70 A2 Yinchuan China
65 B1 Yingchengzi China
71 B3 Yingde China
70 C1 Yingkou China
70 B2 Yingshan Hubei China
70 A2 Yingshan Sichuan China

1 B3 Yingtan China
7 E2 Yining China
7 B4 Yirga Alem Eth.
80 B2 Yishui China
8 C2 Yiwu China
1 B3 Yiyang China
1 A3 Yizhou China
12 J2 Yli-Kitka l. Fin.
2 H2 Ylitornio Fin.
2 H3 Ylivieska Fin.
1 C2 Yogyakarta Indon.
8 B2 Yoko Cameroon
7 D3 Yokohama Japan
5 D4 Yola Nigeria
47 D3 Yonezawa Japan
1 B3 Yong'an China
1 B3 Yongchun China
1 B2 Yongdeng China
5 B2 Yŏngdŏk S. Korea
1 C3 Yongkang China
2 B1 Yongsheng China
1 B3 Yongzhou China
50 A1 Yopal Col.
56 A3 York Austr.
98 E2 York U.K.
47 D2 York NE U.S.A.
91 D3 York PA U.S.A.
51 D1 York, Cape Austr.
56 A3 Yorke Peninsula Austr.
44 B3 Yorketown Austr.
98 C2 Yorkshire Wolds hills U.K.
37 D3 Yorkton Can.
87 D3 Yoshkar-Ola Rus. Fed.
53 C2 Youghal Ireland
52 A3 Younghusband Peninsula
       Austr.
40 C2 Youngstown U.S.A.
44 B3 Youvarou Mali
77 E2 Youyi Feng mt. China/
       Rus. Fed.
80 B2 Yozgat Turkey
34 B2 Yreka U.S.A.
       Yr Wyddfa mt. U.K. see
       Snowdon
05 C2 Yssingeaux France
93 F4 Ystad Sweden
       Ysyk-Köl Kyrg. see Balykchy
77 D2 Ysyk-Köl salt l. Kyrg.
92 A3 Ytri-Rangá r. Iceland
62 B1 Yuanjiang China
62 B1 Yuan Jiang r. China
62 B1 Yuanmou China
35 B3 Yuba City U.S.A.
66 D2 Yūbari Japan
45 C3 Yucatán pen. Mex.
46 B2 Yucatan Channel Cuba/Mex.
50 C2 Yuendumu Austr.
71 B3 Yueyang China
86 F2 Yugorsk Rus. Fed.
       Yugoslavia Europe see Bosnia-
       Herzegovina, Croatia, Kosovo,
       Macedonia, Montenegro,
       Serbia, Slovenia
83 L2 Yukagirskoye Ploskogor'ye
       plat. Rus. Fed.
.26 A2 Yukon r. Can./U.S.A.
.28 A1 Yukon Territory admin. div. Can.
71 B3 Yulin Guangxi China
70 A2 Yulin Shaanxi China
.38 A2 Yulong Xueshan mt. China
.36 C2 Yuma AZ U.S.A.
       Yuma CO U.S.A.
       Yumen China see Laojunmiao
71 B2 Yunak Turkey
70 B2 Yuncheng China
71 B3 Yunfu China

62 B1 Yunnan prov. China
52 A2 Yunta Austr.
70 B2 Yunyang China
150 A2 Yurimaguas Peru
77 E3 Yurungkax He r. China
71 C3 Yü Shan mt. Taiwan
68 C2 Yushu China
       Yushwuan China see Huaihua
81 C1 Yusufeli Turkey
77 E3 Yutian China
62 B1 Yuxi China
66 D2 Yuzhno-Kuril'sk Rus. Fed.
83 K3 Yuzhno-Sakhalinsk Rus. Fed.
91 C2 Yuzhnoukrayins'k Ukr.
69 D2 Yuzhou China
104 C2 Yvetot France

Z

100 B1 Zaandam Neth.
69 D1 Zabaykal'sk Rus. Fed.
78 B3 Zabid Yemen
76 C3 Zābol Iran
79 D2 Zāboli Iran
144 B3 Zacapu Mex.
144 B2 Zacatecas Mex.
145 C3 Zacatepec Mex.
145 C3 Zacatlán Mex.
111 B3 Zacharo Greece
144 B2 Zacoalco Mex.
145 C2 Zacualtipán Mex.
109 C2 Zadar Croatia
63 A3 Zadetkyi Kyun i. Myanmar
89 E3 Zadonsk Rus. Fed.
106 B2 Zafra Spain
109 C1 Zagreb Croatia
       Zagros, Kūhhā-ye mts Iran see
       Zagros Mountains
81 C2 Zagros Mountains Iran
79 D2 Zāhedān Iran
80 B2 Zahlé Lebanon
78 B3 Zahran Saudi Arabia
       Zaire country Africa see Congo,
       Democratic Republic of the
109 D2 Zaječar Serbia
89 E3 Zakharovo Rus. Fed.
81 C2 Zākhō Iraq
111 B3 Zakynthos Greece
111 B3 Zakynthos i. Greece
103 D2 Zalaegerszeg Hungary
110 B1 Zalău Romania
78 B2 Zalim Saudi Arabia
117 A3 Zalingei Sudan
78 A2 Zalmā, Jabal az mt. Saudi
       Arabia
128 C2 Zama City Can.
120 C2 Zambeze r. Moz.
       Zambeze r. Moz. see Zambeze
120 C2 Zambezi r. Africa
120 B2 Zambezi Zambia
120 B2 Zambia country Africa
64 B2 Zamboanga Phil.
64 B2 Zamboanga Peninsula Phil.
106 B1 Zamora Spain
144 B3 Zamora de Hidalgo Mex.
103 E1 Zamość Pol.
75 B1 Zanda China
100 B2 Zandvliet Belgium
140 C3 Zanesville U.S.A.
81 C2 Zanjān Iran
75 B1 Zanskar Mountains India
       Zante i. Greece see Zakynthos
119 D3 Zanzibar Tanz.
119 D3 Zanzibar Island Tanz.
89 E3 Zaokskiy Rus. Fed.

115 C2 Zaouatallaz Alg.
70 B2 Zaozhuang China
89 D2 Zapadnaya Dvina r. Europe
89 D2 Zapadnaya Dvina Rus. Fed.
68 B1 Zapadnyy Sayan reg. Rus. Fed.
139 D3 Zapata U.S.A.
91 C2 Zapolyarnyy Rus. Fed.
91 D2 Zaporizhzhya Ukr.
101 E2 Zappendorf Ger.
80 B2 Zara Turkey
145 B2 Zaragoza Mex.
107 C1 Zaragoza Spain
76 B3 Zarand Iran
76 C3 Zaranj Afgh.
88 C2 Zarasai Lith.
89 E3 Zaraysk Rus. Fed.
150 B1 Zaraza Venez.
115 C3 Zaria Nigeria
81 D3 Zarqān Iran
66 B2 Zarubino Rus. Fed.
103 D1 Zary Pol.
115 D1 Zarzis Tunisia
123 C3 Zastron S. Africa
69 E1 Zavitinsk Rus. Fed.
103 D1 Zawiercie Pol.
77 E2 Zaysan, Lake Kazakh.
       Zaysan, Ozero l. Kazakh. see
       Zaysan, Lake
90 A2 Zdolbuniv Ukr.
93 F4 Zealand i. Denmark
       Zealand i. Denmark see
       Zealand
100 A2 Zeebrugge Belgium
123 C2 Zeerust S. Africa
50 C2 Zeil, Mount Austr.
104 C2 Zeitz Ger.
88 B3 Zelenogradsk Rus. Fed.
82 E1 Zemlya Aleksandry i. Rus. Fed.
82 F1 Zemlya Vil'cheka i. Rus. Fed.
107 D2 Zemmora Alg.
145 C3 Zempoaltépetl, Nudo de mt.
       Mex.
65 B2 Zengfeng Shan mt. China
105 D2 Zermatt Switz.
91 E2 Zernograd Rus. Fed.
101 E2 Zeulenroda Ger.
101 D1 Zeven Ger.
100 C2 Zevenaar Neth.
83 J3 Zeya Rus. Fed.
79 D2 Zeydābād Iran
83 J3 Zeyskoye Vodokhranilishche
       resr Rus. Fed.
103 D1 Zgierz Pol.
88 B3 Zhabinka Belarus
76 A2 Zhalpaktal Kazakh.
77 C1 Zhaltyr Kazakh.
76 B2 Zhanaozen Kazakh.
       Zhangde China see Anyang
71 B3 Zhangjiajie China
70 B1 Zhangjiakou China
71 B3 Zhangping China
71 B3 Zhangshu China
68 C2 Zhangye China
71 B3 Zhangzhou China
77 D4 Zhanibek Kazakh.
71 B3 Zhanjiang China
71 B3 Zhaoqing China
71 A3 Zhaotong China
75 C1 Zhari Namco salt l. China
77 E2 Zharkent Kazakh.
89 D2 Zharkovskiy Rus. Fed.
77 E2 Zharma Kazakh.
90 C2 Zhashkiv Ukr.
71 C3 Zhejiang prov. China
82 F1 Zhelaniya, Mys c. Rus. Fed.

89 E3 **Zheleznogorsk** Rus. Fed.
70 A2 **Zhenba** China
71 A3 **Zheng'an** China
71 B3 **Zhenghe** China
70 B2 **Zhengzhou** China
70 B2 **Zhenjiang** China
71 A3 **Zhenyuan** China
91 E1 **Zherdevka** Rus. Fed.
86 D2 **Zheshart** Rus. Fed.
77 C2 **Zhezkazgan** *Karagandinskaya Oblast'* Kazakh.
77 C2 **Zhezkazgan** *Karagandinskaya Oblast'* Kazakh.
83 J2 **Zhigansk** Rus. Fed.
  Zhi Qu *r.* China *see* Yangtze
76 C1 **Zhitikara** Kazakh.
88 D3 **Zhlobin** Belarus
90 B2 **Zhmerynka** Ukr.
74 A1 **Zhob** Pak.
83 L1 **Zhokhova, Ostrov** *i.* Rus. Fed.
75 C2 **Zhongba** China
  Zhonghe China *see* Xiushan
70 A2 **Zhongning** China
71 B3 **Zhongshan** China
  Zhongshan China *see* Lupanshui
  Zhongxian China
  Zhongxin China *see* Xianggelila
70 A2 **Zhongwei** China
70 B2 **Zhoukou** China
70 C2 **Zhoushan** China
91 C2 **Zhovti Vody** Ukr.
65 A2 **Zhuanghe** China
70 B2 **Zhucheng** China
89 D3 **Zhukovka** Rus. Fed.
89 E2 **Zhukovskiy** Rus. Fed.
70 B2 **Zhumadian** China

  Zhuoyang China *see* Suiping
71 B3 **Zhuzhou** *Hunan* China
71 B3 **Zhuzhou** *Hunan* China
90 A2 **Zhydachiv** Ukr.
88 C3 **Zhytkavichy** Belarus
90 B1 **Zhytomyr** Ukr.
103 D2 **Žiar nad Hronom** Slovakia
70 B2 **Zibo** China
103 D1 **Zielona Góra** Pol.
62 A1 **Zigaing** Myanmar
71 A3 **Zigong** China
114 A3 **Ziguinchor** Senegal
144 B3 **Zihuatanejo** Mex.
103 D2 **Žilina** Slovakia
83 H3 **Zima** Rus. Fed.
145 C2 **Zimapán** Mex.
121 B2 **Zimbabwe** *country* Africa
114 A4 **Zimmi** Sierra Leone
110 C2 **Zimnicea** Romania
115 C3 **Zinder** Niger
78 B3 **Zinjibār** Yemen
103 D2 **Zirc** Hungary
62 A1 **Ziro** India
79 C2 **Zir Rūd** Iran
103 D2 **Zistersdorf** Austria
145 B3 **Zitácuaro** Mex.
103 C1 **Zittau** Ger.
87 E3 **Zlatoust** Rus. Fed.
103 D2 **Zlín** Czech Rep.
89 D3 **Zlynka** Rus. Fed.
89 E3 **Zmiyevka** Rus. Fed.
91 D2 **Zmiyiv** Ukr.
89 E3 **Znamenka** *Orlovskaya Oblast'* Rus. Fed.
91 E1 **Znamenka** *Tambovskaya Oblast'* Rus. Fed.

91 C2 **Znam"yanka** Ukr.
103 D2 **Znojmo** Czech Rep.
91 D1 **Zolochiv** *Kharkivs'ka Oblast'* Ukr.
90 A2 **Zolochiv** *L'vivs'ka Oblast'* Ukr.
91 C2 **Zolotonosha** Ukr.
89 E3 **Zolotukhino** Rus. Fed.
121 C2 **Zomba** Malawi
80 B1 **Zonguldak** Turkey
105 D3 **Zonza** Corse France
114 B4 **Zorzor** Liberia
115 D2 **Zouar** Chad
114 A2 **Zouérat** Maur.
109 D1 **Zrenjanin** Serbia
89 D2 **Zubtsov** Rus. Fed.
105 D2 **Zug** Switz.
81 C1 **Zugdidi** Georgia
106 B2 **Zújar** *r.* Spain
100 C2 **Zülpich** Ger.
121 C2 **Zumbo** Moz.
145 C3 **Zumpango** Mex.
138 B1 **Zuni Mountains** U.S.A.
71 A3 **Zunyi** China
109 C1 **Županja** Croatia
105 D2 **Zürich** Switz.
100 C1 **Zutphen** Neth.
115 D1 **Zuwārah** Libya
90 C2 **Zvenyhorodka** Ukr.
121 C3 **Zvishavane** Zimbabwe
103 D2 **Zvolen** Slovakia
109 C2 **Zvornik** Bos.-Herz.
114 B4 **Zwedru** Liberia
123 C3 **Zwelitsha** S. Africa
103 D2 **Zwettl** Austria
101 F2 **Zwickau** Ger.
100 C1 **Zwolle** Neth.
83 L2 **Zyryanka** Rus. Fed.

Acknowledgements

pages 36–37
Land Cover map data courtesy of
Center for Remote Sensing, Boston University, USA

pages 38–39
Population map data:
Gridded Population of the World (GPW), Version 3.
Palisades, NY: CIESN, Columbia University. Available at
http://sedac.ciesin.columbia.edu/plue/gpw

Cover
View west across the Strait of Gibraltar
with Morocco on the left and Spain on the right.
Image courtesy of the Image Science and Analysis Laboratory,
NASA Johnson Space Center.
http://eol.jsc.nasa.gov